CRIMINAL CODE (CANADA) 2018 EDITION

Updated as of February 26, 2018

THE LAW LIBRARY

TABLE OF CONTENTS

An Act respecting the Criminal Law	18
Criminal Code	18
Short Title	18
Interpretation	18
Part I	25
General	25
Parties to Offences	37
Protection of Persons Administering and Enforcing the Law	38
Suppression of Riots	43
Self-induced Intoxication	44
Defence of Person	44
Defence of Property	45
Protection of Persons in Authority	45
PART II	46
Offences Against Public Order	46
Treason and other Offences against the Queen's Authority and Person	46
Prohibited Acts	47
Official Documents	49
Sedition	51
Unlawful Assemblies and Riots	52
Unlawful Drilling	53
Duels	53
Forcible Entry and Detainer	53
Piracy	54
Offences against Air or Maritime Safety	54
Dangerous Materials and Devices	56
Prize Fights	58
PART II.1	58
Terrorism	58
Interpretation	59
Financing of Terrorism	60
List of Entities	61

Freezing of Property	63
Seizure and Restraint of Property	65
Forfeiture of Property	66
Participating, Facilitating, Instructing and Harbouring	67
Hoax Regarding Terrorist Activity	72
Proceedings and Aggravated Punishment	72
Investigative Hearing	73
Recognizance with Conditions	75
PART III	79
Firearms and Other Weapons	79
Interpretation	79
Use Offences	82
Possession Offences	83
Trafficking Offences	88
Assembling Offence	90
Export and Import Offences	90
Offences relating to Lost, Destroyed or Defaced Weapons, etc.	91
Prohibition Orders	93
Limitations on Access	98
Search and Seizure	99
Exempted Persons	102
General	104
PART IV	105
Offences Against the Administration of Law and Justice	105
Interpretation	105
Corruption and Disobedience	106
Misleading Justice	111
Escapes and Rescues	114
PART V	117
Sexual Offences, Public Morals and Disorderly Conduct	117
Interpretation	117
Sexual Offences	117
Offences Tending to Corrupt Morals	124
Disorderly Conduct	133

Nuisances	136
PART VI	136
Invasion of Privacy	136
Definitions	136
Interception of Communications	141
PART VII	156
Disorderly Houses, Gaming and Betting	156
Interpretation	157
Presumptions	158
Search	158
Obstruction	159
Gaming and Betting	159
Bawdy-houses	167
Offences in Relation to Offering, Providing or Obtaining Sexual Services for Consideration	167
PART VIII	168
Offences Against the Person and Reputation	168
Interpretation	168
Duties Tending to Preservation of Life	169
Criminal Negligence	170
Homicide	170
Murder, Manslaughter and Infanticide	172
Suicide	175
Medical Assistance in Dying	176
Neglect in Child-birth and Concealing Dead Body	180
Bodily Harm and Acts and Omissions Causing Danger to the Person	180
Motor Vehicles, Vessels and Aircraft	183
Assaults	199
Kidnapping, Trafficking in Persons, Hostage Taking and Abduction	211
Commodification of Sexual Activity	216
Abortion	218
Venereal Diseases	220
Offences Against Conjugal Rights	220
Unlawful Solemnization of Marriage	221
Blasphemous Libel	222

Defamatory Libel	222
Verdicts	226
Hate Propaganda	226
PART IX	229
Offences Against Rights of Property	229
Interpretation	229
Theft	229
Offences Resembling Theft	233
Robbery and Extortion	237
Criminal Interest Rate	238
Breaking and Entering	240
Possession and Trafficking	242
False Pretences	245
Forgery and Offences Resembling Forgery	247
PART X	251
Fraudulent Transactions Relating to Contracts and Trade	251
Interpretation	251
Fraud	251
Falsification of Books and Documents	258
Identity Theft and Identity Fraud	259
Forgery of Trade-marks and Trade Descriptions	261
Wreck	262
Public Stores	263
Breach of Contract, Intimidation and Discrimination Against Trade Unionists	264
Secret Commissions	266
Trading Stamps	267
PART XI	267
Wilful and Forbidden Acts in Respect of Certain Property	267
Interpretation	267
Mischief	268
Arson and Other Fires	271
Other Interference with Property	272
Cattle and Other Animals	273
Cruelty to Animals	274

PART XII	276
Offences Relating to Currency	276
Interpretation	276
Making	276
Possession	277
Uttering	277
Defacing or Impairing	277
Instruments or Materials	278
Advertising and Trafficking in Counterfeit Money or Counterfeit Tokens of Value	279
Special Provisions as to Proof	279
Forfeiture	280
PART XII.1	280
Instruments and Literature for Illicit Drug Use	280
Interpretation	280
Offence and Punishment	280
PART XII.2	280
Proceeds of Crime	281
Interpretation	281
Offence	282
Search, Seizure and Detention of Proceeds of Crime	282
Forfeiture of Proceeds of Crime	288
Disclosure Provisions	294
Specific Rules of Forfeiture	297
Regulations	297
PART XIII	297
Attempts — Conspiracies — Accessories	297
PART XIV	301
Jurisdiction	301
General	301
Special Jurisdiction	303
Rules of Court	307
PART XV	309
Special Procedure and Powers	309
General Powers of Certain Officials	309

Forensic DNA Analysis	325
Other Provisions Respecting Search Warrants, Preservation Orders and Production Orders	337
Sex Offender Information	349
Interpretation	349
Order to Comply with the	351
Notice and Obligation to Comply with the	354
Notice and Obligation to Comply with the	359
Disclosure of Information	363
Offences	364
Regulations	365
Forfeiture of Offence-related Property	365
PART XVI	374
Compelling Appearance of Accused Before a Justice and Interim Release	374
Interpretation	374
Arrest without Warrant and Release from Custody	375
Appearance of Accused before Justice	379
Information, Summons and Warrant	382
Judicial Interim Release	386
Arrest of Accused on Interim Release	396
Review of Detention where Trial Delayed	397
Procedure to Procure Attendance of a Prisoner	399
Endorsement of Warrant	400
Powers to Enter Dwelling-houses to Carry out Arrests	400
PART XVII	402
Language of Accused	402
PART XVIII	405
Procedure on Preliminary Inquiry	405
Jurisdiction	405
Procedures before Preliminary Inquiry	407
Powers of Justice	408
Taking Evidence of Witnesses	409
Remand Where Offence Committed in Another Jurisdiction	411
Absconding Accused	412
Procedure where Witness Refuses to Testify	412

Remedial Provisions	413
Adjudication and Recognizances	413
Transmission of Record	414
PART XVIII.1	415
Case Management Judge	415
PART XIX	418
Indictable Offences — Trial Without Jury	418
Interpretation	418
Jurisdiction of Provincial Court Judges	418
Absolute Jurisdiction	418
Provincial Court Judge's Jurisdiction with Consent	419
Jurisdiction of Judges	421
Judge's Jurisdiction with Consent	421
Election	422
Trial	426
General	427
PART XIX.1	428
Nunavut Court of Justice	428
PART XX	430
Procedure in Jury Trials and General Provisions	431
Preferring Indictment	431
General Provisions respecting Counts	433
Special Provisions respecting Counts	434
Particulars	434
Ownership of Property	435
Joinder or Severance of Counts	435
Joinder of Accused in Certain Cases	436
Proceedings when Person Indicted is at Large	437
Change of Venue	438
Amendment	438
Inspection and Copies of Documents	440
Pleas	440
Organizations	443
Record of Proceedings	444

Pre-hearing Conference	444
Juries	445
Challenging the Array	445
Empanelling Jury	446
Trial	451
Evidence on Trial	455
Children and Young Persons	457
Corroboration	457
Verdicts	458
Previous Convictions	459
Jurisdiction	460
Formal Defects in Jury Process	461
PART XX.1	462
Mental Disorder	462
Interpretation	462
Assessment Orders	462
Assessment Reports	465
Protected Statements	465
Fitness to Stand Trial	466
Verdict of Not Criminally Responsible on Account of Mental Disorder	468
Review Boards	469
Disposition Hearings	471
Dispositions by a Court or Review Board	478
Terms of Dispositions	478
High-Risk Accused	480
Dual Status Offenders	481
Appeals	483
Review of Dispositions	485
Power to Compel Appearance	487
Stay of Proceedings	487
Interprovincial Transfers	489
Enforcement of Orders and Regulations	490
PART XXI	491
Appeals — Indictable Offences	492

Interpretation	492
Right of Appeal	492
Procedure on Appeals	494
Powers of the Court of Appeal	499
Appeals to the Supreme Court of Canada	502
Appeals by Attorney General of Canada	504
PART XXI.1	504
Applications for Ministerial Review — Miscarriages of Justice	504
PART XXII	506
Procuring Attendance	506
Application	506
Process	506
Execution or Service of Process	508
Defaulting or Absconding Witness	509
Electronically Transmitted Copies	510
Evidence on Commission	510
Video and Audio Evidence	512
Evidence Previously Taken	513
Video-recorded Evidence	514
PART XXIII	514
Sentencing	514
Interpretation	514
Alternative Measures	515
Purpose and Principles of Sentencing	517
Organizations	518
Punishment Generally	519
Procedure and Evidence	521
Absolute and Conditional Discharges	526
Probation	527
Fines and Forfeiture	533
Restitution	538
Conditional Sentence of Imprisonment	541
Imprisonment	548
Eligibility for Parole	550

Delivery of Offender to Keeper of Prison	551
Imprisonment for Life	551
Pardons and Remissions	557
Disabilities	558
Miscellaneous Provisions	559
PART XXIV	559
Dangerous Offenders and Long-term Offenders	559
Interpretation	559
Dangerous Offenders and Long-Term Offenders	561
PART XXV	568
Effect and Enforcement of Recognizances	568
PART XXVI	571
Extraordinary Remedies	571
PART XXVII	574
Summary Convictions	574
Interpretation	574
Punishment	575
Information	575
Defects and Objections	576
Application	576
Trial	576
Adjudication	578
Sureties to Keep the Peace	579
Appeal	590
Interim Release of Appellant	592
Procedure on Appeal	593
Summary Appeal on Transcript or Agreed Statement of Facts	596
Appeals to Court of Appeal	598
Fees and Allowances	598
PART XXVIII	598
Miscellaneous	598
Electronic Documents	599
Remote Appearance by Incarcerated Accused	599
Forms	600

SCHEDULE TO PART XX.1	600
SCHEDULE [to Part XXV]	600
SCHEDULE [to Part XXVII]	601
Fees and Allowances That May Be Charged by Summary Conviction Courts and Justices	601
Fees and Allowances That May Be Allowed to Peace Officers	601
Fees and Allowances That May Be Allowed to Witnesses	602
Fees and Allowances That May Be Allowed to Interpreters	602
Information To Obtain a Search Warrant	602
Information	602
Heading of Indictment	602
Warrant To Search	603
Preservation Demand	603
Information To Obtain a Preservation Order	603
Preservation Order	604
Information To Obtain a Production Order	604
Production Order for Documents	605
Production Order To Trace a Communication	605
Production Order for Transmission Data or Tracking Data	606
Production Order for Financial Data	606
Information To Revoke or Vary an Order Made Under Any of Sections 487.013 to 487.018 of the Criminal Code	606
Information To Obtain a Non-Disclosure Order	607
Non-Disclosure Order	607
Information To Obtain a Warrant To Take Bodily Substances for Forensic DNA Analysis	607
Warrant Authorizing the Taking of Bodily Substances for Forensic DNA Analysis	608
Order Authorizing the Taking of Bodily Substances for Forensic DNA Analysis	608
Order Authorizing the Taking of Bodily Substances for Forensic DNA Analysis	609
Order to a Person To Have Bodily Substances Taken for Forensic DNA Analysis	610
Application for an Authorization To Take Bodily Substances for Forensic DNA Analysis	610
Authorization To Take Bodily Substances for Forensic DNA Analysis	611
Summons to a Person To Have Bodily Substances Taken for Forensic DNA Analysis	611
Warrant for Arrest	612
Report to a Provincial Court Judge or the Court	612

Application for an Authorization To Take Additional Samples of Bodily Substances for Forensic DNA Analysis	613
Authorization To Take Additional Samples of Bodily Substances for Forensic DNA Analysis	613
Warrant To Search	613
Report to a Justice	614
Report to a Judge of Property Seized	614
Summons to a Person Charged with an Offence	615
Warrant for Arrest	615
Warrant To Enter Dwelling-house	616
Warrant for Committal	616
Appearance Notice Issued by a Peace Officer to a Person Not Yet Charged with an Offence	617
Promise To Appear	618
Recognizance Entered into Before an Officer in Charge or Other Peace Officer	618
Undertaking Given to a Peace Officer or an Officer in Charge	619
Undertaking Given to a Justice or a Judge	620
Undertaking by Appellant (Defendant)	621
Undertaking by Appellant (Prosecutor)	621
Warrant To Convey Accused Before Justice of Another Territorial Division	621
Subpoena to a Witness	622
Subpoena to a Witness in the Case of Proceedings in Respect of an Offence Referred to in Subsection 278.2(1) of the Criminal Code	622
Warrant for Witness	622
Warrant To Arrest an Absconding Witness	623
Warrant Remanding a Prisoner	623
Warrant of Committal of Witness for Refusing To Be Sworn or To Give Evidence	623
Warrant of Committal on Conviction	624
Warrant of Committal on an Order for the Payment of Money	624
Warrant of Committal for Failure To Furnish Recognizance To Keep the Peace	624
Warrant of Committal of Witness for Failure To Enter into Recognizance	625
Warrant of Committal for Contempt	625
Warrant of Committal in Default of Payment of Costs of an Appeal	626
Warrant of Committal on Forfeiture of a Recognizance	626
Endorsement of Warrant	626
Endorsement of Warrant	626

Order for Accused To Be Brought Before Justice Prior to Expiration of Period of Remand	627
Deposition of a Witness	627
Recognizance	627
Certificate of Default To Be Endorsed on Recognizance	628
Writ of Fieri Facias	629
Statement on Restitution	629
Victim Impact Statement	629
Community Impact Statement	631
Conviction	631
Order Against an Offender	632
Order Acquitting Accused	632
Conviction for Contempt	632
Order for Discharge of a Person in Custody	632
Challenge To Array	633
Challenge for Cause	633
Certificate of Non-payment of Costs of Appeal	633
Jailer's Receipt to Peace Officer for Prisoner	633
Probation Order	634
Order To Disclose Income Tax Information	634
Assessment Order of the Court	634
Assessment Order of the Review Board	635
Victim Impact Statement — Not Criminally Responsible	635
Warrant of Committal	636
Disposition of Detention	637
Warrant of Committal	637
Placement Decision	637
Notice of Obligation To Provide Samples of Bodily Substance	637
Order To Comply with Sex Offender Information Registration Act	638
Notice of Obligation To Comply with Sex Offender Information Registration Act	639
Obligation To Comply with Sex Offender Information Registration Act	639
RELATED PROVISIONS	640
— 1991, c. 43, ss. 10(1) to (7), as amended by 2005, c. 22, s. 43	640
— 2004, c. 12, s. 22	640
— 2004, c. 12, s. 23	641

— 2005, c. 32, s. 27.1	641
— 2009, c. 28, s. 12	641
— 2009, c. 29, s. 5	641
— 2011, c. 2, s. 7	641
— 2012, c. 1, par. 163(a)	642
— 2012, c. 1, par. 165(b)	642
— 2014, c. 6, s. 20.1	642
— 2014, c. 25, s. 45.1	642
— 2015, c. 13, s. 37	643
— 2015, c. 13, s. 38	643
— 2015, c. 13, s. 39	643
— 2015, c. 13, s. 40	643
— 2015, c. 13, s. 41	643
— 2015, c. 13, s. 42	643
— 2015, c. 13, s. 42.1	643
— 2015, c. 13, s. 43	643
— 2015, c. 13, s. 44	643
— 2015, c. 20, s. 28	643
— 2016, c. 3, s. 9.1	644
— 2016, c. 3, s. 10	644
AMENDMENTS NOT IN FORCE	644
— 2001, c. 32, ss. 82(1), (3)	644
— 2014, c. 20, s. 366(1)	644
— 2015, c. 16, s. 1	645
— 2015, c. 16, s. 2	645
— 2015, c. 16, s. 3	645
— 2015, c. 16, s. 4	645
— 2015, c. 23, s. 30	645
— 2015, c. 23, s. 31	645
— 2017, c. 7, s. 54	646
— 2017, c. 7, s. 58	646
— 2017, c. 7, s. 59	647
— 2017, c. 7, s. 60(1)	648
— 2017, c. 7, s. 61	648

— 2017, c. 7, s. 64	**648**
— 2017, c. 7, s. 65	**649**
— 2017, c. 7, s. 66	**649**
— 2017, c. 7, s. 67	**649**
— 2017, c. 7, s. 68	**649**
— 2017, c. 27, s. 61	**650**
— 2017, c. 27, s. 62	**650**
— 2017, c. 33, s. 255	**651**

An Act respecting the Criminal Law

Criminal Code

Short Title

Short title
1 This Act may be cited as the
Criminal Code
R.S., c. C-34, s. 1.

Interpretation

Definitions
2 In this Act,
Act
(a) an Act of Parliament,
(b) an Act of the legislature of the former Province of Canada,
(c) an Act of the legislature of a province, and
(d) an Act or ordinance of the legislature of a province, territory or place in force at the time that province, territory or place became a province of Canada;
associated personnel
(a) assigned by a government or an intergovernmental organization with the agreement of the competent organ of the United Nations,
(b) engaged by the Secretary-General of the United Nations, by a specialized agency of the United Nations or by the International Atomic Energy Agency, or
(c) deployed by a humanitarian non-governmental organization or agency under an agreement with the Secretary-General of the United Nations, by a specialized agency of the United Nations or by the International Atomic Energy Agency,
to carry out activities in support of the fulfilment of the mandate of a United Nations operation;
Attorney General
(a) subject to paragraphs (b.1) to (g), with respect to proceedings to which this Act applies, means the Attorney General or Solicitor General of the province in which those proceedings are taken and includes his or her lawful deputy,
(b) with respect to Yukon, the Northwest Territories and Nunavut, or with respect to proceedings commenced at the instance of the Government of Canada and conducted by or on behalf of that Government in respect of a contravention of, a conspiracy or attempt to contravene, or counselling the contravention of, any Act of Parliament other than this Act or any regulation made under such an Act, means the Attorney General of Canada and includes his or her lawful deputy,
(b.1) with respect to proceedings in relation to an offence under subsection 7(2.01), means either the Attorney General of Canada or the Attorney General or Solicitor General of the province in which those proceedings are taken and includes the lawful deputy of any of them,
(c) with respect to proceedings in relation to a terrorism offence or to an offence under section 57, 58, 83.12, 424.1 or 431.1 or in relation to an offence against a member of United Nations personnel or associated personnel under section 235, 236, 266, 267, 268, 269, 269.1, 271, 272, 273, 279 or 279.1, means either the Attorney General of Canada or the Attorney General or Solicitor General of the province in which those proceedings are taken and includes the lawful deputy of any of them,
(d) with respect to proceedings in relation to an offence referred to in subsection 7(3.71), or in relation to an offence referred to in paragraph (a) of the definition
(e) with respect to proceedings in relation to an offence where the act or omission constituting the

offence

(i) constitutes a terrorist activity referred to in paragraph (b) of the definition terrorist activity

(ii) was committed outside Canada but is deemed by virtue of subsection 7(3.74) or (3.75) to have been committed in Canada,

means either the Attorney General of Canada or the Attorney General or Solicitor General of the province in which those proceedings are taken and includes the lawful deputy of any of them,

(f) with respect to proceedings under section 83.13, 83.14, 83.222, 83.223, 83.28, 83.29 or 83.3, means either the Attorney General of Canada or the Attorney General or Solicitor General of the province in which those proceedings are taken and includes the lawful deputy of any of them, and

(g) with respect to proceedings in relation to an offence referred to in sections 121.1, 380, 382, 382.1 and 400, means either the Attorney General of Canada or the Attorney General or Solicitor General of the province in which those proceedings are taken and includes the lawful deputy of any of them;

bank-note

(a) issued by or on behalf of a person carrying on the business of banking in or out of Canada, and

(b) issued under the authority of Parliament or under the lawful authority of the government of a state other than Canada,

intended to be used as money or as the equivalent of money, immediately on issue or at some time subsequent thereto, and includes bank bills and bank post bills;

bodily harm

Canadian Forces

cattle

clerk of the court

common-law partner

complainant

counsel

count

court of appeal

court of criminal jurisdiction

(a) a court of general or quarter sessions of the peace, when presided over by a superior court judge,

(a.1) in the Province of Quebec, the Court of Quebec, the municipal court of Montreal and the municipal court of Quebec,

(b) a provincial court judge or judge acting under Part XIX, and

(c) in the Province of Ontario, the Ontario Court of Justice;

criminal organization

criminal organization offence

(a) an offence under section 467.11, 467.111, 467.12 or 467.13, or a serious offence committed for the benefit of, at the direction of, or in association with, a criminal organization, or

(b) a conspiracy or an attempt to commit, being an accessory after the fact in relation to, or any counselling in relation to, an offence referred to in paragraph (a);

day

document of title to goods

document of title to lands

dwelling-house

(a) a building within the curtilage of a dwelling-house that is connected to it by a doorway or by a covered and enclosed passage-way, and

(b) a unit that is designed to be mobile and to be used as a permanent or temporary residence and that is being used as such a residence;

environment

(a) air, land and water,

(b) all layers of the atmosphere,

(c) all organic and inorganic matter and living organisms, and

(d) the interacting natural systems that include components referred to in paragraphs (a) to (c);

every one

person

owner

every one

person

owner

explosive substance

(a) anything intended to be used to make an explosive substance,

(b) anything, or any part thereof, used or intended to be used, or adapted to cause, or to aid in causing an explosion in or with an explosive substance, and

(c) an incendiary grenade, fire bomb, molotov cocktail or other similar incendiary substance or device and a delaying mechanism or other thing intended for use in connection with such a substance or device;

feeble-minded person

firearm

government or public facility

Her Majesty's Forces

highway

indictment

(a) information or a count therein,

(b) a plea, replication or other pleading, and

(c) any record;

internationally protected person

(a) a head of state, including any member of a collegial body that performs the functions of a head of state under the constitution of the state concerned, a head of a government or a minister of foreign affairs, whenever that person is in a state other than the state in which he holds that position or office,

(b) a member of the family of a person described in paragraph (a) who accompanies that person in a state other than the state in which that person holds that position or office,

(c) a representative or an official of a state or an official or agent of an international organization of an intergovernmental character who, at the time when and at the place where an offence referred to in subsection 7(3) is committed against his person or any property referred to in section 431 that is used by him, is entitled, pursuant to international law, to special protection from any attack on his person, freedom or dignity, or

(d) a member of the family of a representative, official or agent described in paragraph (c) who forms part of his household, if the representative, official or agent, at the time when and at the place where any offence referred to in subsection 7(3) is committed against the member of his family or any property referred to in section 431 that is used by that member, is entitled, pursuant to international law, to special protection from any attack on his person, freedom or dignity;

justice

justice system participant

(a) a member of the Senate, of the House of Commons, of a legislative assembly or of a municipal council,

(b) a person who plays a role in the administration of criminal justice, including

(i) the Minister of Public Safety and Emergency Preparedness and a Minister responsible for policing in a province,

(ii) a prosecutor, a lawyer, a member of the Chambre des notaires du Québec and an officer of a court,

(iii) a judge and a justice,

(iv) a juror and a person who is summoned as a juror,

(v) an informant, a prospective witness, a witness under subpoena and a witness who has testified,

(vi) a peace officer within the meaning of any of paragraphs (b), (c), (d), (e) and (g) of the definition

peace officer
(vii) a civilian employee of a police force,
(viii) a person employed in the administration of a court,
(viii.1) a public officer within the meaning of subsection 25.1(1) and a person acting at the direction of such an officer,
(ix) an employee of the Canada Revenue Agency who is involved in the investigation of an offence under an Act of Parliament,
(ix.1) an employee of the Canada Border Services Agency who is involved in the investigation of an offence under an Act of Parliament,
(x) an employee of a federal or provincial correctional service, a parole supervisor and any other person who is involved in the administration of a sentence under the supervision of such a correctional service and a person who conducts disciplinary hearings under the
Corrections and Conditional Release Act
(xi) an employee and a member of the Parole Board of Canada and of a provincial parole board, and
(c) a person who plays a role in respect of proceedings involving
(i) security information,
(ii) criminal intelligence information,
(iii) information that would endanger the safety of any person if it were disclosed,
(iv) information that is obtained in confidence from a source in Canada, the government of a foreign state, an international organization of states or an institution of such a government or international organization, or
(v) potentially injurious information or sensitive information as those terms are defined in section 38 of the
Canada Evidence Act
magistrate
mental disorder
military
military law
motor vehicle
municipality
newly-born child
night
nuclear facility
(a) any nuclear reactor, including a reactor installed on a vessel, vehicle, aircraft or space object for use as an energy source in order to propel the vessel, vehicle, aircraft or space object or for any other purpose, and
(b) any plant or conveyance used for the production, storage, processing or transport of nuclear material or radioactive material;
nuclear material
(a) plutonium, except plutonium with an isotopic concentration of plutonium-238 that is greater than 80%,
(b) uranium-233,
(c) uranium containing uranium-233 or uranium-235 or both in an amount such that the abundance ratio of the sum of those isotopes to the isotope uranium-238 is greater than 0.72%,
(d) uranium with an isotopic concentration equal to that occurring in nature, except uranium in the form of ore or ore-residue, and
(e) any substance containing any material described in paragraphs (a) to (d);
offence-related property
(a) by means or in respect of which an indictable offence under this Act or the
Corruption of Foreign Public Officials Act
(b) that is used in any manner in connection with the commission of such an offence, or
(c) that is intended to be used for committing such an offence;

offender

offensive weapon

organization

(a) a public body, body corporate, society, company, firm, partnership, trade union or municipality, or
(b) an association of persons that
(i) is created for a common purpose,
(ii) has an operational structure, and
(iii) holds itself out to the public as an association of persons;

peace officer

(a) a mayor, warden, reeve, sheriff, deputy sheriff, sheriff's officer and justice of the peace,
(b) a member of the Correctional Service of Canada who is designated as a peace officer pursuant to Part I of the
Corrections and Conditional Release Act
(c) a police officer, police constable, bailiff, constable, or other person employed for the preservation and maintenance of the public peace or for the service or execution of civil process,
(c.1) a designated officer as defined in section 2 of the
Integrated Cross-border Law Enforcement Operations Act
(i) participating in an integrated cross-border operation, as defined in section 2 of that Act, or
(ii) engaging in an activity incidental to such an operation, including travel for the purpose of participating in the operation and appearances in court arising from the operation,
(d) an officer within the meaning of the
Customs Act
Excise Act
Excise Act, 2001
(d.1) an officer authorized under subsection 138(1) of the
Immigration and Refugee Protection Act
(e) a person designated as a fishery guardian under the
Fisheries Act
Coastal Fisheries Protection Act
(f) the pilot in command of an aircraft
(i) registered in Canada under regulations made under the
Aeronautics Act
(ii) leased without crew and operated by a person who is qualified under regulations made under the
Aeronautics Act
while the aircraft is in flight, and
(g) officers and non-commissioned members of the Canadian Forces who are
(i) appointed for the purposes of section 156 of the
National Defence Act
(ii) employed on duties that the Governor in Council, in regulations made under the
National Defence Act

prison

property

(a) real and personal property of every description and deeds and instruments relating to or evidencing the title or right to property, or giving a right to recover or receive money or goods,
(b) property originally in the possession or under the control of any person, and any property into or for which it has been converted or exchanged and anything acquired at any time by the conversion or exchange, and
(c) any postal card, postage stamp or other stamp issued or prepared for issue under the authority of Parliament or the legislature of a province for the payment to the Crown or a corporate body of any fee, rate or duty, whether or not it is in the possession of the Crown or of any person;

prosecutor

provincial court judge

public department
public officer
(a) an officer of customs or excise,
(b) an officer of the Canadian Forces,
(c) an officer of the Royal Canadian Mounted Police, and
(d) any officer while the officer is engaged in enforcing the laws of Canada relating to revenue, customs, excise, trade or navigation;
public stores
radioactive material
railway equipment
(a) any machine that is constructed for movement exclusively on lines of railway, whether or not the machine is capable of independent motion, or
(b) any vehicle that is constructed for movement both on and off lines of railway while the adaptations of that vehicle for movement on lines of railway are in use;
representative
senior officer
serious offence
steal
street racing
superior court of criminal jurisdiction
(a) in the Province of Ontario, the Court of Appeal or the Superior Court of Justice,
(b) in the Province of Quebec, the Superior Court,
(c) in the Provinces of Nova Scotia, British Columbia and Prince Edward Island, the Court of Appeal or the Supreme Court,
(d) in the Provinces of New Brunswick, Manitoba, Saskatchewan and Alberta, the Court of Appeal or the Court of Queen's Bench,
(e) in the Province of Newfoundland and Labrador, Yukon and the Northwest Territories, the Supreme Court, and
(f) in Nunavut, the Nunavut Court of Justice;
(g) and (h) territorial division
territorial division
terrorism offence
(a) an offence under any of sections 83.02 to 83.04 or 83.18 to 83.23,
(b) an indictable offence under this or any other Act of Parliament committed for the benefit of, at the direction of or in association with a terrorist group,
(c) an indictable offence under this or any other Act of Parliament where the act or omission constituting the offence also constitutes a terrorist activity, or
(d) a conspiracy or an attempt to commit, or being an accessory after the fact in relation to, or any counselling in relation to, an offence referred to in paragraph (a), (b) or (c);
terrorist activity
terrorist group
testamentary instrument
trustee
unfit to stand trial
(a) understand the nature or object of the proceedings,
(b) understand the possible consequences of the proceedings, or
(c) communicate with counsel;
United Nations operation
Convention on the Safety of United Nations and Associated Personnel
United Nations personnel
(a) persons who are engaged or deployed by the Secretary-General of the United Nations as members of the military, police or civilian components of a United Nations operation, or

(b) any other officials or experts who are on mission of the United Nations or one of its specialized agencies or the International Atomic Energy Agency and who are present in an official capacity in the area where a United Nations operation is conducted;
valuable mineral
valuable security
(a) an order, exchequer acquittance or other security that entitles or evidences the title of any person
(i) to a share or interest in a public stock or fund or in any fund of a body corporate, company or society, or
(ii) to a deposit in a financial institution,
(b) any debenture, deed, bond, bill, note, warrant, order or other security for money or for payment of money,
(c) a document of title to lands or goods wherever situated,
(d) a stamp or writing that secures or evidences title to or an interest in a chattel personal, or that evidences delivery of a chattel personal, and
(e) a release, receipt, discharge or other instrument evidencing payment of money;
victim
weapon
(a) in causing death or injury to any person, or
(b) for the purpose of threatening or intimidating any person
and, without restricting the generality of the foregoing, includes a firearm and, for the purposes of sections 88, 267 and 272, any thing used, designed to be used or intended for use in binding or tying up a person against their will;
wreck
writing
R.S., 1985, c. C-46, s. 2;
R.S., 1985, c. 11 (1st Supp.), s. 2, c. 27 (1st Supp.), ss. 2, 203, c. 31 (1st Supp.), s. 61, c. 1 (2nd Supp.), s. 213, c. 27 (2nd Supp.), s. 10, c. 35 (2nd Supp.), s. 34, c. 32 (4th Supp.), s. 55, c. 40 (4th Supp.), s. 2;
1990, c. 17, s. 7;
1991, c. 1, s. 28, c. 40, s. 1, c. 43, ss. 1, 9;
1992, c. 20, s. 216, c. 51, s. 32;
1993, c. 28, s. 78, c. 34, s. 59;
1994, c. 44, s. 2;
1995, c. 29, ss. 39, 40, c. 39, s. 138;
1997, c. 23, s. 1;
1998, c. 30, s. 14;
1999, c. 3, s. 25, c. 5, s. 1, c. 25, s. 1(Preamble), c. 28, s. 155;
2000, c. 12, s. 91, c. 25, s. 1(F);
2001, c. 32, s. 1, c. 41, ss. 2, 131;
2002, c. 7, s. 137, c. 22, s. 324;
2003, c. 21, s. 1;
2004, c. 3, s. 1;
2005, c. 10, s. 34, c. 38, s. 58, c. 40, ss. 1, 7;
2006, c. 14, s. 1;
2007, c. 13, s. 1;
2012, c.1, s. 160, c. 19, s. 371;
2013, c. 13, s. 2;
2014, c. 17, s. 1, c. 23, s. 2, c. 25, s. 2;
2015, c. 3, s. 44, c. 13, s. 3, c. 20, s. 15.
Further definitions — firearms
2.1 In this Act,
ammunition

antique firearm
automatic firearm
cartridge magazine
cross-bow
handgun
imitation firearm
prohibited ammunition
prohibited device
prohibited firearm
prohibited weapon
replica firearm
restricted firearm
restricted weapon
authorization
licence
registration certificate
2009, c. 22, s. 1.

Acting on victim's behalf
2.2 (1) For the purposes of sections 606, 672.5, 722, 737.1 and 745.63, any of the following individuals may act on the victim's behalf if the victim is dead or incapable of acting on their own behalf:
(a) the victim's spouse, or if the victim is dead, their spouse at the time of death;
(b) the victim's common-law partner, or if the victim is dead, their common-law partner at the time of death;
(c) a relative or dependant of the victim;
(d) an individual who has in law or fact custody, or is responsible for the care or support, of the victim; and
(e) an individual who has in law or fact custody, or is responsible for the care or support, of a dependant of the victim.

Exception
(2) An individual is not entitled to act on a victim's behalf if the individual is an accused in relation to the offence or alleged offence that resulted in the victim suffering harm or loss or is an individual who is found guilty of that offence or who is found not criminally responsible on account of mental disorder or unfit to stand trial in respect of that offence.
2015, c. 13, s. 4.

Descriptive cross-references
3 Where, in any provision of this Act, a reference to another provision of this Act or a provision of any other Act is followed by words in parenthesis that are or purport to be descriptive of the subject-matter of the provision referred to, the words in parenthesis form no part of the provision in which they occur but shall be deemed to have been inserted for convenience of reference only.
1976-77, c. 53, s. 2.

Part I

General

Effect of judicial acts
3.1 Unless otherwise provided or ordered, anything done by a court, justice or judge is effective from the moment it is done, whether or not it is reduced to writing.
2002, c. 13, s. 2.

Postcard a chattel, value
4 (1) For the purposes of this Act, a postal card or stamp referred to in paragraph (c) of the definition

property

Value of valuable security

(2) For the purposes of this Act, the following rules apply for the purpose of determining the value of a valuable security where value is material:

(a) where the valuable security is one mentioned in paragraph (a) or (b) of the definition valuable security

(b) where the valuable security is one mentioned in paragraph (c) or (d) of the definition valuable security

(c) where the valuable security is one mentioned in paragraph (e) of the definition valuable security

Possession

(3) For the purposes of this Act,

(a) a person has anything in possession when he has it in his personal possession or knowingly

(i) has it in the actual possession or custody of another person, or

(ii) has it in any place, whether or not that place belongs to or is occupied by him, for the use or benefit of himself or of another person; and

(b) where one of two or more persons, with the knowledge and consent of the rest, has anything in his custody or possession, it shall be deemed to be in the custody and possession of each and all of them.

Expressions taken from other Acts

(4) Where an offence that is dealt with in this Act relates to a subject that is dealt with in another Act, the words and expressions used in this Act with respect to that offence have, subject to this Act, the meaning assigned to them in that other Act.

Sexual intercourse

(5) For the purposes of this Act, sexual intercourse is complete on penetration to even the slightest degree, notwithstanding that seed is not emitted.

Proof of notifications and service of documents

(6) For the purposes of this Act, the service of any document and the giving or sending of any notice may be proved

(a) by oral evidence given under oath by, or by the affidavit or solemn declaration of, the person claiming to have served, given or sent it; or

(b) in the case of a peace officer, by a statement in writing certifying that the document was served or the notice was given or sent by the peace officer, and such a statement is deemed to be a statement made under oath.

Proof of service in accordance with provincial laws

(6.1) Despite subsection (6), the service of documents may be proved in accordance with the laws of a province relating to offences created by the laws of that province.

Attendance for examination

(7) Despite subsection (6) or (6.1), the court may require the person who appears to have signed an affidavit, a solemn declaration or a statement in accordance with that subsection to appear before it for examination or cross-examination in respect of the issue of proof of service or of the giving or sending of any notice.

Means of telecommunication

(8) For greater certainty, for the purposes of this Act, if the elements of an offence contain an explicit or implicit element of communication without specifying the means of communication, the communication may also be made by a means of telecommunication.

R.S., 1985, c. C-46, s. 4;
R.S., 1985, c. 27 (1st Supp.), s. 3;
1994, c. 44, s. 3;
1997, c. 18, s. 2;
2008, c. 18, s. 1;
2014, c. 31, s. 2.

Canadian Forces not affected
5 Nothing in this Act affects any law relating to the government of the Canadian Forces.
R.S., c. C-34, s. 4.
Presumption of innocence
6 (1) Where an enactment creates an offence and authorizes a punishment to be imposed in respect of that offence,
(a) a person shall be deemed not to be guilty of the offence until he is convicted or discharged under section 730 of the offence; and
(b) a person who is convicted or discharged under section 730 of the offence is not liable to any punishment in respect thereof other than the punishment prescribed by this Act or by the enactment that creates the offence.
Offences outside Canada
(2) Subject to this Act or any other Act of Parliament, no person shall be convicted or discharged under section 730 of an offence committed outside Canada.
Definition of
enactment
(3) In this section,
enactment
(a) an Act of Parliament, or
(b) an Act of the legislature of a province that creates an offence to which Part XXVII applies, or any regulation made thereunder.
R.S., 1985, c. C-46, s. 6;
R.S., 1985, c. 27 (1st Supp.), s. 4, c. 1 (4th Supp.), s. 18(F);
1995, c. 22, s. 10.
Offences committed on aircraft
7 (1) Notwithstanding anything in this Act or any other Act, every one who
(a) on or in respect of an aircraft
(i) registered in Canada under regulations made under the
Aeronautics Act
(ii) leased without crew and operated by a person who is qualified under regulations made under the
Aeronautics Act
while the aircraft is in flight, or
(b) on any aircraft, while the aircraft is in flight if the flight terminated in Canada,
commits an act or omission in or outside Canada that if committed in Canada would be an offence punishable by indictment shall be deemed to have committed that act or omission in Canada.
Idem
(2) Notwithstanding this Act or any other Act, every one who
(a) on an aircraft, while the aircraft is in flight, commits an act or omission outside Canada that if committed in Canada or on an aircraft registered in Canada under regulations made under the
Aeronautics Act
(b) in relation to an aircraft in service, commits an act or omission outside Canada that if committed in Canada would be an offence against any of paragraphs 77(c), (d) or (g),
(c) in relation to an air navigation facility used in international air navigation, commits an act or omission outside Canada that if committed in Canada would be an offence against paragraph 77(e),
(d) at or in relation to an airport serving international civil aviation, commits an act or omission outside Canada that if committed in Canada would be an offence against paragraph 77(b) or (f), or
(e) commits an act or omission outside Canada that if committed in Canada would constitute a conspiracy or an attempt to commit an offence referred to in this subsection, or being an accessory after the fact or counselling in relation to such an offence,
shall be deemed to have committed that act or omission in Canada if the person is, after the commission thereof, present in Canada.
Offences in relation to cultural property

(2.01) Despite anything in this Act or any other Act, a person who commits an act or omission outside Canada that if committed in Canada would constitute an offence under section 322, 341, 344, 380, 430 or 434 in relation to cultural property as defined in Article 1 of the Convention, or a conspiracy or an attempt to commit such an offence, or being an accessory after the fact or counselling in relation to such an offence, is deemed to have committed that act or omission in Canada if the person
(a) is a Canadian citizen;
(b) is not a citizen of any state and ordinarily resides in Canada; or
(c) is a permanent resident within the meaning of subsection 2(1) of the
Immigration and Refugee Protection Act
Definition of
Convention
(2.02) For the purpose of subsection (2.01),
Convention
Cultural Property Export and Import Act
Offences against fixed platforms or international maritime navigation
(2.1) Notwithstanding anything in this Act or any other Act, every one who commits an act or omission outside Canada against or on board a fixed platform attached to the continental shelf of any state or against or on board a ship navigating or scheduled to navigate beyond the territorial sea of any state, that if committed in Canada would constitute an offence against, a conspiracy or an attempt to commit an offence against, or being an accessory after the fact or counselling in relation to an offence against, section 78.1, shall be deemed to commit that act or omission in Canada if it is committed
(a) against or on board a fixed platform attached to the continental shelf of Canada;
(b) against or on board a ship registered or licensed, or for which an identification number has been issued, pursuant to any Act of Parliament;
(c) by a Canadian citizen;
(d) by a person who is not a citizen of any state and who ordinarily resides in Canada;
(e) by a person who is, after the commission of the offence, present in Canada;
(f) in such a way as to seize, injure or kill, or threaten to injure or kill, a Canadian citizen; or
(g) in an attempt to compel the Government of Canada to do or refrain from doing any act.
Offences against fixed platforms or navigation in the internal waters or territorial sea of another state
(2.2) Notwithstanding anything in this Act or any other Act, every one who commits an act or omission outside Canada against or on board a fixed platform not attached to the continental shelf of any state or against or on board a ship not navigating or scheduled to navigate beyond the territorial sea of any state, that if committed in Canada would constitute an offence against, a conspiracy or an attempt to commit an offence against, or being an accessory after the fact or counselling in relation to an offence against, section 78.1, shall be deemed to commit that act or omission in Canada
(a) if it is committed as described in any of paragraphs (2.1)(b) to (g); and
(b) if the offender is found in the territory of a state, other than the state in which the act or omission was committed, that is
(i) a party to the Convention for the Suppression of Unlawful Acts against the Safety of Maritime Navigation, done at Rome on March 10, 1988, in respect of an offence committed against or on board a ship, or
(ii) a party to the Protocol for the Suppression of Unlawful Acts against the Safety of Fixed Platforms Located on the Continental Shelf, done at Rome on March 10, 1988, in respect of an offence committed against or on board a fixed platform.
Nuclear terrorism offence committed outside Canada
(2.21) Despite anything in this Act or any other Act, everyone who commits an act or omission outside Canada that if committed in Canada would constitute an offence under any of sections 82.3 to 82.6, or a conspiracy or attempt to commit such an offence, or being an accessory after the fact or

counselling in relation to such an offence, is deemed to have committed that act or omission in Canada if
(a) the act or omission is committed on a ship that is registered or licensed, or for which an identification number has been issued, under any Act of Parliament;
(b) the act or omission is committed on an aircraft that
(i) is registered in Canada under regulations made under the
Aeronautics Act
(ii) is leased without crew and operated by a person who is qualified under regulations made under the
Aeronautics Act
(c) the person who commits the act or omission is a Canadian citizen; or
(d) the person who commits the act or omission is, after the commission of the act or omission, present in Canada.

Space Station — Canadian crew members
(2.3) Despite anything in this Act or any other Act, a Canadian crew member who, during a space flight, commits an act or omission outside Canada that if committed in Canada would constitute an indictable offence is deemed to have committed that act or omission in Canada, if that act or omission is committed
(a) on, or in relation to, a flight element of the Space Station; or
(b) on any means of transportation to or from the Space Station.

Space Station — crew members of Partner States
(2.31) Despite anything in this Act or any other Act, a crew member of a Partner State who commits an act or omission outside Canada during a space flight on, or in relation to, a flight element of the Space Station or on any means of transportation to and from the Space Station that if committed in Canada would constitute an indictable offence is deemed to have committed that act or omission in Canada, if that act or omission
(a) threatens the life or security of a Canadian crew member; or
(b) is committed on or in relation to, or damages, a flight element provided by Canada.

Proceedings by Attorney General of Canada
(2.32) Despite the definition
Attorney General

Consent of Attorney General of Canada
(2.33) No proceedings in relation to an offence referred to in subsection (2.3) or (2.31) may be instituted without the consent of the Attorney General of Canada.

Definitions
(2.34) The definitions in this subsection apply in this subsection and in subsections (2.3) and (2.31).
Agreement
Civil International Space Station Agreement Implementation Act
Canadian crew member
(a) a Canadian citizen; or
(b) a citizen of a foreign state, other than a Partner State, who is authorized by Canada to act as a crew member for a space flight on, or in relation to, a flight element.
crew member of a Partner State
(a) a citizen of a Partner State; or
(b) a citizen of a state, other than that Partner State, who is authorized by that Partner State to act as a crew member for a space flight on, or in relation to, a flight element.
flight element
Partner State
space flight
Space Station

Offence against internationally protected person
(3) Notwithstanding anything in this Act or any other Act, every one who, outside Canada, commits

an act or omission against the person of an internationally protected person or against any property referred to in section 431 used by that person that, if committed in Canada, would be an offence against any of sections 235, 236, 266, 267, 268, 269, 269.1, 271, 272, 273, 279, 279.1, 280 to 283, 424 and 431 is deemed to commit that act or omission in Canada if
(a) the act or omission is committed on a ship that is registered or licensed, or for which an identification number has been issued, pursuant to any Act of Parliament;
(b) the act or omission is committed on an aircraft
(i) registered in Canada under regulations made under the
Aeronautics Act
(ii) leased without crew and operated by a person who is qualified under regulations made under the Aeronautics Act
(c) the person who commits the act or omission is a Canadian citizen or is, after the act or omission has been committed, present in Canada; or
(d) the act or omission is against
(i) a person who enjoys the status of an internationally protected person by virtue of the functions that person performs on behalf of Canada, or
(ii) a member of the family of a person described in subparagraph (i) who qualifies under paragraph (b) or (d) of the definition
internationally protected person

Offence of hostage taking
(3.1) Notwithstanding anything in this Act or any other Act, every one who, outside Canada, commits an act or omission that if committed in Canada would be an offence against section 279.1 shall be deemed to commit that act or omission in Canada if
(a) the act or omission is committed on a ship that is registered or licensed, or for which an identification number has been issued, pursuant to any Act of Parliament;
(b) the act or omission is committed on an aircraft
(i) registered in Canada under regulations made under the
Aeronautics Act
(ii) leased without crew and operated by a person who is qualified under regulations made under the Aeronautics Act
(c) the person who commits the act or omission
(i) is a Canadian citizen, or
(ii) is not a citizen of any state and ordinarily resides in Canada;
(d) the act or omission is committed with intent to induce Her Majesty in right of Canada or of a province to commit or cause to be committed any act or omission;
(e) a person taken hostage by the act or omission is a Canadian citizen; or
(f) the person who commits the act or omission is, after the commission thereof, present in Canada.
(3.2) to (3.6) Jurisdiction
(3.7) Notwithstanding anything in this Act or any other Act, every one who, outside Canada, commits an act or omission that, if committed in Canada, would constitute an offence against, a conspiracy or an attempt to commit an offence against, being an accessory after the fact in relation to an offence against, or any counselling in relation to an offence against, section 269.1 shall be deemed to commit that act or omission in Canada if
(a) the act or omission is committed on a ship that is registered or licensed, or for which an identification number has been issued, pursuant to any Act of Parliament;
(b) the act or omission is committed on an aircraft
(i) registered in Canada under regulations made under the
Aeronautics Act
(ii) leased without crew and operated by a person who is qualified under regulations made under the Aeronautics Act
(c) the person who commits the act or omission is a Canadian citizen;
(d) the complainant is a Canadian citizen; or

(e) the person who commits the act or omission is, after the commission thereof, present in Canada.

Offence against United Nations or associated personnel

(3.71) Notwithstanding anything in this Act or any other Act, every one who, outside Canada, commits an act or omission against a member of United Nations personnel or associated personnel or against property referred to in section 431.1 that, if committed in Canada, would constitute an offence against, a conspiracy or an attempt to commit an offence against, or being an accessory after the fact or counselling in relation to an offence against, section 235, 236, 266, 267, 268, 269, 269.1, 271, 272, 273, 279, 279.1, 424.1 or 431.1 is deemed to commit that act or omission in Canada if
(a) the act or omission is committed on a ship that is registered or licensed, or for which an identification number has been issued, under an Act of Parliament;
(b) the act or omission is committed on an aircraft
(i) registered in Canada under regulations made under the
Aeronautics Act
(ii) leased without crew and operated by a person who is qualified under regulations made under the
Aeronautics Act
(c) the person who commits the act or omission
(i) is a Canadian citizen, or
(ii) is not a citizen of any state and ordinarily resides in Canada;
(d) the person who commits the act or omission is, after the commission of the act or omission, present in Canada;
(e) the act or omission is committed against a Canadian citizen; or
(f) the act or omission is committed with intent to compel the Government of Canada or of a province to do or refrain from doing any act.

Offence involving explosive or other lethal device

(3.72) Notwithstanding anything in this Act or any other Act, every one who, outside Canada, commits an act or omission that, if committed in Canada, would constitute an offence against, a conspiracy or an attempt to commit an offence against, or being an accessory after the fact or counselling in relation to an offence against, section 431.2 is deemed to commit that act or omission in Canada if
(a) the act or omission is committed on a ship that is registered or licensed, or for which an identification number has been issued, under any Act of Parliament;
(b) the act or omission is committed on an aircraft
(i) registered in Canada under regulations made under the
Aeronautics Act
(ii) leased without crew and operated by a person who is qualified under regulations made under the
Aeronautics Act
(iii) operated for or on behalf of the Government of Canada;
(c) the person who commits the act or omission
(i) is a Canadian citizen, or
(ii) is not a citizen of any state and ordinarily resides in Canada;
(d) the person who commits the act or omission is, after the commission of the act or omission, present in Canada;
(e) the act or omission is committed against a Canadian citizen;
(f) the act or omission is committed with intent to compel the Government of Canada or of a province to do or refrain from doing any act; or
(g) the act or omission is committed against a Canadian government or public facility located outside Canada.

Offence relating to financing of terrorism

(3.73) Notwithstanding anything in this Act or any other Act, every one who, outside Canada, commits an act or omission that, if committed in Canada, would constitute an offence against, a conspiracy or an attempt to commit an offence against, or being an accessory after the fact or counselling in relation to an offence against, section 83.02 is deemed to commit the act or omission in Canada if

(a) the act or omission is committed on a ship that is registered or licensed, or for which an identification number has been issued, under an Act of Parliament;

(b) the act or omission is committed on an aircraft

(i) registered in Canada under regulations made under the

Aeronautics Act

(ii) leased without crew and operated by a person who is qualified under regulations made under the Aeronautics Act

(c) the person who commits the act or omission

(i) is a Canadian citizen, or

(ii) is not a citizen of any state and ordinarily resides in Canada;

(d) the person who commits the act or omission is, after its commission, present in Canada;

(e) the act or omission is committed for the purpose of committing an act or omission referred to in paragraph 83.02(a) or (b) in order to compel the Government of Canada or of a province to do or refrain from doing any act;

(f) the act or omission is committed for the purpose of committing an act or omission referred to in paragraph 83.02(a) or (b) against a Canadian government or public facility located outside Canada; or

(g) the act or omission is committed for the purpose of committing an act or omission referred to in paragraph 83.02(a) or (b) in Canada or against a Canadian citizen.

Terrorism offence committed outside Canada

(3.74) Notwithstanding anything in this Act or any other Act, every one who commits an act or omission outside Canada that, if committed in Canada, would be a terrorism offence, other than an offence under section 83.02 or an offence referred to in paragraph (a) of the definition

terrorist activity

(a) is a Canadian citizen;

(b) is not a citizen of any state and ordinarily resides in Canada; or

(c) is a permanent resident within the meaning of subsection 2(1) of the

Immigration and Refugee Protection Act

Terrorist activity committed outside Canada

(3.75) Notwithstanding anything in this Act or any other Act, every one who commits an act or omission outside Canada that, if committed in Canada, would be an indictable offence and would also constitute a terrorist activity referred to in paragraph (b) of the definition

terrorist activity

(a) the act or omission is committed against a Canadian citizen;

(b) the act or omission is committed against a Canadian government or public facility located outside Canada; or

(c) the act or omission is committed with intent to compel the Government of Canada or of a province to do or refrain from doing any act.

(3.76) and (3.77) Offences by Public Service employees

(4) Every one who, while employed as an employee within the meaning of the

Public Service Employment Act

Offence in relation to sexual offences against children

(4.1) Notwithstanding anything in this Act or any other Act, every one who, outside Canada, commits an act or omission that if committed in Canada would be an offence against section 151, 152, 153, 155 or 159, subsection 160(2) or (3), section 163.1, 170, 171, 171.1, 172.1, 172.2 or 173 or subsection 286.1(2) shall be deemed to commit that act or omission in Canada if the person who commits the act or omission is a Canadian citizen or a permanent resident within the meaning of subsection 2(1) of the

Immigration and Refugee Protection Act

Offence in relation to trafficking in persons

(4.11) Notwithstanding anything in this Act or any other Act, every one who, outside Canada,

commits an act or omission that if committed in Canada would be an offence against section 279.01, 279.011, 279.02 or 279.03 shall be deemed to commit that act or omission in Canada if the person who commits the act or omission is a Canadian citizen or a permanent resident within the meaning of subsection 2(1) of the
Immigration and Refugee Protection Act
(4.2) Consent of Attorney General
(4.3) Proceedings with respect to an act or omission deemed to have been committed in Canada under subsection (4.1) may only be instituted with the consent of the Attorney General.
Jurisdiction
(5) Where a person is alleged to have committed an act or omission that is an offence by virtue of this section, proceedings in respect of that offence may, whether or not that person is in Canada, be commenced in any territorial division in Canada and the accused may be tried and punished in respect of that offence in the same manner as if the offence had been committed in that territorial division.
Appearance of accused at trial
(5.1) For greater certainty, the provisions of this Act relating to
(a) requirements that an accused appear at and be present during proceedings, and
(b) the exceptions to those requirements,
apply to proceedings commenced in any territorial division pursuant to subsection (5).
Where previously tried outside Canada
(6) Where a person is alleged to have committed an act or omission that is an offence by virtue of this section and that person has been tried and dealt with outside Canada in respect of the offence in such a manner that, if that person had been tried and dealt with in Canada, he would be able to plead
If accused not Canadian citizen
(7) If the accused is not a Canadian citizen, no proceedings in respect of which courts have jurisdiction by virtue of this section shall be continued unless the consent of the Attorney General of Canada is obtained not later than eight days after the proceedings are commenced.
Definition of
flight
in flight
(8) For the purposes of this section, of the definition
peace officer
flight
(a) the time at which any such door is opened for the purpose of disembarkation, and
(b) where the aircraft makes a forced landing in circumstances in which the owner or operator thereof or a person acting on behalf of either of them is not in control of the aircraft, the time at which control of the aircraft is restored to the owner or operator thereof or a person acting on behalf of either of them.
Definition of
in service
(9) For the purposes of this section and section 77, an aircraft shall be deemed to be in service from the time when pre-flight preparation of the aircraft by ground personnel or the crew thereof begins for a specific flight until
(a) the flight is cancelled before the aircraft is in flight,
(b) twenty-four hours after the aircraft, having commenced the flight, lands, or
(c) the aircraft, having commenced the flight, ceases to be in flight,
whichever is the latest.
Certificate as evidence
(10) In any proceedings under this Act, a certificate purporting to have been issued by or under the authority of the Minister of Foreign Affairs is admissible in evidence without proof of the signature or authority of the person appearing to have signed it and, in the absence of evidence to the contrary, is proof of the facts it states that are relevant to the question of whether any person is a member of

United Nations personnel, a member of associated personnel or a person who is entitled under international law to protection from attack or threat of attack against his or her person, freedom or dignity.

Idem

(11) A certificate purporting to have been issued by or under the authority of the Minister of Foreign Affairs stating

(a) that at a certain time any state was engaged in an armed conflict against Canada or was allied with Canada in an armed conflict,

(b) that at a certain time any convention, treaty or other international agreement was or was not in force and that Canada was or was not a party thereto, or

(c) that Canada agreed or did not agree to accept and apply the provisions of any convention, treaty or other international agreement in an armed conflict in which Canada was involved,

is admissible in evidence in any proceedings without proof of the signature or authority of the person appearing to have issued it, and is proof of the facts so stated.

R.S., 1985, c. C-46, s. 7;
R.S., 1985, c. 27 (1st Supp.), s. 5, c. 10 (3rd Supp.), s. 1, c. 30 (3rd Supp.), s. 1, c. 1 (4th Supp.), s. 18(F);
1992, c. 1, ss. 58, 60(F);
1993, c. 7, s. 1;
1995, c. 5, s. 25;
1997, c. 16, s. 1;
1999, c. 35, s. 11;
2000, c. 24, s. 42;
2001, c. 27, s. 244, c. 41, ss. 3, 126;
2002, c. 13, s. 3;
2004, c. 12, s. 1;
2005, c. 40, s. 2;
2012, c. 1, s. 10, c. 15, s. 1;
2013, c. 9, s. 2, c. 13, s. 3;
2014, c. 25, s. 3.

Application to territories

8 (1) The provisions of this Act apply throughout Canada except

(a) in Yukon, in so far as they are inconsistent with the

Yukon Act

(b) in the Northwest Territories, in so far as they are inconsistent with the

Northwest Territories Act

(c) in Nunavut, in so far as they are inconsistent with the

Nunavut Act

Application of criminal law of England

(2) The criminal law of England that was in force in a province immediately before April 1, 1955 continues in force in the province except as altered, varied, modified or affected by this Act or any other Act of the Parliament of Canada.

Common law principles continued

(3) Every rule and principle of the common law that renders any circumstance a justification or excuse for an act or a defence to a charge continues in force and applies in respect of proceedings for an offence under this Act or any other Act of Parliament except in so far as they are altered by or are inconsistent with this Act or any other Act of Parliament.

R.S., 1985, c. C-46, s. 8;
1993, c. 28, s. 78;
2002, c. 7, s. 138.

Criminal offences to be under law of Canada

9 Notwithstanding anything in this Act or any other Act, no person shall be convicted or discharged under section 730

(a) of an offence at common law,

(b) of an offence under an Act of the Parliament of England, or of Great Britain, or of the United Kingdom of Great Britain and Ireland, or

(c) of an offence under an Act or ordinance in force in any province, territory or place before that province, territory or place became a province of Canada,

but nothing in this section affects the power, jurisdiction or authority that a court, judge, justice or provincial court judge had, immediately before April 1, 1955, to impose punishment for contempt of court.

R.S., 1985, c. C-46, s. 9;
R.S., 1985, c. 27 (1st Supp.), s. 6, c. 1 (4th Supp.), s. 18(F);
1995, c. 22, s. 10.

Appeal

10 (1) Where a court, judge, justice or provincial court judge summarily convicts a person for a contempt of court committed in the face of the court and imposes punishment in respect thereof, that person may appeal

(a) from the conviction; or

(b) against the punishment imposed.

Idem

(2) Where a court or judge summarily convicts a person for a contempt of court not committed in the face of the court and punishment is imposed in respect thereof, that person may appeal

(a) from the conviction; or

(b) against the punishment imposed.

Part XXI applies

(3) An appeal under this section lies to the court of appeal of the province in which the proceedings take place, and, for the purposes of this section, the provisions of Part XXI apply, with such modifications as the circumstances require.

R.S., 1985, c. C-46, s. 10;
R.S., 1985, c. 27 (1st Supp.), s. 203.

Civil remedy not suspended

11 No civil remedy for an act or omission is suspended or affected by reason that the act or omission is a criminal offence.

R.S., c. C-34, s. 10.

Offence punishable under more than one Act

12 Where an act or omission is an offence under more than one Act of Parliament, whether punishable by indictment or on summary conviction, a person who does the act or makes the omission is, unless a contrary intention appears, subject to proceedings under any of those Acts, but is not liable to be punished more than once for the same offence.

R.S., c. C-34, s. 11.

Child under twelve

13 No person shall be convicted of an offence in respect of an act or omission on his part while that person was under the age of twelve years.

R.S., c. C-34, s. 12;
1980-81-82-83, c. 110, s. 72.

Consent to death

14 No person is entitled to consent to have death inflicted on them, and such consent does not affect the criminal responsibility of any person who inflicts death on the person who gave consent.

R.S., 1985, c. C-46, s. 14;
2016, c. 3, s. 1.

Obedience to

15 No person shall be convicted of an offence in respect of an act or omission in obedience to the

laws for the time being made and enforced by persons in
R.S., c. C-34, s. 15.

Defence of mental disorder

16 (1) No person is criminally responsible for an act committed or an omission made while suffering from a mental disorder that rendered the person incapable of appreciating the nature and quality of the act or omission or of knowing that it was wrong.

Presumption

(2) Every person is presumed not to suffer from a mental disorder so as to be exempt from criminal responsibility by virtue of subsection (1), until the contrary is proved on the balance of probabilities.

Burden of proof

(3) The burden of proof that an accused was suffering from a mental disorder so as to be exempt from criminal responsibility is on the party that raises the issue.
R.S., 1985, c. C-46, s. 16;
R.S., 1985, c. 27 (1st Supp.), s. 185(F);
1991, c. 43, s. 2.

Compulsion by threats

17 A person who commits an offence under compulsion by threats of immediate death or bodily harm from a person who is present when the offence is committed is excused for committing the offence if the person believes that the threats will be carried out and if the person is not a party to a conspiracy or association whereby the person is subject to compulsion, but this section does not apply where the offence that is committed is high treason or treason, murder, piracy, attempted murder, sexual assault, sexual assault with a weapon, threats to a third party or causing bodily harm, aggravated sexual assault, forcible abduction, hostage taking, robbery, assault with a weapon or causing bodily harm, aggravated assault, unlawfully causing bodily harm, arson or an offence under sections 280 to 283 (abduction and detention of young persons).
R.S., 1985, c. C-46, s. 17;
R.S., 1985, c. 27 (1st Supp.), s. 40.

Compulsion of spouse

18 No presumption arises that a married person who commits an offence does so under compulsion by reason only that the offence is committed in the presence of the spouse of that married person.
R.S., c. C-34, s. 18;
1980-81-82-83, c. 125, s. 4.

Ignorance of the law

19 Ignorance of the law by a person who commits an offence is not an excuse for committing that offence.
R.S., c. C-34, s. 19.

Certain acts on holidays valid

20 A warrant or summons that is authorized by this Act or an appearance notice, promise to appear, undertaking or recognizance issued, given or entered into in accordance with Part XVI, XXI or XXVII may be issued, executed, given or entered into, as the case may be, on a holiday.
R.S., c. C-34, s. 20;
R.S., c. 2(2nd Supp.), s. 2.

Parties to Offences

Parties to offence

21 (1) Every one is a party to an offence who
(a) actually commits it;
(b) does or omits to do anything for the purpose of aiding any person to commit it; or
(c) abets any person in committing it.

Common intention

(2) Where two or more persons form an intention in common to carry out an unlawful purpose and to

assist each other therein and any one of them, in carrying out the common purpose, commits an offence, each of them who knew or ought to have known that the commission of the offence would be a probable consequence of carrying out the common purpose is a party to that offence.
R.S., c. C-34, s. 21.

Person counselling offence

22 (1) Where a person counsels another person to be a party to an offence and that other person is afterwards a party to that offence, the person who counselled is a party to that offence, notwithstanding that the offence was committed in a way different from that which was counselled.

Idem

(2) Every one who counsels another person to be a party to an offence is a party to every offence that the other commits in consequence of the counselling that the person who counselled knew or ought to have known was likely to be committed in consequence of the counselling.

Definition of
counsel

(3) For the purposes of this Act,
counsel
R.S., 1985, c. C-46, s. 22;
R.S., 1985, c. 27 (1st Supp.), s. 7.

Offences of negligence — organizations

22.1 In respect of an offence that requires the prosecution to prove negligence, an organization is a party to the offence if
(a) acting within the scope of their authority
(i) one of its representatives is a party to the offence, or
(ii) two or more of its representatives engage in conduct, whether by act or omission, such that, if it had been the conduct of only one representative, that representative would have been a party to the offence; and
(b) the senior officer who is responsible for the aspect of the organization's activities that is relevant to the offence departs — or the senior officers, collectively, depart — markedly from the standard of care that, in the circumstances, could reasonably be expected to prevent a representative of the organization from being a party to the offence.
2003, c. 21, s. 2.

Other offences — organizations

22.2 In respect of an offence that requires the prosecution to prove fault — other than negligence — an organization is a party to the offence if, with the intent at least in part to benefit the organization, one of its senior officers
(a) acting within the scope of their authority, is a party to the offence;
(b) having the mental state required to be a party to the offence and acting within the scope of their authority, directs the work of other representatives of the organization so that they do the act or make the omission specified in the offence; or
(c) knowing that a representative of the organization is or is about to be a party to the offence, does not take all reasonable measures to stop them from being a party to the offence.
2003, c. 21, s. 2.

Accessory after the fact

23 (1) An accessory after the fact to an offence is one who, knowing that a person has been a party to the offence, receives, comforts or assists that person for the purpose of enabling that person to escape.
(2) R.S., 1985, c. C-46, s. 23;
2000, c. 12, s. 92.

Where one party cannot be convicted

23.1 For greater certainty, sections 21 to 23 apply in respect of an accused notwithstanding the fact that the person whom the accused aids or abets, counsels or procures or receives, comforts or assists cannot be convicted of the offence.

R.S., 1985, c. 24 (2nd Supp.), s. 45.
Attempts
24 (1) Every one who, having an intent to commit an offence, does or omits to do anything for the purpose of carrying out the intention is guilty of an attempt to commit the offence whether or not it was possible under the circumstances to commit the offence.
Question of law
(2) The question whether an act or omission by a person who has an intent to commit an offence is or is not mere preparation to commit the offence, and too remote to constitute an attempt to commit the offence, is a question of law.
R.S., c. C-34, s. 24.

Protection of Persons Administering and Enforcing the Law

Protection of persons acting under authority
25 (1) Every one who is required or authorized by law to do anything in the administration or enforcement of the law
(a) as a private person,
(b) as a peace officer or public officer,
(c) in aid of a peace officer or public officer, or
(d) by virtue of his office,
is, if he acts on reasonable grounds, justified in doing what he is required or authorized to do and in using as much force as is necessary for that purpose.
Idem
(2) Where a person is required or authorized by law to execute a process or to carry out a sentence, that person or any person who assists him is, if that person acts in good faith, justified in executing the process or in carrying out the sentence notwithstanding that the process or sentence is defective or that it was issued or imposed without jurisdiction or in excess of jurisdiction.
When not protected
(3) Subject to subsections (4) and (5), a person is not justified for the purposes of subsection (1) in using force that is intended or is likely to cause death or grievous bodily harm unless the person believes on reasonable grounds that it is necessary for the self-preservation of the person or the preservation of any one under that person's protection from death or grievous bodily harm.
When protected
(4) A peace officer, and every person lawfully assisting the peace officer, is justified in using force that is intended or is likely to cause death or grievous bodily harm to a person to be arrested, if
(a) the peace officer is proceeding lawfully to arrest, with or without warrant, the person to be arrested;
(b) the offence for which the person is to be arrested is one for which that person may be arrested without warrant;
(c) the person to be arrested takes flight to avoid arrest;
(d) the peace officer or other person using the force believes on reasonable grounds that the force is necessary for the purpose of protecting the peace officer, the person lawfully assisting the peace officer or any other person from imminent or future death or grievous bodily harm; and
(e) the flight cannot be prevented by reasonable means in a less violent manner.
Power in case of escape from penitentiary
(5) A peace officer is justified in using force that is intended or is likely to cause death or grievous bodily harm against an inmate who is escaping from a penitentiary within the meaning of subsection 2(1) of the
Corrections and Conditional Release Act,
(a) the peace officer believes on reasonable grounds that any of the inmates of the penitentiary poses a threat of death or grievous bodily harm to the peace officer or any other person; and
(b) the escape cannot be prevented by reasonable means in a less violent manner.

R.S., 1985, c. C-46, s. 25;
1994, c. 12, s. 1.

Definitions

25.1 (1) The following definitions apply in this section and sections 25.2 to 25.4.

competent authority

(a) in the case of a member of the Royal Canadian Mounted Police, the Minister of Public Safety and Emergency Preparedness, personally;

(b) in the case of a member of a police service constituted under the laws of a province, the Minister responsible for policing in the province, personally; and

(c) in the case of any other public officer or senior official, the Minister who has responsibility for the Act of Parliament that the officer or official has the power to enforce, personally.

public officer

senior official

Principle

(2) It is in the public interest to ensure that public officers may effectively carry out their law enforcement duties in accordance with the rule of law and, to that end, to expressly recognize in law a justification for public officers and other persons acting at their direction to commit acts or omissions that would otherwise constitute offences.

Designation of public officers

(3) A competent authority may designate public officers for the purposes of this section and sections 25.2 to 25.4.

Condition — civilian oversight

(3.1) A competent authority referred to in paragraph (a) or (b) of the definition of that term in subsection (1) may not designate any public officer under subsection (3) unless there is a public authority composed of persons who are not peace officers that may review the public officer's conduct.

Declaration as evidence

(3.2) The Governor in Council or the lieutenant governor in council of a province, as the case may be, may designate a person or body as a public authority for the purposes of subsection (3.1), and that designation is conclusive evidence that the person or body is a public authority described in that subsection.

Considerations

(4) The competent authority shall make designations under subsection (3) on the advice of a senior official and shall consider the nature of the duties performed by the public officer in relation to law enforcement generally, rather than in relation to any particular investigation or enforcement activity.

Designation of senior officials

(5) A competent authority may designate senior officials for the purposes of this section and sections 25.2 to 25.4.

Emergency designation

(6) A senior official may designate a public officer for the purposes of this section and sections 25.2 to 25.4 for a period of not more than 48 hours if the senior official is of the opinion that

(a) by reason of exigent circumstances, it is not feasible for the competent authority to designate a public officer under subsection (3); and

(b) in the circumstances of the case, the public officer would be justified in committing an act or omission that would otherwise constitute an offence.

The senior official shall without delay notify the competent authority of the designation.

Conditions

(7) A designation under subsection (3) or (6) may be made subject to conditions, including conditions limiting

(a) the duration of the designation;

(b) the nature of the conduct in the investigation of which a public officer may be justified in committing, or directing another person to commit, acts or omissions that would otherwise constitute an offence; and

(c) the acts or omissions that would otherwise constitute an offence and that a public officer may be justified in committing or directing another person to commit.

Justification for acts or omissions

(8) A public officer is justified in committing an act or omission — or in directing the commission of an act or omission under subsection (10) — that would otherwise constitute an offence if the public officer

(a) is engaged in the investigation of an offence under, or the enforcement of, an Act of Parliament or in the investigation of criminal activity;

(b) is designated under subsection (3) or (6); and

(c) believes on reasonable grounds that the commission of the act or omission, as compared to the nature of the offence or criminal activity being investigated, is reasonable and proportional in the circumstances, having regard to such matters as the nature of the act or omission, the nature of the investigation and the reasonable availability of other means for carrying out the public officer's law enforcement duties.

Requirements for certain acts

(9) No public officer is justified in committing an act or omission that would otherwise constitute an offence and that would be likely to result in loss of or serious damage to property, or in directing the commission of an act or omission under subsection (10), unless, in addition to meeting the conditions set out in paragraphs (8)(a) to (c), he or she

(a) is personally authorized in writing to commit the act or omission — or direct its commission — by a senior official who believes on reasonable grounds that committing the act or omission, as compared to the nature of the offence or criminal activity being investigated, is reasonable and proportional in the circumstances, having regard to such matters as the nature of the act or omission, the nature of the investigation and the reasonable availability of other means for carrying out the public officer's law enforcement duties; or

(b) believes on reasonable grounds that the grounds for obtaining an authorization under paragraph (a) exist but it is not feasible in the circumstances to obtain the authorization and that the act or omission is necessary to

(i) preserve the life or safety of any person,

(ii) prevent the compromise of the identity of a public officer acting in an undercover capacity, of a confidential informant or of a person acting covertly under the direction and control of a public officer, or

(iii) prevent the imminent loss or destruction of evidence of an indictable offence.

Person acting at direction of public officer

(10) A person who commits an act or omission that would otherwise constitute an offence is justified in committing it if

(a) a public officer directs him or her to commit that act or omission and the person believes on reasonable grounds that the public officer has the authority to give that direction; and

(b) he or she believes on reasonable grounds that the commission of that act or omission is for the purpose of assisting the public officer in the public officer's law enforcement duties.

Limitation

(11) Nothing in this section justifies

(a) the intentional or criminally negligent causing of death or bodily harm to another person;

(b) the wilful attempt in any manner to obstruct, pervert or defeat the course of justice; or

(c) conduct that would violate the sexual integrity of an individual.

Protection, defences and immunities unaffected

(12) Nothing in this section affects the protection, defences and immunities of peace officers and other persons recognized under the law of Canada.

Compliance with requirements

(13) Nothing in this section relieves a public officer of criminal liability for failing to comply with any other requirements that govern the collection of evidence.

Exception: offences under
Controlled Drugs and Substances Act
(14) Nothing in this section justifies a public officer or a person acting at his or her direction in committing an act or omission — or a public officer in directing the commission of an act or omission — that constitutes an offence under a provision of Part I of the
Controlled Drugs and Substances Act
2001, c. 32, s. 2;
2005, c. 10, s. 34.

Public officer to file report
25.2 Every public officer who commits an act or omission — or directs the commission by another person of an act or omission — under paragraph 25.1(9)(a) or (b) shall, as soon as is feasible after the commission of the act or omission, file a written report with the appropriate senior official describing the act or omission.
2001, c. 32, s. 2.

Annual report
25.3 (1) Every competent authority shall publish or otherwise make available to the public an annual report for the previous year that includes, in respect of public officers and senior officials designated by the competent authority,
(a) the number of designations made under subsection 25.1(6) by the senior officials;
(b) the number of authorizations made under paragraph 25.1(9)(a) by the senior officials;
(c) the number of times that acts and omissions were committed in accordance with paragraph 25.1(9)(b) by the public officers;
(d) the nature of the conduct being investigated when the designations referred to in paragraph (a) or the authorizations referred to in paragraph (b) were made or when the acts or omissions referred to in paragraph (c) were committed; and
(e) the nature of the acts or omissions committed under the designations referred to in paragraph (a), under the authorizations referred to in paragraph (b) and in the manner described in paragraph (c).

Limitation
(2) The annual report shall not contain any information the disclosure of which would
(a) compromise or hinder an ongoing investigation of an offence under an Act of Parliament;
(b) compromise the identity of a public officer acting in an undercover capacity, of a confidential informant or of a person acting covertly under the direction and control of a public officer;
(c) endanger the life or safety of any person;
(d) prejudice a legal proceeding; or
(e) otherwise be contrary to the public interest.
2001, c. 32, s. 2.

Written notification to be given
25.4 (1) When a public officer commits an act or omission — or directs the commission by another person of an act or omission — under paragraph 25.1(9)(a) or (b), the senior official with whom the public officer files a written report under section 25.2 shall, as soon as is feasible after the report is filed, and no later than one year after the commission of the act or omission, notify in writing any person whose property was lost or seriously damaged as a result of the act or omission.

Limitation
(2) The competent authority may authorize the senior official not to notify the person under subsection (1) until the competent authority is of the opinion that notification would not
(a) compromise or hinder an ongoing investigation of an offence under an Act of Parliament;
(b) compromise the identity of a public officer acting in an undercover capacity, of a confidential informant or of a person acting covertly under the direction and control of a public officer;
(c) endanger the life or safety of any person;
(d) prejudice a legal proceeding; or
(e) otherwise be contrary to the public interest.
2001, c. 32, s. 2.

Excessive force
26 Every one who is authorized by law to use force is criminally responsible for any excess thereof according to the nature and quality of the act that constitutes the excess.
R.S., c. C-34, s. 26.
Use of force to prevent commission of offence
27 Every one is justified in using as much force as is reasonably necessary
(a) to prevent the commission of an offence
(i) for which, if it were committed, the person who committed it might be arrested without warrant, and
(ii) that would be likely to cause immediate and serious injury to the person or property of anyone; or
(b) to prevent anything being done that, on reasonable grounds, he believes would, if it were done, be an offence mentioned in paragraph (a).
R.S., c. C-34, s. 27.
Use of force on board an aircraft
27.1 (1) Every person on an aircraft in flight is justified in using as much force as is reasonably necessary to prevent the commission of an offence against this Act or another Act of Parliament that the person believes on reasonable grounds, if it were committed, would be likely to cause immediate and serious injury to the aircraft or to any person or property therein.
Application of this section
(2) This section applies in respect of any aircraft in flight in Canadian airspace and in respect of any aircraft registered in Canada in accordance with the regulations made under the
Aeronautics Act
2004, c. 12, s. 2.
Arrest of wrong person
28 (1) Where a person who is authorized to execute a warrant to arrest believes, in good faith and on reasonable grounds, that the person whom he arrests is the person named in the warrant, he is protected from criminal responsibility in respect thereof to the same extent as if that person were the person named in the warrant.
Person assisting
(2) Where a person is authorized to execute a warrant to arrest,
(a) every one who, being called on to assist him, believes that the person in whose arrest he is called on to assist is the person named in the warrant, and
(b) every keeper of a prison who is required to receive and detain a person who he believes has been arrested under the warrant,
is protected from criminal responsibility in respect thereof to the same extent as if that person were the person named in the warrant.
R.S., c. C-34, s. 28.
Duty of person arresting
29 (1) It is the duty of every one who executes a process or warrant to have it with him, where it is feasible to do so, and to produce it when requested to do so.
Notice
(2) It is the duty of every one who arrests a person, whether with or without a warrant, to give notice to that person, where it is feasible to do so, of
(a) the process or warrant under which he makes the arrest; or
(b) the reason for the arrest.
Failure to comply
(3) Failure to comply with subsection (1) or (2) does not of itself deprive a person who executes a process or warrant, or a person who makes an arrest, or those who assist them, of protection from criminal responsibility.
R.S., c. C-34, s. 29.
Preventing breach of peace
30 Every one who witnesses a breach of the peace is justified in interfering to prevent the

continuance or renewal thereof and may detain any person who commits or is about to join in or to renew the breach of the peace, for the purpose of giving him into the custody of a peace officer, if he uses no more force than is reasonably necessary to prevent the continuance or renewal of the breach of the peace or than is reasonably proportioned to the danger to be apprehended from the continuance or renewal of the breach of the peace.
R.S., c. C-34, s. 30.

Arrest for breach of peace
31 (1) Every peace officer who witnesses a breach of the peace and every one who lawfully assists the peace officer is justified in arresting any person whom he finds committing the breach of the peace or who, on reasonable grounds, he believes is about to join in or renew the breach of the peace.

Giving person in charge
(2) Every peace officer is justified in receiving into custody any person who is given into his charge as having been a party to a breach of the peace by one who has, or who on reasonable grounds the peace officer believes has, witnessed the breach of the peace.
R.S., c. C-34, s. 31.

Suppression of Riots

Use of force to suppress riot
32 (1) Every peace officer is justified in using or in ordering the use of as much force as the peace officer believes, in good faith and on reasonable grounds,
(a) is necessary to suppress a riot; and
(b) is not excessive, having regard to the danger to be apprehended from the continuance of the riot.

Person bound by military law
(2) Every one who is bound by military law to obey the command of his superior officer is justified in obeying any command given by his superior officer for the suppression of a riot unless the order is manifestly unlawful.

Obeying order of peace officer
(3) Every one is justified in obeying an order of a peace officer to use force to suppress a riot if
(a) he acts in good faith; and
(b) the order is not manifestly unlawful.

Apprehension of serious mischief
(4) Every one who, in good faith and on reasonable grounds, believes that serious mischief will result from a riot before it is possible to secure the attendance of a peace officer is justified in using as much force as he believes in good faith and on reasonable grounds,
(a) is necessary to suppress the riot; and
(b) is not excessive, having regard to the danger to be apprehended from the continuance of the riot.

Question of law
(5) For the purposes of this section, the question whether an order is manifestly unlawful or not is a question of law.
R.S., c. C-34, s. 32.

Duty of officers if rioters do not disperse
33 (1) Where the proclamation referred to in section 67 has been made or an offence against paragraph 68(a) or (b) has been committed, it is the duty of a peace officer and of a person who is lawfully required by him to assist, to disperse or to arrest persons who do not comply with the proclamation.

Protection of officers
(2) No civil or criminal proceedings lie against a peace officer or a person who is lawfully required by a peace officer to assist him in respect of any death or injury that by reason of resistance is caused as a result of the performance by the peace officer or that person of a duty that is imposed by subsection (1).

Section not restrictive

(3) Nothing in this section limits or affects any powers, duties or functions that are conferred or imposed by this Act with respect to the suppression of riots.
R.S., c. C-34, s. 33.

Self-induced Intoxication

When defence not available
33.1 (1) It is not a defence to an offence referred to in subsection (3) that the accused, by reason of self-induced intoxication, lacked the general intent or the voluntariness required to commit the offence, where the accused departed markedly from the standard of care as described in subsection (2).

Criminal fault by reason of intoxication
(2) For the purposes of this section, a person departs markedly from the standard of reasonable care generally recognized in Canadian society and is thereby criminally at fault where the person, while in a state of self-induced intoxication that renders the person unaware of, or incapable of consciously controlling, their behaviour, voluntarily or involuntarily interferes or threatens to interfere with the bodily integrity of another person.

Application
(3) This section applies in respect of an offence under this Act or any other Act of Parliament that includes as an element an assault or any other interference or threat of interference by a person with the bodily integrity of another person.
1995, c. 32, s. 1.

Defence of Person

Defence — use or threat of force
34 (1) A person is not guilty of an offence if
(a) they believe on reasonable grounds that force is being used against them or another person or that a threat of force is being made against them or another person;
(b) the act that constitutes the offence is committed for the purpose of defending or protecting themselves or the other person from that use or threat of force; and
(c) the act committed is reasonable in the circumstances.

Factors
(2) In determining whether the act committed is reasonable in the circumstances, the court shall consider the relevant circumstances of the person, the other parties and the act, including, but not limited to, the following factors:
(a) the nature of the force or threat;
(b) the extent to which the use of force was imminent and whether there were other means available to respond to the potential use of force;
(c) the person's role in the incident;
(d) whether any party to the incident used or threatened to use a weapon;
(e) the size, age, gender and physical capabilities of the parties to the incident;
(f) the nature, duration and history of any relationship between the parties to the incident, including any prior use or threat of force and the nature of that force or threat;
(f.1) any history of interaction or communication between the parties to the incident;
(g) the nature and proportionality of the person's response to the use or threat of force; and
(h) whether the act committed was in response to a use or threat of force that the person knew was lawful.

No defence
(3) Subsection (1) does not apply if the force is used or threatened by another person for the purpose of doing something that they are required or authorized by law to do in the administration or enforcement of the law, unless the person who commits the act that constitutes the offence believes

on reasonable grounds that the other person is acting unlawfully.
R.S., 1985, c. C-46, s. 34;
1992, c. 1, s. 60(F);
2012, c. 9, s. 2.

Defence of Property

Defence — property
35 (1) A person is not guilty of an offence if
(a) they either believe on reasonable grounds that they are in peaceable possession of property or are acting under the authority of, or lawfully assisting, a person whom they believe on reasonable grounds is in peaceable possession of property;
(b) they believe on reasonable grounds that another person
(i) is about to enter, is entering or has entered the property without being entitled by law to do so,
(ii) is about to take the property, is doing so or has just done so, or
(iii) is about to damage or destroy the property, or make it inoperative, or is doing so;
(c) the act that constitutes the offence is committed for the purpose of
(i) preventing the other person from entering the property, or removing that person from the property, or
(ii) preventing the other person from taking, damaging or destroying the property or from making it inoperative, or retaking the property from that person; and
(d) the act committed is reasonable in the circumstances.
No defence
(2) Subsection (1) does not apply if the person who believes on reasonable grounds that they are, or who is believed on reasonable grounds to be, in peaceable possession of the property does not have a claim of right to it and the other person is entitled to its possession by law.
No defence
(3) Subsection (1) does not apply if the other person is doing something that they are required or authorized by law to do in the administration or enforcement of the law, unless the person who commits the act that constitutes the offence believes on reasonable grounds that the other person is acting unlawfully.
R.S., 1985, c. C-46, s. 35;
2012, c. 9, s. 2.
36 37 38 39 40 41 42

Protection of Persons in Authority

Correction of child by force
43 Every schoolteacher, parent or person standing in the place of a parent is justified in using force by way of correction toward a pupil or child, as the case may be, who is under his care, if the force does not exceed what is reasonable under the circumstances.
R.S., c. C-34, s. 43.
44 Surgical operations
45 Every one is protected from criminal responsibility for performing a surgical operation on any person for the benefit of that person if
(a) the operation is performed with reasonable care and skill; and
(b) it is reasonable to perform the operation, having regard to the state of health of the person at the time the operation is performed and to all the circumstances of the case.
R.S., c. C-34, s. 45.

PART II

PART II

Offences Against Public Order

Treason and other Offences against the Queen's Authority and Person

High treason
46 (1) Every one commits high treason who, in Canada,
(a) kills or attempts to kill Her Majesty, or does her any bodily harm tending to death or destruction, maims or wounds her, or imprisons or restrains her;
(b) levies war against Canada or does any act preparatory thereto; or
(c) assists an enemy at war with Canada, or any armed forces against whom Canadian Forces are engaged in hostilities, whether or not a state of war exists between Canada and the country whose forces they are.
Treason
(2) Every one commits treason who, in Canada,
(a) uses force or violence for the purpose of overthrowing the government of Canada or a province;
(b) without lawful authority, communicates or makes available to an agent of a state other than Canada, military or scientific information or any sketch, plan, model, article, note or document of a military or scientific character that he knows or ought to know may be used by that state for a purpose prejudicial to the safety or defence of Canada;
(c) conspires with any person to commit high treason or to do anything mentioned in paragraph (a);
(d) forms an intention to do anything that is high treason or that is mentioned in paragraph (a) and manifests that intention by an overt act; or
(e) conspires with any person to do anything mentioned in paragraph (b) or forms an intention to do anything mentioned in paragraph (b) and manifests that intention by an overt act.
Canadian citizen
(3) Notwithstanding subsection (1) or (2), a Canadian citizen or a person who owes allegiance to Her Majesty in right of Canada,
(a) commits high treason if, while in or out of Canada, he does anything mentioned in subsection (1); or
(b) commits treason if, while in or out of Canada, he does anything mentioned in subsection (2).
Overt act
(4) Where it is treason to conspire with any person, the act of conspiring is an overt act of treason.
R.S., c. C-34, s. 46;
1974-75-76, c. 105, s. 2.
Punishment for high treason
47 (1) Every one who commits high treason is guilty of an indictable offence and shall be sentenced to imprisonment for life.
Punishment for treason
(2) Every one who commits treason is guilty of an indictable offence and liable
(a) to be sentenced to imprisonment for life if he is guilty of an offence under paragraph 46(2)(a), (c) or (d);
(b) to be sentenced to imprisonment for life if he is guilty of an offence under paragraph 46(2)(b) or (e) committed while a state of war exists between Canada and another country; or
(c) to be sentenced to imprisonment for a term not exceeding fourteen years if he is guilty of an offence under paragraph 46(2)(b) or (e) committed while no state of war exists between Canada and another country.
Corroboration
(3) No person shall be convicted of high treason or treason on the evidence of only one witness, unless the evidence of that witness is corroborated in a material particular by evidence that implicates the accused.
Minimum punishment
(4) For the purposes of Part XXIII, the sentence of imprisonment for life prescribed by subsection (1)

is a minimum punishment.
R.S., c. C-34, s. 47;
1974-75-76, c. 105, s. 2.

Limitation

48 (1) No proceedings for an offence of treason as defined by paragraph 46(2)(a) shall be commenced more than three years after the time when the offence is alleged to have been committed.

Information for treasonable words

(2) No proceedings shall be commenced under section 47 in respect of an overt act of treason expressed or declared by open and considered speech unless

(a) an information setting out the overt act and the words by which it was expressed or declared is laid under oath before a justice within six days after the time when the words are alleged to have been spoken; and

(b) a warrant for the arrest of the accused is issued within ten days after the time when the information is laid.

R.S., c. C-34, s. 48;
1974-75-76, c. 105, s. 29.

Prohibited Acts

Acts intended to alarm Her Majesty or break public peace

49 Every one who wilfully, in the presence of Her Majesty,

(a) does an act with intent to alarm Her Majesty or to break the public peace, or

(b) does an act that is intended or is likely to cause bodily harm to Her Majesty,

is guilty of an indictable offence and liable to imprisonment for a term not exceeding fourteen years.

R.S., c. C-34, s. 49.

Assisting alien enemy to leave Canada, or omitting to prevent treason

50 (1) Every one commits an offence who

(a) incites or wilfully assists a subject of

(i) a state that is at war with Canada, or

(ii) a state against whose forces Canadian Forces are engaged in hostilities, whether or not a state of war exists between Canada and the state whose forces they are,

to leave Canada without the consent of the Crown, unless the accused establishes that assistance to the state referred to in subparagraph (i) or the forces of the state referred to in subparagraph (ii), as the case may be, was not intended thereby; or

(b) knowing that a person is about to commit high treason or treason does not, with all reasonable dispatch, inform a justice of the peace or other peace officer thereof or make other reasonable efforts to prevent that person from committing high treason or treason.

Punishment

(2) Every one who commits an offence under subsection (1) is guilty of an indictable offence and liable to imprisonment for a term not exceeding fourteen years.

R.S., c. C-34, s. 50;
1974-75-76, c. 105, s. 29.

Intimidating Parliament or legislature

51 Every one who does an act of violence in order to intimidate Parliament or the legislature of a province is guilty of an indictable offence and liable to imprisonment for a term not exceeding fourteen years.

R.S., c. C-34, s. 51.

Sabotage

52 (1) Every one who does a prohibited act for a purpose prejudicial to

(a) the safety, security or defence of Canada, or

(b) the safety or security of the naval, army or air forces of any state other than Canada that are lawfully present in Canada, is guilty of an indictable offence and liable to imprisonment for a term not exceeding ten years.

Definition of prohibited act

(2) In this section,

prohibited act

(a) impairs the efficiency or impedes the working of any vessel, vehicle, aircraft, machinery, apparatus or other thing; or

(b) causes property, by whomever it may be owned, to be lost, damaged or destroyed.

Saving

(3) No person does a prohibited act within the meaning of this section by reason only that

(a) he stops work as a result of the failure of his employer and himself to agree on any matter relating to his employment;

(b) he stops work as a result of the failure of his employer and a bargaining agent acting on his behalf to agree on any matter relating to his employment; or

(c) he stops work as a result of his taking part in a combination of workmen or employees for their own reasonable protection as workmen or employees.

Idem

(4) No person does a prohibited act within the meaning of this section by reason only that he attends at or near or approaches a dwelling-house or place for the purpose only of obtaining or communicating information.

R.S., c. C-34, s. 52.

Inciting to mutiny

53 Every one who

(a) attempts, for a traitorous or mutinous purpose, to seduce a member of the Canadian Forces from his duty and allegiance to Her Majesty, or

(b) attempts to incite or to induce a member of the Canadian Forces to commit a traitorous or mutinous act,

is guilty of an indictable offence and liable to imprisonment for a term not exceeding fourteen years.

R.S., c. C-34, s. 53.

Assisting deserter

54 Every one who aids, assists, harbours or conceals a person who he knows is a deserter or absentee without leave from the Canadian Forces is guilty of an offence punishable on summary conviction, but no proceedings shall be instituted under this section without the consent of the Attorney General of Canada.

R.S., c. C-34, s. 54.

Evidence of overt acts

55 In proceedings for an offence against any provision in section 47 or sections 49 to 53, no evidence is admissible of an overt act unless that overt act is set out in the indictment or unless the evidence is otherwise relevant as tending to prove an overt act that is set out therein.

R.S., c. C-34, s. 55.

Offences in relation to members of R.C.M.P.

56 Every one who wilfully

(a) persuades or counsels a member of the Royal Canadian Mounted Police to desert or absent himself without leave,

(b) aids, assists, harbours or conceals a member of the Royal Canadian Mounted Police who he knows is a deserter or absentee without leave, or

(c) aids or assists a member of the Royal Canadian Mounted Police to desert or absent himself without leave, knowing that the member is about to desert or absent himself without leave,

is guilty of an offence punishable on summary conviction.

R.S., 1985, c. C-46, s. 56;

R.S., 1985, c. 27 (1st Supp.), s. 8.

Official Documents

Identity documents
56.1 (1) Every person commits an offence who, without lawful excuse, procures to be made, possesses, transfers, sells or offers for sale an identity document that relates or purports to relate, in whole or in part, to another person.
For greater certainty
(2) For greater certainty, subsection (1) does not prohibit an act that is carried out
(a) in good faith, in the ordinary course of the person's business or employment or in the exercise of the duties of their office;
(b) for genealogical purposes;
(c) with the consent of the person to whom the identity document relates or of a person authorized to consent on behalf of the person to whom the document relates, or of the entity that issued the identity document; or
(d) for a legitimate purpose related to the administration of justice.
Definition of
identity document
(3) For the purposes of this section,
identity document
Punishment
(4) Every person who commits an offence under subsection (1)
(a) is guilty of an indictable offence and liable to imprisonment for a term of not more than five years; or
(b) is guilty of an offence punishable on summary conviction.
2009, c. 28, s. 1.
Forgery of or uttering forged passport
57 (1) Every one who, while in or out of Canada,
(a) forges a passport, or
(b) knowing that a passport is forged
(i) uses, deals with or acts on it, or
(ii) causes or attempts to cause any person to use, deal with or act on it, as if the passport were genuine,
is guilty of an indictable offence and liable to imprisonment for a term not exceeding fourteen years.
False statement in relation to passport
(2) Every one who, while in or out of Canada, for the purpose of procuring a passport for himself or any other person or for the purpose of procuring any material alteration or addition to any such passport, makes a written or an oral statement that he knows is false or misleading
(a) is guilty of an indictable offence and liable to imprisonment for a term not exceeding two years; or
(b) is guilty of an offence punishable on summary conviction.
Possession of forged, etc., passport
(3) Every one who without lawful excuse, the proof of which lies on him, has in his possession a forged passport or a passport in respect of which an offence under subsection (2) has been committed is guilty of an indictable offence and liable to imprisonment for a term not exceeding five years.
Special provisions applicable
(4) For the purposes of proceedings under this section,
(a) the place where a passport was forged is not material; and
(b) the definition
false document
Definition of
passport
(5) In this section,

passport
Canadian Passport Order
Jurisdiction
(6) Where a person is alleged to have committed, while out of Canada, an offence under this section, proceedings in respect of that offence may, whether or not that person is in Canada, be commenced in any territorial division in Canada and the accused may be tried and punished in respect of that offence in the same manner as if the offence had been committed in that territorial division.
Appearance of accused at trial
(7) For greater certainty, the provisions of this Act relating to
(a) requirements that an accused appear at and be present during proceedings, and
(b) the exceptions to those requirements,
apply to proceedings commenced in any territorial division pursuant to subsection (6).
R.S., 1985, c. C-46, s. 57;
R.S., 1985, c. 27 (1st Supp.), s. 9;
1992, c. 1, s. 60(F);
1994, c. 44, s. 4;
1995, c. 5, s. 25;
2013, c. 40, s. 174.
Fraudulent use of certificate of citizenship
58 (1) Every one who, while in or out of Canada,
(a) uses a certificate of citizenship or a certificate of naturalization for a fraudulent purpose, or
(b) being a person to whom a certificate of citizenship or a certificate of naturalization has been granted, knowingly parts with the possession of that certificate with intent that it should be used for a fraudulent purpose,
is guilty of an indictable offence and liable to imprisonment for a term not exceeding two years.
Definition of
certificate of citizenship
certificate of naturalization
(2) In this section,
certificate of citizenship
certificate of naturalization
Citizenship Act
R.S., c. C-34, s. 59;
1974-75-76, c. 108, s. 41.

Sedition

Seditious words
59 (1) Seditious words are words that express a seditious intention.
Seditious libel
(2) A seditious libel is a libel that expresses a seditious intention.
Seditious conspiracy
(3) A seditious conspiracy is an agreement between two or more persons to carry out a seditious intention.
Seditious intention
(4) Without limiting the generality of the meaning of the expression
(a) teaches or advocates, or
(b) publishes or circulates any writing that advocates,
the use, without the authority of law, of force as a means of accomplishing a governmental change within Canada.
R.S., c. C-34, s. 60.
Exception

60 Notwithstanding subsection 59(4), no person shall be deemed to have a seditious intention by reason only that he intends, in good faith,
(a) to show that Her Majesty has been misled or mistaken in her measures;
(b) to point out errors or defects in
(i) the government or constitution of Canada or a province,
(ii) Parliament or the legislature of a province, or
(iii) the administration of justice in Canada;
(c) to procure, by lawful means, the alteration of any matter of government in Canada; or
(d) to point out, for the purpose of removal, matters that produce or tend to produce feelings of hostility and ill-will between different classes of persons in Canada.
R.S., c. C-34, s. 61.

Punishment of seditious offences
61 Every one who
(a) speaks seditious words,
(b) publishes a seditious libel, or
(c) is a party to a seditious conspiracy,
is guilty of an indictable offence and liable to imprisonment for a term not exceeding fourteen years.
R.S., c. C-34, s. 62.

Offences in relation to military forces
62 (1) Every one who wilfully
(a) interferes with, impairs or influences the loyalty or discipline of a member of a force,
(b) publishes, edits, issues, circulates or distributes a writing that advises, counsels or urges insubordination, disloyalty, mutiny or refusal of duty by a member of a force, or
(c) advises, counsels, urges or in any manner causes insubordination, disloyalty, mutiny or refusal of duty by a member of a force,
is guilty of an indictable offence and liable to imprisonment for a term not exceeding five years.

Definition of
member of a force
(2) In this section,
member of a force
(a) the Canadian Forces; or
(b) the naval, army or air forces of a state other than Canada that are lawfully present in Canada.
R.S., c. C-34, s. 63.

Unlawful Assemblies and Riots

Unlawful assembly
63 (1) An unlawful assembly is an assembly of three or more persons who, with intent to carry out any common purpose, assemble in such a manner or so conduct themselves when they are assembled as to cause persons in the neighbourhood of the assembly to fear, on reasonable grounds, that they
(a) will disturb the peace tumultuously; or
(b) will by that assembly needlessly and without reasonable cause provoke other persons to disturb the peace tumultuously.

Lawful assembly becoming unlawful
(2) Persons who are lawfully assembled may become an unlawful assembly if they conduct themselves with a common purpose in a manner that would have made the assembly unlawful if they had assembled in that manner for that purpose.

Exception
(3) Persons are not unlawfully assembled by reason only that they are assembled to protect the dwelling-house of any one of them against persons who are threatening to break and enter it for the purpose of committing an indictable offence therein.
R.S., c. C-34, s. 64.

Riot
64 A riot is an unlawful assembly that has begun to disturb the peace tumultuously.
R.S., c. C-34, s. 65.

Punishment of rioter
65 (1) Every one who takes part in a riot is guilty of an indictable offence and liable to imprisonment for a term not exceeding two years.

Concealment of identity
(2) Every person who commits an offence under subsection (1) while wearing a mask or other disguise to conceal their identity without lawful excuse is guilty of an indictable offence and liable to imprisonment for a term not exceeding 10 years.
R.S., 1985, c. C-46, s. 65;
2013, c. 15, s. 2.

Punishment for unlawful assembly
66 (1) Every one who is a member of an unlawful assembly is guilty of an offence punishable on summary conviction.

Concealment of identity
(2) Every person who commits an offence under subsection (1) while wearing a mask or other disguise to conceal their identity without lawful excuse is guilty of
(a) an indictable offence and liable to imprisonment for a term not exceeding five years; or
(b) an offence punishable on summary conviction.
R.S., 1985, c. C-46, s. 66;
2013, c. 15, s. 3.

Reading proclamation
67 A person who is
(a) a justice, mayor or sheriff, or the lawful deputy of a mayor or sheriff,
(b) a warden or deputy warden of a prison, or
(c) the institutional head of a penitentiary, as those expressions are defined in subsection 2(1) of the Corrections and Conditional Release Act
who receives notice that, at any place within the jurisdiction of the person, twelve or more persons are unlawfully and riotously assembled together shall go to that place and, after approaching as near as is safe, if the person is satisfied that a riot is in progress, shall command silence and thereupon make or cause to be made in a loud voice a proclamation in the following words or to the like effect:
R.S., 1985, c. C-46, s. 67;
1994, c. 44, s. 5.

Offences related to proclamation
68 Every one is guilty of an indictable offence and liable to imprisonment for life who
(a) opposes, hinders or assaults, wilfully and with force, a person who begins to make or is about to begin to make or is making the proclamation referred to in section 67 so that it is not made;
(b) does not peaceably disperse and depart from a place where the proclamation referred to in section 67 is made within thirty minutes after it is made; or
(c) does not depart from a place within thirty minutes when he has reasonable grounds to believe that the proclamation referred to in section 67 would have been made in that place if some person had not opposed, hindered or assaulted, wilfully and with force, a person who would have made it.
R.S., c. C-34, s. 69.

Neglect by peace officer
69 A peace officer who receives notice that there is a riot within his jurisdiction and, without reasonable excuse, fails to take all reasonable steps to suppress the riot is guilty of an indictable offence and liable to imprisonment for a term not exceeding two years.
R.S., c. C-34, s. 70.

Unlawful Drilling

Orders by Governor in Council

70 (1) The Governor in Council may, by proclamation, make orders
(a) to prohibit assemblies, without lawful authority, of persons for the purpose
(i) of training or drilling themselves,
(ii) of being trained or drilled to the use of arms, or
(iii) of practising military exercises; or
(b) to prohibit persons when assembled for any purpose from training or drilling themselves or from being trained or drilled.

General or special order

(2) An order that is made under subsection (1) may be general or may be made applicable to particular places, districts or assemblies to be specified in the order.

Punishment

(3) Every one who contravenes an order made under this section is guilty of an indictable offence and liable to imprisonment for a term not exceeding five years.
R.S., 1985, c. C-46, s. 70;
1992, c. 1, s. 60(F).

Duels

Duelling

71 Every one who
(a) challenges or attempts by any means to provoke another person to fight a duel,
(b) attempts to provoke a person to challenge another person to fight a duel, or
(c) accepts a challenge to fight a duel,
is guilty of an indictable offence and liable to imprisonment for a term not exceeding two years.
R.S., c. C-34, s. 72.

Forcible Entry and Detainer

Forcible entry

72 (1) A person commits forcible entry when that person enters real property that is in the actual and peaceable possession of another in a manner that is likely to cause a breach of the peace or reasonable apprehension of a breach of the peace.

Matters not material

(1.1) For the purposes of subsection (1), it is immaterial whether or not a person is entitled to enter the real property or whether or not that person has any intention of taking possession of the real property.

Forcible detainer

(2) A person commits forcible detainer when, being in actual possession of real property without colour of right, he detains it in a manner that is likely to cause a breach of the peace or reasonable apprehension of a breach of the peace, against a person who is entitled by law to possession of it.

Questions of law

(3) The questions whether a person is in actual and peaceable possession or is in actual possession without colour of right are questions of law.
R.S., 1985, c. C-46, s. 72;
R.S., 1985, c. 27 (1st Supp.), s. 10;
1992, c. 1, s. 60(F).

Punishment

73 Every person who commits forcible entry or forcible detainer is guilty of
(a) an offence punishable on summary conviction; or
(b) an indictable offence and liable to imprisonment for a term not exceeding two years.
R.S., 1985, c. C-46, s. 73;

R.S., 1985, c. 27 (1st Supp.), s. 11;
1992, c. 1, s. 58.

Piracy

Piracy by law of nations
74 (1) Every one commits piracy who does any act that, by the law of nations, is piracy.
Punishment
(2) Every one who commits piracy while in or out of Canada is guilty of an indictable offence and liable to imprisonment for life.
R.S., c. C-34, s. 75;
1974-75-76, c. 105, s. 3.
Piratical acts
75 Every one who, while in or out of Canada,
(a) steals a Canadian ship,
(b) steals or without lawful authority throws overboard, damages or destroys anything that is part of the cargo, supplies or fittings in a Canadian ship,
(c) does or attempts to do a mutinous act on a Canadian ship, or
(d) counsels a person to do anything mentioned in paragraph (a), (b) or (c),
is guilty of an indictable offence and liable to imprisonment for a term not exceeding fourteen years.
R.S., 1985, c. C-46, s. 75;
R.S., 1985, c. 27 (1st Supp.), s. 7.

Offences against Air or Maritime Safety

Hijacking
76 Every one who, unlawfully, by force or threat thereof, or by any other form of intimidation, seizes or exercises control of an aircraft with intent
(a) to cause any person on board the aircraft to be confined or imprisoned against his will,
(b) to cause any person on board the aircraft to be transported against his will to any place other than the next scheduled place of landing of the aircraft,
(c) to hold any person on board the aircraft for ransom or to service against his will, or
(d) to cause the aircraft to deviate in a material respect from its flight plan,
is guilty of an indictable offence and liable to imprisonment for life.
1972, c. 13, s. 6.
Endangering safety of aircraft or airport
77 Every one who
(a) on board an aircraft in flight, commits an act of violence against a person that is likely to endanger the safety of the aircraft,
(b) using a weapon, commits an act of violence against a person at an airport serving international civil aviation that causes or is likely to cause serious injury or death and that endangers or is likely to endanger safety at the airport,
(c) causes damage to an aircraft in service that renders the aircraft incapable of flight or that is likely to endanger the safety of the aircraft in flight,
(d) places or causes to be placed on board an aircraft in service anything that is likely to cause damage to the aircraft, that will render it incapable of flight or that is likely to endanger the safety of the aircraft in flight,
(e) causes damage to or interferes with the operation of any air navigation facility where the damage or interference is likely to endanger the safety of an aircraft in flight,
(f) using a weapon, substance or device, destroys or causes serious damage to the facilities of an airport serving international civil aviation or to any aircraft not in service located there, or causes disruption of services of the airport, that endangers or is likely to endanger safety at the airport, or

(g) endangers the safety of an aircraft in flight by communicating to any other person any information that the person knows to be false,

is guilty of an indictable offence and liable to imprisonment for life.

R.S., 1985, c. C-46, s. 77;
1993, c. 7, s. 3.

Offensive weapons and explosive substances

78 (1) Every one, other than a peace officer engaged in the execution of his duty, who takes on board a civil aircraft an offensive weapon or any explosive substance

(a) without the consent of the owner or operator of the aircraft or of a person duly authorized by either of them to consent thereto, or

(b) with the consent referred to in paragraph (a) but without complying with all terms and conditions on which the consent was given,

is guilty of an indictable offence and liable to imprisonment for a term not exceeding fourteen years.

Definition of
civil aircraft

(2) For the purposes of this section,
civil aircraft
Customs Act
Excise Act
Excise Act, 2001
R.S., 1985, c. C-46, s. 78;
R.S., 1985, c. 1 (2nd Supp.), s. 213;
2002, c. 22, s. 325.

Seizing control of ship or fixed platform

78.1 (1) Every one who seizes or exercises control over a ship or fixed platform by force or threat of force or by any other form of intimidation is guilty of an indictable offence and liable to imprisonment for life.

Endangering safety of ship or fixed platform

(2) Every one who

(a) commits an act of violence against a person on board a ship or fixed platform,

(b) destroys or causes damage to a ship or its cargo or to a fixed platform,

(c) destroys or causes serious damage to or interferes with the operation of any maritime navigational facility, or

(d) places or causes to be placed on board a ship or fixed platform anything that is likely to cause damage to the ship or its cargo or to the fixed platform,

where that act is likely to endanger the safe navigation of a ship or the safety of a fixed platform, is guilty of an indictable offence and liable to imprisonment for life.

False communication

(3) Every one who communicates information that endangers the safe navigation of a ship, knowing the information to be false, is guilty of an indictable offence and liable to imprisonment for life.

Threats causing death or injury

(4) Every one who threatens to commit an offence under paragraph (2)(a), (b) or (c) in order to compel a person to do or refrain from doing any act, where the threat is likely to endanger the safe navigation of a ship or the safety of a fixed platform, is guilty of an indictable offence and liable to imprisonment for life.

Definitions

(5) In this section,
fixed platform
ship
1993, c. 7, s. 4.

Dangerous Materials and Devices

Duty of care re explosive
79 Every one who has an explosive substance in his possession or under his care or control is under a legal duty to use reasonable care to prevent bodily harm or death to persons or damage to property by that explosive substance.
R.S., c. C-34, s. 77.

Breach of duty
80 Every one who, being under a legal duty within the meaning of section 79, fails without lawful excuse to perform that duty, is guilty of an indictable offence and, if as a result an explosion of an explosive substance occurs that
(a) causes death or is likely to cause death to any person, is liable to imprisonment for life; or
(b) causes bodily harm or damage to property or is likely to cause bodily harm or damage to property, is liable to imprisonment for a term not exceeding fourteen years.
R.S., c. C-34, s. 78.

Using explosives
81 (1) Every one commits an offence who
(a) does anything with intent to cause an explosion of an explosive substance that is likely to cause serious bodily harm or death to persons or is likely to cause serious damage to property;
(b) with intent to do bodily harm to any person
(i) causes an explosive substance to explode,
(ii) sends or delivers to a person or causes a person to take or receive an explosive substance or any other dangerous substance or thing, or
(iii) places or throws anywhere or at or on a person a corrosive fluid, explosive substance or any other dangerous substance or thing;
(c) with intent to destroy or damage property without lawful excuse, places or throws an explosive substance anywhere; or
(d) makes or has in his possession or has under his care or control any explosive substance with intent thereby
(i) to endanger life or to cause serious damage to property, or
(ii) to enable another person to endanger life or to cause serious damage to property.

Punishment
(2) Every one who commits an offence under subsection (1) is guilty of an indictable offence and liable
(a) for an offence under paragraph (1)(a) or (b), to imprisonment for life; or
(b) for an offence under paragraph (1)(c) or (d), to imprisonment for a term not exceeding fourteen years.
R.S., c. C-34, s. 79.

Possession without lawful excuse
82 (1) Every person who, without lawful excuse, the proof of which lies on the person, makes or has in the possession or under the care or control of the person any explosive substance is guilty of an indictable offence and liable to imprisonment for a term not exceeding five years.

Possession in association with criminal organization
(2) Every person who, without lawful excuse, the proof of which lies on the person, makes or has in the possession or under the care or control of the person any explosive substance for the benefit of, at the direction of or in association with a criminal organization is guilty of an indictable offence and liable to imprisonment for a term not exceeding fourteen years.
R.S., 1985, c. C-46, s. 82;
R.S., 1985, c. 27 (1st Supp.), s. 12;
1997, c. 23, s. 2;
2001, c. 32, s. 3(F).

Sentences to be served consecutively

82.1 A sentence imposed on a person for an offence under subsection 82(2) shall be served consecutively to any other punishment imposed on the person for an offence arising out of the same event or series of events and to any other sentence to which the person is subject at the time the sentence is imposed on the person for an offence under subsection 82(2).
1997, c. 23, s. 2.

Definition of
device
82.2 For the purposes of sections 82.3 to 82.5,
device
(a) a nuclear explosive device;
(b) a device that disperses radioactive material;
(c) a device that emits ionizing radiation and that is capable of causing death, serious bodily harm or substantial damage to property or the environment.
2013, c. 13, s. 5.

Possession, etc., of nuclear material, radioactive material or device
82.3 Everyone who, with intent to cause death, serious bodily harm or substantial damage to property or the environment, makes a device or possesses, uses, transfers, exports, imports, alters or disposes of nuclear material, radioactive material or a device or commits an act against a nuclear facility or an act that causes serious interference with or serious disruption of its operations, is guilty of an indictable offence and liable to imprisonment for life.
2013, c. 13, s. 5.

Use or alteration of nuclear material, radioactive material or device
82.4 Everyone who, with intent to compel a person, government or international organization to do or refrain from doing any act, uses or alters nuclear material, radioactive material or a device or commits an act against a nuclear facility or an act that causes serious interference with or serious disruption of its operations, is guilty of an indictable offence and liable to imprisonment for life.
2013, c. 13, s. 5.

Commission of indictable offence to obtain nuclear material, etc.
82.5 Everyone who commits an indictable offence under this or any other Act of Parliament, with intent to obtain nuclear material, radioactive material or a device or to obtain access to a nuclear facility, is guilty of an indictable offence and is liable to imprisonment for life.
2013, c. 13, s. 5.

Threats
82.6 Everyone who threatens to commit an offence under any of sections 82.3 to 82.5 is guilty of an indictable offence and is liable to imprisonment for a term of not more than 14 years.
2013, c. 13, s. 5.

Armed forces
82.7 For greater certainty, sections 82.3 to 82.6 do not apply to an act that is committed during an armed conflict and that, at the time and in the place of its commission, is in accordance with customary international law or conventional international law applicable to the conflict, or to activities undertaken by military forces of a state in the exercise of their official duties, to the extent that those activities are governed by other rules of international law.
2013, c. 13, s. 5.

Prize Fights

Engaging in prize fight
83 (1) Every one who
(a) engages as a principal in a prize fight,
(b) advises, encourages or promotes a prize fight, or
(c) is present at a prize fight as an aid, second, surgeon, umpire, backer or reporter,
is guilty of an offence punishable on summary conviction.

Definition of
prize fight
(2) In this section,
prize fight
(a) a contest between amateur athletes in a combative sport with fists, hands or feet held in a province if the sport is on the programme of the International Olympic Committee or the International Paralympic Committee and, in the case where the province's lieutenant governor in council or any other person or body specified by him or her requires it, the contest is held with their permission;
(b) a contest between amateur athletes in a combative sport with fists, hands or feet held in a province if the sport has been designated by the province's lieutenant governor in council or by any other person or body specified by him or her and, in the case where the lieutenant governor in council or other specified person or body requires it, the contest is held with their permission;
(c) a contest between amateur athletes in a combative sport with fists, hands or feet held in a province with the permission of the province's lieutenant governor in council or any other person or body specified by him or her; and
(d) a boxing contest or mixed martial arts contest held in a province with the permission or under the authority of an athletic board, commission or similar body established by or under the authority of the province's legislature for the control of sport within the province.
R.S., 1985, c. C-46, s. 83;
R.S., 1985, c. 27 (1st Supp.), s. 186;
2013, c. 19, s. 1.

PART II.1

PART II.1
Terrorism

Interpretation

Definitions
83.01 (1) The following definitions apply in this Part.
Canadian
Immigration and Refugee Protection Act
entity
listed entity
terrorist activity
(a) an act or omission that is committed in or outside Canada and that, if committed in Canada, is one of the following offences:
(i) the offences referred to in subsection 7(2) that implement the
Convention for the Suppression of Unlawful Seizure of Aircraft
(ii) the offences referred to in subsection 7(2) that implement the
Convention for the Suppression of Unlawful Acts against the Safety of Civil Aviation
(iii) the offences referred to in subsection 7(3) that implement the
Convention on the Prevention and Punishment of Crimes against Internationally Protected Persons, including Diplomatic Agents
(iv) the offences referred to in subsection 7(3.1) that implement the
International Convention against the Taking of Hostages
(v) the offences referred to in subsection 7(2.21) that implement the Convention on the Physical Protection of Nuclear Material, done at Vienna and New York on March 3, 1980, as amended by the Amendment to the Convention on the Physical Protection of Nuclear Material, done at Vienna on July 8, 2005 and the International Convention for the Suppression of Acts of Nuclear Terrorism, done

at New York on September 14, 2005,
(vi) the offences referred to in subsection 7(2) that implement the
Protocol for the Suppression of Unlawful Acts of Violence at Airports Serving International Civil Aviation
Convention for the Suppression of Unlawful Acts against the Safety of Civil Aviation
(vii) the offences referred to in subsection 7(2.1) that implement the
Convention for the Suppression of Unlawful Acts against the Safety of Maritime Navigation
(viii) the offences referred to in subsection 7(2.1) or (2.2) that implement the
Protocol for the Suppression of Unlawful Acts against the Safety of Fixed Platforms Located on the Continental Shelf
(ix) the offences referred to in subsection 7(3.72) that implement the
International Convention for the Suppression of Terrorist Bombings
(x) the offences referred to in subsection 7(3.73) that implement the
International Convention for the Suppression of the Financing of Terrorism
(b) an act or omission, in or outside Canada,
(i) that is committed
(A) in whole or in part for a political, religious or ideological purpose, objective or cause, and
(B) in whole or in part with the intention of intimidating the public, or a segment of the public, with regard to its security, including its economic security, or compelling a person, a government or a domestic or an international organization to do or to refrain from doing any act, whether the public or the person, government or organization is inside or outside Canada, and
(ii) that intentionally
(A) causes death or serious bodily harm to a person by the use of violence,
(B) endangers a person's life,
(C) causes a serious risk to the health or safety of the public or any segment of the public,
(D) causes substantial property damage, whether to public or private property, if causing such damage is likely to result in the conduct or harm referred to in any of clauses (A) to (C), or
(E) causes serious interference with or serious disruption of an essential service, facility or system, whether public or private, other than as a result of advocacy, protest, dissent or stoppage of work that is not intended to result in the conduct or harm referred to in any of clauses (A) to (C),
and includes a conspiracy, attempt or threat to commit any such act or omission, or being an accessory after the fact or counselling in relation to any such act or omission, but, for greater certainty, does not include an act or omission that is committed during an armed conflict and that, at the time and in the place of its commission, is in accordance with customary international law or conventional international law applicable to the conflict, or the activities undertaken by military forces of a state in the exercise of their official duties, to the extent that those activities are governed by other rules of international law.
terrorist group
(a) an entity that has as one of its purposes or activities facilitating or carrying out any terrorist activity, or
(b) a listed entity,
and includes an association of such entities.

For greater certainty

(1.1) For greater certainty, the expression of a political, religious or ideological thought, belief or opinion does not come within paragraph (b) of the definition

For greater certainty

(1.2) For greater certainty, a suicide bombing is an act that comes within paragraph (a) or (b) of the definition

Facilitation

(2) For the purposes of this Part, facilitation shall be construed in accordance with subsection 83.19(2).
2001, c. 41, ss. 4, 126;

2010, c. 19, s. 1;
2013, c. 13, s. 6.

Financing of Terrorism

Providing or collecting property for certain activities

83.02 Every one who, directly or indirectly, wilfully and without lawful justification or excuse, provides or collects property intending that it be used or knowing that it will be used, in whole or in part, in order to carry out

(a) an act or omission that constitutes an offence referred to in subparagraphs (a)(i) to (ix) of the definition of

terrorist activity

(b) any other act or omission intended to cause death or serious bodily harm to a civilian or to any other person not taking an active part in the hostilities in a situation of armed conflict, if the purpose of that act or omission, by its nature or context, is to intimidate the public, or to compel a government or an international organization to do or refrain from doing any act,

is guilty of an indictable offence and is liable to imprisonment for a term of not more than 10 years.
2001, c. 41, s. 4.

Providing, making available, etc., property or services for terrorist purposes

83.03 Every one who, directly or indirectly, collects property, provides or invites a person to provide, or makes available property or financial or other related services

(a) intending that they be used, or knowing that they will be used, in whole or in part, for the purpose of facilitating or carrying out any terrorist activity, or for the purpose of benefiting any person who is facilitating or carrying out such an activity, or

(b) knowing that, in whole or part, they will be used by or will benefit a terrorist group,

is guilty of an indictable offence and is liable to imprisonment for a term of not more than 10 years.
2001, c. 41, s. 4.

Using or possessing property for terrorist purposes

83.04 Every one who

(a) uses property, directly or indirectly, in whole or in part, for the purpose of facilitating or carrying out a terrorist activity, or

(b) possesses property intending that it be used or knowing that it will be used, directly or indirectly, in whole or in part, for the purpose of facilitating or carrying out a terrorist activity,

is guilty of an indictable offence and is liable to imprisonment for a term of not more than 10 years.
2001, c. 41, s. 4.

List of Entities

Establishment of list

83.05 (1) The Governor in Council may, by regulation, establish a list on which the Governor in Council may place any entity if, on the recommendation of the Minister of Public Safety and Emergency Preparedness, the Governor in Council is satisfied that there are reasonable grounds to believe that

(a) the entity has knowingly carried out, attempted to carry out, participated in or facilitated a terrorist activity; or

(b) the entity is knowingly acting on behalf of, at the direction of or in association with an entity referred to in paragraph (a).

Recommendation

(1.1) The Minister may make a recommendation referred to in subsection (1) only if he or she has reasonable grounds to believe that the entity to which the recommendation relates is an entity referred to in paragraph (1)(a) or (b).

Application to Minister

(2) On application in writing by a listed entity, the Minister shall decide whether there are reasonable grounds to recommend to the Governor in Council that the applicant no longer be a listed entity.
Deeming
(3) If the Minister does not make a decision on the application referred to in subsection (2) within 60 days after receipt of the application, he or she is deemed to have decided to recommend that the applicant remain a listed entity.
Notice of the decision to the applicant
(4) The Minister shall give notice without delay to the applicant of any decision taken or deemed to have been taken respecting the application referred to in subsection (2).
Judicial review
(5) Within 60 days after the receipt of the notice of the decision referred to in subsection (4), the applicant may apply to a judge for judicial review of the decision.
Reference
(6) When an application is made under subsection (5), the judge shall, without delay
(a) examine, in private, any security or criminal intelligence reports considered in listing the applicant and hear any other evidence or information that may be presented by or on behalf of the Minister and may, at his or her request, hear all or part of that evidence or information in the absence of the applicant and any counsel representing the applicant, if the judge is of the opinion that the disclosure of the information would injure national security or endanger the safety of any person;
(b) provide the applicant with a statement summarizing the information available to the judge so as to enable the applicant to be reasonably informed of the reasons for the decision, without disclosing any information the disclosure of which would, in the judge's opinion, injure national security or endanger the safety of any person;
(c) provide the applicant with a reasonable opportunity to be heard; and
(d) determine whether the decision is reasonable on the basis of the information available to the judge and, if found not to be reasonable, order that the applicant no longer be a listed entity.
Evidence
(6.1) The judge may receive into evidence anything that, in the opinion of the judge, is reliable and appropriate, even if it would not otherwise be admissible under Canadian law, and may base his or her decision on that evidence.
Publication
(7) The Minister shall cause to be published, without delay, in the
Canada Gazette
New application
(8) A listed entity may not make another application under subsection (2), except if there has been a material change in its circumstances since the time when the entity made its last application or if the Minister has completed the review under subsection (9).
Review of list
(9) Two years after the establishment of the list referred to in subsection (1), and every two years after that, the Minister shall review the list to determine whether there are still reasonable grounds, as set out in subsection (1), for an entity to be a listed entity and make a recommendation to the Governor in Council as to whether the entity should remain a listed entity. The review does not affect the validity of the list.
Completion of review
(10) The Minister shall complete the review as soon as possible and in any event, no later than 120 days after its commencement. After completing the review, he or she shall cause to be published, without delay, in the
Canada Gazette
Definition of
judge
(11) In this section,
judge

2001, c. 41, ss. 4, 143;
2005, c. 10, ss. 18, 34.

Admission of foreign information obtained in confidence

83.06 (1) For the purposes of subsection 83.05(6), in private and in the absence of the applicant or any counsel representing it,

(a) the Minister of Public Safety and Emergency Preparedness may make an application to the judge for the admission of information obtained in confidence from a government, an institution or an agency of a foreign state, from an international organization of states or from an institution or an agency of an international organization of states; and

(b) the judge shall examine the information and provide counsel representing the Minister with a reasonable opportunity to be heard as to whether the information is relevant but should not be disclosed to the applicant or any counsel representing it because the disclosure would injure national security or endanger the safety of any person.

Return of information

(2) The information shall be returned to counsel representing the Minister and shall not be considered by the judge in making the determination under paragraph 83.05(6)(d), if

(a) the judge determines that the information is not relevant;

(b) the judge determines that the information is relevant but should be summarized in the statement to be provided under paragraph 83.05(6)(b); or

(c) the Minister withdraws the application.

Use of information

(3) If the judge decides that the information is relevant but that its disclosure would injure national security or endanger the safety of persons, the information shall not be disclosed in the statement mentioned in paragraph 83.05(6)(b), but the judge may base the determination under paragraph 83.05(6)(d) on it.

2001, c. 41, s. 4;
2005, c. 10, s. 19.

Mistaken identity

83.07 (1) An entity claiming not to be a listed entity may apply to the Minister of Public Safety and Emergency Preparedness for a certificate stating that it is not a listed entity.

Issuance of certificate

(2) The Minister shall, within 15 days after receiving the application, issue a certificate if he or she is satisfied that the applicant is not a listed entity.

2001, c. 41, s. 4;
2005, c. 10, s. 20.

Freezing of Property

Freezing of property

83.08 (1) No person in Canada and no Canadian outside Canada shall knowingly

(a) deal directly or indirectly in any property that is owned or controlled by or on behalf of a terrorist group;

(b) enter into or facilitate, directly or indirectly, any transaction in respect of property referred to in paragraph (a); or

(c) provide any financial or other related services in respect of property referred to in paragraph (a) to, for the benefit of or at the direction of a terrorist group.

No civil liability

(2) A person who acts reasonably in taking, or omitting to take, measures to comply with subsection (1) shall not be liable in any civil action arising from having taken or omitted to take the measures, if they took all reasonable steps to satisfy themselves that the relevant property was owned or controlled by or on behalf of a terrorist group.

2001, c. 41, s. 4;

2013, c. 9, s. 3.
Exemptions
83.09 (1) The Minister of Public Safety and Emergency Preparedness, or a person designated by him or her, may authorize any person in Canada or any Canadian outside Canada to carry out a specified activity or transaction that is prohibited by section 83.08, or a class of such activities or transactions.
Ministerial authorization
(2) The Minister, or a person designated by him or her, may make the authorization subject to any terms and conditions that are required in their opinion and may amend, suspend, revoke or reinstate it.
Existing equities maintained
(3) All secured and unsecured rights and interests in the frozen property that are held by persons, other than terrorist groups or their agents, are entitled to the same ranking that they would have been entitled to had the property not been frozen.
Third party involvement
(4) If a person has obtained an authorization under subsection (1), any other person involved in carrying out the activity or transaction, or class of activities or transactions, to which the authorization relates is not subject to sections 83.08, 83.1 and 83.11 if the terms or conditions of the authorization that are imposed under subsection (2), if any, are met.
2001, c. 41, s. 4;
2005, c. 10, s. 21.
Disclosure
83.1 (1) Every person in Canada and every Canadian outside Canada shall disclose without delay to the Commissioner of the Royal Canadian Mounted Police or to the Director of the Canadian Security Intelligence Service
(a) the existence of property in their possession or control that they know is owned or controlled by or on behalf of a terrorist group; and
(b) information about a transaction or proposed transaction in respect of property referred to in paragraph (a).
Immunity
(2) No criminal or civil proceedings lie against a person for disclosure made in good faith under subsection (1).
2001, c. 41, s. 4;
2013, c. 9, s. 4.
Audit
83.11 (1) The following entities must determine on a continuing basis whether they are in possession or control of property owned or controlled by or on behalf of a listed entity:
(a) authorized foreign banks within the meaning of section 2 of the
Bank Act
(b) cooperative credit societies, savings and credit unions and caisses populaires regulated by a provincial Act and associations regulated by the
Cooperative Credit Associations Act
(c) foreign companies within the meaning of subsection 2(1) of the
Insurance Companies Act
(c.1) companies, provincial companies and societies within the meaning of subsection 2(1) of the
Insurance Companies Act
(c.2) fraternal benefit societies regulated by a provincial Act in respect of their insurance activities, and insurance companies and other entities engaged in the business of insuring risks that are regulated by a provincial Act;
(d) companies to which the
Trust and Loan Companies Act
(e) trust companies regulated by a provincial Act;
(f) loan companies regulated by a provincial Act; and

(g) entities authorized under provincial legislation to engage in the business of dealing in securities, or to provide portfolio management or investment counselling services.

Monthly report

(2) Subject to the regulations, every entity referred to in paragraphs (1)(a) to (g) must report, within the period specified by regulation or, if no period is specified, monthly, to the principal agency or body that supervises or regulates it under federal or provincial law either

(a) that it is not in possession or control of any property referred to in subsection (1), or

(b) that it is in possession or control of such property, in which case it must also report the number of persons, contracts or accounts involved and the total value of the property.

Immunity

(3) No criminal or civil proceedings lie against a person for making a report in good faith under subsection (2).

Regulations

(4) The Governor in Council may make regulations

(a) excluding any entity or class of entities from the requirement to make a report referred to in subsection (2), and specifying the conditions of exclusion; and

(b) specifying a period for the purposes of subsection (2).

2001, c. 41, s. 4.

Offences — freezing of property, disclosure or audit

83.12 (1) Every one who contravenes any of sections 83.08, 83.1 and 83.11 is guilty of an offence and liable

(a) on summary conviction, to a fine of not more than $100,000 or to imprisonment for a term of not more than one year, or to both; or

(b) on conviction on indictment, to imprisonment for a term of not more than 10 years.

(2) 2001, c. 41, s. 4;

2013, c. 9, s. 5.

Seizure and Restraint of Property

Seizure and restraint of assets

83.13 (1) Where a judge of the Federal Court, on an

(a) if the property is situated in Canada, a warrant authorizing a person named therein or a peace officer to search the building, receptacle or place for that property and to seize that property and any other property in respect of which that person or peace officer believes, on reasonable grounds, that an order of forfeiture may be made under that subsection; or

(b) if the property is situated in or outside Canada, a restraint order prohibiting any person from disposing of, or otherwise dealing with any interest in, that property other than as may be specified in the order.

Contents of application

(1.1) An affidavit in support of an application under subsection (1) may be sworn on information and belief, and, notwithstanding the

Appointment of manager

(2) On an application under subsection (1), at the request of the Attorney General, if a judge is of the opinion that the circumstances so require, the judge may

(a) appoint a person to take control of, and to manage or otherwise deal with, all or part of the property in accordance with the directions of the judge; and

(b) require any person having possession of that property to give possession of the property to the person appointed under paragraph (a).

Appointment of Minister of Public Works and Government Services

(3) When the Attorney General of Canada so requests, a judge appointing a person under subsection (2) shall appoint the Minister of Public Works and Government Services.

Power to manage

(4) The power to manage or otherwise deal with property under subsection (2) includes
(a) in the case of perishable or rapidly depreciating property, the power to sell that property; and
(b) in the case of property that has little or no value, the power to destroy that property.

Application for destruction order
(5) Before a person appointed under subsection (2) destroys property referred to in paragraph (4)(b), he or she shall apply to a judge of the Federal Court for a destruction order.

Notice
(6) Before making a destruction order in relation to any property, a judge shall require notice in accordance with subsection (7) to be given to, and may hear, any person who, in the opinion of the judge, appears to have a valid interest in the property.

Manner of giving notice
(7) A notice under subsection (6) shall be given in the manner that the judge directs or as provided in the rules of the Federal Court.

Order
(8) A judge may order that property be destroyed if he or she is satisfied that the property has little or no financial or other value.

When management order ceases to have effect
(9) A management order ceases to have effect when the property that is the subject of the management order is returned to an applicant in accordance with the law or forfeited to Her Majesty.

Application to vary
(10) The Attorney General may at any time apply to a judge of the Federal Court to cancel or vary an order or warrant made under this section, other than an appointment made under subsection (3).

Procedure
(11) Subsections 462.32(4) and (6), sections 462.34 to 462.35 and 462.4, subsections 487(3) and (4) and section 488 apply, with such modifications as the circumstances require, to a warrant issued under paragraph (1)(a).

Procedure
(12) Subsections 462.33(4) and (6) to (11) and sections 462.34 to 462.35 and 462.4 apply, with such modifications as the circumstances require, to an order issued under paragraph (1)(b).
2001, c. 41, s. 4.

Forfeiture of Property

Application for order of forfeiture
83.14 (1) The Attorney General may make an application to a judge of the Federal Court for an order of forfeiture in respect of
(a) property owned or controlled by or on behalf of a terrorist group; or
(b) property that has been or will be used, in whole or in part, to facilitate or carry out a terrorist activity.

Contents of application
(2) An affidavit in support of an application by the Attorney General under subsection (1) may be sworn on information and belief, and, notwithstanding the
Federal Court Rules, 1998

Respondents
(3) The Attorney General is required to name as a respondent to an application under subsection (1) only those persons who are known to own or control the property that is the subject of the application.

Notice
(4) The Attorney General shall give notice of an application under subsection (1) to named respondents in such a manner as the judge directs or as provided in the rules of the Federal Court.

Granting of forfeiture order
(5) If a judge is satisfied on a balance of probabilities that property is property referred to in

paragraph (1)(a) or (b), the judge shall order that the property be forfeited to Her Majesty to be disposed of as the Attorney General directs or otherwise dealt with in accordance with the law.

Use of proceeds

(5.1) Any proceeds that arise from the disposal of property under subsection (5) may be used to compensate victims of terrorist activities and to fund anti-terrorist initiatives in accordance with any regulations made by the Governor in Council under subsection (5.2).

Regulations

(5.2) The Governor in Council may make regulations for the purposes of specifying how the proceeds referred to in subsection (5.1) are to be distributed.

Order refusing forfeiture

(6) Where a judge refuses an application under subsection (1) in respect of any property, the judge shall make an order that describes the property and declares that it is not property referred to in that subsection.

Notice

(7) On an application under subsection (1), a judge may require notice to be given to any person who, in the opinion of the Court, appears to have an interest in the property, and any such person shall be entitled to be added as a respondent to the application.

Third party interests

(8) If a judge is satisfied that a person referred to in subsection (7) has an interest in property that is subject to an application, has exercised reasonable care to ensure that the property would not be used to facilitate or carry out a terrorist activity, and is not a member of a terrorist group, the judge shall order that the interest is not affected by the forfeiture. Such an order shall declare the nature and extent of the interest in question.

Dwelling-house

(9) Where all or part of property that is the subject of an application under subsection (1) is a dwelling-house, the judge shall also consider

(a) the impact of an order of forfeiture on any member of the immediate family of the person who owns or controls the dwelling-house, if the dwelling-house was the member's principal residence at the time the dwelling-house was ordered restrained or at the time the forfeiture application was made and continues to be the member's principal residence; and

(b) whether the member appears innocent of any complicity or collusion in the terrorist activity.

Motion to vary or set aside

(10) A person who claims an interest in property that was forfeited and who did not receive notice under subsection (7) may bring a motion to the Federal Court to vary or set aside an order made under subsection (5) not later than 60 days after the day on which the forfeiture order was made.

No extension of time

(11) The Court may not extend the period set out in subsection (10).

2001, c. 41, s. 4;

2017, c. 7, s. 55(F).

Disposition of property

83.15 Subsection 462.42(6) and sections 462.43 and 462.46 apply, with such modifications as the circumstances require, to property subject to a warrant or restraint order issued under subsection 83.13(1) or ordered forfeited under subsection 83.14(5).

2001, c. 41, s. 4.

Interim preservation rights

83.16 (1) Pending any appeal of an order made under section 83.14, property restrained under an order issued under section 83.13 shall continue to be restrained, property seized under a warrant issued under that section shall continue to be detained, and any person appointed to manage, control or otherwise deal with that property under that section shall continue in that capacity.

Appeal of refusal to grant order

(2) Section 462.34 applies, with such modifications as the circumstances require, to an appeal taken in respect of a refusal to grant an order under subsection 83.14(5).

2001, c. 41, s. 4.
Other forfeiture provisions unaffected
83.17 (1) This Part does not affect the operation of any other provision of this or any other Act of Parliament respecting the forfeiture of property.
Priority for restitution to victims of crime
(2) Property is subject to forfeiture under subsection 83.14(5) only to the extent that it is not required to satisfy the operation of any other provision of this or any other Act of Parliament respecting restitution to, or compensation of, persons affected by the commission of offences.
2001, c. 41, s. 4.

Participating, Facilitating, Instructing and Harbouring

Participation in activity of terrorist group
83.18 (1) Every one who knowingly participates in or contributes to, directly or indirectly, any activity of a terrorist group for the purpose of enhancing the ability of any terrorist group to facilitate or carry out a terrorist activity is guilty of an indictable offence and liable to imprisonment for a term not exceeding ten years.
Prosecution
(2) An offence may be committed under subsection (1) whether or not
(a) a terrorist group actually facilitates or carries out a terrorist activity;
(b) the participation or contribution of the accused actually enhances the ability of a terrorist group to facilitate or carry out a terrorist activity; or
(c) the accused knows the specific nature of any terrorist activity that may be facilitated or carried out by a terrorist group.
Meaning of participating or contributing
(3) Participating in or contributing to an activity of a terrorist group includes
(a) providing, receiving or recruiting a person to receive training;
(b) providing or offering to provide a skill or an expertise for the benefit of, at the direction of or in association with a terrorist group;
(c) recruiting a person in order to facilitate or commit
(i) a terrorism offence, or
(ii) an act or omission outside Canada that, if committed in Canada, would be a terrorism offence;
(d) entering or remaining in any country for the benefit of, at the direction of or in association with a terrorist group; and
(e) making oneself, in response to instructions from any of the persons who constitute a terrorist group, available to facilitate or commit
(i) a terrorism offence, or
(ii) an act or omission outside Canada that, if committed in Canada, would be a terrorism offence.
Factors
(4) In determining whether an accused participates in or contributes to any activity of a terrorist group, the court may consider, among other factors, whether the accused
(a) uses a name, word, symbol or other representation that identifies, or is associated with, the terrorist group;
(b) frequently associates with any of the persons who constitute the terrorist group;
(c) receives any benefit from the terrorist group; or
(d) repeatedly engages in activities at the instruction of any of the persons who constitute the terrorist group.
2001, c. 41, s. 4.
Leaving Canada to participate in activity of terrorist group
83.181 Everyone who leaves or attempts to leave Canada, or goes or attempts to go on board a conveyance with the intent to leave Canada, for the purpose of committing an act or omission outside Canada that, if committed in Canada, would be an offence under subsection 83.18(1) is guilty of an

indictable offence and liable to imprisonment for a term of not more than 10 years.
2013, c. 9, s. 6.

Facilitating terrorist activity

83.19 (1) Every one who knowingly facilitates a terrorist activity is guilty of an indictable offence and liable to imprisonment for a term not exceeding fourteen years.

Facilitation

(2) For the purposes of this Part, a terrorist activity is facilitated whether or not
(a) the facilitator knows that a particular terrorist activity is facilitated;
(b) any particular terrorist activity was foreseen or planned at the time it was facilitated; or
(c) any terrorist activity was actually carried out.
2001, c. 41, s. 4.

Leaving Canada to facilitate terrorist activity

83.191 Everyone who leaves or attempts to leave Canada, or goes or attempts to go on board a conveyance with the intent to leave Canada, for the purpose of committing an act or omission outside Canada that, if committed in Canada, would be an offence under subsection 83.19(1) is guilty of an indictable offence and liable to imprisonment for a term of not more than 14 years.
2013, c. 9, s. 7.

Commission of offence for terrorist group

83.2 Every one who commits an indictable offence under this or any other Act of Parliament for the benefit of, at the direction of or in association with a terrorist group is guilty of an indictable offence and liable to imprisonment for life.
2001, c. 41, s. 4.

Leaving Canada to commit offence for terrorist group

83.201 Everyone who leaves or attempts to leave Canada, or goes or attempts to go on board a conveyance with the intent to leave Canada, for the purpose of committing an act or omission outside Canada that, if committed in Canada, would be an indictable offence under this or any other Act of Parliament for the benefit of, at the direction of or in association with a terrorist group is guilty of an indictable offence and liable to imprisonment for a term of not more than 14 years.
2013, c. 9, s. 8.

Leaving Canada to commit offence that is terrorist activity

83.202 Everyone who leaves or attempts to leave Canada, or goes or attempts to go on board a conveyance with the intent to leave Canada, for the purpose of committing an act or omission outside Canada that, if committed in Canada, would be an indictable offence under this or any other Act of Parliament if the act or omission constituting the offence also constitutes a terrorist activity is guilty of an indictable offence and liable to imprisonment for a term of not more than 14 years.
2013, c. 9, s. 8.

Instructing to carry out activity for terrorist group

83.21 (1) Every person who knowingly instructs, directly or indirectly, any person to carry out any activity for the benefit of, at the direction of or in association with a terrorist group, for the purpose of enhancing the ability of any terrorist group to facilitate or carry out a terrorist activity, is guilty of an indictable offence and liable to imprisonment for life.

Prosecution

(2) An offence may be committed under subsection (1) whether or not
(a) the activity that the accused instructs to be carried out is actually carried out;
(b) the accused instructs a particular person to carry out the activity referred to in paragraph (a);
(c) the accused knows the identity of the person whom the accused instructs to carry out the activity referred to in paragraph (a);
(d) the person whom the accused instructs to carry out the activity referred to in paragraph (a) knows that it is to be carried out for the benefit of, at the direction of or in association with a terrorist group;
(e) a terrorist group actually facilitates or carries out a terrorist activity;
(f) the activity referred to in paragraph (a) actually enhances the ability of a terrorist group to facilitate or carry out a terrorist activity; or

(g) the accused knows the specific nature of any terrorist activity that may be facilitated or carried out by a terrorist group.
2001, c. 41, s. 4.
Instructing to carry out terrorist activity
83.22 (1) Every person who knowingly instructs, directly or indirectly, any person to carry out a terrorist activity is guilty of an indictable offence and liable to imprisonment for life.
Prosecution
(2) An offence may be committed under subsection (1) whether or not
(a) the terrorist activity is actually carried out;
(b) the accused instructs a particular person to carry out the terrorist activity;
(c) the accused knows the identity of the person whom the accused instructs to carry out the terrorist activity; or
(d) the person whom the accused instructs to carry out the terrorist activity knows that it is a terrorist activity.
2001, c. 41, s. 4.
Advocating or promoting commission of terrorism offences
83.221 (1) Every person who, by communicating statements, knowingly advocates or promotes the commission of terrorism offences in general — other than an offence under this section — while knowing that any of those offences will be committed or being reckless as to whether any of those offences may be committed, as a result of such communication, is guilty of an indictable offence and is liable to imprisonment for a term of not more than five years.
Definitions
(2) The following definitions apply in this section.
communicating
statements
2015, c. 20, s. 16.
Warrant of seizure
83.222 (1) A judge who is satisfied by information on oath that there are reasonable grounds to believe that any publication, copies of which are kept for sale or distribution in premises within the court's jurisdiction, is terrorist propaganda may issue a warrant authorizing seizure of the copies.
Summons to occupier
(2) Within seven days after the day on which the warrant is issued, the judge shall issue a summons to the premises' occupier requiring the occupier to appear before the court and to show cause why the matter seized should not be forfeited to Her Majesty.
Owner and author may appear
(3) The owner and the author of the matter seized and alleged to be terrorist propaganda may appear and be represented before the court in order to oppose the making of an order for the forfeiture of the matter.
Order of forfeiture
(4) If the court is satisfied, on a balance of probabilities, that the publication is terrorist propaganda, it may make an order declaring that the matter be forfeited to Her Majesty, for disposal as the Attorney General may direct.
Disposal of matter
(5) If the court is not satisfied that the publication is terrorist propaganda, it may order that the matter be restored to the person from whom it was seized without delay after the time for final appeal has expired.
Appeal
(6) An appeal lies from an order made under subsection (4) or (5) by any person who appeared before the court, on any ground of appeal that involves a question of law or fact alone, or a question of mixed law and fact, as if it were an appeal against conviction or against a judgment or verdict of acquittal, as the case may be, on a question of law alone under Part XXI, and sections 673 to 696 apply with any modifications that the circumstances require.

Consent
(7) No proceeding under this section shall be instituted without the Attorney General's consent.
Definitions
(8) The following definitions apply in this section.
court
judge
terrorist propaganda
2015, c. 20, s. 16.
Order to computer system's custodian
83.223 (1) If a judge is satisfied by information on oath that there are reasonable grounds to believe that there is material — that is terrorist propaganda or computer data that makes terrorist propaganda available — stored on and made available to the public through a computer system that is within the court's jurisdiction, the judge may order the computer system's custodian to
(a) give an electronic copy of the material to the court;
(b) ensure that the material is no longer stored on and made available through the computer system; and
(c) provide the information that is necessary to identify and locate the person who posted the material.
Notice to person who posted material
(2) Within a reasonable time after receiving the information referred to in paragraph (1)(c), the judge shall cause notice to be given to the person who posted the material, giving that person the opportunity to appear and be represented before the court and to show cause why the material should not be deleted. If the person cannot be identified or located or does not reside in Canada, the judge may order the computer system's custodian to post the text of the notice at the location where the material was previously stored and made available, until the time set for the appearance.
Person who posted material may appear
(3) The person who posted the material may appear and be represented before the court in order to oppose the making of an order under subsection (5).
Non-appearance
(4) If the person who posted the material does not appear before the court, the court may proceed to hear and determine the proceedings in the absence of the person as fully and effectually as if the person had appeared.
Order of deletion
(5) If the court is satisfied, on a balance of probabilities, that the material is available to the public and is terrorist propaganda or computer data that makes terrorist propaganda available, it may order the computer system's custodian to delete the material.
Destruction of electronic copy
(6) When the court makes the order for the deletion of the material, it may order the destruction of the electronic copy in the court's possession.
Return of material
(7) If the court is not satisfied that the material is available to the public and is terrorist propaganda or computer data that makes terrorist propaganda available, the court shall order that the electronic copy be returned to the computer system's custodian and terminate the order under paragraph (1)(b).
Appeal
(8) An appeal lies from an order made under subsection (5) or (6) by any person who appeared before the court, on any ground of appeal that involves a question of law or fact alone, or a question of mixed law and fact, as if it were an appeal against conviction or against a judgment or verdict of acquittal, as the case may be, on a question of law alone under Part XXI, and sections 673 to 696 apply with any modifications that the circumstances require.
Consent
(9) No proceeding under this section shall be instituted without the Attorney General's consent.
When order takes effect

(10) No order made under any of subsections (5) to (7) takes effect until the time for final appeal has expired.
Definitions
(11) The following definitions apply in this section.
computer data
computer system
court
data
judge
terrorist propaganda
2015, c. 20, ss. 16, 35.
Concealing person who carried out terrorist activity
83.23 (1) Everyone who knowingly harbours or conceals any person whom they know to be a person who has carried out a terrorist activity, for the purpose of enabling the person to facilitate or carry out any terrorist activity, is guilty of an indictable offence and liable to imprisonment
(a) for a term of not more than 14 years, if the person who is harboured or concealed carried out a terrorist activity that is a terrorism offence for which that person is liable to imprisonment for life; and
(b) for a term of not more than 10 years, if the person who is harboured or concealed carried out a terrorist activity that is a terrorism offence for which that person is liable to any other punishment.
Concealing person who is likely to carry out terrorist activity
(2) Everyone who knowingly harbours or conceals any person whom they know to be a person who is likely to carry out a terrorist activity, for the purpose of enabling the person to facilitate or carry out any terrorist activity, is guilty of an indictable offence and liable to imprisonment for a term of not more than 10 years.
2001, c. 41, s. 4;
2013, c. 9, s. 9.

Hoax Regarding Terrorist Activity

Hoax — terrorist activity
83.231 (1) Every one commits an offence who, without lawful excuse and with intent to cause any person to fear death, bodily harm, substantial damage to property or serious interference with the lawful use or operation of property,
(a) conveys or causes or procures to be conveyed information that, in all the circumstances, is likely to cause a reasonable apprehension that terrorist activity is occurring or will occur, without believing the information to be true; or
(b) commits an act that, in all the circumstances, is likely to cause a reasonable apprehension that terrorist activity is occurring or will occur, without believing that such activity is occurring or will occur.
Punishment
(2) Every one who commits an offence under subsection (1) is guilty of
(a) an indictable offence and liable to imprisonment for a term not exceeding five years; or
(b) an offence punishable on summary conviction.
Causing bodily harm
(3) Every one who commits an offence under subsection (1) and thereby causes bodily harm to any other person is guilty of
(a) an indictable offence and liable to imprisonment for a term not exceeding ten years; or
(b) an offence punishable on summary conviction and liable to imprisonment for a term not exceeding eighteen months.
Causing death
(4) Every one who commits an offence under subsection (1) and thereby causes the death of any

other person is guilty of an indictable offence and liable to imprisonment for life.
2004, c. 15, s. 32.

Proceedings and Aggravated Punishment

Attorney General's consent
83.24 Proceedings in respect of a terrorism offence or an offence under section 83.12 shall not be commenced without the consent of the Attorney General.
2001, c. 41, s. 4.
Jurisdiction
83.25 (1) Where a person is alleged to have committed a terrorism offence or an offence under section 83.12, proceedings in respect of that offence may, whether or not that person is in Canada, be commenced at the instance of the Government of Canada and conducted by the Attorney General of Canada or counsel acting on his or her behalf in any territorial division in Canada, if the offence is alleged to have occurred outside the province in which the proceedings are commenced, whether or not proceedings have previously been commenced elsewhere in Canada.
Trial and punishment
(2) An accused may be tried and punished in respect of an offence referred to in subsection (1) in the same manner as if the offence had been committed in the territorial division where the proceeding is conducted.
2001, c. 41, s. 4.
Sentences to be served consecutively
83.26 A sentence, other than one of life imprisonment, imposed on a person for an offence under any of sections 83.02 to 83.04 and 83.18 to 83.23 shall be served consecutively to
(a) any other punishment imposed on the person, other than a sentence of life imprisonment, for an offence arising out of the same event or series of events; and
(b) any other sentence, other than one of life imprisonment, to which the person is subject at the time the sentence is imposed on the person for an offence under any of those sections.
2001, c. 41, s. 4.
Punishment for terrorist activity
83.27 (1) Notwithstanding anything in this Act, a person convicted of an indictable offence, other than an offence for which a sentence of imprisonment for life is imposed as a minimum punishment, where the act or omission constituting the offence also constitutes a terrorist activity, is liable to imprisonment for life.
Offender must be notified
(2) Subsection (1) does not apply unless the prosecutor satisfies the court that the offender, before making a plea, was notified that the application of that subsection would be sought.
2001, c. 41, s. 4.

Investigative Hearing

Definition of
judge
83.28 (1) In this section and section 83.29,
judge
Order for gathering information
(2) Subject to subsection (3), a peace officer may, for the purposes of an investigation of a terrorism offence, apply
Attorney General's consent
(3) A peace officer may make an application under subsection (2) only if the Attorney General's prior consent was obtained.
Making of order

(4) The judge to whom the application is made may make an order for the gathering of information if they are satisfied that the Attorney General's consent was obtained as required by subsection (3), and
(a) that there are reasonable grounds to believe that
(i) a terrorism offence has been committed,
(ii) information concerning the offence, or information that may reveal the whereabouts of a person suspected by the peace officer of having committed the offence, is likely to be obtained as a result of the order, and
(iii) reasonable attempts have been made to obtain the information referred to in subparagraph (ii) by other means; or
(b) that
(i) there are reasonable grounds to believe that a terrorism offence will be committed,
(ii) there are reasonable grounds to believe that a person has direct and material information that relates to the offence referred to in subparagraph (i), or that may reveal the whereabouts of an individual who the peace officer suspects may commit the offence referred to in that subparagraph, and
(iii) reasonable attempts have been made to obtain the information referred to in subparagraph (ii) by other means.

Contents of order
(5) An order made under subsection (4) shall order the examination, on oath or not, of the person named in the order and require the person to attend at the place fixed by the judge, or by the judge designated under paragraph (b), as the case may be, for the examination and to remain in attendance until excused by the presiding judge, and may
(a) order the person to bring to the examination any thing in their possession or control, and produce it to the presiding judge;
(b) designate another judge as the judge before whom the examination is to take place; and
(c) include any other terms or conditions that the judge considers desirable, including terms or conditions for the protection of the interests of the person named in the order and of third parties or for the protection of any ongoing investigation.

Execution of order
(6) The order may be executed anywhere in Canada.

Variation of order
(7) The judge who made the order, or another judge of the same court, may vary its terms and conditions.

Obligation to answer questions and produce things
(8) A person named in an order made under subsection (4) shall answer questions put to them by the Attorney General or the Attorney General's agent, and shall produce to the presiding judge things that the person was ordered to bring, but may refuse if answering a question or producing a thing would disclose information that is protected by any law relating to privilege or to disclosure of information.

Judge to rule
(9) The presiding judge shall rule on any objection or other issue relating to a refusal to answer a question or to produce a thing.

No person excused from complying with subsection (8)
(10) No person shall be excused from answering a question or producing a thing under subsection (8) on the ground that the answer or thing may tend to incriminate them or subject them to any proceeding or penalty, but
(a) no answer given or thing produced under subsection (8) shall be used or received against the person in any criminal proceedings against them, other than a prosecution under section 132 or 136; and
(b) no evidence derived from the evidence obtained from the person shall be used or received against the person in any criminal proceedings against them, other than a prosecution under section 132 or 136.

Right to counsel
(11) A person has the right to retain and instruct counsel at any stage of the proceedings.
Order for custody of thing
(12) The presiding judge, if satisfied that any thing produced during the course of the examination will likely be relevant to the investigation of any terrorism offence, may order that the thing be given into the custody of the peace officer or someone acting on the peace officer's behalf.
2001, c. 41, s. 4;
2013, c. 9, s. 10.
Arrest warrant
83.29 (1) The judge who made the order under subsection 83.28(4), or another judge of the same court, may issue a warrant for the arrest of the person named in the order if the judge is satisfied, on an information in writing and under oath, that the person
(a) is evading service of the order;
(b) is about to abscond; or
(c) did not attend the examination, or did not remain in attendance, as required by the order.
Execution of warrant
(2) The warrant may be executed at any place in Canada by any peace officer having jurisdiction in that place.
Person to be brought before judge
(3) A peace officer who arrests a person in the execution of the warrant shall, without delay, bring the person, or cause them to be brought, before the judge who issued the warrant or another judge of the same court. The judge in question may, to ensure compliance with the order, order that the person be detained in custody or released on recognizance, with or without sureties.
Application of section 707
(4) Section 707 applies, with any necessary modifications, to persons detained in custody under this section.
2001, c. 41, s. 4;
2013, c. 9, s. 10.

Recognizance with Conditions

Attorney General's consent
83.3 (1) The Attorney General's consent is required before a peace officer may lay an information under subsection (2).
Terrorist activity
(2) Subject to subsection (1), a peace officer may lay an information before a provincial court judge if the peace officer
(a) believes on reasonable grounds that a terrorist activity may be carried out; and
(b) suspects on reasonable grounds that the imposition of a recognizance with conditions on a person, or the arrest of a person, is likely to prevent the carrying out of the terrorist activity.
Appearance
(3) The judge who receives the information may cause the person to appear before any provincial court judge.
Arrest without warrant
(4) Despite subsections (2) and (3), a peace officer may arrest a person without a warrant and cause the person to be detained in custody, in order to bring them before a provincial court judge in accordance with subsection (6), if
(a) either
(i) the grounds for laying an information referred to in paragraphs (2)(a) and (b) exist but, by reason of exigent circumstances, it would be impracticable to lay an information under subsection (2), or
(ii) an information has been laid under subsection (2) and a summons has been issued; and
(b) the peace officer suspects on reasonable grounds that the detention of the person in custody is

likely to prevent a terrorist activity.
Duty of peace officer
(5) If a peace officer arrests a person without a warrant in the circumstance described in subparagraph (4)(a)(i), the peace officer shall, within the time prescribed by paragraph (6)(a) or (b),
(a) lay an information in accordance with subsection (2); or
(b) release the person.
When person to be taken before judge
(6) Unless a peace officer, or an officer in charge as defined in Part XVI, is satisfied that a person should be released from custody unconditionally before their appearance before a provincial court judge in accordance with the rules in paragraph (a) or (b), and so releases the person, the person detained in custody shall be taken before a provincial court judge in accordance with the following rules:
(a) if a provincial court judge is available within 24 hours after the person has been arrested, the person shall be taken before a provincial court judge without unreasonable delay and in any event within that period; and
(b) if a provincial court judge is not available within 24 hours after the person has been arrested, the person shall be taken before a provincial court judge as soon as feasible.
How person dealt with
(7) When a person is taken before a provincial court judge under subsection (6),
(a) if an information has not been laid under subsection (2), the judge shall order that the person be released; or
(b) if an information has been laid under subsection (2),
(i) the judge shall order that the person be released unless the peace officer who laid the information shows cause why the person's detention in custody is justified on one or more of the following grounds:
(A) the detention is necessary to ensure the person's appearance before a provincial court judge in order to be dealt with in accordance with subsection (8),
(B) the detention is necessary for the protection or safety of the public, including any witness, having regard to all the circumstances including
(I) the likelihood that, if the person is released from custody, a terrorist activity will be carried out, and
(II) any substantial likelihood that the person will, if released from custody, interfere with the administration of justice, and
(C) the detention is necessary to maintain confidence in the administration of justice, having regard to all the circumstances, including the apparent strength of the peace officer's grounds under subsection (2), and the gravity of any terrorist activity that may be carried out, and
(ii) the judge may adjourn the matter for a hearing under subsection (8) but, if the person is not released under subparagraph (i), the adjournment may not exceed 48 hours.
Adjournment under subparagraph (7)(b)(ii)
(7.1) If a judge has adjourned the matter under subparagraph (7)(b)(ii) and the person remains in custody at the end of the period of adjournment, the person shall be taken before a provincial court judge who
(a) shall order that the person be released unless a peace officer shows cause why the person's detention in custody is justified on one or more of the grounds set out in clauses (7)(b)(i)(A) to (C) and satisfies the judge that the investigation in relation to which the person is detained is being conducted diligently and expeditiously; and
(b) may adjourn the matter for a hearing under subsection (8) but, if the person is not released under paragraph (a), the adjournment may not exceed 48 hours.
Adjournment under paragraph (7.1)(b)
(7.2) If a judge has adjourned the matter under paragraph (7.1)(b) and the person remains in custody at the end of the period of adjournment, the person shall be taken before a provincial court judge who
(a) shall order that the person be released unless a peace officer shows cause why the person's

detention in custody is justified on one or more of the grounds set out in clauses (7)(b)(i)(A) to (C) and satisfies the judge that the investigation in relation to which the person is detained is being conducted diligently and expeditiously; and

(b) may adjourn the matter for a hearing under subsection (8) but, if the person is not released under paragraph (a), the adjournment may not exceed 48 hours.

Hearing before judge

(8) The judge before whom the person appears in accordance with subsection (3)

(a) may, if the judge is satisfied by the evidence adduced that the peace officer has reasonable grounds for the suspicion, order that the person enter into a recognizance, with or without sureties, to keep the peace and be of good behaviour for a period of not more than 12 months and to comply with any other reasonable conditions prescribed in the recognizance, including the conditions set out in subsections (10), (11.1) and (11.2), that the judge considers desirable for preventing the carrying out of a terrorist activity; and

(b) if the person was not released under subparagraph (7)(b)(i) or paragraph (7.1)(a) or (7.2)(a), shall order that the person be released, subject to the recognizance, if any, ordered under paragraph (a).

Duration extended

(8.1) However, if the judge is also satisfied that the person was convicted previously of a terrorism offence, the judge may order that the person enter into the recognizance for a period of not more than two years.

Refusal to enter into recognizance

(9) The judge may commit the person to prison for a term not exceeding 12 months if the person fails or refuses to enter into the recognizance.

Conditions — firearms

(10) Before making an order under paragraph (8)(a), the judge shall consider whether it is desirable, in the interests of the safety of the person or of any other person, to include as a condition of the recognizance that the person be prohibited from possessing any firearm, cross-bow, prohibited weapon, restricted weapon, prohibited device, ammunition, prohibited ammunition or explosive substance, or all of those things, for any period specified in the recognizance, and if the judge decides that it is so desirable, they shall add the condition to the recognizance.

Surrender, etc.

(11) If the judge adds the condition described in subsection (10) to a recognizance, they shall specify in it the manner and method by which

(a) the things referred to in that subsection that are in the person's possession shall be surrendered, disposed of, detained, stored or dealt with; and

(b) the authorizations, licences and registration certificates that are held by the person shall be surrendered.

Condition — passport

(11.1) The judge shall consider whether it is desirable, to prevent the carrying out of a terrorist activity, to include in the recognizance a condition that the person deposit, in the specified manner, any passport or other travel document issued in their name that is in their possession or control. If the judge decides that it is desirable, the judge shall add the condition to the recognizance and specify the period during which it applies.

Condition — specified geographic area

(11.2) The judge shall consider whether it is desirable, to prevent the carrying out of a terrorist activity, to include in the recognizance a condition that the person remain within a specified geographic area unless written permission to leave that area is obtained from the judge or any individual designated by the judge. If the judge decides that it is desirable, the judge shall add the condition to the recognizance and specify the period during which it applies.

Reasons

(12) If the judge does not add a condition described in subsection (10), (11.1) or (11.2) to a recognizance, the judge shall include in the record a statement of the reasons for not adding it.

Variance of conditions

(13) The judge, or any other judge of the same court, may, on application of the peace officer, the Attorney General or the person, vary the conditions fixed in the recognizance.
Other provisions to apply
(14) Subsections 810(4) and (5) apply, with any necessary modifications, to proceedings under this section.
2001, c. 41, s. 4;
2013, c. 9, s. 10;
2015, c. 20, s. 17.
Annual report (sections 83.28 and 83.29)
83.31 (1) The Attorney General of Canada shall prepare and cause to be laid before Parliament and the Attorney General of every province shall publish or otherwise make available to the public an annual report for the previous year on the operation of sections 83.28 and 83.29 that includes
(a) the number of consents to make an application that were sought, and the number that were obtained, by virtue of subsections 83.28(2) and (3);
(b) the number of orders for the gathering of information that were made under subsection 83.28(4); and
(c) the number of arrests that were made with a warrant issued under section 83.29.
Attorney General's opinion
(1.1) The Attorney General of Canada shall include in the annual report under subsection (1) his or her opinion, supported by reasons, on whether the operation of sections 83.28 and 83.29 should be extended.
Annual report (section 83.3)
(2) The Attorney General of Canada shall prepare and cause to be laid before Parliament and the Attorney General of every province shall publish or otherwise make available to the public an annual report for the previous year on the operation of section 83.3 that includes
(a) the number of consents to lay an information that were sought, and the number that were obtained, by virtue of subsections 83.3(1) and (2);
(b) the number of cases in which a summons or a warrant of arrest was issued for the purposes of subsection 83.3(3);
(c) the number of cases in which a person was not released under subsection 83.3(7), (7.1) or (7.2) pending a hearing;
(d) the number of cases in which an order to enter into a recognizance was made under paragraph 83.3(8)(a), and the types of conditions that were imposed;
(e) the number of times that a person failed or refused to enter into a recognizance, and the term of imprisonment imposed under subsection 83.3(9) in each case; and
(f) the number of cases in which the conditions fixed in a recognizance were varied under subsection 83.3(13).
Annual report (section 83.3)
(3) The Minister of Public Safety and Emergency Preparedness shall prepare and cause to be laid before Parliament and the Minister responsible for policing in every province shall publish or otherwise make available to the public an annual report for the previous year on the operation of section 83.3 that includes
(a) the number of arrests without warrant that were made under subsection 83.3(4) and the period of the arrested person's detention in custody in each case; and
(b) the number of cases in which a person was arrested without warrant under subsection 83.3(4) and was released
(i) by a peace officer under paragraph 83.3(5)(b), or
(ii) by a judge under paragraph 83.3(7)(a), (7.1)(a) or (7.2)(a).
Opinions
(3.1) The Attorney General of Canada and the Minister of Public Safety and Emergency Preparedness shall include in their annual reports under subsections (2) and (3), respectively, their opinion, supported by reasons, on whether the operation of section 83.3 should be extended.

Limitation

(4) The annual report shall not contain any information the disclosure of which would
(a) compromise or hinder an ongoing investigation of an offence under an Act of Parliament;
(b) endanger the life or safety of any person;
(c) prejudice a legal proceeding; or
(d) otherwise be contrary to the public interest.
2001, c. 41, s. 4;
2005, c. 10, s. 34;
2013, c. 9, s. 11;
2015, c. 20, s. 18.

Sunset provision

83.32 (1) Sections 83.28, 83.29 and 83.3 cease to have effect at the end of the 15th sitting day of Parliament after the fifth anniversary of the coming into force of this subsection unless, before the end of that day, the operation of those sections is extended by resolution — whose text is established under subsection (2) — passed by both Houses of Parliament in accordance with the rules set out in subsection (3).

Review

(1.1) A comprehensive review of sections 83.28, 83.29 and 83.3 and their operation shall be undertaken by any committee of the Senate, of the House of Commons or of both Houses of Parliament that may be designated or established by the Senate or the House of Commons, or by both Houses of Parliament, as the case may be, for that purpose.

Report

(1.2) The committee referred to in subsection (1.1) shall, within a year after a review is undertaken under that subsection or within any further time that may be authorized by the Senate, the House of Commons or both Houses of Parliament, as the case may be, submit a report on the review to Parliament, including its recommendation with respect to extending the operation of section 83.28, 83.29 or 83.3.

Order in council

(2) The Governor in Council may, by order, establish the text of a resolution that provides for the extension of the operation of section 83.28, 83.29 or 83.3 and that specifies the period of the extension, which may not exceed five years from the first day on which the resolution has been passed by both Houses of Parliament.

Rules

(3) A motion for the adoption of the resolution may be debated in both Houses of Parliament but may not be amended. At the conclusion of the debate, the Speaker of the House of Parliament shall immediately put every question necessary to determine whether or not the motion is concurred in.

Subsequent extensions

(4) The operation of section 83.28, 83.29 or 83.3 may be further extended in accordance with the procedure set out in this section, but the reference to "the fifth anniversary of the coming into force of this subsection" in subsection (1) is to be read as a reference to "the expiry of the most recent extension under this section".

Definition of
sitting day of Parliament
(5) In subsection (1),
sitting day of Parliament
2001, c. 41, s. 4;
2013, c. 9, s. 12.

Transitional provision — sections 83.28 and 83.29

83.33 (1) In the event that sections 83.28 and 83.29 cease to have effect in accordance with section 83.32, proceedings commenced under those sections shall be completed if the hearing before the judge of the application made under subsection 83.28(2) began before those sections ceased to have effect.

Transitional provision — section 83.3
(2) In the event that section 83.3 ceases to have effect in accordance with section 83.32, a person detained in custody under section 83.3 shall be released when that section ceases to have effect, except that subsections 83.3(7) to (14) continue to apply to a person who was taken before a judge under subsection 83.3(6) before section 83.3 ceased to have effect.
2001, c. 41, s. 4;
2013, c. 9, s. 13.

PART III

PART III
Firearms and Other Weapons

Interpretation

Definitions
84 (1) In this Part,
ammunition
antique firearm
(a) any firearm manufactured before 1898 that was not designed to discharge rim-fire or centre-fire ammunition and that has not been redesigned to discharge such ammunition, or
(b) any firearm that is prescribed to be an antique firearm;
authorization
Firearms Act
automatic firearm
cartridge magazine
chief firearms officer
Firearms Act
Commissioner of Firearms
Firearms Act
cross-bow
export
firearms officer
Firearms Act
handgun
imitation firearm
import
licence
Firearms Act
non-restricted firearm
(a) a firearm that is neither a prohibited firearm nor a restricted firearm, or
(b) a firearm that is prescribed to be a non-restricted firearm;
prescribed
prohibited ammunition
prohibited device
(a) any component or part of a weapon, or any accessory for use with a weapon, that is prescribed to be a prohibited device,
(b) a handgun barrel that is equal to or less than 105 mm in length, but does not include any such handgun barrel that is prescribed, where the handgun barrel is for use in international sporting competitions governed by the rules of the International Shooting Union,
(c) a device or contrivance designed or intended to muffle or stop the sound or report of a firearm,
(d) a cartridge magazine that is prescribed to be a prohibited device, or

(e) a replica firearm;
prohibited firearm
(a) a handgun that
(i) has a barrel equal to or less than 105 mm in length, or
(ii) is designed or adapted to discharge a 25 or 32 calibre cartridge,
but does not include any such handgun that is prescribed, where the handgun is for use in international sporting competitions governed by the rules of the International Shooting Union,
(b) a firearm that is adapted from a rifle or shotgun, whether by sawing, cutting or any other alteration, and that, as so adapted,
(i) is less than 660 mm in length, or
(ii) is 660 mm or greater in length and has a barrel less than 457 mm in length,
(c) an automatic firearm, whether or not it has been altered to discharge only one projectile with one pressure of the trigger, or
(d) any firearm that is prescribed to be a prohibited firearm;
prohibited weapon
(a) a knife that has a blade that opens automatically by gravity or centrifugal force or by hand pressure applied to a button, spring or other device in or attached to the handle of the knife, or
(b) any weapon, other than a firearm, that is prescribed to be a prohibited weapon;
prohibition order
Registrar
Firearms Act
registration certificate
Firearms Act
replica firearm
restricted firearm
(a) a handgun that is not a prohibited firearm,
(b) a firearm that
(i) is not a prohibited firearm,
(ii) has a barrel less than 470 mm in length, and
(iii) is capable of discharging centre-fire ammunition in a semi-automatic manner,
(c) a firearm that is designed or adapted to be fired when reduced to a length of less than 660 mm by folding, telescoping or otherwise, or
(d) a firearm of any other kind that is prescribed to be a restricted firearm;
restricted weapon
superior court
(a) in Ontario, the Superior Court of Justice, sitting in the region, district or county or group of counties where the relevant adjudication was made,
(b) in Quebec, the Superior Court,
(c) in New Brunswick, Manitoba, Saskatchewan and Alberta, the Court of Queen's Bench,
(d) in Nova Scotia, British Columbia, Prince Edward Island and a territory, the Supreme Court, and
(e) in Newfoundland and Labrador, the Trial Division of the Supreme Court;
transfer

Barrel length
(2) For the purposes of this Part, the length of a barrel of a firearm is
(a) in the case of a revolver, the distance from the muzzle of the barrel to the breach end immediately in front of the cylinder, and
(b) in any other case, the distance from the muzzle of the barrel to and including the chamber,
but does not include the length of any component, part or accessory including any component, part or accessory designed or intended to suppress the muzzle flash or reduce recoil.

Certain weapons deemed not to be firearms
(3) For the purposes of sections 91 to 95, 99 to 101, 103 to 107 and 117.03 of this Act and the provisions of the

Firearms Act
(a) any antique firearm;
(b) any device that is
(i) designed exclusively for signalling, for notifying of distress, for firing blank cartridges or for firing stud cartridges, explosive-driven rivets or other industrial projectiles, and
(ii) intended by the person in possession of it to be used exclusively for the purpose for which it is designed;
(c) any shooting device that is
(i) designed exclusively for the slaughtering of domestic animals, the tranquillizing of animals or the discharging of projectiles with lines attached to them, and
(ii) intended by the person in possession of it to be used exclusively for the purpose for which it is designed; and
(d) any other barrelled weapon, where it is proved that the weapon is not designed or adapted to discharge
(i) a shot, bullet or other projectile at a muzzle velocity exceeding 152.4 m per second or at a muzzle energy exceeding 5.7 Joules, or
(ii) a shot, bullet or other projectile that is designed or adapted to attain a velocity exceeding 152.4 m per second or an energy exceeding 5.7 Joules.

Exception — antique firearms
(3.1) Notwithstanding subsection (3), an antique firearm is a firearm for the purposes of regulations made under paragraph 117(h) of the
Firearms Act

Meaning of
holder
(4) For the purposes of this Part, a person is the holder of
(a) an authorization or a licence if the authorization or licence has been issued to the person and the person continues to hold it; and
(b) a registration certificate for a firearm if
(i) the registration certificate has been issued to the person and the person continues to hold it, or
(ii) the person possesses the registration certificate with the permission of its lawful holder.

Subsequent offences
(5) In determining, for the purpose of subsection 85(3), 95(2), 99(2), 100(2) or 103(2), whether a convicted person has committed a second or subsequent offence, if the person was earlier convicted of any of the following offences, that offence is to be considered as an earlier offence:
(a) an offence under section 85, 95, 96, 98, 98.1, 99, 100, 102 or 103 or subsection 117.01(1);
(b) an offence under section 244 or 244.2; or
(c) an offence under section 220, 236, 239, 272 or 273, subsection 279(1) or section 279.1, 344 or 346 if a firearm was used in the commission of the offence.
However, an earlier offence shall not be taken into account if 10 years have elapsed between the day on which the person was convicted of the earlier offence and the day on which the person was convicted of the offence for which sentence is being imposed, not taking into account any time in custody.

Sequence of convictions only
(6) For the purposes of subsection (5), the only question to be considered is the sequence of convictions and no consideration shall be given to the sequence of commission of offences or whether any offence occurred before or after any conviction.
R.S., 1985, c. C-46, s. 84;
R.S., 1985, c. 27 (1st Supp.), ss. 185(F), 186;
1991, c. 40, s. 2;
1995, c. 39, s. 139;
1998, c. 30, s. 16;
2003, c. 8, s. 2;

2008, c. 6, s. 2;
2009, c. 22, s. 2;
2015, c. 3, s. 45, c. 27, s. 18.

Use Offences

Using firearm in commission of offence
85 (1) Every person commits an offence who uses a firearm, whether or not the person causes or means to cause bodily harm to any person as a result of using the firearm,
(a) while committing an indictable offence, other than an offence under section 220 (criminal negligence causing death), 236 (manslaughter), 239 (attempted murder), 244 (discharging firearm with intent), 244.2 (discharging firearm — recklessness), 272 (sexual assault with a weapon) or 273 (aggravated sexual assault), subsection 279(1) (kidnapping) or section 279.1 (hostage taking), 344 (robbery) or 346 (extortion);
(b) while attempting to commit an indictable offence; or
(c) during flight after committing or attempting to commit an indictable offence.
Using imitation firearm in commission of offence
(2) Every person commits an offence who uses an imitation firearm
(a) while committing an indictable offence,
(b) while attempting to commit an indictable offence, or
(c) during flight after committing or attempting to commit an indictable offence,
whether or not the person causes or means to cause bodily harm to any person as a result of using the imitation firearm.
Punishment
(3) Every person who commits an offence under subsection (1) or (2) is guilty of an indictable offence and liable
(a) in the case of a first offence, except as provided in paragraph (b), to imprisonment for a term not exceeding fourteen years and to a minimum punishment of imprisonment for a term of one year; and
(b) in the case of a second or subsequent offence, to imprisonment for a term not exceeding 14 years and to a minimum punishment of imprisonment for a term of three years.
(c) Sentences to be served consecutively
(4) A sentence imposed on a person for an offence under subsection (1) or (2) shall be served consecutively to any other punishment imposed on the person for an offence arising out of the same event or series of events and to any other sentence to which the person is subject at the time the sentence is imposed on the person for an offence under subsection (1) or (2).
R.S., 1985, c. C-46, s. 85;
1995, c. 39, s. 139;
2003, c. 8, s. 3;
2008, c. 6, s. 3;
2009, c. 22, s. 3.
Careless use of firearm, etc.
86 (1) Every person commits an offence who, without lawful excuse, uses, carries, handles, ships, transports or stores a firearm, a prohibited weapon, a restricted weapon, a prohibited device or any ammunition or prohibited ammunition in a careless manner or without reasonable precautions for the safety of other persons.
Contravention of storage regulations, etc.
(2) Every person commits an offence who contravenes a regulation made under paragraph 117(h) of the
Firearms Act
Punishment
(3) Every person who commits an offence under subsection (1) or (2)
(a) is guilty of an indictable offence and liable to imprisonment

(i) in the case of a first offence, for a term not exceeding two years, and
(ii) in the case of a second or subsequent offence, for a term not exceeding five years; or
(b) is guilty of an offence punishable on summary conviction.
R.S., 1985, c. C-46, s. 86;
1991, c. 40, s. 3;
1995, c. 39, s. 139.

Pointing a firearm

87 (1) Every person commits an offence who, without lawful excuse, points a firearm at another person, whether the firearm is loaded or unloaded.

Punishment

(2) Every person who commits an offence under subsection (1)
(a) is guilty of an indictable offence and liable to imprisonment for a term not exceeding five years; or
(b) is guilty of an offence punishable on summary conviction.
R.S., 1985, c. C-46, s. 87;
1995, c. 39, s. 139.

Possession Offences

Possession of weapon for dangerous purpose

88 (1) Every person commits an offence who carries or possesses a weapon, an imitation of a weapon, a prohibited device or any ammunition or prohibited ammunition for a purpose dangerous to the public peace or for the purpose of committing an offence.

Punishment

(2) Every person who commits an offence under subsection (1)
(a) is guilty of an indictable offence and liable to imprisonment for a term not exceeding ten years; or
(b) is guilty of an offence punishable on summary conviction.
R.S., 1985, c. C-46, s. 88;
1995, c. 39, s. 139.

Carrying weapon while attending public meeting

89 (1) Every person commits an offence who, without lawful excuse, carries a weapon, a prohibited device or any ammunition or prohibited ammunition while the person is attending or is on the way to attend a public meeting.

Punishment

(2) Every person who commits an offence under subsection (1) is guilty of an offence punishable on summary conviction.
R.S., 1985, c. C-46, s. 89;
1995, c. 39, s. 139.

Carrying concealed weapon

90 (1) Every person commits an offence who carries a weapon, a prohibited device or any prohibited ammunition concealed, unless the person is authorized under the
Firearms Act

Punishment

(2) Every person who commits an offence under subsection (1)
(a) is guilty of an indictable offence and liable to imprisonment for a term not exceeding five years; or
(b) is guilty of an offence punishable on summary conviction.
R.S., 1985, c. C-46, s. 90;
1991, c. 28, s. 6, c. 40, ss. 4, 35;
1994, c. 44, s. 6;
1995, c. 39, s. 139.

Unauthorized possession of firearm

91 (1) Subject to subsection (4), every person commits an offence who possesses a prohibited firearm, a restricted firearm or a non-restricted firearm without being the holder of
(a) a licence under which the person may possess it; and
(b) in the case of a prohibited firearm or a restricted firearm, a registration certificate for it.
Unauthorized possession of prohibited weapon or restricted weapon
(2) Subject to subsection (4), every person commits an offence who possesses a prohibited weapon, a restricted weapon, a prohibited device, other than a replica firearm, or any prohibited ammunition, without being the holder of a licence under which the person may possess it.
Punishment
(3) Every person who commits an offence under subsection (1) or (2)
(a) is guilty of an indictable offence and liable to imprisonment for a term not exceeding five years; or
(b) is guilty of an offence punishable on summary conviction.
Exceptions
(4) Subsections (1) and (2) do not apply to
(a) a person who possesses a prohibited firearm, a restricted firearm, a non-restricted firearm, a prohibited weapon, a restricted weapon, a prohibited device or any prohibited ammunition while the person is under the direct and immediate supervision of a person who may lawfully possess it, for the purpose of using it in a manner in which the supervising person may lawfully use it; or
(b) a person who comes into possession of a prohibited firearm, a restricted firearm, a non-restricted firearm, a prohibited weapon, a restricted weapon, a prohibited device or any prohibited ammunition by the operation of law and who, within a reasonable period after acquiring possession of it,
(i) lawfully disposes of it, or
(ii) obtains a licence under which the person may possess it and, in the case of a prohibited firearm or a restricted firearm, a registration certificate for it.
(5) R.S., 1985, c. C-46, s. 91;
1991, c. 28, s. 7, c. 40, ss. 5, 36;
1995, c. 22, s. 10, c. 39, s. 139;
2008, c. 6, s. 4;
2012, c. 6, s. 2;
2015, c. 27, s. 19.
Possession of firearm knowing its possession is unauthorized
92 (1) Subject to subsection (4), every person commits an offence who possesses a prohibited firearm, a restricted firearm or a non-restricted firearm knowing that the person is not the holder of
(a) a licence under which the person may possess it; and
(b) in the case of a prohibited firearm or a restricted firearm, a registration certificate for it.
Possession of prohibited weapon, device or ammunition knowing its possession is unauthorized
(2) Subject to subsection (4), every person commits an offence who possesses a prohibited weapon, a restricted weapon, a prohibited device, other than a replica firearm, or any prohibited ammunition knowing that the person is not the holder of a licence under which the person may possess it.
Punishment
(3) Every person who commits an offence under subsection (1) or (2) is guilty of an indictable offence and liable
(a) in the case of a first offence, to imprisonment for a term not exceeding ten years;
(b) in the case of a second offence, to imprisonment for a term not exceeding ten years and to a minimum punishment of imprisonment for a term of one year; and
(c) in the case of a third or subsequent offence, to imprisonment for a term not exceeding ten years and to a minimum punishment of imprisonment for a term of two years less a day.
Exceptions
(4) Subsections (1) and (2) do not apply to
(a) a person who possesses a prohibited firearm, a restricted firearm, a non-restricted firearm, a prohibited weapon, a restricted weapon, a prohibited device or any prohibited ammunition while the

person is under the direct and immediate supervision of a person who may lawfully possess it, for the purpose of using it in a manner in which the supervising person may lawfully use it; or
(b) a person who comes into possession of a prohibited firearm, a restricted firearm, a non-restricted firearm, a prohibited weapon, a restricted weapon, a prohibited device or any prohibited ammunition by the operation of law and who, within a reasonable period after acquiring possession of it,
(i) lawfully disposes of it, or
(ii) obtains a licence under which the person may possess it and, in the case of a prohibited firearm or a restricted firearm, a registration certificate for it.
(5) and (6) R.S., 1985, c. C-46, s. 92;
R.S., 1985, c. 1 (2nd Supp.), s. 213;
1991, c. 40, s. 7;
1995, c. 39, s. 139;
2008, c. 6, s. 5;
2012, c. 6, s. 3;
2015, c. 27, s. 20.

Possession at unauthorized place
93 (1) Subject to subsection (3), every person commits an offence who, being the holder of an authorization or a licence under which the person may possess a prohibited firearm, a restricted firearm, a non-restricted firearm, a prohibited weapon, a restricted weapon, a prohibited device or prohibited ammunition, possesses them at a place that is
(a) indicated on the authorization or licence as being a place where the person may not possess it;
(b) other than a place indicated on the authorization or licence as being a place where the person may possess it; or
(c) other than a place where it may be possessed under the
Firearms Act

Punishment
(2) Every person who commits an offence under subsection (1)
(a) is guilty of an indictable offence and liable to imprisonment for a term not exceeding five years; or
(b) is guilty of an offence punishable on summary conviction.

Exception
(3) Subsection (1) does not apply to a person who possesses a replica firearm.
R.S., 1985, c. C-46, s. 93;
1991, c. 40, s. 8;
1995, c. 39, s. 139;
2008, c. 6, s. 6;
2015, c. 27, s. 21.

Unauthorized possession in motor vehicle
94 (1) Subject to subsections (3) and (4), every person commits an offence who is an occupant of a motor vehicle in which the person knows there is a prohibited firearm, a restricted firearm, a non-restricted firearm, a prohibited weapon, a restricted weapon, a prohibited device, other than a replica firearm, or any prohibited ammunition, unless
(a) in the case of a prohibited firearm, a restricted firearm or a non-restricted firearm,
(i) the person or any other occupant of the motor vehicle is the holder of
(A) a licence under which the person or other occupant may possess the firearm, and
(B) in the case of a prohibited firearm or a restricted firearm, an authorization and a registration certificate for it,
(ii) the person had reasonable grounds to believe that any other occupant of the motor vehicle was the holder of
(A) a licence under which that other occupant may possess the firearm, and
(B) in the case of a prohibited firearm or a restricted firearm, an authorization and a registration certificate for it, or

(iii) the person had reasonable grounds to believe that any other occupant of the motor vehicle was a person who could not be convicted of an offence under this Act by reason of sections 117.07 to 117.1 or any other Act of Parliament; and
(b) in the case of a prohibited weapon, a restricted weapon, a prohibited device or any prohibited ammunition,
(i) the person or any other occupant of the motor vehicle is the holder of an authorization or a licence under which the person or other occupant may transport the prohibited weapon, restricted weapon, prohibited device or prohibited ammunition, or
(ii) the person had reasonable grounds to believe that any other occupant of the motor vehicle was
(A) the holder of an authorization or a licence under which the other occupant may transport the prohibited weapon, restricted weapon, prohibited device or prohibited ammunition, or
(B) a person who could not be convicted of an offence under this Act by reason of sections 117.07 to 117.1 or any other Act of Parliament.
Punishment
(2) Every person who commits an offence under subsection (1)
(a) is guilty of an indictable offence and liable to imprisonment for a term not exceeding ten years; or
(b) is guilty of an offence punishable on summary conviction.
Exception
(3) Subsection (1) does not apply to an occupant of a motor vehicle who, on becoming aware of the presence of the firearm, weapon, device or ammunition in the motor vehicle, attempted to leave the motor vehicle, to the extent that it was feasible to do so, or actually left the motor vehicle.
Exception
(4) Subsection (1) does not apply to an occupant of a motor vehicle when the occupant or any other occupant of the motor vehicle is a person who came into possession of the firearm, weapon, device or ammunition by the operation of law.
(5) R.S., 1985, c. C-46, s. 94;
1995, c. 39, s. 139;
2008, c. 6, s. 7;
2012, c. 6, s. 4;
2015, c. 27, s. 22.
Possession of prohibited or restricted firearm with ammunition
95 (1) Subject to subsection (3), every person commits an offence who, in any place, possesses a loaded prohibited firearm or restricted firearm, or an unloaded prohibited firearm or restricted firearm together with readily accessible ammunition that is capable of being discharged in the firearm, without being the holder of
(a) an authorization or a licence under which the person may possess the firearm in that place; and
(b) the registration certificate for the firearm.
Punishment
(2) Every person who commits an offence under subsection (1)
(a) is guilty of an indictable offence and liable to imprisonment for a term not exceeding 10 years and to a minimum punishment of imprisonment for a term of
(i) in the case of a first offence, three years, and
(ii) in the case of a second or subsequent offence, five years; or
(b) is guilty of an offence punishable on summary conviction and liable to imprisonment for a term not exceeding one year.
Exception
(3) Subsection (1) does not apply to a person who is using the firearm under the direct and immediate supervision of another person who is lawfully entitled to possess it and is using the firearm in a manner in which that other person may lawfully use it.
R.S., 1985, c. C-46, s. 95;
1991, c. 28, s. 8, c. 40, ss. 9, 37;
1993, c. 25, s. 93;

1995, c. 39, s. 139;
2008, c. 6, s. 8;
2012, c. 6, s. 5(E).

Possession of weapon obtained by commission of offence

96 (1) Subject to subsection (3), every person commits an offence who possesses a firearm, a prohibited weapon, a restricted weapon, a prohibited device or any prohibited ammunition that the person knows was obtained by the commission in Canada of an offence or by an act or omission anywhere that, if it had occurred in Canada, would have constituted an offence.

Punishment

(2) Every person who commits an offence under subsection (1)

(a) is guilty of an indictable offence and liable to imprisonment for a term not exceeding ten years and to a minimum punishment of imprisonment for a term of one year; or

(b) is guilty of an offence punishable on summary conviction and liable to imprisonment for a term not exceeding one year.

Exception

(3) Subsection (1) does not apply to a person who comes into possession of anything referred to in that subsection by the operation of law and who lawfully disposes of it within a reasonable period after acquiring possession of it.

R.S., 1985, c. C-46, s. 96;
1995, c. 39, s. 139.

97 [Repealed before coming into force, 2008, c. 20, s. 3]

Breaking and entering to steal firearm

98 (1) Every person commits an offence who

(a) breaks and enters a place with intent to steal a firearm located in it;

(b) breaks and enters a place and steals a firearm located in it; or

(c) breaks out of a place after

(i) stealing a firearm located in it, or

(ii) entering the place with intent to steal a firearm located in it.

Definitions of

break

place

(2) In this section,

break

place

Entrance

(3) For the purposes of this section,

(a) a person enters as soon as any part of his or her body or any part of an instrument that he or she uses is within any thing that is being entered; and

(b) a person is deemed to have broken and entered if he or she

(i) obtained entrance by a threat or an artifice or by collusion with a person within, or

(ii) entered without lawful justification or excuse by a permanent or temporary opening.

Punishment

(4) Every person who commits an offence under subsection (1) is guilty of an indictable offence and liable to imprisonment for life.

R.S., 1985, c. C-46, s. 98;
R.S., 1985, c. 27 (1st Supp.), s. 13;
1991, c. 40, s. 11;
1995, c. 39, s. 139;
2008, c. 6, s. 9.

Robbery to steal firearm

98.1 Every person who commits a robbery within the meaning of section 343 with intent to steal a firearm or in the course of which he or she steals a firearm commits an indictable offence and is

liable to imprisonment for life.
2008, c. 6, s. 9.

Trafficking Offences

Weapons trafficking
99 (1) Every person commits an offence who
(a) manufactures or transfers, whether or not for consideration, or
(b) offers to do anything referred to in paragraph (a) in respect of
a prohibited firearm, a restricted firearm, a non-restricted firearm, a prohibited weapon, a restricted weapon, a prohibited device, any ammunition or any prohibited ammunition knowing that the person is not authorized to do so under the
Firearms Act
Punishment — firearm
(2) Every person who commits an offence under subsection (1) when the object in question is a prohibited firearm, a restricted firearm, a non-restricted firearm, a prohibited device, any ammunition or any prohibited ammunition is guilty of an indictable offence and liable to imprisonment for a term not exceeding 10 years and to a minimum punishment of imprisonment for a term of
(a) in the case of a first offence, three years; and
(b) in the case of a second or subsequent offence, five years.
Punishment — other cases
(3) In any other case, a person who commits an offence under subsection (1) is guilty of an indictable offence and liable to imprisonment for a term not exceeding 10 years and to a minimum punishment of imprisonment for a term of one year.
R.S., 1985, c. C-46, s. 99;
1995, c. 39, s. 139;
2008, c. 6, s. 10;
2015, c. 27, s. 23.
Possession for purpose of weapons trafficking
100 (1) Every person commits an offence who possesses a prohibited firearm, a restricted firearm, a non-restricted firearm, a prohibited weapon, a restricted weapon, a prohibited device, any ammunition or any prohibited ammunition for the purpose of
(a) transferring it, whether or not for consideration, or
(b) offering to transfer it,
knowing that the person is not authorized to transfer it under the
Firearms Act
Punishment — firearm
(2) Every person who commits an offence under subsection (1) when the object in question is a prohibited firearm, a restricted firearm, a non-restricted firearm, a prohibited device, any ammunition or any prohibited ammunition is guilty of an indictable offence and liable to imprisonment for a term not exceeding 10 years and to a minimum punishment of imprisonment for a term of
(a) in the case of a first offence, three years; and
(b) in the case of a second or subsequent offence, five years.
Punishment — other cases
(3) In any other case, a person who commits an offence under subsection (1) is guilty of an indictable offence and liable to imprisonment for a term not exceeding 10 years and to a minimum punishment of imprisonment for a term of one year.
R.S., 1985, c. C-46, s. 100;
R.S., 1985, c. 11 (1st Supp.), s. 2, c. 27 (1st Supp.), ss. 14, 203, c. 27 (2nd Supp.), s. 10, c. 1 (4th Supp.), s. 18(F);
1990, c. 16, s. 2, c. 17, s. 8;
1991, c. 40, s. 12;

1992, c. 51, s. 33;
1995, c. 22, ss. 10, 18(F), c. 39, s. 139;
1996, c. 19, s. 65;
2008, c. 6, s. 11;
2015, c. 27, s. 24.

Transfer without authority

101 (1) Every person commits an offence who transfers a prohibited firearm, a restricted firearm, a non-restricted firearm, a prohibited weapon, a restricted weapon, a prohibited device, any ammunition or any prohibited ammunition to any person otherwise than under the authority of the Firearms Act

Punishment

(2) Every person who commits an offence under subsection (1)
(a) is guilty of an indictable offence and liable to imprisonment for a term not exceeding five years; or
(b) is guilty of an offence punishable on summary conviction.
R.S., 1985, c. C-46, s. 101;
1991, c. 40, s. 13;
1995, c. 39, s. 139;
2015, c. 27, s. 25.

Assembling Offence

Making automatic firearm

102 (1) Every person commits an offence who, without lawful excuse, alters a firearm so that it is capable of, or manufactures or assembles any firearm that is capable of, discharging projectiles in rapid succession during one pressure of the trigger.

Punishment

(2) Every person who commits an offence under subsection (1)
(a) is guilty of an indictable offence and liable to imprisonment for a term not exceeding ten years and to a minimum punishment of imprisonment for a term of one year; or
(b) is guilty of an offence punishable on summary conviction and liable to imprisonment for a term not exceeding one year.
R.S., 1985, c. C-46, s. 102;
R.S., 1985, c. 27 (1st Supp.), s. 203;
1991, c. 28, s. 9, c. 40, s. 14;
1995, c. 39, s. 139.

Export and Import Offences

Importing or exporting knowing it is unauthorized

103 (1) Every person commits an offence who imports or exports
(a) a prohibited firearm, a restricted firearm, a non-restricted firearm, a prohibited weapon, a restricted weapon, a prohibited device or any prohibited ammunition, or
(b) any component or part designed exclusively for use in the manufacture of or assembly into an automatic firearm,
knowing that the person is not authorized to do so under the
Firearms Act

Punishment — firearm

(2) Every person who commits an offence under subsection (1) when the object in question is a prohibited firearm, a restricted firearm, a non-restricted firearm, a prohibited device or any prohibited ammunition is guilty of an indictable offence and liable to imprisonment for a term not exceeding 10 years and to a minimum punishment of imprisonment for a term of

(a) in the case of a first offence, three years; and
(b) in the case of a second or subsequent offence, five years.
Punishment — other cases
(2.1) In any other case, a person who commits an offence under subsection (1) is guilty of an indictable offence and liable to imprisonment for a term not exceeding 10 years and to a minimum punishment of imprisonment for a term of one year.
Attorney General of Canada may act
(3) Any proceedings in respect of an offence under subsection (1) may be commenced at the instance of the Government of Canada and conducted by or on behalf of that government.
R.S., 1985, c. C-46, s. 103;
1991, c. 40, s. 15;
1995, c. 39, s. 139;
2008, c. 6, s. 12;
2015, c. 27, s. 26.
Unauthorized importing or exporting
104 (1) Every person commits an offence who imports or exports
(a) a prohibited firearm, a restricted firearm, a non-restricted firearm, a prohibited weapon, a restricted weapon, a prohibited device or any prohibited ammunition, or
(b) any component or part designed exclusively for use in the manufacture of or assembly into an automatic firearm,
otherwise than under the authority of the
Firearms Act
Punishment
(2) Every person who commits an offence under subsection (1)
(a) is guilty of an indictable offence and liable to imprisonment for a term not exceeding five years; or
(b) is guilty of an offence punishable on summary conviction.
Attorney General of Canada may act
(3) Any proceedings in respect of an offence under subsection (1) may be commenced at the instance of the Government of Canada and conducted by or on behalf of that government.
R.S., 1985, c. C-46, s. 104;
1991, c. 40, s. 16;
1995, c. 39, s. 139;
2015, c. 27, s. 27.

Offences relating to Lost, Destroyed or Defaced Weapons, etc.

Losing or finding
105 (1) Every person commits an offence who
(a) having lost a prohibited firearm, a restricted firearm, a non-restricted firearm, a prohibited weapon, a restricted weapon, a prohibited device, any prohibited ammunition, an authorization, a licence or a registration certificate, or having had it stolen from the person's possession, does not with reasonable despatch report the loss to a peace officer, to a firearms officer or a chief firearms officer; or
(b) on finding a prohibited firearm, a restricted firearm, a non-restricted firearm, a prohibited weapon, a restricted weapon, a prohibited device or any prohibited ammunition that the person has reasonable grounds to believe has been lost or abandoned, does not with reasonable despatch deliver it to a peace officer, a firearms officer or a chief firearms officer or report the finding to a peace officer, a firearms officer or a chief firearms officer.
Punishment
(2) Every person who commits an offence under subsection (1)
(a) is guilty of an indictable offence and liable to imprisonment for a term not exceeding five years;

or
(b) is guilty of an offence punishable on summary conviction.

R.S., 1985, c. C-46, s. 105;
1991, c. 28, s. 10, c. 40, ss. 18, 39;
1994, c. 44, s. 7;
1995, c. 39, s. 139;
2015, c. 27, s. 28.

Destroying

106 (1) Every person commits an offence who
(a) after destroying any prohibited firearm, restricted firearm, prohibited weapon, restricted weapon, prohibited device or prohibited ammunition, or
(b) on becoming aware of the destruction of any prohibited firearm, restricted firearm, prohibited weapon, restricted weapon, prohibited device or prohibited ammunition that was in the person's possession before its destruction,
does not with reasonable despatch report the destruction to a peace officer, firearms officer or chief firearms officer.

Punishment

(2) Every person who commits an offence under subsection (1)
(a) is guilty of an indictable offence and liable to imprisonment for a term not exceeding five years; or
(b) is guilty of an offence punishable on summary conviction.

R.S., 1985, c. C-46, s. 106;
R.S., 1985, c. 27 (1st Supp.), s. 203;
1991, c. 40, s. 19;
1995, c. 22, s. 10, c. 39, s. 139;
2012, c. 6, s. 6.

False statements

107 (1) Every person commits an offence who knowingly makes, before a peace officer, firearms officer or chief firearms officer, a false report or statement concerning the loss, theft or destruction of a prohibited firearm, a restricted firearm, a non-restricted firearm, a prohibited weapon, a restricted weapon, a prohibited device, any prohibited ammunition, an authorization, a licence or a registration certificate.

Punishment

(2) Every person who commits an offence under subsection (1)
(a) is guilty of an indictable offence and liable to imprisonment for a term not exceeding five years; or
(b) is guilty of an offence punishable on summary conviction.

Definition of

report
statement

(3) In this section,
report
statement

R.S., 1985, c. C-46, s. 107;
1991, c. 40, s. 20;
1995, c. 39, s. 139;
2015, c. 27, s. 29.

Tampering with serial number

108 (1) Every person commits an offence who, without lawful excuse, the proof of which lies on the person,
(a) alters, defaces or removes a serial number on a firearm; or
(b) possesses a firearm knowing that the serial number on it has been altered, defaced or removed.

Punishment
(2) Every person who commits an offence under subsection (1)
(a) is guilty of an indictable offence and liable to imprisonment for a term not exceeding five years; or
(b) is guilty of an offence punishable on summary conviction.

Exception
(3) No person is guilty of an offence under paragraph (1)(b) by reason only of possessing a prohibited firearm or restricted firearm the serial number on which has been altered, defaced or removed, if that serial number has been replaced and a registration certificate in respect of the firearm has been issued setting out a new serial number for the firearm.

Evidence
(4) In proceedings for an offence under subsection (1), evidence that a person possesses a firearm the serial number on which has been wholly or partially obliterated otherwise than through normal use over time is, in the absence of evidence to the contrary, proof that the person possesses the firearm knowing that the serial number on it has been altered, defaced or removed.

R.S., 1985, c. C-46, s. 108;
1991, c. 40, s. 20;
1995, c. 39, s. 139;
2012, c. 6, s. 7.

Prohibition Orders

Mandatory prohibition order
109 (1) Where a person is convicted, or discharged under section 730, of
(a) an indictable offence in the commission of which violence against a person was used, threatened or attempted and for which the person may be sentenced to imprisonment for ten years or more,
(a.1) an indictable offence in the commission of which violence was used, threatened or attempted against
(i) the person's current or former intimate partner,
(ii) a child or parent of the person or of anyone referred to in subparagraph (i), or
(iii) any person who resides with the person or with anyone referred to in subparagraph (i) or (ii),
(b) an offence under subsection 85(1) (using firearm in commission of offence), subsection 85(2) (using imitation firearm in commission of offence), 95(1) (possession of prohibited or restricted firearm with ammunition), 99(1) (weapons trafficking), 100(1) (possession for purpose of weapons trafficking), 102(1) (making automatic firearm), 103(1) (importing or exporting knowing it is unauthorized) or section 264 (criminal harassment),
(c) an offence relating to the contravention of subsection 5(1) or (2), 6(1) or (2) or 7(1) of the Controlled Drugs and Substances Act
(d) an offence that involves, or the subject-matter of which is, a firearm, a cross-bow, a prohibited weapon, a restricted weapon, a prohibited device, any ammunition, any prohibited ammunition or an explosive substance and, at the time of the offence, the person was prohibited by any order made under this Act or any other Act of Parliament from possessing any such thing,
the court that sentences the person or directs that the person be discharged, as the case may be, shall, in addition to any other punishment that may be imposed for that offence or any other condition prescribed in the order of discharge, make an order prohibiting the person from possessing any firearm, cross-bow, prohibited weapon, restricted weapon, prohibited device, ammunition, prohibited ammunition and explosive substance during the period specified in the order as determined in accordance with subsection (2) or (3), as the case may be.

Duration of prohibition order — first offence
(2) An order made under subsection (1) shall, in the case of a first conviction for or discharge from the offence to which the order relates, prohibit the person from possessing
(a) any firearm, other than a prohibited firearm or restricted firearm, and any crossbow, restricted

weapon, ammunition and explosive substance during the period that
(i) begins on the day on which the order is made, and
(ii) ends not earlier than ten years after the person's release from imprisonment after conviction for the offence or, if the person is not then imprisoned or subject to imprisonment, after the person's conviction for or discharge from the offence; and
(b) any prohibited firearm, restricted firearm, prohibited weapon, prohibited device and prohibited ammunition for life.

Duration of prohibition order — subsequent offences
(3) An order made under subsection (1) shall, in any case other than a case described in subsection (2), prohibit the person from possessing any firearm, cross-bow, restricted weapon, ammunition and explosive substance for life.

Definition of
release from imprisonment
(4) In subparagraph (2)(a)(ii),
release from imprisonment

Application of ss. 113 to 117
(5) Sections 113 to 117 apply in respect of every order made under subsection (1).
R.S., 1985, c. C-46, s. 109;
R.S., 1985, c. 27 (1st Supp.), s. 185(F);
1991, c. 40, s. 21;
1995, c. 39, ss. 139, 190;
1996, c. 19, s. 65.1;
2003, c. 8, s. 4;
2015, c. 27, s. 30.

Discretionary prohibition order
110 (1) Where a person is convicted, or discharged under section 730, of
(a) an offence, other than an offence referred to in any of paragraphs 109(1)(a) to (c), in the commission of which violence against a person was used, threatened or attempted, or
(b) an offence that involves, or the subject-matter of which is, a firearm, a cross-bow, a prohibited weapon, a restricted weapon, a prohibited device, ammunition, prohibited ammunition or an explosive substance and, at the time of the offence, the person was not prohibited by any order made under this Act or any other Act of Parliament from possessing any such thing,
the court that sentences the person or directs that the person be discharged, as the case may be, shall, in addition to any other punishment that may be imposed for that offence or any other condition prescribed in the order of discharge, consider whether it is desirable, in the interests of the safety of the person or of any other person, to make an order prohibiting the person from possessing any firearm, cross-bow, prohibited weapon, restricted weapon, prohibited device, ammunition, prohibited ammunition or explosive substance, or all such things, and where the court decides that it is so desirable, the court shall so order.

Duration of prohibition order
(2) An order made under subsection (1) against a person begins on the day on which the order is made and ends not later than ten years after the person's release from imprisonment after conviction for the offence to which the order relates or, if the person is not then imprisoned or subject to imprisonment, after the person's conviction for or discharge from the offence.

Exception
(2.1) Despite subsection (2), an order made under subsection (1) may be imposed for life or for any shorter duration if, in the commission of the offence, violence was used, threatened or attempted against
(a) the person's current or former intimate partner;
(b) a child or parent of the person or of anyone referred to in paragraph (a); or
(c) any person who resides with the person or with anyone referred to in paragraph (a) or (b).

Reasons

(3) Where the court does not make an order under subsection (1), or where the court does make such an order but does not prohibit the possession of everything referred to in that subsection, the court shall include in the record a statement of the court's reasons for not doing so.

Definition of
release from imprisonment
(4) In subsection (2),
release from imprisonment

Application of ss. 113 to 117
(5) Sections 113 to 117 apply in respect of every order made under subsection (1).
R.S., 1985, c. C-46, s. 110;
1991, c. 40, ss. 23, 40;
1995, c. 39, ss. 139, 190;
2015, c. 27, s. 31.

Definition of
intimate partner
110.1 In sections 109 and 110,
intimate partner
2015, c. 27, s. 32.

Application for prohibition order
111 (1) A peace officer, firearms officer or chief firearms officer may apply to a provincial court judge for an order prohibiting a person from possessing any firearm, cross-bow, prohibited weapon, restricted weapon, prohibited device, ammunition, prohibited ammunition or explosive substance, or all such things, where the peace officer, firearms officer or chief firearms officer believes on reasonable grounds that it is not desirable in the interests of the safety of the person against whom the order is sought or of any other person that the person against whom the order is sought should possess any such thing.

Date for hearing and notice
(2) On receipt of an application made under subsection (1), the provincial court judge shall fix a date for the hearing of the application and direct that notice of the hearing be given, in such manner as the provincial court judge may specify, to the person against whom the order is sought.

Hearing of application
(3) Subject to subsection (4), at the hearing of an application made under subsection (1), the provincial court judge shall hear all relevant evidence presented by or on behalf of the applicant and the person against whom the order is sought.

Where hearing may proceed
(4) A provincial court judge may proceed

Prohibition order
(5) Where, at the conclusion of a hearing of an application made under subsection (1), the provincial court judge is satisfied that the circumstances referred to in that subsection exist, the provincial court judge shall make an order prohibiting the person from possessing any firearm, cross-bow, prohibited weapon, restricted weapon, prohibited device, ammunition, prohibited ammunition or explosive substance, or all such things, for such period, not exceeding five years, as is specified in the order, beginning on the day on which the order is made.

Reasons
(6) Where a provincial court judge does not make an order under subsection (1), or where a provincial court judge does make such an order but does not prohibit the possession of everything referred to in that subsection, the provincial court judge shall include in the record a statement of the court's reasons.

Application of ss. 113 to 117
(7) Sections 113 to 117 apply in respect of every order made under subsection (5).

Appeal by person or Attorney General
(8) Where a provincial court judge makes an order under subsection (5), the person to whom the

order relates, or the Attorney General, may appeal to the superior court against the order.

Appeal by Attorney General

(9) Where a provincial court judge does not make an order under subsection (5), the Attorney General may appeal to the superior court against the decision not to make an order.

Application of Part XXVII to appeals

(10) The provisions of Part XXVII, except sections 785 to 812, 816 to 819 and 829 to 838, apply in respect of an appeal made under subsection (8) or (9), with such modifications as the circumstances require and as if each reference in that Part to the appeal court were a reference to the superior court.

Definition of

provincial court judge

(11) In this section and sections 112, 117.011 and 117.012,

provincial court judge

R.S., 1985, c. C-46, s. 111;
1991, c. 40, s. 24;
1995, c. 39, s. 139.

Revocation of prohibition order under s. 111(5)

112 A provincial court judge may, on application by the person against whom an order is made under subsection 111(5), revoke the order if satisfied that the circumstances for which it was made have ceased to exist.

R.S., 1985, c. C-46, s. 112;
R.S., 1985, c. 27 (1st Supp.), s. 203;
1991, c. 40, s. 26;
1995, c. 39, s. 139.

Lifting of prohibition order for sustenance or employment

113 (1) Where a person who is or will be a person against whom a prohibition order is made establishes to the satisfaction of a competent authority that

(a) the person needs a firearm or restricted weapon to hunt or trap in order to sustain the person or the person's family, or

(b) a prohibition order against the person would constitute a virtual prohibition against employment in the only vocation open to the person,

the competent authority may, notwithstanding that the person is or will be subject to a prohibition order, make an order authorizing a chief firearms officer or the Registrar to issue, in accordance with such terms and conditions as the competent authority considers appropriate, an authorization, a licence or a registration certificate, as the case may be, to the person for sustenance or employment purposes.

Factors

(2) A competent authority may make an order under subsection (1) only after taking the following factors into account:

(a) the criminal record, if any, of the person;

(b) the nature and circumstances of the offence, if any, in respect of which the prohibition order was or will be made; and

(c) the safety of the person and of other persons.

Effect of order

(3) Where an order is made under subsection (1),

(a) an authorization, a licence or a registration certificate may not be denied to the person in respect of whom the order was made solely on the basis of a prohibition order against the person or the commission of an offence in respect of which a prohibition order was made against the person; and

(b) an authorization and a licence may, for the duration of the order, be issued to the person in respect of whom the order was made only for sustenance or employment purposes and, where the order sets out terms and conditions, only in accordance with those terms and conditions, but, for greater certainty, the authorization or licence may also be subject to terms and conditions set by the chief firearms officer that are not inconsistent with the purpose for which it is issued and any terms and conditions set out in the order.

When order can be made

(4) For greater certainty, an order under subsection (1) may be made during proceedings for an order under subsection 109(1), 110(1), 111(5), 117.05(4) or 515(2), paragraph 732.1(3)(d) or subsection 810(3).

Meaning of
competent authority

(5) In this section,
competent authority

R.S., 1985, c. C-46, s. 113;
1991, c. 40, s. 27(E);
1995, c. 22, s. 10, c. 39, ss. 139, 190.

Requirement to surrender

114 A competent authority that makes a prohibition order against a person may, in the order, require the person to surrender to a peace officer, a firearms officer or a chief firearms officer

(a) any thing the possession of which is prohibited by the order that is in the possession of the person on the commencement of the order, and

(b) every authorization, licence and registration certificate relating to any thing the possession of which is prohibited by the order that is held by the person on the commencement of the order,

and where the competent authority does so, it shall specify in the order a reasonable period for surrendering such things and documents and during which section 117.01 does not apply to that person.

R.S., 1985, c. C-46, s. 114;
R.S., 1985, c. 27 (1st Supp.), s. 203;
1995, c. 22, s. 10, c. 39, s. 139.

Forfeiture

115 (1) Unless a prohibition order against a person specifies otherwise, every thing the possession of which is prohibited by the order that, on the commencement of the order, is in the possession of the person is forfeited to Her Majesty.

Exception

(1.1) Subsection (1) does not apply in respect of an order made under section 515.

Disposal

(2) Every thing forfeited to Her Majesty under subsection (1) shall be disposed of or otherwise dealt with as the Attorney General directs.

R.S., 1985, c. C-46, s. 115;
1995, c. 39, s. 139;
2003, c. 8, s. 5.

Authorizations revoked or amended

116 (1) Subject to subsection (2), every authorization, licence and registration certificate relating to any thing the possession of which is prohibited by a prohibition order and issued to a person against whom the prohibition order is made is, on the commencement of the prohibition order, revoked, or amended, as the case may be, to the extent of the prohibitions in the order.

Duration of revocation or amendment — orders under section 515

(2) An authorization, a licence and a registration certificate relating to a thing the possession of which is prohibited by an order made under section 515 is revoked, or amended, as the case may be, only in respect of the period during which the order is in force.

R.S., 1985, c. C-46, s. 116;
1991, c. 28, s. 11, c. 40, ss. 28, 41;
1995, c. 39, s. 139;
2003, c. 8, s. 6.

Return to owner

117 Where the competent authority that makes a prohibition order or that would have had

jurisdiction to make the order is, on application for an order under this section, satisfied that a person, other than the person against whom a prohibition order was or will be made,
(a) is the owner of any thing that is or may be forfeited to Her Majesty under subsection 115(1) and is lawfully entitled to possess it, and
(b) in the case of a prohibition order under subsection 109(1) or 110(1), had no reasonable grounds to believe that the thing would or might be used in the commission of the offence in respect of which the prohibition order was made,
the competent authority shall order that the thing be returned to the owner or the proceeds of any sale of the thing be paid to that owner or, if the thing was destroyed, that an amount equal to the value of the thing be paid to the owner.
R.S., 1985, c. C-46, s. 117;
1991, c. 40, s. 29;
1995, c. 39, s. 139.

Possession contrary to order
117.01 (1) Subject to subsection (4), every person commits an offence who possesses a firearm, a cross-bow, a prohibited weapon, a restricted weapon, a prohibited device, any ammunition, any prohibited ammunition or an explosive substance while the person is prohibited from doing so by any order made under this Act or any other Act of Parliament.

Failure to surrender authorization, etc.
(2) Every person commits an offence who wilfully fails to surrender to a peace officer, a firearms officer or a chief firearms officer any authorization, licence or registration certificate held by the person when the person is required to do so by any order made under this Act or any other Act of Parliament.

Punishment
(3) Every person who commits an offence under subsection (1) or (2)
(a) is guilty of an indictable offence and liable to imprisonment for a term not exceeding ten years; or
(b) is guilty of an offence punishable on summary conviction.

Exception
(4) Subsection (1) does not apply to a person who possessed a firearm in accordance with an authorization or licence issued to the person as the result of an order made under subsection 113(1).
1995, c. 39, s. 139.

Limitations on Access

Application for order
117.011 (1) A peace officer, firearms officer or chief firearms officer may apply to a provincial court judge for an order under this section where the peace officer, firearms officer or chief firearms officer believes on reasonable grounds that
(a) the person against whom the order is sought cohabits with, or is an associate of, another person who is prohibited by any order made under this Act or any other Act of Parliament from possessing any firearm, cross-bow, prohibited weapon, restricted weapon, prohibited device, ammunition, prohibited ammunition or explosive substance, or all such things; and
(b) the other person would or might have access to any such thing that is in the possession of the person against whom the order is sought.

Date for hearing and notice
(2) On receipt of an application made under subsection (1), the provincial court judge shall fix a date for the hearing of the application and direct that notice of the hearing be given, in such manner as the provincial court judge may specify, to the person against whom the order is sought.

Hearing of application
(3) Subject to subsection (4), at the hearing of an application made under subsection (1), the provincial court judge shall hear all relevant evidence presented by or on behalf of the applicant and the person against whom the order is sought.

Where hearing may proceed
(4) A provincial court judge may proceed
Order
(5) Where, at the conclusion of a hearing of an application made under subsection (1), the provincial court judge is satisfied that the circumstances referred to in that subsection exist, the provincial court judge shall make an order in respect of the person against whom the order was sought imposing such terms and conditions on the person's use and possession of anything referred to in subsection (1) as the provincial court judge considers appropriate.
Terms and conditions
(6) In determining terms and conditions under subsection (5), the provincial court judge shall impose terms and conditions that are the least intrusive as possible, bearing in mind the purpose of the order.
Appeal by person or Attorney General
(7) Where a provincial court judge makes an order under subsection (5), the person to whom the order relates, or the Attorney General, may appeal to the superior court against the order.
Appeal by Attorney General
(8) Where a provincial court judge does not make an order under subsection (5), the Attorney General may appeal to the superior court against the decision not to make an order.
Application of Part XXVII to appeals
(9) The provisions of Part XXVII, except sections 785 to 812, 816 to 819 and 829 to 838, apply in respect of an appeal made under subsection (7) or (8), with such modifications as the circumstances require and as if each reference in that Part to the appeal court were a reference to the superior court.
1995, c. 39, s. 139.
Revocation of order under s. 117.011
117.012 A provincial court judge may, on application by the person against whom an order is made under subsection 117.011(5), revoke the order if satisfied that the circumstances for which it was made have ceased to exist.
1995, c. 39, s. 139.

Search and Seizure

Search and seizure without warrant where offence committed
117.02 (1) Where a peace officer believes on reasonable grounds
(a) that a weapon, an imitation firearm, a prohibited device, any ammunition, any prohibited ammunition or an explosive substance was used in the commission of an offence, or
(b) that an offence is being committed, or has been committed, under any provision of this Act that involves, or the subject-matter of which is, a firearm, an imitation firearm, a cross-bow, a prohibited weapon, a restricted weapon, a prohibited device, ammunition, prohibited ammunition or an explosive substance,
and evidence of the offence is likely to be found on a person, in a vehicle or in any place or premises other than a dwelling-house, the peace officer may, where the conditions for obtaining a warrant exist but, by reason of exigent circumstances, it would not be practicable to obtain a warrant, search, without warrant, the person, vehicle, place or premises, and seize any thing by means of or in relation to which that peace officer believes on reasonable grounds the offence is being committed or has been committed.
Disposition of seized things
(2) Any thing seized pursuant to subsection (1) shall be dealt with in accordance with sections 490 and 491.
1995, c. 39, s. 139.
Seizure on failure to produce authorization
117.03 (1) Despite section 117.02, a peace officer who finds
(a) a person in possession of a prohibited firearm, a restricted firearm or a non-restricted firearm who fails, on demand, to produce, for inspection by the peace officer, an authorization or a licence under

which the person may lawfully possess the firearm and, in the case of a prohibited firearm or a restricted firearm, a registration certificate for it, or

(b) a person in possession of a prohibited weapon, a restricted weapon, a prohibited device or any prohibited ammunition who fails, on demand, to produce, for inspection by the peace officer, an authorization or a licence under which the person may lawfully possess it,

may seize the firearm, prohibited weapon, restricted weapon, prohibited device or prohibited ammunition unless its possession by the person in the circumstances in which it is found is authorized by any provision of this Part, or the person is under the direct and immediate supervision of another person who may lawfully possess it.

Return of seized thing on production of authorization

(2) If a person from whom any thing is seized under subsection (1) claims the thing within 14 days after the seizure and produces for inspection by the peace officer by whom it was seized, or any other peace officer having custody of it,

(a) a licence under which the person is lawfully entitled to possess it, and

(b) in the case of a prohibited firearm or a restricted firearm, an authorization and registration certificate for it,

the thing shall without delay be returned to that person.

Forfeiture of seized thing

(3) Where any thing seized pursuant to subsection (1) is not claimed and returned as and when provided by subsection (2), a peace officer shall forthwith take the thing before a provincial court judge, who may, after affording the person from whom it was seized or its owner, if known, an opportunity to establish that the person is lawfully entitled to possess it, declare it to be forfeited to Her Majesty, to be disposed of or otherwise dealt with as the Attorney General directs.

1995, c. 39, s. 139;

2012, c. 6, s. 8;

2015, c. 27, s. 33.

Application for warrant to search and seize

117.04 (1) Where, pursuant to an application made by a peace officer with respect to any person, a justice is satisfied by information on oath that there are reasonable grounds to believe that the person possesses a weapon, a prohibited device, ammunition, prohibited ammunition or an explosive substance in a building, receptacle or place and that it is not desirable in the interests of the safety of the person, or of any other person, for the person to possess the weapon, prohibited device, ammunition, prohibited ammunition or explosive substance, the justice may issue a warrant authorizing a peace officer to search the building, receptacle or place and seize any such thing, and any authorization, licence or registration certificate relating to any such thing, that is held by or in the possession of the person.

Search and seizure without warrant

(2) Where, with respect to any person, a peace officer is satisfied that there are reasonable grounds to believe that it is not desirable, in the interests of the safety of the person or any other person, for the person to possess any weapon, prohibited device, ammunition, prohibited ammunition or explosive substance, the peace officer may, where the grounds for obtaining a warrant under subsection (1) exist but, by reason of a possible danger to the safety of that person or any other person, it would not be practicable to obtain a warrant, search for and seize any such thing, and any authorization, licence or registration certificate relating to any such thing, that is held by or in the possession of the person.

Return to justice

(3) A peace officer who executes a warrant referred to in subsection (1) or who conducts a search without a warrant under subsection (2) shall forthwith make a return to the justice who issued the warrant or, if no warrant was issued, to a justice who might otherwise have issued a warrant, showing

(a) in the case of an execution of a warrant, the things or documents, if any, seized and the date of execution of the warrant; and

(b) in the case of a search conducted without a warrant, the grounds on which it was concluded that

the peace officer was entitled to conduct the search, and the things or documents, if any, seized.
Authorizations, etc., revoked
(4) Where a peace officer who seizes any thing under subsection (1) or (2) is unable at the time of the seizure to seize an authorization or a licence under which the person from whom the thing was seized may possess the thing and, in the case of a seized firearm, a registration certificate for the firearm, every authorization, licence and registration certificate held by the person is, as at the time of the seizure, revoked.
1995, c. 39, s. 139;
2004, c. 12, s. 3.
Application for disposition
117.05 (1) Where any thing or document has been seized under subsection 117.04(1) or (2), the justice who issued the warrant authorizing the seizure or, if no warrant was issued, a justice who might otherwise have issued a warrant, shall, on application for an order for the disposition of the thing or document so seized made by a peace officer within thirty days after the date of execution of the warrant or of the seizure without a warrant, as the case may be, fix a date for the hearing of the application and direct that notice of the hearing be given to such persons or in such manner as the justice may specify.
(2) A justice may proceed
Hearing of application
(3) At the hearing of an application made under subsection (1), the justice shall hear all relevant evidence, including evidence respecting the value of the thing in respect of which the application was made.
Forfeiture and prohibition order on finding
(4) Where, following the hearing of an application made under subsection (1), the justice finds that it is not desirable in the interests of the safety of the person from whom the thing was seized or of any other person that the person should possess any weapon, prohibited device, ammunition, prohibited ammunition and explosive substance, or any such thing, the justice shall
(a) order that any thing seized be forfeited to Her Majesty or be otherwise disposed of; and
(b) where the justice is satisfied that the circumstances warrant such an action, order that the possession by that person of any weapon, prohibited device, ammunition, prohibited ammunition and explosive substance, or of any such thing, be prohibited during any period, not exceeding five years, that is specified in the order, beginning on the making of the order.
Reasons
(5) Where a justice does not make an order under subsection (4), or where a justice does make such an order but does not prohibit the possession of all of the things referred to in that subsection, the justice shall include in the record a statement of the justice's reasons.
Application of ss. 113 to 117
(6) Sections 113 to 117 apply in respect of every order made under subsection (4).
Appeal by person
(7) Where a justice makes an order under subsection (4) in respect of a person, or in respect of any thing that was seized from a person, the person may appeal to the superior court against the order.
Appeal by Attorney General
(8) Where a justice does not make a finding as described in subsection (4) following the hearing of an application under subsection (1), or makes the finding but does not make an order to the effect described in paragraph (4)(b), the Attorney General may appeal to the superior court against the failure to make the finding or to make an order to the effect so described.
Application of Part XXVII to appeals
(9) The provisions of Part XXVII, except sections 785 to 812, 816 to 819 and 829 to 838, apply in respect of an appeal made under subsection (7) or (8) with such modifications as the circumstances require and as if each reference in that Part to the appeal court were a reference to the superior court.
1995, c. 39, s. 139.
Where no finding or application

117.06 (1) Any thing or document seized pursuant to subsection 117.04(1) or (2) shall be returned to the person from whom it was seized if
(a) no application is made under subsection 117.05(1) within thirty days after the date of execution of the warrant or of the seizure without a warrant, as the case may be; or
(b) an application is made under subsection 117.05(1) within the period referred to in paragraph (a), and the justice does not make a finding as described in subsection 117.05(4).
Restoration of authorizations
(2) Where, pursuant to subsection (1), any thing is returned to the person from whom it was seized and an authorization, a licence or a registration certificate, as the case may be, is revoked pursuant to subsection 117.04(4), the justice referred to in paragraph (1)(b) may order that the revocation be reversed and that the authorization, licence or registration certificate be restored.
1995, c. 39, s. 139.

Exempted Persons

Public officers
117.07 (1) Notwithstanding any other provision of this Act, but subject to section 117.1, no public officer is guilty of an offence under this Act or the
Firearms Act
(a) possesses a firearm, a prohibited weapon, a restricted weapon, a prohibited device, any prohibited ammunition or an explosive substance in the course of or for the purpose of the public officer's duties or employment;
(b) manufactures or transfers, or offers to manufacture or transfer, a firearm, a prohibited weapon, a restricted weapon, a prohibited device, any ammunition or any prohibited ammunition in the course of the public officer's duties or employment;
(c) exports or imports a firearm, a prohibited weapon, a restricted weapon, a prohibited device or any prohibited ammunition in the course of the public officer's duties or employment;
(d) exports or imports a component or part designed exclusively for use in the manufacture of or assembly into an automatic firearm in the course of the public officer's duties or employment;
(e) in the course of the public officer's duties or employment, alters a firearm so that it is capable of, or manufactures or assembles any firearm with intent to produce a firearm that is capable of, discharging projectiles in rapid succession during one pressure of the trigger;
(f) fails to report the loss, theft or finding of any firearm, prohibited weapon, restricted weapon, prohibited device, ammunition, prohibited ammunition or explosive substance that occurs in the course of the public officer's duties or employment or the destruction of any such thing in the course of the public officer's duties or employment; or
(g) alters a serial number on a firearm in the course of the public officer's duties or employment.
Definition of
public officer
(2) In this section,
public officer
(a) a peace officer;
(b) a member of the Canadian Forces or of the armed forces of a state other than Canada who is attached or seconded to any of the Canadian Forces;
(c) an operator of a museum established by the Chief of the Defence Staff or a person employed in any such museum;
(d) a member of a cadet organization under the control and supervision of the Canadian Forces;
(e) a person training to become a police officer or a peace officer under the control and supervision of
(i) a police force, or
(ii) a police academy or similar institution designated by the Attorney General of Canada or the lieutenant governor in council of a province;

(f) a member of a visiting force, within the meaning of section 2 of the
Visiting Forces Act
(g) a person, or member of a class of persons, employed in the federal public administration or by the government of a province or municipality who is prescribed to be a public officer; or
(h) the Commissioner of Firearms, the Registrar, a chief firearms officer, any firearms officer and any person designated under section 100 of the
Firearms Act
1995, c. 39, s. 139;
2003, c. 8, s. 7, c. 22, s. 224(E).

Individuals acting for police force, Canadian Forces and visiting forces
117.08 Notwithstanding any other provision of this Act, but subject to section 117.1, no individual is guilty of an offence under this Act or the
Firearms Act
(a) possesses a firearm, a prohibited weapon, a restricted weapon, a prohibited device, any prohibited ammunition or an explosive substance,
(b) manufactures or transfers, or offers to manufacture or transfer, a firearm, a prohibited weapon, a restricted weapon, a prohibited device, any ammunition or any prohibited ammunition,
(c) exports or imports a firearm, a prohibited weapon, a restricted weapon, a prohibited device or any prohibited ammunition,
(d) exports or imports a component or part designed exclusively for use in the manufacture of or assembly into an automatic firearm,
(e) alters a firearm so that it is capable of, or manufactures or assembles any firearm with intent to produce a firearm that is capable of, discharging projectiles in rapid succession during one pressure of the trigger,
(f) fails to report the loss, theft or finding of any firearm, prohibited weapon, restricted weapon, prohibited device, ammunition, prohibited ammunition or explosive substance or the destruction of any such thing, or
(g) alters a serial number on a firearm,
if the individual does so on behalf of, and under the authority of, a police force, the Canadian Forces, a visiting force, within the meaning of section 2 of the
Visiting Forces Act
1995, c. 39, s. 139.

Employees of business with licence
117.09 (1) Notwithstanding any other provision of this Act, but subject to section 117.1, no individual who is the holder of a licence to possess and acquire restricted firearms and who is employed by a business as defined in subsection 2(1) of the
Firearms Act
(a) possesses a prohibited firearm, a prohibited weapon, a prohibited device or any prohibited ammunition;
(b) manufactures or transfers, or offers to manufacture or transfer, a prohibited weapon, a prohibited device or any prohibited ammunition;
(c) alters a firearm so that it is capable of, or manufactures or assembles any firearm with intent to produce a firearm that is capable of, discharging projectiles in rapid succession during one pressure of the trigger; or
(d) alters a serial number on a firearm.

Employees of business with licence
(2) Notwithstanding any other provision of this Act, but subject to section 117.1, no individual who is employed by a business as defined in subsection 2(1) of the
Firearms Act

Employees of carriers
(3) Notwithstanding any other provision of this Act, but subject to section 117.1, no individual who is employed by a carrier, as defined in subsection 2(1) of the

Firearms Act
Employees of museums handling functioning imitation antique firearm
(4) Notwithstanding any other provision of this Act, but subject to section 117.1, no individual who is employed by a museum as defined in subsection 2(1) of the
Firearms Act
Employees of museums handling firearms generally
(5) Notwithstanding any other provision of this Act, but subject to section 117.1, no individual who is employed by a museum as defined in subsection 2(1) of the
Firearms Act
Public safety
(6) A provincial minister shall not designate an individual for the purpose of subsection (5) where it is not desirable, in the interests of the safety of any person, to designate the individual.
Conditions
(7) A provincial minister may attach to a designation referred to in subsection (5) any reasonable condition that the provincial minister considers desirable in the particular circumstances and in the interests of the safety of any person.
1995, c. 39, s. 139.
Restriction
117.1 Sections 117.07 to 117.09 do not apply if the public officer or the individual is subject to a prohibition order and acts contrary to that order or to an authorization or a licence issued under the authority of an order made under subsection 113(1).
1995, c. 39, s. 139.

General

Onus on the accused
117.11 Where, in any proceedings for an offence under any of sections 89, 90, 91, 93, 97, 101, 104 and 105, any question arises as to whether a person is the holder of an authorization, a licence or a registration certificate, the onus is on the accused to prove that the person is the holder of the authorization, licence or registration certificate.
1995, c. 39, s. 139.
Authorizations, etc., as evidence
117.12 (1) In any proceedings under this Act or any other Act of Parliament, a document purporting to be an authorization, a licence or a registration certificate is evidence of the statements contained therein.
Certified copies
(2) In any proceedings under this Act or any other Act of Parliament, a copy of any authorization, licence or registration certificate is, if certified as a true copy by the Registrar or a chief firearms officer, admissible in evidence and, in the absence of evidence to the contrary, has the same probative force as the authorization, licence or registration certificate would have had if it had been proved in the ordinary way.
1995, c. 39, s. 139.
Certificate of analyst
117.13 (1) A certificate purporting to be signed by an analyst stating that the analyst has analyzed any weapon, prohibited device, ammunition, prohibited ammunition or explosive substance, or any part or component of such a thing, and stating the results of the analysis is evidence in any proceedings in relation to any of those things under this Act or under section 19 of the
Export and Import Permits Act
Attendance of analyst
(2) The party against whom a certificate of an analyst is produced may, with leave of the court, require the attendance of the analyst for the purposes of cross-examination.
Notice of intention to produce certificate

(3) No certificate of an analyst may be admitted in evidence unless the party intending to produce it has, before the trial, given to the party against whom it is intended to be produced reasonable notice of that intention together with a copy of the certificate.

(4) and (5) 1995, c. 39, s. 139;

2008, c. 18, s. 2.

Amnesty period

117.14 (1) The Governor in Council may, by order, declare for any purpose referred to in subsection (2) any period as an amnesty period with respect to any weapon, prohibited device, prohibited ammunition, explosive substance or component or part designed exclusively for use in the manufacture of or assembly into an automatic firearm.

Purposes of amnesty period

(2) An order made under subsection (1) may declare an amnesty period for the purpose of

(a) permitting any person in possession of any thing to which the order relates to do anything provided in the order, including, without restricting the generality of the foregoing, delivering the thing to a peace officer, a firearms officer or a chief firearms officer, registering it, destroying it or otherwise disposing of it; or

(b) permitting alterations to be made to any prohibited firearm, prohibited weapon, prohibited device or prohibited ammunition to which the order relates so that it no longer qualifies as a prohibited firearm, a prohibited weapon, a prohibited device or prohibited ammunition, as the case may be.

Reliance on amnesty period

(3) No person who, during an amnesty period declared by an order made under subsection (1) and for a purpose described in the order, does anything provided for in the order, is, by reason only of the fact that the person did that thing, guilty of an offence under this Part.

Proceedings are a nullity

(4) Any proceedings taken under this Part against any person for anything done by the person in reliance of this section are a nullity.

1995, c. 39, s. 139.

Regulations

117.15 (1) Subject to subsection (2), the Governor in Council may make regulations prescribing anything that by this Part is to be or may be prescribed.

Restriction

(2) In making regulations, the Governor in Council may not prescribe any thing to be a prohibited firearm, a restricted firearm, a prohibited weapon, a restricted weapon, a prohibited device or prohibited ammunition if, in the opinion of the Governor in Council, the thing to be prescribed is reasonable for use in Canada for hunting or sporting purposes.

Non-restricted firearm

(3) Despite the definitions

prohibited firearm

restricted firearm

Restricted firearm

(4) Despite the definition

prohibited firearm

1995, c. 39, s. 139;

2015, c. 27, s. 34.

PART IV

PART IV

Offences Against the Administration of Law and Justice

Interpretation

Definitions
118 In this Part,
evidence
statement
evidence
statement
government
(a) the Government of Canada,
(b) the government of a province, or
(c) Her Majesty in right of Canada or a province;
judicial proceeding
(a) in or under the authority of a court of justice,
(b) before the Senate or House of Commons or a committee of the Senate or House of Commons, or before a legislative council, legislative assembly or house of assembly or a committee thereof that is authorized by law to administer an oath,
(c) before a court, judge, justice, provincial court judge or coroner,
(d) before an arbitrator or umpire, or a person or body of persons authorized by law to make an inquiry and take evidence therein under oath, or
(e) before a tribunal by which a legal right or legal liability may be established,
whether or not the proceeding is invalid for want of jurisdiction or for any other reason;
office
(a) an office or appointment under the government,
(b) a civil or military commission, and
(c) a position or an employment in a public department;
official
(a) holds an office, or
(b) is appointed or elected to discharge a public duty;
witness
R.S., 1985, c. C-46, s. 118;
R.S., 1985, c. 27 (1st Supp.), ss. 15, 203;
2007, c. 13, s. 2.

Corruption and Disobedience

Bribery of judicial officers, etc.
119 (1) Every one is guilty of an indictable offence and liable to imprisonment for a term not exceeding fourteen years who
(a) being the holder of a judicial office, or being a member of Parliament or of the legislature of a province, directly or indirectly, corruptly accepts, obtains, agrees to accept or attempts to obtain, for themselves or another person, any money, valuable consideration, office, place or employment in respect of anything done or omitted or to be done or omitted by them in their official capacity, or
(b) directly or indirectly, corruptly gives or offers to a person mentioned in paragraph (a), or to anyone for the benefit of that person, any money, valuable consideration, office, place or employment in respect of anything done or omitted or to be done or omitted by that person in their official capacity.
Consent of Attorney General
(2) No proceedings against a person who holds a judicial office shall be instituted under this section without the consent in writing of the Attorney General of Canada.
R.S., 1985, c. C-46, s. 119;
2007, c. 13, s. 3.
Bribery of officers
120 Every one is guilty of an indictable offence and liable to imprisonment for a term not exceeding

fourteen years who

(a) being a justice, police commissioner, peace officer, public officer or officer of a juvenile court, or being employed in the administration of criminal law, directly or indirectly, corruptly accepts, obtains, agrees to accept or attempts to obtain, for themselves or another person, any money, valuable consideration, office, place or employment with intent

(i) to interfere with the administration of justice,

(ii) to procure or facilitate the commission of an offence, or

(iii) to protect from detection or punishment a person who has committed or who intends to commit an offence; or

(b) directly or indirectly, corruptly gives or offers to a person mentioned in paragraph (a), or to anyone for the benefit of that person, any money, valuable consideration, office, place or employment with intent that the person should do anything mentioned in subparagraph (a)(i), (ii) or (iii).

R.S., 1985, c. C-46, s. 120;
2007, c. 13, s. 4.

Frauds on the government

121 (1) Every one commits an offence who

(a) directly or indirectly

(i) gives, offers or agrees to give or offer to an official or to any member of his family, or to any one for the benefit of an official, or

(ii) being an official, demands, accepts or offers or agrees to accept from any person for himself or another person,

a loan, reward, advantage or benefit of any kind as consideration for cooperation, assistance, exercise of influence or an act or omission in connection with

(iii) the transaction of business with or any matter of business relating to the government, or

(iv) a claim against Her Majesty or any benefit that Her Majesty is authorized or is entitled to bestow,

whether or not, in fact, the official is able to cooperate, render assistance, exercise influence or do or omit to do what is proposed, as the case may be;

(b) having dealings of any kind with the government, directly or indirectly pays a commission or reward to or confers an advantage or benefit of any kind on an employee or official of the government with which the dealings take place, or to any member of the employee's or official's family, or to anyone for the benefit of the employee or official, with respect to those dealings, unless the person has the consent in writing of the head of the branch of government with which the dealings take place;

(c) being an official or employee of the government, directly or indirectly demands, accepts or offers or agrees to accept from a person who has dealings with the government a commission, reward, advantage or benefit of any kind for themselves or another person, unless they have the consent in writing of the head of the branch of government that employs them or of which they are an official;

(d) having or pretending to have influence with the government or with a minister of the government or an official, directly or indirectly demands, accepts or offers or agrees to accept, for themselves or another person, a reward, advantage or benefit of any kind as consideration for cooperation, assistance, exercise of influence or an act or omission in connection with

(i) anything mentioned in subparagraph (a)(iii) or (iv), or

(ii) the appointment of any person, including themselves, to an office;

(e) directly or indirectly gives or offers, or agrees to give or offer, to a minister of the government or an official, or to anyone for the benefit of a minister or an official, a reward, advantage or benefit of any kind as consideration for cooperation, assistance, exercise of influence, or an act or omission, by that minister or official, in connection with

(i) anything mentioned in subparagraph (a)(iii) or (iv), or

(ii) the appointment of any person, including themselves, to an office; or

(f) having made a tender to obtain a contract with the government,

(i) directly or indirectly gives or offers, or agrees to give or offer, to another person who has made a tender, to a member of that person's family or to another person for the benefit of that person, a reward, advantage or benefit of any kind as consideration for the withdrawal of the tender of that person, or

(ii) directly or indirectly demands, accepts or offers or agrees to accept from another person who has made a tender a reward, advantage or benefit of any kind for themselves or another person as consideration for the withdrawal of their own tender.

Contractor subscribing to election fund

(2) Every one commits an offence who, in order to obtain or retain a contract with the government, or as a term of any such contract, whether express or implied, directly or indirectly subscribes or gives, or agrees to subscribe or give, to any person any valuable consideration

(a) for the purpose of promoting the election of a candidate or a class or party of candidates to Parliament or the legislature of a province; or

(b) with intent to influence or affect in any way the result of an election conducted for the purpose of electing persons to serve in Parliament or the legislature of a province.

Punishment

(3) Every one who commits an offence under this section is guilty of an indictable offence and liable to imprisonment for a term not exceeding five years.

R.S., 1985, c. C-46, s. 121;

2007, c. 13, s. 5.

Selling, etc., of tobacco products and raw leaf tobacco

121.1 (1) No person shall sell, offer for sale, transport, deliver, distribute or have in their possession for the purpose of sale a tobacco product, or raw leaf tobacco that is not packaged, unless it is stamped. The terms

tobacco product

raw leaf tobacco

packaged

stamped

Excise Act, 2001

Exceptions — subsections 30(2) and 32(2) and (3) of

Excise Act, 2001

(2) Subsection (1) does not apply in any of the circumstances described in any of subsections 30(2) and 32(2) and (3) of the

Excise Act, 2001

Exception — section 31 of

Excise Act, 2001

(3) A tobacco grower does not contravene subsection (1) by reason only that they have in their possession raw leaf tobacco described in paragraph 31(a), (b) or (c) of the

Excise Act, 2001

Punishment

(4) Every person who contravenes subsection (1)

(a) is guilty of an indictable offence and liable to imprisonment for a term of not more than five years and, if the amount of tobacco product is 10,000 cigarettes or more or 10 kg or more of any other tobacco product, or the amount of raw leaf tobacco is 10 kg or more,

(i) in the case of a second offence, to a minimum punishment of imprisonment for a term of 90 days,

(ii) in the case of a third offence, to a minimum punishment of imprisonment for a term of 180 days, and

(iii) in the case of a fourth or subsequent offence, to a minimum punishment of imprisonment for a term of two years less a day; or

(b) is guilty of an offence punishable on summary conviction and liable to imprisonment for a term of not more than six months.

Subsequent offences

(5) For the purpose of determining whether a convicted person has committed a second or subsequent offence, an offence under this section for which the person was previously convicted is considered to be an earlier offence whether it was prosecuted by indictment or by way of summary conviction proceedings.
2014, c. 23, s. 3.
Breach of trust by public officer
122 Every official who, in connection with the duties of his office, commits fraud or a breach of trust is guilty of an indictable offence and liable to imprisonment for a term not exceeding five years, whether or not the fraud or breach of trust would be an offence if it were committed in relation to a private person.
R.S., c. C-34, s. 111.
Municipal corruption
123 (1) Every one is guilty of an indictable offence and liable to imprisonment for a term not exceeding five years who directly or indirectly gives, offers or agrees to give or offer to a municipal official or to anyone for the benefit of a municipal official — or, being a municipal official, directly or indirectly demands, accepts or offers or agrees to accept from any person for themselves or another person — a loan, reward, advantage or benefit of any kind as consideration for the official
(a) to abstain from voting at a meeting of the municipal council or a committee of the council;
(b) to vote in favour of or against a measure, motion or resolution;
(c) to aid in procuring or preventing the adoption of a measure, motion or resolution; or
(d) to perform or fail to perform an official act.
Influencing municipal official
(2) Every one is guilty of an indictable offence and liable to imprisonment for a term not exceeding five years who influences or attempts to influence a municipal official to do anything mentioned in paragraphs (1)(a) to (d) by
(a) suppression of the truth, in the case of a person who is under a duty to disclose the truth;
(b) threats or deceit; or
(c) any unlawful means.
Definition of
municipal official
(3) In this section,
municipal official
R.S., 1985, c. C-46, s. 123;
R.S., 1985, c. 27 (1st Supp.), s. 16;
2007, c. 13, s. 6.
Selling or purchasing office
124 Every one who
(a) purports to sell or agrees to sell an appointment to or a resignation from an office, or a consent to any such appointment or resignation, or receives or agrees to receive a reward or profit from the purported sale thereof, or
(b) purports to purchase or gives a reward or profit for the purported purchase of any such appointment, resignation or consent, or agrees or promises to do so,
is guilty of an indictable offence and liable to imprisonment for a term not exceeding five years.
R.S., c. C-34, s. 113.
Influencing or negotiating appointments or dealing in offices
125 Every one who
(a) receives, agrees to receive, gives or procures to be given, directly or indirectly, a reward, advantage or benefit of any kind as consideration for cooperation, assistance or exercise of influence to secure the appointment of any person to an office,
(b) solicits, recommends or negotiates in any manner with respect to an appointment to or resignation from an office, in expectation of a direct or indirect reward, advantage or benefit, or
(c) keeps without lawful authority, the proof of which lies on him, a place for transacting or

negotiating any business relating to
(i) the filling of vacancies in offices,
(ii) the sale or purchase of offices, or
(iii) appointments to or resignations from offices,
is guilty of an indictable offence and liable to imprisonment for a term not exceeding five years.
R.S., c. C-34, s. 114.

Disobeying a statute

126 (1) Every one who, without lawful excuse, contravenes an Act of Parliament by wilfully doing anything that it forbids or by wilfully omitting to do anything that it requires to be done is, unless a punishment is expressly provided by law, guilty of an indictable offence and liable to imprisonment for a term not exceeding two years.

Attorney General of Canada may act

(2) Any proceedings in respect of a contravention of or conspiracy to contravene an Act mentioned in subsection (1), other than this Act, may be instituted at the instance of the Government of Canada and conducted by or on behalf of that Government.
R.S., 1985, c. C-46, s. 126;
R.S., 1985, c. 27 (1st Supp.), s. 185(F).

Disobeying order of court

127 (1) Every one who, without lawful excuse, disobeys a lawful order made by a court of justice or by a person or body of persons authorized by any Act to make or give the order, other than an order for the payment of money, is, unless a punishment or other mode of proceeding is expressly provided by law, guilty of
(a) an indictable offence and liable to imprisonment for a term not exceeding two years; or
(b) an offence punishable on summary conviction.

Attorney General of Canada may act

(2) Where the order referred to in subsection (1) was made in proceedings instituted at the instance of the Government of Canada and conducted by or on behalf of that Government, any proceedings in respect of a contravention of or conspiracy to contravene that order may be instituted and conducted in like manner.
R.S., 1985, c. C-46, s. 127;
R.S., 1985, c. 27 (1st Supp.), s. 185(F);
2005, c. 32, s. 1.

Misconduct of officers executing process

128 Every peace officer or coroner who, being entrusted with the execution of a process, wilfully
(a) misconducts himself in the execution of the process, or
(b) makes a false return to the process,
is guilty of an indictable offence and liable to imprisonment for a term not exceeding two years.
R.S., c. C-34, s. 117.

Offences relating to public or peace officer

129 Every one who
(a) resists or wilfully obstructs a public officer or peace officer in the execution of his duty or any person lawfully acting in aid of such an officer,
(b) omits, without reasonable excuse, to assist a public officer or peace officer in the execution of his duty in arresting a person or in preserving the peace, after having reasonable notice that he is required to do so, or
(c) resists or wilfully obstructs any person in the lawful execution of a process against lands or goods or in making a lawful distress or seizure,
is guilty of
(d) an indictable offence and is liable to imprisonment for a term not exceeding two years, or
(e) an offence punishable on summary conviction.
R.S., c. C-34, s. 118;
1972, c. 13, s. 7.

Personating peace officer
130 (1) Everyone commits an offence who
(a) falsely represents himself to be a peace officer or a public officer; or
(b) not being a peace officer or public officer, uses a badge or article of uniform or equipment in a manner that is likely to cause persons to believe that he is a peace officer or a public officer, as the case may be.
Punishment
(2) Everyone who commits an offence under subsection (1)
(a) is guilty of an indictable offence and liable to imprisonment for a term of not more than five years; or
(b) is guilty of an offence punishable on summary conviction.
R.S., 1985, c. C-46, s. 130;
2009, c. 28, s. 2.
Aggravating circumstance
130.1 If a person is convicted of an offence under section 130, the court imposing the sentence on the person shall consider as an aggravating circumstance the fact that the accused personated a peace officer or a public officer, as the case may be, for the purpose of facilitating the commission of another offence.
2014, c. 10, s. 1.

Misleading Justice

Perjury
131 (1) Subject to subsection (3), every one commits perjury who, with intent to mislead, makes before a person who is authorized by law to permit it to be made before him a false statement under oath or solemn affirmation, by affidavit, solemn declaration or deposition or orally, knowing that the statement is false.
Video links, etc.
(1.1) Subject to subsection (3), every person who gives evidence under subsection 46(2) of the Canada Evidence Act
Mutual Legal Assistance in Criminal Matters Act
Idem
(2) Subsection (1) applies, whether or not a statement referred to in that subsection is made in a judicial proceeding.
Application
(3) Subsections (1) and (1.1) do not apply to a statement referred to in either of those subsections that is made by a person who is not specially permitted, authorized or required by law to make that statement.
R.S., 1985, c. C-46, s. 131;
R.S., 1985, c. 27 (1st Supp.), s. 17;
1999, c. 18, s. 92.
Punishment
132 Every one who commits perjury is guilty of an indictable offence and liable to imprisonment for a term not exceeding fourteen years.
R.S., 1985, c. C-46, s. 132;
R.S., 1985, c. 27 (1st Supp.), s. 17;
1998, c. 35, s. 119.
Corroboration
133 No person shall be convicted of an offence under section 132 on the evidence of only one witness unless the evidence of that witness is corroborated in a material particular by evidence that implicates the accused.
R.S., 1985, c. C-46, s. 133;

R.S., 1985, c. 27 (1st Supp.), s. 17.
Idem
134 (1) Subject to subsection (2), every one who, not being specially permitted, authorized or required by law to make a statement under oath or solemn affirmation, makes such a statement, by affidavit, solemn declaration or deposition or orally before a person who is authorized by law to permit it to be made before him, knowing that the statement is false, is guilty of an offence punishable on summary conviction.
Application
(2) Subsection (1) does not apply to a statement referred to in that subsection that is made in the course of a criminal investigation.

R.S., 1985, c. C-46, s. 134;

R.S., 1985, c. 27 (1st Supp.), s. 17.

135 Witness giving contradictory evidence
136 (1) Every one who, being a witness in a judicial proceeding, gives evidence with respect to any matter of fact or knowledge and who subsequently, in a judicial proceeding, gives evidence that is contrary to his previous evidence is guilty of an indictable offence and liable to imprisonment for a term not exceeding fourteen years, whether or not the prior or later evidence or either is true, but no person shall be convicted under this section unless the court, judge or provincial court judge, as the case may be, is satisfied beyond a reasonable doubt that the accused, in giving evidence in either of the judicial proceedings, intended to mislead.
Evidence in specific cases
(1.1) Evidence given under section 714.1, 714.2, 714.3 or 714.4 or under subsection 46(2) of the Canada Evidence Act

Mutual Legal Assistance in Criminal Matters Act
Definition of
evidence

(2) Notwithstanding the definition

evidence
Proof of former trial
(2.1) Where a person is charged with an offence under this section, a certificate specifying with reasonable particularity the proceeding in which that person is alleged to have given the evidence in respect of which the offence is charged, is evidence that it was given in a judicial proceeding, without proof of the signature or official character of the person by whom the certificate purports to be signed if it purports to be signed by the clerk of the court or other official having the custody of the record of that proceeding or by his lawful deputy.
Consent required
(3) No proceedings shall be instituted under this section without the consent of the Attorney General.

R.S., 1985, c. C-46, s. 136;

R.S., 1985, c. 27 (1st Supp.), ss. 18, 203;

1999, c. 18, s. 93.
Fabricating evidence
137 Every one who, with intent to mislead, fabricates anything with intent that it shall be used as evidence in a judicial proceeding, existing or proposed, by any means other than perjury or incitement to perjury is guilty of an indictable offence and liable to imprisonment for a term not exceeding fourteen years.

R.S., c. C-34, s. 125.
Offences relating to affidavits
138 Every one who

(a) signs a writing that purports to be an affidavit or statutory declaration and to have been sworn or declared before him when the writing was not so sworn or declared or when he knows that he has no authority to administer the oath or declaration,

(b) uses or offers for use any writing purporting to be an affidavit or statutory declaration that he knows was not sworn or declared, as the case may be, by the affiant or declarant or before a person authorized in that behalf, or

(c) signs as affiant or declarant a writing that purports to be an affidavit or statutory declaration and to have been sworn or declared by him, as the case may be, when the writing was not so sworn or declared,

is guilty of an indictable offence and liable to imprisonment for a term not exceeding two years. R.S., c. C-34, s. 126.

Obstructing justice

139 (1) Every one who wilfully attempts in any manner to obstruct, pervert or defeat the course of justice in a judicial proceeding,

(a) by indemnifying or agreeing to indemnify a surety, in any way and either in whole or in part, or

(b) where he is a surety, by accepting or agreeing to accept a fee or any form of indemnity whether in whole or in part from or in respect of a person who is released or is to be released from custody,

is guilty of

(c) an indictable offence and is liable to imprisonment for a term not exceeding two years, or

(d) an offence punishable on summary conviction.

Idem

(2) Every one who wilfully attempts in any manner other than a manner described in subsection (1) to obstruct, pervert or defeat the course of justice is guilty of an indictable offence and liable to imprisonment for a term not exceeding ten years.

Idem

(3) Without restricting the generality of subsection (2), every one shall be deemed wilfully to attempt to obstruct, pervert or defeat the course of justice who in a judicial proceeding, existing or proposed,

(a) dissuades or attempts to dissuade a person by threats, bribes or other corrupt means from giving evidence;

(b) influences or attempts to influence by threats, bribes or other corrupt means a person in his conduct as a juror; or

(c) accepts or obtains, agrees to accept or attempts to obtain a bribe or other corrupt consideration to abstain from giving evidence, or to do or to refrain from doing anything as a juror.

R.S., c. C-34, s. 127;
R.S., c. 2(2nd Supp.), s. 3;
1972, c. 13, s. 8.

Public mischief

140 (1) Every one commits public mischief who, with intent to mislead, causes a peace officer to enter on or continue an investigation by

(a) making a false statement that accuses some other person of having committed an offence;

(b) doing anything intended to cause some other person to be suspected of having committed an offence that the other person has not committed, or to divert suspicion from himself;

(c) reporting that an offence has been committed when it has not been committed; or

(d) reporting or in any other way making it known or causing it to be made known that he or some other person has died when he or that other person has not died.

Punishment

(2) Every one who commits public mischief

(a) is guilty of an indictable offence and liable to imprisonment for a term not exceeding five years; or

(b) is guilty of an offence punishable on summary conviction.

R.S., 1985, c. C-46, s. 140;
R.S., 1985, c. 27 (1st Supp.), s. 19.

Compounding indictable offence

141 (1) Every one who asks for or obtains or agrees to receive or obtain any valuable consideration for himself or any other person by agreeing to compound or conceal an indictable offence is guilty of an indictable offence and liable to imprisonment for a term not exceeding two years.

Exception for diversion agreements
(2) No offence is committed under subsection (1) where valuable consideration is received or obtained or is to be received or obtained under an agreement for compensation or restitution or personal services that is
(a) entered into with the consent of the Attorney General; or
(b) made as part of a program, approved by the Attorney General, to divert persons charged with indictable offences from criminal proceedings.
R.S., 1985, c. C-46, s. 141;
R.S., 1985, c. 27 (1st Supp.), s. 19.

Corruptly taking reward for recovery of goods
142 Every one who corruptly accepts any valuable consideration, directly or indirectly, under pretence or on account of helping any person to recover anything obtained by the commission of an indictable offence is guilty of an indictable offence and liable to imprisonment for a term not exceeding five years.
R.S., c. C-34, s. 130.

Advertising reward and immunity
143 Every one who
(a) publicly advertises a reward for the return of anything that has been stolen or lost, and in the advertisement uses words to indicate that no questions will be asked if it is returned,
(b) uses words in a public advertisement to indicate that a reward will be given or paid for anything that has been stolen or lost, without interference with or inquiry about the person who produces it,
(c) promises or offers in a public advertisement to return to a person who has advanced money by way of loan on, or has bought, anything that has been stolen or lost, the money so advanced or paid, or any other sum of money for the return of that thing, or
(d) prints or publishes any advertisement referred to in paragraph (a), (b) or (c),
is guilty of an offence punishable on summary conviction.
R.S., c. C-34, s. 131.

Escapes and Rescues

Prison breach
144 Every one who
(a) by force or violence breaks a prison with intent to set at liberty himself or any other person confined therein, or
(b) with intent to escape forcibly breaks out of, or makes any breach in, a cell or other place within a prison in which he is confined,
is guilty of an indictable offence and liable to imprisonment for a term not exceeding ten years.
R.S., c. C-34, s. 132;
1976-77, c. 53, s. 5.

Escape and being at large without excuse
145 (1) Every one who
(a) escapes from lawful custody, or
(b) is, before the expiration of a term of imprisonment to which he was sentenced, at large in or out of Canada without lawful excuse, the proof of which lies on him,
is guilty of an indictable offence and liable to imprisonment for a term not exceeding two years or is guilty of an offence punishable on summary conviction.

Failure to attend court
(2) Every one who,
(a) being at large on his undertaking or recognizance given to or entered into before a justice or judge, fails, without lawful excuse, the proof of which lies on him, to attend court in accordance with the undertaking or recognizance, or
(b) having appeared before a court, justice or judge, fails, without lawful excuse, the proof of which

lies on him, to attend court as thereafter required by the court, justice or judge,
or to surrender himself in accordance with an order of the court, justice or judge, as the case may be, is guilty of an indictable offence and liable to imprisonment for a term not exceeding two years or is guilty of an offence punishable on summary conviction.

Failure to comply with condition of undertaking or recognizance
(3) Every person who is at large on an undertaking or recognizance given to or entered into before a justice or judge and is bound to comply with a condition of that undertaking or recognizance, and every person who is bound to comply with a direction under subsection 515(12) or 522(2.1) or an order under subsection 516(2), and who fails, without lawful excuse, the proof of which lies on them, to comply with the condition, direction or order is guilty of
(a) an indictable offence and is liable to imprisonment for a term not exceeding two years; or
(b) an offence punishable on summary conviction.

Failure to appear or to comply with summons
(4) Every one who is served with a summons and who fails, without lawful excuse, the proof of which lies on him, to appear at a time and place stated therein, if any, for the purposes of the Identification of Criminals Act
(a) an indictable offence and is liable to imprisonment for a term not exceeding two years; or
(b) an offence punishable on summary conviction.

Failure to comply with appearance notice or promise to appear
(5) Every person who is named in an appearance notice or promise to appear, or in a recognizance entered into before an officer in charge or another peace officer, that has been confirmed by a justice under section 508 and who fails, without lawful excuse, the proof of which lies on the person, to appear at the time and place stated therein, if any, for the purposes of the
Identification of Criminals Act
(a) an indictable offence and is liable to imprisonment for a term not exceeding two years; or
(b) an offence punishable on summary conviction.

Failure to comply with conditions of undertaking
(5.1) Every person who, without lawful excuse, the proof of which lies on the person, fails to comply with any condition of an undertaking entered into pursuant to subsection 499(2) or 503(2.1)
(a) is guilty of an indictable offence and is liable to imprisonment for a term not exceeding two years; or
(b) is guilty of an offence punishable on summary conviction.

Idem
(6) For the purposes of subsection (5), it is not a lawful excuse that an appearance notice, promise to appear or recognizance states defectively the substance of the alleged offence.

(7) Election of Crown under
Contraventions Act
(8) For the purposes of subsections (3) to (5), it is a lawful excuse to fail to comply with a condition of an undertaking or recognizance or to fail to appear at a time and place stated in a summons, an appearance notice, a promise to appear or a recognizance for the purposes of the
Identification of Criminals Act
Contraventions Act

Proof of certain facts by certificate
(9) In any proceedings under subsection (2), (4) or (5), a certificate of the clerk of the court or a judge of the court before which the accused is alleged to have failed to attend or of the person in charge of the place at which it is alleged the accused failed to attend for the purposes of the Identification of Criminals Act
(a) in the case of proceedings under subsection (2), the accused gave or entered into an undertaking or recognizance before a justice or judge and failed to attend court in accordance therewith or, having attended court, failed to attend court thereafter as required by the court, justice or judge or to surrender in accordance with an order of the court, justice or judge, as the case may be,
(b) in the case of proceedings under subsection (4), a summons was issued to and served on the

accused and the accused failed to attend court in accordance therewith or failed to appear at the time and place stated therein for the purposes of the
Identification of Criminals Act

(c) in the case of proceedings under subsection (5), the accused was named in an appearance notice, a promise to appear or a recognizance entered into before an officer in charge or another peace officer, that was confirmed by a justice under section 508, and the accused failed to appear at the time and place stated therein for the purposes of the
Identification of Criminals Act

is evidence of the statements contained in the certificate without proof of the signature or the official character of the person appearing to have signed the certificate.

Attendance and right to cross-examination

(10) An accused against whom a certificate described in subsection (9) is produced may, with leave of the court, require the attendance of the person making the certificate for the purposes of cross-examination.

Notice of intention to produce

(11) No certificate shall be received in evidence pursuant to subsection (9) unless the party intending to produce it has, before the trial, given to the accused reasonable notice of his intention together with a copy of the certificate.

R.S., 1985, c. C-46, s. 145;
R.S., 1985, c. 27 (1st Supp.), s. 20;
1992, c. 47, s. 68;
1994, c. 44, s. 8;
1996, c. 7, s. 38;
1997, c. 18, s. 3;
2008, c. 18, s. 3.

Permitting or assisting escape

146 Every one who

(a) permits a person whom he has in lawful custody to escape, by failing to perform a legal duty,
(b) conveys or causes to be conveyed into a prison anything, with intent to facilitate the escape of a person imprisoned therein, or
(c) directs or procures, under colour of pretended authority, the discharge of a prisoner who is not entitled to be discharged,

is guilty of an indictable offence and liable to imprisonment for a term not exceeding two years.
R.S., c. C-34, s. 134.

Rescue or permitting escape

147 Every one who

(a) rescues any person from lawful custody or assists any person in escaping or attempting to escape from lawful custody,
(b) being a peace officer, wilfully permits a person in his lawful custody to escape, or
(c) being an officer of or an employee in a prison, wilfully permits a person to escape from lawful custody therein,

is guilty of an indictable offence and liable to imprisonment for a term not exceeding five years.
R.S., c. C-34, s. 135.

Assisting prisoner of war to escape

148 Every one who knowingly and wilfully

(a) assists a prisoner of war in Canada to escape from a place where he is detained, or
(b) assists a prisoner of war, who is permitted to be at large on parole in Canada, to escape from the place where he is at large on parole,

is guilty of an indictable offence and liable to imprisonment for a term not exceeding five years.
R.S., c. C-34, s. 136.

Service of term for escape

149 (1) Notwithstanding section 743.1, a court that convicts a person for an escape committed while

undergoing imprisonment may order that the term of imprisonment be served in a penitentiary, even if the time to be served is less than two years.

Definition of
escape
(2) In this section,
escape
R.S., 1985, c. C-46, s. 149;
R.S., 1985, c. 27 (1st Supp.), s. 203;
1992, c. 20, s. 199;
1995, c. 22, s. 1.

PART V

PART V
Sexual Offences, Public Morals and Disorderly Conduct

Interpretation

Definitions
150 In this Part,
guardian
public place
theatre
R.S., c. C-34, s. 138.

Sexual Offences

Consent no defence
150.1 (1) Subject to subsections (2) to (2.2), when an accused is charged with an offence under section 151 or 152 or subsection 153(1), 160(3) or 173(2) or is charged with an offence under section 271, 272 or 273 in respect of a complainant under the age of 16 years, it is not a defence that the complainant consented to the activity that forms the subject-matter of the charge.

Exception — complainant aged 12 or 13
(2) When an accused is charged with an offence under section 151 or 152, subsection 173(2) or section 271 in respect of a complainant who is 12 years of age or more but under the age of 14 years, it is a defence that the complainant consented to the activity that forms the subject-matter of the charge if the accused
(a) is less than two years older than the complainant; and
(b) is not in a position of trust or authority towards the complainant, is not a person with whom the complainant is in a relationship of dependency and is not in a relationship with the complainant that is exploitative of the complainant.

Exception — complainant aged 14 or 15
(2.1) If an accused is charged with an offence under section 151 or 152, subsection 173(2) or section 271 in respect of a complainant who is 14 years of age or more but under the age of 16 years, it is a defence that the complainant consented to the activity that forms the subject-matter of the charge if the accused
(a) is less than five years older than the complainant; and
(b) is not in a position of trust or authority towards the complainant, is not a person with whom the complainant is in a relationship of dependency and is not in a relationship with the complainant that is exploitative of the complainant.

Exception for transitional purposes
(2.2) When the accused referred to in subsection (2.1) is five or more years older than the

complainant, it is a defence that the complainant consented to the activity that forms the subject-matter of the charge if, on the day on which this subsection comes into force,
(a) the accused is the common-law partner of the complainant, or has been cohabiting with the complainant in a conjugal relationship for a period of less than one year and they have had or are expecting to have a child as a result of the relationship; and
(b) the accused is not in a position of trust or authority towards the complainant, is not a person with whom the complainant is in a relationship of dependency and is not in a relationship with the complainant that is exploitative of the complainant.

Exception for transitional purposes
(2.3) If, immediately before the day on which this subsection comes into force, the accused referred to in subsection (2.1) is married to the complainant, it is a defence that the complainant consented to the activity that forms the subject-matter of the charge.

Exemption for accused aged twelve or thirteen
(3) No person aged twelve or thirteen years shall be tried for an offence under section 151 or 152 or subsection 173(2) unless the person is in a position of trust or authority towards the complainant, is a person with whom the complainant is in a relationship of dependency or is in a relationship with the complainant that is exploitative of the complainant.

Mistake of age
(4) It is not a defence to a charge under section 151 or 152, subsection 160(3) or 173(2), or section 271, 272 or 273 that the accused believed that the complainant was 16 years of age or more at the time the offence is alleged to have been committed unless the accused took all reasonable steps to ascertain the age of the complainant.

Idem
(5) It is not a defence to a charge under section 153, 159, 170, 171 or 172 or subsection 286.1(2), 286.2(2) or 286.3(2) that the accused believed that the complainant was eighteen years of age or more at the time the offence is alleged to have been committed unless the accused took all reasonable steps to ascertain the age of the complainant.

Mistake of age
(6) An accused cannot raise a mistaken belief in the age of the complainant in order to invoke a defence under subsection (2) or (2.1) unless the accused took all reasonable steps to ascertain the age of the complainant.
R.S., 1985, c. 19 (3rd Supp.), s. 1;
2005, c. 32, s. 2;
2008, c. 6, ss. 13, 54;
2014, c. 25, s. 4;
2015, c. 29, s. 6.

Sexual interference
151 Every person who, for a sexual purpose, touches, directly or indirectly, with a part of the body or with an object, any part of the body of a person under the age of 16 years
(a) is guilty of an indictable offence and is liable to imprisonment for a term of not more than 14 years and to a minimum punishment of imprisonment for a term of one year; or
(b) is guilty of an offence punishable on summary conviction and is liable to imprisonment for a term of not more than two years less a day and to a minimum punishment of imprisonment for a term of 90 days.
R.S., 1985, c. C-46, s. 151;
R.S., 1985, c. 19 (3rd Supp.), s. 1;
2005, c. 32, s. 3;
2008, c. 6, s. 54;
2012, c. 1, s. 11;
2015, c. 23, s. 2.

Invitation to sexual touching
152 Every person who, for a sexual purpose, invites, counsels or incites a person under the age of 16

years to touch, directly or indirectly, with a part of the body or with an object, the body of any person, including the body of the person who so invites, counsels or incites and the body of the person under the age of 16 years,
(a) is guilty of an indictable offence and is liable to imprisonment for a term of not more than 14 years and to a minimum punishment of imprisonment for a term of one year; or
(b) is guilty of an offence punishable on summary conviction and is liable to imprisonment for a term of not more than two years less a day and to a minimum punishment of imprisonment for a term of 90 days.
R.S., 1985, c. C-46, s. 152;
R.S., 1985, c. 19 (3rd Supp.), s. 1;
2005, c. 32, s. 3;
2008, c. 6, s. 54;
2012, c. 1, s. 12;
2015, c. 23, s. 3.

Sexual exploitation
153 (1) Every person commits an offence who is in a position of trust or authority towards a young person, who is a person with whom the young person is in a relationship of dependency or who is in a relationship with a young person that is exploitative of the young person, and who
(a) for a sexual purpose, touches, directly or indirectly, with a part of the body or with an object, any part of the body of the young person; or
(b) for a sexual purpose, invites, counsels or incites a young person to touch, directly or indirectly, with a part of the body or with an object, the body of any person, including the body of the person who so invites, counsels or incites and the body of the young person.

Punishment
(1.1) Every person who commits an offence under subsection (1)
(a) is guilty of an indictable offence and is liable to imprisonment for a term of not more than 14 years and to a minimum punishment of imprisonment for a term of one year; or
(b) is guilty of an offence punishable on summary conviction and is liable to imprisonment for a term of not more than two years less a day and to a minimum punishment of imprisonment for a term of 90 days.

Inference of sexual exploitation
(1.2) A judge may infer that a person is in a relationship with a young person that is exploitative of the young person from the nature and circumstances of the relationship, including
(a) the age of the young person;
(b) the age difference between the person and the young person;
(c) the evolution of the relationship; and
(d) the degree of control or influence by the person over the young person.

Definition of
young person
(2) In this section,
young person
R.S., 1985, c. C-46, s. 153;
R.S., 1985, c. 19 (3rd Supp.), s. 1;
2005, c. 32, s. 4;
2008, c. 6, s. 54;
2012, c. 1, s. 13;
2015, c. 23, s. 4.

Sexual exploitation of person with disability
153.1 (1) Every person who is in a position of trust or authority towards a person with a mental or physical disability or who is a person with whom a person with a mental or physical disability is in a relationship of dependency and who, for a sexual purpose, counsels or incites that person to touch, without that person's consent, his or her own body, the body of the person who so counsels or incites,

or the body of any other person, directly or indirectly, with a part of the body or with an object, is guilty of
(a) an indictable offence and liable to imprisonment for a term not exceeding five years; or
(b) an offence punishable on summary conviction and liable to imprisonment for a term not exceeding eighteen months.

Definition of
consent
(2) Subject to subsection (3),
consent

When no consent obtained
(3) No consent is obtained, for the purposes of this section, if
(a) the agreement is expressed by the words or conduct of a person other than the complainant;
(b) the complainant is incapable of consenting to the activity;
(c) the accused counsels or incites the complainant to engage in the activity by abusing a position of trust, power or authority;
(d) the complainant expresses, by words or conduct, a lack of agreement to engage in the activity; or
(e) the complainant, having consented to engage in sexual activity, expresses, by words or conduct, a lack of agreement to continue to engage in the activity.

Subsection (3) not limiting
(4) Nothing in subsection (3) shall be construed as limiting the circumstances in which no consent is obtained.

When belief in consent not a defence
(5) It is not a defence to a charge under this section that the accused believed that the complainant consented to the activity that forms the subject-matter of the charge if
(a) the accused's belief arose from the accused's
(i) self-induced intoxication, or
(ii) recklessness or wilful blindness; or
(b) the accused did not take reasonable steps, in the circumstances known to the accused at the time, to ascertain that the complainant was consenting.

Accused's belief as to consent
(6) If an accused alleges that he or she believed that the complainant consented to the conduct that is the subject-matter of the charge, a judge, if satisfied that there is sufficient evidence and that, if believed by the jury, the evidence would constitute a defence, shall instruct the jury, when reviewing all the evidence relating to the determination of the honesty of the accused's belief, to consider the presence or absence of reasonable grounds for that belief.
1998, c. 9, s. 2.

154 Incest
155 (1) Every one commits incest who, knowing that another person is by blood relationship his or her parent, child, brother, sister, grandparent or grandchild, as the case may be, has sexual intercourse with that person.

Punishment
(2) Everyone who commits incest is guilty of an indictable offence and is liable to imprisonment for a term of not more than 14 years and, if the other person is under the age of 16 years, to a minimum punishment of imprisonment for a term of five years.

Defence
(3) No accused shall be determined by a court to be guilty of an offence under this section if the accused was under restraint, duress or fear of the person with whom the accused had the sexual intercourse at the time the sexual intercourse occurred.

Definition of
brother
sister
(4) In this section,

brother
sister
R.S., 1985, c. C-46, s. 155;
R.S., 1985, c. 27 (1st Supp.), s. 21;
2012, c. 1, s. 14.
156 to 158 Anal intercourse
159 (1) Every person who engages in an act of anal intercourse is guilty of an indictable offence and liable to imprisonment for a term not exceeding ten years or is guilty of an offence punishable on summary conviction.
Exception
(2) Subsection (1) does not apply to any act engaged in, in private, between
(a) husband and wife, or
(b) any two persons, each of whom is eighteen years of age or more,
both of whom consent to the act.
Idem
(3) For the purposes of subsection (2),
(a) an act shall be deemed not to have been engaged in in private if it is engaged in in a public place or if more than two persons take part or are present; and
(b) a person shall be deemed not to consent to an act
(i) if the consent is extorted by force, threats or fear of bodily harm or is obtained by false and fraudulent misrepresentations respecting the nature and quality of the act, or
(ii) if the court is satisfied beyond a reasonable doubt that the person could not have consented to the act by reason of mental disability.
R.S., 1985, c. C-46, s. 159;
R.S., 1985, c. 19 (3rd Supp.), s. 3.
Bestiality
160 (1) Every person who commits bestiality is guilty of an indictable offence and liable to imprisonment for a term not exceeding ten years or is guilty of an offence punishable on summary conviction.
Compelling the commission of bestiality
(2) Every person who compels another to commit bestiality is guilty of an indictable offence and liable to imprisonment for a term not exceeding ten years or is guilty of an offence punishable on summary conviction.
Bestiality in presence of or by child
(3) Despite subsection (1), every person who commits bestiality in the presence of a person under the age of 16 years, or who incites a person under the age of 16 years to commit bestiality,
(a) is guilty of an indictable offence and is liable to imprisonment for a term of not more than 14 years and to a minimum punishment of imprisonment for a term of one year; or
(b) is guilty of an offence punishable on summary conviction and is liable to imprisonment for a term of not more than two years less a day and to a minimum punishment of imprisonment for a term of six months.
R.S., 1985, c. C-46, s. 160;
R.S., 1985, c. 19 (3rd Supp.), s. 3;
2008, c. 6, s. 54;
2012, c. 1, s. 15;
2015, c. 23, s. 5.
Order of prohibition
161 (1) When an offender is convicted, or is discharged on the conditions prescribed in a probation order under section 730, of an offence referred to in subsection (1.1) in respect of a person who is under the age of 16 years, the court that sentences the offender or directs that the accused be discharged, as the case may be, in addition to any other punishment that may be imposed for that offence or any other condition prescribed in the order of discharge, shall consider making and may

make, subject to the conditions or exemptions that the court directs, an order prohibiting the offender from
(a) attending a public park or public swimming area where persons under the age of 16 years are present or can reasonably be expected to be present, or a daycare centre, schoolground, playground or community centre;
(a.1) being within two kilometres, or any other distance specified in the order, of any dwelling-house where the victim identified in the order ordinarily resides or of any other place specified in the order;
(b) seeking, obtaining or continuing any employment, whether or not the employment is remunerated, or becoming or being a volunteer in a capacity, that involves being in a position of trust or authority towards persons under the age of 16 years;
(c) having any contact — including communicating by any means — with a person who is under the age of 16 years, unless the offender does so under the supervision of a person whom the court considers appropriate; or
(d) using the Internet or other digital network, unless the offender does so in accordance with conditions set by the court.

Offences
(1.1) The offences for the purpose of subsection (1) are
(a) an offence under section 151, 152, 155 or 159, subsection 160(2) or (3), section 163.1, 170, 171, 171.1, 172.1 or 172.2, subsection 173(2), section 271, 272, 273 or 279.011, subsection 279.02(2) or 279.03(2), section 280 or 281 or subsection 286.1(2), 286.2(2) or 286.3(2);
(b) an offence under section 144 (rape), 145 (attempt to commit rape), 149 (indecent assault on female), 156 (indecent assault on male) or 245 (common assault) or subsection 246(1) (assault with intent) of the
Criminal Code
(c) an offence under subsection 146(1) (sexual intercourse with a female under 14) or section 153 (sexual intercourse with step-daughter), 155 (buggery or bestiality), 157 (gross indecency), 166 (parent or guardian procuring defilement) or 167 (householder permitting defilement) of the
Criminal Code
(d) an offence under subsection 212(1) (procuring), 212(2) (living on the avails of prostitution of person under 18 years), 212(2.1) (aggravated offence in relation to living on the avails of prostitution of person under 18 years) or 212(4) (prostitution of person under 18 years) of this Act, as it read from time to time before the day on which this paragraph comes into force.

Duration of prohibition
(2) The prohibition may be for life or for any shorter duration that the court considers desirable and, in the case of a prohibition that is not for life, the prohibition begins on the later of
(a) the date on which the order is made; and
(b) where the offender is sentenced to a term of imprisonment, the date on which the offender is released from imprisonment for the offence, including release on parole, mandatory supervision or statutory release.

Court may vary order
(3) A court that makes an order of prohibition or, where the court is for any reason unable to act, another court of equivalent jurisdiction in the same province, may, on application of the offender or the prosecutor, require the offender to appear before it at any time and, after hearing the parties, that court may vary the conditions prescribed in the order if, in the opinion of the court, the variation is desirable because of changed circumstances after the conditions were prescribed.

Offence
(4) Every person who is bound by an order of prohibition and who does not comply with the order is guilty of
(a) an indictable offence and is liable to imprisonment for a term of not more than four years; or
(b) an offence punishable on summary conviction and is liable to imprisonment for a term of not more than 18 months.
R.S., 1985, c. C-46, s. 161;

R.S., 1985, c. 19 (3rd Supp.), s. 4;
1993, c. 45, s. 1;
1995, c. 22, s. 18;
1997, c. 18, s. 4;
1999, c. 31, s. 67;
2002, c. 13, s. 4;
2005, c. 32, s. 5;
2008, c. 6, s. 54;
2012, c. 1, s. 16;
2014, c. 21, s. 1, c. 25, s. 5;
2015, c. 23, s. 6.

Voyeurism

162 (1) Every one commits an offence who, surreptitiously, observes — including by mechanical or electronic means — or makes a visual recording of a person who is in circumstances that give rise to a reasonable expectation of privacy, if

(a) the person is in a place in which a person can reasonably be expected to be nude, to expose his or her genital organs or anal region or her breasts, or to be engaged in explicit sexual activity;

(b) the person is nude, is exposing his or her genital organs or anal region or her breasts, or is engaged in explicit sexual activity, and the observation or recording is done for the purpose of observing or recording a person in such a state or engaged in such an activity; or

(c) the observation or recording is done for a sexual purpose.

Definition of
visual recording
(2) In this section,
visual recording

Exemption

(3) Paragraphs (1)(a) and (b) do not apply to a peace officer who, under the authority of a warrant issued under section 487.01, is carrying out any activity referred to in those paragraphs.

Printing, publication, etc., of voyeuristic recordings

(4) Every one commits an offence who, knowing that a recording was obtained by the commission of an offence under subsection (1), prints, copies, publishes, distributes, circulates, sells, advertises or makes available the recording, or has the recording in his or her possession for the purpose of printing, copying, publishing, distributing, circulating, selling or advertising it or making it available.

Punishment

(5) Every one who commits an offence under subsection (1) or (4)

(a) is guilty of an indictable offence and liable to imprisonment for a term not exceeding five years; or

(b) is guilty of an offence punishable on summary conviction.

Defence

(6) No person shall be convicted of an offence under this section if the acts that are alleged to constitute the offence serve the public good and do not extend beyond what serves the public good.

Question of law, motives

(7) For the purposes of subsection (6),

(a) it is a question of law whether an act serves the public good and whether there is evidence that the act alleged goes beyond what serves the public good, but it is a question of fact whether the act does or does not extend beyond what serves the public good; and

(b) the motives of an accused are irrelevant.

R.S., 1985, c. C-46, s. 162;
R.S., 1985, c. 19 (3rd Supp.), s. 4;
2005, c. 32, s. 6.

Publication, etc., of an intimate image without consent

162.1 (1) Everyone who knowingly publishes, distributes, transmits, sells, makes available or

advertises an intimate image of a person knowing that the person depicted in the image did not give their consent to that conduct, or being reckless as to whether or not that person gave their consent to that conduct, is guilty
(a) of an indictable offence and liable to imprisonment for a term of not more than five years; or
(b) of an offence punishable on summary conviction.

Definition of
intimate image
(2) In this section,
(a) in which the person is nude, is exposing his or her genital organs or anal region or her breasts or is engaged in explicit sexual activity;
(b) in respect of which, at the time of the recording, there were circumstances that gave rise to a reasonable expectation of privacy; and
(c) in respect of which the person depicted retains a reasonable expectation of privacy at the time the offence is committed.

Defence
(3) No person shall be convicted of an offence under this section if the conduct that forms the subject-matter of the charge serves the public good and does not extend beyond what serves the public good.

Question of fact and law, motives
(4) For the purposes of subsection (3),
(a) it is a question of law whether the conduct serves the public good and whether there is evidence that the conduct alleged goes beyond what serves the public good, but it is a question of fact whether the conduct does or does not extend beyond what serves the public good; and
(b) the motives of an accused are irrelevant.
2014, c. 31, s. 3.

Prohibition order
162.2 (1) When an offender is convicted, or is discharged on the conditions prescribed in a probation order under section 730, of an offence referred to in subsection 162.1(1), the court that sentences or discharges the offender, in addition to any other punishment that may be imposed for that offence or any other condition prescribed in the order of discharge, may make, subject to the conditions or exemptions that the court directs, an order prohibiting the offender from using the Internet or other digital network, unless the offender does so in accordance with conditions set by the court.

Duration of prohibition
(2) The prohibition may be for any period that the court considers appropriate, including any period to which the offender is sentenced to imprisonment.

Court may vary order
(3) A court that makes an order of prohibition or, if the court is for any reason unable to act, another court of equivalent jurisdiction in the same province may, on application of the offender or the prosecutor, require the offender to appear before it at any time and, after hearing the parties, that court may vary the conditions prescribed in the order if, in the opinion of the court, the variation is desirable because of changed circumstances after the conditions were prescribed.

Offence
(4) Every person who is bound by an order of prohibition and who does not comply with the order is guilty of
(a) an indictable offence and is liable to imprisonment for a term of not more than four years; or
(b) an offence punishable on summary conviction and is liable to imprisonment for a term of not more than 18 months.
2014, c. 31, s. 3;
2015, c. 23, s. 33.

Offences Tending to Corrupt Morals

Corrupting morals

163 (1) Every one commits an offence who

(a) makes, prints, publishes, distributes, circulates, or has in his possession for the purpose of publication, distribution or circulation any obscene written matter, picture, model, phonograph record or other thing whatever; or

(b) makes, prints, publishes, distributes, sells or has in his possession for the purpose of publication, distribution or circulation a crime comic.

Idem

(2) Every one commits an offence who knowingly, without lawful justification or excuse,

(a) sells, exposes to public view or has in his possession for such a purpose any obscene written matter, picture, model, phonograph record or other thing whatever;

(b) publicly exhibits a disgusting object or an indecent show;

(c) offers to sell, advertises or publishes an advertisement of, or has for sale or disposal, any means, instructions, medicine, drug or article intended or represented as a method of causing abortion or miscarriage; or

(d) advertises or publishes an advertisement of any means, instructions, medicine, drug or article intended or represented as a method for restoring sexual virility or curing venereal diseases or diseases of the generative organs.

Defence of public good

(3) No person shall be convicted of an offence under this section if the public good was served by the acts that are alleged to constitute the offence and if the acts alleged did not extend beyond what served the public good.

Question of law and question of fact

(4) For the purposes of this section, it is a question of law whether an act served the public good and whether there is evidence that the act alleged went beyond what served the public good, but it is a question of fact whether the acts did or did not extend beyond what served the public good.

Motives irrelevant

(5) For the purposes of this section, the motives of an accused are irrelevant.

(6) Definition of

crime comic

(7) In this section,

crime comic

(a) the commission of crimes, real or fictitious; or

(b) events connected with the commission of crimes, real or fictitious, whether occurring before or after the commission of the crime.

Obscene publication

(8) For the purposes of this Act, any publication a dominant characteristic of which is the undue exploitation of sex, or of sex and any one or more of the following subjects, namely, crime, horror, cruelty and violence, shall be deemed to be obscene.

R.S., 1985, c. C-46, s. 163;

1993, c. 46, s. 1.

Definition of

child pornography

163.1 (1) In this section,

child pornography

(a) a photographic, film, video or other visual representation, whether or not it was made by electronic or mechanical means,

(i) that shows a person who is or is depicted as being under the age of eighteen years and is engaged in or is depicted as engaged in explicit sexual activity, or

(ii) the dominant characteristic of which is the depiction, for a sexual purpose, of a sexual organ or the anal region of a person under the age of eighteen years;

(b) any written material, visual representation or audio recording that advocates or counsels sexual

activity with a person under the age of eighteen years that would be an offence under this Act;
(c) any written material whose dominant characteristic is the description, for a sexual purpose, of sexual activity with a person under the age of eighteen years that would be an offence under this Act; or
(d) any audio recording that has as its dominant characteristic the description, presentation or representation, for a sexual purpose, of sexual activity with a person under the age of eighteen years that would be an offence under this Act.

Making child pornography
(2) Every person who makes, prints, publishes or possesses for the purpose of publication any child pornography is guilty of an indictable offence and liable to imprisonment for a term of not more than 14 years and to a minimum punishment of imprisonment for a term of one year.

Distribution, etc. of child pornography
(3) Every person who transmits, makes available, distributes, sells, advertises, imports, exports or possesses for the purpose of transmission, making available, distribution, sale, advertising or exportation any child pornography is guilty of an indictable offence and liable to imprisonment for a term of not more than 14 years and to a minimum punishment of imprisonment for a term of one year.

Possession of child pornography
(4) Every person who possesses any child pornography is guilty of
(a) an indictable offence and is liable to imprisonment for a term of not more than 10 years and to a minimum punishment of imprisonment for a term of one year; or
(b) an offence punishable on summary conviction and is liable to imprisonment for a term of not more than two years less a day and to a minimum punishment of imprisonment for a term of six months.

Accessing child pornography
(4.1) Every person who accesses any child pornography is guilty of
(a) an indictable offence and is liable to imprisonment for a term of not more than 10 years and to a minimum punishment of imprisonment for a term of one year; or
(b) an offence punishable on summary conviction and is liable to imprisonment for a term of not more than two years less a day and to a minimum punishment of imprisonment for a term of six months.

Interpretation
(4.2) For the purposes of subsection (4.1), a person accesses child pornography who knowingly causes child pornography to be viewed by, or transmitted to, himself or herself.

Aggravating factor
(4.3) If a person is convicted of an offence under this section, the court that imposes the sentence shall consider as an aggravating factor the fact that the person committed the offence with intent to make a profit.

Defence
(5) It is not a defence to a charge under subsection (2) in respect of a visual representation that the accused believed that a person shown in the representation that is alleged to constitute child pornography was or was depicted as being eighteen years of age or more unless the accused took all reasonable steps to ascertain the age of that person and took all reasonable steps to ensure that, where the person was eighteen years of age or more, the representation did not depict that person as being under the age of eighteen years.

Defence
(6) No person shall be convicted of an offence under this section if the act that is alleged to constitute the offence
(a) has a legitimate purpose related to the administration of justice or to science, medicine, education or art; and
(b) does not pose an undue risk of harm to persons under the age of eighteen years.

Question of law

(7) For greater certainty, for the purposes of this section, it is a question of law whether any written material, visual representation or audio recording advocates or counsels sexual activity with a person under the age of eighteen years that would be an offence under this Act.

1993, c. 46, s. 2;
2002, c. 13, s. 5;
2005, c. 32, s. 7;
2012, c. 1, s. 17;
2015, c. 23, s. 7.

Warrant of seizure

164 (1) A judge may issue a warrant authorizing seizure of copies of a recording, a publication, a representation or any written material, if the judge is satisfied by information on oath that there are reasonable grounds to believe that

(a) the recording, copies of which are kept for sale or distribution in premises within the jurisdiction of the court, is a voyeuristic recording;

(b) the recording, copies of which are kept for sale or distribution in premises within the jurisdiction of the court, is an intimate image;

(c) the publication, copies of which are kept for sale or distribution in premises within the jurisdiction of the court, is obscene or a crime comic, as defined in section 163;

(d) the representation, written material or recording, copies of which are kept in premises within the jurisdiction of the court, is child pornography as defined in section 163.1; or

(e) the representation, written material or recording, copies of which are kept in premises within the jurisdiction of the court, is an advertisement of sexual services.

Summons to occupier

(2) Within seven days of the issue of a warrant under subsection (1), the judge shall issue a summons to the occupier of the premises requiring him to appear before the court and show cause why the matter seized should not be forfeited to Her Majesty.

Owner and maker may appear

(3) The owner and the maker of the matter seized under subsection (1), and alleged to be obscene, a crime comic, child pornography, a voyeuristic recording, an intimate image or an advertisement of sexual services, may appear and be represented in the proceedings to oppose the making of an order for the forfeiture of the matter.

Order of forfeiture

(4) If the court is satisfied, on a balance of probabilities, that the publication, representation, written material or recording referred to in subsection (1) is obscene, a crime comic, child pornography, a voyeuristic recording, an intimate image or an advertisement of sexual services, it may make an order declaring the matter forfeited to Her Majesty in right of the province in which the proceedings take place, for disposal as the Attorney General may direct.

Disposal of matter

(5) If the court is not satisfied that the publication, representation, written material or recording referred to in subsection (1) is obscene, a crime comic, child pornography, a voyeuristic recording, an intimate image or an advertisement of sexual services, it shall order that the matter be restored to the person from whom it was seized without delay after the time for final appeal has expired.

Appeal

(6) An appeal lies from an order made under subsection (4) or (5) by any person who appeared in the proceedings

(a) on any ground of appeal that involves a question of law alone,

(b) on any ground of appeal that involves a question of fact alone, or

(c) on any ground of appeal that involves a question of mixed law and fact,

as if it were an appeal against conviction or against a judgment or verdict of acquittal, as the case may be, on a question of law alone under Part XXI and sections 673 to 696 apply with such modifications as the circumstances require.

Consent

(7) If an order is made under this section by a judge in a province with respect to one or more copies of a publication, a representation, written material or a recording, no proceedings shall be instituted or continued in that province under section 162, 162.1, 163, 163.1 or 286.4 with respect to those or other copies of the same publication, representation, written material or recording without the consent of the Attorney General.

Definitions

(8) In this section,

advertisement of sexual services

court

(a) in the Province of Quebec, the Court of Quebec, the municipal court of Montreal and the municipal court of Quebec,

(a.1) in the Province of Ontario, the Superior Court of Justice,

(b) in the Provinces of New Brunswick, Manitoba, Saskatchewan and Alberta, the Court of Queen's Bench,

(c) in the Province of Newfoundland and Labrador, the Trial Division of the Supreme Court,

(c.1) (d) in the Provinces of Nova Scotia, British Columbia and Prince Edward Island, in Yukon and in the Northwest Territories, the Supreme Court, and

(e) in Nunavut, the Nunavut Court of Justice;

crime comic

intimate image

judge

voyeuristic recording

R.S., 1985, c. C-46, s. 164;
R.S., 1985, c. 27 (2nd Supp.), s. 10, c. 40 (4th Supp.), s. 2;
1990, c. 16, s. 3, c. 17, s. 9;
1992, c. 1, s. 58, c. 51, s. 34;
1993, c. 46, s. 3;
1997, c. 18, s. 5;
1998, c. 30, s. 14;
1999, c. 3, s. 27;
2002, c. 7, s. 139, c. 13, s. 6;
2005, c. 32, s. 8;
2014, c. 25, ss. 6, 46, c. 31, s. 4;
2015, c. 3, s. 46.

Warrant of seizure

164.1 (1) If a judge is satisfied by information on oath that there are reasonable grounds to believe that there is material — namely, child pornography as defined in section 163.1, a voyeuristic recording, an intimate image or an advertisement of sexual services as defined in 164(8) or computer data as defined in subsection 342.1(2) that makes child pornography, a voyeuristic recording, an intimate image or an advertisement of sexual services available — that is stored on and made available through a computer system as defined in subsection 342.1(2) that is within the jurisdiction of the court, the judge may order the custodian of the computer system to

(a) give an electronic copy of the material to the court;

(b) ensure that the material is no longer stored on and made available through the computer system; and

(c) provide the information necessary to identify and locate the person who posted the material.

Notice to person who posted the material

(2) Within a reasonable time after receiving the information referred to in paragraph (1)(c), the judge shall cause notice to be given to the person who posted the material, giving that person the opportunity to appear and be represented before the court, and show cause why the material should not be deleted. If the person cannot be identified or located or does not reside in Canada, the judge may order the custodian of the computer system to post the text of the notice at the location where

the material was previously stored and made available, until the time set for the appearance.
Person who posted the material may appear
(3) The person who posted the material may appear and be represented in the proceedings in order to oppose the making of an order under subsection (5).
Non-appearance
(4) If the person who posted the material does not appear for the proceedings, the court may proceed
Order
(5) If the court is satisfied, on a balance of probabilities, that the material is child pornography as defined in section 163.1, a voyeuristic recording, an intimate image or an advertisement of sexual services as defined in subsection 164(8) or computer data as defined in subsection 342.1(2) that makes child pornography, the voyeuristic recording, the intimate image or the advertisement of sexual services available, it may order the custodian of the computer system to delete the material.
Destruction of copy
(6) When the court makes the order for the deletion of the material, it may order the destruction of the electronic copy in the court's possession.
Return of material
(7) If the court is not satisfied that the material is child pornography as defined in 163.1, a voyeuristic recording, an intimate image or an advertisement of sexual services as defined in subsection 164(8) or computer data as defined in subsection 342.1(2) that makes child pornography, the voyeuristic recording, the intimate image or the advertisement of sexual services available, the court shall order that the electronic copy be returned to the custodian of the computer system and terminate the order under paragraph (1)(b).
Other provisions to apply
(8) Subsections 164(6) to (8) apply, with any modifications that the circumstances require, to this section.
When order takes effect
(9) No order made under subsections (5) to (7) takes effect until the time for final appeal has expired.
2002, c. 13, s. 7;
2005, c. 32, s. 9;
2014, c. 25, ss. 7, 46, c. 31, s. 5.
Forfeiture after conviction
164.2 (1) On application of the Attorney General, a court that convicts a person of an offence under section 162.1, 163.1, 172.1 or 172.2, in addition to any other punishment that it may impose, may order that anything — other than real property — be forfeited to Her Majesty and disposed of as the Attorney General directs if it is satisfied, on a balance of probabilities, that the thing
(a) was used in the commission of the offence; and
(b) is the property of
(i) the convicted person or another person who was a party to the offence, or
(ii) a person who acquired the thing from a person referred to in subparagraph (i) under circumstances that give rise to a reasonable inference that it was transferred for the purpose of avoiding forfeiture.
Third party rights
(2) Before making an order under subsection (1), the court shall cause notice to be given to, and may hear, any person whom it considers to have an interest in the thing, and may declare the nature and extent of the person's interest in it.
Right of appeal — third party
(3) A person who was heard in response to a notice given under subsection (2) may appeal to the court of appeal against an order made under subsection (1).
Right of appeal — Attorney General
(4) The Attorney General may appeal to the court of appeal against the refusal of a court to make an order under subsection (1).
Application of Part XXI

(5) Part XXI applies, with any modifications that the circumstances require, with respect to the procedure for an appeal under subsections (3) and (4).

2002, c. 13, s. 7;
2008, c. 18, s. 4;
2012, c. 1, s. 18;
2014, c. 31, s. 6.

Relief from forfeiture
164.3 (1) Within thirty days after an order under subsection 164.2(1) is made, a person who claims an interest in the thing forfeited may apply in writing to a judge for an order under subsection (4).

Hearing of application
(2) The judge shall fix a day — not less than thirty days after the application is made — for its hearing.

Notice to Attorney General
(3) At least fifteen days before the hearing, the applicant shall cause notice of the application and of the hearing day to be served on the Attorney General.

Order
(4) The judge may make an order declaring that the applicant's interest in the thing is not affected by the forfeiture and declaring the nature and extent of the interest if the judge is satisfied that the applicant

(a) was not a party to the offence; and

(b) did not acquire the thing from a person who was a party to the offence under circumstances that give rise to a reasonable inference that it was transferred for the purpose of avoiding forfeiture.

Appeal to court of appeal
(5) A person referred to in subsection (4) or the Attorney General may appeal to the court of appeal against an order made under that subsection. Part XXI applies, with any modifications that the circumstances require, with respect to the procedure for an appeal under this subsection.

Powers of Attorney General
(6) On application by a person who obtained an order under subsection (4), made after the expiration of the time allowed for an appeal against the order and, if an appeal is taken, after it has been finally disposed of, the Attorney General shall direct that

(a) the thing be returned to the person; or

(b) an amount equal to the value of the extent of the person's interest, as declared in the order, be paid to the person.

2002, c. 13, s. 7.

Tied sale
165 Every one commits an offence who refuses to sell or supply to any other person copies of any publication for the reason only that the other person refuses to purchase or acquire from him copies of any other publication that the other person is apprehensive may be obscene or a crime comic.

R.S., c. C-34, s. 161.

166 Immoral theatrical performance
167 (1) Every one commits an offence who, being the lessee, manager, agent or person in charge of a theatre, presents or gives or allows to be presented or given therein an immoral, indecent or obscene performance, entertainment or representation.

Person taking part
(2) Every one commits an offence who takes part or appears as an actor, a performer or an assistant in any capacity, in an immoral, indecent or obscene performance, entertainment or representation in a theatre.

R.S., c. C-34, s. 163.

Mailing obscene matter
168 (1) Every one commits an offence who makes use of the mails for the purpose of transmitting or delivering anything that is obscene, indecent, immoral or scurrilous.

Exceptions

(2) Subsection (1) does not apply to a person who
(a) prints or publishes any matter for use in connection with any judicial proceedings or communicates it to persons who are concerned in the proceedings;
(b) prints or publishes a notice or report under the direction of a court; or
(c) prints or publishes any matter
(i) in a volume or part of a genuine series of law reports that does not form part of any other publication and consists solely of reports of proceedings in courts of law, or
(ii) in a publication of a technical character that is intended, in good faith, for circulation among members of the legal or medical profession.
R.S., 1985, c. C-46, s. 168;
1999, c. 5, s. 2.

Punishment

169 Every one who commits an offence under section 163, 165, 167 or 168 is guilty of
(a) an indictable offence and is liable to imprisonment for a term not exceeding two years; or
(b) an offence punishable on summary conviction.
R.S., 1985, c. C-46, s. 169;
1999, c. 5, s. 3.

Parent or guardian procuring sexual activity

170 Every parent or guardian of a person under the age of 18 years who procures the person for the purpose of engaging in any sexual activity prohibited by this Act with a person other than the parent or guardian is guilty of an indictable offence and liable to imprisonment for a term of not more than 14 years and to a minimum punishment of imprisonment for a term of one year.
R.S., 1985, c. C-46, s. 170;
R.S., 1985, c. 19 (3rd Supp.), s. 5;
2005, c. 32, s. 9.1;
2008, c. 6, s. 54;
2012, c. 1, s. 19;
2015, c. 23, s. 8.

Householder permitting prohibited sexual activity

171 Every owner, occupier or manager of premises, or any other person who has control of premises or assists in the management or control of premises, who knowingly permits a person under the age of 18 years to resort to or to be in or on the premises for the purpose of engaging in any sexual activity prohibited by this Act is guilty of an indictable offence and liable to imprisonment for a term of not more than 14 years and to a minimum punishment of imprisonment for a term of one year.
R.S., 1985, c. C-46, s. 171;
R.S., 1985, c. 19 (3rd Supp.), s. 5;
2005, c. 32, s. 9.1;
2008, c. 6, s. 54;
2012, c. 1, s. 20;
2015, c. 23, s. 9.

Making sexually explicit material available to child

171.1 (1) Every person commits an offence who transmits, makes available, distributes or sells sexually explicit material to
(a) a person who is, or who the accused believes is, under the age of 18 years, for the purpose of facilitating the commission of an offence with respect to that person under subsection 153(1), section 155, 163.1, 170, 171 or 279.011 or subsection 279.02(2), 279.03(2), 286.1(2), 286.2(2) or 286.3(2);
(b) a person who is, or who the accused believes is, under the age of 16 years, for the purpose of facilitating the commission of an offence under section 151 or 152, subsection 160(3) or 173(2) or section 271, 272, 273 or 280 with respect to that person; or
(c) a person who is, or who the accused believes is, under the age of 14 years, for the purpose of facilitating the commission of an offence under section 281 with respect to that person.

Punishment

(2) Every person who commits an offence under subsection (1)
(a) is guilty of an indictable offence and is liable to imprisonment for a term of not more than 14 years and to a minimum punishment of imprisonment for a term of six months; or
(b) is guilty of an offence punishable on summary conviction and is liable to imprisonment for a term of not more than two years less a day and to a minimum punishment of imprisonment for a term of 90 days.

Presumption
(3) Evidence that the person referred to in paragraph (1)(a), (b) or (c) was represented to the accused as being under the age of 18, 16 or 14 years, as the case may be, is, in the absence of evidence to the contrary, proof that the accused believed that the person was under that age.

No defence
(4) It is not a defence to a charge under paragraph (1)(a), (b) or (c) that the accused believed that the person referred to in that paragraph was at least 18, 16 or 14 years of age, as the case may be, unless the accused took reasonable steps to ascertain the age of the person.

Definition of
sexually explicit material
(5) In subsection (1),
sexually explicit material
(a) a photographic, film, video or other visual representation, whether or not it was made by electronic or mechanical means,
(i) that shows a person who is engaged in or is depicted as engaged in explicit sexual activity, or
(ii) the dominant characteristic of which is the depiction, for a sexual purpose, of a person's genital organs or anal region or, if the person is female, her breasts;
(b) written material whose dominant characteristic is the description, for a sexual purpose, of explicit sexual activity with a person; or
(c) an audio recording whose dominant characteristic is the description, presentation or representation, for a sexual purpose, of explicit sexual activity with a person.
2012, c. 1, s. 21;
2014, c. 25, s. 8;
2015, c. 23, s. 10.

Corrupting children
172 (1) Every one who, in the home of a child, participates in adultery or sexual immorality or indulges in habitual drunkenness or any other form of vice, and thereby endangers the morals of the child or renders the home an unfit place for the child to be in, is guilty of an indictable offence and liable to imprisonment for a term not exceeding two years.

(2) Definition of
child
(3) For the purposes of this section,
child

Who may institute prosecutions
(4) No proceedings shall be commenced under subsection (1) without the consent of the Attorney General, unless they are instituted by or at the instance of a recognized society for the protection of children or by an officer of a juvenile court.
R.S., 1985, c. C-46, s. 172;
R.S., 1985, c. 19 (3rd Supp.), s. 6.

Luring a child
172.1 (1) Every person commits an offence who, by a means of telecommunication, communicates with
(a) a person who is, or who the accused believes is, under the age of 18 years, for the purpose of facilitating the commission of an offence with respect to that person under subsection 153(1), section 155, 163.1, 170, 171 or 279.011 or subsection 279.02(2), 279.03(2), 286.1(2), 286.2(2) or 286.3(2);
(b) a person who is, or who the accused believes is, under the age of 16 years, for the purpose of

facilitating the commission of an offence under section 151 or 152, subsection 160(3) or 173(2) or section 271, 272, 273 or 280 with respect to that person; or

(c) a person who is, or who the accused believes is, under the age of 14 years, for the purpose of facilitating the commission of an offence under section 281 with respect to that person.

Punishment

(2) Every person who commits an offence under subsection (1)

(a) is guilty of an indictable offence and is liable to imprisonment for a term of not more than 14 years and to a minimum punishment of imprisonment for a term of one year; or

(b) is guilty of an offence punishable on summary conviction and is liable to imprisonment for a term of not more than two years less a day and to a minimum punishment of imprisonment for a term of six months.

Presumption re age

(3) Evidence that the person referred to in paragraph (1)(a), (b) or (c) was represented to the accused as being under the age of eighteen years, sixteen years or fourteen years, as the case may be, is, in the absence of evidence to the contrary, proof that the accused believed that the person was under that age.

No defence

(4) It is not a defence to a charge under paragraph (1)(a), (b) or (c) that the accused believed that the person referred to in that paragraph was at least eighteen years of age, sixteen years or fourteen years of age, as the case may be, unless the accused took reasonable steps to ascertain the age of the person.

2002, c. 13, s. 8;
2007, c. 20, s. 1;
2008, c. 6, s. 14;
2012, c. 1, s. 22;
2014, c. 25, s. 9;
2015, c. 23, s. 11.

Disorderly Conduct

Agreement or arrangement — sexual offence against child

172.2 (1) Every person commits an offence who, by a means of telecommunication, agrees with a person, or makes an arrangement with a person, to commit an offence

(a) under subsection 153(1), section 155, 163.1, 170, 171 or 279.011 or subsection 279.02(2), 279.03(2), 286.1(2), 286.2(2) or 286.3(2) with respect to another person who is, or who the accused believes is, under the age of 18 years;

(b) under section 151 or 152, subsection 160(3) or 173(2) or section 271, 272, 273 or 280 with respect to another person who is, or who the accused believes is, under the age of 16 years; or

(c) under section 281 with respect to another person who is, or who the accused believes is, under the age of 14 years.

Punishment

(2) Every person who commits an offence under subsection (1)

(a) is guilty of an indictable offence and is liable to imprisonment for a term of not more than 14 years and to a minimum punishment of imprisonment for a term of one year; or

(b) is guilty of an offence punishable on summary conviction and is liable to imprisonment for a term of not more than two years less a day and to a minimum punishment of imprisonment for a term of six months.

Presumption

(3) Evidence that the person referred to in paragraph (1)(a), (b) or (c) was represented to the accused as being under the age of 18, 16 or 14 years, as the case may be, is, in the absence of evidence to the contrary, proof that the accused believed that the person was under that age.

No defence

(4) It is not a defence to a charge under paragraph (1)(a), (b) or (c) that the accused believed that the person referred to in that paragraph was at least 18, 16 or 14 years of age, as the case may be, unless the accused took reasonable steps to ascertain the age of the person.

No defence

(5) It is not a defence to a charge under paragraph (1)(a), (b) or (c)

(a) that the person with whom the accused agreed or made an arrangement was a peace officer or a person acting under the direction of a peace officer; or

(b) that, if the person with whom the accused agreed or made an arrangement was a peace officer or a person acting under the direction of a peace officer, the person referred to in paragraph (1)(a), (b) or (c) did not exist.

2012, c. 1, s. 23;
2014, c. 25, s. 10;
2015, c. 23, s. 12.

Indecent acts

173 (1) Everyone who wilfully does an indecent act in a public place in the presence of one or more persons, or in any place with intent to insult or offend any person,

(a) is guilty of an indictable offence and is liable to imprisonment for a term of not more than two years; or

(b) is guilty of an offence punishable on summary conviction and is liable to imprisonment for a term of not more than six months.

Exposure

(2) Every person who, in any place, for a sexual purpose, exposes his or her genital organs to a person who is under the age of 16 years

(a) is guilty of an indictable offence and is liable to imprisonment for a term of not more than two years and to a minimum punishment of imprisonment for a term of 90 days; or

(b) is guilty of an offence punishable on summary conviction and is liable to imprisonment for a term of not more than six months and to a minimum punishment of imprisonment for a term of 30 days.

R.S., 1985, c. C-46, s. 173;
R.S., 1985, c. 19 (3rd Supp.), s. 7;
2008, c. 6, s. 54;
2010, c. 17, s. 2;
2012, c. 1, s. 23.

Nudity

174 (1) Every one who, without lawful excuse,

(a) is nude in a public place, or

(b) is nude and exposed to public view while on private property, whether or not the property is his own,

is guilty of an offence punishable on summary conviction.

Nude

(2) For the purposes of this section, a person is nude who is so clad as to offend against public decency or order.

Consent of Attorney General

(3) No proceedings shall be commenced under this section without the consent of the Attorney General.

R.S., c. C-34, s. 170.

Causing disturbance, indecent exhibition, loitering, etc.

175 (1) Every one who

(a) not being in a dwelling-house, causes a disturbance in or near a public place,

(i) by fighting, screaming, shouting, swearing, singing or using insulting or obscene language,

(ii) by being drunk, or

(iii) by impeding or molesting other persons,

(b) openly exposes or exhibits an indecent exhibition in a public place,

(c) loiters in a public place and in any way obstructs persons who are in that place, or
(d) disturbs the peace and quiet of the occupants of a dwelling-house by discharging firearms or by other disorderly conduct in a public place or who, not being an occupant of a dwelling-house comprised in a particular building or structure, disturbs the peace and quiet of the occupants of a dwelling-house comprised in the building or structure by discharging firearms or by other disorderly conduct in any part of a building or structure to which, at the time of such conduct, the occupants of two or more dwelling-houses comprised in the building or structure have access as of right or by invitation, express or implied,
is guilty of an offence punishable on summary conviction.

Evidence of peace officer

(2) In the absence of other evidence, or by way of corroboration of other evidence, a summary conviction court may infer from the evidence of a peace officer relating to the conduct of a person or persons, whether ascertained or not, that a disturbance described in paragraph (1)(a) or (d) or an obstruction described in paragraph (1)(c) was caused or occurred.
R.S., 1985, c. C-46, s. 175;
1997, c. 18, s. 6.

Obstructing or violence to or arrest of officiating clergyman

176 (1) Every one who
(a) by threats or force, unlawfully obstructs or prevents or endeavours to obstruct or prevent a clergyman or minister from celebrating divine service or performing any other function in connection with his calling, or
(b) knowing that a clergyman or minister is about to perform, is on his way to perform or is returning from the performance of any of the duties or functions mentioned in paragraph (a)
(i) assaults or offers any violence to him, or
(ii) arrests him on a civil process, or under the pretence of executing a civil process,
is guilty of an indictable offence and liable to imprisonment for a term not exceeding two years.

Disturbing religious worship or certain meetings

(2) Every one who wilfully disturbs or interrupts an assemblage of persons met for religious worship or for a moral, social or benevolent purpose is guilty of an offence punishable on summary conviction.

Idem

(3) Every one who, at or near a meeting referred to in subsection (2), wilfully does anything that disturbs the order or solemnity of the meeting is guilty of an offence punishable on summary conviction.
R.S., c. C-34, s. 172.

Trespassing at night

177 Every one who, without lawful excuse, the proof of which lies on him, loiters or prowls at night on the property of another person near a dwelling-house situated on that property is guilty of an offence punishable on summary conviction.
R.S., c. C-34, s. 173.

Offensive volatile substance

178 Every one other than a peace officer engaged in the discharge of his duty who has in his possession in a public place or who deposits, throws or injects or causes to be deposited, thrown or injected in, into or near any place,
(a) an offensive volatile substance that is likely to alarm, inconvenience, discommode or cause discomfort to any person or to cause damage to property, or
(b) a stink or stench bomb or device from which any substance mentioned in paragraph (a) is or is capable of being liberated,
is guilty of an offence punishable on summary conviction.
R.S., c. C-34, s. 174.

Vagrancy

179 (1) Every one commits vagrancy who

(a) supports himself in whole or in part by gaming or crime and has no lawful profession or calling by which to maintain himself; or
(b) having at any time been convicted of an offence under section 151, 152 or 153, subsection 160(3) or 173(2) or section 271, 272 or 273, or of an offence under a provision referred to in paragraph (b) of the definition
Criminal Code
Punishment
(2) Every one who commits vagrancy is guilty of an offence punishable on summary conviction.
R.S., 1985, c. C-46, s. 179;
R.S., 1985, c. 27 (1st Supp.), s. 22, c. 19 (3rd Supp.), s. 8.

Nuisances

Common nuisance
180 (1) Every one who commits a common nuisance and thereby
(a) endangers the lives, safety or health of the public, or
(b) causes physical injury to any person,
is guilty of an indictable offence and liable to imprisonment for a term not exceeding two years.
Definition
(2) For the purposes of this section, every one commits a common nuisance who does an unlawful act or fails to discharge a legal duty and thereby
(a) endangers the lives, safety, health, property or comfort of the public; or
(b) obstructs the public in the exercise or enjoyment of any right that is common to all the subjects of Her Majesty in Canada.
R.S., c. C-34, s. 176.
Spreading false news
181 Every one who wilfully publishes a statement, tale or news that he knows is false and that causes or is likely to cause injury or mischief to a public interest is guilty of an indictable offence and liable to imprisonment for a term not exceeding two years.
R.S., c. C-34, s. 177.
Dead body
182 Every one who
(a) neglects, without lawful excuse, to perform any duty that is imposed on him by law or that he undertakes with reference to the burial of a dead human body or human remains, or
(b) improperly or indecently interferes with or offers any indignity to a dead human body or human remains, whether buried or not,
is guilty of an indictable offence and liable to imprisonment for a term not exceeding five years.
R.S., c. C-34, s. 178.

PART VI

PART VI
Invasion of Privacy

Definitions

Definitions
183 In this Part,
authorization
electro-magnetic, acoustic, mechanical or other device
intercept
offence

(a) any of the following provisions of this Act, namely,
(i) section 47 (high treason),
(ii) section 51 (intimidating Parliament or a legislature),
(iii) section 52 (sabotage),
(iii.1) section 56.1 (identity documents),
(iv) section 57 (forgery, etc.),
(v) section 61 (sedition),
(vi) section 76 (hijacking),
(vii) section 77 (endangering safety of aircraft or airport),
(viii) section 78 (offensive weapons, etc., on aircraft),
(ix) section 78.1 (offences against maritime navigation or fixed platforms),
(x) section 80 (breach of duty),
(xi) section 81 (using explosives),
(xii) section 82 (possessing explosives),
(xii.01) section 82.3 (possession, etc., of nuclear material, radioactive material or device),
(xii.02) section 82.4 (use or alteration of nuclear material, radioactive material or device),
(xii.03) section 82.5 (commission of indictable offence to obtain nuclear material, etc.),
(xii.04) section 82.6 (threats),
(xii.1) section 83.02 (providing or collecting property for certain activities),
(xii.2) section 83.03 (providing, making available, etc., property or services for terrorist purposes),
(xii.3) section 83.04 (using or possessing property for terrorist purposes),
(xii.4) section 83.18 (participation in activity of terrorist group),
(xii.41) section 83.181 (leaving Canada to participate in activity of terrorist group),
(xii.5) section 83.19 (facilitating terrorist activity),
(xii.51) section 83.191 (leaving Canada to facilitate terrorist activity),
(xii.6) section 83.2 (commission of offence for terrorist group),
(xii.61) section 83.201 (leaving Canada to commit offence for terrorist group),
(xii.62) section 83.202 (leaving Canada to commit offence that is terrorist activity),
(xii.7) section 83.21 (instructing to carry out activity for terrorist group),
(xii.8) section 83.22 (instructing to carry out terrorist activity),
(xii.81) subsection 83.221(1) (advocating or promoting commission of terrorism offences),
(xii.9) section 83.23 (harbouring or concealing),
(xii.91) section 83.231 (hoax — terrorist activity),
(xiii) section 96 (possession of weapon obtained by commission of offence),
(xiii.1) section 98 (breaking and entering to steal firearm),
(xiii.2) section 98.1 (robbery to steal firearm),
(xiv) section 99 (weapons trafficking),
(xv) section 100 (possession for purpose of weapons trafficking),
(xvi) section 102 (making automatic firearm),
(xvii) section 103 (importing or exporting knowing it is unauthorized),
(xviii) section 104 (unauthorized importing or exporting),
(xix) section 119 (bribery, etc.),
(xx) section 120 (bribery, etc.),
(xxi) section 121 (fraud on government),
(xxii) section 122 (breach of trust),
(xxiii) section 123 (municipal corruption),
(xxiv) section 132 (perjury),
(xxv) section 139 (obstructing justice),
(xxvi) section 144 (prison breach),
(xxvii) subsection 145(1) (escape, etc.),
(xxvii.1) section 162 (voyeurism),
(xxvii.2) section 162.1 (intimate image),

(xxviii) paragraph 163(1)(a) (obscene materials),
(xxix) section 163.1 (child pornography),
(xxix.1) section 170 (parent or guardian procuring sexual activity),
(xxix.2) section 171 (householder permitting sexual activity),
(xxix.3) section 171.1 (making sexually explicit material available to child),
(xxix.4) section 172.1 (luring a child),
(xxix.5) section 172.2 (agreement or arrangement — sexual offence against child),
(xxx) section 184 (unlawful interception),
(xxxi) section 191 (possession of intercepting device),
(xxxii) subsection 201(1) (keeping gaming or betting house),
(xxxiii) paragraph 202(1)(e) (pool-selling, etc.),
(xxxiv) subsection 210(1) (keeping common bawdy house),
(xxxv) to (xxxviii) (xxxix) section 235 (murder),
(xxxix.1) section 244 (discharging firearm with intent),
(xxxix.2) section 244.2 (discharging firearm — recklessness),
(xl) section 264.1 (uttering threats),
(xli) section 267 (assault with a weapon or causing bodily harm),
(xlii) section 268 (aggravated assault),
(xliii) section 269 (unlawfully causing bodily harm),
(xliii.1) section 270.01 (assaulting peace officer with weapon or causing bodily harm),
(xliii.2) section 270.02 (aggravated assault of peace officer),
(xliv) section 271 (sexual assault),
(xlv) section 272 (sexual assault with a weapon, threats to a third party or causing bodily harm),
(xlvi) section 273 (aggravated sexual assault),
(xlvii) section 279 (kidnapping),
(xlvii.1) section 279.01 (trafficking in persons),
(xlvii.11) section 279.011 (trafficking of a person under the age of eighteen years),
(xlvii.2) section 279.02 (material benefit),
(xlvii.3) section 279.03 (withholding or destroying documents),
(xlviii) section 279.1 (hostage taking),
(xlix) section 280 (abduction of person under sixteen),
(l) section 281 (abduction of person under fourteen),
(li) section 282 (abduction in contravention of custody order),
(lii) section 283 (abduction),
(lii.1) 286.1 (obtaining sexual services for consideration),
(lii.2) 286.2 (material benefit from sexual services),
(lii.3) 286.3 (procuring),
(lii.4) 286.4 (advertising sexual services),
(liii) section 318 (advocating genocide),
(liv) section 327 (possession of device to obtain telecommunication facility or service),
(liv.1) section 333.1 (motor vehicle theft),
(lv) section 334 (theft),
(lvi) section 342 (theft, forgery, etc., of credit card),
(lvi.1) section 342.01 (instruments for copying credit card data or forging or falsifying credit cards),
(lvii) section 342.1 (unauthorized use of computer),
(lviii) section 342.2 (possession of device to obtain unauthorized use of computer system or to commit mischief),
(lix) section 344 (robbery),
(lx) section 346 (extortion),
(lxi) section 347 (criminal interest rate),
(lxii) section 348 (breaking and entering),
(lxii.1) section 353.1 (tampering with vehicle identification number),

(lxiii) section 354 (possession of property obtained by crime),
(lxiii.1) section 355.2 (trafficking in property obtained by crime),
(lxiii.2) section 355.4 (possession of property obtained by crime — trafficking),
(lxiv) section 356 (theft from mail),
(lxv) section 367 (forgery),
(lxvi) section 368 (use, trafficking or possession of forged document),
(lxvi.1) section 368.1 (forgery instruments),
(lxvii) section 372 (false information),
(lxviii) section 380 (fraud),
(lxix) section 381 (using mails to defraud),
(lxx) section 382 (fraudulent manipulation of stock exchange transactions),
(lxx.1) subsection 402.2(1) (identity theft),
(lxx.2) subsection 402.2(2) (trafficking in identity information),
(lxx.3) section 403 (identity fraud),
(lxxi) section 423.1 (intimidation of justice system participant or journalist),
(lxxii) section 424 (threat to commit offences against internationally protected person),
(lxxii.1) section 424.1 (threat against United Nations or associated personnel),
(lxxiii) section 426 (secret commissions),
(lxxiv) section 430 (mischief),
(lxxv) section 431 (attack on premises, residence or transport of internationally protected person),
(lxxv.1) section 431.1 (attack on premises, accommodation or transport of United Nations or associated personnel),
(lxxv.2) subsection 431.2(2) (explosive or other lethal device),
(lxxvi) section 433 (arson),
(lxxvii) section 434 (arson),
(lxxviii) section 434.1 (arson),
(lxxix) section 435 (arson for fraudulent purpose),
(lxxx) section 449 (making counterfeit money),
(lxxxi) section 450 (possession, etc., of counterfeit money),
(lxxxii) section 452 (uttering, etc., counterfeit money),
(lxxxiii) section 462.31 (laundering proceeds of crime),
(lxxxiv) subsection 462.33(11) (acting in contravention of restraint order),
(lxxxv) section 467.11 (participation in criminal organization),
(lxxxv.1) section 467.111 (recruitment of members — criminal organization),
(lxxxvi) section 467.12 (commission of offence for criminal organization), or
(lxxxvii) section 467.13 (instructing commission of offence for criminal organization),
(b) section 198 (fraudulent bankruptcy) of the
Bankruptcy and Insolvency Act
(b.1) any of the following provisions of the
Biological and Toxin Weapons Convention Implementation Act
(i) section 6 (production, etc., of biological agents and means of delivery), or
(ii) section 7 (unauthorized production, etc., of biological agents),
(c) any of the following provisions of the
Competition Act
(i) section 45 (conspiracies, agreements or arrangements between competitors),
(ii) section 47 (bid-rigging), or
(iii) subsection 52.1(3) (deceptive telemarketing),
(d) any of the following provisions of the
Controlled Drugs and Substances Act
(i) section 5 (trafficking),
(ii) section 6 (importing and exporting),
(iii) section 7 (production), or

(iv) section 7.1 (possession, sale, etc., for use in production or trafficking),
(d.1) section 42 (offences related to infringement of copyright) of the
Copyright Act
(e) section 3 (bribing a foreign public official) of the
Corruption of Foreign Public Officials Act
(e.1) the
Crimes Against Humanity and War Crimes Act
(f) either of the following provisions of the
Customs Act
(i) section 153 (false statements), or
(ii) section 159 (smuggling),
(g) any of the following provisions of the
Excise Act, 2001
(i) section 214 (unlawful production, sale, etc., of tobacco or alcohol),
(ii) section 216 (unlawful possession of tobacco product),
(iii) section 218 (unlawful possession, sale, etc., of alcohol),
(iv) section 219 (falsifying or destroying records),
(v) section 230 (possession of property obtained by excise offences), or
(vi) section 231 (laundering proceeds of excise offences),
(h) any of the following provisions of the
Export and Import Permits Act
(i) section 13 (export or attempt to export),
(ii) section 14 (import or attempt to import),
(iii) section 15 (diversion, etc.),
(iv) section 16 (no transfer of permits),
(v) section 17 (false information), or
(vi) section 18 (aiding and abetting),
(i) any of the following provisions of the
Immigration and Refugee Protection Act
(i) section 117 (organizing entry into Canada),
(ii) section 118 (trafficking in persons),
(iii) section 119 (disembarking persons at sea),
(iv) section 122 (offences related to documents),
(v) section 126 (counselling misrepresentation), or
(vi) section 129 (offences relating to officers),
(j) any offence under the
Security of Information Act
(k) section 51.01 (offences related to goods, labels, packaging or services) of the
Trade-marks Act
and includes any other offence that there are reasonable grounds to believe is a criminal organization offence or any other offence that there are reasonable grounds to believe is an offence described in paragraph (b) or (c) of the definition
police officer
private communication
public switched telephone network
radio-based telephone communication
Radiocommunication Act
sell
solicitor
R.S., 1985, c. C-46, s. 183;
R.S., 1985, c. 27 (1st Supp.), ss. 7, 23, c. 1 (2nd Supp.), s. 213, c. 1 (4th Supp.), s. 13, c. 29 (4th Supp.), s. 17, c. 42 (4th Supp.), s. 1;

1991, c. 28, s. 12;
1992, c. 27, s. 90;
1993, c. 7, s. 5, c. 25, s. 94, c. 40, s. 1, c. 46, s. 4;
1995, c. 39, s. 140;
1996, c. 19, s. 66;
1997, c. 18, s. 7, c. 23, s. 3;
1998, c. 34, s. 8;
1999, c. 2, s. 47, c. 5, s. 4;
2000, c. 24, s. 43;
2001, c. 32, s. 4, c. 41, ss. 5, 31, 133;
2002, c. 22, s. 409;
2004, c. 15, s. 108;
2005, c. 32, s. 10, c. 43, s. 1;
2008, c. 6, s. 15;
2009, c. 2, s. 442, c. 22, s. 4, c. 28, s. 3;
2010, c. 3, s. 1, c. 14, s. 2;
2012, c. 1, s. 24;
2013, c. 8, s. 2, c. 9, s. 14, c. 13, s. 7;
2014, c. 17, s. 2, c. 25, s. 11, c. 31, s. 7, c. 32, s. 59;
2015, c. 20, s. 19;
2017, c. 7, s. 56.

Consent to interception

183.1 Where a private communication is originated by more than one person or is intended by the originator thereof to be received by more than one person, a consent to the interception thereof by any one of those persons is sufficient consent for the purposes of any provision of this Part.
1993, c. 40, s. 2.

Interception of Communications

Interception

184 (1) Every one who, by means of any electro-magnetic, acoustic, mechanical or other device, wilfully intercepts a private communication is guilty of an indictable offence and liable to imprisonment for a term not exceeding five years.

Saving provision

(2) Subsection (1) does not apply to
(a) a person who has the consent to intercept, express or implied, of the originator of the private communication or of the person intended by the originator thereof to receive it;
(b) a person who intercepts a private communication in accordance with an authorization or pursuant to section 184.4 or any person who in good faith aids in any way another person who the aiding person believes on reasonable grounds is acting with an authorization or pursuant to section 184.4;
(c) a person engaged in providing a telephone, telegraph or other communication service to the public who intercepts a private communication,
(i) if the interception is necessary for the purpose of providing the service,
(ii) in the course of service observing or random monitoring necessary for the purpose of mechanical or service quality control checks, or
(iii) if the interception is necessary to protect the person's rights or property directly related to providing the service;
(d) an officer or servant of Her Majesty in right of Canada who engages in radio frequency spectrum management, in respect of a private communication intercepted by that officer or servant for the purpose of identifying, isolating or preventing an unauthorized or interfering use of a frequency or of a transmission; or
(e) a person, or any person acting on their behalf, in possession or control of a computer system, as

defined in subsection 342.1(2), who intercepts a private communication originating from, directed to or transmitting through that computer system, if the interception is reasonably necessary for
(i) managing the quality of service of the computer system as it relates to performance factors such as the responsiveness and capacity of the system as well as the integrity and availability of the system and data, or
(ii) protecting the computer system against any act that would be an offence under subsection 342.1(1) or 430(1.1).

Use or retention
(3) A private communication intercepted by a person referred to in paragraph (2)(e) can be used or retained only if
(a) it is essential to identify, isolate or prevent harm to the computer system; or
(b) it is to be disclosed in circumstances referred to in subsection 193(2).
R.S., 1985, c. C-46, s. 184;
1993, c. 40, s. 3;
2004, c. 12, s. 4.

Interception to prevent bodily harm
184.1 (1) An agent of the state may intercept, by means of any electro-magnetic, acoustic, mechanical or other device, a private communication if
(a) either the originator of the private communication or the person intended by the originator to receive it has consented to the interception;
(b) the agent of the state believes on reasonable grounds that there is a risk of bodily harm to the person who consented to the interception; and
(c) the purpose of the interception is to prevent the bodily harm.

Admissibility of intercepted communication
(2) The contents of a private communication that is obtained from an interception pursuant to subsection (1) are inadmissible as evidence except for the purposes of proceedings in which actual, attempted or threatened bodily harm is alleged, including proceedings in respect of an application for an authorization under this Part or in respect of a search warrant or a warrant for the arrest of any person.

Destruction of recordings and transcripts
(3) The agent of the state who intercepts a private communication pursuant to subsection (1) shall, as soon as is practicable in the circumstances, destroy any recording of the private communication that is obtained from an interception pursuant to subsection (1), any full or partial transcript of the recording and any notes made by that agent of the private communication if nothing in the private communication suggests that bodily harm, attempted bodily harm or threatened bodily harm has occurred or is likely to occur.

Definition of
agent of the state
(4) For the purposes of this section,
agent of the state
(a) a peace officer; and
(b) a person acting under the authority of, or in cooperation with, a peace officer.
1993, c. 40, s. 4.

Interception with consent
184.2 (1) A person may intercept, by means of any electro-magnetic, acoustic, mechanical or other device, a private communication where either the originator of the private communication or the person intended by the originator to receive it has consented to the interception and an authorization has been obtained pursuant to subsection (3).

Application for authorization
(2) An application for an authorization under this section shall be made by a peace officer, or a public officer who has been appointed or designated to administer or enforce any federal or provincial law and whose duties include the enforcement of this or any other Act of Parliament,

(a) that there are reasonable grounds to believe that an offence against this or any other Act of Parliament has been or will be committed;
(b) the particulars of the offence;
(c) the name of the person who has consented to the interception;
(d) the period for which the authorization is requested; and
(e) in the case of an application for an authorization where an authorization has previously been granted under this section or section 186, the particulars of the authorization.

Judge to be satisfied
(3) An authorization may be given under this section if the judge to whom the application is made is satisfied that
(a) there are reasonable grounds to believe that an offence against this or any other Act of Parliament has been or will be committed;
(b) either the originator of the private communication or the person intended by the originator to receive it has consented to the interception; and
(c) there are reasonable grounds to believe that information concerning the offence referred to in paragraph (a) will be obtained through the interception sought.

Content and limitation of authorization
(4) An authorization given under this section shall
(a) state the offence in respect of which private communications may be intercepted;
(b) state the type of private communication that may be intercepted;
(c) state the identity of the persons, if known, whose private communications are to be intercepted, generally describe the place at which private communications may be intercepted, if a general description of that place can be given, and generally describe the manner of interception that may be used;
(d) contain the terms and conditions that the judge considers advisable in the public interest; and
(e) be valid for the period, not exceeding sixty days, set out therein.

Related warrant or order
(5) A judge who gives an authorization under this section may, at the same time, issue a warrant or make an order under any of sections 487, 487.01, 487.014 to 487.018, 487.02, 492.1 and 492.2 if the judge is of the opinion that the requested warrant or order is related to the execution of the authorization.
1993, c. 40, s. 4;
2014, c. 31, s. 8.

Application by means of telecommunication
184.3 (1) Notwithstanding section 184.2, an application for an authorization under subsection 184.2(2) may be made

Application
(2) An application for an authorization made under this section shall be on oath and shall be accompanied by a statement that includes the matters referred to in paragraphs 184.2(2)(a) to (e) and that states the circumstances that make it impracticable for the applicant to appear personally before a judge.

Recording
(3) The judge shall record, in writing or otherwise, the application for an authorization made under this section and, on determination of the application, shall cause the writing or recording to be placed in the packet referred to in subsection 187(1) and sealed in that packet, and a recording sealed in a packet shall be treated as if it were a document for the purposes of section 187.

Oath
(4) For the purposes of subsection (2), an oath may be administered by telephone or other means of telecommunication.

Alternative to oath
(5) An applicant who uses a means of telecommunication that produces a writing may, instead of swearing an oath for the purposes of subsection (2), make a statement in writing stating that all

matters contained in the application are true to the knowledge or belief of the applicant and such a statement shall be deemed to be a statement made under oath.

Authorization

(6) Where the judge to whom an application is made under this section is satisfied that the circumstances referred to in paragraphs 184.2(3)(a) to (c) exist and that the circumstances referred to in subsection (2) make it impracticable for the applicant to appear personally before a judge, the judge may, on such terms and conditions, if any, as are considered advisable, give an authorization by telephone or other means of telecommunication for a period of up to thirty-six hours.

Giving authorization

(7) Where a judge gives an authorization by telephone or other means of telecommunication, other than a means of telecommunication that produces a writing,

(a) the judge shall complete and sign the authorization in writing, noting on its face the time, date and place at which it is given;

(b) the applicant shall, on the direction of the judge, complete a facsimile of the authorization in writing, noting on its face the name of the judge who gave it and the time, date and place at which it was given; and

(c) the judge shall, as soon as is practicable after the authorization has been given, cause the authorization to be placed in the packet referred to in subsection 187(1) and sealed in that packet.

Giving authorization where telecommunication produces writing

(8) Where a judge gives an authorization by a means of telecommunication that produces a writing, the judge shall

(a) complete and sign the authorization in writing, noting on its face the time, date and place at which it is given;

(b) transmit the authorization by the means of telecommunication to the applicant, and the copy received by the applicant shall be deemed to be a facsimile referred to in paragraph (7)(b); and

(c) as soon as is practicable after the authorization has been given, cause the authorization to be placed in the packet referred to in subsection 187(1) and sealed in that packet.

1993, c. 40, s. 4.

Immediate interception — imminent harm

184.4 A police officer may intercept, by means of any electro-magnetic, acoustic, mechanical or other device, a private communication if the police officer has reasonable grounds to believe that

(a) the urgency of the situation is such that an authorization could not, with reasonable diligence, be obtained under any other provision of this Part;

(b) the interception is immediately necessary to prevent an offence that would cause serious harm to any person or to property; and

(c) either the originator of the private communication or the person intended by the originator to receive it is the person who would commit the offence that is likely to cause the harm or is the victim, or intended victim, of the harm.

1993, c. 40, s. 4;

2013, c. 8, s. 3.

Interception of radio-based telephone communications

184.5 (1) Every person who intercepts, by means of any electro-magnetic, acoustic, mechanical or other device, maliciously or for gain, a radio-based telephone communication, if the originator of the communication or the person intended by the originator of the communication to receive it is in Canada, is guilty of an indictable offence and liable to imprisonment for a term not exceeding five years.

Other provisions to apply

(2) Section 183.1, subsection 184(2) and sections 184.1 to 190 and 194 to 196 apply, with such modifications as the circumstances require, to interceptions of radio-based telephone communications referred to in subsection (1).

1993, c. 40, s. 4.

One application for authorization sufficient

184.6 For greater certainty, an application for an authorization under this Part may be made with respect to both private communications and radio-based telephone communications at the same time.
1993, c. 40, s. 4.

Application for authorization

185 (1) An application for an authorization to be given under section 186 shall be made

(a) the Minister personally or the Deputy Minister of Public Safety and Emergency Preparedness personally, if the offence under investigation is one in respect of which proceedings, if any, may be instituted at the instance of the Government of Canada and conducted by or on behalf of the Attorney General of Canada, or

(b) the Attorney General of a province personally or the Deputy Attorney General of a province personally, in any other case,

and shall be accompanied by an affidavit, which may be sworn on the information and belief of a peace officer or public officer deposing to the following matters:

(c) the facts relied on to justify the belief that an authorization should be given together with particulars of the offence,

(d) the type of private communication proposed to be intercepted,

(e) the names, addresses and occupations, if known, of all persons, the interception of whose private communications there are reasonable grounds to believe may assist the investigation of the offence, a general description of the nature and location of the place, if known, at which private communications are proposed to be intercepted and a general description of the manner of interception proposed to be used,

(f) the number of instances, if any, on which an application has been made under this section in relation to the offence and a person named in the affidavit pursuant to paragraph (e) and on which the application was withdrawn or no authorization was given, the date on which each application was made and the name of the judge to whom each application was made,

(g) the period for which the authorization is requested, and

(h) whether other investigative procedures have been tried and have failed or why it appears they are unlikely to succeed or that the urgency of the matter is such that it would be impractical to carry out the investigation of the offence using only other investigative procedures.

Exception for criminal organizations and terrorist groups

(1.1) Notwithstanding paragraph (1)(h), that paragraph does not apply where the application for an authorization is in relation to

(a) an offence under section 467.11, 467.111, 467.12 or 467.13;

(b) an offence committed for the benefit of, at the direction of or in association with a criminal organization; or

(c) a terrorism offence.

Extension of period for notification

(2) An application for an authorization may be accompanied by an application, personally signed by the Attorney General of the province in which the application for the authorization is made or the Minister of Public Safety and Emergency Preparedness if the application for the authorization is made by him or on his behalf, to substitute for the period mentioned in subsection 196(1) such longer period not exceeding three years as is set out in the application.

Where extension to be granted

(3) Where an application for an authorization is accompanied by an application referred to in subsection (2), the judge to whom the applications are made shall first consider the application referred to in subsection (2) and where, on the basis of the affidavit in support of the application for the authorization and any other affidavit evidence submitted in support of the application referred to in subsection (2), the judge is of the opinion that the interests of justice warrant the granting of the application, he shall fix a period, not exceeding three years, in substitution for the period mentioned in subsection 196(1).

Where extension not granted

(4) Where the judge to whom an application for an authorization and an application referred to in

subsection (2) are made refuses to fix a period in substitution for the period mentioned in subsection 196(1) or where the judge fixes a period in substitution therefor that is less than the period set out in the application referred to in subsection (2), the person appearing before the judge on the application for the authorization may withdraw the application for the authorization and thereupon the judge shall not proceed to consider the application for the authorization or to give the authorization and shall return to the person appearing before him on the application for the authorization both applications and all other material pertaining thereto.
R.S., 1985, c. C-46, s. 185;
1993, c. 40, s. 5;
1997, c. 18, s. 8, c. 23, s. 4;
2001, c. 32, s. 5, c. 41, ss. 6, 133;
2005, c. 10, ss. 22, 34;
2014, c. 17, s. 3.

Judge to be satisfied

186 (1) An authorization under this section may be given if the judge to whom the application is made is satisfied
(a) that it would be in the best interests of the administration of justice to do so; and
(b) that other investigative procedures have been tried and have failed, other investigative procedures are unlikely to succeed or the urgency of the matter is such that it would be impractical to carry out the investigation of the offence using only other investigative procedures.

Exception for criminal organizations and terrorism offences

(1.1) Notwithstanding paragraph (1)(b), that paragraph does not apply where the judge is satisfied that the application for an authorization is in relation to
(a) an offence under section 467.11, 467.111, 467.12 or 467.13;
(b) an offence committed for the benefit of, at the direction of or in association with a criminal organization; or
(c) a terrorism offence.

Where authorization not to be given

(2) No authorization may be given to intercept a private communication at the office or residence of a solicitor, or at any other place ordinarily used by a solicitor and by other solicitors for the purpose of consultation with clients, unless the judge to whom the application is made is satisfied that there are reasonable grounds to believe that the solicitor, any other solicitor practising with him, any person employed by him or any other such solicitor or a member of the solicitor's household has been or is about to become a party to an offence.

Terms and conditions

(3) Where an authorization is given in relation to the interception of private communications at a place described in subsection (2), the judge by whom the authorization is given shall include therein such terms and conditions as he considers advisable to protect privileged communications between solicitors and clients.

Content and limitation of authorization

(4) An authorization shall
(a) state the offence in respect of which private communications may be intercepted;
(b) state the type of private communication that may be intercepted;
(c) state the identity of the persons, if known, whose private communications are to be intercepted, generally describe the place at which private communications may be intercepted, if a general description of that place can be given, and generally describe the manner of interception that may be used;
(d) contain such terms and conditions as the judge considers advisable in the public interest; and
(e) be valid for the period, not exceeding sixty days, set out therein.

Persons designated

(5) The Minister of Public Safety and Emergency Preparedness or the Attorney General, as the case may be, may designate a person or persons who may intercept private communications under

authorizations.
Installation and removal of device
(5.1) For greater certainty, an authorization that permits interception by means of an electro-magnetic, acoustic, mechanical or other device includes the authority to install, maintain or remove the device covertly.
Removal after expiry of authorization
(5.2) On an
(a) under any terms or conditions that the judge considers advisable in the public interest; and
(b) during any specified period of not more than sixty days.
Renewal of authorization
(6) Renewals of an authorization may be given by a judge of a superior court of criminal jurisdiction or a judge as defined in section 552 on receipt by him or her of an
(a) the reason and period for which the renewal is required,
(b) full particulars, together with times and dates, when interceptions, if any, were made or attempted under the authorization, and any information that has been obtained by any interception, and
(c) the number of instances, if any, on which, to the knowledge and belief of the deponent, an application has been made under this subsection in relation to the same authorization and on which the application was withdrawn or no renewal was given, the date on which each application was made and the name of the judge to whom each application was made,
and supported by such other information as the judge may require.
Renewal
(7) A renewal of an authorization may be given if the judge to whom the application is made is satisfied that any of the circumstances described in subsection (1) still obtain, but no renewal shall be for a period exceeding sixty days.
Related warrant or order
(8) A judge who gives an authorization under this section may, at the same time, issue a warrant or make an order under any of sections 487, 487.01, 487.014 to 487.018, 487.02, 492.1 and 492.2 if the judge is of the opinion that the requested warrant or order is related to the execution of the authorization.
R.S., 1985, c. C-46, s. 186;
1993, c. 40, s. 6;
1997, c. 23, s. 5;
1999, c. 5, s. 5;
2001, c. 32, s. 6, c. 41, ss. 6.1, 133;
2005, c. 10, ss. 23, 34;
2014, c. 17, s. 4, c. 31, s. 9.
Time limitation in relation to criminal organizations and terrorism offences
186.1 Notwithstanding paragraphs 184.2(4)(e) and 186(4)(e) and subsection 186(7), an authorization or any renewal of an authorization may be valid for one or more periods specified in the authorization exceeding sixty days, each not exceeding one year, where the authorization is in relation to
(a) an offence under section 467.11, 467.111, 467.12 or 467.13;
(b) an offence committed for the benefit of, at the direction of or in association with a criminal organization; or
(c) a terrorism offence.
1997, c. 23, s. 6;
2001, c. 32, s. 7, c. 41, ss. 7, 133;
2014, c. 17, s. 5.
Manner in which application to be kept secret
187 (1) All documents relating to an application made pursuant to any provision of this Part are confidential and, subject to subsection (1.1), shall be placed in a packet and sealed by the judge to whom the application is made immediately on determination of the application, and that packet shall

be kept in the custody of the court in a place to which the public has no access or in such other place as the judge may authorize and shall not be dealt with except in accordance with subsections (1.2) to (1.5).

Exception

(1.1) An authorization given under this Part need not be placed in the packet except where, pursuant to subsection 184.3(7) or (8), the original authorization is in the hands of the judge, in which case that judge must place it in the packet and the facsimile remains with the applicant.

Opening for further applications

(1.2) The sealed packet may be opened and its contents removed for the purpose of dealing with an application for a further authorization or with an application for renewal of an authorization.

Opening on order of judge

(1.3) A provincial court judge, a judge of a superior court of criminal jurisdiction or a judge as defined in section 552 may order that the sealed packet be opened and its contents removed for the purpose of copying and examining the documents contained in the packet.

Opening on order of trial judge

(1.4) A judge or provincial court judge before whom a trial is to be held and who has jurisdiction in the province in which an authorization was given may order that the sealed packet be opened and its contents removed for the purpose of copying and examining the documents contained in the packet if
(a) any matter relevant to the authorization or any evidence obtained pursuant to the authorization is in issue in the trial; and
(b) the accused applies for such an order for the purpose of consulting the documents to prepare for trial.

Order for destruction of documents

(1.5) Where a sealed packet is opened, its contents shall not be destroyed except pursuant to an order of a judge of the same court as the judge who gave the authorization.

Order of judge

(2) An order under subsection (1.2), (1.3), (1.4) or (1.5) made with respect to documents relating to an application made pursuant to section 185 or subsection 186(6) or 196(2) may only be made after the Attorney General or the Minister of Public Safety and Emergency Preparedness by whom or on whose authority the application for the authorization to which the order relates was made has been given an opportunity to be heard.

Idem

(3) An order under subsection (1.2), (1.3), (1.4) or (1.5) made with respect to documents relating to an application made pursuant to subsection 184.2(2) or section 184.3 may only be made after the Attorney General has been given an opportunity to be heard.

Editing of copies

(4) Where a prosecution has been commenced and an accused applies for an order for the copying and examination of documents pursuant to subsection (1.3) or (1.4), the judge shall not, notwithstanding those subsections, provide any copy of any document to the accused until the prosecutor has deleted any part of the copy of the document that the prosecutor believes would be prejudicial to the public interest, including any part that the prosecutor believes could
(a) compromise the identity of any confidential informant;
(b) compromise the nature and extent of ongoing investigations;
(c) endanger persons engaged in particular intelligence-gathering techniques and thereby prejudice future investigations in which similar techniques would be used; or
(d) prejudice the interests of innocent persons.

Accused to be provided with copies

(5) After the prosecutor has deleted the parts of the copy of the document to be given to the accused under subsection (4), the accused shall be provided with an edited copy of the document.

Original documents to be returned

(6) After the accused has received an edited copy of a document, the prosecutor shall keep a copy of the original document, and an edited copy of the document and the original document shall be

returned to the packet and the packet resealed.
Deleted parts
(7) An accused to whom an edited copy of a document has been provided pursuant to subsection (5) may request that the judge before whom the trial is to be held order that any part of the document deleted by the prosecutor be made available to the accused, and the judge shall order that a copy of any part that, in the opinion of the judge, is required in order for the accused to make full answer and defence and for which the provision of a judicial summary would not be sufficient, be made available to the accused.
Documents to be kept secret — related warrant or order
(8) The rules provided for in this section apply to all documents relating to a request for a related warrant or order referred to in subsection 184.2(5), 186(8) or 188(6) with any necessary modifications.
R.S., 1985, c. C-46, s. 187;
R.S., 1985, c. 27 (1st Supp.), s. 24;
1993, c. 40, s. 7;
2005, c. 10, s. 24;
2014, c. 31, s. 10.
Applications to specially appointed judges
188 (1) Notwithstanding section 185, an application made under that section for an authorization may be made
(a) the Minister of Public Safety and Emergency Preparedness, if the offence is one in respect of which proceedings, if any, may be instituted by the Government of Canada and conducted by or on behalf of the Attorney General of Canada, or
(b) the Attorney General of a province, in respect of any other offence in the province,
if the urgency of the situation requires interception of private communications to commence before an authorization could, with reasonable diligence, be obtained under section 186.
Authorizations in emergency
(2) Where the judge to whom an application is made pursuant to subsection (1) is satisfied that the urgency of the situation requires that interception of private communications commence before an authorization could, with reasonable diligence, be obtained under section 186, he may, on such terms and conditions, if any, as he considers advisable, give an authorization in writing for a period of up to thirty-six hours.
(3) Definition of
Chief Justice
(4) In this section,
Chief Justice
(a) in the Province of Ontario, the Chief Justice of the Ontario Court;
(b) in the Province of Quebec, the Chief Justice of the Superior Court;
(c) in the Provinces of Nova Scotia, British Columbia and Prince Edward Island, the Chief Justice of the Supreme Court;
(d) in the Provinces of New Brunswick, Manitoba, Saskatchewan and Alberta, the Chief Justice of the Court of Queen's Bench;
(e) in the Province of Newfoundland and Labrador, the Chief Justice of the Supreme Court, Trial Division; and
(f) in Yukon, the Northwest Territories and Nunavut, the senior judge within the meaning of subsection 22(3) of the
Judges Act
Inadmissibility of evidence
(5) The trial judge may deem inadmissible the evidence obtained by means of an interception of a private communication pursuant to a subsequent authorization given under this section, where he finds that the application for the subsequent authorization was based on the same facts, and involved the interception of the private communications of the same person or persons, or related to the same

offence, on which the application for the original authorization was based.
Related warrant or order
(6) A judge who gives an authorization under this section may, at the same time, issue a warrant or make an order under any of sections 487, 487.01, 487.014 to 487.018, 487.02, 492.1 and 492.2 if the judge is of the opinion that the requested warrant or order is related to the execution of the authorization, that the urgency of the situation requires the warrant or the order and that it can be reasonably executed or complied with within 36 hours.
R.S., 1985, c. C-46, s. 188;
R.S., 1985, c. 27 (1st Supp.), ss. 25, 185(F), c. 27 (2nd Supp.), s. 10;
1990, c. 17, s. 10;
1992, c. 1, s. 58, c. 51, s. 35;
1993, c. 40, s. 8;
1999, c. 3, s. 28;
2002, c. 7, s. 140;
2005, c. 10, s. 34;
2014, c. 31, s. 11;
2015, c. 3, s. 47.
Execution of authorizations
188.1 (1) Subject to subsection (2), the interception of a private communication authorized pursuant to section 184.2, 184.3, 186 or 188 may be carried out anywhere in Canada.
Execution in another province
(2) Where an authorization is given under section 184.2, 184.3, 186 or 188 in one province but it may reasonably be expected that it is to be executed in another province and the execution of the authorization would require entry into or upon the property of any person in the other province or would require that an order under section 487.02 be made with respect to any person in that other province, a judge in the other province may, on application, confirm the authorization and when the authorization is so confirmed, it shall have full force and effect in that other province as though it had originally been given in that other province.
1993, c. 40, s. 9.
No civil or criminal liability
188.2 No person who acts in accordance with an authorization or under section 184.1 or 184.4 or who aids, in good faith, a person who he or she believes on reasonable grounds is acting in accordance with an authorization or under one of those sections incurs any criminal or civil liability for anything reasonably done further to the authorization or to that section.
1993, c. 40, s. 9.
189 (1) to (4) Notice of intention to produce evidence
(5) The contents of a private communication that is obtained from an interception of the private communication pursuant to any provision of, or pursuant to an authorization given under, this Part shall not be received in evidence unless the party intending to adduce it has given to the accused reasonable notice of the intention together with
(a) a transcript of the private communication, where it will be adduced in the form of a recording, or a statement setting out full particulars of the private communication, where evidence of the private communication will be given
(b) a statement respecting the time, place and date of the private communication and the parties thereto, if known.
Privileged evidence
(6) Any information obtained by an interception that, but for the interception, would have been privileged remains privileged and inadmissible as evidence without the consent of the person enjoying the privilege.
R.S., 1985, c. C-46, s. 189;
1993, c. 40, s. 10.
Further particulars

190 Where an accused has been given notice pursuant to subsection 189(5), any judge of the court in which the trial of the accused is being or is to be held may at any time order that further particulars be given of the private communication that is intended to be adduced in evidence.
1973-74, c. 50, s. 2.

Possession, etc.

191 (1) Every one who possesses, sells or purchases any electro-magnetic, acoustic, mechanical or other device or any component thereof knowing that the design thereof renders it primarily useful for surreptitious interception of private communications is guilty of an indictable offence and liable to imprisonment for a term not exceeding two years.

Exemptions

(2) Subsection (1) does not apply to

(a) a police officer in possession of a device or component described in subsection (1) in the course of his employment;

(b) a person in possession of such a device or component for the purpose of using it in an interception made or to be made in accordance with an authorization;

(b.1) a person in possession of such a device or component under the direction of a police officer in order to assist that officer in the course of his duties as a police officer;

(c) an officer or a servant of Her Majesty in right of Canada or a member of the Canadian Forces in possession of such a device or component in the course of his duties as such an officer, servant or member, as the case may be; and

(d) any other person in possession of such a device or component under the authority of a licence issued by the Minister of Public Safety and Emergency Preparedness.

Terms and conditions of licence

(3) A licence issued for the purpose of paragraph (2)(d) may contain such terms and conditions relating to the possession, sale or purchase of a device or component described in subsection (1) as the Minister of Public Safety and Emergency Preparedness may prescribe.

R.S., 1985, c. C-46, s. 191;

R.S., 1985, c. 27 (1st Supp.), s. 26;

2005, c. 10, s. 34;

2013, c. 8, s. 4.

Forfeiture

192 (1) Where a person is convicted of an offence under section 184 or 191, any electro-magnetic, acoustic, mechanical or other device by means of which the offence was committed or the possession of which constituted the offence, on the conviction, in addition to any punishment that is imposed, may be ordered forfeited to Her Majesty whereupon it may be disposed of as the Attorney General directs.

Limitation

(2) No order for forfeiture shall be made under subsection (1) in respect of telephone, telegraph or other communication facilities or equipment owned by a person engaged in providing telephone, telegraph or other communication service to the public or forming part of the telephone, telegraph or other communication service or system of that person by means of which an offence under section 184 has been committed if that person was not a party to the offence.
1973-74, c. 50, s. 2.

Disclosure of information

193 (1) Where a private communication has been intercepted by means of an electro-magnetic, acoustic, mechanical or other device without the consent, express or implied, of the originator thereof or of the person intended by the originator thereof to receive it, every one who, without the express consent of the originator thereof or of the person intended by the originator thereof to receive it, wilfully

(a) uses or discloses the private communication or any part thereof or the substance, meaning or purport thereof or of any part thereof, or

(b) discloses the existence thereof,

is guilty of an indictable offence and liable to imprisonment for a term not exceeding two years.
Exemptions
(2) Subsection (1) does not apply to a person who discloses a private communication or any part thereof or the substance, meaning or purport thereof or of any part thereof or who discloses the existence of a private communication
(a) in the course of or for the purpose of giving evidence in any civil or criminal proceedings or in any other proceedings in which the person may be required to give evidence on oath;
(b) in the course of or for the purpose of any criminal investigation if the private communication was lawfully intercepted;
(c) in giving notice under section 189 or furnishing further particulars pursuant to an order under section 190;
(d) in the course of the operation of
(i) a telephone, telegraph or other communication service to the public,
(ii) a department or an agency of the Government of Canada, or
(iii) services relating to the management or protection of a computer system, as defined in subsection 342.1(2),
if the disclosure is necessarily incidental to an interception described in paragraph 184(2)(c), (d) or (e);
(e) where disclosure is made to a peace officer or prosecutor in Canada or to a person or authority with responsibility in a foreign state for the investigation or prosecution of offences and is intended to be in the interests of the administration of justice in Canada or elsewhere; or
(f) where the disclosure is made to the Director of the Canadian Security Intelligence Service or to an employee of the Service for the purpose of enabling the Service to perform its duties and functions under section 12 of the
Canadian Security Intelligence Service Act
Publishing of prior lawful disclosure
(3) Subsection (1) does not apply to a person who discloses a private communication or any part thereof or the substance, meaning or purport thereof or of any part thereof or who discloses the existence of a private communication where that which is disclosed by him was, prior to the disclosure, lawfully disclosed in the course of or for the purpose of giving evidence in proceedings referred to in paragraph (2)(a).
R.S., 1985, c. C-46, s. 193;
R.S., 1985, c. 30 (4th Supp.), s. 45;
1993, c. 40, s. 11;
2004, c. 12, s. 5.
Disclosure of information received from interception of radio-based telephone communications
193.1 (1) Every person who wilfully uses or discloses a radio-based telephone communication or who wilfully discloses the existence of such a communication is guilty of an indictable offence and liable to imprisonment for a term not exceeding two years, if
(a) the originator of the communication or the person intended by the originator of the communication to receive it was in Canada when the communication was made;
(b) the communication was intercepted by means of an electromagnetic, acoustic, mechanical or other device without the consent, express or implied, of the originator of the communication or of the person intended by the originator to receive the communication; and
(c) the person does not have the express or implied consent of the originator of the communication or of the person intended by the originator to receive the communication.
Other provisions to apply
(2) Subsections 193(2) and (3) apply, with such modifications as the circumstances require, to disclosures of radio-based telephone communications.
1993, c. 40, s. 12.
Damages
194 (1) Subject to subsection (2), a court that convicts an accused of an offence under section 184,

184.5, 193 or 193.1 may, on the application of a person aggrieved, at the time sentence is imposed, order the accused to pay to that person an amount not exceeding five thousand dollars as punitive damages.

No damages where civil proceedings commenced

(2) No amount shall be ordered to be paid under subsection (1) to a person who has commenced an action under Part II of the

Crown Liability Act

Judgment may be registered

(3) Where an amount that is ordered to be paid under subsection (1) is not paid forthwith, the applicant may, by filing the order, enter as a judgment, in the superior court of the province in which the trial was held, the amount ordered to be paid, and that judgment is enforceable against the accused in the same manner as if it were a judgment rendered against the accused in that court in civil proceedings.

Moneys in possession of accused may be taken

(4) All or any part of an amount that is ordered to be paid under subsection (1) may be taken out of moneys found in the possession of the accused at the time of his arrest, except where there is a dispute respecting ownership of or right of possession to those moneys by claimants other than the accused.

R.S., 1985, c. C-46, s. 194;

1993, c. 40, s. 13.

Annual report

195 (1) The Minister of Public Safety and Emergency Preparedness shall, as soon as possible after the end of each year, prepare a report relating to

(a) authorizations for which that Minister and agents specially designated in writing by that Minister for the purposes of section 185 applied and the interceptions made under those authorizations in the immediately preceding year;

(b) authorizations given under section 188 for which peace officers specially designated by that Minister for the purposes of that section applied and the interceptions made under those authorizations in the immediately preceding year; and

(c) interceptions made under section 184.4 in the immediately preceding year if the interceptions relate to an offence for which proceedings may be commenced by the Attorney General of Canada.

Information respecting authorizations — sections 185 and 188

(2) The report shall, in relation to the authorizations and interceptions referred to in paragraphs (1)(a) and (b), set out

(a) the number of applications made for authorizations;

(b) the number of applications made for renewal of authorizations;

(c) the number of applications referred to in paragraphs (a) and (b) that were granted, the number of those applications that were refused and the number of applications referred to in paragraph (a) that were granted subject to terms and conditions;

(d) the number of persons identified in an authorization against whom proceedings were commenced at the instance of the Attorney General of Canada in respect of

(i) an offence specified in the authorization,

(ii) an offence other than an offence specified in the authorization but in respect of which an authorization may be given, and

(iii) an offence in respect of which an authorization may not be given;

(e) the number of persons not identified in an authorization against whom proceedings were commenced at the instance of the Attorney General of Canada in respect of

(i) an offence specified in such an authorization,

(ii) an offence other than an offence specified in such an authorization but in respect of which an authorization may be given, and

(iii) an offence other than an offence specified in such an authorization and for which no such authorization may be given,

and whose commission or alleged commission of the offence became known to a peace officer as a result of an interception of a private communication under an authorization;
(f) the average period for which authorizations were given and for which renewals thereof were granted;
(g) the number of authorizations that, by virtue of one or more renewals thereof, were valid for more than sixty days, for more than one hundred and twenty days, for more than one hundred and eighty days and for more than two hundred and forty days;
(h) the number of notifications given pursuant to section 196;
(i) the offences in respect of which authorizations were given, specifying the number of authorizations given in respect of each of those offences;
(j) a description of all classes of places specified in authorizations and the number of authorizations in which each of those classes of places was specified;
(k) a general description of the methods of interception involved in each interception under an authorization;
(l) the number of persons arrested whose identity became known to a peace officer as a result of an interception under an authorization;
(m) the number of criminal proceedings commenced at the instance of the Attorney General of Canada in which private communications obtained by interception under an authorization were adduced in evidence and the number of those proceedings that resulted in a conviction; and
(n) the number of criminal investigations in which information obtained as a result of the interception of a private communication under an authorization was used although the private communication was not adduced in evidence in criminal proceedings commenced at the instance of the Attorney General of Canada as a result of the investigations.

Information respecting interceptions — section 184.4
(2.1) The report shall, in relation to the interceptions referred to in paragraph (1)(c), set out
(a) the number of interceptions made;
(b) the number of parties to each intercepted private communication against whom proceedings were commenced in respect of the offence that the police officer sought to prevent in intercepting the private communication or in respect of any other offence that was detected as a result of the interception;
(c) the number of persons who were not parties to an intercepted private communication but whose commission or alleged commission of an offence became known to a police officer as a result of the interception of a private communication, and against whom proceedings were commenced in respect of the offence that the police officer sought to prevent in intercepting the private communication or in respect of any other offence that was detected as a result of the interception;
(d) the number of notifications given under section 196.1;
(e) the offences in respect of which interceptions were made and any other offences for which proceedings were commenced as a result of an interception, as well as the number of interceptions made with respect to each offence;
(f) a general description of the methods of interception used for each interception;
(g) the number of persons arrested whose identity became known to a police officer as a result of an interception;
(h) the number of criminal proceedings commenced in which private communications obtained by interception were adduced in evidence and the number of those proceedings that resulted in a conviction;
(i) the number of criminal investigations in which information obtained as a result of the interception of a private communication was used even though the private communication was not adduced in evidence in criminal proceedings commenced as a result of the investigations; and
(j) the duration of each interception and the aggregate duration of all the interceptions related to the investigation of the offence that the police officer sought to prevent in intercepting the private communication.

Other information

(3) The report shall, in addition to the information referred to in subsections (2) and (2.1), set out
(a) the number of prosecutions commenced against officers or servants of Her Majesty in right of Canada or members of the Canadian Forces for offences under section 184 or 193; and
(b) a general assessment of the importance of interception of private communications for the investigation, detection, prevention and prosecution of offences in Canada.

Report to be laid before Parliament
(4) The Minister of Public Safety and Emergency Preparedness shall cause a copy of each report prepared by him under subsection (1) to be laid before Parliament forthwith on completion thereof, or if Parliament is not then sitting, on any of the first fifteen days next thereafter that Parliament is sitting.

Report by Attorneys General
(5) The Attorney General of each province shall, as soon as possible after the end of each year, prepare and publish or otherwise make available to the public a report relating to
(a) authorizations for which the Attorney General and agents specially designated in writing by the Attorney General for the purposes of section 185 applied and to the interceptions made under those authorizations in the immediately preceding year;
(b) authorizations given under section 188 for which peace officers specially designated by the Attorney General for the purposes of that section applied and to the interceptions made under those authorizations in the immediately preceding year; and
(c) interceptions made under section 184.4 in the immediately preceding year, if the interceptions relate to an offence not referred to in paragraph (1)(c).
The report must set out, with any modifications that the circumstances require, the information described in subsections (2) to (3).
R.S., 1985, c. C-46, s. 195;
R.S., 1985, c. 27 (1st Supp.), s. 27;
2005, c. 10, s. 34;
2013, c. 8, s. 5;
2015, c. 20, s. 20.

Written notification to be given
196 (1) The Attorney General of the province in which an application under subsection 185(1) was made or the Minister of Public Safety and Emergency Preparedness if the application was made by or on behalf of that Minister shall, within 90 days after the period for which the authorization was given or renewed or within such other period as is fixed pursuant to subsection 185(3) or subsection (3) of this section, notify in writing the person who was the object of the interception pursuant to the authorization and shall, in a manner prescribed by regulations made by the Governor in Council, certify to the court that gave the authorization that the person has been so notified.

Extension of period for notification
(2) The running of the 90 days referred to in subsection (1), or of any other period fixed pursuant to subsection 185(3) or subsection (3) of this section, is suspended until any application made by the Attorney General or the Minister to a judge of a superior court of criminal jurisdiction or a judge as defined in section 552 for an extension or a subsequent extension of the period for which the authorization was given or renewed has been heard and disposed of.

Where extension to be granted
(3) Where the judge to whom an application referred to in subsection (2) is made, on the basis of an affidavit submitted in support of the application, is satisfied that
(a) the investigation of the offence to which the authorization relates, or
(b) a subsequent investigation of an offence listed in section 183 commenced as a result of information obtained from the investigation referred to in paragraph (a),
is continuing and is of the opinion that the interests of justice warrant the granting of the application, the judge shall grant an extension, or a subsequent extension, of the period, each extension not to exceed three years.

Application to be accompanied by affidavit

(4) An application pursuant to subsection (2) shall be accompanied by an affidavit deposing to
(a) the facts known or believed by the deponent and relied on to justify the belief that an extension should be granted; and
(b) the number of instances, if any, on which an application has, to the knowledge or belief of the deponent, been made under that subsection in relation to the particular authorization and on which the application was withdrawn or the application was not granted, the date on which each application was made and the judge to whom each application was made.

Exception for criminal organizations and terrorist groups
(5) Notwithstanding subsections (3) and 185(3), where the judge to whom an application referred to in subsection (2) or 185(2) is made, on the basis of an affidavit submitted in support of the application, is satisfied that the investigation is in relation to
(a) an offence under section 467.11, 467.111, 467.12 or 467.13,
(b) an offence committed for the benefit of, at the direction of or in association with a criminal organization, or
(c) a terrorism offence,
and is of the opinion that the interests of justice warrant the granting of the application, the judge shall grant an extension, or a subsequent extension, of the period, but no extension may exceed three years.
R.S., 1985, c. C-46, s. 196;
R.S., 1985, c. 27 (1st Supp.), s. 28;
1993, c. 40, s. 14;
1997, c. 23, s. 7;
2001, c. 32, s. 8, c. 41, ss. 8, 133;
2005, c. 10, s. 25;
2014, c. 17, s. 6.

Written notice — interception in accordance with section 184.4
196.1 (1) Subject to subsections (3) and (5), the Attorney General of the province in which a police officer intercepts a private communication under section 184.4 or, if the interception relates to an offence for which proceedings may be commenced by the Attorney General of Canada, the Minister of Public Safety and Emergency Preparedness shall give notice in writing of the interception to any person who was the object of the interception within 90 days after the day on which it occurred.

Extension of period for notification
(2) The running of the 90-day period or of any extension granted under subsection (3) or (5) is suspended until any application made by the Attorney General of the province or the Minister to a judge of a superior court of criminal jurisdiction or a judge as defined in section 552 for an extension or a subsequent extension of the period has been heard and disposed of.

Where extension to be granted
(3) The judge to whom an application under subsection (2) is made shall grant an extension or a subsequent extension of the 90-day period — each extension not to exceed three years — if the judge is of the opinion that the interests of justice warrant granting the application and is satisfied, on the basis of an affidavit submitted in support of the application, that one of the following investigations is continuing:
(a) the investigation of the offence to which the interception relates; or
(b) a subsequent investigation of an offence commenced as a result of information obtained from the investigation referred to in paragraph (a).

Application to be accompanied by affidavit
(4) An application shall be accompanied by an affidavit deposing to
(a) the facts known or believed by the deponent and relied on to justify the belief that an extension should be granted; and
(b) the number of instances, if any, on which an application has, to the knowledge or belief of the deponent, been made under subsection (2) in relation to the particular interception and on which the application was withdrawn or the application was not granted, the date on which each application

was made and the judge to whom each application was made.
Exception — criminal organization or terrorism offence
(5) Despite subsection (3), the judge to whom an application under subsection (2) is made shall grant an extension or a subsequent extension of the 90-day period — each extension not to exceed three years — if the judge is of the opinion that the interests of justice warrant granting the application and is satisfied, on the basis of an affidavit submitted in support of the application, that the interception of the communication relates to an investigation of

(a) an offence under section 467.11, 467.12 or 467.13;

(b) an offence committed for the benefit of, at the direction of or in association with a criminal organization; or

(c) a terrorism offence.
2013, c. 8, s. 6.

PART VII

PART VII
Disorderly Houses, Gaming and Betting

Interpretation

Definitions
197 (1) In this Part,
bet
common bawdy-house
common betting house
(a) enabling, encouraging or assisting persons who resort thereto to bet between themselves or with the keeper, or

(b) enabling any person to receive, record, register, transmit or pay bets or to announce the results of betting;

common gaming house
(a) kept for gain to which persons resort for the purpose of playing games, or

(b) kept or used for the purpose of playing games

(i) in which a bank is kept by one or more but not all of the players,

(ii) in which all or any portion of the bets on or proceeds from a game is paid, directly or indirectly, to the keeper of the place,

(iii) in which, directly or indirectly, a fee is charged to or paid by the players for the privilege of playing or participating in a game or using gaming equipment, or

(iv) in which the chances of winning are not equally favourable to all persons who play the game, including the person, if any, who conducts the game;

disorderly house
game
gaming equipment
keeper
(a) is an owner or occupier of a place,

(b) assists or acts on behalf of an owner or occupier of a place,

(c) appears to be, or to assist or act on behalf of an owner or occupier of a place,

(d) has the care or management of a place, or

(e) uses a place permanently or temporarily, with or without the consent of the owner or occupier thereof;

place
(a) it is covered or enclosed,

(b) it is used permanently or temporarily, or

(c) any person has an exclusive right of user with respect to it;
prostitute
public place
Exception
(2) A place is not a common gaming house within the meaning of paragraph (a) or subparagraph (b) (ii) or (iii) of the definition
(a) the whole or any portion of the bets on or proceeds from games played therein is not directly or indirectly paid to the keeper thereof; and
(b) no fee is charged to persons for the right or privilege of participating in the games played therein other than under the authority of and in accordance with the terms of a licence issued by the Attorney General of the province in which the place is situated or by such other person or authority in the province as may be specified by the Attorney General thereof.
Onus
(3) The onus of proving that, by virtue of subsection (2), a place is not a common gaming house is on the accused.
Effect when game partly played on premises
(4) A place may be a common gaming house notwithstanding that
(a) it is used for the purpose of playing part of a game and another part of the game is played elsewhere;
(b) the stake that is played for is in some other place; or
(c) it is used on only one occasion in the manner described in paragraph (b) of the definition
R.S., 1985, c. C-46, s. 197;
R.S., 1985, c. 27 (1st Supp.), s. 29;
2014, c. 25, s. 12.

Presumptions

Presumptions
198 (1) In proceedings under this Part,
(a) evidence that a peace officer who was authorized to enter a place was wilfully prevented from entering or was wilfully obstructed or delayed in entering is, in the absence of any evidence to the contrary, proof that the place is a disorderly house;
(b) evidence that a place was found to be equipped with gaming equipment or any device for concealing, removing or destroying gaming equipment is, in the absence of any evidence to the contrary, proof that the place is a common gaming house or a common betting house, as the case may be;
(c) evidence that gaming equipment was found in a place entered under a warrant issued pursuant to this Part, or on or about the person of anyone found therein, is, in the absence of any evidence to the contrary, proof that the place is a common gaming house and that the persons found therein were playing games, whether or not any person acting under the warrant observed any persons playing games therein; and
(d) evidence that a person was convicted of keeping a disorderly house is, for the purpose of proceedings against any one who is alleged to have been an inmate or to have been found in that house at the time the person committed the offence of which he was convicted, in the absence of any evidence to the contrary, proof that the house was, at that time, a disorderly house.
Conclusive presumption from slot machine
(2) For the purpose of proceedings under this Part, a place that is found to be equipped with a slot machine shall be conclusively presumed to be a common gaming house.
Definition of
slot machine
(3) In subsection (2),
slot machine

(a) that is used or intended to be used for any purpose other than vending merchandise or services, or
(b) that is used or intended to be used for the purpose of vending merchandise or services if
(i) the result of one of any number of operations of the machine is a matter of chance or uncertainty to the operator,
(ii) as a result of a given number of successive operations by the operator the machine produces different results, or
(iii) on any operation of the machine it discharges or emits a slug or token,
but does not include an automatic machine or slot machine that dispenses as prizes only one or more free games on that machine.
R.S., c. C-34, s. 180;
1974-75-76, c. 93, s. 10.

Search

Warrant to search
199 (1) A justice who is satisfied by information on oath that there are reasonable grounds to believe that an offence under section 201, 202, 203, 206, 207 or 210 is being committed at any place within the jurisdiction of the justice may issue a warrant authorizing a peace officer to enter and search the place by day or night and seize anything found therein that may be evidence that an offence under section 201, 202, 203, 206, 207 or 210, as the case may be, is being committed at that place, and to take into custody all persons who are found in or at that place and requiring those persons and things to be brought before that justice or before another justice having jurisdiction, to be dealt with according to law.

Search without warrant, seizure and arrest
(2) A peace officer may, whether or not he is acting under a warrant issued pursuant to this section, take into custody any person whom he finds keeping a common gaming house and any person whom he finds therein, and may seize anything that may be evidence that such an offence is being committed and shall bring those persons and things before a justice having jurisdiction, to be dealt with according to law.

Disposal of property seized
(3) Except where otherwise expressly provided by law, a court, judge, justice or provincial court judge before whom anything that is seized under this section is brought may declare that the thing is forfeited, in which case it shall be disposed of or dealt with as the Attorney General may direct if no person shows sufficient cause why it should not be forfeited.

When declaration or direction may be made
(4) No declaration or direction shall be made pursuant to subsection (3) in respect of anything seized under this section until
(a) it is no longer required as evidence in any proceedings that are instituted pursuant to the seizure; or
(b) the expiration of thirty days from the time of seizure where it is not required as evidence in any proceedings.

Conversion into money
(5) The Attorney General may, for the purpose of converting anything forfeited under this section into money, deal with it in all respects as if he were the owner thereof.

Telephones exempt from seizure
(6) Nothing in this section or in section 489 authorizes the seizure, forfeiture or destruction of telephone, telegraph or other communication facilities or equipment that may be evidence of or that may have been used in the commission of an offence under section 201, 202, 203, 206, 207 or 210 and that is owned by a person engaged in providing telephone, telegraph or other communication service to the public or forming part of the telephone, telegraph or other communication service or system of that person.

Exception

(7) Subsection (6) does not apply to prohibit the seizure, for use as evidence, of any facility or equipment described in that subsection that is designed or adapted to record a communication.
R.S., 1985, c. C-46, s. 199;
R.S., 1985, c. 27 (1st Supp.), s. 203;
1994, c. 44, s. 10.

Obstruction

200
Gaming and Betting

Keeping gaming or betting house
201 (1) Every one who keeps a common gaming house or common betting house is guilty of an indictable offence and liable to imprisonment for a term not exceeding two years.
Person found in or owner permitting use
(2) Every one who
(a) is found, without lawful excuse, in a common gaming house or common betting house, or
(b) as owner, landlord, lessor, tenant, occupier or agent, knowingly permits a place to be let or used for the purposes of a common gaming house or common betting house,
is guilty of an offence punishable on summary conviction.
R.S., c. C-34, s. 185.
Betting, pool-selling, book-making, etc.
202 (1) Every one commits an offence who
(a) uses or knowingly allows a place under his control to be used for the purpose of recording or registering bets or selling a pool;
(b) imports, makes, buys, sells, rents, leases, hires or keeps, exhibits, employs or knowingly allows to be kept, exhibited or employed in any place under his control any device or apparatus for the purpose of recording or registering bets or selling a pool, or any machine or device for gambling or betting;
(c) has under his control any money or other property relating to a transaction that is an offence under this section;
(d) records or registers bets or sells a pool;
(e) engages in book-making or pool-selling, or in the business or occupation of betting, or makes any agreement for the purchase or sale of betting or gaming privileges, or for the purchase or sale of information that is intended to assist in book-making, pool-selling or betting;
(f) prints, provides or offers to print or provide information intended for use in connection with book-making, pool-selling or betting on any horse-race, fight, game or sport, whether or not it takes place in or outside Canada or has or has not taken place;
(g) imports or brings into Canada any information or writing that is intended or is likely to promote or be of use in gambling, book-making, pool-selling or betting on a horse-race, fight, game or sport, and where this paragraph applies it is immaterial
(i) whether the information is published before, during or after the race, fight game or sport, or
(ii) whether the race, fight, game or sport takes place in Canada or elsewhere,
but this paragraph does not apply to a newspaper, magazine or other periodical published in good faith primarily for a purpose other than the publication of such information;
(h) advertises, prints, publishes, exhibits, posts up, or otherwise gives notice of any offer, invitation or inducement to bet on, to guess or to foretell the result of a contest, or a result of or contingency relating to any contest;
(i) wilfully and knowingly sends, transmits, delivers or receives any message that conveys any information relating to book-making, pool-selling, betting or wagering, or that is intended to assist in book-making, pool-selling, betting or wagering; or
(j) aids or assists in any manner in anything that is an offence under this section.

Punishment
(2) Every one who commits an offence under this section is guilty of an indictable offence and liable
(a) for a first offence, to imprisonment for not more than two years;
(b) for a second offence, to imprisonment for not more than two years and not less than fourteen days; and
(c) for each subsequent offence, to imprisonment for not more than two years and not less than three months.
R.S., 1985, c. C-46, s. 202;
2008, c. 18, s. 5.
Placing bets on behalf of others
203 Every one who
(a) places or offers or agrees to place a bet on behalf of another person for a consideration paid or to be paid by or on behalf of that other person,
(b) engages in the business or practice of placing or agreeing to place bets on behalf of other persons, whether for a consideration or otherwise, or
(c) holds himself out or allows himself to be held out as engaging in the business or practice of placing or agreeing to place bets on behalf of other persons, whether for a consideration or otherwise,
is guilty of an indictable offence and liable
(d) for a first offence, to imprisonment for not more than two years,
(e) for a second offence, to imprisonment for not more than two years and not less than fourteen days, and
(f) for each subsequent offence, to imprisonment for not more than two years and not less than three months.
R.S., c. C-34, s. 187;
1974-75-76, c. 93, s. 11.
Exemption
204 (1) Sections 201 and 202 do not apply to
(a) any person or association by reason of his or their becoming the custodian or depository of any money, property or valuable thing staked, to be paid to
(i) the winner of a lawful race, sport, game or exercise,
(ii) the owner of a horse engaged in a lawful race, or
(iii) the winner of any bets between not more than ten individuals;
(b) a private bet between individuals not engaged in any way in the business of betting;
(c) bets made or records of bets made through the agency of a pari-mutuel system on running, trotting or pacing horse-races if
(i) the bets or records of bets are made on the race-course of an association in respect of races conducted at that race-course or another race-course in or out of Canada, and, in the case of a race conducted on a race-course situated outside Canada, the governing body that regulates the race has been certified as acceptable by the Minister of Agriculture and Agri-Food or a person designated by that Minister pursuant to subsection (8.1) and that Minister or person has permitted pari-mutuel betting in Canada on the race pursuant to that subsection, and
(ii) the provisions of this section and the regulations are complied with.
Exception
(1.1) For greater certainty, a person may, in accordance with the regulations, do anything described in section 201 or 202, if the person does it for the purposes of legal pari-mutuel betting.
Presumption
(2) For the purposes of paragraph (1)(c), bets made, in accordance with the regulations, in a betting theatre referred to in paragraph (8)(e), or by any means of telecommunication to the race-course of an association or to such a betting theatre, are deemed to be made on the race-course of the association.
Operation of pari-mutuel system
(3) No person or association shall use a pari-mutuel system of betting in respect of a horse-race

unless the system has been approved by and its operation is carried on under the supervision of an officer appointed by the Minister of Agriculture and Agri-Food.

Supervision of pari-mutuel system

(4) Every person or association operating a pari-mutuel system of betting in accordance with this section in respect of a horse-race, whether or not the person or association is conducting the race-meeting at which the race is run, shall pay to the Receiver General in respect of each individual pool of the race and each individual feature pool one-half of one per cent, or such greater fraction not exceeding one per cent as may be fixed by the Governor in Council, of the total amount of money that is bet through the agency of the pari-mutuel system of betting.

Percentage that may be deducted and retained

(5) Where any person or association becomes a custodian or depository of any money, bet or stakes under a pari-mutuel system in respect of a horse-race, that person or association shall not deduct or retain any amount from the total amount of money, bets or stakes unless it does so pursuant to subsection (6).

Percentage that may be deducted and retained

(6) An association operating a pari-mutuel system of betting in accordance with this section in respect of a horse-race, or any other association or person acting on its behalf, may deduct and retain from the total amount of money that is bet through the agency of the pari-mutuel system, in respect of each individual pool of each race or each individual feature pool, a percentage not exceeding the percentage prescribed by the regulations plus any odd cents over any multiple of five cents in the amount calculated in accordance with the regulations to be payable in respect of each dollar bet.

Stopping of betting

(7) Where an officer appointed by the Minister of Agriculture and Agri-Food is not satisfied that the provisions of this section and the regulations are being carried out in good faith by any person or association in relation to a race meeting, he may, at any time, order any betting in relation to the race meeting to be stopped for any period that he considers proper.

Regulations

(8) The Minister of Agriculture and Agri-Food may make regulations

(a) prescribing the maximum number of races for each race-course on which a race meeting is conducted, in respect of which a pari-mutuel system of betting may be used for the race meeting or on any one calendar day during the race meeting, and the circumstances in which the Minister of Agriculture and Agri-Food or a person designated by him for that purpose may approve of the use of that system in respect of additional races on any race-course for a particular race meeting or on a particular day during the race meeting;

(b) prohibiting any person or association from using a pari-mutuel system of betting for any race-course on which a race meeting is conducted in respect of more than the maximum number of races prescribed pursuant to paragraph (a) and the additional races, if any, in respect of which the use of a pari-mutuel system of betting has been approved pursuant to that paragraph;

(c) prescribing the maximum percentage that may be deducted and retained pursuant to subsection (6) by or on behalf of a person or association operating a pari-mutuel system of betting in respect of a horse-race in accordance with this section and providing for the determination of the percentage that each such person or association may deduct and retain;

(d) respecting pari-mutuel betting in Canada on horse-races conducted on a race-course situated outside Canada; and

(e) authorizing pari-mutuel betting and governing the conditions for pari-mutuel betting, including the granting of licences therefor, that is conducted by an association in a betting theatre owned or leased by the association in a province in which the Lieutenant Governor in Council, or such other person or authority in the province as may be specified by the Lieutenant Governor in Council thereof, has issued a licence to that association for the betting theatre.

Approvals

(8.1) The Minister of Agriculture and Agri-Food or a person designated by that Minister may, with respect to a horse-race conducted on a race-course situated outside Canada,

(a) certify as acceptable, for the purposes of this section, the governing body that regulates the race; and
(b) permit pari-mutuel betting in Canada on the race.

Idem
(9) The Minister of Agriculture and Agri-Food may make regulations respecting
(a) the supervision and operation of pari-mutuel systems related to race meetings, and the fixing of the dates on which and the places at which an association may conduct those meetings;
(b) the method of calculating the amount payable in respect of each dollar bet;
(c) the conduct of race-meetings in relation to the supervision and operation of pari-mutuel systems, including photo-finishes, video patrol and the testing of bodily substances taken from horses entered in a race at such meetings, including, in the case of a horse that dies while engaged in racing or immediately before or after the race, the testing of any tissue taken from its body;
(d) the prohibition, restriction or regulation of
(i) the possession of drugs or medicaments or of equipment used in the administering of drugs or medicaments at or near race-courses, or
(ii) the administering of drugs or medicaments to horses participating in races run at a race meeting during which a pari-mutuel system of betting is used; and
(e) the provision, equipment and maintenance of accommodation, services or other facilities for the proper supervision and operation of pari-mutuel systems related to race meetings, by associations conducting those meetings or by other associations.

900 metre zone
(9.1) For the purposes of this section, the Minister of Agriculture and Agri-Food may designate, with respect to any race-course, a zone that shall be deemed to be part of the race-course, if
(a) the zone is immediately adjacent to the race-course;
(b) the farthest point of that zone is not more than 900 metres from the nearest point on the race track of the race-course; and
(c) all real property situated in that zone is owned or leased by the person or association that owns or leases the race-course.

Contravention
(10) Every person who contravenes or fails to comply with any of the provisions of this section or of any regulations made under this section is guilty of
(a) an indictable offence and is liable to imprisonment for a term not exceeding two years; or
(b) an offence punishable on summary conviction.

Definition of
(11) For the purposes of this section,
association
R.S., 1985, c. C-46, s. 204;
R.S., 1985, c. 47 (1st Supp.), s. 1;
1989, c. 2, s. 1;
1994, c. 38, ss. 14, 25;
2008, c. 18, s. 6.

205 Offence in relation to lotteries and games of chance
206 (1) Every one is guilty of an indictable offence and liable to imprisonment for a term not exceeding two years who
(a) makes, prints, advertises or publishes, or causes or procures to be made, printed, advertised or published, any proposal, scheme or plan for advancing, lending, giving, selling or in any way disposing of any property by lots, cards, tickets or any mode of chance whatever;
(b) sells, barters, exchanges or otherwise disposes of, or causes or procures, or aids or assists in, the sale, barter, exchange or other disposal of, or offers for sale, barter or exchange, any lot, card, ticket or other means or device for advancing, lending, giving, selling or otherwise disposing of any property by lots, tickets or any mode of chance whatever;
(c) knowingly sends, transmits, mails, ships, delivers or allows to be sent, transmitted, mailed,

shipped or delivered, or knowingly accepts for carriage or transport or conveys any article that is used or intended for use in carrying out any device, proposal, scheme or plan for advancing, lending, giving, selling or otherwise disposing of any property by any mode of chance whatever;

(d) conducts or manages any scheme, contrivance or operation of any kind for the purpose of determining who, or the holders of what lots, tickets, numbers or chances, are the winners of any property so proposed to be advanced, lent, given, sold or disposed of;

(e) conducts, manages or is a party to any scheme, contrivance or operation of any kind by which any person, on payment of any sum of money, or the giving of any valuable security, or by obligating himself to pay any sum of money or give any valuable security, shall become entitled under the scheme, contrivance or operation to receive from the person conducting or managing the scheme, contrivance or operation, or any other person, a larger sum of money or amount of valuable security than the sum or amount paid or given, or to be paid or given, by reason of the fact that other persons have paid or given, or obligated themselves to pay or give any sum of money or valuable security under the scheme, contrivance or operation;

(f) disposes of any goods, wares or merchandise by any game of chance or any game of mixed chance and skill in which the contestant or competitor pays money or other valuable consideration;

(g) induces any person to stake or hazard any money or other valuable property or thing on the result of any dice game, three-card monte, punch board, coin table or on the operation of a wheel of fortune;

(h) for valuable consideration carries on or plays or offers to carry on or to play, or employs any person to carry on or play in a public place or a place to which the public have access, the game of three-card monte;

(i) receives bets of any kind on the outcome of a game of three-card monte; or

(j) being the owner of a place, permits any person to play the game of three-card monte therein.

Definition of
three-card monte

(2) In this section,
three-card monte

Exemption for fairs

(3) Paragraphs (1)(f) and (g), in so far as they do not relate to a dice game, three-card monte, punch board or coin table, do not apply to the board of an annual fair or exhibition, or to any operator of a concession leased by that board within its own grounds and operated during the fair or exhibition on those grounds.

Definition of
fair or exhibition

(3.1) For the purposes of this section,
fair or exhibition

Offence

(4) Every one who buys, takes or receives a lot, ticket or other device mentioned in subsection (1) is guilty of an offence punishable on summary conviction.

Lottery sale void

(5) Every sale, loan, gift, barter or exchange of any property, by any lottery, ticket, card or other mode of chance depending on or to be determined by chance or lot, is void, and all property so sold, lent, given, bartered or exchanged is forfeited to Her Majesty.

(6) Subsection (5) does not affect any right or title to property acquired by any

Foreign lottery included

(7) This section applies to the printing or publishing, or causing to be printed or published, of any advertisement, scheme, proposal or plan of any foreign lottery, and the sale or offer for sale of any ticket, chance or share, in any such lottery, or the advertisement for sale of such ticket, chance or share, and the conducting or managing of any such scheme, contrivance or operation for determining the winners in any such lottery.

Saving

(8) This section does not apply to
(a) the division by lot or chance of any property by joint tenants or tenants in common, or persons having joint interests in any such property; or
(b) (c) bonds, debentures, debenture stock or other securities recallable by drawing of lots and redeemable with interest and providing for payment of premiums on redemption or otherwise.
R.S., 1985, c. C-46, s. 206;
R.S., 1985, c. 52 (1st Supp.), s. 2;
1999, c. 28, s. 156.

Permitted lotteries

207 (1) Notwithstanding any of the provisions of this Part relating to gaming and betting, it is lawful
(a) for the government of a province, either alone or in conjunction with the government of another province, to conduct and manage a lottery scheme in that province, or in that and the other province, in accordance with any law enacted by the legislature of that province;
(b) for a charitable or religious organization, pursuant to a licence issued by the Lieutenant Governor in Council of a province or by such other person or authority in the province as may be specified by the Lieutenant Governor in Council thereof, to conduct and manage a lottery scheme in that province if the proceeds from the lottery scheme are used for a charitable or religious object or purpose;
(c) for the board of a fair or of an exhibition, or an operator of a concession leased by that board, to conduct and manage a lottery scheme in a province where the Lieutenant Governor in Council of the province or such other person or authority in the province as may be specified by the Lieutenant Governor in Council thereof has
(i) designated that fair or exhibition as a fair or exhibition where a lottery scheme may be conducted and managed, and
(ii) issued a licence for the conduct and management of a lottery scheme to that board or operator;
(d) for any person, pursuant to a licence issued by the Lieutenant Governor in Council of a province or by such other person or authority in the province as may be specified by the Lieutenant Governor in Council thereof, to conduct and manage a lottery scheme at a public place of amusement in that province if
(i) the amount or value of each prize awarded does not exceed five hundred dollars, and
(ii) the money or other valuable consideration paid to secure a chance to win a prize does not exceed two dollars;
(e) for the government of a province to agree with the government of another province that lots, cards or tickets in relation to a lottery scheme that is by any of paragraphs (a) to (d) authorized to be conducted and managed in that other province may be sold in the province;
(f) for any person, pursuant to a licence issued by the Lieutenant Governor in Council of a province or such other person or authority in the province as may be designated by the Lieutenant Governor in Council thereof, to conduct and manage in the province a lottery scheme that is authorized to be conducted and managed in one or more other provinces where the authority by which the lottery scheme was first authorized to be conducted and managed consents thereto;
(g) for any person, for the purpose of a lottery scheme that is lawful in a province under any of paragraphs (a) to (f), to do anything in the province, in accordance with the applicable law or licence, that is required for the conduct, management or operation of the lottery scheme or for the person to participate in the scheme; and
(h) for any person to make or print anywhere in Canada or to cause to be made or printed anywhere in Canada anything relating to gaming and betting that is to be used in a place where it is or would, if certain conditions provided by law are met, be lawful to use such a thing, or to send, transmit, mail, ship, deliver or allow to be sent, transmitted, mailed, shipped or delivered or to accept for carriage or transport or convey any such thing where the destination thereof is such a place.

Terms and conditions of licence

(2) Subject to this Act, a licence issued by or under the authority of the Lieutenant Governor in Council of a province as described in paragraph (1)(b), (c), (d) or (f) may contain such terms and conditions relating to the conduct, management and operation of or participation in the lottery

scheme to which the licence relates as the Lieutenant Governor in Council of that province, the person or authority in the province designated by the Lieutenant Governor in Council thereof or any law enacted by the legislature of that province may prescribe.

Offence

(3) Every one who, for the purposes of a lottery scheme, does anything that is not authorized by or pursuant to a provision of this section
(a) in the case of the conduct, management or operation of that lottery scheme,
(i) is guilty of an indictable offence and liable to imprisonment for a term not exceeding two years, or
(ii) is guilty of an offence punishable on summary conviction; or
(b) in the case of participating in that lottery scheme, is guilty of an offence punishable on summary conviction.

Definition of
lottery scheme

(4) In this section,
lottery scheme
(a) three-card monte, punch board or coin table;
(b) bookmaking, pool selling or the making or recording of bets, including bets made through the agency of a pool or pari-mutuel system, on any race or fight, or on a single sport event or athletic contest; or
(c) for the purposes of paragraphs (1)(b) to (f), a game or proposal, scheme, plan, means, device, contrivance or operation described in any of paragraphs 206(1)(a) to (g) that is operated on or through a computer, video device or slot machine, within the meaning of subsection 198(3), or a dice game.

Exception — charitable or religious organization

(4.1) The use of a computer for the sale of a ticket, selection of a winner or the distribution of a prize in a raffle, including a 50/50 draw, is excluded from paragraph (4)(c) in so far as the raffle is authorized under paragraph (1)(b) and the proceeds are used for a charitable or religious object or purpose.

Exception re: pari-mutuel betting

(5) For greater certainty, nothing in this section shall be construed as authorizing the making or recording of bets on horse-races through the agency of a pari-mutuel system other than in accordance with section 204.

R.S., 1985, c. C-46, s. 207;
R.S., 1985, c. 27 (1st Supp.), s. 31, c. 52 (1st Supp.), s. 3;
1999, c. 5, s. 6;
2014, c. 39, s. 171.

Exemption — lottery scheme on an international cruise ship

207.1 (1) Despite any of the provisions of this Part relating to gaming and betting, it is lawful for the owner or operator of an international cruise ship, or their agent, to conduct, manage or operate and for any person to participate in a lottery scheme during a voyage on an international cruise ship when all of the following conditions are satisfied:
(a) all the people participating in the lottery scheme are located on the ship;
(b) the lottery scheme is not linked, by any means of communication, with any lottery scheme, betting, pool selling or pool system of betting located off the ship;
(c) the lottery scheme is not operated within five nautical miles of a Canadian port at which the ship calls or is scheduled to call; and
(d) the ship is registered
(i) in Canada and its entire voyage is scheduled to be outside Canada, or
(ii) anywhere, including Canada, and its voyage includes some scheduled voyaging within Canada and the voyage
(A) is of at least forty-eight hours duration and includes some voyaging in international waters and at least one non-Canadian port of call including the port at which the voyage begins or ends, and

(B) is not scheduled to disembark any passengers at a Canadian port who have embarked at another Canadian port, without calling on at least one non-Canadian port between the two Canadian ports.

Paragraph 207(1)(h) and subsection 207(5) apply

(2) For greater certainty, paragraph 207(1)(h) and subsection 207(5) apply for the purposes of this section.

Offence

(3) Every one who, for the purpose of a lottery scheme, does anything that is not authorized by this section

(a) in the case of the conduct, management or operation of the lottery scheme,

(i) is guilty of an indictable offence and liable to imprisonment for a term of not more than two years, or

(ii) is guilty of an offence punishable on summary conviction; and

(b) in the case of participating in the lottery scheme, is guilty of an offence punishable on summary conviction.

Definitions

(4) The definitions in this subsection apply in this section.

international cruise ship

lottery scheme

(a) three-card monte, punch board or coin table; or

(b) bookmaking, pool selling or the making or recording of bets, including bets made through the agency of a pool or pari-mutuel system, on any race or fight, or on a single sporting event or athletic contest.

1999, c. 5, s. 7.

208 Cheating at play

209 Every one who, with intent to defraud any person, cheats while playing a game or in holding the stakes for a game or in betting is guilty of an indictable offence and liable to imprisonment for a term not exceeding two years.

R.S., c. C-34, s. 192.

Bawdy-houses

Keeping common bawdy-house

210 (1) Every one who keeps a common bawdy-house is guilty of an indictable offence and liable to imprisonment for a term not exceeding two years.

Landlord, inmate, etc.

(2) Every one who

(a) is an inmate of a common bawdy-house,

(b) is found, without lawful excuse, in a common bawdy-house, or

(c) as owner, landlord, lessor, tenant, occupier, agent or otherwise having charge or control of any place, knowingly permits the place or any part thereof to be let or used for the purposes of a common bawdy-house,

is guilty of an offence punishable on summary conviction.

Notice of conviction to be served on owner

(3) Where a person is convicted of an offence under subsection (1), the court shall cause a notice of the conviction to be served on the owner, landlord or lessor of the place in respect of which the person is convicted or his agent, and the notice shall contain a statement to the effect that it is being served pursuant to this section.

Duty of landlord on notice

(4) Where a person on whom a notice is served under subsection (3) fails forthwith to exercise any right he may have to determine the tenancy or right of occupation of the person so convicted, and thereafter any person is convicted of an offence under subsection (1) in respect of the same premises, the person on whom the notice was served shall be deemed to have committed an offence under

subsection (1) unless he proves that he has taken all reasonable steps to prevent the recurrence of the offence.
R.S., c. C-34, s. 193.
Transporting person to bawdy-house
211 Every one who knowingly takes, transports, directs, or offers to take, transport or direct, any other person to a common bawdy-house is guilty of an offence punishable on summary conviction.
R.S., c. C-34, s. 194.
212

Offences in Relation to Offering, Providing or Obtaining Sexual Services for Consideration

Stopping or impeding traffic
213 (1) Everyone is guilty of an offence punishable on summary conviction who, in a public place or in any place open to public view, for the purpose of offering, providing or obtaining sexual services for consideration,
(a) stops or attempts to stop any motor vehicle; or
(b) impedes the free flow of pedestrian or vehicular traffic or ingress to or egress from premises adjacent to that place.
(c) Communicating to provide sexual services for consideration
(1.1) Everyone is guilty of an offence punishable on summary conviction who communicates with any person — for the purpose of offering or providing sexual services for consideration — in a public place, or in any place open to public view, that is or is next to a school ground, playground or daycare centre.
Definition of
public place
(2) In this section,
public place
R.S., 1985, c. C-46, s. 213;
R.S., 1985, c. 51 (1st Supp.), s. 1;
2014, c. 25, s. 15.

PART VIII

PART VIII
Offences Against the Person and Reputation

Interpretation

Definitions
214 In this Part,
abandon
expose
abandon
expose
(a) a wilful omission to take charge of a child by a person who is under a legal duty to do so, and
(b) dealing with a child in a manner that is likely to leave that child exposed to risk without protection;
aircraft
child
form of marriage
(a) by the law of the place where it was celebrated, or

(b) by the law of the place where an accused is tried, notwithstanding that it is not recognized as valid by the law of the place where it was celebrated;
guardian
operate
(a) means, in respect of a motor vehicle, to drive the vehicle,
(b) means, in respect of railway equipment, to participate in the direct control of its motion, whether
(i) as a member of the crew of the equipment,
(ii) as a person who, by remote control, acts in lieu of such crew, or
(iii) as other than a member or person described in subparagraphs (i) and (ii), and
(c) includes, in respect of a vessel or an aircraft, to navigate the vessel or aircraft;
vessel
R.S., 1985, c. C-46, s. 214;
R.S., 1985, c. 27 (1st Supp.), s. 33, c. 32 (4th Supp.), s. 56;
2002, c. 13, s. 9.

Duties Tending to Preservation of Life

Duty of persons to provide necessaries
215 (1) Every one is under a legal duty
(a) as a parent, foster parent, guardian or head of a family, to provide necessaries of life for a child under the age of sixteen years;
(b) to provide necessaries of life to their spouse or common-law partner; and
(c) to provide necessaries of life to a person under his charge if that person
(i) is unable, by reason of detention, age, illness, mental disorder or other cause, to withdraw himself from that charge, and
(ii) is unable to provide himself with necessaries of life.
Offence
(2) Every one commits an offence who, being under a legal duty within the meaning of subsection (1), fails without lawful excuse, the proof of which lies on him, to perform that duty, if
(a) with respect to a duty imposed by paragraph (1)(a) or (b),
(i) the person to whom the duty is owed is in destitute or necessitous circumstances, or
(ii) the failure to perform the duty endangers the life of the person to whom the duty is owed, or causes or is likely to cause the health of that person to be endangered permanently; or
(b) with respect to a duty imposed by paragraph (1)(c), the failure to perform the duty endangers the life of the person to whom the duty is owed or causes or is likely to cause the health of that person to be injured permanently.
Punishment
(3) Every one who commits an offence under subsection (2)
(a) is guilty of an indictable offence and liable to imprisonment for a term not exceeding five years; or
(b) is guilty of an offence punishable on summary conviction and liable to imprisonment for a term not exceeding eighteen months.
Presumptions
(4) For the purpose of proceedings under this section,
(a) (b) evidence that a person has in any way recognized a child as being his child is, in the absence of any evidence to the contrary, proof that the child is his child;
(c) evidence that a person has failed for a period of one month to make provision for the maintenance of any child of theirs under the age of sixteen years is, in the absence of any evidence to the contrary, proof that the person has failed without lawful excuse to provide necessaries of life for the child; and
(d) the fact that a spouse or common-law partner or child is receiving or has received necessaries of life from another person who is not under a legal duty to provide them is not a defence.
R.S., 1985, c. C-46, s. 215;

1991, c. 43, s. 9;
2000, c. 12, ss. 93, 95;
2005, c. 32, s. 11.

Duty of persons undertaking acts dangerous to life

216 Every one who undertakes to administer surgical or medical treatment to another person or to do any other lawful act that may endanger the life of another person is, except in cases of necessity, under a legal duty to have and to use reasonable knowledge, skill and care in so doing.
R.S., c. C-34, s. 198.

Duty of persons undertaking acts

217 Every one who undertakes to do an act is under a legal duty to do it if an omission to do the act is or may be dangerous to life.
R.S., c. C-34, s. 199.

Duty of persons directing work

217.1 Every one who undertakes, or has the authority, to direct how another person does work or performs a task is under a legal duty to take reasonable steps to prevent bodily harm to that person, or any other person, arising from that work or task.
2003, c. 21, s. 3.

Abandoning child

218 Every one who unlawfully abandons or exposes a child who is under the age of ten years, so that its life is or is likely to be endangered or its health is or is likely to be permanently injured,
(a) is guilty of an indictable offence and liable to imprisonment for a term not exceeding five years; or
(b) is guilty of an offence punishable on summary conviction and liable to imprisonment for a term not exceeding eighteen months.
R.S., 1985, c. C-46, s. 218;
2005, c. 32, s. 12.

Criminal Negligence

Criminal negligence

219 (1) Every one is criminally negligent who
(a) in doing anything, or
(b) in omitting to do anything that it is his duty to do,
shows wanton or reckless disregard for the lives or safety of other persons.

Definition of
duty
(2) For the purposes of this section,
duty
R.S., c. C-34, s. 202.

Causing death by criminal negligence

220 Every person who by criminal negligence causes death to another person is guilty of an indictable offence and liable
(a) where a firearm is used in the commission of the offence, to imprisonment for life and to a minimum punishment of imprisonment for a term of four years; and
(b) in any other case, to imprisonment for life.
R.S., 1985, c. C-46, s. 220;
1995, c. 39, s. 141.

Causing bodily harm by criminal negligence

221 Every one who by criminal negligence causes bodily harm to another person is guilty of an indictable offence and liable to imprisonment for a term not exceeding ten years.
R.S., c. C-34, s. 204.

Homicide

Homicide
222 (1) A person commits homicide when, directly or indirectly, by any means, he causes the death of a human being.

Kinds of homicide
(2) Homicide is culpable or not culpable.

Non culpable homicide
(3) Homicide that is not culpable is not an offence.

Culpable homicide
(4) Culpable homicide is murder or manslaughter or infanticide.

Idem
(5) A person commits culpable homicide when he causes the death of a human being,
(a) by means of an unlawful act;
(b) by criminal negligence;
(c) by causing that human being, by threats or fear of violence or by deception, to do anything that causes his death; or
(d) by wilfully frightening that human being, in the case of a child or sick person.

Exception
(6) Notwithstanding anything in this section, a person does not commit homicide within the meaning of this Act by reason only that he causes the death of a human being by procuring, by false evidence, the conviction and death of that human being by sentence of the law.
R.S., c. C-34, s. 205.

When child becomes human being
223 (1) A child becomes a human being within the meaning of this Act when it has completely proceeded, in a living state, from the body of its mother, whether or not
(a) it has breathed;
(b) it has an independent circulation; or
(c) the navel string is severed.

Killing child
(2) A person commits homicide when he causes injury to a child before or during its birth as a result of which the child dies after becoming a human being.
R.S., c. C-34, s. 206.

Death that might have been prevented
224 Where a person, by an act or omission, does any thing that results in the death of a human being, he causes the death of that human being notwithstanding that death from that cause might have been prevented by resorting to proper means.
R.S., c. C-34, s. 207.

Death from treatment of injury
225 Where a person causes to a human being a bodily injury that is of itself of a dangerous nature and from which death results, he causes the death of that human being notwithstanding that the immediate cause of death is proper or improper treatment that is applied in good faith.
R.S., c. C-34, s. 208.

Acceleration of death
226 Where a person causes to a human being a bodily injury that results in death, he causes the death of that human being notwithstanding that the effect of the bodily injury is only to accelerate his death from a disease or disorder arising from some other cause.
R.S., c. C-34, s. 209.

Exemption for medical assistance in dying
227 (1) No medical practitioner or nurse practitioner commits culpable homicide if they provide a person with medical assistance in dying in accordance with section 241.2.

Exemption for person aiding practitioner

(2) No person is a party to culpable homicide if they do anything for the purpose of aiding a medical practitioner or nurse practitioner to provide a person with medical assistance in dying in accordance with section 241.2.
Reasonable but mistaken belief
(3) For greater certainty, the exemption set out in subsection (1) or (2) applies even if the person invoking it has a reasonable but mistaken belief about any fact that is an element of the exemption.
Non-application of section 14
(4) Section 14 does not apply with respect to a person who consents to have death inflicted on them by means of medical assistance in dying provided in accordance with section 241.2.
Definitions
(5) In this section,
medical assistance in dying
medical practitioner
nurse practitioner
R.S., 1985, c. C-46, s. 227;
R.S., 1985, c. 27 (1st Supp.), s. 34;
1997, c. 18, s. 9;
1999, c. 5, s. 9;
2016, c. 3, s. 2.
Killing by influence on the mind
228 No person commits culpable homicide where he causes the death of a human being
(a) by any influence on the mind alone, or
(b) by any disorder or disease resulting from influence on the mind alone,
but this section does not apply where a person causes the death of a child or sick person by wilfully frightening him.
R.S., c. C-34, s. 211.

Murder, Manslaughter and Infanticide

Murder
229 Culpable homicide is murder
(a) where the person who causes the death of a human being
(i) means to cause his death, or
(ii) means to cause him bodily harm that he knows is likely to cause his death, and is reckless whether death ensues or not;
(b) where a person, meaning to cause death to a human being or meaning to cause him bodily harm that he knows is likely to cause his death, and being reckless whether death ensues or not, by accident or mistake causes death to another human being, notwithstanding that he does not mean to cause death or bodily harm to that human being; or
(c) where a person, for an unlawful object, does anything that he knows or ought to know is likely to cause death, and thereby causes death to a human being, notwithstanding that he desires to effect his object without causing death or bodily harm to any human being.
R.S., c. C-34, s. 212.
Murder in commission of offences
230 Culpable homicide is murder where a person causes the death of a human being while committing or attempting to commit high treason or treason or an offence mentioned in section 52 (sabotage), 75 (piratical acts), 76 (hijacking an aircraft), 144 or subsection 145(1) or sections 146 to 148 (escape or rescue from prison or lawful custody), section 270 (assaulting a peace officer), section 271 (sexual assault), 272 (sexual assault with a weapon, threats to a third party or causing bodily harm), 273 (aggravated sexual assault), 279 (kidnapping and forcible confinement), 279.1 (hostage taking), 343 (robbery), 348 (breaking and entering) or 433 or 434 (arson), whether or not the person means to cause death to any human being and whether or not he knows that death is likely to be

caused to any human being, if
(a) he means to cause bodily harm for the purpose of
(i) facilitating the commission of the offence, or
(ii) facilitating his flight after committing or attempting to commit the offence,
and the death ensues from the bodily harm;
(b) he administers a stupefying or overpowering thing for a purpose mentioned in paragraph (a), and the death ensues therefrom; or
(c) he wilfully stops, by any means, the breath of a human being for a purpose mentioned in paragraph (a), and the death ensues therefrom.
(d) R.S., 1985, c. C-46, s. 230;
R.S., 1985, c. 27 (1st Supp.), s. 40;
1991, c. 4, s. 1.

Classification of murder

231 (1) Murder is first degree murder or second degree murder.

Planned and deliberate murder

(2) Murder is first degree murder when it is planned and deliberate.

Contracted murder

(3) Without limiting the generality of subsection (2), murder is planned and deliberate when it is committed pursuant to an arrangement under which money or anything of value passes or is intended to pass from one person to another, or is promised by one person to another, as consideration for that other's causing or assisting in causing the death of anyone or counselling another person to do any act causing or assisting in causing that death.

Murder of peace officer, etc.

(4) Irrespective of whether a murder is planned and deliberate on the part of any person, murder is first degree murder when the victim is
(a) a police officer, police constable, constable, sheriff, deputy sheriff, sheriff's officer or other person employed for the preservation and maintenance of the public peace, acting in the course of his duties;
(b) a warden, deputy warden, instructor, keeper, jailer, guard or other officer or a permanent employee of a prison, acting in the course of his duties; or
(c) a person working in a prison with the permission of the prison authorities and acting in the course of his work therein.

Hijacking, sexual assault or kidnapping

(5) Irrespective of whether a murder is planned and deliberate on the part of any person, murder is first degree murder in respect of a person when the death is caused by that person while committing or attempting to commit an offence under one of the following sections:
(a) section 76 (hijacking an aircraft);
(b) section 271 (sexual assault);
(c) section 272 (sexual assault with a weapon, threats to a third party or causing bodily harm);
(d) section 273 (aggravated sexual assault);
(e) section 279 (kidnapping and forcible confinement); or
(f) section 279.1 (hostage taking).

Criminal harassment

(6) Irrespective of whether a murder is planned and deliberate on the part of any person, murder is first degree murder when the death is caused by that person while committing or attempting to commit an offence under section 264 and the person committing that offence intended to cause the person murdered to fear for the safety of the person murdered or the safety of anyone known to the person murdered.

Murder — terrorist activity

(6.01) Irrespective of whether a murder is planned and deliberate on the part of a person, murder is first degree murder when the death is caused by that person while committing or attempting to commit an indictable offence under this or any other Act of Parliament if the act or omission

constituting the offence also constitutes a terrorist activity.
Murder — criminal organization
(6.1) Irrespective of whether a murder is planned and deliberate on the part of a person, murder is first degree murder when
(a) the death is caused by that person for the benefit of, at the direction of or in association with a criminal organization; or
(b) the death is caused by that person while committing or attempting to commit an indictable offence under this or any other Act of Parliament for the benefit of, at the direction of or in association with a criminal organization.
Intimidation
(6.2) Irrespective of whether a murder is planned and deliberate on the part of a person, murder is first degree murder when the death is caused by that person while committing or attempting to commit an offence under section 423.1.
Second degree murder
(7) All murder that is not first degree murder is second degree murder.
R.S., 1985, c. C-46, s. 231;
R.S., 1985, c. 27 (1st Supp.), ss. 7, 35, 40, 185(F), c. 1 (4th Supp.), s. 18(F);
1997, c. 16, s. 3, c. 23, s. 8;
2001, c. 32, s. 9, c. 41, s. 9;
2009, c. 22, s. 5.
Murder reduced to manslaughter
232 (1) Culpable homicide that otherwise would be murder may be reduced to manslaughter if the person who committed it did so in the heat of passion caused by sudden provocation.
What is provocation
(2) Conduct of the victim that would constitute an indictable offence under this Act that is punishable by five or more years of imprisonment and that is of such a nature as to be sufficient to deprive an ordinary person of the power of self-control is provocation for the purposes of this section, if the accused acted on it on the sudden and before there was time for their passion to cool.
Questions of fact
(3) For the purposes of this section, the questions
(a) whether the conduct of the victim amounted to provocation under subsection (2), and
(b) whether the accused was deprived of the power of self-control by the provocation that he alleges he received,
are questions of fact, but no one shall be deemed to have given provocation to another by doing anything that he had a legal right to do, or by doing anything that the accused incited him to do in order to provide the accused with an excuse for causing death or bodily harm to any human being.
Death during illegal arrest
(4) Culpable homicide that otherwise would be murder is not necessarily manslaughter by reason only that it was committed by a person who was being arrested illegally, but the fact that the illegality of the arrest was known to the accused may be evidence of provocation for the purpose of this section.
R.S., 1985, c. C-46, s. 232;
2015, c. 29, s. 7.
Infanticide
233 A female person commits infanticide when by a wilful act or omission she causes the death of her newly-born child, if at the time of the act or omission she is not fully recovered from the effects of giving birth to the child and by reason thereof or of the effect of lactation consequent on the birth of the child her mind is then disturbed.
R.S., c. C-34, s. 216.
Manslaughter
234 Culpable homicide that is not murder or infanticide is manslaughter.
R.S., c. C-34, s. 217.

Punishment for murder
235 (1) Every one who commits first degree murder or second degree murder is guilty of an indictable offence and shall be sentenced to imprisonment for life.
Minimum punishment
(2) For the purposes of Part XXIII, the sentence of imprisonment for life prescribed by this section is a minimum punishment.
R.S., c. C-34, s. 218;
1973-74, c. 38, s. 3;
1974-75-76, c. 105, s. 5.
Manslaughter
236 Every person who commits manslaughter is guilty of an indictable offence and liable
(a) where a firearm is used in the commission of the offence, to imprisonment for life and to a minimum punishment of imprisonment for a term of four years; and
(b) in any other case, to imprisonment for life.
R.S., 1985, c. C-46, s. 236;
1995, c. 39, s. 142.
Punishment for infanticide
237 Every female person who commits infanticide is guilty of an indictable offence and liable to imprisonment for a term not exceeding five years.
R.S., c. C-34, s. 220.
Killing unborn child in act of birth
238 (1) Every one who causes the death, in the act of birth, of any child that has not become a human being, in such a manner that, if the child were a human being, he would be guilty of murder, is guilty of an indictable offence and liable to imprisonment for life.
Saving
(2) This section does not apply to a person who, by means that, in good faith, he considers necessary to preserve the life of the mother of a child, causes the death of that child.
R.S., c. C-34, s. 221.
Attempt to commit murder
239 (1) Every person who attempts by any means to commit murder is guilty of an indictable offence and liable
(a) if a restricted firearm or prohibited firearm is used in the commission of the offence or if any firearm is used in the commission of the offence and the offence is committed for the benefit of, at the direction of, or in association with, a criminal organization, to imprisonment for life and to a minimum punishment of imprisonment for a term of
(i) in the case of a first offence, five years, and
(ii) in the case of a second or subsequent offence, seven years;
(a.1) in any other case where a firearm is used in the commission of the offence, to imprisonment for life and to a minimum punishment of imprisonment for a term of four years; and
(b) in any other case, to imprisonment for life.
Subsequent offences
(2) In determining, for the purpose of paragraph (1)(a), whether a convicted person has committed a second or subsequent offence, if the person was earlier convicted of any of the following offences, that offence is to be considered as an earlier offence:
(a) an offence under this section;
(b) an offence under subsection 85(1) or (2) or section 244 or 244.2; or
(c) an offence under section 220, 236, 272 or 273, subsection 279(1) or section 279.1, 344 or 346 if a firearm was used in the commission of the offence.
However, an earlier offence shall not be taken into account if 10 years have elapsed between the day on which the person was convicted of the earlier offence and the day on which the person was convicted of the offence for which sentence is being imposed, not taking into account any time in custody.

Sequence of convictions only
(3) For the purposes of subsection (2), the only question to be considered is the sequence of convictions and no consideration shall be given to the sequence of commission of offences or whether any offence occurred before or after any conviction.
R.S., 1985, c. C-46, s. 239;
1995, c. 39, s. 143;
2008, c. 6, s. 16;
2009, c. 22, s. 6.

Accessory after fact to murder
240 Every one who is an accessory after the fact to murder is guilty of an indictable offence and liable to imprisonment for life.
R.S., c. C-34, s. 223.

Suicide

Counselling or aiding suicide
241 (1) Everyone is guilty of an indictable offence and liable to imprisonment for a term of not more than 14 years who, whether suicide ensues or not,
(a) counsels a person to die by suicide or abets a person in dying by suicide; or
(b) aids a person to die by suicide.

Exemption for medical assistance in dying
(2) No medical practitioner or nurse practitioner commits an offence under paragraph (1)(b) if they provide a person with medical assistance in dying in accordance with section 241.2.

Exemption for person aiding practitioner
(3) No person is a party to an offence under paragraph (1)(b) if they do anything for the purpose of aiding a medical practitioner or nurse practitioner to provide a person with medical assistance in dying in accordance with section 241.2.

Exemption for pharmacist
(4) No pharmacist who dispenses a substance to a person other than a medical practitioner or nurse practitioner commits an offence under paragraph (1)(b) if the pharmacist dispenses the substance further to a prescription that is written by such a practitioner in providing medical assistance in dying in accordance with section 241.2.

Exemption for person aiding patient
(5) No person commits an offence under paragraph (1)(b) if they do anything, at another person's explicit request, for the purpose of aiding that other person to self-administer a substance that has been prescribed for that other person as part of the provision of medical assistance in dying in accordance with section 241.2.

Clarification
(5.1) For greater certainty, no social worker, psychologist, psychiatrist, therapist, medical practitioner, nurse practitioner or other health care professional commits an offence if they provide information to a person on the lawful provision of medical assistance in dying.

Reasonable but mistaken belief
(6) For greater certainty, the exemption set out in any of subsections (2) to (5) applies even if the person invoking the exemption has a reasonable but mistaken belief about any fact that is an element of the exemption.

Definitions
(7) In this section,
medical assistance in dying
medical practitioner
nurse practitioner
pharmacist
R.S., 1985, c. C-46, s. 241;

R.S., 1985, c. 27 (1st Supp.), s. 7;
2016, c. 3, s. 3.

Medical Assistance in Dying

Definitions
241.1 The following definitions apply in this section and in sections 241.2 to 241.4.
medical assistance in dying
(a) the administering by a medical practitioner or nurse practitioner of a substance to a person, at their request, that causes their death; or
(b) the prescribing or providing by a medical practitioner or nurse practitioner of a substance to a person, at their request, so that they may self-administer the substance and in doing so cause their own death. (
medical practitioner
nurse practitioner
pharmacist
2016, c. 3, s. 3.

Eligibility for medical assistance in dying
241.2 (1) A person may receive medical assistance in dying only if they meet all of the following criteria:
(a) they are eligible — or, but for any applicable minimum period of residence or waiting period, would be eligible — for health services funded by a government in Canada;
(b) they are at least 18 years of age and capable of making decisions with respect to their health;
(c) they have a grievous and irremediable medical condition;
(d) they have made a voluntary request for medical assistance in dying that, in particular, was not made as a result of external pressure; and
(e) they give informed consent to receive medical assistance in dying after having been informed of the means that are available to relieve their suffering, including palliative care.

Grievous and irremediable medical condition
(2) A person has a grievous and irremediable medical condition only if they meet all of the following criteria:
(a) they have a serious and incurable illness, disease or disability;
(b) they are in an advanced state of irreversible decline in capability;
(c) that illness, disease or disability or that state of decline causes them enduring physical or psychological suffering that is intolerable to them and that cannot be relieved under conditions that they consider acceptable; and
(d) their natural death has become reasonably foreseeable, taking into account all of their medical circumstances, without a prognosis necessarily having been made as to the specific length of time that they have remaining.

Safeguards
(3) Before a medical practitioner or nurse practitioner provides a person with medical assistance in dying, the medical practitioner or nurse practitioner must
(a) be of the opinion that the person meets all of the criteria set out in subsection (1);
(b) ensure that the person's request for medical assistance in dying was
(i) made in writing and signed and dated by the person or by another person under subsection (4), and
(ii) signed and dated after the person was informed by a medical practitioner or nurse practitioner that the person has a grievous and irremediable medical condition;
(c) be satisfied that the request was signed and dated by the person — or by another person under subsection (4) — before two independent witnesses who then also signed and dated the request;
(d) ensure that the person has been informed that they may, at any time and in any manner, withdraw their request;

(e) ensure that another medical practitioner or nurse practitioner has provided a written opinion confirming that the person meets all of the criteria set out in subsection (1);

(f) be satisfied that they and the other medical practitioner or nurse practitioner referred to in paragraph (e) are independent;

(g) ensure that there are at least 10 clear days between the day on which the request was signed by or on behalf of the person and the day on which the medical assistance in dying is provided or — if they and the other medical practitioner or nurse practitioner referred to in paragraph (e) are both of the opinion that the person's death, or the loss of their capacity to provide informed consent, is imminent — any shorter period that the first medical practitioner or nurse practitioner considers appropriate in the circumstances;

(h) immediately before providing the medical assistance in dying, give the person an opportunity to withdraw their request and ensure that the person gives express consent to receive medical assistance in dying; and

(i) if the person has difficulty communicating, take all necessary measures to provide a reliable means by which the person may understand the information that is provided to them and communicate their decision.

Unable to sign

(4) If the person requesting medical assistance in dying is unable to sign and date the request, another person — who is at least 18 years of age, who understands the nature of the request for medical assistance in dying and who does not know or believe that they are a beneficiary under the will of the person making the request, or a recipient, in any other way, of a financial or other material benefit resulting from that person's death — may do so in the person's presence, on the person's behalf and under the person's express direction.

Independent witness

(5) Any person who is at least 18 years of age and who understands the nature of the request for medical assistance in dying may act as an independent witness, except if they

(a) know or believe that they are a beneficiary under the will of the person making the request, or a recipient, in any other way, of a financial or other material benefit resulting from that person's death;

(b) are an owner or operator of any health care facility at which the person making the request is being treated or any facility in which that person resides;

(c) are directly involved in providing health care services to the person making the request; or

(d) directly provide personal care to the person making the request.

Independence — medical practitioners and nurse practitioners

(6) The medical practitioner or nurse practitioner providing medical assistance in dying and the medical practitioner or nurse practitioner who provides the opinion referred to in paragraph (3)(e) are independent if they

(a) are not a mentor to the other practitioner or responsible for supervising their work;

(b) do not know or believe that they are a beneficiary under the will of the person making the request, or a recipient, in any other way, of a financial or other material benefit resulting from that person's death, other than standard compensation for their services relating to the request; or

(c) do not know or believe that they are connected to the other practitioner or to the person making the request in any other way that would affect their objectivity.

Reasonable knowledge, care and skill

(7) Medical assistance in dying must be provided with reasonable knowledge, care and skill and in accordance with any applicable provincial laws, rules or standards.

Informing pharmacist

(8) The medical practitioner or nurse practitioner who, in providing medical assistance in dying, prescribes or obtains a substance for that purpose must, before any pharmacist dispenses the substance, inform the pharmacist that the substance is intended for that purpose.

Clarification

(9) For greater certainty, nothing in this section compels an individual to provide or assist in providing medical assistance in dying.

2016, c. 3, s. 3.
Failure to comply with safeguards
241.3 A medical practitioner or nurse practitioner who, in providing medical assistance in dying, knowingly fails to comply with all of the requirements set out in paragraphs 241.2(3)(b) to (i) and subsection 241.2(8) is guilty of an offence and is liable

(a) on conviction on indictment, to a term of imprisonment of not more than five years; or

(b) on summary conviction, to a term of imprisonment of not more than 18 months.

2016, c. 3, s. 3.

Filing information — medical practitioner or nurse practitioner
241.31 (1) Unless they are exempted under regulations made under subsection (3), a medical practitioner or nurse practitioner who receives a written request for medical assistance in dying must, in accordance with those regulations, provide the information required by those regulations to the recipient designated in those regulations.

Filing information — pharmacist
(2) Unless they are exempted under regulations made under subsection (3), a pharmacist who dispenses a substance in connection with the provision of medical assistance in dying must, in accordance with those regulations, provide the information required by those regulations to the recipient designated in those regulations.

Regulations
(3) The Minister of Health must make regulations that he or she considers necessary

(a) respecting the provision and collection, for the purpose of monitoring medical assistance in dying, of information relating to requests for, and the provision of, medical assistance in dying, including

(i) the information to be provided, at various stages, by medical practitioners or nurse practitioners and by pharmacists, or by a class of any of them,

(ii) the form, manner and time in which the information must be provided,

(iii) the designation of a person as the recipient of the information, and

(iv) the collection of information from coroners and medical examiners;

(b) respecting the use of that information, including its analysis and interpretation, its protection and its publication and other disclosure;

(c) respecting the disposal of that information; and

(d) exempting, on any terms that may be specified, a class of persons from the requirement set out in subsection (1) or (2).

Guidelines — information on death certificates
(3.1) The Minister of Health, after consultation with representatives of the provincial governments responsible for health, must establish guidelines on the information to be included on death certificates in cases where medical assistance in dying has been provided, which may include the way in which to clearly identify medical assistance in dying as the manner of death, as well as the illness, disease or disability that prompted the request for medical assistance in dying.

Offence and punishment
(4) A medical practitioner or nurse practitioner who knowingly fails to comply with subsection (1), or a pharmacist who knowingly fails to comply with subsection (2),

(a) is guilty of an indictable offence and liable to a term of imprisonment of not more than two years; or

(b) is guilty of an offence punishable on summary conviction.

Offence and punishment
(5) Everyone who knowingly contravenes the regulations made under subsection (3)

(a) is guilty of an indictable offence and liable to a term of imprisonment of not more than two years; or

(b) is guilty of an offence punishable on summary conviction.

2016, c. 3, s. 4.

Forgery

241.4 (1) Everyone commits an offence who commits forgery in relation to a request for medical assistance in dying.
Destruction of documents
(2) Everyone commits an offence who destroys a document that relates to a request for medical assistance in dying with intent to interfere with
(a) another person's access to medical assistance in dying;
(b) the lawful assessment of a request for medical assistance in dying;
(c) another person invoking an exemption under any of subsections 227(1) or (2), 241(2) to (5) or 245(2); or
(d) the provision by a person of information under section 241.31.
Punishment
(3) Everyone who commits an offence under subsection (1) or (2) is liable
(a) on conviction on indictment, to a term of imprisonment of not more than five years; or
(b) on summary conviction, to a term of imprisonment of not more than 18 months.
Definition of
(4) In subsection (2),
2016, c. 3, ss. 3, 5.

Neglect in Child-birth and Concealing Dead Body

Neglect to obtain assistance in child-birth
242 A female person who, being pregnant and about to be delivered, with intent that the child shall not live or with intent to conceal the birth of the child, fails to make provision for reasonable assistance in respect of her delivery is, if the child is permanently injured as a result thereof or dies immediately before, during or in a short time after birth, as a result thereof, guilty of an indictable offence and is liable to imprisonment for a term not exceeding five years.
R.S., c. C-34, s. 226.
Concealing body of child
243 Every one who in any manner disposes of the dead body of a child, with intent to conceal the fact that its mother has been delivered of it, whether the child died before, during or after birth, is guilty of an indictable offence and liable to imprisonment for a term not exceeding two years.
R.S., c. C-34, s. 227.

Bodily Harm and Acts and Omissions Causing Danger to the Person

Discharging firearm with intent
244 (1) Every person commits an offence who discharges a firearm at a person with intent to wound, maim or disfigure, to endanger the life of or to prevent the arrest or detention of any person — whether or not that person is the one at whom the firearm is discharged.
Punishment
(2) Every person who commits an offence under subsection (1) is guilty of an indictable offence and liable
(a) if a restricted firearm or prohibited firearm is used in the commission of the offence or if the offence is committed for the benefit of, at the direction of, or in association with, a criminal organization, to imprisonment for a term not exceeding 14 years and to a minimum punishment of imprisonment for a term of
(i) in the case of a first offence, five years, and
(ii) in the case of a second or subsequent offence, seven years; and
(b) in any other case, to imprisonment for a term not exceeding 14 years and to a minimum punishment of imprisonment for a term of four years.
Subsequent offences
(3) In determining, for the purpose of paragraph (2)(a), whether a convicted person has committed a

second or subsequent offence, if the person was earlier convicted of any of the following offences, that offence is to be considered as an earlier offence:
(a) an offence under this section;
(b) an offence under subsection 85(1) or (2) or section 244.2; or
(c) an offence under section 220, 236, 239, 272 or 273, subsection 279(1) or section 279.1, 344 or 346 if a firearm was used in the commission of the offence.

However, an earlier offence shall not be taken into account if 10 years have elapsed between the day on which the person was convicted of the earlier offence and the day on which the person was convicted of the offence for which sentence is being imposed, not taking into account any time in custody.

Sequence of convictions only
(4) For the purposes of subsection (3), the only question to be considered is the sequence of convictions and no consideration shall be given to the sequence of commission of offences or whether any offence occurred before or after any conviction.
R.S., 1985, c. C-46, s. 244;
1995, c. 39, s. 144;
2008, c. 6, s. 17;
2009, c. 22, s. 7.

Causing bodily harm with intent — air gun or pistol
244.1 Every person who, with intent
(a) to wound, maim or disfigure any person,
(b) to endanger the life of any person, or
(c) to prevent the arrest or detention of any person,
discharges an air or compressed gas gun or pistol at any person, whether or not that person is the person mentioned in paragraph (a), (b) or (c), is guilty of an indictable offence and liable to imprisonment for a term not exceeding fourteen years.
1995, c. 39, s. 144.

Discharging firearm — recklessness
244.2 (1) Every person commits an offence
(a) who intentionally discharges a firearm into or at a place, knowing that or being reckless as to whether another person is present in the place; or
(b) who intentionally discharges a firearm while being reckless as to the life or safety of another person.

Definition of
place
(2) For the purpose of paragraph (1)(a),
place

Punishment
(3) Every person who commits an offence under subsection (1) is guilty of an indictable offence and
(a) if a restricted firearm or prohibited firearm is used in the commission of the offence or if the offence is committed for the benefit of, at the direction of or in association with a criminal organization, is liable to imprisonment for a term of not more than 14 years and to a minimum punishment of imprisonment for a term of
(i) five years, in the case of a first offence, and
(ii) seven years, in the case of a second or subsequent offence; and
(b) in any other case, is liable to imprisonment for a term of not more than 14 years and to a minimum punishment of imprisonment for a term of four years.

Subsequent offences
(4) In determining, for the purpose of paragraph (3)(a), whether a convicted person has committed a second or subsequent offence, if the person was earlier convicted of any of the following offences, that offence is to be considered as an earlier offence:
(a) an offence under this section;

(b) an offence under subsection 85(1) or (2) or section 244; or

(c) an offence under section 220, 236, 239, 272 or 273, subsection 279(1) or section 279.1, 344 or 346 if a firearm was used in the commission of the offence.

However, an earlier offence shall not be taken into account if 10 years have elapsed between the day on which the person was convicted of the earlier offence and the day on which the person was convicted of the offence for which sentence is being imposed, not taking into account any time in custody.

Sequence of convictions only

(5) For the purpose of subsection (4), the only question to be considered is the sequence of convictions and no consideration shall be given to the sequence of commission of offences or whether any offence occurred before or after any conviction.

2009, c. 22, s. 8.

Administering noxious thing

245 (1) Every one who administers or causes to be administered to any person or causes any person to take poison or any other destructive or noxious thing is guilty of an indictable offence and liable

(a) to imprisonment for a term not exceeding fourteen years, if he intends thereby to endanger the life of or to cause bodily harm to that person; or

(b) to imprisonment for a term not exceeding two years, if he intends thereby to aggrieve or annoy that person.

Exemption

(2) Subsection (1) does not apply to

(a) a medical practitioner or nurse practitioner who provides medical assistance in dying in accordance with section 241.2; and

(b) a person who does anything for the purpose of aiding a medical practitioner or nurse practitioner to provide medical assistance in dying in accordance with section 241.2.

Definitions

(3) In subsection (2),

medical assistance in dying

medical practitioner

nurse practitioner

R.S., 1985, c. C-46, s. 245;

2016, c. 3, s. 6.

Overcoming resistance to commission of offence

246 Every one who, with intent to enable or assist himself or another person to commit an indictable offence,

(a) attempts, by any means, to choke, suffocate or strangle another person, or by any means calculated to choke, suffocate or strangle, attempts to render another person insensible, unconscious or incapable of resistance, or

(b) administers or causes to be administered to any person, or attempts to administer to any person, or causes or attempts to cause any person to take a stupefying or overpowering drug, matter or thing,

is guilty of an indictable offence and liable to imprisonment for life.

R.S., c. C-34, s. 230;

1972, c. 13, s. 70.

Traps likely to cause bodily harm

247 (1) Every one is guilty of an indictable offence and is liable to imprisonment for a term not exceeding five years, who with intent to cause death or bodily harm to a person, whether ascertained or not,

(a) sets or places a trap, device or other thing that is likely to cause death or bodily harm to a person; or

(b) being in occupation or possession of a place, knowingly permits such a trap, device or other thing to remain in that place.

Bodily harm

(2) Every one who commits an offence under subsection (1) and thereby causes bodily harm to any other person is guilty of an indictable offence and liable to imprisonment for a term not exceeding ten years.

Offence-related place

(3) Every one who commits an offence under subsection (1), in a place kept or used for the purpose of committing another indictable offence, is guilty of an indictable offence and is liable to a term of imprisonment not exceeding ten years.

Offence-related place — bodily harm

(4) Every one who commits an offence under subsection (1), in a place kept or used for the purpose of committing another indictable offence, and thereby causes bodily harm to a person is guilty of an indictable offence and liable to a term of imprisonment not exceeding fourteen years.

Death

(5) Every one who commits an offence under subsection (1) and thereby causes the death of any other person is guilty of an indictable offence and liable to imprisonment for life.

R.S., 1985, c. C-46, s. 247;

2004, c. 12, s. 6.

Interfering with transportation facilities

248 Every one who, with intent to endanger the safety of any person, places anything on or does anything to any property that is used for or in connection with the transportation of persons or goods by land, water or air that is likely to cause death or bodily harm to persons is guilty of an indictable offence and liable to imprisonment for life.

R.S., c. C-34, s. 232.

Motor Vehicles, Vessels and Aircraft

Dangerous operation of motor vehicles, vessels and aircraft

249 (1) Every one commits an offence who operates

(a) a motor vehicle in a manner that is dangerous to the public, having regard to all the circumstances, including the nature, condition and use of the place at which the motor vehicle is being operated and the amount of traffic that at the time is or might reasonably be expected to be at that place;

(b) a vessel or any water skis, surf-board, water sled or other towed object on or over any of the internal waters of Canada or the territorial sea of Canada, in a manner that is dangerous to the public, having regard to all the circumstances, including the nature and condition of those waters or sea and the use that at the time is or might reasonably be expected to be made of those waters or sea;

(c) an aircraft in a manner that is dangerous to the public, having regard to all the circumstances, including the nature and condition of that aircraft or the place or air space in or through which the aircraft is operated; or

(d) railway equipment in a manner that is dangerous to the public, having regard to all the circumstances, including the nature and condition of the equipment or the place in or through which the equipment is operated.

Punishment

(2) Every one who commits an offence under subsection (1)

(a) is guilty of an indictable offence and liable to imprisonment for a term not exceeding five years; or

(b) is guilty of an offence punishable on summary conviction.

Dangerous operation causing bodily harm

(3) Every one who commits an offence under subsection (1) and thereby causes bodily harm to any other person is guilty of an indictable offence and liable to imprisonment for a term not exceeding ten years.

Dangerous operation causing death

(4) Every one who commits an offence under subsection (1) and thereby causes the death of any

other person is guilty of an indictable offence and liable to imprisonment for a term not exceeding fourteen years.
R.S., 1985, c. C-46, s. 249;
R.S., 1985, c. 27 (1st Supp.), s. 36, c. 32 (4th Supp.), s. 57;
1994, c. 44, s. 11.

Flight
249.1 (1) Every one commits an offence who, operating a motor vehicle while being pursued by a peace officer operating a motor vehicle, fails, without reasonable excuse and in order to evade the peace officer, to stop the vehicle as soon as is reasonable in the circumstances.

Punishment
(2) Every one who commits an offence under subsection (1)
(a) is guilty of an indictable offence and liable to imprisonment for a term not exceeding five years; or
(b) is guilty of an offence punishable on summary conviction.

Flight causing bodily harm or death
(3) Every one commits an offence who causes bodily harm to or the death of another person by operating a motor vehicle in a manner described in paragraph 249(1)(a), if the person operating the motor vehicle was being pursued by a peace officer operating a motor vehicle and failed, without reasonable excuse and in order to evade the police officer, to stop the vehicle as soon as is reasonable in the circumstances.

Punishment
(4) Every person who commits an offence under subsection (3)
(a) if bodily harm was caused, is guilty of an indictable offence and liable to imprisonment for a term not exceeding 14 years; and
(b) if death was caused, is guilty of an indictable offence and liable to imprisonment for life.
2000, c. 2, s. 1.

Causing death by criminal negligence (street racing)
249.2 Everyone who by criminal negligence causes death to another person while street racing is guilty of an indictable offence and liable to imprisonment for life.
2006, c. 14, s. 2.

Causing bodily harm by criminal negligence (street racing)
249.3 Everyone who by criminal negligence causes bodily harm to another person while street racing is guilty of an indictable offence and liable to imprisonment for a term not exceeding fourteen years.
2006, c. 14, s. 2.

Dangerous operation of motor vehicle while street racing
249.4 (1) Everyone commits an offence who, while street racing, operates a motor vehicle in a manner described in paragraph 249(1)(a).

Punishment
(2) Everyone who commits an offence under subsection (1)
(a) is guilty of an indictable offence and liable to imprisonment for a term not exceeding five years; or
(b) is guilty of an offence punishable on summary conviction.

Dangerous operation causing bodily harm
(3) Everyone who commits an offence under subsection (1) and thereby causes bodily harm to another person is guilty of an indictable offence and liable to imprisonment for a term not exceeding fourteen years.

Dangerous operation causing death
(4) Everyone who commits an offence under subsection (1) and thereby causes the death of another person is guilty of an indictable offence and liable to imprisonment for life.
2006, c. 14, s. 2.

Failure to keep watch on person towed
250 (1) Every one who operates a vessel while towing a person on any water skis, surf-board, water

sled or other object, when there is not on board such vessel another responsible person keeping watch on the person being towed, is guilty of an offence punishable on summary conviction.
Towing of person after dark
(2) Every one who operates a vessel while towing a person on any water skis, surf-board, water sled or other object during the period from one hour after sunset to sunrise is guilty of an offence punishable on summary conviction.
R.S., 1985, c. C-46, s. 250;
R.S., 1985, c. 27 (1st Supp.), s. 36.
Unseaworthy vessel and unsafe aircraft
251 (1) Every one who knowingly
(a) sends or being the master takes a vessel that is registered or licensed, or for which an identification number has been issued, pursuant to any Act of Parliament and that is unseaworthy
(i) on a voyage from a place in Canada to any other place in or out of Canada, or
(ii) on a voyage from a place on the inland waters of the United States to a place in Canada,
(b) sends an aircraft on a flight or operates an aircraft that is not fit and safe for flight, or
(c) sends for operation or operates railway equipment that is not fit and safe for operation
and thereby endangers the life of any person, is guilty of an indictable offence and liable to imprisonment for a term not exceeding five years.
Defences
(2) An accused shall not be convicted of an offence under this section where the accused establishes that,
(a) in the case of an offence under paragraph (1)(a),
(i) the accused used all reasonable means to ensure that the vessel was seaworthy, or
(ii) to send or take the vessel while it was unseaworthy was, under the circumstances, reasonable and justifiable;
(b) in the case of an offence under paragraph (1)(b),
(i) the accused used all reasonable means to ensure that the aircraft was fit and safe for flight, or
(ii) to send or operate the aircraft while it was not fit and safe for flight was, under the circumstances, reasonable and justifiable; and
(c) in the case of an offence under paragraph (1)(c),
(i) the accused used all reasonable means to ensure that the railway equipment was fit and safe for operation, or
(ii) to send the railway equipment for operation or to operate it while it was not fit and safe for operation was, under the circumstances, reasonable and justifiable.
Consent of Attorney General
(3) No proceedings shall be instituted under this section in respect of a vessel or aircraft, or in respect of railway equipment sent for operation or operated on a line of railway that is within the legislative authority of Parliament, without the consent in writing of the Attorney General of Canada.
R.S., 1985, c. C-46, s. 251;
R.S., 1985, c. 27 (1st Supp.), s. 36, c. 32 (4th Supp.), s. 58.
Failure to stop at scene of accident
252 (1) Every person commits an offence who has the care, charge or control of a vehicle, vessel or aircraft that is involved in an accident with
(a) another person,
(b) a vehicle, vessel or aircraft, or
(c) in the case of a vehicle, cattle in the charge of another person,
and with intent to escape civil or criminal liability fails to stop the vehicle, vessel or, if possible, the aircraft, give his or her name and address and, where any person has been injured or appears to require assistance, offer assistance.
Punishment
(1.1) Every person who commits an offence under subsection (1) in a case not referred to in subsection (1.2) or (1.3) is guilty of an indictable offence and liable to imprisonment for a term not

exceeding five years or is guilty of an offence punishable on summary conviction.

Offence involving bodily harm

(1.2) Every person who commits an offence under subsection (1) knowing that bodily harm has been caused to another person involved in the accident is guilty of an indictable offence and liable to imprisonment for a term not exceeding ten years.

Offence involving bodily harm or death

(1.3) Every person who commits an offence under subsection (1) is guilty of an indictable offence and liable to imprisonment for life if

(a) the person knows that another person involved in the accident is dead; or

(b) the person knows that bodily harm has been caused to another person involved in the accident and is reckless as to whether the death of the other person results from that bodily harm, and the death of that other person so results.

Evidence

(2) In proceedings under subsection (1), evidence that an accused failed to stop his vehicle, vessel or, where possible, his aircraft, as the case may be, offer assistance where any person has been injured or appears to require assistance and give his name and address is, in the absence of evidence to the contrary, proof of an intent to escape civil or criminal liability.

R.S., 1985, c. C-46, s. 252;

R.S., 1985, c. 27 (1st Supp.), s. 36;

1994, c. 44, s. 12;

1999, c. 32, s. 1(Preamble).

Operation while impaired

253 (1) Every one commits an offence who operates a motor vehicle or vessel or operates or assists in the operation of an aircraft or of railway equipment or has the care or control of a motor vehicle, vessel, aircraft or railway equipment, whether it is in motion or not,

(a) while the person's ability to operate the vehicle, vessel, aircraft or railway equipment is impaired by alcohol or a drug; or

(b) having consumed alcohol in such a quantity that the concentration in the person's blood exceeds eighty milligrams of alcohol in one hundred millilitres of blood.

For greater certainty

(2) For greater certainty, the reference to impairment by alcohol or a drug in paragraph (1)(a) includes impairment by a combination of alcohol and a drug.

R.S., 1985, c. C-46, s. 253;

R.S., 1985, c. 27 (1st Supp.), s. 36, c. 32 (4th Supp.), s. 59;

2008, c. 6, s. 18.

Definitions

254 (1) In this section and sections 254.1 to 258.1,

analyst

approved container

(a) in respect of breath samples, a container of a kind that is designed to receive a sample of the breath of a person for analysis and is approved as suitable for the purposes of section 258 by order of the Attorney General of Canada, and

(b) in respect of blood samples, a container of a kind that is designed to receive a sample of the blood of a person for analysis and is approved as suitable for the purposes of section 258 by order of the Attorney General of Canada;

approved instrument

approved screening device

evaluating officer

qualified medical practitioner

qualified technician

(a) in respect of breath samples, a person designated by the Attorney General as being qualified to operate an approved instrument, and

(b) in respect of blood samples, any person or person of a class of persons designated by the Attorney General as being qualified to take samples of blood for the purposes of this section and sections 256 and 258.

Testing for presence of alcohol or a drug

(2) If a peace officer has reasonable grounds to suspect that a person has alcohol or a drug in their body and that the person has, within the preceding three hours, operated a motor vehicle or vessel, operated or assisted in the operation of an aircraft or railway equipment or had the care or control of a motor vehicle, a vessel, an aircraft or railway equipment, whether it was in motion or not, the peace officer may, by demand, require the person to comply with paragraph (a), in the case of a drug, or with either or both of paragraphs (a) and (b), in the case of alcohol:

(a) to perform forthwith physical coordination tests prescribed by regulation to enable the peace officer to determine whether a demand may be made under subsection (3) or (3.1) and, if necessary, to accompany the peace officer for that purpose; and

(b) to provide forthwith a sample of breath that, in the peace officer's opinion, will enable a proper analysis to be made by means of an approved screening device and, if necessary, to accompany the peace officer for that purpose.

Video recording

(2.1) For greater certainty, a peace officer may make a video recording of a performance of the physical coordination tests referred to in paragraph (2)(a).

Samples of breath or blood

(3) If a peace officer has reasonable grounds to believe that a person is committing, or at any time within the preceding three hours has committed, an offence under section 253 as a result of the consumption of alcohol, the peace officer may, by demand made as soon as practicable, require the person

(a) to provide, as soon as practicable,

(i) samples of breath that, in a qualified technician's opinion, will enable a proper analysis to be made to determine the concentration, if any, of alcohol in the person's blood, or

(ii) if the peace officer has reasonable grounds to believe that, because of their physical condition, the person may be incapable of providing a sample of breath or it would be impracticable to obtain a sample of breath, samples of blood that, in the opinion of the qualified medical practitioner or qualified technician taking the samples, will enable a proper analysis to be made to determine the concentration, if any, of alcohol in the person's blood; and

(b) if necessary, to accompany the peace officer for that purpose.

Evaluation

(3.1) If a peace officer has reasonable grounds to believe that a person is committing, or at any time within the preceding three hours has committed, an offence under paragraph 253(1)(a) as a result of the consumption of a drug or of a combination of alcohol and a drug, the peace officer may, by demand made as soon as practicable, require the person to submit, as soon as practicable, to an evaluation conducted by an evaluating officer to determine whether the person's ability to operate a motor vehicle, a vessel, an aircraft or railway equipment is impaired by a drug or by a combination of alcohol and a drug, and to accompany the peace officer for that purpose.

Video recording

(3.2) For greater certainty, a peace officer may make a video recording of an evaluation referred to in subsection (3.1).

Testing for presence of alcohol

(3.3) If the evaluating officer has reasonable grounds to suspect that the person has alcohol in their body and if a demand was not made under paragraph (2)(b) or subsection (3), the evaluating officer may, by demand made as soon as practicable, require the person to provide, as soon as practicable, a sample of breath that, in the evaluating officer's opinion, will enable a proper analysis to be made by means of an approved instrument.

Samples of bodily substances

(3.4) If, on completion of the evaluation, the evaluating officer has reasonable grounds to believe, based on the evaluation, that the person's ability to operate a motor vehicle, a vessel, an aircraft or railway equipment is impaired by a drug or by a combination of alcohol and a drug, the evaluating officer may, by demand made as soon as practicable, require the person to provide, as soon as practicable,

(a) a sample of either oral fluid or urine that, in the evaluating officer's opinion, will enable a proper analysis to be made to determine whether the person has a drug in their body; or

(b) samples of blood that, in the opinion of the qualified medical practitioner or qualified technician taking the samples, will enable a proper analysis to be made to determine whether the person has a drug in their body.

Condition

(4) Samples of blood may be taken from a person under subsection (3) or (3.4) only by or under the direction of a qualified medical practitioner who is satisfied that taking the samples would not endanger the person's life or health.

Failure or refusal to comply with demand

(5) Everyone commits an offence who, without reasonable excuse, fails or refuses to comply with a demand made under this section.

Only one determination of guilt

(6) A person who is convicted of an offence under subsection (5) for a failure or refusal to comply with a demand may not be convicted of another offence under that subsection in respect of the same transaction.

R.S., 1985, c. C-46, s. 254;
R.S., 1985, c. 27 (1st Supp.), s. 36, c. 1 (4th Supp.), ss. 14, 18(F), c. 32 (4th Supp.), s. 60;
1999, c. 32, s. 2(Preamble);
2008, c. 6, s. 19.

Regulations

254.1 (1) The Governor in Council may make regulations

(a) respecting the qualifications and training of evaluating officers;

(b) prescribing the physical coordination tests to be conducted under paragraph 254(2)(a); and

(c) prescribing the tests to be conducted and procedures to be followed during an evaluation under subsection 254(3.1).

Incorporated material

(2) A regulation may incorporate any material by reference either as it exists on a specified date or as amended from time to time.

Incorporated material is not a regulation

(3) For greater certainty, material does not become a regulation for the purposes of the Statutory Instruments Act

2008, c. 6, s. 20.

Punishment

255 (1) Every one who commits an offence under section 253 or 254 is guilty of an indictable offence or an offence punishable on summary conviction and is liable,

(a) whether the offence is prosecuted by indictment or punishable on summary conviction, to the following minimum punishment, namely,

(i) for a first offence, to a fine of not less than $1,000,

(ii) for a second offence, to imprisonment for not less than 30 days, and

(iii) for each subsequent offence, to imprisonment for not less than 120 days;

(b) where the offence is prosecuted by indictment, to imprisonment for a term not exceeding five years; and

(c) if the offence is punishable on summary conviction, to imprisonment for a term of not more than 18 months.

Impaired driving causing bodily harm

(2) Everyone who commits an offence under paragraph 253(1)(a) and causes bodily harm to another person as a result is guilty of an indictable offence and liable to imprisonment for a term of not more

than 10 years.
Blood alcohol level over legal limit — bodily harm
(2.1) Everyone who, while committing an offence under paragraph 253(1)(b), causes an accident resulting in bodily harm to another person is guilty of an indictable offence and liable to imprisonment for a term of not more than 10 years.
Failure or refusal to provide sample — bodily harm
(2.2) Everyone who commits an offence under subsection 254(5) and, at the time of committing the offence, knows or ought to know that their operation of the motor vehicle, vessel, aircraft or railway equipment, their assistance in the operation of the aircraft or railway equipment or their care or control of the motor vehicle, vessel, aircraft or railway equipment caused an accident resulting in bodily harm to another person is guilty of an indictable offence and liable to imprisonment for a term of not more than 10 years.
Impaired driving causing death
(3) Everyone who commits an offence under paragraph 253(1)(a) and causes the death of another person as a result is guilty of an indictable offence and liable to imprisonment for life.
Blood alcohol level over legal limit — death
(3.1) Everyone who, while committing an offence under paragraph 253(1)(b), causes an accident resulting in the death of another person is guilty of an indictable offence and liable to imprisonment for life.
Failure or refusal to provide sample — death
(3.2) Everyone who commits an offence under subsection 254(5) and, at the time of committing the offence, knows or ought to know that their operation of the motor vehicle, vessel, aircraft or railway equipment, their assistance in the operation of the aircraft or railway equipment or their care or control of the motor vehicle, vessel, aircraft or railway equipment caused an accident resulting in the death of another person, or in bodily harm to another person whose death ensues, is guilty of an indictable offence and liable to imprisonment for life.
Interpretation
(3.3) For greater certainty, everyone who is liable to the punishment described in any of subsections (2) to (3.2) is also liable to the minimum punishment described in paragraph (1)(a).
Previous convictions
(4) A person who is convicted of an offence committed under section 253 or subsection 254(5) is, for the purposes of this Act, deemed to be convicted for a second or subsequent offence, as the case may be, if they have previously been convicted of
(a) an offence committed under either of those provisions;
(b) an offence under subsection (2) or (3); or
(c) an offence under section 250, 251, 252, 253, 259 or 260 or subsection 258(4) of this Act as this Act read immediately before the coming into force of this subsection.
Conditional discharge
Notwithstanding subsection 730(1), a court may, instead of convicting a person of an offence committed under section 253, after hearing medical or other evidence, if it considers that the person is in need of curative treatment in relation to his consumption of alcohol or drugs and that it would not be contrary to the public interest, by order direct that the person be discharged under section 730 on the conditions prescribed in a probation order, including a condition respecting the person's attendance for curative treatment in relation to that consumption of alcohol or drugs.
* [Note: In force in the provinces of Nova Scotia, New Brunswick, Manitoba, Prince Edward Island, Saskatchewan and Alberta and in the Yukon Territory, the Northwest Territories and the Nunavut Territory,
R.S., 1985, c. C-46, s. 255;
R.S., 1985, c. 27 (1st Supp.), s. 36;
R.S., 1985, c. 1 (4th Supp.), s. 18(F);
1995, c. 22, s. 18;
1999, c. 32, s. 3(Preamble);

2000, c. 25, s. 2;
2008, c. 6, s. 21, c. 18, ss. 7, 45.2.
Aggravating circumstances for sentencing purposes
255.1 Without limiting the generality of section 718.2, where a court imposes a sentence for an offence committed under this Act by means of a motor vehicle, vessel or aircraft or of railway equipment, evidence that the concentration of alcohol in the blood of the offender at the time when the offence was committed exceeded one hundred and sixty milligrams of alcohol in one hundred millilitres of blood shall be deemed to be aggravating circumstances relating to the offence that the court shall consider under paragraph 718.2(a).
1999, c. 32, s. 4(Preamble).
Warrants to obtain blood samples
256 (1) Subject to subsection (2), if a justice is satisfied, on an information on oath in Form 1 or on an information on oath submitted to the justice under section 487.1 by telephone or other means of telecommunication, that there are reasonable grounds to believe that
(a) a person has, within the preceding four hours, committed, as a result of the consumption of alcohol or a drug, an offence under section 253 and the person was involved in an accident resulting in the death of another person or in bodily harm to himself or herself or to any other person, and
(b) a qualified medical practitioner is of the opinion that
(i) by reason of any physical or mental condition of the person that resulted from the consumption of alcohol or a drug, the accident or any other occurrence related to or resulting from the accident, the person is unable to consent to the taking of samples of his or her blood, and
(ii) the taking of samples of blood from the person would not endanger the life or health of the person,
the justice may issue a warrant authorizing a peace officer to require a qualified medical practitioner to take, or to cause to be taken by a qualified technician under the direction of the qualified medical practitioner, the samples of the blood of the person that in the opinion of the person taking the samples are necessary to enable a proper analysis to be made in order to determine the concentration, if any, of alcohol or drugs in the person's blood.
Form
(2) A warrant issued pursuant to subsection (1) may be in Form 5 or 5.1 varied to suit the case.
Information on oath
(3) Notwithstanding paragraphs 487.1(4)(b) and (c), an information on oath submitted by telephone or other means of telecommunication for the purposes of this section shall include, instead of the statements referred to in those paragraphs, a statement setting out the offence alleged to have been committed and identifying the person from whom blood samples are to be taken.
Duration of warrant
(4) Samples of blood may be taken from a person pursuant to a warrant issued pursuant to subsection (1) only during such time as a qualified medical practitioner is satisfied that the conditions referred to in subparagraphs (1)(b)(i) and (ii) continue to exist in respect of that person.
Copy or facsimile to person
(5) When a warrant issued under subsection (1) is executed, the peace officer shall, as soon as practicable, give a copy of it — or, in the case of a warrant issued by telephone or other means of telecommunication, a facsimile — to the person from whom the blood samples are taken.
R.S., 1985, c. C-46, s. 256;
R.S., 1985, c. 27 (1st Supp.), s. 36;
1992, c. 1, s. 58;
1994, c. 44, s. 13;
2000, c. 25, s. 3;
2008, c. 6, s. 22.
No offence committed
257 (1) No qualified medical practitioner or qualified technician is guilty of an offence only by reason of his refusal to take a sample of blood from a person for the purposes of section 254 or 256

and no qualified medical practitioner is guilty of an offence only by reason of his refusal to cause to be taken by a qualified technician under his direction a sample of blood from a person for those purposes.

No criminal or civil liability

(2) No qualified medical practitioner by whom or under whose direction a sample of blood is taken from a person under subsection 254(3) or (3.4) or section 256, and no qualified technician acting under the direction of a qualified medical practitioner, incurs any criminal or civil liability for anything necessarily done with reasonable care and skill when taking the sample.

R.S., 1985, c. C-46, s. 257;

R.S., 1985, c. 27 (1st Supp.), s. 36;

2008, c. 6, s. 23.

Proceedings under section 255

258 (1) In any proceedings under subsection 255(1) in respect of an offence committed under section 253 or subsection 254(5) or in any proceedings under any of subsections 255(2) to (3.2),

(a) where it is proved that the accused occupied the seat or position ordinarily occupied by a person who operates a motor vehicle, vessel or aircraft or any railway equipment or who assists in the operation of an aircraft or of railway equipment, the accused shall be deemed to have had the care or control of the vehicle, vessel, aircraft or railway equipment, as the case may be, unless the accused establishes that the accused did not occupy that seat or position for the purpose of setting the vehicle, vessel, aircraft or railway equipment in motion or assisting in the operation of the aircraft or railway equipment, as the case may be;

(b) the result of an analysis of a sample of the accused's breath, blood, urine or other bodily substance — other than a sample taken under subsection 254(3), (3.3) or (3.4) — may be admitted in evidence even if the accused was not warned before they gave the sample that they need not give the sample or that the result of the analysis of the sample might be used in evidence;

(c) where samples of the breath of the accused have been taken pursuant to a demand made under subsection 254(3), if

(i) [Repealed before coming into force, 2008, c. 20, s. 3]

(ii) each sample was taken as soon as practicable after the time when the offence was alleged to have been committed and, in the case of the first sample, not later than two hours after that time, with an interval of at least fifteen minutes between the times when the samples were taken,

(iii) each sample was received from the accused directly into an approved container or into an approved instrument operated by a qualified technician, and

(iv) an analysis of each sample was made by means of an approved instrument operated by a qualified technician,

evidence of the results of the analyses so made is conclusive proof that the concentration of alcohol in the accused's blood both at the time when the analyses were made and at the time when the offence was alleged to have been committed was, if the results of the analyses are the same, the concentration determined by the analyses and, if the results of the analyses are different, the lowest of the concentrations determined by the analyses, in the absence of evidence tending to show all of the following three things — that the approved instrument was malfunctioning or was operated improperly, that the malfunction or improper operation resulted in the determination that the concentration of alcohol in the accused's blood exceeded 80 mg of alcohol in 100 mL of blood, and that the concentration of alcohol in the accused's blood would not in fact have exceeded 80 mg of alcohol in 100 mL of blood at the time when the offence was alleged to have been committed;

(d) if a sample of the accused's blood has been taken under subsection 254(3) or section 256 or with the accused's consent and if

(i) at the time the sample was taken, the person taking the sample took an additional sample of the blood of the accused and one of the samples was retained to permit an analysis of it to be made by or on behalf of the accused and, in the case where the accused makes a request within six months from the taking of the samples, one of the samples was ordered to be released under subsection (4),

(ii) both samples referred to in subparagraph (i) were taken as soon as practicable and in any event

not later than two hours after the time when the offence was alleged to have been committed,
(iii) both samples referred to in subparagraph (i) were taken by a qualified medical practitioner or a qualified technician under the direction of a qualified medical practitioner,
(iv) both samples referred to in subparagraph (i) were received from the accused directly into, or placed directly into, approved containers that were subsequently sealed, and
(v) an analysis was made by an analyst of at least one of the samples,
evidence of the result of the analysis is conclusive proof that the concentration of alcohol in the accused's blood both at the time when the samples were taken and at the time when the offence was alleged to have been committed was the concentration determined by the analysis or, if more than one sample was analyzed and the results of the analyses are the same, the concentration determined by the analyses and, if the results of the analyses are different, the lowest of the concentrations determined by the analyses, in the absence of evidence tending to show all of the following three things — that the analysis was performed improperly, that the improper performance resulted in the determination that the concentration of alcohol in the accused's blood exceeded 80 mg of alcohol in 100 mL of blood, and that the concentration of alcohol in the accused's blood would not in fact have exceeded 80 mg of alcohol in 100 mL of blood at the time when the offence was alleged to have been committed;
(d.01) for greater certainty, evidence tending to show that an approved instrument was malfunctioning or was operated improperly, or that an analysis of a sample of the accused's blood was performed improperly, does not include evidence of
(i) the amount of alcohol that the accused consumed,
(ii) the rate at which the alcohol that the accused consumed would have been absorbed and eliminated by the accused's body, or
(iii) a calculation based on that evidence of what the concentration of alcohol in the accused's blood would have been at the time when the offence was alleged to have been committed;
(d.1) if samples of the accused's breath or a sample of the accused's blood have been taken as described in paragraph (c) or (d) under the conditions described in that paragraph and the results of the analyses show a concentration of alcohol in blood exceeding 80 mg of alcohol in 100 mL of blood, evidence of the results of the analyses is proof that the concentration of alcohol in the accused's blood at the time when the offence was alleged to have been committed exceeded 80 mg of alcohol in 100 mL of blood, in the absence of evidence tending to show that the accused's consumption of alcohol was consistent with both
(i) a concentration of alcohol in the accused's blood that did not exceed 80 mg of alcohol in 100 mL of blood at the time when the offence was alleged to have been committed, and
(ii) the concentration of alcohol in the accused's blood as determined under paragraph (c) or (d), as the case may be, at the time when the sample or samples were taken;
(e) a certificate of an analyst stating that the analyst has made an analysis of a sample of the blood, urine, breath or other bodily substance of the accused and stating the result of that analysis is evidence of the facts alleged in the certificate without proof of the signature or the official character of the person appearing to have signed the certificate;
(f) a certificate of an analyst stating that the analyst has made an analysis of a sample of an alcohol standard that is identified in the certificate and intended for use with an approved instrument and that the sample of the standard analyzed by the analyst was found to be suitable for use with an approved instrument, is evidence that the alcohol standard so identified is suitable for use with an approved instrument without proof of the signature or the official character of the person appearing to have signed the certificate;
(f.1) the document printed out from an approved instrument and signed by a qualified technician who certifies it to be the printout produced by the approved instrument when it made the analysis of a sample of the accused's breath is evidence of the facts alleged in the document without proof of the signature or official character of the person appearing to have signed it;
(g) where samples of the breath of the accused have been taken pursuant to a demand made under subsection 254(3), a certificate of a qualified technician stating

(i) that the analysis of each of the samples has been made by means of an approved instrument operated by the technician and ascertained by the technician to be in proper working order by means of an alcohol standard, identified in the certificate, that is suitable for use with an approved instrument,
(ii) the results of the analyses so made, and
(iii) if the samples were taken by the technician,
(A) [Repealed before coming into force, 2008, c. 20, s. 3]
(B) the time when and place where each sample and any specimen described in clause (A) was taken, and
(C) that each sample was received from the accused directly into an approved container or into an approved instrument operated by the technician,
is evidence of the facts alleged in the certificate without proof of the signature or the official character of the person appearing to have signed the certificate;
(h) if a sample of the accused's blood has been taken under subsection 254(3) or (3.4) or section 256 or with the accused's consent,
(i) a certificate of a qualified medical practitioner stating that
(A) they took the sample and before the sample was taken they were of the opinion that taking it would not endanger the accused's life or health and, in the case of a demand made under section 256, that by reason of any physical or mental condition of the accused that resulted from the consumption of alcohol or a drug, the accident or any other occurrence related to or resulting from the accident, the accused was unable to consent to the taking of the sample,
(B) at the time the sample was taken, an additional sample of the blood of the accused was taken to permit analysis of one of the samples to be made by or on behalf of the accused,
(C) the time when and place where both samples referred to in clause (B) were taken, and
(D) both samples referred to in clause (B) were received from the accused directly into, or placed directly into, approved containers that were subsequently sealed and that are identified in the certificate,
(ii) a certificate of a qualified medical practitioner stating that the medical practitioner caused the sample to be taken by a qualified technician under his direction and that before the sample was taken the qualified medical practitioner was of the opinion referred to in clause (i)(A), or
(iii) a certificate of a qualified technician stating that the technician took the sample and the facts referred to in clauses (i)(B) to (D)
is evidence of the facts alleged in the certificate without proof of the signature or official character of the person appearing to have signed the certificate; and
(i) a certificate of an analyst stating that the analyst has made an analysis of a sample of the blood of the accused that was contained in a sealed approved container identified in the certificate, the date on which and place where the sample was analyzed and the result of that analysis is evidence of the facts alleged in the certificate without proof of the signature or official character of the person appearing to have signed it.

Evidence of failure to give sample
(2) Unless a person is required to give a sample of a bodily substance under paragraph 254(2)(b) or subsection 254(3), (3.3) or (3.4), evidence that they failed or refused to give a sample for analysis for the purposes of this section or that a sample was not taken is not admissible and the failure, refusal or fact that a sample was not taken shall not be the subject of comment by any person in the proceedings.

Evidence of failure to comply with demand
(3) In any proceedings under subsection 255(1) in respect of an offence committed under paragraph 253(1)(a) or in any proceedings under subsection 255(2) or (3), evidence that the accused, without reasonable excuse, failed or refused to comply with a demand made under section 254 is admissible and the court may draw an inference adverse to the accused from that evidence.

Release of sample for analysis
(4) If, at the time a sample of an accused's blood is taken, an additional sample is taken and retained,

a judge of a superior court of criminal jurisdiction or a court of criminal jurisdiction shall, on the summary application of the accused made within six months after the day on which the samples were taken, order the release of one of the samples for the purpose of examination or analysis, subject to any terms that appear to be necessary or desirable to ensure that the sample is safeguarded and preserved for use in any proceedings in respect of which it was taken.

Testing of blood for concentration of a drug

(5) A sample of an accused's blood taken under subsection 254(3) or section 256 or with the accused's consent for the purpose of analysis to determine the concentration, if any, of alcohol in the blood may be tested to determine the concentration, if any, of a drug in the blood.

Attendance and right to cross-examine

(6) A party against whom a certificate described in paragraph (1)(e), (f), (f.1), (g), (h) or (i) is produced may, with leave of the court, require the attendance of the qualified medical practitioner, analyst or qualified technician, as the case may be, for the purposes of cross-examination.

Notice of intention to produce certificate

(7) No certificate shall be received in evidence pursuant to paragraph (1)(e), (f), (g), (h) or (i) unless the party intending to produce it has, before the trial, given to the other party reasonable notice of his intention and a copy of the certificate.

R.S., 1985, c. C-46, s. 258;
R.S., 1985, c. 27 (1st Supp.), s. 36, c. 32 (4th Supp.), s. 61;
1992, c. 1, s. 60(F);
1994, c. 44, s. 14(E);
1997, c. 18, s. 10;
2008, c. 6, s. 24.

Unauthorized use of bodily substance

258.1 (1) Subject to subsections 258(4) and (5) and subsection (3), no person shall use a bodily substance taken under paragraph 254(2)(b), subsection 254(3), (3.3) or (3.4) or section 256 or with the consent of the person from whom it was taken after a request by a peace officer or medical samples that are provided by consent and subsequently seized under a warrant, except for the purpose of an analysis that is referred to in that provision or for which the consent is given.

Unauthorized use or disclosure of results

(2) Subject to subsections (3) and (4), no person shall use, disclose or allow the disclosure of the results of physical coordination tests under paragraph 254(2)(a), the results of an evaluation under subsection 254(3.1), the results of the analysis of a bodily substance taken under paragraph 254(2)(b), subsection 254(3), (3.3) or (3.4) or section 256 or with the consent of the person from whom it was taken after a request by a peace officer, or the results of the analysis of medical samples that are provided by consent and subsequently seized under a warrant, except

(a) in the course of an investigation of, or in a proceeding for, an offence under any of sections 220, 221, 236 and 249 to 255, an offence under Part I of the
Aeronautics Act
Railway Safety Act

(b) for the purpose of the administration or enforcement of the law of a province.

Exception

(3) Subsections (1) and (2) do not apply to persons who for medical purposes use samples or use or disclose the results of tests, taken for medical purposes, that are subsequently seized under a warrant.

Exception

(4) The results of physical coordination tests, an evaluation or an analysis referred to in subsection (2) may be disclosed to the person to whom they relate, and may be disclosed to any other person if the results are made anonymous and the disclosure is made for statistical or other research purposes.

Offence

(5) Every person who contravenes subsection (1) or (2) is guilty of an offence punishable on summary conviction.

2008, c. 6, s. 25.

Mandatory order of prohibition
259 (1) When an offender is convicted of an offence committed under section 253 or 254 or this section or discharged under section 730 of an offence committed under section 253 and, at the time the offence was committed or, in the case of an offence committed under section 254, within the three hours preceding that time, was operating or had the care or control of a motor vehicle, vessel or aircraft or of railway equipment or was assisting in the operation of an aircraft or of railway equipment, the court that sentences the offender shall, in addition to any other punishment that may be imposed for that offence, make an order prohibiting the offender from operating a motor vehicle on any street, road, highway or other public place, or from operating a vessel or an aircraft or railway equipment, as the case may be,
(a) for a first offence, during a period of not more than three years plus any period to which the offender is sentenced to imprisonment, and not less than one year;
(b) for a second offence, during a period of not more than five years plus any period to which the offender is sentenced to imprisonment, and not less than two years; and
(c) for each subsequent offence, during a period of not less than three years plus any period to which the offender is sentenced to imprisonment.

Alcohol ignition interlock device program
(1.1) If the offender is registered in an alcohol ignition interlock device program established under the law of the province in which the offender resides and complies with the conditions of the program, the offender may, subject to subsection (1.2), operate a motor vehicle equipped with an alcohol ignition interlock device during the prohibition period, unless the court orders otherwise.

Minimum absolute prohibition period
(1.2) An offender who is registered in a program referred to in subsection (1.1) may not operate a motor vehicle equipped with an alcohol ignition interlock device until
(a) the expiry of a period of
(i) for a first offence, 3 months after the day on which sentence is imposed,
(ii) for a second offence, 6 months after the day on which sentence is imposed, and
(iii) for each subsequent offence, 12 months after the day on which sentence is imposed; or
(b) the expiry of any period that may be fixed by order of the court that is greater than a period referred to in paragraph (a).

(1.3) and (1.4) Discretionary order of prohibition
(2) If an offender is convicted or discharged under section 730 of an offence under section 220, 221, 236, 249, 249.1, 250, 251 or 252 or any of subsections 255(2) to (3.2) committed by means of a motor vehicle, a vessel, an aircraft or railway equipment, the court that sentences the offender may, in addition to any other punishment that may be imposed for that offence, make an order prohibiting the offender from operating a motor vehicle on any street, road, highway or other public place, or from operating a vessel, an aircraft or railway equipment, as the case may be,
(a) during any period that the court considers proper, if the offender is sentenced to imprisonment for life in respect of that offence;
(a.1) during any period that the court considers proper, plus any period to which the offender is sentenced to imprisonment, if the offender is liable to imprisonment for life in respect of that offence and if the sentence imposed is other than imprisonment for life;
(b) during any period not exceeding ten years plus any period to which the offender is sentenced to imprisonment, if the offender is liable to imprisonment for more than five years but less than life in respect of that offence; and
(c) during any period not exceeding three years plus any period to which the offender is sentenced to imprisonment, in any other case.

Consecutive prohibition periods
(2.1) The court may, when it makes an order under this section prohibiting the operation of a motor vehicle, a vessel, an aircraft or railway equipment, as the case may be, order that the time served under that order be served consecutively to the time served under any other order made under this section that prohibits the operation of the same means of transport and that is in force.

Saving
(3) No order made under subsection (1) or (2) shall operate to prevent any person from acting as master, mate or engineer of a vessel that is required to carry officers holding certificates as master, mate or engineer.
Mandatory order of prohibition — street racing
(3.1) When an offender is convicted or discharged under section 730 of an offence committed under subsection 249.4(1), the court that sentences the offender shall, in addition to any other punishment that may be imposed for that offence, make an order prohibiting the offender from operating a motor vehicle on any street, road, highway or other public place
(a) for a first offence, during a period of not more than three years plus any period to which the offender is sentenced to imprisonment, and not less than one year;
(b) for a second offence, during a period of not more than five years plus any period to which the offender is sentenced to imprisonment, and not less than two years; and
(c) for each subsequent offence, during a period of not less than three years plus any period to which the offender is sentenced to imprisonment.
Mandatory order of prohibition — bodily harm
(3.2) When an offender is convicted or discharged under section 730 of an offence committed under section 249.3 or subsection 249.4(3), the court that sentences the offender shall, in addition to any other punishment that may be imposed for that offence, make an order prohibiting the offender from operating a motor vehicle on any street, road, highway or other public place
(a) for a first offence, during a period of not more than ten years plus any period to which the offender is sentenced to imprisonment, and not less than one year;
(b) for a second offence, during a period of not more than ten years plus any period to which the offender is sentenced to imprisonment, and not less than two years; and
(c) for each subsequent offence, during a period of not less than three years plus any period to which the offender is sentenced to imprisonment.
Mandatory order of prohibition — death
(3.3) When an offender is convicted or discharged under section 730 of a first offence committed under section 249.2 or subsection 249.4(4), the court that sentences the offender shall, in addition to any other punishment that may be imposed for that offence, make an order prohibiting the offender from operating a motor vehicle on any street, road, highway or other public place
(a) for an offence under section 249.2, during a period of not less than one year plus any period to which the offender is sentenced to imprisonment; and
(b) for an offence under subsection 249.4(4), during a period of not more than ten years plus any period to which the offender is sentenced to imprisonment, and not less than one year.
Mandatory life prohibition
(3.4) When an offender is convicted or discharged under section 730 of an offence committed under section 249.2 or 249.3 or subsection 249.4(3) or (4), the offender has previously been convicted or discharged under section 730 of one of those offences and at least one of the convictions or discharges is under section 249.2 or subsection 249.4(4), the court that sentences the offender shall make an order prohibiting the offender from operating a motor vehicle on any street, road, highway or other public place for life.
Operation while disqualified
(4) Every offender who operates a motor vehicle, vessel or aircraft or any railway equipment in Canada while disqualified from doing so, other than an offender who is registered in an alcohol ignition interlock device program established under the law of the province in which the offender resides and who complies with the conditions of the program,
(a) is guilty of an indictable offence and liable to imprisonment for a term not exceeding five years; or
(b) is guilty of an offence punishable on summary conviction.
Definition of
disqualification

(5) For the purposes of this section,
disqualification
(a) a prohibition from operating a motor vehicle, vessel or aircraft or any railway equipment ordered pursuant to any of subsections (1), (2) and (3.1) to (3.4); or
(b) a disqualification or any other form of legal restriction of the right or privilege to operate a motor vehicle, vessel or aircraft imposed
(i) in the case of a motor vehicle, under the law of a province, or
(ii) in the case of a vessel or an aircraft, under an Act of Parliament,
in respect of a conviction or discharge under section 730 of any offence referred to in any of subsections (1), (2) and (3.1) to (3.4).
R.S., 1985, c. C-46, s. 259;
R.S., 1985, c. 27 (1st Supp.), s. 36, c. 1 (4th Supp.), s. 18(F), c. 32 (4th Supp.), s. 62;
1995, c. 22, ss. 10, 18;
1997, c. 18, s. 11;
1999, c. 32, s. 5(Preamble);
2000, c. 2, s. 2;
2001, c. 37, s. 1;
2006, c. 14, s. 3;
2008, c. 6, s. 26, c. 18, s. 8.

Proceedings on making of prohibition order
260 (1) If a court makes a prohibition order under section 259 in relation to an offender, it shall cause
(a) the order to be read by or to the offender;
(b) a copy of the order to be given to the offender; and
(c) the offender to be informed of subsection 259(4).

Endorsement by offender
(2) After subsection (1) has been complied with in relation to an offender who is bound by an order referred to in that subsection, the offender shall endorse the order, acknowledging receipt of a copy thereof and that the order has been explained to him.

Validity of order not affected
(3) The failure of an offender to endorse an order pursuant to subsection (2) does not affect the validity of the order.

Onus
(4) In the absence of evidence to the contrary, where it is proved that a disqualification referred to in paragraph 259(5)(b) has been imposed on a person and that notice of the disqualification has been mailed by registered or certified mail to that person, that person shall, after five days following the mailing of the notice, be deemed to have received the notice and to have knowledge of the disqualification, of the date of its commencement and of its duration.

Certificate admissible in evidence
(5) In proceedings under section 259, a certificate setting out with reasonable particularity that a person is disqualified from
(a) driving a motor vehicle in a province, purporting to be signed by the registrar of motor vehicles for that province, or
(b) operating a vessel or aircraft, purporting to be signed by the Minister of Transport or any person authorized by the Minister of Transport for that purpose
is evidence of the facts alleged therein without proof of the signature or official character of the person by whom it purports to be signed.

Notice to accused
(6) Subsection (5) does not apply in any proceedings unless at least seven days notice in writing is given to the accused that it is intended to tender the certificate in evidence.

Definition of
registrar of motor vehicles
(7) In subsection (5),

registrar of motor vehicles
R.S., 1985, c. C-46, s. 260;
R.S., 1985, c. 27 (1st Supp.), s. 36, c. 1 (4th Supp.), s. 18(F);
2006, c. 14, s. 4.
Stay of order pending appeal
261 (1) Subject to subsection (1.1), if an appeal is taken against a conviction or discharge under section 730 for an offence committed under any of sections 220, 221, 236, 249 to 255 and 259, a judge of the court being appealed to may direct that any prohibition order under section 259 arising out of the conviction or discharge shall, on any conditions that the judge or court imposes, be stayed pending the final disposition of the appeal or until otherwise ordered by that court.
Appeals to Supreme Court of Canada
(1.1) In the case of an appeal to the Supreme Court of Canada, the direction referred to in subsection (1) may be made only by a judge of the court being appealed from and not by a judge of the Supreme Court of Canada.
Effect of conditions
(2) If conditions are imposed under a direction made under subsection (1) or (1.1) that a prohibition order be stayed, the direction shall not operate to decrease the period of prohibition provided in the order.
R.S., 1985, c. C-46, s. 261;
R.S., 1985, c. 27 (1st Supp.), s. 36, c. 1 (4th Supp.), s. 18(F);
1994, c. 44, ss. 15, 103;
1995, c. 22, s. 10;
1997, c. 18, ss. 12, 141;
2006, c. 14, s. 5;
2008, c. 6, s. 27.
Impeding attempt to save life
262 Every one who
(a) prevents or impedes or attempts to prevent or impede any person who is attempting to save his own life, or
(b) without reasonable cause prevents or impedes or attempts to prevent or impede any person who is attempting to save the life of another person,
is guilty of an indictable offence and liable to imprisonment for a term not exceeding ten years.
R.S., c. C-34, s. 241.
Duty to safeguard opening in ice
263 (1) Every one who makes or causes to be made an opening in ice that is open to or frequented by the public is under a legal duty to guard it in a manner that is adequate to prevent persons from falling in by accident and is adequate to warn them that the opening exists.
Excavation on land
(2) Every one who leaves an excavation on land that he owns or of which he has charge or supervision is under a legal duty to guard it in a manner that is adequate to prevent persons from falling in by accident and is adequate to warn them that the excavation exists.
Offences
(3) Every one who fails to perform a duty imposed by subsection (1) or (2) is guilty of
(a) manslaughter, if the death of any person results therefrom;
(b) an offence under section 269, if bodily harm to any person results therefrom; or
(c) an offence punishable on summary conviction.
R.S., c. C-34, s. 242;
1980-81-82-83, c. 125, s. 18.
Criminal harassment
264 (1) No person shall, without lawful authority and knowing that another person is harassed or recklessly as to whether the other person is harassed, engage in conduct referred to in subsection (2) that causes that other person reasonably, in all the circumstances, to fear for their safety or the safety

of anyone known to them.
Prohibited conduct
(2) The conduct mentioned in subsection (1) consists of
(a) repeatedly following from place to place the other person or anyone known to them;
(b) repeatedly communicating with, either directly or indirectly, the other person or anyone known to them;
(c) besetting or watching the dwelling-house, or place where the other person, or anyone known to them, resides, works, carries on business or happens to be; or
(d) engaging in threatening conduct directed at the other person or any member of their family.
Punishment
(3) Every person who contravenes this section is guilty of
(a) an indictable offence and is liable to imprisonment for a term not exceeding ten years; or
(b) an offence punishable on summary conviction.
Factors to be considered
(4) Where a person is convicted of an offence under this section, the court imposing the sentence on the person shall consider as an aggravating factor that, at the time the offence was committed, the person contravened
(a) the terms or conditions of an order made pursuant to section 161 or a recognizance entered into pursuant to section 810, 810.1 or 810.2; or
(b) the terms or conditions of any other order or recognizance made or entered into under the common law or a provision of this or any other Act of Parliament or of a province that is similar in effect to an order or recognizance referred to in paragraph (a).
Reasons
(5) Where the court is satisfied of the existence of an aggravating factor referred to in subsection (4), but decides not to give effect to it for sentencing purposes, the court shall give reasons for its decision.
R.S., 1985, c. C-46, s. 264;
R.S., 1985, c. 27 (1st Supp.), s. 37;
1993, c. 45, s. 2;
1997, c. 16, s. 4, c. 17, s. 9;
2002, c. 13, s. 10.

Assaults

Uttering threats
264.1 (1) Every one commits an offence who, in any manner, knowingly utters, conveys or causes any person to receive a threat
(a) to cause death or bodily harm to any person;
(b) to burn, destroy or damage real or personal property; or
(c) to kill, poison or injure an animal or bird that is the property of any person.
Punishment
(2) Every one who commits an offence under paragraph (1)(a) is guilty of
(a) an indictable offence and liable to imprisonment for a term not exceeding five years; or
(b) an offence punishable on summary conviction and liable to imprisonment for a term not exceeding eighteen months.
Idem
(3) Every one who commits an offence under paragraph (1)(b) or (c)
(a) is guilty of an indictable offence and liable to imprisonment for a term not exceeding two years; or
(b) is guilty of an offence punishable on summary conviction.
R.S., 1985, c. 27 (1st Supp.), s. 38;
1994, c. 44, s. 16.

Assault
265 (1) A person commits an assault when
(a) without the consent of another person, he applies force intentionally to that other person, directly or indirectly;
(b) he attempts or threatens, by an act or a gesture, to apply force to another person, if he has, or causes that other person to believe on reasonable grounds that he has, present ability to effect his purpose; or
(c) while openly wearing or carrying a weapon or an imitation thereof, he accosts or impedes another person or begs.
Application
(2) This section applies to all forms of assault, including sexual assault, sexual assault with a weapon, threats to a third party or causing bodily harm and aggravated sexual assault.
Consent
(3) For the purposes of this section, no consent is obtained where the complainant submits or does not resist by reason of
(a) the application of force to the complainant or to a person other than the complainant;
(b) threats or fear of the application of force to the complainant or to a person other than the complainant;
(c) fraud; or
(d) the exercise of authority.
Accused's belief as to consent
(4) Where an accused alleges that he believed that the complainant consented to the conduct that is the subject-matter of the charge, a judge, if satisfied that there is sufficient evidence and that, if believed by the jury, the evidence would constitute a defence, shall instruct the jury, when reviewing all the evidence relating to the determination of the honesty of the accused's belief, to consider the presence or absence of reasonable grounds for that belief.
R.S., c. C-34, s. 244;
1974-75-76, c. 93, s. 21;
1980-81-82-83, c. 125, s. 19.
Assault
266 Every one who commits an assault is guilty of
(a) an indictable offence and is liable to imprisonment for a term not exceeding five years; or
(b) an offence punishable on summary conviction.
R.S., c. C-34, s. 245;
1972, c. 13, s. 21;
1974-75-76, c. 93, s. 22;
1980-81-82-83, c. 125, s. 19.
Assault with a weapon or causing bodily harm
267 Every one who, in committing an assault,
(a) carries, uses or threatens to use a weapon or an imitation thereof, or
(b) causes bodily harm to the complainant,
is guilty of an indictable offence and liable to imprisonment for a term not exceeding ten years or an offence punishable on summary conviction and liable to imprisonment for a term not exceeding eighteen months.
R.S., 1985, c. C-46, s. 267;
1994, c. 44, s. 17.
Aggravated assault
268 (1) Every one commits an aggravated assault who wounds, maims, disfigures or endangers the life of the complainant.
Punishment
(2) Every one who commits an aggravated assault is guilty of an indictable offence and liable to imprisonment for a term not exceeding fourteen years.

Excision

(3) For greater certainty, in this section, "wounds" or "maims" includes to excise, infibulate or mutilate, in whole or in part, the labia majora, labia minora or clitoris of a person, except where
(a) a surgical procedure is performed, by a person duly qualified by provincial law to practise medicine, for the benefit of the physical health of the person or for the purpose of that person having normal reproductive functions or normal sexual appearance or function; or
(b) the person is at least eighteen years of age and there is no resulting bodily harm.

Consent

(4) For the purposes of this section and section 265, no consent to the excision, infibulation or mutilation, in whole or in part, of the labia majora, labia minora or clitoris of a person is valid, except in the cases described in paragraphs (3)(a) and (b).
R.S., 1985, c. C-46, s. 268;
1997, c. 16, s. 5.

Unlawfully causing bodily harm

269 Every one who unlawfully causes bodily harm to any person is guilty of
(a) an indictable offence and liable to imprisonment for a term not exceeding ten years; or
(b) an offence punishable on summary conviction and liable to imprisonment for a term not exceeding eighteen months.
R.S., 1985, c. C-46, s. 269;
1994, c. 44, s. 18.

Aggravating circumstance — assault against a public transit operator

269.01 (1) When a court imposes a sentence for an offence referred to in paragraph 264.1(1)(a) or any of sections 266 to 269, it shall consider as an aggravating circumstance the fact that the victim of the offence was, at the time of the commission of the offence, a public transit operator engaged in the performance of his or her duty.

Definitions

(2) The following definitions apply in this section.
public transit operator
vehicle
2015, c. 1, s. 1.

Torture

269.1 (1) Every official, or every person acting at the instigation of or with the consent or acquiescence of an official, who inflicts torture on any other person is guilty of an indictable offence and liable to imprisonment for a term not exceeding fourteen years.

Definitions

(2) For the purposes of this section,
official
(a) a peace officer,
(b) a public officer,
(c) a member of the Canadian Forces, or
(d) any person who may exercise powers, pursuant to a law in force in a foreign state, that would, in Canada, be exercised by a person referred to in paragraph (a), (b), or (c),
whether the person exercises powers in Canada or outside Canada;
torture
(a) for a purpose including
(i) obtaining from the person or from a third person information or a statement,
(ii) punishing the person for an act that the person or a third person has committed or is suspected of having committed, and
(iii) intimidating or coercing the person or a third person, or
(b) for any reason based on discrimination of any kind,
but does not include any act or omission arising only from, inherent in or incidental to lawful sanctions.

No defence

(3) It is no defence to a charge under this section that the accused was ordered by a superior or a public authority to perform the act or omission that forms the subject-matter of the charge or that the act or omission is alleged to have been justified by exceptional circumstances, including a state of war, a threat of war, internal political instability or any other public emergency.

Evidence

(4) In any proceedings over which Parliament has jurisdiction, any statement obtained as a result of the commission of an offence under this section is inadmissible in evidence, except as evidence that the statement was so obtained.

R.S., 1985, c. 10 (3rd Supp.), s. 2.

Assaulting a peace officer

270 (1) Every one commits an offence who

(a) assaults a public officer or peace officer engaged in the execution of his duty or a person acting in aid of such an officer;

(b) assaults a person with intent to resist or prevent the lawful arrest or detention of himself or another person; or

(c) assaults a person

(i) who is engaged in the lawful execution of a process against lands or goods or in making a lawful distress or seizure, or

(ii) with intent to rescue anything taken under lawful process, distress or seizure.

Punishment

(2) Every one who commits an offence under subsection (1) is guilty of

(a) an indictable offence and is liable to imprisonment for a term not exceeding five years; or

(b) an offence punishable on summary conviction.

R.S., c. C-34, s. 246;

1972, c. 13, s. 22;

1980-81-82-83, c. 125, s. 19.

Assaulting peace officer with weapon or causing bodily harm

270.01 (1) Everyone commits an offence who, in committing an assault referred to in section 270,

(a) carries, uses or threatens to use a weapon or an imitation of one; or

(b) causes bodily harm to the complainant.

Punishment

(2) Everyone who commits an offence under subsection (1) is guilty of

(a) an indictable offence and liable to imprisonment for a term of not more than 10 years; or

(b) an offence punishable on summary conviction and liable to imprisonment for a term of not more than 18 months.

2009, c. 22, s. 9.

Aggravated assault of peace officer

270.02 Everyone who, in committing an assault referred to in section 270, wounds, maims, disfigures or endangers the life of the complainant is guilty of an indictable offence and liable to imprisonment for a term of not more than 14 years.

2009, c. 22, s. 9.

Sentences to be served consecutively

270.03 A sentence imposed on a person for an offence under subsection 270(1) or 270.01(1) or section 270.02 committed against a law enforcement officer, as defined in subsection 445.01(4), shall be served consecutively to any other punishment imposed on the person for an offence arising out of the same event or series of events.

2015, c. 34, s. 2.

Disarming a peace officer

270.1 (1) Every one commits an offence who, without the consent of a peace officer, takes or attempts to take a weapon that is in the possession of the peace officer when the peace officer is engaged in the execution of his or her duty.

Definition of
(2) For the purpose of subsection (1),
weapon
Punishment
(3) Every one who commits an offence under subsection (1) is guilty of
(a) an indictable offence and liable to imprisonment for a term of not more than five years; or
(b) an offence punishable on summary conviction and liable to imprisonment for a term of not more than eighteen months.
2002, c. 13, s. 11.
Sexual assault
271 Everyone who commits a sexual assault is guilty of
(a) an indictable offence and is liable to imprisonment for a term of not more than 10 years or, if the complainant is under the age of 16 years, to imprisonment for a term of not more than 14 years and to a minimum punishment of imprisonment for a term of one year; or
(b) an offence punishable on summary conviction and is liable to imprisonment for a term of not more than 18 months or, if the complainant is under the age of 16 years, to imprisonment for a term of not more than two years less a day and to a minimum punishment of imprisonment for a term of six months.
R.S., 1985, c. C-46, s. 271;
R.S., 1985, c. 19 (3rd Supp.), s. 10;
1994, c. 44, s. 19;
2012, c. 1, s. 25;
2015, c. 23, s. 14.
Sexual assault with a weapon, threats to a third party or causing bodily harm
272 (1) Every person commits an offence who, in committing a sexual assault,
(a) carries, uses or threatens to use a weapon or an imitation of a weapon;
(b) threatens to cause bodily harm to a person other than the complainant;
(c) causes bodily harm to the complainant; or
(d) is a party to the offence with any other person.
Punishment
(2) Every person who commits an offence under subsection (1) is guilty of an indictable offence and liable
(a) if a restricted firearm or prohibited firearm is used in the commission of the offence or if any firearm is used in the commission of the offence and the offence is committed for the benefit of, at the direction of, or in association with, a criminal organization, to imprisonment for a term not exceeding 14 years and to a minimum punishment of imprisonment for a term of
(i) in the case of a first offence, five years, and
(ii) in the case of a second or subsequent offence, seven years;
(a.1) in any other case where a firearm is used in the commission of the offence, to imprisonment for a term not exceeding 14 years and to a minimum punishment of imprisonment for a term of four years; and
(a.2) if the complainant is under the age of 16 years, to imprisonment for life and to a minimum punishment of imprisonment for a term of five years; and
(b) in any other case, to imprisonment for a term not exceeding fourteen years.
Subsequent offences
(3) In determining, for the purpose of paragraph (2)(a), whether a convicted person has committed a second or subsequent offence, if the person was earlier convicted of any of the following offences, that offence is to be considered as an earlier offence:
(a) an offence under this section;
(b) an offence under subsection 85(1) or (2) or section 244 or 244.2; or
(c) an offence under section 220, 236, 239 or 273, subsection 279(1) or section 279.1, 344 or 346 if a firearm was used in the commission of the offence.

However, an earlier offence shall not be taken into account if 10 years have elapsed between the day on which the person was convicted of the earlier offence and the day on which the person was convicted of the offence for which sentence is being imposed, not taking into account any time in custody.

Sequence of convictions only

(4) For the purposes of subsection (3), the only question to be considered is the sequence of convictions and no consideration shall be given to the sequence of commission of offences or whether any offence occurred before or after any conviction.

R.S., 1985, c. C-46, s. 272;
1995, c. 39, s. 145;
2008, c. 6, s. 28;
2009, c. 22, s. 10;
2012, c. 1, s. 26;
2015, c. 23, s. 15.

Aggravated sexual assault

273 (1) Every one commits an aggravated sexual assault who, in committing a sexual assault, wounds, maims, disfigures or endangers the life of the complainant.

Aggravated sexual assault

(2) Every person who commits an aggravated sexual assault is guilty of an indictable offence and liable
(a) if a restricted firearm or prohibited firearm is used in the commission of the offence or if any firearm is used in the commission of the offence and the offence is committed for the benefit of, at the direction of, or in association with, a criminal organization, to imprisonment for life and to a minimum punishment of imprisonment for a term of
(i) in the case of a first offence, five years, and
(ii) in the case of a second or subsequent offence, seven years;
(a.1) in any other case where a firearm is used in the commission of the offence, to imprisonment for life and to a minimum punishment of imprisonment for a term of four years; and
(a.2) if the complainant is under the age of 16 years, to imprisonment for life and to a minimum punishment of imprisonment for a term of five years; and
(b) in any other case, to imprisonment for life.

Subsequent offences

(3) In determining, for the purpose of paragraph (2)(a), whether a convicted person has committed a second or subsequent offence, if the person was earlier convicted of any of the following offences, that offence is to be considered as an earlier offence:
(a) an offence under this section;
(b) an offence under subsection 85(1) or (2) or section 244 or 244.2; or
(c) an offence under section 220, 236, 239 or 272, subsection 279(1) or section 279.1, 344 or 346 if a firearm was used in the commission of the offence.

However, an earlier offence shall not be taken into account if 10 years have elapsed between the day on which the person was convicted of the earlier offence and the day on which the person was convicted of the offence for which sentence is being imposed, not taking into account any time in custody.

Sequence of convictions only

(4) For the purposes of subsection (3), the only question to be considered is the sequence of convictions and no consideration shall be given to the sequence of commission of offences or whether any offence occurred before or after any conviction.

R.S., 1985, c. C-46, s. 273;
1995, c. 39, s. 146;
2008, c. 6, s. 29;
2009, c. 22, s. 11;
2012, c. 1, s. 27.

Meaning of
273.1 (1) Subject to subsection (2) and subsection 265(3),
consent
Where no consent obtained
(2) No consent is obtained, for the purposes of sections 271, 272 and 273, where
(a) the agreement is expressed by the words or conduct of a person other than the complainant;
(b) the complainant is incapable of consenting to the activity;
(c) the accused induces the complainant to engage in the activity by abusing a position of trust, power or authority;
(d) the complainant expresses, by words or conduct, a lack of agreement to engage in the activity; or
(e) the complainant, having consented to engage in sexual activity, expresses, by words or conduct, a lack of agreement to continue to engage in the activity.
Subsection (2) not limiting
(3) Nothing in subsection (2) shall be construed as limiting the circumstances in which no consent is obtained.
1992, c. 38, s. 1.
Where belief in consent not a defence
273.2 It is not a defence to a charge under section 271, 272 or 273 that the accused believed that the complainant consented to the activity that forms the subject-matter of the charge, where
(a) the accused's belief arose from the accused's
(i) self-induced intoxication, or
(ii) recklessness or wilful blindness; or
(b) the accused did not take reasonable steps, in the circumstances known to the accused at the time, to ascertain that the complainant was consenting.
1992, c. 38, s. 1.
Removal of child from Canada
273.3 (1) No person shall do anything for the purpose of removing from Canada a person who is ordinarily resident in Canada and who is
(a) under the age of 16 years, with the intention that an act be committed outside Canada that if it were committed in Canada would be an offence against section 151 or 152 or subsection 160(3) or 173(2) in respect of that person;
(b) 16 years of age or more but under the age of eighteen years, with the intention that an act be committed outside Canada that if it were committed in Canada would be an offence against section 153 in respect of that person;
(c) under the age of eighteen years, with the intention that an act be committed outside Canada that if it were committed in Canada would be an offence against section 155 or 159, subsection 160(2) or section 170, 171, 267, 268, 269, 271, 272 or 273 in respect of that person; or
(d) under the age of 18 years, with the intention that an act be committed outside Canada that, if it were committed in Canada, would be an offence against section 293.1 in respect of that person or under the age of 16 years, with the intention that an act be committed outside Canada that, if it were committed in Canada, would be an offence against section 293.2 in respect of that person.
Punishment
(2) Every person who contravenes this section is guilty of
(a) an indictable offence and is liable to imprisonment for a term not exceeding five years; or
(b) an offence punishable on summary conviction.
1993, c. 45, s. 3;
1997, c. 18, s. 13;
2008, c. 6, s. 54;
2015, c. 29, s. 8.
Corroboration not required
274 If an accused is charged with an offence under section 151, 152, 153, 153.1, 155, 159, 160, 170, 171, 172, 173, 271, 272, 273, 286.1, 286.2 or 286.3, no corroboration is required for a conviction

and the judge shall not instruct the jury that it is unsafe to find the accused guilty in the absence of corroboration.
R.S., 1985, c. C-46, s. 274;
R.S., 1985, c. 19 (3rd Supp.), s. 11;
2002, c. 13, s. 12;
2014, c. 25, s. 16.

Rules respecting recent complaint abrogated

275 The rules relating to evidence of recent complaint are hereby abrogated with respect to offences under sections 151, 152, 153, 153.1, 155 and 159, subsections 160(2) and (3) and sections 170, 171, 172, 173, 271, 272 and 273.
R.S., 1985, c. C-46, s. 275;
R.S., 1985, c. 19 (3rd Supp.), s. 11;
2002, c. 13, s. 12.

Evidence of complainant's sexual activity

276 (1) In proceedings in respect of an offence under section 151, 152, 153, 153.1, 155 or 159, subsection 160(2) or (3) or section 170, 171, 172, 173, 271, 272 or 273, evidence that the complainant has engaged in sexual activity, whether with the accused or with any other person, is not admissible to support an inference that, by reason of the sexual nature of that activity, the complainant

(a) is more likely to have consented to the sexual activity that forms the subject-matter of the charge; or
(b) is less worthy of belief.

Idem

(2) In proceedings in respect of an offence referred to in subsection (1), no evidence shall be adduced by or on behalf of the accused that the complainant has engaged in sexual activity other than the sexual activity that forms the subject-matter of the charge, whether with the accused or with any other person, unless the judge, provincial court judge or justice determines, in accordance with the procedures set out in sections 276.1 and 276.2, that the evidence

(a) is of specific instances of sexual activity;
(b) is relevant to an issue at trial; and
(c) has significant probative value that is not substantially outweighed by the danger of prejudice to the proper administration of justice.

Factors that judge must consider

(3) In determining whether evidence is admissible under subsection (2), the judge, provincial court judge or justice shall take into account

(a) the interests of justice, including the right of the accused to make a full answer and defence;
(b) society's interest in encouraging the reporting of sexual assault offences;
(c) whether there is a reasonable prospect that the evidence will assist in arriving at a just determination in the case;
(d) the need to remove from the fact-finding process any discriminatory belief or bias;
(e) the risk that the evidence may unduly arouse sentiments of prejudice, sympathy or hostility in the jury;
(f) the potential prejudice to the complainant's personal dignity and right of privacy;
(g) the right of the complainant and of every individual to personal security and to the full protection and benefit of the law; and
(h) any other factor that the judge, provincial court judge or justice considers relevant.
R.S., 1985, c. C-46, s. 276;
R.S., 1985, c. 19 (3rd Supp.), s. 12;
1992, c. 38, s. 2;
2002, c. 13, s. 13.

Application for hearing

276.1 (1) Application may be made to the judge, provincial court judge or justice by or on behalf of the accused for a hearing under section 276.2 to determine whether evidence is admissible under subsection 276(2).

Form and content of application

(2) An application referred to in subsection (1) must be made in writing and set out

(a) detailed particulars of the evidence that the accused seeks to adduce, and

(b) the relevance of that evidence to an issue at trial,

and a copy of the application must be given to the prosecutor and to the clerk of the court.

Jury and public excluded

(3) The judge, provincial court judge or justice shall consider the application with the jury and the public excluded.

Judge may decide to hold hearing

(4) Where the judge, provincial court judge or justice is satisfied

(a) that the application was made in accordance with subsection (2),

(b) that a copy of the application was given to the prosecutor and to the clerk of the court at least seven days previously, or such shorter interval as the judge, provincial court judge or justice may allow where the interests of justice so require, and

(c) that the evidence sought to be adduced is capable of being admissible under subsection 276(2),

the judge, provincial court judge or justice shall grant the application and hold a hearing under section 276.2 to determine whether the evidence is admissible under subsection 276(2).

1992, c. 38, s. 2.

Jury and public excluded

276.2 (1) At a hearing to determine whether evidence is admissible under subsection 276(2), the jury and the public shall be excluded.

Complainant not compellable

(2) The complainant is not a compellable witness at the hearing.

Judge's determination and reasons

(3) At the conclusion of the hearing, the judge, provincial court judge or justice shall determine whether the evidence, or any part thereof, is admissible under subsection 276(2) and shall provide reasons for that determination, and

(a) where not all of the evidence is to be admitted, the reasons must state the part of the evidence that is to be admitted;

(b) the reasons must state the factors referred to in subsection 276(3) that affected the determination; and

(c) where all or any part of the evidence is to be admitted, the reasons must state the manner in which that evidence is expected to be relevant to an issue at trial.

Record of reasons

(4) The reasons provided under subsection (3) shall be entered in the record of the proceedings or, where the proceedings are not recorded, shall be provided in writing.

1992, c. 38, s. 2.

Publication prohibited

276.3 (1) No person shall publish in any document, or broadcast or transmit in any way, any of the following:

(a) the contents of an application made under section 276.1;

(b) any evidence taken, the information given and the representations made at an application under section 276.1 or at a hearing under section 276.2;

(c) the decision of a judge or justice under subsection 276.1(4), unless the judge or justice, after taking into account the complainant's right of privacy and the interests of justice, orders that the decision may be published, broadcast or transmitted; and

(d) the determination made and the reasons provided under section 276.2, unless

(i) that determination is that evidence is admissible, or

(ii) the judge or justice, after taking into account the complainant's right of privacy and the interests of justice, orders that the determination and reasons may be published, broadcast or transmitted.

Offence
(2) Every person who contravenes subsection (1) is guilty of an offence punishable on summary conviction.
1992, c. 38, s. 2;
2005, c. 32, s. 13.
Judge to instruct jury re use of evidence
276.4 Where evidence is admitted at trial pursuant to a determination made under section 276.2, the judge shall instruct the jury as to the uses that the jury may and may not make of that evidence.
1992, c. 38, s. 2.
Appeal
276.5 For the purposes of sections 675 and 676, a determination made under section 276.2 shall be deemed to be a question of law.
1992, c. 38, s. 2.
Reputation evidence
277 In proceedings in respect of an offence under section 151, 152, 153, 153.1, 155 or 159, subsection 160(2) or (3) or section 170, 171, 172, 173, 271, 272 or 273, evidence of sexual reputation, whether general or specific, is not admissible for the purpose of challenging or supporting the credibility of the complainant.
R.S., 1985, c. C-46, s. 277;
R.S., 1985, c. 19 (3rd Supp.), s. 13;
2002, c. 13, s. 14.
Spouse may be charged
278 A husband or wife may be charged with an offence under section 271, 272 or 273 in respect of his or her spouse, whether or not the spouses were living together at the time the activity that forms the subject-matter of the charge occurred.
1980-81-82-83, c. 125, s. 19.
Definition of
278.1 For the purposes of sections 278.2 to 278.9,
record
1997, c. 30, s. 1.
Production of record to accused
278.2 (1) Except in accordance with sections 278.3 to 278.91, no record relating to a complainant or a witness shall be produced to an accused in any proceedings in respect of any of the following offences or in any proceedings in respect of two or more offences at least one of which is any of the following offences:
(a) an offence under section 151, 152, 153, 153.1, 155, 159, 160, 170, 171, 172, 173, 210, 211, 213, 271, 272, 273, 279.01, 279.011, 279.02, 279.03, 286.1, 286.2 or 286.3; or
(b) any offence under this Act, as it read from time to time before the day on which this paragraph comes into force, if the conduct alleged would be an offence referred to in paragraph (a) if it occurred on or after that day.
Application of provisions
(2) Section 278.1, this section and sections 278.3 to 278.91 apply where a record is in the possession or control of any person, including the prosecutor in the proceedings, unless, in the case of a record in the possession or control of the prosecutor, the complainant or witness to whom the record relates has expressly waived the application of those sections.
Duty of prosecutor to give notice
(3) In the case of a record in respect of which this section applies that is in the possession or control of the prosecutor, the prosecutor shall notify the accused that the record is in the prosecutor's possession but, in doing so, the prosecutor shall not disclose the record's contents.
1997, c. 30, s. 1;
1998, c. 9, s. 3;
2014, c. 25, ss. 17, 48;

2015, c. 13, s. 5.
Application for production
278.3 (1) An accused who seeks production of a record referred to in subsection 278.2(1) must make an application to the judge before whom the accused is to be, or is being, tried.
No application in other proceedings
(2) For greater certainty, an application under subsection (1) may not be made to a judge or justice presiding at any other proceedings, including a preliminary inquiry.
Form and content of application
(3) An application must be made in writing and set out
(a) particulars identifying the record that the accused seeks to have produced and the name of the person who has possession or control of the record; and
(b) the grounds on which the accused relies to establish that the record is likely relevant to an issue at trial or to the competence of a witness to testify.
Insufficient grounds
(4) Any one or more of the following assertions by the accused are not sufficient on their own to establish that the record is likely relevant to an issue at trial or to the competence of a witness to testify:
(a) that the record exists;
(b) that the record relates to medical or psychiatric treatment, therapy or counselling that the complainant or witness has received or is receiving;
(c) that the record relates to the incident that is the subject-matter of the proceedings;
(d) that the record may disclose a prior inconsistent statement of the complainant or witness;
(e) that the record may relate to the credibility of the complainant or witness;
(f) that the record may relate to the reliability of the testimony of the complainant or witness merely because the complainant or witness has received or is receiving psychiatric treatment, therapy or counselling;
(g) that the record may reveal allegations of sexual abuse of the complainant by a person other than the accused;
(h) that the record relates to the sexual activity of the complainant with any person, including the accused;
(i) that the record relates to the presence or absence of a recent complaint;
(j) that the record relates to the complainant's sexual reputation; or
(k) that the record was made close in time to a complaint or to the activity that forms the subject-matter of the charge against the accused.
Service of application and subpoena
(5) The accused shall serve the application on the prosecutor, on the person who has possession or control of the record, on the complainant or witness, as the case may be, and on any other person to whom, to the knowledge of the accused, the record relates, at least 14 days before the hearing referred to in subsection 278.4(1) or any shorter interval that the judge may allow in the interests of justice. The accused shall also serve a subpoena issued under Part XXII in Form 16.1 on the person who has possession or control of the record at the same time as the application is served.
Service on other persons
(6) The judge may at any time order that the application be served on any person to whom the judge considers the record may relate.
1997, c. 30, s. 1;
2015, c. 13, s. 6.
Hearing
278.4 (1) The judge shall hold a hearing
Persons who may appear at hearing
(2) The person who has possession or control of the record, the complainant or witness, as the case may be, and any other person to whom the record relates may appear and make submissions at the hearing, but they are not compellable as witnesses at the hearing.

Right to counsel
(2.1) The judge shall, as soon as feasible, inform any person referred to in subsection (2) who participates in the hearing of their right to be represented by counsel.
Costs
(3) No order for costs may be made against a person referred to in subsection (2) in respect of their participation in the hearing.
1997, c. 30, s. 1;
2015, c. 13, s. 7.
Judge may order production of record for review
278.5 (1) The judge may order the person who has possession or control of the record to produce the record or part of the record to the court for review by the judge if, after the hearing referred to in subsection 278.4(1), the judge is satisfied that
(a) the application was made in accordance with subsections 278.3(2) to (6);
(b) the accused has established that the record is likely relevant to an issue at trial or to the competence of a witness to testify; and
(c) the production of the record is necessary in the interests of justice.
Factors to be considered
(2) In determining whether to order the production of the record or part of the record for review pursuant to subsection (1), the judge shall consider the salutary and deleterious effects of the determination on the accused's right to make a full answer and defence and on the right to privacy, personal security and equality of the complainant or witness, as the case may be, and of any other person to whom the record relates. In particular, the judge shall take the following factors into account:
(a) the extent to which the record is necessary for the accused to make a full answer and defence;
(b) the probative value of the record;
(c) the nature and extent of the reasonable expectation of privacy with respect to the record;
(d) whether production of the record is based on a discriminatory belief or bias;
(e) the potential prejudice to the personal dignity and right to privacy of any person to whom the record relates;
(f) society's interest in encouraging the reporting of sexual offences;
(g) society's interest in encouraging the obtaining of treatment by complainants of sexual offences; and
(h) the effect of the determination on the integrity of the trial process.
1997, c. 30, s. 1;
2015, c. 13, s. 8.
Review of record by judge
278.6 (1) Where the judge has ordered the production of the record or part of the record for review, the judge shall review it in the absence of the parties in order to determine whether the record or part of the record should be produced to the accused.
Hearing
(2) The judge may hold a hearing
Provisions re hearing
(3) Subsections 278.4(2) to (3) apply in the case of a hearing under subsection (2).
1997, c. 30, s. 1;
2015, c. 13, s. 9.
Judge may order production of record to accused
278.7 (1) Where the judge is satisfied that the record or part of the record is likely relevant to an issue at trial or to the competence of a witness to testify and its production is necessary in the interests of justice, the judge may order that the record or part of the record that is likely relevant be produced to the accused, subject to any conditions that may be imposed pursuant to subsection (3).
Factors to be considered
(2) In determining whether to order the production of the record or part of the record to the accused,

the judge shall consider the salutary and deleterious effects of the determination on the accused's right to make a full answer and defence and on the right to privacy, personal security and equality of the complainant or witness, as the case may be, and of any other person to whom the record relates and, in particular, shall take the factors specified in paragraphs 278.5(2)(a) to (h) into account.

Conditions on production

(3) If the judge orders the production of the record or part of the record to the accused, the judge may impose conditions on the production to protect the interests of justice and, to the greatest extent possible, the privacy, personal security and equality interests of the complainant or witness, as the case may be, and of any other person to whom the record relates, including, for example, the following conditions:

(a) that the record be edited as directed by the judge;

(b) that a copy of the record, rather than the original, be produced;

(c) that the accused and counsel for the accused not disclose the contents of the record to any other person, except with the approval of the court;

(d) that the record be viewed only at the offices of the court;

(e) that no copies of the record be made or that restrictions be imposed on the number of copies of the record that may be made; and

(f) that information regarding any person named in the record, such as their address, telephone number and place of employment, be severed from the record.

Copy to prosecutor

(4) Where the judge orders the production of the record or part of the record to the accused, the judge shall direct that a copy of the record or part of the record be provided to the prosecutor, unless the judge determines that it is not in the interests of justice to do so.

Record not to be used in other proceedings

(5) The record or part of the record that is produced to the accused pursuant to an order under subsection (1) shall not be used in any other proceedings.

Retention of record by court

(6) Where the judge refuses to order the production of the record or part of the record to the accused, the record or part of the record shall, unless a court orders otherwise, be kept in a sealed package by the court until the later of the expiration of the time for any appeal and the completion of any appeal in the proceedings against the accused, whereupon the record or part of the record shall be returned to the person lawfully entitled to possession or control of it.

1997, c. 30, s. 1;

2015, c. 13, s. 10.

Reasons for decision

278.8 (1) The judge shall provide reasons for ordering or refusing to order the production of the record or part of the record pursuant to subsection 278.5(1) or 278.7(1).

Record of reasons

(2) The reasons referred to in subsection (1) shall be entered in the record of the proceedings or, where the proceedings are not recorded, shall be provided in writing.

1997, c. 30, s. 1.

Publication prohibited

278.9 (1) No person shall publish in any document, or broadcast or transmit in any way, any of the following:

(a) the contents of an application made under section 278.3;

(b) any evidence taken, information given or submissions made at a hearing under subsection 278.4(1) or 278.6(2); or

(c) the determination of the judge pursuant to subsection 278.5(1) or 278.7(1) and the reasons provided pursuant to section 278.8, unless the judge, after taking into account the interests of justice and the right to privacy of the person to whom the record relates, orders that the determination may be published.

Offence

(2) Every person who contravenes subsection (1) is guilty of an offence punishable on summary conviction.
1997, c. 30, s. 1;
2005, c. 32, s. 14.
Appeal
278.91 For the purposes of sections 675 and 676, a determination to make or refuse to make an order pursuant to subsection 278.5(1) or 278.7(1) is deemed to be a question of law.
1997, c. 30, s. 1.

Kidnapping, Trafficking in Persons, Hostage Taking and Abduction

Kidnapping
279 (1) Every person commits an offence who kidnaps a person with intent
(a) to cause the person to be confined or imprisoned against the person's will;
(b) to cause the person to be unlawfully sent or transported out of Canada against the person's will; or
(c) to hold the person for ransom or to service against the person's will.
Punishment
(1.1) Every person who commits an offence under subsection (1) is guilty of an indictable offence and liable
(a) if a restricted firearm or prohibited firearm is used in the commission of the offence or if any firearm is used in the commission of the offence and the offence is committed for the benefit of, at the direction of, or in association with, a criminal organization, to imprisonment for life and to a minimum punishment of imprisonment for a term of
(i) in the case of a first offence, five years, and
(ii) in the case of a second or subsequent offence, seven years;
(a.1) in any other case where a firearm is used in the commission of the offence, to imprisonment for life and to a minimum punishment of imprisonment for a term of four years;
(a.2) if the person referred to in paragraph (1)(a), (b) or (c) is under 16 years of age, to imprisonment for life and, unless the person who commits the offence is a parent, guardian or person having the lawful care or charge of the person referred to in that paragraph, to a minimum punishment of imprisonment for a term of five years; and
(b) in any other case, to imprisonment for life.
Subsequent offences
(1.2) In determining, for the purpose of paragraph (1.1)(a), whether a convicted person has committed a second or subsequent offence, if the person was earlier convicted of any of the following offences, that offence is to be considered as an earlier offence:
(a) an offence under subsection (1);
(b) an offence under subsection 85(1) or (2) or section 244 or 244.2; or
(c) an offence under section 220, 236, 239, 272, 273, 279.1, 344 or 346 if a firearm was used in the commission of the offence.
However, an earlier offence shall not be taken into account if 10 years have elapsed between the day on which the person was convicted of the earlier offence and the day on which the person was convicted of the offence for which sentence is being imposed, not taking into account any time in custody.
Factors to consider
(1.21) In imposing a sentence under paragraph (1.1)(a.2), the court shall take into account the age and vulnerability of the victim.
Sequence of convictions only
(1.3) For the purposes of subsection (1.2), the only question to be considered is the sequence of convictions and no consideration shall be given to the sequence of commission of offences or whether any offence occurred before or after any conviction.

Forcible confinement
(2) Every one who, without lawful authority, confines, imprisons or forcibly seizes another person is guilty of
(a) an indictable offence and liable to imprisonment for a term not exceeding ten years; or
(b) an offence punishable on summary conviction and liable to imprisonment for a term not exceeding eighteen months.
Non-resistance
(3) In proceedings under this section, the fact that the person in relation to whom the offence is alleged to have been committed did not resist is not a defence unless the accused proves that the failure to resist was not caused by threats, duress, force or exhibition of force.
R.S., 1985, c. C-46, s. 279;
R.S., 1985, c. 27 (1st Supp.), s. 39;
1995, c. 39, s. 147;
1997, c. 18, s. 14;
2008, c. 6, s. 30;
2009, c. 22, s. 12;
2013, c. 32, s. 1.
Trafficking in persons
279.01 (1) Every person who recruits, transports, transfers, receives, holds, conceals or harbours a person, or exercises control, direction or influence over the movements of a person, for the purpose of exploiting them or facilitating their exploitation is guilty of an indictable offence and liable
(a) to imprisonment for life and to a minimum punishment of imprisonment for a term of five years if they kidnap, commit an aggravated assault or aggravated sexual assault against, or cause death to, the victim during the commission of the offence; or
(b) to imprisonment for a term of not more than 14 years and to a minimum punishment of imprisonment for a term of four years in any other case.
Consent
(2) No consent to the activity that forms the subject-matter of a charge under subsection (1) is valid.
2005, c. 43, s. 3;
2014, c. 25, s. 18.
Trafficking of a person under the age of eighteen years
279.011 (1) Every person who recruits, transports, transfers, receives, holds, conceals or harbours a person under the age of eighteen years, or exercises control, direction or influence over the movements of a person under the age of eighteen years, for the purpose of exploiting them or facilitating their exploitation is guilty of an indictable offence and liable
(a) to imprisonment for life and to a minimum punishment of imprisonment for a term of six years if they kidnap, commit an aggravated assault or aggravated sexual assault against, or cause death to, the victim during the commission of the offence; or
(b) to imprisonment for a term of not more than fourteen years and to a minimum punishment of imprisonment for a term of five years, in any other case.
Consent
(2) No consent to the activity that forms the subject-matter of a charge under subsection (1) is valid.
2010, c. 3, s. 2.
Material benefit — trafficking
279.02 (1) Everyone who receives a financial or other material benefit, knowing that it is obtained by or derived directly or indirectly from the commission of an offence under subsection 279.01(1), is guilty of an indictable offence and liable to imprisonment for a term of not more than 10 years.
Material benefit — trafficking of person under 18 years
(2) Everyone who receives a financial or other material benefit, knowing that it is obtained by or derived directly or indirectly from the commission of an offence under subsection 279.011(1), is guilty of an indictable offence and liable to imprisonment for a term of not more than 14 years and to a minimum punishment of imprisonment for a term of two years.

2005, c. 43, s. 3;
2010, c. 3, s. 3;
2014, c. 25, s. 19.

Withholding or destroying documents — trafficking

279.03 (1) Everyone who, for the purpose of committing or facilitating an offence under subsection 279.01(1), conceals, removes, withholds or destroys any travel document that belongs to another person or any document that establishes or purports to establish another person's identity or immigration status — whether or not the document is of Canadian origin or is authentic — is guilty of an indictable offence and liable to imprisonment for a term of not more than five years.

Withholding or destroying documents — trafficking of person under 18 years

(2) Everyone who, for the purpose of committing or facilitating an offence under subsection 279.011(1), conceals, removes, withholds or destroys any travel document that belongs to another person or any document that establishes or purports to establish another person's identity or immigration status — whether or not the document is of Canadian origin or is authentic — is guilty of an indictable offence and liable to imprisonment for a term of not more than 10 years and to a minimum punishment of imprisonment for a term of one year.

2005, c. 43, s. 3;
2010, c. 3, s. 3;
2014, c. 25, s. 19.

Exploitation

279.04 (1) For the purposes of sections 279.01 to 279.03, a person exploits another person if they cause them to provide, or offer to provide, labour or a service by engaging in conduct that, in all the circumstances, could reasonably be expected to cause the other person to believe that their safety or the safety of a person known to them would be threatened if they failed to provide, or offer to provide, the labour or service.

Factors

(2) In determining whether an accused exploits another person under subsection (1), the Court may consider, among other factors, whether the accused
(a) used or threatened to use force or another form of coercion;
(b) used deception; or
(c) abused a position of trust, power or authority.

Organ or tissue removal

(3) For the purposes of sections 279.01 to 279.03, a person exploits another person if they cause them, by means of deception or the use or threat of force or of any other form of coercion, to have an organ or tissue removed.

2005, c. 43, s. 3;
2012, c. 15, s. 2.

Hostage taking

279.1 (1) Everyone takes a person hostage who — with intent to induce any person, other than the hostage, or any group of persons or any state or international or intergovernmental organization to commit or cause to be committed any act or omission as a condition, whether express or implied, of the release of the hostage —
(a) confines, imprisons, forcibly seizes or detains that person; and
(b) in any manner utters, conveys or causes any person to receive a threat that the death of, or bodily harm to, the hostage will be caused or that the confinement, imprisonment or detention of the hostage will be continued.

Hostage-taking

(2) Every person who takes a person hostage is guilty of an indictable offence and liable
(a) if a restricted firearm or prohibited firearm is used in the commission of the offence or if any firearm is used in the commission of the offence and the offence is committed for the benefit of, at the direction of, or in association with, a criminal organization, to imprisonment for life and to a minimum punishment of imprisonment for a term of

(i) in the case of a first offence, five years, and
(ii) in the case of a second or subsequent offence, seven years;
(a.1) in any other case where a firearm is used in the commission of the offence, to imprisonment for life and to a minimum punishment of imprisonment for a term of four years; and
(b) in any other case, to imprisonment for life.

Subsequent offences

(2.1) In determining, for the purpose of paragraph (2)(a), whether a convicted person has committed a second or subsequent offence, if the person was earlier convicted of any of the following offences, that offence is to be considered as an earlier offence:

(a) an offence under this section;
(b) an offence under subsection 85(1) or (2) or section 244 or 244.2; or
(c) an offence under section 220, 236, 239, 272 or 273, subsection 279(1) or section 344 or 346 if a firearm was used in the commission of the offence.

However, an earlier offence shall not be taken into account if 10 years have elapsed between the day on which the person was convicted of the earlier offence and the day on which the person was convicted of the offence for which sentence is being imposed, not taking into account any time in custody.

Sequence of convictions only

(2.2) For the purposes of subsection (2.1), the only question to be considered is the sequence of convictions and no consideration shall be given to the sequence of commission of offences or whether any offence occurred before or after any conviction.

Non-resistance

(3) Subsection 279(3) applies to proceedings under this section as if the offence under this section were an offence under section 279.

R.S., 1985, c. 27 (1st Supp.), s. 40;
1995, c. 39, s. 148;
2008, c. 6, s. 31;
2009, c. 22, s. 13.

Abduction of person under sixteen

280 (1) Every one who, without lawful authority, takes or causes to be taken an unmarried person under the age of sixteen years out of the possession of and against the will of the parent or guardian of that person or of any other person who has the lawful care or charge of that person is guilty of an indictable offence and liable to imprisonment for a term not exceeding five years.

Definition of

guardian

(2) In this section and sections 281 to 283,

guardian

R.S., c. C-34, s. 249;
1980-81-82-83, c. 125, s. 20.

Abduction of person under fourteen

281 Every one who, not being the parent, guardian or person having the lawful care or charge of a person under the age of fourteen years, unlawfully takes, entices away, conceals, detains, receives or harbours that person with intent to deprive a parent or guardian, or any other person who has the lawful care or charge of that person, of the possession of that person is guilty of an indictable offence and liable to imprisonment for a term not exceeding ten years.

R.S., c. C-34, s. 250;
1980-81-82-83, c. 125, s. 20.

Abduction in contravention of custody order

282 (1) Every one who, being the parent, guardian or person having the lawful care or charge of a person under the age of fourteen years, takes, entices away, conceals, detains, receives or harbours that person, in contravention of the custody provisions of a custody order in relation to that person made by a court anywhere in Canada, with intent to deprive a parent or guardian, or any other person

who has the lawful care or charge of that person, of the possession of that person is guilty of
(a) an indictable offence and is liable to imprisonment for a term not exceeding ten years; or
(b) an offence punishable on summary conviction.

Where no belief in validity of custody order

(2) Where a count charges an offence under subsection (1) and the offence is not proven only because the accused did not believe that there was a valid custody order but the evidence does prove an offence under section 283, the accused may be convicted of an offence under section 283.

R.S., 1985, c. C-46, s. 282;
1993, c. 45, s. 4.

Abduction

283 (1) Every one who, being the parent, guardian or person having the lawful care or charge of a person under the age of fourteen years, takes, entices away, conceals, detains, receives or harbours that person, whether or not there is a custody order in relation to that person made by a court anywhere in Canada, with intent to deprive a parent or guardian, or any other person who has the lawful care or charge of that person, of the possession of that person, is guilty of
(a) an indictable offence and is liable to imprisonment for a term not exceeding ten years; or
(b) an offence punishable on summary conviction.

Consent required

(2) No proceedings may be commenced under subsection (1) without the consent of the Attorney General or counsel instructed by him for that purpose.

R.S., 1985, c. C-46, s. 283;
1993, c. 45, s. 5.

Defence

284 No one shall be found guilty of an offence under sections 281 to 283 if he establishes that the taking, enticing away, concealing, detaining, receiving or harbouring of any young person was done with the consent of the parent, guardian or other person having the lawful possession, care or charge of that young person.

1980-81-82-83, c. 125, s. 20.

Defence

285 No one shall be found guilty of an offence under sections 280 to 283 if the court is satisfied that the taking, enticing away, concealing, detaining, receiving or harbouring of any young person was necessary to protect the young person from danger of imminent harm or if the person charged with the offence was escaping from danger of imminent harm.

R.S., 1985, c. C-46, s. 285;
1993, c. 45, s. 6.

No defence

286 In proceedings in respect of an offence under sections 280 to 283, it is not a defence to any charge that a young person consented to or suggested any conduct of the accused.

1980-81-82-83, c. 125, s. 20.

Commodification of Sexual Activity

Obtaining sexual services for consideration

286.1 (1) Everyone who, in any place, obtains for consideration, or communicates with anyone for the purpose of obtaining for consideration, the sexual services of a person is guilty of
(a) an indictable offence and liable to imprisonment for a term of not more than five years and a minimum punishment of,
(i) in the case where the offence is committed in a public place, or in any place open to public view, that is or is next to a park or the grounds of a school or religious institution or that is or is next to any other place where persons under the age of 18 can reasonably be expected to be present,
(A) for a first offence, a fine of $2,000, and
(B) for each subsequent offence, a fine of $4,000, or

(ii) in any other case,
(A) for a first offence, a fine of $1,000, and
(B) for each subsequent offence, a fine of $2,000; or
(b) an offence punishable on summary conviction and liable to imprisonment for a term of not more than 18 months and a minimum punishment of,
(i) in the case referred to in subparagraph (a)(i),
(A) for a first offence, a fine of $1,000, and
(B) for each subsequent offence, a fine of $2,000, or
(ii) in any other case,
(A) for a first offence, a fine of $500, and
(B) for each subsequent offence, a fine of $1,000.

Obtaining sexual services for consideration from person under 18 years

(2) Everyone who, in any place, obtains for consideration, or communicates with anyone for the purpose of obtaining for consideration, the sexual services of a person under the age of 18 years is guilty of an indictable offence and liable to imprisonment for a term of not more than 10 years and to a minimum punishment of imprisonment for a term of
(a) for a first offence, six months; and
(b) for each subsequent offence, one year.

Subsequent offences

(3) In determining, for the purpose of subsection (2), whether a convicted person has committed a subsequent offence, if the person was earlier convicted of any of the following offences, that offence is to be considered as an earlier offence:
(a) an offence under that subsection; or
(b) an offence under subsection 212(4) of this Act, as it read from time to time before the day on which this subsection comes into force.

Sequence of convictions only

(4) In determining, for the purposes of this section, whether a convicted person has committed a subsequent offence, the only question to be considered is the sequence of convictions and no consideration shall be given to the sequence of commission of offences, whether any offence occurred before or after any conviction or whether offences were prosecuted by indictment or by way of summary conviction proceedings.

Definitions of
place
public place
(5) For the purposes of this section,
place
public place
2014, c. 25, s. 20.

Material benefit from sexual services

286.2 (1) Everyone who receives a financial or other material benefit, knowing that it is obtained by or derived directly or indirectly from the commission of an offence under subsection 286.1(1), is guilty of an indictable offence and liable to imprisonment for a term of not more than 10 years.

Material benefit from sexual services provided by person under 18 years

(2) Everyone who receives a financial or other material benefit, knowing that it is obtained by or derived directly or indirectly from the commission of an offence under subsection 286.1(2), is guilty of an indictable offence and liable to imprisonment for a term of not more than 14 years and to a minimum punishment of imprisonment for a term of two years.

Presumption

(3) For the purposes of subsections (1) and (2), evidence that a person lives with or is habitually in the company of a person who offers or provides sexual services for consideration is, in the absence of evidence to the contrary, proof that the person received a financial or other material benefit from those services.

Exception

(4) Subject to subsection (5), subsections (1) and (2) do not apply to a person who receives the benefit

(a) in the context of a legitimate living arrangement with the person from whose sexual services the benefit is derived;

(b) as a result of a legal or moral obligation of the person from whose sexual services the benefit is derived;

(c) in consideration for a service or good that they offer, on the same terms and conditions, to the general public; or

(d) in consideration for a service or good that they do not offer to the general public but that they offered or provided to the person from whose sexual services the benefit is derived, if they did not counsel or encourage that person to provide sexual services and the benefit is proportionate to the value of the service or good.

No exception

(5) Subsection (4) does not apply to a person who commits an offence under subsection (1) or (2) if that person

(a) used, threatened to use or attempted to use violence, intimidation or coercion in relation to the person from whose sexual services the benefit is derived;

(b) abused a position of trust, power or authority in relation to the person from whose sexual services the benefit is derived;

(c) provided a drug, alcohol or any other intoxicating substance to the person from whose sexual services the benefit is derived for the purpose of aiding or abetting that person to offer or provide sexual services for consideration;

(d) engaged in conduct, in relation to any person, that would constitute an offence under section 286.3; or

(e) received the benefit in the context of a commercial enterprise that offers sexual services for consideration.

Aggravating factor

(6) If a person is convicted of an offence under this section, the court that imposes the sentence shall consider as an aggravating factor the fact that that person received the benefit in the context of a commercial enterprise that offers sexual services for consideration.

2014, c. 25, s. 20.

Procuring

286.3 (1) Everyone who procures a person to offer or provide sexual services for consideration or, for the purpose of facilitating an offence under subsection 286.1(1), recruits, holds, conceals or harbours a person who offers or provides sexual services for consideration, or exercises control, direction or influence over the movements of that person, is guilty of an indictable offence and liable to imprisonment for a term of not more than 14 years.

Procuring — person under 18 years

(2) Everyone who procures a person under the age of 18 years to offer or provide sexual services for consideration or, for the purpose of facilitating an offence under subsection 286.1(2), recruits, holds, conceals or harbours a person under the age of 18 who offers or provides sexual services for consideration, or exercises control, direction or influence over the movements of that person, is guilty of an indictable offence and liable to imprisonment for a term of not more than 14 years and to a minimum punishment of imprisonment for a term of five years.

2014, c. 25, s. 20.

Advertising sexual services

286.4 Everyone who knowingly advertises an offer to provide sexual services for consideration is guilty of

(a) an indictable offence and liable to imprisonment for a term of not more than five years; or

(b) an offence punishable on summary conviction and liable to imprisonment for a term of not more than 18 months.

2014, c. 25, s. 20.
Immunity — material benefit and advertising
286.5 (1) No person shall be prosecuted for
(a) an offence under section 286.2 if the benefit is derived from the provision of their own sexual services; or
(b) an offence under section 286.4 in relation to the advertisement of their own sexual services.
Immunity — aiding, abetting, etc.
(2) No person shall be prosecuted for aiding, abetting, conspiring or attempting to commit an offence under any of sections 286.1 to 286.4 or being an accessory after the fact or counselling a person to be a party to such an offence, if the offence relates to the offering or provision of their own sexual services.
2014, c. 25, s. 20.

Abortion

Procuring miscarriage
287 (1) Every one who, with intent to procure the miscarriage of a female person, whether or not she is pregnant, uses any means for the purpose of carrying out his intention is guilty of an indictable offence and liable to imprisonment for life.
Woman procuring her own miscarriage
(2) Every female person who, being pregnant, with intent to procure her own miscarriage, uses any means or permits any means to be used for the purpose of carrying out her intention is guilty of an indictable offence and liable to imprisonment for a term not exceeding two years.
Definition of
means
(3) In this section,
means
(a) the administration of a drug or other noxious thing;
(b) the use of an instrument; and
(c) manipulation of any kind.
Exceptions
(4) Subsections (1) and (2) do not apply to
(a) a qualified medical practitioner, other than a member of a therapeutic abortion committee for any hospital, who in good faith uses in an accredited or approved hospital any means for the purpose of carrying out his intention to procure the miscarriage of a female person, or
(b) a female person who, being pregnant, permits a qualified medical practitioner to use in an accredited or approved hospital any means for the purpose of carrying out her intention to procure her own miscarriage,
if, before the use of those means, the therapeutic abortion committee for that accredited or approved hospital, by a majority of the members of the committee and at a meeting of the committee at which the case of the female person has been reviewed,
(c) has by certificate in writing stated that in its opinion the continuation of the pregnancy of the female person would or would be likely to endanger her life or health, and
(d) has caused a copy of that certificate to be given to the qualified medical practitioner.
Information requirement
(5) The Minister of Health of a province may by order
(a) require a therapeutic abortion committee for any hospital in that province, or any member thereof, to furnish him with a copy of any certificate described in paragraph (4)(c) issued by that committee, together with such other information relating to the circumstances surrounding the issue of that certificate as he may require; or
(b) require a medical practitioner who, in that province, has procured the miscarriage of any female person named in a certificate described in paragraph (4)(c), to furnish him with a copy of that

certificate, together with such other information relating to the procuring of the miscarriage as he may require.
Definitions
(6) For the purposes of subsections (4) and (5) and this subsection,
accredited hospital
approved hospital
board
Minister of Health
(a) in the Provinces of Ontario, Quebec, New Brunswick, Manitoba, Prince Edward Island and Newfoundland and Labrador, the Minister of Health,
(b) in the Provinces of Nova Scotia and Saskatchewan, the Minister of Public Health, and
(c) in the Province of British Columbia, the Minister of Health Services and Hospital Insurance,
(d) in the Province of Alberta, the Minister of Hospitals and Medical Care,
(e) in Yukon, the Northwest Territories and Nunavut, the Minister of Health;
qualified medical practitioner
therapeutic abortion committee
Requirement of consent not affected
(7) Nothing in subsection (4) shall be construed as making unnecessary the obtaining of any authorization or consent that is or may be required, otherwise than under this Act, before any means are used for the purpose of carrying out an intention to procure the miscarriage of a female person.
R.S., 1985, c. C-46, s. 287;
1993, c. 28, s. 78;
1996, c. 8, s. 32;
2002, c. 7, s. 141;
2015, c. 3, s. 48.
Supplying noxious things
288 Every one who unlawfully supplies or procures a drug or other noxious thing or an instrument or thing, knowing that it is intended to be used or employed to procure the miscarriage of a female person, whether or not she is pregnant, is guilty of an indictable offence and liable to imprisonment for a term not exceeding two years.
R.S., c. C-34, s. 252.

Venereal Diseases

289
Offences Against Conjugal Rights

Bigamy
290 (1) Every one commits bigamy who
(a) in Canada,
(i) being married, goes through a form of marriage with another person,
(ii) knowing that another person is married, goes through a form of marriage with that person, or
(iii) on the same day or simultaneously, goes through a form of marriage with more than one person; or
(b) being a Canadian citizen resident in Canada leaves Canada with intent to do anything mentioned in subparagraphs (a)(i) to (iii) and, pursuant thereto, does outside Canada anything mentioned in those subparagraphs in circumstances mentioned therein.
Matters of defence
(2) No person commits bigamy by going through a form of marriage if
(a) that person in good faith and on reasonable grounds believes that his spouse is dead;
(b) the spouse of that person has been continuously absent from him for seven years immediately preceding the time when he goes through the form of marriage, unless he knew that his spouse was

alive at any time during those seven years;

(c) that person has been divorced from the bond of the first marriage; or

(d) the former marriage has been declared void by a court of competent jurisdiction.

Incompetency no defence

(3) Where a person is alleged to have committed bigamy, it is not a defence that the parties would, if unmarried, have been incompetent to contract marriage under the law of the place where the offence is alleged to have been committed.

Validity presumed

(4) Every marriage or form of marriage shall, for the purpose of this section, be deemed to be valid unless the accused establishes that it was invalid.

Act or omission by accused

(5) No act or omission on the part of an accused who is charged with bigamy invalidates a marriage or form of marriage that is otherwise valid.

R.S., c. C-34, s. 254.

Punishment

291 (1) Every one who commits bigamy is guilty of an indictable offence and liable to imprisonment for a term not exceeding five years.

Certificate of marriage

(2) For the purposes of this section, a certificate of marriage issued under the authority of law is evidence of the marriage or form of marriage to which it relates without proof of the signature or official character of the person by whom it purports to be signed.

R.S., c. C-34, s. 255.

Procuring feigned marriage

292 (1) Every person who procures or knowingly aids in procuring a feigned marriage between himself and another person is guilty of an indictable offence and liable to imprisonment for a term not exceeding five years.

Corroboration

(2) No person shall be convicted of an offence under this section on the evidence of only one witness unless the evidence of that witness is corroborated in a material particular by evidence that implicates the accused.

R.S., c. C-34, s. 256;

1980-81-82-83, c. 125, s. 21.

Polygamy

293 (1) Every one who

(a) practises or enters into or in any manner agrees or consents to practise or enter into

(i) any form of polygamy, or

(ii) any kind of conjugal union with more than one person at the same time,

whether or not it is by law recognized as a binding form of marriage, or

(b) celebrates, assists or is a party to a rite, ceremony, contract or consent that purports to sanction a relationship mentioned in subparagraph (a)(i) or (ii),

is guilty of an indictable offence and liable to imprisonment for a term not exceeding five years.

Evidence in case of polygamy

(2) Where an accused is charged with an offence under this section, no averment or proof of the method by which the alleged relationship was entered into, agreed to or consented to is necessary in the indictment or on the trial of the accused, nor is it necessary on the trial to prove that the persons who are alleged to have entered into the relationship had or intended to have sexual intercourse.

R.S., c. C-34, s. 257.

Forced marriage

293.1 Everyone who celebrates, aids or participates in a marriage rite or ceremony knowing that one of the persons being married is marrying against their will is guilty of an indictable offence and liable to imprisonment for a term not exceeding five years.

2015, c. 29, s. 9.

Marriage under age of 16 years
293.2 Everyone who celebrates, aids or participates in a marriage rite or ceremony knowing that one of the persons being married is under the age of 16 years is guilty of an indictable offence and liable to imprisonment for a term not exceeding five years.
2015, c. 29, s. 9.

Unlawful Solemnization of Marriage

Pretending to solemnize marriage
294 Every one who
(a) solemnizes or pretends to solemnize a marriage without lawful authority, the proof of which lies on him, or
(b) procures a person to solemnize a marriage knowing that he is not lawfully authorized to solemnize the marriage,
is guilty of an indictable offence and liable to imprisonment for a term not exceeding two years.
R.S., c. C-34, s. 258.
Marriage contrary to law
295 Everyone who, being lawfully authorized to solemnize marriage, knowingly solemnizes a marriage in contravention of federal law or the laws of the province in which the marriage is solemnized is guilty of an indictable offence and liable to imprisonment for a term not exceeding two years.
R.S., 1985, c. C-46, s. 295;
2015, c. 29, s. 10.

Blasphemous Libel

Offence
296 (1) Every one who publishes a blasphemous libel is guilty of an indictable offence and liable to imprisonment for a term not exceeding two years.
Question of fact
(2) It is a question of fact whether or not any matter that is published is a blasphemous libel.
Saving
(3) No person shall be convicted of an offence under this section for expressing in good faith and in decent language, or attempting to establish by argument used in good faith and conveyed in decent language, an opinion on a religious subject.
R.S., c. C-34, s. 260.

Defamatory Libel

Definition of
newspaper
297 In sections 303, 304 and 308,
newspaper
R.S., c. C-34, s. 261.
Definition
298 (1) A defamatory libel is matter published, without lawful justification or excuse, that is likely to injure the reputation of any person by exposing him to hatred, contempt or ridicule, or that is designed to insult the person of or concerning whom it is published.
Mode of expression
(2) A defamatory libel may be expressed directly or by insinuation or irony
(a) in words legibly marked on any substance; or
(b) by any object signifying a defamatory libel otherwise than by words.

R.S., c. C-34, s. 262.
Publishing
299 A person publishes a libel when he
(a) exhibits it in public;
(b) causes it to be read or seen; or
(c) shows or delivers it, or causes it to be shown or delivered, with intent that it should be read or seen by the person whom it defames or by any other person.
R.S., c. C-34, s. 263.
Punishment of libel known to be false
300 Every one who publishes a defamatory libel that he knows is false is guilty of an indictable offence and liable to imprisonment for a term not exceeding five years.
R.S., c. C-34, s. 264.
Punishment for defamatory libel
301 Every one who publishes a defamatory libel is guilty of an indictable offence and liable to imprisonment for a term not exceeding two years.
R.S., c. C-34, s. 265.
Extortion by libel
302 (1) Every one commits an offence who, with intent
(a) to extort money from any person, or
(b) to induce a person to confer on or procure for another person an appointment or office of profit or trust,
publishes or threatens to publish or offers to abstain from publishing or to prevent the publication of a defamatory libel.
Idem
(2) Every one commits an offence who, as the result of the refusal of any person to permit money to be extorted or to confer or procure an appointment or office of profit or trust, publishes or threatens to publish a defamatory libel.
Punishment
(3) Every one who commits an offence under this section is guilty of an indictable offence and liable to imprisonment for a term not exceeding five years.
R.S., c. C-34, s. 266.
Proprietor of newspaper presumed responsible
303 (1) The proprietor of a newspaper shall be deemed to publish defamatory matter that is inserted and published therein, unless he proves that the defamatory matter was inserted in the newspaper without his knowledge and without negligence on his part.
General authority to manager when negligence
(2) Where the proprietor of a newspaper gives to a person general authority to manage or conduct the newspaper as editor or otherwise, the insertion by that person of defamatory matter in the newspaper shall, for the purposes of subsection (1), be deemed not to be negligence on the part of the proprietor unless it is proved that
(a) he intended the general authority to include authority to insert defamatory matter in the newspaper; or
(b) he continued to confer general authority after he knew that it had been exercised by the insertion of defamatory matter in the newspaper.
Selling newspapers
(3) No person shall be deemed to publish a defamatory libel by reason only that he sells a number or part of a newspaper that contains a defamatory libel, unless he knows that the number or part contains defamatory matter or that defamatory matter is habitually contained in the newspaper.
R.S., c. C-34, s. 267.
Selling book containing defamatory libel
304 (1) No person shall be deemed to publish a defamatory libel by reason only that he sells a book, magazine, pamphlet or other thing, other than a newspaper that contains defamatory matter, if, at the

time of the sale, he does not know that it contains the defamatory matter.
Sale by servant
(2) Where a servant, in the course of his employment, sells a book, magazine, pamphlet or other thing, other than a newspaper, the employer shall be deemed not to publish any defamatory matter contained therein unless it is proved that the employer authorized the sale knowing that
(a) defamatory matter was contained therein; or
(b) defamatory matter was habitually contained therein, in the case of a periodical.
R.S., c. C-34, s. 268.
Publishing proceedings of courts of justice
305 No person shall be deemed to publish a defamatory libel by reason only that he publishes defamatory matter
(a) in a proceeding held before or under the authority of a court exercising judicial authority; or
(b) in an inquiry made under the authority of an Act or by order of Her Majesty, or under the authority of a public department or a department of the government of a province.
R.S., c. C-34, s. 269.
Parliamentary papers
306 No person shall be deemed to publish a defamatory libel by reason only that he
(a) publishes to the Senate or House of Commons or to the legislature of a province defamatory matter contained in a petition to the Senate or House of Commons or to the legislature of a province, as the case may be;
(b) publishes by order or under the authority of the Senate or House of Commons or of the legislature of a province a paper containing defamatory matter; or
(c) publishes, in good faith and without ill-will to the person defamed, an extract from or abstract of a petition or paper mentioned in paragraph (a) or (b).
R.S., c. C-34, s. 270.
Fair reports of parliamentary or judicial proceedings
307 (1) No person shall be deemed to publish a defamatory libel by reason only that he publishes in good faith, for the information of the public, a fair report of the proceedings of the Senate or House of Commons or the legislature of a province, or a committee thereof, or of the public proceedings before a court exercising judicial authority, or publishes, in good faith, any fair comment on any such proceedings.
Divorce proceedings an exception
(2) This section does not apply to a person who publishes a report of evidence taken or offered in any proceeding before the Senate or House of Commons or any committee thereof, on a petition or bill relating to any matter of marriage or divorce, if the report is published without authority from or leave of the House in which the proceeding is held or is contrary to any rule, order or practice of that House.
R.S., c. C-34, s. 271.
Fair report of public meeting
308 No person shall be deemed to publish a defamatory libel by reason only that he publishes in good faith, in a newspaper, a fair report of the proceedings of any public meeting if
(a) the meeting is lawfully convened for a lawful purpose and is open to the public;
(b) the report is fair and accurate;
(c) the publication of the matter complained of is for the public benefit; and
(d) he does not refuse to publish in a conspicuous place in the newspaper a reasonable explanation or contradiction by the person defamed in respect of the defamatory matter.
R.S., c. C-34, s. 272.
Public benefit
309 No person shall be deemed to publish a defamatory libel by reason only that he publishes defamatory matter that, on reasonable grounds, he believes is true, and that is relevant to any subject of public interest, the public discussion of which is for the public benefit.
R.S., c. C-34, s. 273.

Fair comment on public person or work of art
310 No person shall be deemed to publish a defamatory libel by reason only that he publishes fair comments
(a) on the public conduct of a person who takes part in public affairs; or
(b) on a published book or other literary production, or on any composition or work of art or performance publicly exhibited, or on any other communication made to the public on any subject, if the comments are confined to criticism thereof.
R.S., c. C-34, s. 274.

When truth a defence
311 No person shall be deemed to publish a defamatory libel where he proves that the publication of the defamatory matter in the manner in which it was published was for the public benefit at the time when it was published and that the matter itself was true.
R.S., c. C-34, s. 275.

Publication invited or necessary
312 No person shall be deemed to publish a defamatory libel by reason only that he publishes defamatory matter
(a) on the invitation or challenge of the person in respect of whom it is published, or
(b) that it is necessary to publish in order to refute defamatory matter published in respect of him by another person,
if he believes that the defamatory matter is true and it is relevant to the invitation, challenge or necessary refutation, as the case may be, and does not in any respect exceed what is reasonably sufficient in the circumstances.
R.S., c. C-34, s. 276.

Answer to inquiries
313 No person shall be deemed to publish a defamatory libel by reason only that he publishes, in answer to inquiries made to him, defamatory matter relating to a subject-matter in respect of which the person by whom or on whose behalf the inquiries are made has an interest in knowing the truth or who, on reasonable grounds, the person who publishes the defamatory matter believes has such an interest, if
(a) the matter is published, in good faith, for the purpose of giving information in answer to the inquiries;
(b) the person who publishes the defamatory matter believes that it is true;
(c) the defamatory matter is relevant to the inquiries; and
(d) the defamatory matter does not in any respect exceed what is reasonably sufficient in the circumstances.
R.S., c. C-34, s. 277.

Giving information to person interested
314 No person shall be deemed to publish a defamatory libel by reason only that he publishes to another person defamatory matter for the purpose of giving information to that person with respect to a subject-matter in which the person to whom the information is given has, or is believed on reasonable grounds by the person who gives it to have, an interest in knowing the truth with respect to that subject-matter if
(a) the conduct of the person who gives the information is reasonable in the circumstances;
(b) the defamatory matter is relevant to the subject-matter; and
(c) the defamatory matter is true, or if it is not true, is made without ill-will toward the person who is defamed and is made in the belief, on reasonable grounds, that it is true.
R.S., c. C-34, s. 278.

Publication in good faith for redress of wrong
315 No person shall be deemed to publish a defamatory libel by reason only that he publishes defamatory matter in good faith for the purpose of seeking remedy or redress for a private or public wrong or grievance from a person who has, or who on reasonable grounds he believes has, the right or is under an obligation to remedy or redress the wrong or grievance, if

(a) he believes that the defamatory matter is true;
(b) the defamatory matter is relevant to the remedy or redress that is sought; and
(c) the defamatory matter does not in any respect exceed what is reasonably sufficient in the circumstances.
R.S., c. C-34, s. 279.

Proving publication by order of legislature
316 (1) An accused who is alleged to have published a defamatory libel may, at any stage of the proceedings, adduce evidence to prove that the matter that is alleged to be defamatory was contained in a paper published by order or under the authority of the Senate or House of Commons or the legislature of a province.

Directing verdict
(2) Where at any stage in proceedings referred to in subsection (1) the court, judge, justice or provincial court judge is satisfied that the matter alleged to be defamatory was contained in a paper published by order or under the authority of the Senate or House of Commons or the legislature of a province, he shall direct a verdict of not guilty to be entered and shall discharge the accused.

Certificate of order
(3) For the purposes of this section, a certificate under the hand of the Speaker or clerk of the Senate or House of Commons or the legislature of a province to the effect that the matter that is alleged to be defamatory was contained in a paper published by order or under the authority of the Senate, House of Commons or the legislature of a province, as the case may be, is conclusive evidence thereof.
R.S., 1985, c. C-46, s. 316;
R.S., 1985, c. 27 (1st Supp.), s. 203.

Verdicts

Verdicts in cases of defamatory libel
317 Where, on the trial of an indictment for publishing a defamatory libel, a plea of not guilty is pleaded, the jury that is sworn to try the issue may give a general verdict of guilty or not guilty on the whole matter put in issue on the indictment, and shall not be required or directed by the judge to find the defendant guilty merely on proof of publication by the defendant of the alleged defamatory libel, and of the sense ascribed thereto in the indictment, but the judge may, in his discretion, give a direction or opinion to the jury on the matter in issue as in other criminal proceedings, and the jury may, on the issue, find a special verdict.
R.S., c. C-34, s. 281.

Hate Propaganda

Advocating genocide
318 (1) Every one who advocates or promotes genocide is guilty of an indictable offence and liable to imprisonment for a term not exceeding five years.

Definition of
(2) In this section,
genocide
(a) killing members of the group; or
(b) deliberately inflicting on the group conditions of life calculated to bring about its physical destruction.

Consent
(3) No proceeding for an offence under this section shall be instituted without the consent of the Attorney General.

Definition of
(4) In this section,

identifiable group
R.S., 1985, c. C-46, s. 318;
2004, c. 14, s. 1;
2014, c. 31, s. 12;
2017, c. 13, s. 3.

Public incitement of hatred

319 (1) Every one who, by communicating statements in any public place, incites hatred against any identifiable group where such incitement is likely to lead to a breach of the peace is guilty of
(a) an indictable offence and is liable to imprisonment for a term not exceeding two years; or
(b) an offence punishable on summary conviction.

Wilful promotion of hatred

(2) Every one who, by communicating statements, other than in private conversation, wilfully promotes hatred against any identifiable group is guilty of
(a) an indictable offence and is liable to imprisonment for a term not exceeding two years; or
(b) an offence punishable on summary conviction.

Defences

(3) No person shall be convicted of an offence under subsection (2)
(a) if he establishes that the statements communicated were true;
(b) if, in good faith, the person expressed or attempted to establish by an argument an opinion on a religious subject or an opinion based on a belief in a religious text;
(c) if the statements were relevant to any subject of public interest, the discussion of which was for the public benefit, and if on reasonable grounds he believed them to be true; or
(d) if, in good faith, he intended to point out, for the purpose of removal, matters producing or tending to produce feelings of hatred toward an identifiable group in Canada.

Forfeiture

(4) Where a person is convicted of an offence under section 318 or subsection (1) or (2) of this section, anything by means of or in relation to which the offence was committed, on such conviction, may, in addition to any other punishment imposed, be ordered by the presiding provincial court judge or judge to be forfeited to Her Majesty in right of the province in which that person is convicted, for disposal as the Attorney General may direct.

Exemption from seizure of communication facilities

(5) Subsections 199(6) and (7) apply with such modifications as the circumstances require to section 318 or subsection (1) or (2) of this section.

Consent

(6) No proceeding for an offence under subsection (2) shall be instituted without the consent of the Attorney General.

Definitions

(7) In this section,
communicating
identifiable group
public place
statements
R.S., 1985, c. C-46, s. 319;
R.S., 1985, c. 27 (1st Supp.), s. 203;
2004, c. 14, s. 2.

Warrant of seizure

320 (1) A judge who is satisfied by information on oath that there are reasonable grounds for believing that any publication, copies of which are kept for sale or distribution in premises within the jurisdiction of the court, is hate propaganda shall issue a warrant under his hand authorizing seizure of the copies.

Summons to occupier

(2) Within seven days of the issue of a warrant under subsection (1), the judge shall issue a summons

to the occupier of the premises requiring him to appear before the court and show cause why the matter seized should not be forfeited to Her Majesty.

Owner and author may appear

(3) The owner and the author of the matter seized under subsection (1) and alleged to be hate propaganda may appear and be represented in the proceedings in order to oppose the making of an order for the forfeiture of the matter.

Order of forfeiture

(4) If the court is satisfied that the publication referred to in subsection (1) is hate propaganda, it shall make an order declaring the matter forfeited to Her Majesty in right of the province in which the proceedings take place, for disposal as the Attorney General may direct.

Disposal of matter

(5) If the court is not satisfied that the publication referred to in subsection (1) is hate propaganda, it shall order that the matter be restored to the person from whom it was seized forthwith after the time for final appeal has expired.

Appeal

(6) An appeal lies from an order made under subsection (4) or (5) by any person who appeared in the proceedings

(a) on any ground of appeal that involves a question of law alone,

(b) on any ground of appeal that involves a question of fact alone, or

(c) on any ground of appeal that involves a question of mixed law and fact,

as if it were an appeal against conviction or against a judgment or verdict of acquittal, as the case may be, on a question of law alone under Part XXI, and sections 673 to 696 apply with such modifications as the circumstances require.

Consent

(7) No proceeding under this section shall be instituted without the consent of the Attorney General.

Definitions

(8) In this section,

court

(a) in the Province of Quebec, the Court of Quebec,

(a.1) in the Province of Ontario, the Superior Court of Justice,

(b) in the Provinces of New Brunswick, Manitoba, Saskatchewan and Alberta, the Court of Queen's Bench,

(c) in the Province of Newfoundland and Labrador, the Supreme Court, Trial Division,

(c.1) (d) in the Provinces of Nova Scotia, British Columbia and Prince Edward Island, in Yukon and in the Northwest Territories, the Supreme Court, and

(e) in Nunavut, the Nunavut Court of Justice;

genocide

hate propaganda

judge

R.S., 1985, c. C-46, s. 320;

R.S., 1985, c. 27 (2nd Supp.), s. 10, c. 40 (4th Supp.), s. 2;

1990, c. 16, s. 4, c. 17, s. 11;

1992, c. 1, s. 58, c. 51, s. 36;

1998, c. 30, s. 14;

1999, c. 3, s. 29;

2002, c. 7, s. 142;

2015, c. 3, s. 49.

Warrant of seizure

320.1 (1) If a judge is satisfied by information on oath that there are reasonable grounds to believe that there is material that is hate propaganda within the meaning of subsection 320(8) or computer data within the meaning of subsection 342.1(2) that makes hate propaganda available, that is stored on and made available to the public through a computer system within the meaning of subsection

342.1(2) that is within the jurisdiction of the court, the judge may order the custodian of the computer system to

(a) give an electronic copy of the material to the court;

(b) ensure that the material is no longer stored on and made available through the computer system; and

(c) provide the information necessary to identify and locate the person who posted the material.

Notice to person who posted the material

(2) Within a reasonable time after receiving the information referred to in paragraph (1)(c), the judge shall cause notice to be given to the person who posted the material, giving that person the opportunity to appear and be represented before the court and show cause why the material should not be deleted. If the person cannot be identified or located or does not reside in Canada, the judge may order the custodian of the computer system to post the text of the notice at the location where the material was previously stored and made available, until the time set for the appearance.

Person who posted the material may appear

(3) The person who posted the material may appear and be represented in the proceedings in order to oppose the making of an order under subsection (5).

Non-appearance

(4) If the person who posted the material does not appear for the proceedings, the court may proceed

Order

(5) If the court is satisfied, on a balance of probabilities, that the material is available to the public and is hate propaganda within the meaning of subsection 320(8) or computer data within the meaning of subsection 342.1(2) that makes hate propaganda available, it may order the custodian of the computer system to delete the material.

Destruction of copy

(6) When the court makes the order for the deletion of the material, it may order the destruction of the electronic copy in the court's possession.

Return of material

(7) If the court is not satisfied that the material is available to the public and is hate propaganda within the meaning of subsection 320(8) or computer data within the meaning of subsection 342.1(2) that makes hate propaganda available, the court shall order that the electronic copy be returned to the custodian and terminate the order under paragraph (1)(b).

Other provisions to apply

(8) Subsections 320(6) to (8) apply, with any modifications that the circumstances require, to this section.

When order takes effect

(9) No order made under subsections (5) to (7) takes effect until the time for final appeal has expired.

2001, c. 41, s. 10;

2014, c. 31, s. 13.

PART IX

PART IX

Offences Against Rights of Property

Interpretation

Definitions

321 In this Part,

break

(a) to break any part, internal or external, or

(b) to open any thing that is used or intended to be used to close or to cover an internal or external opening;

credit card
(a) on presentation to obtain, on credit, money, goods, services or any other thing of value, or
(b) in an automated teller machine, a remote service unit or a similar automated banking device to obtain any of the services offered through the machine, unit or device;
document
exchequer bill
exchequer bill paper
false document
(a) the whole or a material part of which purports to be made by or on behalf of a person
(i) who did not make it or authorize it to be made, or
(ii) who did not in fact exist,
(b) that is made by or on behalf of the person who purports to make it but is false in some material particular,
(c) that is made in the name of an existing person, by him or under his authority, with a fraudulent intention that it should pass as being made by a person, real or fictitious, other than the person who makes it or under whose authority it is made;
revenue paper
R.S., 1985, c. C-46, s. 321;
R.S., 1985, c. 27 (1st Supp.), s. 42.

Theft

Theft
322 (1) Every one commits theft who fraudulently and without colour of right takes, or fraudulently and without colour of right converts to his use or to the use of another person, anything, whether animate or inanimate, with intent
(a) to deprive, temporarily or absolutely, the owner of it, or a person who has a special property or interest in it, of the thing or of his property or interest in it;
(b) to pledge it or deposit it as security;
(c) to part with it under a condition with respect to its return that the person who parts with it may be unable to perform; or
(d) to deal with it in such a manner that it cannot be restored in the condition in which it was at the time it was taken or converted.

Time when theft completed
(2) A person commits theft when, with intent to steal anything, he moves it or causes it to move or to be moved, or begins to cause it to become movable.

Secrecy
(3) A taking or conversion of anything may be fraudulent notwithstanding that it is effected without secrecy or attempt at concealment.

Purpose of taking
(4) For the purposes of this Act, the question whether anything that is converted is taken for the purpose of conversion, or whether it is, at the time it is converted, in the lawful possession of the person who converts it is not material.

Wild living creature
(5) For the purposes of this section, a person who has a wild living creature in captivity shall be deemed to have a special property or interest in it while it is in captivity and after it has escaped from captivity.
R.S., c. C-34, s. 283.

Oysters
323 (1) Where oysters and oyster brood are in oyster beds, layings or fisheries that are the property of any person and are sufficiently marked out or known as the property of that person, that person shall be deemed to have a special property or interest in them.

Oyster bed
(2) An indictment is sufficient if it describes an oyster bed, laying or fishery by name or in any other way, without stating that it is situated in a particular territorial division.
R.S., c. C-34, s. 284.

Theft by bailee of things under seizure
324 Every one who is a bailee of anything that is under lawful seizure by a peace officer or public officer in the execution of the duties of his office, and who is obliged by law or agreement to produce and deliver it to that officer or to another person entitled thereto at a certain time and place, or on demand, steals it if he does not produce and deliver it in accordance with his obligation, but he does not steal it if his failure to produce and deliver it is not the result of a wilful act or omission by him.
R.S., c. C-34, s. 285.

Agent pledging goods, when not theft
325 A factor or an agent does not commit theft by pledging or giving a lien on goods or documents of title to goods that are entrusted to him for the purpose of sale or for any other purpose, if the pledge or lien is for an amount that does not exceed the sum of

(a) the amount due to him from his principal at the time the goods or documents are pledged or the lien is given; and

(b) the amount of any bill of exchange that he has accepted for or on account of his principal.
R.S., c. C-34, s. 286.

Theft of telecommunication service
326 (1) Every one commits theft who fraudulently, maliciously, or without colour of right,

(a) abstracts, consumes or uses electricity or gas or causes it to be wasted or diverted; or

(b) uses any telecommunication facility or obtains any telecommunication service.

(2) R.S., 1985, c. C-46, s. 326;
2014, c. 31, s. 14.

Possession, etc., of device to obtain use of telecommunication facility or telecommunication service
327 (1) Everyone who, without lawful excuse, makes, possesses, sells, offers for sale, imports, obtains for use, distributes or makes available a device that is designed or adapted primarily to use a telecommunication facility or obtain a telecommunication service without payment of a lawful charge, under circumstances that give rise to a reasonable inference that the device has been used or is or was intended to be used for that purpose, is

(a) guilty of an indictable offence and liable to imprisonment for a term of not more than two years; or

(b) guilty of an offence punishable on summary conviction.

Forfeiture
(2) If a person is convicted of an offence under subsection (1) or paragraph 326(1)(b), in addition to any punishment that is imposed, any device in relation to which the offence was committed or the possession of which constituted the offence may be ordered forfeited to Her Majesty and may be disposed of as the Attorney General directs.

Limitation
(3) No order for forfeiture is to be made in respect of telecommunication facilities or equipment by means of which an offence under subsection (1) is committed if they are owned by a person engaged in providing a telecommunication service to the public or form part of such a person's telecommunication service or system and that person is not a party to the offence.

Definition of
device
(4) In this section,
device
(a) a component of a device; and
(b) a computer program within the meaning of subsection 342.1(2).
R.S., 1985, c. C-46, s. 327;

2014, c. 31, s. 15.
Theft by or from person having special property or interest
328 A person may be convicted of theft notwithstanding that anything that is alleged to have been stolen was stolen

(a) by the owner of it from a person who has a special property or interest in it;

(b) by a person who has a special property or interest in it from the owner of it;

(c) by a lessee of it from his reversioner;

(d) by one of several joint owners, tenants in common or partners of or in it from the other persons who have an interest in it; or

(e) by the representatives of an organization from the organization.

R.S., 1985, c. C-46, s. 328;

2003, c. 21, s. 4.

329 Theft by person required to account
330 (1) Every one commits theft who, having received anything from any person on terms that require him to account for or pay it or the proceeds of it or a part of the proceeds to that person or another person, fraudulently fails to account for or pay it or the proceeds of it or the part of the proceeds of it accordingly.

Effect of entry in account
(2) Where subsection (1) otherwise applies, but one of the terms is that the thing received or the proceeds or part of the proceeds of it shall be an item in a debtor and creditor account between the person who receives the thing and the person to whom he is to account for or to pay it, and that the latter shall rely only on the liability of the other as his debtor in respect thereof, a proper entry in that account of the thing received or the proceeds or part of the proceeds of it, as the case may be, is a sufficient accounting therefor, and no fraudulent conversion of the thing or the proceeds or part of the proceeds of it thereby accounted for shall be deemed to have taken place.

R.S., c. C-34, s. 290.

Theft by person holding power of attorney
331 Every one commits theft who, being entrusted, whether solely or jointly with another person, with a power of attorney for the sale, mortgage, pledge or other disposition of real or personal property, fraudulently sells, mortgages, pledges or otherwise disposes of the property or any part of it, or fraudulently converts the proceeds of a sale, mortgage, pledge or other disposition of the property, or any part of the proceeds, to a purpose other than that for which he was entrusted by the power of attorney.

R.S., c. C-34, s. 291.

Misappropriation of money held under direction
332 (1) Every one commits theft who, having received, either solely or jointly with another person, money or valuable security or a power of attorney for the sale of real or personal property, with a direction that the money or a part of it, or the proceeds or a part of the proceeds of the security or the property shall be applied to a purpose or paid to a person specified in the direction, fraudulently and contrary to the direction applies to any other purpose or pays to any other person the money or proceeds or any part of it.

Effect of entry in account
(2) This section does not apply where a person who receives anything mentioned in subsection (1) and the person from whom he receives it deal with each other on such terms that all money paid to the former would, in the absence of any such direction, be properly treated as an item in a debtor and creditor account between them, unless the direction is in writing.

R.S., c. C-34, s. 292.

Taking ore for scientific purpose
333 No person commits theft by reason only that he takes, for the purpose of exploration or scientific investigation, a specimen of ore or mineral from land that is not enclosed and is not occupied or worked as a mine, quarry or digging.

R.S., c. C-34, s. 293.

Motor vehicle theft
333.1 (1) Everyone who commits theft is, if the property stolen is a motor vehicle, guilty of an offence and liable
(a) on proceedings by way of indictment, to imprisonment for a term of not more than 10 years, and to a minimum punishment of imprisonment for a term of six months in the case of a third or subsequent offence under this subsection; or
(b) on summary conviction, to imprisonment for a term of not more than 18 months.
Subsequent offences
(2) For the purpose of determining whether a convicted person has committed a third or subsequent offence, an offence for which the person was previously convicted is considered to be an earlier offence whether it was prosecuted by indictment or by way of summary conviction proceedings.
2010, c. 14, s. 3.
Punishment for theft
334 Except where otherwise provided by law, every one who commits theft
(a) is guilty of an indictable offence and liable to imprisonment for a term not exceeding ten years, where the property stolen is a testamentary instrument or the value of what is stolen exceeds five thousand dollars; or
(b) is guilty
(i) of an indictable offence and is liable to imprisonment for a term not exceeding two years, or
(ii) of an offence punishable on summary conviction,
where the value of what is stolen does not exceed five thousand dollars.
R.S., 1985, c. C-46, s. 334;
R.S., 1985, c. 27 (1st Supp.), s. 43;
1994, c. 44, s. 20.

Offences Resembling Theft

Taking motor vehicle or vessel or found therein without consent
335 (1) Subject to subsection (1.1), every one who, without the consent of the owner, takes a motor vehicle or vessel with intent to drive, use, navigate or operate it or cause it to be driven, used, navigated or operated, or is an occupant of a motor vehicle or vessel knowing that it was taken without the consent of the owner, is guilty of an offence punishable on summary conviction.
Exception
(1.1) Subsection (1) does not apply to an occupant of a motor vehicle or vessel who, on becoming aware that it was taken without the consent of the owner, attempted to leave the motor vehicle or vessel, to the extent that it was feasible to do so, or actually left the motor vehicle or vessel.
Definition of
vessel
(2) For the purposes of subsection (1),
vessel
R.S., 1985, c. C-46, s. 335;
R.S., 1985, c. 1 (4th Supp.), s. 15;
1997, c. 18, s. 15.
Criminal breach of trust
336 Every one who, being a trustee of anything for the use or benefit, whether in whole or in part, of another person, or for a public or charitable purpose, converts, with intent to defraud and in contravention of his trust, that thing or any part of it to a use that is not authorized by the trust is guilty of an indictable offence and liable to imprisonment for a term not exceeding fourteen years.
R.S., c. C-34, s. 296.
Public servant refusing to deliver property
337 Every one who, being or having been employed in the service of Her Majesty in right of Canada or a province, or in the service of a municipality, and entrusted by virtue of that employment with the

receipt, custody, management or control of anything, refuses or fails to deliver it to a person who is authorized to demand it and does demand it is guilty of an indictable offence and liable to imprisonment for a term not exceeding fourteen years.
R.S., c. C-34, s. 297.

Fraudulently taking cattle or defacing brand
338 (1) Every one who, without the consent of the owner,
(a) fraudulently takes, holds, keeps in his possession, conceals, receives, appropriates, purchases or sells cattle that are found astray, or
(b) fraudulently, in whole or in part,
(i) obliterates, alters or defaces a brand or mark on cattle, or
(ii) makes a false or counterfeit brand or mark on cattle,
is guilty of an indictable offence and liable to imprisonment for a term not exceeding five years.

Punishment for theft of cattle
(2) Every one who commits theft of cattle is guilty of an indictable offence and liable to imprisonment for a term not exceeding ten years.

Evidence of property in cattle
(3) In any proceedings under this Act, evidence that cattle are marked with a brand or mark that is recorded or registered in accordance with any Act is, in the absence of any evidence to the contrary, proof that the cattle are owned by the registered owner of that brand or mark.

Presumption from possession
(4) Where an accused is charged with an offence under subsection (1) or (2), the burden of proving that the cattle came lawfully into the possession of the accused or his employee or into the possession of another person on behalf of the accused is on the accused, if the accused is not the registered owner of the brand or mark with which the cattle are marked, unless it appears that possession of the cattle by an employee of the accused or by another person on behalf of the accused was without the knowledge and authority, sanction or approval of the accused.
R.S., c. C-34, s. 298;
1974-75-76, c. 93, s. 26.

Taking possession, etc., of drift timber
339 (1) Every one is guilty of an indictable offence and liable to imprisonment for a term not exceeding five years who, without the consent of the owner,
(a) fraudulently takes, holds, keeps in his possession, conceals, receives, appropriates, purchases or sells,
(b) removes, alters, obliterates or defaces a mark or number on, or
(c) refuses to deliver up to the owner or to the person in charge thereof on behalf of the owner or to a person authorized by the owner to receive it,
any lumber or lumbering equipment that is found adrift, cast ashore or lying on or embedded in the bed or bottom, or on the bank or beach, of a river, stream or lake in Canada, or in the harbours or any of the coastal waters of Canada.

Dealer in second-hand goods
(2) Every one who, being a dealer in second-hand goods of any kind, trades or traffics in or has in his possession for sale or traffic any lumbering equipment that is marked with the mark, brand, registered timber mark, name or initials of a person, without the written consent of that person, is guilty of an offence punishable on summary conviction.

Search for timber unlawfully detained
(3) A peace officer who suspects, on reasonable grounds, that any lumber owned by any person and bearing the registered timber mark of that person is kept or detained in or on any place without the knowledge or consent of that person, may enter into or on that place to ascertain whether or not it is detained there without the knowledge or consent of that person.

Evidence of property in timber
(4) Where any lumber or lumbering equipment is marked with a timber mark or a boom chain brand registered under any Act, the mark or brand is, in proceedings under subsection (1), and, in the

absence of any evidence to the contrary, proof that it is the property of the registered owner of the mark or brand.

Presumption from possession

(5) Where an accused or his servants or agents are in possession of lumber or lumbering equipment marked with the mark, brand, registered timber mark, name or initials of another person, the burden of proving that it came lawfully into his possession or into possession of his servants or agents is, in proceedings under subsection (1), on the accused.

Definitions

(6) In this section,

coastal waters of Canada

lumber

lumbering equipment

R.S., c. C-34, s. 299.

Destroying documents of title

340 Every one who, for a fraudulent purpose, destroys, cancels, conceals or obliterates

(a) a document of title to goods or lands,

(b) a valuable security or testamentary instrument, or

(c) a judicial or official document,

is guilty of an indictable offence and liable to imprisonment for a term not exceeding ten years.

R.S., c. C-34, s. 300.

Fraudulent concealment

341 Every one who, for a fraudulent purpose, takes, obtains, removes or conceals anything is guilty of an indictable offence and liable to imprisonment for a term not exceeding two years.

R.S., c. C-34, s. 301.

Theft, forgery, etc., of credit card

342 (1) Every person who

(a) steals a credit card,

(b) forges or falsifies a credit card,

(c) possesses, uses or traffics in a credit card or a forged or falsified credit card, knowing that it was obtained, made or altered

(i) by the commission in Canada of an offence, or

(ii) by an act or omission anywhere that, if it had occurred in Canada, would have constituted an offence, or

(d) uses a credit card knowing that it has been revoked or cancelled,

is guilty of

(e) an indictable offence and is liable to imprisonment for a term not exceeding ten years, or

(f) an offence punishable on summary conviction.

Jurisdiction

(2) An accused who is charged with an offence under subsection (1) may be tried and punished by any court having jurisdiction to try that offence in the place where the offence is alleged to have been committed or in the place where the accused is found, is arrested or is in custody, but where the place where the accused is found, is arrested or is in custody is outside the province in which the offence is alleged to have been committed, no proceedings in respect of that offence shall be commenced in that place without the consent of the Attorney General of that province.

Unauthorized use of credit card data

(3) Every person who, fraudulently and without colour of right, possesses, uses, traffics in or permits another person to use credit card data, including personal authentication information, whether or not the data is authentic, that would enable a person to use a credit card or to obtain the services that are provided by the issuer of a credit card to credit card holders is guilty of

(a) an indictable offence and is liable to imprisonment for a term not exceeding ten years; or

(b) an offence punishable on summary conviction.

Definitions

(4) In this section,
personal authentication information
traffic
R.S., 1985, c. C-46, s. 342;
R.S., 1985, c. 27 (1st Supp.), ss. 44, 185(F);
1997, c. 18, s. 16;
2009, c. 28, s. 4.

Instruments for copying credit card data or forging or falsifying credit cards

342.01 (1) Every person is guilty of an indictable offence and liable to imprisonment for a term of not more than 10 years, or is guilty of an offence punishable on summary conviction, who, without lawful justification or excuse, makes, repairs, buys, sells, exports from Canada, imports into Canada or possesses any instrument, device, apparatus, material or thing that they know has been used or know is adapted or intended for use

(a) in the copying of credit card data for use in the commission of an offence under subsection 342(3); or

(b) in the forging or falsifying of credit cards.

Forfeiture

(2) Where a person is convicted of an offence under subsection (1), any instrument, device, apparatus, material or thing in relation to which the offence was committed or the possession of which constituted the offence may, in addition to any other punishment that may be imposed, be ordered forfeited to Her Majesty, whereupon it may be disposed of as the Attorney General directs.

Limitation

(3) No order of forfeiture may be made under subsection (2) in respect of any thing that is the property of a person who was not a party to the offence under subsection (1).

1997, c. 18, s. 17;
2009, c. 28, s. 5.

Unauthorized use of computer

342.1 (1) Everyone is guilty of an indictable offence and liable to imprisonment for a term of not more than 10 years, or is guilty of an offence punishable on summary conviction who, fraudulently and without colour of right,

(a) obtains, directly or indirectly, any computer service;

(b) by means of an electro-magnetic, acoustic, mechanical or other device, intercepts or causes to be intercepted, directly or indirectly, any function of a computer system;

(c) uses or causes to be used, directly or indirectly, a computer system with intent to commit an offence under paragraph (a) or (b) or under section 430 in relation to computer data or a computer system; or

(d) uses, possesses, traffics in or permits another person to have access to a computer password that would enable a person to commit an offence under paragraph (a), (b) or (c).

Definitions

(2) In this section,
computer data
computer password
computer program
computer service
computer system

(a) contains computer programs or other computer data, and

(b) by means of computer programs,

(i) performs logic and control, and

(ii) may perform any other function;

data
electro-magnetic, acoustic, mechanical or other device
function

intercept
traffic
R.S., 1985, c. 27 (1st Supp.), s. 45;
1997, c. 18, s. 18;
2014, c. 31, s. 16.

Possession of device to obtain unauthorized use of computer system or to commit mischief
342.2 (1) Everyone who, without lawful excuse, makes, possesses, sells, offers for sale, imports, obtains for use, distributes or makes available a device that is designed or adapted primarily to commit an offence under section 342.1 or 430, under circumstances that give rise to a reasonable inference that the device has been used or is or was intended to be used to commit such an offence, is
(a) guilty of an indictable offence and liable to imprisonment for a term of not more than two years; or
(b) guilty of an offence punishable on summary conviction.

Forfeiture
(2) If a person is convicted of an offence under subsection (1), in addition to any punishment that is imposed, any device in relation to which the offence was committed or the possession of which constituted the offence may be ordered forfeited to Her Majesty and may be disposed of as the Attorney General directs.

Limitation
(3) No order of forfeiture may be made under subsection (2) in respect of any thing that is the property of a person who was not a party to the offence under subsection (1).

Definition of
device
(4) In this section,
device
(a) a component of a device; and
(b) a computer program within the meaning of subsection 342.1(2).
1997, c. 18, s. 19;
2014, c. 31, s. 17.

Robbery and Extortion

Robbery
343 Every one commits robbery who
(a) steals, and for the purpose of extorting whatever is stolen or to prevent or overcome resistance to the stealing, uses violence or threats of violence to a person or property;
(b) steals from any person and, at the time he steals or immediately before or immediately thereafter, wounds, beats, strikes or uses any personal violence to that person;
(c) assaults any person with intent to steal from him; or
(d) steals from any person while armed with an offensive weapon or imitation thereof.
R.S., c. C-34, s. 302.

Robbery
344 (1) Every person who commits robbery is guilty of an indictable offence and liable
(a) if a restricted firearm or prohibited firearm is used in the commission of the offence or if any firearm is used in the commission of the offence and the offence is committed for the benefit of, at the direction of, or in association with, a criminal organization, to imprisonment for life and to a minimum punishment of imprisonment for a term of
(i) in the case of a first offence, five years, and
(ii) in the case of a second or subsequent offence, seven years;
(a.1) in any other case where a firearm is used in the commission of the offence, to imprisonment for life and to a minimum punishment of imprisonment for a term of four years; and
(b) in any other case, to imprisonment for life.

Subsequent offences
(2) In determining, for the purpose of paragraph (1)(a), whether a convicted person has committed a second or subsequent offence, if the person was earlier convicted of any of the following offences, that offence is to be considered as an earlier offence:
(a) an offence under this section;
(b) an offence under subsection 85(1) or (2) or section 244 or 244.2; or
(c) an offence under section 220, 236, 239, 272 or 273, subsection 279(1) or section 279.1 or 346 if a firearm was used in the commission of the offence.
However, an earlier offence shall not be taken into account if 10 years have elapsed between the day on which the person was convicted of the earlier offence and the day on which the person was convicted of the offence for which sentence is being imposed, not taking into account any time in custody.

Sequence of convictions only
(3) For the purposes of subsection (2), the only question to be considered is the sequence of convictions and no consideration shall be given to the sequence of commission of offences or whether any offence occurred before or after any conviction.
R.S., 1985, c. C-46, s. 344;
1995, c. 39, s. 149;
2008, c. 6, s. 32;
2009, c. 22, s. 14.

Stopping mail with intent
345 Every one who stops a mail conveyance with intent to rob or search it is guilty of an indictable offence and liable to imprisonment for life.
R.S., c. C-34, s. 304.

Extortion
346 (1) Every one commits extortion who, without reasonable justification or excuse and with intent to obtain anything, by threats, accusations, menaces or violence induces or attempts to induce any person, whether or not he is the person threatened, accused or menaced or to whom violence is shown, to do anything or cause anything to be done.

Extortion
(1.1) Every person who commits extortion is guilty of an indictable offence and liable
(a) if a restricted firearm or prohibited firearm is used in the commission of the offence or if any firearm is used in the commission of the offence and the offence is committed for the benefit of, at the direction of, or in association with, a criminal organization, to imprisonment for life and to a minimum punishment of imprisonment for a term of
(i) in the case of a first offence, five years, and
(ii) in the case of a second or subsequent offence, seven years;
(a.1) in any other case where a firearm is used in the commission of the offence, to imprisonment for life and to a minimum punishment of imprisonment for a term of four years; and
(b) in any other case, to imprisonment for life.

Subsequent offences
(1.2) In determining, for the purpose of paragraph (1.1)(a), whether a convicted person has committed a second or subsequent offence, if the person was earlier convicted of any of the following offences, that offence is to be considered as an earlier offence:
(a) an offence under this section;
(b) an offence under subsection 85(1) or (2) or section 244 or 244.2; or
(c) an offence under section 220, 236, 239, 272 or 273, subsection 279(1) or section 279.1 or 344 if a firearm was used in the commission of the offence.
However, an earlier offence shall not be taken into account if 10 years have elapsed between the day on which the person was convicted of the earlier offence and the day on which the person was convicted of the offence for which sentence is being imposed, not taking into account any time in custody.

Sequence of convictions only
(1.3) For the purposes of subsection (1.2), the only question to be considered is the sequence of convictions and no consideration shall be given to the sequence of commission of offences or whether any offence occurred before or after any conviction.
Saving
(2) A threat to institute civil proceedings is not a threat for the purposes of this section.
R.S., 1985, c. C-46, s. 346;
R.S., 1985, c. 27 (1st Supp.), s. 46;
1995, c. 39, s. 150;
2008, c. 6, s. 33;
2009, c. 22, s. 15.

Criminal Interest Rate

Criminal interest rate
347 (1) Despite any other Act of Parliament, every one who enters into an agreement or arrangement to receive interest at a criminal rate, or receives a payment or partial payment of interest at a criminal rate, is
(a) guilty of an indictable offence and liable to imprisonment for a term not exceeding five years; or
(b) guilty of an offence punishable on summary conviction and liable to a fine not exceeding $25,000 or to imprisonment for a term not exceeding six months or to both.
Definitions
(2) In this section,
credit advanced
criminal rate
insurance charge
interest
official fee
overdraft charge
required deposit balance
Presumption
(3) Where a person receives a payment or partial payment of interest at a criminal rate, he shall, in the absence of evidence to the contrary, be deemed to have knowledge of the nature of the payment and that it was received at a criminal rate.
Proof of effective annual rate
(4) In any proceedings under this section, a certificate of a Fellow of the Canadian Institute of Actuaries stating that he has calculated the effective annual rate of interest on any credit advanced under an agreement or arrangement and setting out the calculations and the information on which they are based is, in the absence of evidence to the contrary, proof of the effective annual rate without proof of the signature or official character of the person appearing to have signed the certificate.
Notice
(5) A certificate referred to in subsection (4) shall not be received in evidence unless the party intending to produce it has given to the accused or defendant reasonable notice of that intention together with a copy of the certificate.
Cross-examination with leave
(6) An accused or a defendant against whom a certificate referred to in subsection (4) is produced may, with leave of the court, require the attendance of the actuary for the purposes of cross-examination.
Consent required for proceedings
(7) No proceedings shall be commenced under this section without the consent of the Attorney General.

Application
(8) This section does not apply to any transaction to which the
Tax Rebate Discounting Act
R.S., 1985, c. C-46, s. 347;
1992, c. 1, s. 60(F);
2007, c. 9, s. 1.
Definitions
347.1 (1) The following definitions apply in subsection (2).
interest
payday loan
Non-application
(2) Section 347 and section 2 of the
Interest Act
financial institution
Bank Act
(a) the amount of money advanced under the agreement is $1,500 or less and the term of the agreement is 62 days or less;
(b) the person is licensed or otherwise specifically authorized under the laws of a province to enter into the agreement; and
(c) the province is designated under subsection (3).
Designation of province
(3) The Governor in Council shall, by order and at the request of the lieutenant governor in council of a province, designate the province for the purposes of this section if the province has legislative measures that protect recipients of payday loans and that provide for limits on the total cost of borrowing under the agreements.
Revocation
(4) The Governor in Council shall, by order, revoke the designation made under subsection (3) if requested to do so by the lieutenant governor in council of the province or if the legislative measures described in that subsection are no longer in force in that province.
2007, c. 9, s. 2.

Breaking and Entering

Breaking and entering with intent, committing offence or breaking out
348 (1) Every one who
(a) breaks and enters a place with intent to commit an indictable offence therein,
(b) breaks and enters a place and commits an indictable offence therein, or
(c) breaks out of a place after
(i) committing an indictable offence therein, or
(ii) entering the place with intent to commit an indictable offence therein,
is guilty
(d) if the offence is committed in relation to a dwelling-house, of an indictable offence and liable to imprisonment for life, and
(e) if the offence is committed in relation to a place other than a dwelling-house, of an indictable offence and liable to imprisonment for a term not exceeding ten years or of an offence punishable on summary conviction.
Presumptions
(2) For the purposes of proceedings under this section, evidence that an accused
(a) broke and entered a place or attempted to break and enter a place is, in the absence of evidence to the contrary, proof that he broke and entered the place or attempted to do so, as the case may be, with intent to commit an indictable offence therein; or
(b) broke out of a place is, in the absence of any evidence to the contrary, proof that he broke out

after
(i) committing an indictable offence therein, or
(ii) entering with intent to commit an indictable offence therein.

Definition of
(3) For the purposes of this section and section 351,
place
(a) a dwelling-house;
(b) a building or structure or any part thereof, other than a dwelling-house;
(c) a railway vehicle, a vessel, an aircraft or a trailer; or
(d) a pen or an enclosure in which fur-bearing animals are kept in captivity for breeding or commercial purposes.
R.S., 1985, c. C-46, s. 348;
R.S., 1985, c. 27 (1st Supp.), s. 47;
1997, c. 18, s. 20.

Aggravating circumstance — home invasion
348.1 If a person is convicted of an offence under section 98 or 98.1, subsection 279(2) or section 343, 346 or 348 in relation to a dwelling-house, the court imposing the sentence on the person shall consider as an aggravating circumstance the fact that the dwelling-house was occupied at the time of the commission of the offence and that the person, in committing the offence,
(a) knew that or was reckless as to whether the dwelling-house was occupied; and
(b) used violence or threats of violence to a person or property.
2002, c. 13, s. 15;
2008, c. 6, s. 34.

Being unlawfully in dwelling-house
349 (1) Every person who, without lawful excuse, the proof of which lies on that person, enters or is in a dwelling-house with intent to commit an indictable offence in it is guilty of an indictable offence and liable to imprisonment for a term not exceeding ten years or of an offence punishable on summary conviction.

Presumption
(2) For the purposes of proceedings under this section, evidence that an accused, without lawful excuse, entered or was in a dwelling-house is, in the absence of any evidence to the contrary, proof that he entered or was in the dwelling-house with intent to commit an indictable offence therein.
R.S., 1985, c. C-46, s. 349;
1997, c. 18, s. 21.

Entrance
350 For the purposes of sections 348 and 349,
(a) a person enters as soon as any part of his body or any part of an instrument that he uses is within any thing that is being entered; and
(b) a person shall be deemed to have broken and entered if
(i) he obtained entrance by a threat or an artifice or by collusion with a person within, or
(ii) he entered without lawful justification or excuse, the proof of which lies on him, by a permanent or temporary opening.
R.S., c. C-34, s. 308.

Possession of break-in instrument
351 (1) Every one who, without lawful excuse, the proof of which lies on them, has in their possession any instrument suitable for the purpose of breaking into any place, motor vehicle, vault or safe under circumstances that give rise to a reasonable inference that the instrument has been used or is or was intended to be used for such a purpose,
(a) is guilty of an indictable offence and liable to imprisonment for a term not exceeding ten years; or
(b) is guilty of an offence punishable on summary conviction.

Disguise with intent
(2) Every one who, with intent to commit an indictable offence, has his face masked or coloured or is

otherwise disguised is guilty of an indictable offence and liable to imprisonment for a term not exceeding ten years.
R.S., 1985, c. C-46, s. 351;
R.S., 1985, c. 27 (1st Supp.), s. 48;
2008, c. 18, s. 9.

Possession of instruments for breaking into coin-operated or currency exchange devices

352 Every one who, without lawful excuse, the proof of which lies on him, has in his possession any instrument suitable for breaking into a coin-operated device or a currency exchange device, under circumstances that give rise to a reasonable inference that the instrument has been used or is or was intended to be used for breaking into a coin-operated device or a currency exchange device, is guilty of an indictable offence and liable to imprisonment for a term not exceeding two years.
R.S., c. C-34, s. 310;
1972, c. 13, s. 26;
1974-75-76, c. 93, s. 28.

Selling, etc., automobile master key

353 (1) Every one who
(a) sells, offers for sale or advertises in a province an automobile master key otherwise than under the authority of a licence issued by the Attorney General of that province, or
(b) purchases or has in his possession in a province an automobile master key otherwise than under the authority of a licence issued by the Attorney General of that province,
is guilty of an indictable offence and liable to imprisonment for a term not exceeding two years.

Exception

(1.1) A police officer specially authorized by the chief of the police force to possess an automobile master key is not guilty of an offence under subsection (1) by reason only that the police officer possesses an automobile master key for the purposes of the execution of the police officer's duties.

Terms and conditions of licence

(2) A licence issued by the Attorney General of a province as described in paragraph (1)(a) or (b) may contain such terms and conditions relating to the sale, offering for sale, advertising, purchasing, having in possession or use of an automobile master key as the Attorney General of that province may prescribe.

Fees

(2.1) The Attorney General of a province may prescribe fees for the issue or renewal of licences as described in paragraph (1)(a) or (b).

Record to be kept

(3) Every one who sells an automobile master key
(a) shall keep a record of the transaction showing the name and address of the purchaser and particulars of the licence issued to the purchaser as described in paragraph (1)(b); and
(b) shall produce the record for inspection at the request of a peace officer.

Failure to comply with subsection (3)

(4) Every one who fails to comply with subsection (3) is guilty of an offence punishable on summary conviction.

Definitions

(5) The definitions in this subsection apply in this section.
automobile master key
licence
R.S., 1985, c. C-46, s. 353;
1997, c. 18, s. 22.

Tampering with vehicle identification number

353.1 (1) Every person commits an offence who, without lawful excuse, wholly or partially alters, removes or obliterates a vehicle identification number on a motor vehicle.

Definition of

vehicle identification number

(2) For the purpose of this section,
vehicle identification number
Exception
(3) Despite subsection (1), it is not an offence to wholly or partially alter, remove or obliterate a vehicle identification number on a motor vehicle during regular maintenance or any repair or other work done on the vehicle for a legitimate purpose, including a modification of the vehicle.
Punishment
(4) Every person who commits an offence under subsection (1)
(a) is guilty of an indictable offence and liable to imprisonment for a term of not more than five years; or
(b) is guilty of an offence punishable on summary conviction.
2010, c. 14, s. 4.

Possession and Trafficking

Possession of property obtained by crime
354 (1) Every one commits an offence who has in his possession any property or thing or any proceeds of any property or thing knowing that all or part of the property or thing or of the proceeds was obtained by or derived directly or indirectly from
(a) the commission in Canada of an offence punishable by indictment; or
(b) an act or omission anywhere that, if it had occurred in Canada, would have constituted an offence punishable by indictment.
Obliterated vehicle identification number
(2) In proceedings in respect of an offence under subsection (1), evidence that a person has in his possession a motor vehicle the vehicle identification number of which has been wholly or partially removed or obliterated or a part of a motor vehicle being a part bearing a vehicle identification number that has been wholly or partially removed or obliterated is, in the absence of any evidence to the contrary, proof that the motor vehicle or part, as the case may be, was obtained, and that such person had the motor vehicle or part, as the case may be, in his possession knowing that it was obtained,
(a) by the commission in Canada of an offence punishable by indictment; or
(b) by an act or omission anywhere that, if it had occurred in Canada, would have constituted an offence punishable by indictment.
Definition of
vehicle identification number
(3) For the purposes of subsection (2),
vehicle identification number
Exception
(4) A peace officer or a person acting under the direction of a peace officer is not guilty of an offence under this section by reason only that the peace officer or person possesses property or a thing or the proceeds of property or a thing mentioned in subsection (1) for the purposes of an investigation or otherwise in the execution of the peace officer's duties.
R.S., 1985, c. C-46, s. 354;
1997, c. 18, s. 23.
Punishment
355 Every one who commits an offence under section 354
(a) is guilty of an indictable offence and liable to imprisonment for a term not exceeding ten years, where the subject-matter of the offence is a testamentary instrument or the value of the subject-matter of the offence exceeds five thousand dollars; or
(b) is guilty
(i) of an indictable offence and is liable to imprisonment for a term not exceeding two years, or
(ii) of an offence punishable on summary conviction,

where the value of the subject-matter of the offence does not exceed five thousand dollars.
R.S., 1985, c. C-46, s. 355;
R.S., 1985, c. 27 (1st Supp.), s. 49;
1994, c. 44, s. 21.

Definition of
traffic
355.1 For the purposes of sections 355.2 and 355.4,
traffic
2010, c. 14, s. 6.

Trafficking in property obtained by crime
355.2 Everyone commits an offence who traffics in any property or thing or any proceeds of any property or thing knowing that all or part of the property, thing or proceeds was obtained by or derived directly or indirectly from
(a) the commission in Canada of an offence punishable by indictment; or
(b) an act or omission anywhere that, if it had occurred in Canada, would have constituted an offence punishable by indictment.
2010, c. 14, s. 6.

355.3 The importation into Canada or exportation from Canada of any property or thing or any proceeds of any property or thing is prohibited if all or part of the property, thing or proceeds was obtained by or derived directly or indirectly from
(a) the commission in Canada of an offence punishable by indictment; or
(b) an act or omission anywhere that, if it had occurred in Canada, would have constituted an offence punishable by indictment.
2010, c. 14, s. 6.

Possession of property obtained by crime — trafficking
355.4 Everyone commits an offence who has in their possession, for the purpose of trafficking, any property or thing or any proceeds of any property or thing knowing that all or part of the property, thing or proceeds was obtained by or derived directly or indirectly from
(a) the commission in Canada of an offence punishable by indictment; or
(b) an act or omission anywhere that, if it had occurred in Canada, would have constituted an offence punishable by indictment.
2010, c. 14, s. 6.

Punishment
355.5 Everyone who commits an offence under section 355.2 or 355.4
(a) is, if the value of the subject matter of the offence is more than $5,000, guilty of an indictable offence and liable to imprisonment for a term of not more than 14 years; or
(b) is, if the value of the subject matter of the offence is not more than $5,000,
(i) guilty of an indictable offence and liable to imprisonment for a term of not more than five years, or
(ii) guilty of an offence punishable on summary conviction.
2010, c. 14, s. 6.

Theft from mail
356 (1) Everyone commits an offence who
(a) steals
(i) anything sent by post, after it is deposited at a post office and before it is delivered, or after it is delivered but before it is in the possession of the addressee or of a person who may reasonably be considered to be authorized by the addressee to receive mail,
(ii) a bag, sack or other container or covering in which mail is conveyed, whether or not it contains mail, or
(iii) a key suited to a lock adopted for use by the Canada Post Corporation;
(a.1) with intent to commit an offence under paragraph (a), makes, possesses or uses a copy of a key suited to a lock adopted for use by the Canada Post Corporation, or a key suited to obtaining access

to a receptacle or device provided for the receipt of mail;

(b) has in their possession anything that they know has been used to commit an offence under paragraph (a) or (a.1) or anything in respect of which they know that such an offence has been committed; or

(c) fraudulently redirects, or causes to be redirected, anything sent by post.

Allegation of value not necessary

(2) In proceedings for an offence under this section it is not necessary to allege in the indictment or to prove on the trial that anything in respect of which the offence was committed had any value.

Punishment

(3) Everyone who commits an offence under subsection (1)

(a) is guilty of an indictable offence and liable to imprisonment for a term of not more than 10 years; or

(b) is guilty of an offence punishable on summary conviction.

R.S., 1985, c. C-46, s. 356;
2009, c. 28, s. 6.

Bringing into Canada property obtained by crime

357 Every one who brings into or has in Canada anything that he has obtained outside Canada by an act that, if it had been committed in Canada, would have been the offence of theft or an offence under section 342 or 354 is guilty of an indictable offence and liable to a term of imprisonment not exceeding ten years.

R.S., 1985, c. C-46, s. 357;
R.S., 1985, c. 27 (1st Supp.), s. 50.

Having in possession when complete

358 For the purposes of sections 342 and 354 and paragraph 356(1)(b), the offence of having in possession is complete when a person has, alone or jointly with another person, possession of or control over anything mentioned in those sections or when he aids in concealing or disposing of it, as the case may be.

R.S., 1985, c. C-46, s. 358;
R.S., 1985, c. 27 (1st Supp.), s. 50.

Evidence

359 (1) Where an accused is charged with an offence under section 342 or 354 or paragraph 356(1)(b), evidence is admissible at any stage of the proceedings to show that property other than the property that is the subject-matter of the proceedings

(a) was found in the possession of the accused, and

(b) was stolen within twelve months before the proceedings were commenced,

and that evidence may be considered for the purpose of proving that the accused knew that the property that forms the subject-matter of the proceedings was stolen property.

Notice to accused

(2) Subsection (1) does not apply unless

(a) at least three days notice in writing is given to the accused that in the proceedings it is intended to prove that property other than the property that is the subject-matter of the proceedings was found in his possession; and

(b) the notice sets out the nature or description of the property and describes the person from whom it is alleged to have been stolen.

R.S., 1985, c. C-46, s. 359;
R.S., 1985, c. 27 (1st Supp.), s. 51.

Evidence of previous conviction

360 (1) Where an accused is charged with an offence under section 354 or paragraph 356(1)(b) and evidence is adduced that the subject-matter of the proceedings was found in his possession, evidence that the accused was, within five years before the proceedings were commenced, convicted of an offence involving theft or an offence under section 354 is admissible at any stage of the proceedings and may be taken into consideration for the purpose of proving that the accused knew that the

property that forms the subject-matter of the proceedings was unlawfully obtained.
Notice to accused
(2) Subsection (1) does not apply unless at least three days notice in writing is given to the accused that in the proceedings it is intended to prove the previous conviction.
R.S., c. C-34, s. 318.

False Pretences

False pretence
361 (1) A false pretence is a representation of a matter of fact either present or past, made by words or otherwise, that is known by the person who makes it to be false and that is made with a fraudulent intent to induce the person to whom it is made to act on it.
Exaggeration
(2) Exaggerated commendation or depreciation of the quality of anything is not a false pretence unless it is carried to such an extent that it amounts to a fraudulent misrepresentation of fact.
Question of fact
(3) For the purposes of subsection (2), it is a question of fact whether commendation or depreciation amounts to a fraudulent misrepresentation of fact.
R.S., c. C-34, s. 319.
False pretence or false statement
362 (1) Every one commits an offence who
(a) by a false pretence, whether directly or through the medium of a contract obtained by a false pretence, obtains anything in respect of which the offence of theft may be committed or causes it to be delivered to another person;
(b) obtains credit by a false pretence or by fraud;
(c) knowingly makes or causes to be made, directly or indirectly, a false statement in writing with intent that it should be relied on, with respect to the financial condition or means or ability to pay of himself or herself or any person or organization that he or she is interested in or that he or she acts for, for the purpose of procuring, in any form whatever, whether for his or her benefit or the benefit of that person or organization,
(i) the delivery of personal property,
(ii) the payment of money,
(iii) the making of a loan,
(iv) the grant or extension of credit,
(v) the discount of an account receivable, or
(vi) the making, accepting, discounting or endorsing of a bill of exchange, cheque, draft or promissory note; or
(d) knowing that a false statement in writing has been made with respect to the financial condition or means or ability to pay of himself or herself or another person or organization that he or she is interested in or that he or she acts for, procures on the faith of that statement, whether for his or her benefit or for the benefit of that person or organization, anything mentioned in subparagraphs (c)(i) to (vi).
Punishment
(2) Every one who commits an offence under paragraph (1)(a)
(a) is guilty of an indictable offence and liable to a term of imprisonment not exceeding ten years, where the property obtained is a testamentary instrument or the value of what is obtained exceeds five thousand dollars; or
(b) is guilty
(i) of an indictable offence and is liable to imprisonment for a term not exceeding two years, or
(ii) of an offence punishable on summary conviction,
where the value of what is obtained does not exceed five thousand dollars.
Idem

(3) Every one who commits an offence under paragraph (1)(b), (c) or (d) is guilty of an indictable offence and liable to imprisonment for a term not exceeding ten years.

Presumption from cheque issued without funds

(4) Where, in proceedings under paragraph (1)(a), it is shown that anything was obtained by the accused by means of a cheque that, when presented for payment within a reasonable time, was dishonoured on the ground that no funds or insufficient funds were on deposit to the credit of the accused in the bank or other institution on which the cheque was drawn, it shall be presumed to have been obtained by a false pretence, unless the court is satisfied by evidence that when the accused issued the cheque he believed on reasonable grounds that it would be honoured if presented for payment within a reasonable time after it was issued.

Definition of

cheque

(5) In this section,

cheque

R.S., 1985, c. C-46, s. 362;
R.S., 1985, c. 27 (1st Supp.), s. 52;
1994, c. 44, s. 22;
2003, c. 21, s. 5.

Obtaining execution of valuable security by fraud

363 Every one who, with intent to defraud or injure another person, by a false pretence causes or induces any person

(a) to execute, make, accept, endorse or destroy the whole or any part of a valuable security, or

(b) to write, impress or affix a name or seal on any paper or parchment in order that it may afterwards be made or converted into or used or dealt with as a valuable security,

is guilty of an indictable offence and liable to imprisonment for a term not exceeding five years.
R.S., c. C-34, s. 321.

Fraudulently obtaining food, beverage or accommodation

364 (1) Every one who fraudulently obtains food, a beverage or accommodation at any place that is in the business of providing those things is guilty of an offence punishable on summary conviction.

Presumption

(2) In proceedings under this section, evidence that the accused obtained food, a beverage or accommodation at a place that is in the business of providing those things and did not pay for it and

(a) made a false or fictitious show or pretence of having baggage,

(b) had any false or pretended baggage,

(c) surreptitiously removed or attempted to remove his baggage or any material part of it,

(d) absconded or surreptitiously left the premises,

(e) knowingly made a false statement to obtain credit or time for payment, or

(f) offered a worthless cheque, draft or security in payment for the food, beverage or accommodation,

is, in the absence of any evidence to the contrary, proof of fraud.

Definition of

cheque

(3) In this section,

cheque

R.S., 1985, c. C-46, s. 364;
1994, c. 44, s. 23.

Pretending to practise witchcraft, etc.

365 Every one who fraudulently

(a) pretends to exercise or to use any kind of witchcraft, sorcery, enchantment or conjuration,

(b) undertakes, for a consideration, to tell fortunes, or

(c) pretends from his skill in or knowledge of an occult or crafty science to discover where or in what manner anything that is supposed to have been stolen or lost may be found,

is guilty of an offence punishable on summary conviction.
R.S., c. C-34, s. 323.

Forgery and Offences Resembling Forgery

Forgery
366 (1) Every one commits forgery who makes a false document, knowing it to be false, with intent
(a) that it should in any way be used or acted on as genuine, to the prejudice of any one whether within Canada or not; or
(b) that a person should be induced, by the belief that it is genuine, to do or to refrain from doing anything, whether within Canada or not.

Making false document
(2) Making a false document includes
(a) altering a genuine document in any material part;
(b) making a material addition to a genuine document or adding to it a false date, attestation, seal or other thing that is material; or
(c) making a material alteration in a genuine document by erasure, obliteration, removal or in any other way.

When forgery complete
(3) Forgery is complete as soon as a document is made with the knowledge and intent referred to in subsection (1), notwithstanding that the person who makes it does not intend that any particular person should use or act on it as genuine or be induced, by the belief that it is genuine, to do or refrain from doing anything.

Forgery complete though document incomplete
(4) Forgery is complete notwithstanding that the false document is incomplete or does not purport to be a document that is binding in law, if it is such as to indicate that it was intended to be acted on as genuine.

Exception
(5) No person commits forgery by reason only that the person, in good faith, makes a false document at the request of a police force, the Canadian Forces or a department or agency of the federal government or of a provincial government.
R.S., 1985, c. C-46, s. 366;
2009, c. 28, s. 7.

Punishment for forgery
367 Every one who commits forgery
(a) is guilty of an indictable offence and liable to imprisonment for a term not exceeding ten years; or
(b) is guilty of an offence punishable on summary conviction.
R.S., 1985, c. C-46, s. 367;
1994, c. 44, s. 24;
1997, c. 18, s. 24.

Use, trafficking or possession of forged document
368 (1) Everyone commits an offence who, knowing or believing that a document is forged,
(a) uses, deals with or acts on it as if it were genuine;
(b) causes or attempts to cause any person to use, deal with or act on it as if it were genuine;
(c) transfers, sells or offers to sell it or makes it available, to any person, knowing that or being reckless as to whether an offence will be committed under paragraph (a) or (b); or
(d) possesses it with intent to commit an offence under any of paragraphs (a) to (c).

Punishment
(1.1) Everyone who commits an offence under subsection (1)
(a) is guilty of an indictable offence and liable to imprisonment for a term of not more than 10 years; or
(b) is guilty of an offence punishable on summary conviction.

Wherever forged
(2) For the purposes of proceedings under this section, the place where a document was forged is not material.
R.S., 1985, c. C-46, s. 368;
1992, c. 1, s. 60(F);
1997, c. 18, s. 25;
2009, c. 28, s. 8.
Forgery instruments
368.1 Everyone is guilty of an indictable offence and liable to imprisonment for a term of not more than 14 years, or is guilty of an offence punishable on summary conviction, who, without lawful authority or excuse, makes, repairs, buys, sells, exports from Canada, imports into Canada or possesses any instrument, device, apparatus, material or thing that they know has been used or know is adapted or intended for use by any person to commit forgery.
2009, c. 28, s. 9.
Public officers acting in the course of their duties or employment
368.2 No public officer, as defined in subsection 25.1(1), is guilty of an offence under any of sections 366 to 368.1 if the acts alleged to constitute the offence were committed by the public officer for the sole purpose of establishing or maintaining a covert identity for use in the course of the public officer's duties or employment.
2009, c. 28, s. 9.
Exchequer bill paper, public seals, etc.
369 Everyone is guilty of an indictable offence and liable to imprisonment for a term of not more than 14 years who, without lawful authority or excuse,
(a) makes, uses or possesses
(i) any exchequer bill paper, revenue paper or paper that is used to make bank-notes, or
(ii) any paper that is intended to resemble paper mentioned in subparagraph (i); or
(b) makes, reproduces or uses a public seal of Canada or of a province, or the seal of a public body or authority in Canada or of a court of law.
R.S., 1985, c. C-46, s. 369;
2009, c. 28, s. 9.
Counterfeit proclamation, etc.
370 Every one who knowingly
(a) prints any proclamation, order, regulation or appointment, or notice thereof, and causes it falsely to purport to have been printed by the Queen's Printer for Canada or the Queen's Printer for a province, or
(b) tenders in evidence a copy of any proclamation, order, regulation or appointment that falsely purports to have been printed by the Queen's Printer for Canada or the Queen's Printer for a province,
is guilty of an indictable offence and liable to imprisonment for a term not exceeding five years.
R.S., c. C-34, s. 328.
Message in false name
371 Everyone who, with intent to defraud, causes a message to be sent as if it were sent under the authority of another person, knowing that it is not sent under that authority and with intent that it should be acted on as if it were, is guilty of an indictable offence and liable to imprisonment for a term of not more than five years.
R.S., 1985, c. C-46, s. 371;
2014, c. 31, s. 18.
False information
372 (1) Everyone commits an offence who, with intent to injure or alarm a person, conveys information that they know is false, or causes such information to be conveyed by letter or any means of telecommunication.
Indecent communications

(2) Everyone commits an offence who, with intent to alarm or annoy a person, makes an indecent communication to that person or to any other person by a means of telecommunication.

Harassing communications

(3) Everyone commits an offence who, without lawful excuse and with intent to harass a person, repeatedly communicates, or causes repeated communications to be made, with them by a means of telecommunication.

Punishment

(4) Everyone who commits an offence under this section is

(a) guilty of an indictable offence and liable to imprisonment for a term of not more than two years; or

(b) guilty of an offence punishable on summary conviction.

R.S., 1985, c. C-46, s. 372;

2014, c. 31, s. 18.

373 Drawing document without authority, etc.

374 Every one who

(a) with intent to defraud and without lawful authority makes, executes, draws, signs, accepts or endorses a document in the name or on the account of another person by procuration or otherwise, or

(b) makes use of or utters a document knowing that it has been made, executed, signed, accepted or endorsed with intent to defraud and without lawful authority, in the name or on the account of another person, by procuration or otherwise,

is guilty of an indictable offence and liable to imprisonment for a term not exceeding fourteen years.

R.S., c. C-34, s. 332.

Obtaining, etc., by instrument based on forged document

375 Every one who demands, receives or obtains anything, or causes or procures anything to be delivered or paid to any person under, on or by virtue of any instrument issued under the authority of law, knowing that it is based on a forged document, is guilty of an indictable offence and liable to imprisonment for a term not exceeding fourteen years.

R.S., c. C-34, s. 333.

Counterfeiting stamp, etc.

376 (1) Every one who

(a) fraudulently uses, mutilates, affixes, removes or counterfeits a stamp or part thereof,

(b) knowingly and without lawful excuse, the proof of which lies on him, has in his possession

(i) a counterfeit stamp or a stamp that has been fraudulently mutilated, or

(ii) anything bearing a stamp of which a part has been fraudulently erased, removed or concealed, or

(c) without lawful excuse, the proof of which lies on him, makes or knowingly has in his possession a die or instrument that is capable of making the impression of a stamp or part thereof,

is guilty of an indictable offence and liable to imprisonment for a term not exceeding fourteen years.

Counterfeiting mark

(2) Every one who, without lawful authority,

(a) makes a mark,

(b) sells, or exposes for sale, or has in his possession a counterfeit mark,

(c) affixes a mark to anything that is required by law to be marked, branded, sealed or wrapped other than the thing to which the mark was originally affixed or was intended to be affixed, or

(d) affixes a counterfeit mark to anything that is required by law to be marked, branded, sealed or wrapped,

is guilty of an indictable offence and liable to imprisonment for a term not exceeding fourteen years.

Definitions

(3) In this section,

mark

(a) the government of Canada or a province,

(b) the government of a state other than Canada, or

(c) any department, board, commission or agent established by a government mentioned in paragraph

(a) or (b) in connection with the service or business of that government;
stamp
R.S., c. C-34, s. 334.

Damaging documents

377 (1) Every one who unlawfully
(a) destroys, defaces or injures a register, or any part of a register, of births, baptisms, marriages, deaths or burials that is required or authorized by law to be kept in Canada, or a copy or any part of a copy of such a register that is required by law to be transmitted to a registrar or other officer,
(b) inserts or causes to be inserted in a register or copy referred to in paragraph (a) an entry, that he knows is false, of any matter relating to a birth, baptism, marriage, death or burial, or erases any material part from that register or copy,
(c) destroys, damages or obliterates an election document or causes an election document to be destroyed, damaged or obliterated, or
(d) makes or causes to be made an erasure, alteration or interlineation in or on an election document, is guilty of an indictable offence and liable to imprisonment for a term not exceeding five years.

Definition of

(2) In this section,
election document
R.S., c. C-34, s. 335.

Offences in relation to registers

378 Every one who
(a) being authorized or required by law to make or issue a certified copy of, extract from or certificate in respect of a register, record or document, knowingly makes or issues a false certified copy, extract or certificate,
(b) not being authorized or required by law to make or issue a certified copy of, extract from or certificate in respect of a register, record or document, fraudulently makes or issues a copy, extract or certificate that purports to be certified as authorized or required by law, or
(c) being authorized or required by law to make a certificate or declaration concerning any particular required for the purpose of making entries in a register, record or document, knowingly and falsely makes the certificate or declaration,
is guilty of an indictable offence and liable to imprisonment for a term not exceeding five years.
R.S., c. C-34, s. 336.

PART X

PART X
Fraudulent Transactions Relating to Contracts and Trade

Interpretation

Definitions
379 In this Part,
goods
trading stamps
(a) that may be redeemed
(i) by any person other than the vendor, the person from whom the vendor purchased the goods or the manufacturer of the goods,
(ii) by the vendor, the person from whom the vendor purchased the goods or the manufacturer of the goods in cash or in goods that are not his property in whole or in part, or
(iii) by the vendor elsewhere than in the premises where the goods are purchased, or
(b) that does not show on its face the place where it is delivered and the merchantable value thereof, or

(c) that may not be redeemed on demand at any time,
but an offer, endorsed by the manufacturer on a wrapper or container in which goods are sold, of a premium or reward for the return of that wrapper or container to the manufacturer is not a trading stamp.
R.S., c. C-34, s. 337.

Fraud

Fraud
380 (1) Every one who, by deceit, falsehood or other fraudulent means, whether or not it is a false pretence within the meaning of this Act, defrauds the public or any person, whether ascertained or not, of any property, money or valuable security or any service,
(a) is guilty of an indictable offence and liable to a term of imprisonment not exceeding fourteen years, where the subject-matter of the offence is a testamentary instrument or the value of the subject-matter of the offence exceeds five thousand dollars; or
(b) is guilty
(i) of an indictable offence and is liable to imprisonment for a term not exceeding two years, or
(ii) of an offence punishable on summary conviction,
where the value of the subject-matter of the offence does not exceed five thousand dollars.
Minimum punishment
(1.1) When a person is prosecuted on indictment and convicted of one or more offences referred to in subsection (1), the court that imposes the sentence shall impose a minimum punishment of imprisonment for a term of two years if the total value of the subject-matter of the offences exceeds one million dollars.
Affecting public market
(2) Every one who, by deceit, falsehood or other fraudulent means, whether or not it is a false pretence within the meaning of this Act, with intent to defraud, affects the public market price of stocks, shares, merchandise or anything that is offered for sale to the public is guilty of an indictable offence and liable to imprisonment for a term not exceeding fourteen years.
R.S., 1985, c. C-46, s. 380;
R.S., 1985, c. 27 (1st Supp.), s. 54;
1994, c. 44, s. 25;
1997, c. 18, s. 26;
2004, c. 3, s. 2;
2011, c. 6, s. 2.
Sentencing — aggravating circumstances
380.1 (1) Without limiting the generality of section 718.2, where a court imposes a sentence for an offence referred to in section 380, 382, 382.1 or 400, it shall consider the following as aggravating circumstances:
(a) the magnitude, complexity, duration or degree of planning of the fraud committed was significant;
(b) the offence adversely affected, or had the potential to adversely affect, the stability of the Canadian economy or financial system or any financial market in Canada or investor confidence in such a financial market;
(c) the offence involved a large number of victims;
(c.1) the offence had a significant impact on the victims given their personal circumstances including their age, health and financial situation;
(d) in committing the offence, the offender took advantage of the high regard in which the offender was held in the community;
(e) the offender did not comply with a licensing requirement, or professional standard, that is normally applicable to the activity or conduct that forms the subject-matter of the offence; and
(f) the offender concealed or destroyed records related to the fraud or to the disbursement of the

proceeds of the fraud.

Aggravating circumstance — value of the fraud

(1.1) Without limiting the generality of section 718.2, when a court imposes a sentence for an offence referred to in section 382, 382.1 or 400, it shall also consider as an aggravating circumstance the fact that the value of the fraud committed exceeded one million dollars.

Non-mitigating factors

(2) When a court imposes a sentence for an offence referred to in section 380, 382, 382.1 or 400, it shall not consider as mitigating circumstances the offender's employment, employment skills or status or reputation in the community if those circumstances were relevant to, contributed to, or were used in the commission of the offence.

Record of proceedings

(3) The court shall cause to be stated in the record the aggravating and mitigating circumstances it took into account when determining the sentence.

2004, c. 3, s. 3;

2011, c. 6, s. 3.

Prohibition order

380.2 (1) When an offender is convicted, or is discharged on the conditions prescribed in a probation order under section 730, of an offence referred to in subsection 380(1), the court that sentences or discharges the offender, in addition to any other punishment that may be imposed for that offence or any other condition prescribed in the order of discharge, may make, subject to the conditions or exemptions that the court directs, an order prohibiting the offender from seeking, obtaining or continuing any employment, or becoming or being a volunteer in any capacity, that involves having authority over the real property, money or valuable security of another person.

Duration

(2) The prohibition may be for any period that the court considers appropriate, including any period to which the offender is sentenced to imprisonment.

Court may vary order

(3) A court that makes an order of prohibition or, if the court is for any reason unable to act, another court of equivalent jurisdiction in the same province, may, on application of the offender or the prosecutor, require the offender to appear before it at any time and, after hearing the parties, that court may vary the conditions prescribed in the order if, in the opinion of the court, the variation is desirable because of changed circumstances.

Offence

(4) Every person who is bound by an order of prohibition and who does not comply with the order is guilty of

(a) an indictable offence and is liable to imprisonment for a term not exceeding two years; or

(b) an offence punishable on summary conviction.

2011, c. 6, s. 4.

380.3 380.4 Using mails to defraud

381 Every one who makes use of the mails for the purpose of transmitting or delivering letters or circulars concerning schemes devised or intended to deceive or defraud the public, or for the purpose of obtaining money under false pretences, is guilty of an indictable offence and liable to imprisonment for a term not exceeding two years.

R.S., c. C-34, s. 339.

Fraudulent manipulation of stock exchange transactions

382 Every one who, through the facility of a stock exchange, curb market or other market, with intent to create a false or misleading appearance of active public trading in a security or with intent to create a false or misleading appearance with respect to the market price of a security,

(a) effects a transaction in the security that involves no change in the beneficial ownership thereof,

(b) enters an order for the purchase of the security, knowing that an order of substantially the same size at substantially the same time and at substantially the same price for the sale of the security has been or will be entered by or for the same or different persons, or

(c) enters an order for the sale of the security, knowing that an order of substantially the same size at substantially the same time and at substantially the same price for the purchase of the security has been or will be entered by or for the same or different persons,

is guilty of an indictable offence and liable to imprisonment for a term not exceeding ten years.

R.S., 1985, c. C-46, s. 382;

2004, c. 3, s. 4.

Prohibited insider trading

382.1 (1) A person is guilty of an indictable offence and liable to imprisonment for a term not exceeding ten years who, directly or indirectly, buys or sells a security, knowingly using inside information that they

(a) possess by virtue of being a shareholder of the issuer of that security;

(b) possess by virtue of, or obtained in the course of, their business or professional relationship with that issuer;

(c) possess by virtue of, or obtained in the course of, a proposed takeover or reorganization of, or amalgamation, merger or similar business combination with, that issuer;

(d) possess by virtue of, or obtained in the course of, their employment, office, duties or occupation with that issuer or with a person referred to in paragraphs (a) to (c); or

(e) obtained from a person who possesses or obtained the information in a manner referred to in paragraphs (a) to (d).

Tipping

(2) Except when necessary in the course of business, a person who knowingly conveys inside information that they possess or obtained in a manner referred to in subsection (1) to another person, knowing that there is a risk that the person will use the information to buy or sell, directly or indirectly, a security to which the information relates, or that they may convey the information to another person who may buy or sell such a security, is guilty of

(a) an indictable offence and liable to imprisonment for a term not exceeding five years; or

(b) an offence punishable on summary conviction.

Saving

(3) For greater certainty, an act is not an offence under this section if it is authorized or required, or is not prohibited, by any federal or provincial Act or regulation applicable to it.

Definition of

inside information

(4) In this section,

inside information

(a) has not been generally disclosed; and

(b) could reasonably be expected to significantly affect the market price or value of a security of the issuer.

2004, c. 3, s. 5.

Gaming in stocks or merchandise

383 (1) Every one is guilty of an indictable offence and liable to imprisonment for a term not exceeding five years who, with intent to make gain or profit by the rise or fall in price of the stock of an incorporated or unincorporated company or undertaking, whether in or outside Canada, or of any goods, wares or merchandise,

(a) makes or signs, or authorizes to be made or signed, any contract or agreement, oral or written, purporting to be for the purchase or sale of shares of stock or goods, wares or merchandise, without the

(b) makes or signs, or authorizes to be made or signed, any contract or agreement, oral or written, purporting to be for the sale or purchase of shares of stock or goods, wares or merchandise in respect of which no delivery of the thing sold or purchased is made or received, and without the

but this section does not apply where a broker, on behalf of a purchaser, receives delivery, notwithstanding that the broker retains or pledges what is delivered as security for the advance of the purchase money or any part thereof.

Onus
(2) Where, in proceedings under this section, it is established that the accused made or signed a contract or an agreement for the sale or purchase of shares of stock or goods, wares or merchandise, or acted, aided or abetted in the making or signing thereof, the burden of proof of a
R.S., c. C-34, s. 341.

Broker reducing stock by selling for his own account
384 Every one is guilty of an indictable offence and liable to imprisonment for a term not exceeding five years who, being an individual, or a member or an employee of a partnership, or a director, an officer or an employee of a corporation, where he or the partnership or corporation is employed as a broker by any customer to buy and carry on margin any shares of an incorporated or unincorporated company or undertaking, whether in or out of Canada, thereafter sells or causes to be sold shares of the company or undertaking for any account in which
(a) he or his firm or a partner thereof, or
(b) the corporation or a director thereof,
has a direct or indirect interest, if the effect of the sale is, otherwise than unintentionally, to reduce the amount of those shares in the hands of the broker or under his control in the ordinary course of business below the amount of those shares that the broker should be carrying for all customers.
R.S., c. C-34, s. 342.

Fraudulent concealment of title documents
385 (1) Every one who, being a vendor or mortgagor of property or of a chose in action or being a solicitor for or agent of a vendor or mortgagor of property or a chose in action, is served with a written demand for an abstract of title by or on behalf of the purchaser or mortgagee before the completion of the purchase or mortgage, and who
(a) with intent to defraud and for the purpose of inducing the purchaser or mortgagee to accept the title offered or produced to him, conceals from him any settlement, deed, will or other instrument material to the title, or any encumbrance on the title, or
(b) falsifies any pedigree on which the title depends,
is guilty of an indictable offence and liable to imprisonment for a term not exceeding two years.

Consent required
(2) No proceedings shall be instituted under this section without the consent of the Attorney General.
R.S., c. C-34, s. 343.

Fraudulent registration of title
386 Every one who, as principal or agent, in a proceeding to register title to real property, or in a transaction relating to real property that is or is proposed to be registered, knowingly and with intent to deceive,
(a) makes a material false statement or representation,
(b) suppresses or conceals from a judge or registrar, or any person employed by or assisting the registrar, any material document, fact, matter or information, or
(c) is privy to anything mentioned in paragraph (a) or (b),
is guilty of an indictable offence and liable to imprisonment for a term not exceeding five years.
R.S., c. C-34, s. 344.

Fraudulent sale of real property
387 Every one who, knowing of an unregistered prior sale or of an existing unregistered grant, mortgage, hypothec, privilege or encumbrance of or on real property, fraudulently sells the property or any part thereof is guilty of an indictable offence and liable to imprisonment for a term not exceeding two years.
R.S., c. C-34, s. 345.

Misleading receipt
388 Every one who wilfully
(a) with intent to mislead, injure or defraud any person, whether or not that person is known to him, gives to a person anything in writing that purports to be a receipt for or an acknowledgment of property that has been delivered to or received by him, before the property referred to in the

purported receipt or acknowledgment has been delivered to or received by him, or
(b) accepts, transmits or uses a purported receipt or acknowledgment to which paragraph (a) applies,
is guilty of an indictable offence and liable to imprisonment for a term not exceeding two years.
R.S., c. C-34, s. 346.
Fraudulent disposal of goods on which money advanced
389 (1) Every one who
(a) having shipped or delivered to the keeper of a warehouse or to a factor, an agent or a carrier anything on which the consignee thereof has advanced money or has given valuable security, thereafter, with intent to deceive, defraud or injure the consignee, disposes of it in a manner that is different from and inconsistent with any agreement that has been made in that behalf between him and the consignee, or
(b) knowingly and wilfully aids or assists any person to make a disposition of anything to which paragraph (a) applies for the purpose of deceiving, defrauding or injuring the consignee,
is guilty of an indictable offence and liable to imprisonment for a term not exceeding two years.
Saving
(2) No person is guilty of an offence under this section where, before disposing of anything in a manner that is different from and inconsistent with any agreement that has been made in that behalf between him and the consignee, he pays or tenders to the consignee the full amount of money or valuable security that the consignee has advanced.
R.S., c. C-34, s. 347.
Fraudulent receipts under
Bank Act
390 Every one is guilty of an indictable offence and liable to imprisonment for a term not exceeding two years who
(a) wilfully makes a false statement in any receipt, certificate or acknowledgment for anything that may be used for a purpose mentioned in the
Bank Act
(b) wilfully,
(i) after giving to another person,
(ii) after a person employed by him has, to his knowledge, given to another person, or
(iii) after obtaining and endorsing or assigning to another person,
any receipt, certificate or acknowledgment for anything that may be used for a purpose mentioned in the
Bank Act
R.S., c. C-34, s. 348.
391 Disposal of property to defraud creditors
392 Every one who,
(a) with intent to defraud his creditors,
(i) makes or causes to be made any gift, conveyance, assignment, sale, transfer or delivery of his property, or
(ii) removes, conceals or disposes of any of his property, or
(b) with intent that any one should defraud his creditors, receives any property by means of or in relation to which an offence has been committed under paragraph (a),
is guilty of an indictable offence and liable to imprisonment for a term not exceeding two years.
R.S., c. C-34, s. 350.
Fraud in relation to fares, etc.
393 (1) Every one whose duty it is to collect a fare, toll, ticket or admission who wilfully
(a) fails to collect it,
(b) collects less than the proper amount payable in respect thereof, or
(c) accepts any valuable consideration for failing to collect it or for collecting less than the proper amount payable in respect thereof,
is guilty of an indictable offence and liable to imprisonment for a term not exceeding two years.

Idem
(2) Every one who gives or offers to a person whose duty it is to collect a fare, toll, ticket or admission fee any valuable consideration
(a) for failing to collect it, or
(b) for collecting an amount less than the amount payable in respect thereof,
is guilty of an indictable offence and liable to imprisonment for a term not exceeding two years.
Fraudulently obtaining transportation
(3) Every one who, by any false pretence or fraud, unlawfully obtains transportation by land, water or air is guilty of an offence punishable on summary conviction.
R.S., c. C-34, s. 351.
Fraud in relation to valuable minerals
394 (1) No person who is the holder of a lease or licence issued under an Act relating to the mining of valuable minerals, or by the owner of land that is supposed to contain valuable minerals, shall
(a) by a fraudulent device or contrivance, defraud or attempt to defraud any person of
(i) any valuable minerals obtained under or reserved by the lease or licence, or
(ii) any money or valuable interest or thing payable in respect of valuable minerals obtained or rights reserved by the lease or licence; or
(b) fraudulently conceal or make a false statement with respect to the amount of valuable minerals obtained under the lease or licence.
Sale of valuable minerals
(2) No person, other than the owner or the owner's agent or someone otherwise acting under lawful authority, shall sell any valuable mineral that is unrefined, partly refined, uncut or otherwise unprocessed.
Purchase of valuable minerals
(3) No person shall buy any valuable mineral that is unrefined, partly refined, uncut or otherwise unprocessed from anyone who the person has reason to believe is not the owner or the owner's agent or someone otherwise acting under lawful authority.
Presumption
(4) In any proceeding in relation to subsection (2) or (3), in the absence of evidence raising a reasonable doubt to the contrary, it is presumed that
(a) in the case of a sale, the seller is not the owner of the valuable mineral or the owner's agent or someone otherwise acting under lawful authority; and
(b) in the case of a purchase, the purchaser, when buying the valuable mineral, had reason to believe that the seller was not the owner of the mineral or the owner's agent or someone otherwise acting under lawful authority.
Offence
(5) A person who contravenes subsection (1), (2) or (3) is guilty of an indictable offence and liable to imprisonment for a term of not more than five years.
Forfeiture
(6) If a person is convicted of an offence under this section, the court may order anything by means of or in relation to which the offence was committed, on such conviction, to be forfeited to Her Majesty.
Exception
(7) Subsection (6) does not apply to real property other than real property built or significantly modified for the purpose of facilitating the commission of an offence under this section.
R.S., 1985, c. C-46, s. 394;
R.S., 1985, c. 27 (1st Supp.), s. 186;
1999, c. 5, s. 10.
Possession of stolen or fraudulently obtained valuable minerals
394.1 (1) No person shall possess any valuable mineral that is unrefined, partly refined, uncut or otherwise unprocessed that has been stolen or dealt with contrary to section 394.
Evidence

(2) Reasonable grounds to believe that the valuable mineral has been stolen or dealt with contrary to section 394 are, in the absence of evidence raising a reasonable doubt to the contrary, proof that the valuable mineral has been stolen or dealt with contrary to section 394.

Offence

(3) A person who contravenes subsection (1) is guilty of an indictable offence and liable to imprisonment for a term of not more than five years.

Forfeiture

(4) If a person is convicted of an offence under this section, the court may, on that conviction, order that anything by means of or in relation to which the offence was committed be forfeited to Her Majesty.

Exception

(5) Subsection (4) does not apply to real property, other than real property built or significantly modified for the purpose of facilitating the commission of an offence under subsection (3).
1999, c. 5, s. 10.

Search for valuable minerals

395 (1) If an information in writing is laid under oath before a justice by a peace officer or by a public officer who has been appointed or designated to administer or enforce a federal or provincial law and whose duties include the enforcement of this Act or any other Act of Parliament and the justice is satisfied that there are reasonable grounds to believe that, contrary to this Act or any other Act of Parliament, any valuable mineral is deposited in a place or held by a person, the justice may issue a warrant authorizing a peace officer or a public officer, if the public officer is named in it, to search any of the places or persons mentioned in the information.

Power to seize

(2) Where, on search, anything mentioned in subsection (1) is found, it shall be seized and carried before the justice who shall order

(a) that it be detained for the purposes of an inquiry or a trial; or

(b) if it is not detained for the purposes of an inquiry or a trial,

(i) that it be restored to the owner, or

(ii) that it be forfeited to Her Majesty in right of the province in which the proceedings take place if the owner cannot be ascertained.

Appeal

(3) An appeal lies from an order made under paragraph (2)(b) in the manner in which an appeal lies in summary conviction proceedings under Part XXVII and the provisions of that Part relating to appeals apply to appeals under this subsection.
R.S., 1985, c. C-46, s. 395;
1999, c. 5, s. 11.

Offences in relation to mines

396 (1) Every one who

(a) adds anything to or removes anything from any existing or prospective mine, mining claim or oil well with a fraudulent intent to affect the result of an assay, a test or a valuation that has been made or is to be made with respect to the mine, mining claim or oil well, or

(b) adds anything to, removes anything from or tampers with a sample or material that has been taken or is being or is about to be taken from any existing or prospective mine, mining claim or oil well for the purpose of being assayed, tested or otherwise valued, with a fraudulent intent to affect the result of the assay, test or valuation,

is guilty of an indictable offence and liable to imprisonment for a term not exceeding ten years.

Presumption

(2) For the purposes of proceedings under subsection (1), evidence that

(a) something has been added to or removed from anything to which subsection (1) applies, or

(b) anything to which subsection (1) applies has been tampered with,

is, in the absence of any evidence to the contrary, proof of a fraudulent intent to affect the result of an assay, a test or a valuation.

R.S., c. C-34, s. 354.

Falsification of Books and Documents

Books and documents
397 (1) Every one who, with intent to defraud,
(a) destroys, mutilates, alters, falsifies or makes a false entry in, or
(b) omits a material particular from, or alters a material particular in,
a book, paper, writing, valuable security or document is guilty of an indictable offence and liable to imprisonment for a term not exceeding five years.
Privy
(2) Every one who, with intent to defraud his creditors, is privy to the commission of an offence under subsection (1) is guilty of an indictable offence and liable to imprisonment for a term not exceeding five years.
R.S., c. C-34, s. 355.
Falsifying employment record
398 Every one who, with intent to deceive, falsifies an employment record by any means, including the punching of a time clock, is guilty of an offence punishable on summary conviction.
R.S., 1985, c. C-46, s. 398;
1992, c. 1, s. 60(F).
False return by public officer
399 Every one who, being entrusted with the receipt, custody or management of any part of the public revenues, knowingly furnishes a false statement or return of
(a) any sum of money collected by him or entrusted to his care, or
(b) any balance of money in his hands or under his control,
is guilty of an indictable offence and liable to imprisonment for a term not exceeding five years.
R.S., c. C-34, s. 357.
False prospectus, etc.
400 (1) Every one who makes, circulates or publishes a prospectus, a statement or an account, whether written or oral, that he knows is false in a material particular, with intent
(a) to induce persons, whether ascertained or not, to become shareholders or partners in a company,
(b) to deceive or defraud the members, shareholders or creditors, whether ascertained or not, of a company, or
(c) to induce any person to
(i) entrust or advance anything to a company, or
(ii) enter into any security for the benefit of a company,
(d) is guilty of an indictable offence and liable to imprisonment for a term not exceeding ten years.
Definition of
(2) In this section,
company
R.S., 1985, c. C-46, s. 400;
1994, c. 44, s. 26.
Obtaining carriage by false billing
401 (1) Every one who, by means of a false or misleading representation, knowingly obtains or attempts to obtain the carriage of anything by any person into a country, province, district or other place, whether or not within Canada, where the importation or transportation of it is, in the circumstances of the case, unlawful is guilty of an offence punishable on summary conviction.
Forfeiture
(2) Where a person is convicted of an offence under subsection (1), anything by means of or in relation to which the offence was committed, on such conviction, in addition to any punishment that is imposed, is forfeited to Her Majesty and shall be disposed of as the court may direct.
R.S., c. C-34, s. 359.

Trader failing to keep accounts
402 (1) Every one who, being a trader or in business,
(a) is indebted in an amount exceeding one thousand dollars,
(b) is unable to pay his creditors in full, and
(c) has not kept books of account that, in the ordinary course of the trade or business in which he is engaged, are necessary to exhibit or explain his transactions,
is guilty of an indictable offence and liable to imprisonment for a term not exceeding two years.
Saving
(2) No person shall be convicted of an offence under this section
(a) where, to the satisfaction of the court or judge, he
(i) accounts for his losses, and
(ii) shows that his failure to keep books was not intended to defraud his creditors; or
(b) where his failure to keep books occurred at a time more than five years prior to the day on which he was unable to pay his creditors in full.
R.S., c. C-34, s. 360.

Identity Theft and Identity Fraud

Definition of
identity information
402.1 For the purposes of sections 402.2 and 403,
identity information
2009, c. 28, s. 10.
Identity theft
402.2 (1) Everyone commits an offence who knowingly obtains or possesses another person's identity information in circumstances giving rise to a reasonable inference that the information is intended to be used to commit an indictable offence that includes fraud, deceit or falsehood as an element of the offence.
Trafficking in identity information
(2) Everyone commits an offence who transmits, makes available, distributes, sells or offers for sale another person's identity information, or has it in their possession for any of those purposes, knowing that or being reckless as to whether the information will be used to commit an indictable offence that includes fraud, deceit or falsehood as an element of the offence.
Clarification
(3) For the purposes of subsections (1) and (2), an indictable offence referred to in either of those subsections includes an offence under any of the following sections:
(a) section 57 (forgery of or uttering forged passport);
(b) section 58 (fraudulent use of certificate of citizenship);
(c) section 130 (personating peace officer);
(d) section 131 (perjury);
(e) section 342 (theft, forgery, etc., of credit card);
(f) section 362 (false pretence or false statement);
(g) section 366 (forgery);
(h) section 368 (use, trafficking or possession of forged document);
(i) section 380 (fraud); and
(j) section 403 (identity fraud).
Jurisdiction
(4) An accused who is charged with an offence under subsection (1) or (2) may be tried and punished by any court having jurisdiction to try that offence in the place where the offence is alleged to have been committed or in the place where the accused is found, is arrested or is in custody. However, no proceeding in respect of the offence shall be commenced in a province without the consent of the Attorney General of that province if the offence is alleged to have been committed outside that

province.
Punishment
(5) Everyone who commits an offence under subsection (1) or (2)
(a) is guilty of an indictable offence and liable to imprisonment for a term of not more than five years; or
(b) is guilty of an offence punishable on summary conviction.
2009, c. 28, s. 10.
Identity fraud
403 (1) Everyone commits an offence who fraudulently personates another person, living or dead,
(a) with intent to gain advantage for themselves or another person;
(b) with intent to obtain any property or an interest in any property;
(c) with intent to cause disadvantage to the person being personated or another person; or
(d) with intent to avoid arrest or prosecution or to obstruct, pervert or defeat the course of justice.
Clarification
(2) For the purposes of subsection (1), personating a person includes pretending to be the person or using the person's identity information — whether by itself or in combination with identity information pertaining to any person — as if it pertains to the person using it.
Punishment
(3) Everyone who commits an offence under subsection (1)
(a) is guilty of an indictable offence and liable to imprisonment for a term of not more than 10 years; or
(b) is guilty of an offence punishable on summary conviction.
R.S., 1985, c. C-46, s. 403;
1994, c. 44, s. 27;
2009, c. 28, s. 10.
Personation at examination
404 Every one who falsely, with intent to gain advantage for himself or some other person, personates a candidate at a competitive or qualifying examination held under the authority of law or in connection with a university, college or school or who knowingly avails himself of the results of such personation is guilty of an offence punishable on summary conviction.
R.S., c. C-34, s. 362.
Acknowledging instrument in false name
405 Every one who, without lawful authority or excuse, the proof of which lies on him, acknowledges, in the name of another person before a court or a judge or other person authorized to receive the acknowledgment, a recognizance of bail, a confession of judgment, a consent to judgment or a judgment, deed or other instrument is guilty of an indictable offence and liable to imprisonment for a term not exceeding five years.
R.S., c. C-34, s. 363.

Forgery of Trade-marks and Trade Descriptions

Forging trade-mark
406 For the purposes of this Part, every one forges a trade-mark who
(a) without the consent of the proprietor of the trade-mark, makes or reproduces in any manner that trade-mark or a mark so nearly resembling it as to be calculated to deceive; or
(b) falsifies, in any manner, a genuine trade-mark.
R.S., c. C-34, s. 364.
Offence
407 Every one commits an offence who, with intent to deceive or defraud the public or any person, whether ascertained or not, forges a trade-mark.
R.S., c. C-34, s. 365.
Passing off

408 Every one commits an offence who, with intent to deceive or defraud the public or any person, whether ascertained or not,
(a) passes off other wares or services as and for those ordered or required; or
(b) makes use, in association with wares or services, of any description that is false in a material respect regarding
(i) the kind, quality, quantity or composition,
(ii) the geographical origin, or
(iii) the mode of the manufacture, production or performance
of those wares or services.
R.S., 1985, c. C-46, s. 408;
1992, c. 1, s. 60(F).

Instruments for forging trade-mark
409 (1) Every one commits an offence who makes, has in his possession or disposes of a die, block, machine or other instrument designed or intended to be used in forging a trade-mark.

Saving
(2) No person shall be convicted of an offence under this section where he proves that he acted in good faith in the ordinary course of his business or employment.
R.S., c. C-34, s. 367.

Other offences in relation to trade-marks
410 Every one commits an offence who, with intent to deceive or defraud,
(a) defaces, conceals or removes a trade-mark or the name of another person from anything without the consent of that other person; or
(b) being a manufacturer, dealer, trader or bottler, fills any bottle or siphon that bears the trade-mark or name of another person, without the consent of that other person, with a beverage, milk, by-product of milk or other liquid commodity for the purpose of sale or traffic.
R.S., c. C-34, s. 368.

Used goods sold without disclosure
411 Every one commits an offence who sells, exposes or has in his possession for sale, or advertises for sale, goods that have been used, reconditioned or remade and that bear the trade-mark or the trade-name of another person, without making full disclosure that the goods have been reconditioned, rebuilt or remade for sale and that they are not then in the condition in which they were originally made or produced.
R.S., c. C-34, s. 369.

Punishment
412 (1) Every one who commits an offence under section 407, 408, 409, 410 or 411 is guilty of
(a) an indictable offence and is liable to imprisonment for a term not exceeding two years; or
(b) an offence punishable on summary conviction.

Forfeiture
(2) Anything by means of or in relation to which a person commits an offence under section 407, 408, 409, 410 or 411 is, unless the court otherwise orders, forfeited on the conviction of that person for that offence.
R.S., c. C-34, s. 370.

Falsely claiming royal warrant
413 Every one who falsely represents that goods are made by a person holding a royal warrant, or for the service of Her Majesty, a member of the Royal Family or a public department is guilty of an offence punishable on summary conviction.
R.S., c. C-34, s. 371.

Presumption from port of shipment
414 Where, in proceedings under this Part, the alleged offence relates to imported goods, evidence that the goods were shipped to Canada from a place outside Canada is, in the absence of any evidence to the contrary, proof that the goods were made or produced in the country from which they were shipped.

R.S., c. C-34, s. 372.

Wreck

Offences in relation to wreck
415 Every one who
(a) secretes wreck, defaces or obliterates the marks on wreck or uses any means to disguise or conceal the fact that anything is wreck, or in any manner conceals the character of wreck, from a person who is entitled to inquire into the wreck,
(b) receives wreck, knowing that it is wreck, from a person other than the owner thereof or a receiver of wreck, and does not within forty-eight hours thereafter inform the receiver of wreck thereof,
(c) offers wreck for sale or otherwise deals with it, knowing that it is wreck, and not having a lawful authority to sell or deal with it,
(d) keeps wreck in his possession knowing that it is wreck, without lawful authority to keep it, for any time longer than the time reasonably necessary to deliver it to the receiver of wreck, or
(e) boards, against the will of the master, a vessel that is wrecked, stranded or in distress unless he is a receiver of wreck or a person acting under orders of a receiver of wreck,
is guilty of
(f) an indictable offence and is liable to imprisonment for a term not exceeding two years, or
(g) an offence punishable on summary conviction.
R.S., c. C-34, s. 373.

Public Stores

Distinguishing mark on public stores
416 The Governor in Council may, by notice to be published in the
Canada Gazette
R.S., c. C-34, s. 374.
Applying or removing marks without authority
417 (1) Every one who,
(a) without lawful authority, the proof of which lies on him, applies a distinguishing mark to anything, or
(b) with intent to conceal the property of Her Majesty in public stores, removes, destroys or obliterates, in whole or in part, a distinguishing mark,
is guilty of an indictable offence and liable to imprisonment for a term not exceeding two years.
Unlawful transactions in public stores
(2) Every one who, without lawful authority, the proof of which lies on him, receives, possesses, keeps, sells or delivers public stores that he knows bear a distinguishing mark is guilty of
(a) an indictable offence and is liable to imprisonment for a term not exceeding two years; or
(b) an offence punishable on summary conviction.
Definition of
(3) For the purposes of this section,
distinguishing mark
R.S., c. C-34, s. 375.
Selling defective stores to Her Majesty
418 (1) Every one who knowingly sells or delivers defective stores to Her Majesty or commits fraud in connection with the sale, lease or delivery of stores to Her Majesty or the manufacture of stores for Her Majesty is guilty of an indictable offence and liable to imprisonment for a term not exceeding fourteen years.
Offences by representatives
(2) Every one who, being a representative of an organization that commits, by fraud, an offence under subsection (1),

(a) knowingly takes part in the fraud, or
(b) knows or has reason to suspect that the fraud is being committed or has been or is about to be committed and does not inform the responsible government, or a department thereof, of Her Majesty,
is guilty of an indictable offence and liable to imprisonment for a term not exceeding fourteen years.
R.S., 1985, c. C-46, s. 418;
2003, c. 21, s. 6.1.

Unlawful use of military uniforms or certificates
419 Every one who without lawful authority, the proof of which lies on him,
(a) wears a uniform of the Canadian Forces or any other naval, army or air force or a uniform that is so similar to the uniform of any of those forces that it is likely to be mistaken therefor,
(b) wears a distinctive mark relating to wounds received or service performed in war, or a military medal, ribbon, badge, chevron or any decoration or order that is awarded for war services, or any imitation thereof, or any mark or device or thing that is likely to be mistaken for any such mark, medal, ribbon, badge, chevron, decoration or order,
(c) has in his possession a certificate of discharge, certificate of release, statement of service or identity card from the Canadian Forces or any other naval, army or air force that has not been issued to and does not belong to him, or
(d) has in his possession a commission or warrant or a certificate of discharge, certificate of release, statement of service or identity card, issued to an officer or a person in or who has been in the Canadian Forces or any other naval, army or air force, that contains any alteration that is not verified by the initials of the officer who issued it, or by the initials of an officer thereto lawfully authorized,
is guilty of an offence punishable on summary conviction.
R.S., c. C-34, s. 377.

Military stores
420 (1) Every one who buys, receives or detains from a member of the Canadian Forces or a deserter or an absentee without leave therefrom any military stores that are owned by Her Majesty or for which the member, deserter or absentee without leave is accountable to Her Majesty is guilty of
(a) an indictable offence and is liable to imprisonment for a term not exceeding five years; or
(b) an offence punishable on summary conviction.

Exception
(2) No person shall be convicted of an offence under this section where he establishes that he did not know and had no reason to suspect that the military stores in respect of which the offence was committed were owned by Her Majesty or were military stores for which the member, deserter or absentee without leave was accountable to Her Majesty.
R.S., c. C-34, s. 378.

Evidence of enlistment
421 (1) In proceedings under sections 417 to 420, evidence that a person was at any time performing duties in the Canadian Forces is, in the absence of any evidence to the contrary, proof that his enrolment in the Canadian Forces prior to that time was regular.

Presumption when accused a dealer in stores
(2) An accused who is charged with an offence under subsection 417(2) shall be presumed to have known that the stores in respect of which the offence is alleged to have been committed bore a distinguishing mark within the meaning of that subsection at the time the offence is alleged to have been committed if he was, at that time, in the service or employment of Her Majesty or was a dealer in marine stores or in old metals.
R.S., c. C-34, s. 379.

Breach of Contract, Intimidation and Discrimination Against Trade Unionists

Criminal breach of contract
422 (1) Every one who wilfully breaks a contract, knowing or having reasonable cause to believe that the probable consequences of doing so, whether alone or in combination with others, will be

(a) to endanger human life,
(b) to cause serious bodily injury,
(c) to expose valuable property, real or personal, to destruction or serious injury,
(d) to deprive the inhabitants of a city or place, or part thereof, wholly or to a great extent, of their supply of light, power, gas or water, or
(e) to delay or prevent the running of any locomotive engine, tender, freight or passenger train or car, on a railway that is a common carrier,
is guilty of
(f) an indictable offence and is liable to imprisonment for a term not exceeding five years, or
(g) an offence punishable on summary conviction.

Saving

(2) No person wilfully breaks a contract within the meaning of subsection (1) by reason only that
(a) being the employee of an employer, he stops work as a result of the failure of his employer and himself to agree on any matter relating to his employment, or,
(b) being a member of an organization of employees formed for the purpose of regulating relations between employers and employees, he stops work as a result of the failure of the employer and a bargaining agent acting on behalf of the organization to agree on any matter relating to the employment of members of the organization,
if, before the stoppage of work occurs, all steps provided by law with respect to the settlement of industrial disputes are taken and any provision for the final settlement of differences, without stoppage of work, contained in or by law deemed to be contained in a collective agreement is complied with and effect given thereto.

Consent required

(3) No proceedings shall be instituted under this section without the consent of the Attorney General.
R.S., c. C-34, s. 380.

Intimidation

423 (1) Every one is guilty of an indictable offence and liable to imprisonment for a term of not more than five years or is guilty of an offence punishable on summary conviction who, wrongfully and without lawful authority, for the purpose of compelling another person to abstain from doing anything that he or she has a lawful right to do, or to do anything that he or she has a lawful right to abstain from doing,
(a) uses violence or threats of violence to that person or his or her spouse or common-law partner or children, or injures his or her property;
(b) intimidates or attempts to intimidate that person or a relative of that person by threats that, in Canada or elsewhere, violence or other injury will be done to or punishment inflicted on him or her or a relative of his or hers, or that the property of any of them will be damaged;
(c) persistently follows that person;
(d) hides any tools, clothes or other property owned or used by that person, or deprives him or her of them or hinders him or her in the use of them;
(e) with one or more other persons, follows that person, in a disorderly manner, on a highway;
(f) besets or watches the place where that person resides, works, carries on business or happens to be; or
(g) blocks or obstructs a highway.

Exception

(2) A person who attends at or near or approaches a dwelling-house or place, for the purpose only of obtaining or communicating information, does not watch or beset within the meaning of this section.
R.S., 1985, c. C-46, s. 423;
2000, c. 12, s. 95;
2001, c. 32, s. 10.

Intimidation of a justice system participant or a journalist

423.1 (1) No person shall, without lawful authority, engage in any conduct with the intent to provoke a state of fear in

(a) a group of persons or the general public in order to impede the administration of criminal justice;
(b) a justice system participant in order to impede him or her in the performance of his or her duties; or
(c) a journalist in order to impede him or her in the transmission to the public of information in relation to a criminal organization.

(2) Punishment

(3) Every person who contravenes this section is guilty of an indictable offence and is liable to imprisonment for a term of not more than fourteen years.

2001, c. 32, s. 11;
2015, c. 13, s. 12.

Threat against internationally protected person

424 Every one who threatens to commit an offence under section 235, 236, 266, 267, 268, 269, 269.1, 271, 272, 273, 279 or 279.1 against an internationally protected person or who threatens to commit an offence under section 431 is guilty of an indictable offence and liable to imprisonment for a term of not more than five years.

R.S., 1985, c. C-46, s. 424;
R.S., 1985, c. 27 (1st Supp.), s. 55;
2001, c. 41, s. 11.

Threat against United Nations or associated personnel

424.1 Every one who, with intent to compel any person, group of persons, state or any international or intergovernmental organization to do or refrain from doing any act, threatens to commit an offence under section 235, 236, 266, 267, 268, 269, 269.1, 271, 272, 273, 279 or 279.1 against a member of United Nations personnel or associated personnel or threatens to commit an offence under section 431.1 is guilty of an indictable offence and liable to imprisonment for a term of not more than ten years.

2001, c. 41, s. 11.

Offences by employers

425 Every one who, being an employer or the agent of an employer, wrongfully and without lawful authority
(a) refuses to employ or dismisses from his employment any person for the reason only that the person is a member of a lawful trade union or of a lawful association or combination of workmen or employees formed for the purpose of advancing, in a lawful manner, their interests and organized for their protection in the regulation of wages and conditions of work,
(b) seeks by intimidation, threat of loss of position or employment, or by causing actual loss of position or employment, or by threatening or imposing any pecuniary penalty, to compel workmen or employees to abstain from belonging to any trade union, association or combination to which they have a lawful right to belong, or
(c) conspires, combines, agrees or arranges with any other employer or his agent to do anything mentioned in paragraph (a) or (b),
is guilty of an offence punishable on summary conviction.

R.S., c. C-34, s. 382.

Threats and retaliation against employees

425.1 (1) No employer or person acting on behalf of an employer or in a position of authority in respect of an employee of the employer shall take a disciplinary measure against, demote, terminate or otherwise adversely affect the employment of such an employee, or threaten to do so,
(a) with the intent to compel the employee to abstain from providing information to a person whose duties include the enforcement of federal or provincial law, respecting an offence that the employee believes has been or is being committed contrary to this or any other federal or provincial Act or regulation by the employer or an officer or employee of the employer or, if the employer is a corporation, by one or more of its directors; or
(b) with the intent to retaliate against the employee because the employee has provided information referred to in paragraph (a) to a person whose duties include the enforcement of federal or provincial

law.
Punishment
(2) Any one who contravenes subsection (1) is guilty of
(a) an indictable offence and liable to imprisonment for a term not exceeding five years; or
(b) an offence punishable on summary conviction.
2004, c. 3, s. 6.

Secret Commissions

Secret commissions
426 (1) Every one commits an offence who
(a) directly or indirectly, corruptly gives, offers or agrees to give or offer to an agent or to anyone for the benefit of the agent — or, being an agent, directly or indirectly, corruptly demands, accepts or offers or agrees to accept from any person, for themselves or another person — any reward, advantage or benefit of any kind as consideration for doing or not doing, or for having done or not done, any act relating to the affairs or business of the agent's principal, or for showing or not showing favour or disfavour to any person with relation to the affairs or business of the agent's principal; or
(b) with intent to deceive a principal, gives to an agent of that principal, or, being an agent, uses with intent to deceive his principal, a receipt, an account or other writing
(i) in which the principal has an interest,
(ii) that contains any statement that is false or erroneous or defective in any material particular, and
(iii) that is intended to mislead the principal.
Privity to offence
(2) Every one commits an offence who is knowingly privy to the commission of an offence under subsection (1).
Punishment
(3) A person who commits an offence under this section is guilty of an indictable offence and liable to imprisonment for a term not exceeding five years.
Definition of
agent
principal
(4) In this section,
agent
principal
R.S., 1985, c. C-46, s. 426;
R.S., 1985, c. 27 (1st Supp.), s. 56;
2007, c. 13, s. 7.

Trading Stamps

Issuing trading stamps
427 (1) Every one who, by himself or his employee or agent, directly or indirectly issues, gives, sells or otherwise disposes of, or offers to issue, give, sell or otherwise dispose of trading stamps to a merchant or dealer in goods for use in his business is guilty of an offence punishable on summary conviction.
Giving to purchaser of goods
(2) Every one who, being a merchant or dealer in goods, by himself or his employee or agent, directly or indirectly gives or in any way disposes of, or offers to give or in any way dispose of, trading stamps to a person who purchases goods from him is guilty of an offence punishable on summary conviction.
R.S., c. C-34, s. 384.

PART XI

PART XI
Wilful and Forbidden Acts in Respect of Certain Property

Interpretation

Definition of
property
428 In this Part,
property
R.S., c. C-34, s. 385.

Wilfully causing event to occur

429 (1) Every one who causes the occurrence of an event by doing an act or by omitting to do an act that it is his duty to do, knowing that the act or omission will probably cause the occurrence of the event and being reckless whether the event occurs or not, shall be deemed, for the purposes of this Part, wilfully to have caused the occurrence of the event.

Colour of right

(2) No person shall be convicted of an offence under sections 430 to 446 where he proves that he acted with legal justification or excuse and with colour of right.

Interest

(3) Where it is an offence to destroy or to damage anything,

(a) the fact that a person has a partial interest in what is destroyed or damaged does not prevent him from being guilty of the offence if he caused the destruction or damage; and

(b) the fact that a person has a total interest in what is destroyed or damaged does not prevent him from being guilty of the offence if he caused the destruction or damage with intent to defraud.

R.S., c. C-34, s. 386.

Mischief

Mischief

430 (1) Every one commits mischief who wilfully

(a) destroys or damages property;

(b) renders property dangerous, useless, inoperative or ineffective;

(c) obstructs, interrupts or interferes with the lawful use, enjoyment or operation of property; or

(d) obstructs, interrupts or interferes with any person in the lawful use, enjoyment or operation of property.

Mischief in relation to computer data

(1.1) Everyone commits mischief who wilfully

(a) destroys or alters computer data;

(b) renders computer data meaningless, useless or ineffective;

(c) obstructs, interrupts or interferes with the lawful use of computer data; or

(d) obstructs, interrupts or interferes with a person in the lawful use of computer data or denies access to computer data to a person who is entitled to access to it.

Punishment

(2) Every one who commits mischief that causes actual danger to life is guilty of an indictable offence and liable to imprisonment for life.

Punishment

(3) Every one who commits mischief in relation to property that is a testamentary instrument or the value of which exceeds five thousand dollars

(a) is guilty of an indictable offence and liable to imprisonment for a term not exceeding ten years; or

(b) is guilty of an offence punishable on summary conviction.
Idem
(4) Every one who commits mischief in relation to property, other than property described in subsection (3),
(a) is guilty of an indictable offence and liable to imprisonment for a term not exceeding two years; or
(b) is guilty of an offence punishable on summary conviction.
Mischief relating to religious property, educational institutions, etc.
(4.1) Everyone who commits mischief in relation to property described in any of paragraphs (4.101)(a) to (d), if the commission of the mischief is motivated by bias, prejudice or hate based on colour, race, religion, national or ethnic origin, age, sex, sexual orientation, gender identity or expression or mental or physical disability,
(a) is guilty of an indictable offence and liable to imprisonment for a term not exceeding ten years; or
(b) is guilty of an offence punishable on summary conviction and liable to imprisonment for a term not exceeding eighteen months.
Definition of
(4.101) For the purposes of subsection (4.1),
property
(a) a building or structure, or part of a building or structure, that is primarily used for religious worship — including a church, mosque, synagogue or temple —, an object associated with religious worship located in or on the grounds of such a building or structure, or a cemetery;
(b) a building or structure, or part of a building or structure, that is primarily used by an
(c) a building or structure, or part of a building or structure, that is primarily used by an
(d) a building or structure, or part of a building or structure, that is primarily used by an
Mischief relating to war memorials
(4.11) Everyone who commits mischief in relation to property that is a building, structure or part thereof that primarily serves as a monument to honour persons who were killed or died as a consequence of a war, including a war memorial or cenotaph, or an object associated with honouring or remembering those persons that is located in or on the grounds of such a building or structure, or a cemetery is guilty of an indictable offence or an offence punishable on summary conviction and is liable,
(a) whether the offence is prosecuted by indictment or punishable on summary conviction, to the following minimum punishment, namely,
(i) for a first offence, to a fine of not less than $1,000,
(ii) for a second offence, to imprisonment for not less than 14 days, and
(iii) for each subsequent offence, to imprisonment for not less than 30 days;
(b) if the offence is prosecuted by indictment, to imprisonment for a term not exceeding 10 years; and
(c) if the offence is punishable on summary conviction, to imprisonment for a term not exceeding 18 months.
Mischief in relation to cultural property
(4.2) Every one who commits mischief in relation to cultural property as defined in Article 1 of the Convention for the Protection of Cultural Property in the Event of Armed Conflict, done at The Hague on May 14, 1954, as set out in the schedule to the
Cultural Property Export and Import Act
(a) is guilty of an indictable offence and liable to imprisonment for a term not exceeding ten years; or
(b) is guilty of an offence punishable on summary conviction.
Mischief in relation to computer data
(5) Everyone who commits mischief in relation to computer data
(a) is guilty of an indictable offence and liable to imprisonment for a term not exceeding ten years; or
(b) is guilty of an offence punishable on summary conviction.
Offence

(5.1) Everyone who wilfully does an act or wilfully omits to do an act that it is their duty to do, if that act or omission is likely to constitute mischief causing actual danger to life, or to constitute mischief in relation to property or computer data,
(a) is guilty of an indictable offence and liable to imprisonment for a term not exceeding five years; or
(b) is guilty of an offence punishable on summary conviction.

Saving
(6) No person commits mischief within the meaning of this section by reason only that
(a) he stops work as a result of the failure of his employer and himself to agree on any matter relating to his employment;
(b) he stops work as a result of the failure of his employer and a bargaining agent acting on his behalf to agree on any matter relating to his employment; or
(c) he stops work as a result of his taking part in a combination of workmen or employees for their own reasonable protection as workmen or employees.

Idem
(7) No person commits mischief within the meaning of this section by reason only that he attends at or near or approaches a dwelling-house or place for the purpose only of obtaining or communicating information.

Definition of
(8) In this section,
R.S., 1985, c. C-46, s. 430;
R.S., 1985, c. 27 (1st Supp.), s. 57;
1994, c. 44, s. 28;
2001, c. 41, s. 12;
2005, c. 40, s. 3;
2014, c. 9, s. 1, c. 31, s. 19;
2017, c. 23, ss. 1, 2.

Attack on premises, residence or transport of internationally protected person
431 Every one who commits a violent attack on the official premises, private accommodation or means of transport of an internationally protected person that is likely to endanger the life or liberty of such a person is guilty of an indictable offence and liable to imprisonment for a term of not more than fourteen years.
R.S., 1985, c. C-46, s. 431;
R.S., 1985, c. 27 (1st Supp.), s. 58;
2001, c. 41, s. 13.

Attack on premises, accommodation or transport of United Nations or associated personnel
431.1 Every one who commits a violent attack on the official premises, private accommodation or means of transport of a member of United Nations personnel or associated personnel that is likely to endanger the life or liberty of such a person is guilty of an indictable offence and liable to imprisonment for a term of not more than fourteen years.
2001, c. 41, s. 13.

Definitions
431.2 (1) The following definitions apply in this section.
explosive or other lethal device
(a) an explosive or incendiary weapon or device that is designed to cause, or is capable of causing, death, serious bodily injury or substantial material damage; or
(b) a weapon or device that is designed to cause, or is capable of causing, death, serious bodily injury or substantial material damage through the release, dissemination or impact of toxic chemicals, biological agents or toxins or similar substances, or radiation or radioactive material.
infrastructure facility
military forces of a state
place of public use

public transportation system
Explosive or other lethal device
(2) Every one who delivers, places, discharges or detonates an explosive or other lethal device to, into, in or against a place of public use, a government or public facility, a public transportation system or an infrastructure facility, either with intent to cause death or serious bodily injury or with intent to cause extensive destruction of such a place, system or facility that results in or is likely to result in major economic loss, is guilty of an indictable offence and liable to imprisonment for life.
Armed forces
(3) For greater certainty, subsection (2) does not apply to an act or omission that is committed during an armed conflict and that, at the time and in the place of its commission, is in accordance with customary international law or conventional international law applicable to the conflict, or to activities undertaken by military forces of a state in the exercise of their official duties, to the extent that those activities are governed by other rules of international law.
2001, c. 41, s. 13.
Unauthorized recording of a movie
432 (1) A person who, without the consent of the theatre manager, records in a movie theatre a performance of a cinematographic work within the meaning of section 2 of the
Copyright Act
(a) is guilty of an indictable offence and liable to imprisonment for a term of not more than two years; or
(b) is guilty of an offence punishable on summary conviction.
Unauthorized recording for purpose of sale, etc.
(2) A person who, without the consent of the theatre manager, records in a movie theatre a performance of a cinematographic work within the meaning of section 2 of the
Copyright Act
(a) is guilty of an indictable offence and liable to imprisonment for a term of not more than five years; or
(b) is guilty of an offence punishable on summary conviction.
Forfeiture
(3) In addition to any punishment that is imposed on a person who is convicted of an offence under this section, the court may order that anything that is used in the commission of the offence be forfeited to Her Majesty in right of the province in which the proceedings are taken. Anything that is forfeited may be disposed of as the Attorney General directs.
Forfeiture — limitation
(4) No order may be made under subsection (3) in respect of anything that is the property of a person who is not a party to the offence.
R.S., 1985, c. C-46, s. 432;
R.S., 1985, c. 27 (1st Supp.), s. 58;
2007, c. 28, s. 1.

Arson and Other Fires

Arson — disregard for human life
433 Every person who intentionally or recklessly causes damage by fire or explosion to property, whether or not that person owns the property, is guilty of an indictable offence and liable to imprisonment for life where
(a) the person knows that or is reckless with respect to whether the property is inhabited or occupied; or
(b) the fire or explosion causes bodily harm to another person.
R.S., 1985, c. C-46, s. 433;
1990, c. 15, s. 1.
Arson — damage to property

434 Every person who intentionally or recklessly causes damage by fire or explosion to property that is not wholly owned by that person is guilty of an indictable offence and liable to imprisonment for a term not exceeding fourteen years.
R.S., 1985, c. C-46, s. 434;
1990, c. 15, s. 1.

Arson — own property

434.1 Every person who intentionally or recklessly causes damage by fire or explosion to property that is owned, in whole or in part, by that person is guilty of an indictable offence and liable to imprisonment for a term not exceeding fourteen years, where the fire or explosion seriously threatens the health, safety or property of another person.
1990, c. 15, s. 1.

Arson for fraudulent purpose

435 (1) Every person who, with intent to defraud any other person, causes damage by fire or explosion to property, whether or not that person owns, in whole or in part, the property, is guilty of an indictable offence and liable to imprisonment for a term not exceeding ten years.

Holder or beneficiary of fire insurance policy

(2) Where a person is charged with an offence under subsection (1), the fact that the person was the holder of or was named as a beneficiary under a policy of fire insurance relating to the property in respect of which the offence is alleged to have been committed is a fact from which intent to defraud may be inferred by the court.
R.S., 1985, c. C-46, s. 435;
1990, c. 15, s. 1.

Arson by negligence

436 (1) Every person who owns, in whole or in part, or controls property is guilty of an indictable offence and liable to imprisonment for a term not exceeding five years where, as a result of a marked departure from the standard of care that a reasonably prudent person would use to prevent or control the spread of fires or to prevent explosions, that person is a cause of a fire or explosion in that property that causes bodily harm to another person or damage to property.

Non-compliance with prevention laws

(2) Where a person is charged with an offence under subsection (1), the fact that the person has failed to comply with any law respecting the prevention or control of fires or explosions in the property is a fact from which a marked departure from the standard of care referred to in that subsection may be inferred by the court.
R.S., 1985, c. C-46, s. 436;
1990, c. 15, s. 1.

Possession of incendiary material

436.1 Every person who possesses any incendiary material, incendiary device or explosive substance for the purpose of committing an offence under any of sections 433 to 436 is guilty of an indictable offence and liable to imprisonment for a term not exceeding five years.
1990, c. 15, s. 1.

Other Interference with Property

False alarm of fire

437 Every one who wilfully, without reasonable cause, by outcry, ringing bells, using a fire alarm, telephone or telegraph, or in any other manner, makes or circulates or causes to be made or circulated an alarm of fire is guilty of
(a) an indictable offence and is liable to imprisonment for a term not exceeding two years; or
(b) an offence punishable on summary conviction.
R.S., c. C-34, s. 393;
1972, c. 13, s. 31.

Interfering with saving of wrecked vessel

438 (1) Every one who wilfully prevents or impedes, or who wilfully endeavours to prevent or impede,
(a) the saving of a vessel that is wrecked, stranded, abandoned or in distress, or
(b) a person who attempts to save a vessel that is wrecked, stranded, abandoned or in distress,
is guilty of an indictable offence and liable to imprisonment for a term not exceeding five years.

Interfering with saving of wreck

(2) Every one who wilfully prevents or impedes or wilfully endeavours to prevent or impede the saving of wreck is guilty of an offence punishable on summary conviction.
R.S., c. C-34, s. 394.

Interfering with marine signal, etc.

439 (1) Every one who makes fast a vessel or boat to a signal, buoy or other sea-mark that is used for purposes of navigation is guilty of an offence punishable on summary conviction.

Idem

(2) Every one who wilfully alters, removes or conceals a signal, buoy or other sea-mark that is used for purposes of navigation is guilty of an indictable offence and liable to imprisonment for a term not exceeding ten years.
R.S., c. C-34, s. 395.

Removing natural bar without permission

440 Every one who wilfully and without the written permission of the Minister of Transport, the burden of proof of which lies on the accused, removes any stone, wood, earth or other material that forms a natural bar necessary to the existence of a public harbour, or that forms a natural protection to such a bar, is guilty of an indictable offence and liable to imprisonment for a term not exceeding two years.
R.S., c. C-34, s. 396.

Occupant injuring building

441 Every one who, wilfully and to the prejudice of a mortgagee or an owner, pulls down, demolishes or removes all or any part of a dwelling-house or other building of which he is in possession or occupation, or severs from the freehold any fixture fixed therein or thereto, is guilty of an indictable offence and liable to imprisonment for a term not exceeding five years.
R.S., c. C-34, s. 397.

Interfering with boundary lines

442 Every one who wilfully pulls down, defaces, alters or removes anything planted or set up as the boundary line or part of the boundary line of land is guilty of an offence punishable on summary conviction.
R.S., c. C-34, s. 398.

Interfering with international boundary marks, etc.

443 (1) Every one who wilfully pulls down, defaces, alters or removes
(a) a boundary mark lawfully placed to mark any international, provincial, county or municipal boundary, or
(b) a boundary mark lawfully placed by a land surveyor to mark any limit, boundary or angle of a concession, range, lot or parcel of land,
is guilty of an indictable offence and liable to imprisonment for a term not exceeding five years.

Saving provision

(2) A land surveyor does not commit an offence under subsection (1) where, in his operations as a land surveyor,
(a) he takes up, when necessary, a boundary mark mentioned in paragraph (1)(b) and carefully replaces it as it was before he took it up; or
(b) he takes up a boundary mark mentioned in paragraph (1)(b) in the course of surveying for a highway or other work that, when completed, will make it impossible or impracticable for that boundary mark to occupy its original position, and he establishes a permanent record of the original position sufficient to permit that position to be ascertained.
R.S., c. C-34, s. 399.

Cattle and Other Animals

Injuring or endangering cattle
444 (1) Every one commits an offence who wilfully
(a) kills, maims, wounds, poisons or injures cattle; or
(b) places poison in such a position that it may easily be consumed by cattle.

Punishment
(2) Every one who commits an offence under subsection (1) is guilty of
(a) an indictable offence and liable to imprisonment for a term of not more than five years; or
(b) an offence punishable on summary conviction and liable to a fine not exceeding ten thousand dollars or to imprisonment for a term of not more than eighteen months or to both.
R.S., 1985, c. C-46, s. 444;
2008, c. 12, s. 1.

Injuring or endangering other animals
445 (1) Every one commits an offence who, wilfully and without lawful excuse,
(a) kills, maims, wounds, poisons or injures dogs, birds or animals that are not cattle and are kept for a lawful purpose; or
(b) places poison in such a position that it may easily be consumed by dogs, birds or animals that are not cattle and are kept for a lawful purpose.

Punishment
(2) Every one who commits an offence under subsection (1) is guilty of
(a) an indictable offence and liable to imprisonment for a term of not more than five years; or
(b) an offence punishable on summary conviction and liable to a fine not exceeding ten thousand dollars or to imprisonment for a term of not more than eighteen months or to both.
R.S., 1985, c. C-46, s. 445;
2008, c. 12, s. 1.

Killing or injuring certain animals
445.01 (1) Every one commits an offence who, wilfully and without lawful excuse, kills, maims, wounds, poisons or injures a law enforcement animal while it is aiding a law enforcement officer in carrying out that officer's duties, a military animal while it is aiding a member of the Canadian Forces in carrying out that member's duties or a service animal.

Punishment
(2) Every one who commits an offence under subsection (1) is guilty of
(a) an indictable offence and liable to imprisonment for a term of not more than five years and, if a law enforcement animal is killed in the commission of the offence, to a minimum punishment of imprisonment for a term of six months; or
(b) an offence punishable on summary conviction and liable to a fine of not more than $10,000 or to imprisonment for a term of not more than 18 months or to both.

Sentences to be served consecutively
(3) A sentence imposed on a person for an offence under subsection (1) committed against a law enforcement animal shall be served consecutively to any other punishment imposed on the person for an offence arising out of the same event or series of events.

Definitions
(4) The following definitions apply in this section.
law enforcement animal
law enforcement officer
peace officer
military animal
service animal
2015, c. 34, s. 3.

Cruelty to Animals

Causing unnecessary suffering

445.1 (1) Every one commits an offence who

(a) wilfully causes or, being the owner, wilfully permits to be caused unnecessary pain, suffering or injury to an animal or a bird;

(b) in any manner encourages, aids or assists at the fighting or baiting of animals or birds;

(c) wilfully, without reasonable excuse, administers a poisonous or an injurious drug or substance to a domestic animal or bird or an animal or a bird wild by nature that is kept in captivity or, being the owner of such an animal or a bird, wilfully permits a poisonous or an injurious drug or substance to be administered to it;

(d) promotes, arranges, conducts, assists in, receives money for or takes part in any meeting, competition, exhibition, pastime, practice, display or event at or in the course of which captive birds are liberated by hand, trap, contrivance or any other means for the purpose of being shot when they are liberated; or

(e) being the owner, occupier or person in charge of any premises, permits the premises or any part thereof to be used for a purpose mentioned in paragraph (d).

Punishment

(2) Every one who commits an offence under subsection (1) is guilty of

(a) an indictable offence and liable to imprisonment for a term of not more than five years; or

(b) an offence punishable on summary conviction and liable to a fine not exceeding ten thousand dollars or to imprisonment for a term of not more than eighteen months or to both.

Failure to exercise reasonable care as evidence

(3) For the purposes of proceedings under paragraph (1)(a), evidence that a person failed to exercise reasonable care or supervision of an animal or a bird thereby causing it pain, suffering or injury is, in the absence of any evidence to the contrary, proof that the pain, suffering or injury was caused or was permitted to be caused wilfully, as the case may be.

Presence at baiting as evidence

(4) For the purpose of proceedings under paragraph (1)(b), evidence that an accused was present at the fighting or baiting of animals or birds is, in the absence of any evidence to the contrary, proof that he or she encouraged, aided or assisted at the fighting or baiting.

2008, c. 12, s. 1.

Causing damage or injury

446 (1) Every one commits an offence who

(a) by wilful neglect causes damage or injury to animals or birds while they are being driven or conveyed; or

(b) being the owner or the person having the custody or control of a domestic animal or a bird or an animal or a bird wild by nature that is in captivity, abandons it in distress or wilfully neglects or fails to provide suitable and adequate food, water, shelter and care for it.

Punishment

(2) Every one who commits an offence under subsection (1) is guilty of

(a) an indictable offence and liable to imprisonment for a term of not more than two years; or

(b) an offence punishable on summary conviction and liable to a fine not exceeding five thousand dollars or to imprisonment for a term of not more than six months or to both.

Failure to exercise reasonable care as evidence

(3) For the purposes of proceedings under paragraph (1)(a), evidence that a person failed to exercise reasonable care or supervision of an animal or a bird thereby causing it damage or injury is, in the absence of any evidence to the contrary, proof that the damage or injury was caused by wilful neglect.

R.S., 1985, c. C-46, s. 446;
2008, c. 12, s. 1.

Keeping cockpit

447 (1) Every one commits an offence who builds, makes, maintains or keeps a cockpit on premises that he or she owns or occupies, or allows a cockpit to be built, made, maintained or kept on such premises.
Punishment
(2) Every one who commits an offence under subsection (1) is guilty of
(a) an indictable offence and liable to imprisonment for a term of not more than five years; or
(b) an offence punishable on summary conviction and liable to a fine not exceeding ten thousand dollars or to imprisonment for a term of not more than eighteen months or to both.
Confiscation
(3) A peace officer who finds cocks in a cockpit or on premises where a cockpit is located shall seize them and take them before a justice who shall order them to be destroyed.
R.S., 1985, c. C-46, s. 447;
2008, c. 12, s. 1.
Order of prohibition or restitution
447.1 (1) The court may, in addition to any other sentence that it may impose under subsection 444(2), 445(2), 445.1(2), 446(2) or 447(2),
(a) make an order prohibiting the accused from owning, having the custody or control of or residing in the same premises as an animal or a bird during any period that the court considers appropriate but, in the case of a second or subsequent offence, for a minimum of five years; and
(b) on application of the Attorney General or on its own motion, order that the accused pay to a person or an organization that has taken care of an animal or a bird as a result of the commission of the offence the reasonable costs that the person or organization incurred in respect of the animal or bird, if the costs are readily ascertainable.
Breach of order
(2) Every one who contravenes an order made under paragraph (1)(a) is guilty of an offence punishable on summary conviction.
Application
(3) Sections 740 to 741.2 apply, with any modifications that the circumstances require, to orders made under paragraph (1)(b).
2008, c. 12, s. 1.

PART XII

PART XII
Offences Relating to Currency

Interpretation

Definitions
448 In this Part,
counterfeit money
(a) a false coin or false paper money that resembles or is apparently intended to resemble or pass for a current coin or current paper money,
(b) a forged bank-note or forged blank bank-note, whether complete or incomplete,
(c) a genuine coin or genuine paper money that is prepared or altered to resemble or pass for a current coin or current paper money of a higher denomination,
(d) a current coin from which the milling is removed by filing or cutting the edges and on which new milling is made to restore its appearance,
(e) a coin cased with gold, silver or nickel, as the case may be, that is intended to resemble or pass for a current gold, silver or nickel coin, and
(f) a coin or a piece of metal or mixed metals that is washed or coloured by any means with a wash or material capable of producing the appearance of gold, silver or nickel and that is intended to

resemble or pass for a current gold, silver or nickel coin;
counterfeit token of value
current
utter
R.S., c. C-34, s. 406.

Making

Making
449 Every one who makes or begins to make counterfeit money is guilty of an indictable offence and liable to imprisonment for a term not exceeding fourteen years.
R.S., c. C-34, s. 407.

Possession

Possession, etc., of counterfeit money
450 Every one who, without lawful justification or excuse, the proof of which lies on him,
(a) buys, receives or offers to buy or receive,
(b) has in his custody or possession, or
(c) introduces into Canada,
counterfeit money is guilty of an indictable offence and liable to imprisonment for a term not exceeding fourteen years.
R.S., c. C-34, s. 408.

Having clippings, etc.
451 Every one who, without lawful justification or excuse, the proof of which lies on him, has in his custody or possession
(a) gold or silver filings or clippings,
(b) gold or silver bullion, or
(c) gold or silver in dust, solution or otherwise,
produced or obtained by impairing, diminishing or lightening a current gold or silver coin, knowing that it has been so produced or obtained, is guilty of an indictable offence and liable to imprisonment for a term not exceeding five years.
R.S., c. C-34, s. 409.

Uttering

Uttering, etc., counterfeit money
452 Every one who, without lawful justification or excuse, the proof of which lies on him,
(a) utters or offers to utter counterfeit money or uses counterfeit money as if it were genuine, or
(b) exports, sends or takes counterfeit money out of Canada,
is guilty of an indictable offence and liable to imprisonment for a term not exceeding fourteen years.
R.S., c. C-34, s. 410.

Uttering coin
453 Every one who, with intent to defraud, knowingly utters
(a) a coin that is not current, or
(b) a piece of metal or mixed metals that resembles in size, figure or colour a current coin for which it is uttered,
is guilty of an indictable offence and liable to imprisonment for a term not exceeding two years.
R.S., c. C-34, s. 411.

Slugs and tokens
454 Every one who without lawful excuse, the proof of which lies on him,
(a) manufactures, produces or sells, or

(b) has in his possession
anything that is intended to be fraudulently used in substitution for a coin or token of value that any coin or token-operated device is designed to receive is guilty of an offence punishable on summary conviction.
R.S., c. C-34, s. 412;
1972, c. 13, s. 32.

Defacing or Impairing

Clipping and uttering clipped coin
455 Every one who
(a) impairs, diminishes or lightens a current gold or silver coin with intent that it should pass for a current gold or silver coin, or
(b) utters a coin knowing that it has been impaired, diminished or lightened contrary to paragraph (a),
is guilty of an indictable offence and liable to imprisonment for a term not exceeding fourteen years.
R.S., c. C-34, s. 413.

Defacing current coins
456 Every one who
(a) defaces a current coin, or
(b) utters a current coin that has been defaced,
is guilty of an offence punishable on summary conviction.
R.S., c. C-34, s. 414.

Likeness of bank-notes
457 (1) No person shall make, publish, print, execute, issue, distribute or circulate, including by electronic or computer-assisted means, anything in the likeness of
(a) a current bank-note; or
(b) an obligation or a security of a government or bank.

Exception
(2) Subsection (1) does not apply to
(a) the Bank of Canada or its employees when they are carrying out their duties;
(b) the Royal Canadian Mounted Police or its members or employees when they are carrying out their duties; or
(c) any person acting under a contract or licence from the Bank of Canada or Royal Canadian Mounted Police.

Offence
(3) A person who contravenes subsection (1) is guilty of an offence punishable on summary conviction.

Defence
(4) No person shall be convicted of an offence under subsection (3) in relation to the printed likeness of a Canadian bank-note if it is established that the length or width of the likeness is less than three-fourths or greater than one-and-one-half times the length or width, as the case may be, of the bank-note and
(a) the likeness is in black-and-white only; or
(b) the likeness of the bank-note appears on only one side of the likeness.
R.S., 1985, c. C-46, s. 457;
1999, c. 5, s. 12.

Instruments or Materials

Making, having or dealing in instruments for counterfeiting
458 Every one who, without lawful justification or excuse, the proof of which lies on him,
(a) makes or repairs,

(b) begins or proceeds to make or repair,
(c) buys or sells, or
(d) has in his custody or possession,

any machine, engine, tool, instrument, material or thing that he knows has been used or that he knows is adapted and intended for use in making counterfeit money or counterfeit tokens of value is guilty of an indictable offence and liable to imprisonment for a term not exceeding fourteen years.
R.S., c. C-34, s. 416.

Conveying instruments for coining out of mint
459 Every one who, without lawful justification or excuse, the proof of which lies on him, knowingly conveys out of any of Her Majesty's mints in Canada,
(a) any machine, engine, tool, instrument, material or thing used or employed in connection with the manufacture of coins,
(b) a useful part of anything mentioned in paragraph (a), or
(c) coin, bullion, metal or a mixture of metals,
is guilty of an indictable offence and liable to imprisonment for a term not exceeding fourteen years.
R.S., c. C-34, s. 417.

Advertising and Trafficking in Counterfeit Money or Counterfeit Tokens of Value

Advertising and dealing in counterfeit money, etc.
460 (1) Every one who
(a) by an advertisement or any other writing, offers to sell, procure or dispose of counterfeit money or counterfeit tokens of value or to give information with respect to the manner in which or the means by which counterfeit money or counterfeit tokens of value may be sold, procured or disposed of, or
(b) purchases, obtains, negotiates or otherwise deals with counterfeit tokens of value, or offers to negotiate with a view to purchasing or obtaining them,
is guilty of an indictable offence and liable to imprisonment for a term not exceeding five years.

Fraudulent use of money genuine but valueless
(2) No person shall be convicted of an offence under subsection (1) in respect of genuine coin or genuine paper money that has no value as money unless, at the time when the offence is alleged to have been committed, he knew that the coin or paper money had no value as money and he had a fraudulent intent in his dealings with or with respect to the coin or paper money.
R.S., c. C-34, s. 418.

Special Provisions as to Proof

When counterfeit complete
461 (1) Every offence relating to counterfeit money or counterfeit tokens of value shall be deemed to be complete notwithstanding that the money or tokens of value in respect of which the proceedings are taken are not finished or perfected or do not copy exactly the money or tokens of value that they are apparently intended to resemble or for which they are apparently intended to pass.

Certificate of examiner of counterfeit
(2) In any proceedings under this Part, a certificate signed by a person designated as an examiner of counterfeit by the Minister of Public Safety and Emergency Preparedness, stating that any coin, paper money or bank-note described therein is counterfeit money or that any coin, paper money or bank-note described therein is genuine and is or is not, as the case may be, current in Canada or elsewhere, is evidence of the statements contained in the certificate without proof of the signature or official character of the person appearing to have signed the certificate.

Cross-examination and notice
(3) Subsections 258(6) and (7) apply, with such modifications as the circumstances require, in

respect of a certificate described in subsection (2).
R.S., 1985, c. C-46, s. 461;
1992, c. 1, s. 58;
2005, c. 10, s. 34.

Forfeiture

Ownership
462 (1) Counterfeit money, counterfeit tokens of value and anything that is used or is intended to be used to make counterfeit money or counterfeit tokens of value belong to Her Majesty.
Seizure
(2) A peace officer may seize and detain
(a) counterfeit money,
(b) counterfeit tokens of value, and
(c) machines, engines, tools, instruments, materials or things that have been used or that have been adapted and are intended for use in making counterfeit money or counterfeit tokens of value,
and anything seized shall be sent to the Minister of Finance to be disposed of or dealt with as he may direct, but anything that is required as evidence in any proceedings shall not be sent to the Minister until it is no longer required in those proceedings.
R.S., c. C-34, s. 420.

PART XII.1

PART XII.1
Instruments and Literature for Illicit Drug Use

Interpretation

Definitions
462.1 In this Part,
consume
illicit drug
Controlled Drugs and Substances Act
illicit drug use
Controlled Drugs and Substances Act
instrument for illicit drug use
Food and Drugs Act
literature for illicit drug use
sell
R.S., 1985, c. 50 (4th Supp.), s. 1;
1996, c. 19, s. 67.

Offence and Punishment

Offence
462.2 Every one who knowingly imports into Canada, exports from Canada, manufactures, promotes or sells instruments or literature for illicit drug use is guilty of an offence and liable on summary conviction
(a) for a first offence, to a fine not exceeding one hundred thousand dollars or to imprisonment for a term not exceeding six months or to both; or
(b) for a second or subsequent offence, to a fine not exceeding three hundred thousand dollars or to

imprisonment for a term not exceeding one year or to both.
R.S., 1985, c. 50 (4th Supp.), s. 1.

PART XII.2

PART XII.2
Proceeds of Crime

Interpretation

Definitions
462.3 (1) In this Part,
designated drug offence
designated offence
(a) any offence that may be prosecuted as an indictable offence under this or any other Act of Parliament, other than an indictable offence prescribed by regulation, or
(b) a conspiracy or an attempt to commit, being an accessory after the fact in relation to, or any counselling in relation to, an offence referred to in paragraph (a);
designated substance offence
enterprise crime offence
judge
proceeds of crime
(a) the commission in Canada of a designated offence, or
(b) an act or omission anywhere that, if it had occurred in Canada, would have constituted a designated offence.
Regulations
(2) The Governor in Council may make regulations prescribing indictable offences that are excluded from the definition
Powers of Attorney General of Canada
(3) Despite the definition
(a) exercise all the powers and perform all the duties and functions assigned to the Attorney General by or under this Act in respect of a designated offence if the alleged offence arises out of conduct that in whole or in part is in relation to an alleged contravention of an Act of Parliament or a regulation made under such an Act, other than this Act or a regulation made under this Act; and
(b) conduct proceedings and exercise all the powers and perform all the duties and functions assigned to the Attorney General by or under this Act in respect of
(i) an offence referred to in section 354, 355.2, 355.4 or 462.31, if the alleged offence arises out of conduct that in whole or in part is in relation to an alleged contravention of an Act of Parliament, other than this Act, or a regulation made under such an Act, and
(ii) an offence under subsection 462.33(11) if the restraint order was made on application of the Attorney General of Canada.
Powers of Attorney General of a province
(4) Subsection (3) does not affect the authority of the Attorney General of a province to conduct proceedings in respect of a designated offence or to exercise any of the powers or perform any of the duties and functions assigned to the Attorney General by or under this Act.
R.S., 1985, c. 42 (4th Supp.), s. 2;
1993, c. 25, s. 95, c. 37, s. 32, c. 46, s. 5;
1994, c. 44, s. 29;
1995, c. 39, s. 151;
1996, c. 19, ss. 68, 70;
1997, c. 18, s. 27, c. 23, s. 9;
1998, c. 34, ss. 9, 11;

1999, c. 5, ss. 13, 52;
2001, c. 32, s. 12, c. 41, ss. 14, 33;
2005, c. 44, s. 1;
2010, c. 14, s. 7.

Offence

Laundering proceeds of crime
462.31 (1) Every one commits an offence who uses, transfers the possession of, sends or delivers to any person or place, transports, transmits, alters, disposes of or otherwise deals with, in any manner and by any means, any property or any proceeds of any property with intent to conceal or convert that property or those proceeds, knowing or believing that all or a part of that property or of those proceeds was obtained or derived directly or indirectly as a result of
(a) the commission in Canada of a designated offence; or
(b) an act or omission anywhere that, if it had occurred in Canada, would have constituted a designated offence.
Punishment
(2) Every one who commits an offence under subsection (1)
(a) is guilty of an indictable offence and liable to imprisonment for a term not exceeding ten years; or
(b) is guilty of an offence punishable on summary conviction.
Exception
(3) A peace officer or a person acting under the direction of a peace officer is not guilty of an offence under subsection (1) if the peace officer or person does any of the things mentioned in that subsection for the purposes of an investigation or otherwise in the execution of the peace officer's duties.
R.S., 1985, c. 42 (4th Supp.), s. 2;
1996, c. 19, s. 70;
1997, c. 18, s. 28;
2001, c. 32, s. 13;
2005, c. 44, s. 2(F).

Search, Seizure and Detention of Proceeds of Crime

Special search warrant
462.32 (1) Subject to subsection (3), if a judge, on application of the Attorney General, is satisfied by information on oath in Form 1 that there are reasonable grounds to believe that there is in any building, receptacle or place, within the province in which the judge has jurisdiction or any other province, any property in respect of which an order of forfeiture may be made under subsection 462.37(1) or (2.01) or 462.38(2), in respect of a designated offence alleged to have been committed within the province in which the judge has jurisdiction, the judge may issue a warrant authorizing a person named in the warrant or a peace officer to search the building, receptacle or place for that property and to seize that property and any other property in respect of which that person or peace officer believes, on reasonable grounds, that an order of forfeiture may be made under that subsection.
Procedure
(2) An application for a warrant under subsection (1) may be made
Execution of warrant
(2.1) Subject to subsection (2.2), a warrant issued pursuant to subsection (1) may be executed anywhere in Canada.
Execution in another province
(2.2) Where a warrant is issued under subsection (1) in one province but it may be reasonably expected that it is to be executed in another province and the execution of the warrant would require

entry into or on the property of any person in the other province, a judge in the other province may, on

Execution of warrant in other territorial jurisdictions

(3) Subsections 487(2) to (4) and section 488 apply, with such modifications as the circumstances require, to a warrant issued under this section.

Detention and record of property seized

(4) Every person who executes a warrant issued by a judge under this section shall
(a) detain or cause to be detained the property seized, taking reasonable care to ensure that the property is preserved so that it may be dealt with in accordance with the law;
(b) as soon as practicable after the execution of the warrant but within a period not exceeding seven days thereafter, prepare a report in Form 5.3, identifying the property seized and the location where the property is being detained, and cause the report to be filed with the clerk of the court; and
(c) cause a copy of the report to be provided, on request, to the person from whom the property was seized and to any other person who, in the opinion of the judge, appears to have a valid interest in the property.

Return of proceeds

(4.1) Subject to this or any other Act of Parliament, a peace officer who has seized anything under a warrant issued by a judge under this section may, with the written consent of the Attorney General, on being issued a receipt for it, return the thing seized to the person lawfully entitled to its possession, if
(a) the peace officer is satisfied that there is no dispute as to who is lawfully entitled to possession of the thing seized;
(b) the peace officer is satisfied that the continued detention of the thing seized is not required for the purpose of forfeiture; and
(c) the thing seized is returned before a report is filed with the clerk of the court under paragraph (4)(b).

Notice

(5) Before issuing a warrant under this section in relation to any property, a judge may require notice to be given to and may hear any person who, in the opinion of the judge, appears to have a valid interest in the property unless the judge is of the opinion that giving such notice before the issuance of the warrant would result in the disappearance, dissipation or reduction in value of the property or otherwise affect the property so that all or a part thereof could not be seized pursuant to the warrant.

Undertakings by Attorney General

(6) Before issuing a warrant under this section, a judge shall require the Attorney General to give such undertakings as the judge considers appropriate with respect to the payment of damages or costs, or both, in relation to the issuance and execution of the warrant.

R.S., 1985, c. 42 (4th Supp.), s. 2;
1997, c. 18, s. 29;
2001, c. 32, s. 14;
2005, c. 44, s. 3;
2017, c. 7, s. 57(F).

Application for restraint order

462.33 (1) The Attorney General may make an application in accordance with subsection (2) for a restraint order under subsection (3) in respect of any property.

Procedure

(2) An application made under subsection (1) for a restraint order under subsection (3) in respect of any property may be made
(a) the offence or matter under investigation;
(b) the person who is believed to be in possession of the property;
(c) the grounds for the belief that an order of forfeiture may be made under subsection 462.37(1) or (2.01) or 462.38(2) in respect of the property;
(d) a description of the property; and

(e) whether any previous applications have been made under this section with respect to the property.
Restraint order
(3) A judge who hears an application for a restraint order made under subsection (1) may — if the judge is satisfied that there are reasonable grounds to believe that there exists, within the province in which the judge has jurisdiction or any other province, any property in respect of which an order of forfeiture may be made under subsection 462.37(1) or (2.01) or 462.38(2), in respect of a designated offence alleged to have been committed within the province in which the judge has jurisdiction — make an order prohibiting any person from disposing of, or otherwise dealing with any interest in, the property specified in the order otherwise than in the manner that may be specified in the order.
Execution in another province
(3.01) Subsections 462.32(2.1) and (2.2) apply, with such modifications as the circumstances require, in respect of a restraint order.
Property outside Canada
(3.1) A restraint order may be issued under this section in respect of property situated outside Canada, with any modifications that the circumstances require.
Idem
(4) An order made by a judge under subsection (3) may be subject to such reasonable conditions as the judge thinks fit.
Notice
(5) Before making an order under subsection (3) in relation to any property, a judge may require notice to be given to and may hear any person who, in the opinion of the judge, appears to have a valid interest in the property unless the judge is of the opinion that giving such notice before making the order would result in the disappearance, dissipation or reduction in value of the property or otherwise affect the property so that all or a part thereof could not be subject to an order of forfeiture under subsection 462.37(1) or (2.01) or 462.38(2).
Order in writing
(6) An order made under subsection (3) shall be made in writing.
Undertakings by Attorney General
(7) Before making an order under subsection (3), a judge shall require the Attorney General to give such undertakings as the judge considers appropriate with respect to the payment of damages or costs, or both, in relation to
(a) the making of an order in respect of property situated within or outside Canada; and
(b) the execution of an order in respect of property situated within Canada.
Service of order
(8) A copy of an order made by a judge under subsection (3) shall be served on the person to whom the order is addressed in such manner as the judge directs or as may be prescribed by rules of court.
Registration of order
(9) A copy of an order made under subsection (3) shall be registered against any property in accordance with the laws of the province in which the property is situated.
Continues in force
(10) An order made under subsection (3) remains in effect until
(a) it is revoked or varied under subsection 462.34(4) or revoked under paragraph 462.43(a);
(b) it ceases to be in force under section 462.35; or
(c) an order of forfeiture or restoration of the property is made under subsection 462.37(1) or (2.01), 462.38(2) or 462.41(3) or any other provision of this or any other Act of Parliament.
Offence
(11) Any person on whom an order made under subsection (3) is served in accordance with this section and who, while the order is in force, acts in contravention of or fails to comply with the order is guilty of an indictable offence or an offence punishable on summary conviction.
R.S., 1985, c. 42 (4th Supp.), s. 2;
1993, c. 37, s. 21;
1996, c. 16, s. 60;

1997, c. 18, s. 30;
2001, c. 32, s. 15;
2005, c. 44, s. 4.

Management order

462.331 (1) With respect to property seized under section 462.32 or restrained under section 462.33, other than a controlled substance within the meaning of the
Controlled Drugs and Substances Act
(a) appoint a person to take control of and to manage or otherwise deal with all or part of the property in accordance with the directions of the judge; and
(b) require any person having possession of that property to give possession of the property to the person appointed under paragraph (a).

Appointment of Minister of Public Works and Government Services

(2) When the Attorney General of Canada so requests, a judge appointing a person under subsection (1) shall appoint the Minister of Public Works and Government Services.

Power to manage

(3) The power to manage or otherwise deal with property under subsection (1) includes
(a) in the case of perishable or rapidly depreciating property, the power to make an interlocutory sale of that property; and
(b) in the case of property that has little or no value, the power to destroy that property.

Application for destruction order

(4) Before a person appointed to manage property destroys property that has little or no value, he or she shall apply to a court for a destruction order.

Notice

(5) Before making a destruction order in relation to any property, a court shall require notice in accordance with subsection (6) to be given to, and may hear, any person who, in the opinion of the court, appears to have a valid interest in the property.

Manner of giving notice

(6) A notice shall
(a) be given or served in the manner that the court directs or that may be specified in the rules of the court; and
(b) be of any duration that the court considers reasonable or that may be specified in the rules of the court.

Order

(7) A court may order that the property be destroyed if it is satisfied that the property has little or no value, whether financial or other.

When management order ceases to have effect

(8) A management order ceases to have effect when the property that is the subject of the management order is returned in accordance with the law to an applicant or forfeited to Her Majesty.

Application to vary conditions

(9) The Attorney General may at any time apply to the judge to cancel or vary any condition to which a management order is subject but may not apply to vary an appointment made under subsection (2).
2001, c. 32, s. 16.

Application for review of special warrants and restraint orders

462.34 (1) Any person who has an interest in property that was seized under a warrant issued pursuant to section 462.32 or in respect of which a restraint order was made under subsection 462.33(3) may, at any time, apply to a judge
(a) for an order under subsection (4); or
(b) for permission to examine the property.

Notice to Attorney General

(2) Where an application is made under paragraph (1)(a),
(a) the application shall not, without the consent of the Attorney General, be heard by a judge unless the applicant has given to the Attorney General at least two clear days notice in writing of the

application; and

(b) the judge may require notice of the application to be given to and may hear any person who, in the opinion of the judge, appears to have a valid interest in the property.

Terms of examination order

(3) A judge may, on an application made to the judge under paragraph (1)(b), order that the applicant be permitted to examine property subject to such terms as appear to the judge to be necessary or desirable to ensure that the property is safeguarded and preserved for any purpose for which it may subsequently be required.

Order of restoration of property or revocation or variation of order

(4) On an application made to a judge under paragraph (1)(a) in respect of any property and after hearing the applicant and the Attorney General and any other person to whom notice was given pursuant to paragraph (2)(b), the judge may order that the property or a part thereof be returned to the applicant or, in the case of a restraint order made under subsection 462.33(3), revoke the order, vary the order to exclude the property or any interest in the property or part thereof from the application of the order or make the order subject to such reasonable conditions as the judge thinks fit,

(a) if the applicant enters into a recognizance before the judge, with or without sureties, in such amount and with such conditions, if any, as the judge directs and, where the judge considers it appropriate, deposits with the judge such sum of money or other valuable security as the judge directs;

(b) if the conditions referred to in subsection (6) are satisfied; or

(c) for the purpose of

(i) meeting the reasonable living expenses of the person who was in possession of the property at the time the warrant was executed or the order was made or any person who, in the opinion of the judge, has a valid interest in the property and of the dependants of that person,

(ii) meeting the reasonable business and legal expenses of a person referred to in subparagraph (i), or

(iii) permitting the use of the property in order to enter into a recognizance under Part XVI,

if the judge is satisfied that the applicant has no other assets or means available for the purposes set out in this paragraph and that no other person appears to be the lawful owner of or lawfully entitled to possession of the property.

Hearing

(5) For the purpose of determining the reasonableness of legal expenses referred to in subparagraph (4)(c)(ii), a judge shall hold an

Expenses

(5.1) For the purpose of determining the reasonableness of expenses referred to in paragraph (4)(c), the Attorney General may

(a) at the hearing of the application, make representations as to what would constitute the reasonableness of the expenses, other than legal expenses; and

(b) before or after the hearing of the application held

Taxing legal fees

(5.2) The judge who made an order under paragraph (4)(c) may, and on the application of the Attorney General shall, tax the legal fees forming part of the legal expenses referred to in subparagraph (4)(c)(ii) and, in so doing, shall take into account

(a) the value of property in respect of which an order of forfeiture may be made;

(b) the complexity of the proceedings giving rise to those legal expenses;

(c) the importance of the issues involved in those proceedings;

(d) the duration of any hearings held in respect of those proceedings;

(e) whether any stage of those proceedings was improper or vexatious;

(f) any representations made by the Attorney General; and

(g) any other relevant matter.

Conditions to be satisfied

(6) An order under paragraph (4)(b) in respect of property may be made by a judge if the judge is

satisfied

(a) where the application is made by

(i) a person charged with a designated offence, or

(ii) any person who acquired title to or a right of possession of that property from a person referred to in subparagraph (i) under circumstances that give rise to a reasonable inference that the title or right was transferred from that person for the purpose of avoiding the forfeiture of the property,

that a warrant should not have been issued pursuant to section 462.32 or a restraint order under subsection 462.33(3) should not have been made in respect of that property, or

(b) in any other case, that the applicant is the lawful owner of or lawfully entitled to possession of the property and appears innocent of any complicity in a designated offence or of any collusion in relation to such an offence, and that no other person appears to be the lawful owner of or lawfully entitled to possession of the property,

and that the property will no longer be required for the purpose of any investigation or as evidence in any proceeding.

Saving provision

(7) Sections 354, 355.2 and 355.4 do not apply to a person who comes into possession of any property that, by virtue of an order made under paragraph (4)(c), was returned to any person after having been seized or was excluded from the application of a restraint order made under subsection 462.33(3).

Form of recognizance

(8) A recognizance entered into pursuant to paragraph (4)(a) may be in Form 32.

R.S., 1985, c. 42 (4th Supp.), s. 2;

1996, c. 19, ss. 69, 70;

1997, c. 18, ss. 31, 140;

2001, c. 32, s. 17;

2010, c. 14, s. 8.

Application of property restitution provisions

462.341 Subsection 462.34(2), paragraph 462.34(4)(c) and subsections 462.34(5), (5.1) and (5.2) apply, with any modifications that the circumstances require, to a person who has an interest in money or bank-notes that are seized under this Act or the

Controlled Drugs and Substances Act

1997, c. 18, ss. 32, 140;

1999, c. 5, s. 14;

2005, c. 44, s. 5.

Expiration of special warrants and restraint orders

462.35 (1) Subject to this section, where property has been seized under a warrant issued pursuant to section 462.32 or a restraint order has been made under section 462.33 in relation to property, the property may be detained or the order may continue in force, as the case may be, for a period not exceeding six months from the seizure or the making of the order, as the case may be.

Where proceedings instituted

(2) The property may continue to be detained, or the order may continue in force, for a period that exceeds six months if proceedings are instituted in respect of which the thing detained may be forfeited.

Where application made

(3) The property may continue to be detained or the order may continue in force for a period or periods that exceed six months if the continuation is, on application made by the Attorney General, ordered by a judge, where the judge is satisfied that the property is required, after the expiration of the period or periods, for the purpose of section 462.37 or 462.38 or any other provision of this or any other Act of Parliament respecting forfeiture or for the purpose of any investigation or as evidence in any proceeding.

R.S., 1985, c. 42 (4th Supp.), s. 2;

1997, c. 18, s. 33.

Forwarding to clerk where accused to stand trial
462.36 Where a judge issues a warrant under section 462.32 or makes a restraint order under section 462.33 in respect of any property, the clerk of the court shall, when an accused is ordered to stand trial for a designated offence, cause to be forwarded to the clerk of the court to which the accused has been ordered to stand trial a copy of the report filed pursuant to paragraph 462.32(4)(b) or of the restraint order in respect of the property.
R.S., 1985, c. 42 (4th Supp.), s. 2;
2001, c. 32, s. 18.

Forfeiture of Proceeds of Crime

Order of forfeiture of property on conviction
462.37 (1) Subject to this section and sections 462.39 to 462.41, where an offender is convicted, or discharged under section 730, of a designated offence and the court imposing sentence on the offender, on application of the Attorney General, is satisfied, on a balance of probabilities, that any property is proceeds of crime and that the designated offence was committed in relation to that property, the court shall order that the property be forfeited to Her Majesty to be disposed of as the Attorney General directs or otherwise dealt with in accordance with the law.
Proceeds of crime derived from other offences
(2) Where the evidence does not establish to the satisfaction of the court that the designated offence of which the offender is convicted, or discharged under section 730, was committed in relation to property in respect of which an order of forfeiture would otherwise be made under subsection (1) but the court is satisfied, beyond a reasonable doubt, that that property is proceeds of crime, the court may make an order of forfeiture under subsection (1) in relation to that property.
Order of forfeiture — particular circumstances
(2.01) A court imposing sentence on an offender convicted of an offence described in subsection (2.02) shall, on application of the Attorney General and subject to this section and sections 462.4 and 462.41, order that any property of the offender that is identified by the Attorney General in the application be forfeited to Her Majesty to be disposed of as the Attorney General directs or otherwise dealt with in accordance with the law if the court is satisfied, on a balance of probabilities, that
(a) within 10 years before the proceedings were commenced in respect of the offence for which the offender is being sentenced, the offender engaged in a pattern of criminal activity for the purpose of directly or indirectly receiving a material benefit, including a financial benefit; or
(b) the income of the offender from sources unrelated to designated offences cannot reasonably account for the value of all the property of the offender.
Offences
(2.02) The offences are the following:
(a) a criminal organization offence punishable by five or more years of imprisonment; and
(b) an offence under section 5, 6 or 7 of the
Controlled Drugs and Substances Act
Offender may establish that property is not proceeds of crime
(2.03) A court shall not make an order of forfeiture under subsection (2.01) in respect of any property that the offender establishes, on a balance of probabilities, is not proceeds of crime.
Pattern of criminal activity
(2.04) In determining whether the offender has engaged in a pattern of criminal activity described in paragraph (2.01)(a), the court shall consider
(a) the circumstances of the offence for which the offender is being sentenced;
(b) any act or omission — other than an act or omission that constitutes the offence for which the offender is being sentenced — that the court is satisfied, on a balance of probabilities, was committed by the offender and constitutes an offence punishable by indictment under any Act of Parliament;
(c) any act or omission that the court is satisfied, on a balance of probabilities, was committed by the

offender and is an offence in the place where it was committed and, if committed in Canada, would constitute an offence punishable by indictment under any Act of Parliament; and
(d) any other factor that the court considers relevant.

Conditions — pattern of criminal activity

(2.05) A court shall not determine that an offender has engaged in a pattern of criminal activity unless the court is satisfied, on a balance of probabilities, that the offender committed, within the period referred to in paragraph (2.01)(a),
(a) acts or omissions — other than an act or omission that constitutes the offence for which the offender is being sentenced — that constitute at least two serious offences or one criminal organization offence;
(b) acts or omissions that are offences in the place where they were committed and, if committed in Canada, would constitute at least two serious offences or one criminal organization offence; or
(c) an act or omission described in paragraph (a) that constitutes a serious offence and an act or omission described in paragraph (b) that, if committed in Canada, would constitute a serious offence.

Application under subsection (1) not prevented

(2.06) Nothing in subsection (2.01) shall be interpreted as preventing the Attorney General from making an application under subsection (1) in respect of any property.

Exception

(2.07) A court may, if it considers it in the interests of justice, decline to make an order of forfeiture against any property that would otherwise be subject to forfeiture under subsection (2.01). The court shall give reasons for its decision.

Property outside Canada

(2.1) An order may be issued under this section in respect of property situated outside Canada, with any modifications that the circumstances require.

Fine instead of forfeiture

(3) If a court is satisfied that an order of forfeiture under subsection (1) or (2.01) should be made in respect of any property of an offender but that the property or any part of or interest in the property cannot be made subject to an order, the court may, instead of ordering the property or any part of or interest in the property to be forfeited, order the offender to pay a fine in an amount equal to the value of the property or the part of or interest in the property. In particular, a court may order the offender to pay a fine if the property or any part of or interest in the property
(a) cannot, on the exercise of due diligence, be located;
(b) has been transferred to a third party;
(c) is located outside Canada;
(d) has been substantially diminished in value or rendered worthless; or
(e) has been commingled with other property that cannot be divided without difficulty.

Imprisonment in default of payment of fine

(4) Where a court orders an offender to pay a fine pursuant to subsection (3), the court shall
(a) impose, in default of payment of that fine, a term of imprisonment
(i) not exceeding six months, where the amount of the fine does not exceed ten thousand dollars,
(ii) of not less than six months and not exceeding twelve months, where the amount of the fine exceeds ten thousand dollars but does not exceed twenty thousand dollars,
(iii) of not less than twelve months and not exceeding eighteen months, where the amount of the fine exceeds twenty thousand dollars but does not exceed fifty thousand dollars,
(iv) of not less than eighteen months and not exceeding two years, where the amount of the fine exceeds fifty thousand dollars but does not exceed one hundred thousand dollars,
(v) of not less than two years and not exceeding three years, where the amount of the fine exceeds one hundred thousand dollars but does not exceed two hundred and fifty thousand dollars,
(vi) of not less than three years and not exceeding five years, where the amount of the fine exceeds two hundred and fifty thousand dollars but does not exceed one million dollars, or
(vii) of not less than five years and not exceeding ten years, where the amount of the fine exceeds one million dollars; and

(b) direct that the term of imprisonment imposed pursuant to paragraph (a) be served consecutively to any other term of imprisonment imposed on the offender or that the offender is then serving.

Fine option program not available to offender

(5) Section 736 does not apply to an offender against whom a fine is imposed pursuant to subsection (3).

R.S., 1985, c. 42 (4th Supp.), s. 2;
1992, c. 1, s. 60(F);
1995, c. 22, s. 10;
1999, c. 5, s. 15(F);
2001, c. 32, s. 19;
2005, c. 44, s. 6.

Definition of

462.371 (1) In this section,

order

Execution

(2) An order may be executed anywhere in Canada.

Filing of order from another province

(3) Where the Attorney General of a province in which property that is the subject of an order made in another province is situated receives a certified copy of the order and files it with the superior court of criminal jurisdiction of the province in which the property is situated, the order shall be entered as a judgment of that court.

Attorney General of Canada

(4) Where the Attorney General of Canada receives a certified copy of an order made in a province in respect of property situated in another province and files the order with the superior court of criminal jurisdiction of the province in which the property is situated, the order shall be entered as a judgment of that court.

Effect of registered order

(5) An order has, from the date it is filed in a court of a province under subsection (3) or (4), the same effect as if it had been an order originally made by that court.

Notice

(6) Where an order has been filed in a court under subsection (3) or (4), it shall not be executed before notice in accordance with subsection 462.41(2) is given to every person who, in the opinion of the court, appears to have a valid interest in the property.

Application of section 462.42

(7) Section 462.42 applies, with such modifications as the circumstances require, in respect of a person who claims an interest in property that is the subject of an order filed under subsection (3) or (4).

Application under section 462.42 to be made in one province

(8) No person may make an application under section 462.42 in relation to property that is the subject of an order filed under subsection (3) or (4) if that person has previously made an application in respect of the same property in another province.

Finding in one court binding

(9) The finding by a court of a province in relation to property that is the subject of an order filed under subsection (3) or (4) as to whether or not an applicant referred to in subsection 462.42(4) is affected by the forfeiture referred to in that subsection or declaring the nature and extent of the interest of the applicant under that subsection is binding on the superior court of criminal jurisdiction of the province where the order is entered as a judgment.

1997, c. 18, s. 34.

Application for forfeiture

462.38 (1) Where an information has been laid in respect of a designated offence, the Attorney General may make an application to a judge for an order of forfeiture under subsection (2) in respect of any property.

Order of forfeiture of property
(2) Subject to sections 462.39 to 462.41, where an application is made to a judge under subsection (1), the judge shall, if the judge is satisfied that
(a) any property is, beyond a reasonable doubt, proceeds of crime,
(b) proceedings in respect of a designated offence committed in relation to that property were commenced, and
(c) the accused charged with the offence referred to in paragraph (b) has died or absconded,
order that the property be forfeited to Her Majesty to be disposed of as the Attorney General directs or otherwise dealt with in accordance with the law.

Property outside Canada
(2.1) An order may be issued under this section in respect of property situated outside Canada, with any modifications that the circumstances require.

Person deemed absconded
(3) For the purposes of this section, a person shall be deemed to have absconded in connection with a designated offence if
(a) an information has been laid alleging the commission of the offence by the person,
(b) a warrant for the arrest of the person or a summons in respect of an organization has been issued in relation to that information, and
(c) reasonable attempts to arrest the person pursuant to the warrant or to serve the summons have been unsuccessful during the period of six months commencing on the day the warrant or summons was issued, or, in the case of a person who is not or never was in Canada, the person cannot be brought within that period to the jurisdiction in which the warrant or summons was issued,
and the person shall be deemed to have so absconded on the last day of that period of six months.
R.S., 1985, c. 42 (4th Supp.), s. 2;
1997, c. 18, s. 35;
2001, c. 32, s. 20;
2003, c. 21, s. 7;
2017, c. 7, s. 60(F).

Inference
462.39 For the purpose of subsection 462.37(1) or 462.38(2), the court may infer that property was obtained or derived as a result of the commission of a designated offence where evidence establishes that the value, after the commission of that offence, of all the property of the person alleged to have committed the offence exceeds the value of all the property of that person before the commission of that offence and the court is satisfied that the income of that person from sources unrelated to designated offences committed by that person cannot reasonably account for such an increase in value.
R.S., 1985, c. 42 (4th Supp.), s. 2;
1996, c. 19, s. 70;
2001, c. 32, s. 21.

Voidable transfers
462.4 A court may,
(a) prior to ordering property to be forfeited under subsection 462.37(1) or (2.01) or 462.38(2), and
(b) in the case of property in respect of which a restraint order was made under section 462.33, where the order was served in accordance with subsection 462.33(8),
set aside any conveyance or transfer of the property that occurred after the seizure of the property or the service of the order under section 462.33, unless the conveyance or transfer was for valuable consideration to a person acting in good faith.
R.S., 1985, c. 42 (4th Supp.), s. 2;
1997, c. 18, s. 36(E);
2005, c. 44, s. 7.

Notice
462.41 (1) Before making an order under subsection 462.37(1) or (2.01) or 462.38(2) in relation to

any property, a court shall require notice in accordance with subsection (2) to be given to and may hear any person who, in the opinion of the court, appears to have a valid interest in the property.
Service, duration and contents of notice
(2) A notice given under subsection (1) shall
(a) be given or served in such manner as the court directs or as may be prescribed by the rules of the court;
(b) be of such duration as the court considers reasonable or as may be prescribed by the rules of the court; and
(c) set out the designated offence charged and a description of the property.
Order of restoration of property
(3) Where a court is satisfied that any person, other than
(a) a person who is charged with, or was convicted of, a designated offence, or
(b) a person who acquired title to or a right of possession of that property from a person referred to in paragraph (a) under circumstances that give rise to a reasonable inference that the title or right was transferred for the purpose of avoiding the forfeiture of the property,
is the lawful owner or is lawfully entitled to possession of any property or any part thereof that would otherwise be forfeited pursuant to subsection 462.37(1) or (2.01) or 462.38(2) and that the person appears innocent of any complicity in an offence referred to in paragraph (a) or of any collusion in relation to such an offence, the court may order that the property or part thereof be returned to that person.
R.S., 1985, c. 42 (4th Supp.), s. 2;
1996, c. 19, s. 70;
1997, c. 18, ss. 37, 140;
2001, c. 32, s. 22;
2005, c. 44, s. 8.
Application by person claiming interest for relief from forfeiture
462.42 (1) Any person who claims an interest in property that is forfeited to Her Majesty under subsection 462.37(1) or (2.01) or 462.38(2) may, within thirty days after the forfeiture, apply by notice in writing to a judge for an order under subsection (4) unless the person is
(a) a person who is charged with, or was convicted of, a designated offence that resulted in the forfeiture; or
(b) a person who acquired title to or a right of possession of the property from a person referred to in paragraph (a) under circumstances that give rise to a reasonable inference that the title or right was transferred from that person for the purpose of avoiding the forfeiture of the property.
Fixing day for hearing
(2) The judge to whom an application is made under subsection (1) shall fix a day not less than thirty days after the date of filing of the application for the hearing thereof.
Notice
(3) An applicant shall serve a notice of the application made under subsection (1) and of the hearing thereof on the Attorney General at least fifteen days before the day fixed for the hearing.
Order declaring interest not subject to forfeiture
(4) Where, on the hearing of an application made under subsection (1), the judge is satisfied that the applicant is not a person referred to in paragraph (1)(a) or (b) and appears innocent of any complicity in any designated offence that resulted in the forfeiture or of any collusion in relation to any such offence, the judge may make an order declaring that the interest of the applicant is not affected by the forfeiture and declaring the nature and extent of the interest.
Appeal from order under subsection (4)
(5) An applicant or the Attorney General may appeal to the court of appeal from an order under subsection (4) and the provisions of Part XXI with respect to procedure on appeals apply, with such modifications as the circumstances require, to appeals under this subsection.
Return of property
(6) The Attorney General shall, on application made to the Attorney General by any person who has

obtained an order under subsection (4) and where the periods with respect to the taking of appeals from that order have expired and any appeal from that order taken under subsection (5) has been determined,

(a) direct that the property or the part thereof to which the interest of the applicant relates be returned to the applicant; or

(b) direct that an amount equal to the value of the interest of the applicant, as declared in the order, be paid to the applicant.

R.S., 1985, c. 42 (4th Supp.), s. 2;
1996, c. 19, s. 70;
1997, c. 18, ss. 38, 140;
2001, c. 32, s. 23;
2005, c. 44, s. 9.

Residual disposal of property seized or dealt with pursuant to special warrants or restraint orders

462.43 (1) Where property has been seized under a warrant issued pursuant to section 462.32, a restraint order has been made under section 462.33 in relation to any property or a recognizance has been entered into pursuant to paragraph 462.34(4)(a) in relation to any property and a judge, on application made to the judge by the Attorney General or any person having an interest in the property or on the judge's own motion, after notice given to the Attorney General and any other person having an interest in the property, is satisfied that the property will no longer be required for the purpose of section 462.37, 462.38 or any other provision of this or any other Act of Parliament respecting forfeiture or for the purpose of any investigation or as evidence in any proceeding, the judge

(a) in the case of a restraint order, shall revoke the order;

(b) in the case of a recognizance, shall cancel the recognizance; and

(c) in the case of property seized under a warrant issued pursuant to section 462.32 or property under the control of a person appointed pursuant to paragraph 462.331(1)(a),

(i) if possession of it by the person from whom it was taken is lawful, shall order that it be returned to that person,

(ii) if possession of it by the person from whom it was taken is unlawful and the lawful owner or person who is lawfully entitled to its possession is known, shall order that it be returned to the lawful owner or the person who is lawfully entitled to its possession, or

(iii) if possession of it by the person from whom it was taken is unlawful and the lawful owner or person who is lawfully entitled to its possession is not known, may order that it be forfeited to Her Majesty, to be disposed of as the Attorney General directs, or otherwise dealt with in accordance with the law.

Property outside Canada

(2) An order may be issued under this section in respect of property situated outside Canada, with any modifications that the circumstances require.

R.S., 1985, c. 42 (4th Supp.), s. 2;
2001, c. 32, s. 24;
2004, c. 12, s. 7;
2017, c. 7, s. 62(F).

Appeals from certain orders

462.44 Any person who considers that they are aggrieved by an order made under subsection 462.38(2) or 462.41(3) or section 462.43 may appeal from the order as if the order were an appeal against conviction or against a judgment or verdict of acquittal, as the case may be, under Part XXI, and that Part applies, with such modifications as the circumstances require, to such an appeal.

R.S., 1985, c. 42 (4th Supp.), s. 2;
1997, c. 18, s. 39.

Suspension of forfeiture pending appeal

462.45 Despite anything in this Part, the operation of an order of forfeiture or restoration of property

under subsection 462.34(4), 462.37(1) or (2.01), 462.38(2) or 462.41(3) or section 462.43 is suspended pending
(a) any application made in respect of the property under any of those provisions or any other provision of this or any other Act of Parliament that provides for the restoration or forfeiture of such property,
(b) any appeal taken from an order of forfeiture or restoration in respect of the property, or
(c) any other proceeding in which the right of seizure of the property is questioned,
and property shall not be disposed of within thirty days after an order of forfeiture is made under any of those provisions.
R.S., 1985, c. 42 (4th Supp.), s. 2;
2005, c. 44, s. 10.

Copies of documents returned or forfeited
462.46 (1) If any document is returned or ordered to be returned, forfeited or otherwise dealt with under subsection 462.34(3) or (4), 462.37(1) or (2.01), 462.38(2) or 462.41(3) or section 462.43, the Attorney General may, before returning the document or complying with the order, cause a copy of the document to be made and retained.

Probative force
(2) Every copy made under subsection (1) shall, if certified as a true copy by the Attorney General, be admissible in evidence and, in the absence of evidence to the contrary, shall have the same probative force as the original document would have had if it had been proved in the ordinary way.
R.S., 1985, c. 42 (4th Supp.), s. 2;
2005, c. 44, s. 11.

Disclosure Provisions

No civil or criminal liability incurred by informants
462.47 For greater certainty but subject to section 241 of the
Income Tax Act
R.S., 1985, c. 42 (4th Supp.), s. 2;
1996, c. 19, s. 70;
2001, c. 32, ss. 25, 82;
2002, c. 13, s. 16(F);
2004, c. 12, s. 8(F).

Definition of
designated substance offence
462.48 (1) In this section,
designated substance offence
(a) an offence under Part I of the
Controlled Drugs and Substances Act
(b) a conspiracy or an attempt to commit, being an accessory after the fact in relation to, or any counselling in relation to, an offence referred to in paragraph (a).

Disclosure of income tax information
(1.1) The Attorney General may make an application in accordance with subsection (2) for an order for disclosure of information under subsection (3), for the purposes of an investigation in relation to
(a) a designated substance offence;
(b) an offence against section 354, 355.2, 355.4 or 462.31 if the offence is alleged to have been committed in relation to any property, thing or proceeds obtained or derived directly or indirectly as a result of
(i) the commission in Canada of a designated substance offence, or
(ii) an act or omission anywhere that, if it had occurred in Canada, would have constituted a designated substance offence;
(c) an offence against section 467.11, 467.111, 467.12 or 467.13, or a conspiracy or an attempt to

commit, or being an accessory after the fact in relation to, such an offence; or
(d) a terrorism offence.
Application
(2) An application under subsection (1.1) shall be made
(a) the offence or matter under investigation;
(b) the person in relation to whom the information or documents referred to in paragraph (c) are required;
(c) the type of information or book, record, writing, return or other document obtained by or on behalf of the Minister of National Revenue for the purposes of the
Income Tax Act
(d) the facts relied on to justify the belief, on reasonable grounds, that the person referred to in paragraph (b) has committed or benefited from the commission of any of the offences referred to in subsection (1.1) and that the information or documents referred to in paragraph (c) are likely to be of substantial value, whether alone or together with other material, to the investigation for the purposes of which the application is made.
Order for disclosure of information
(3) Where the judge to whom an application under subsection (1.1) is made is satisfied
(a) of the matters referred to in paragraph (2)(d), and
(b) that there are reasonable grounds for believing that it is in the public interest to allow access to the information or documents to which the application relates, having regard to the benefit likely to accrue to the investigation if the access is obtained,
the judge may, subject to any conditions that the judge considers advisable in the public interest, order the Commissioner of Revenue or any person specially designated in writing by the Commissioner for the purposes of this section
(c) to allow a police officer named in the order access to all such information and documents and to examine them, or
(d) where the judge considers it necessary in the circumstances, to produce all such information and documents to the police officer and allow the police officer to remove the information and documents,
within such period after the expiration of seven clear days following the service of the order pursuant to subsection (4) as the judge may specify.
Service of order
(4) A copy of an order made by a judge under subsection (3) shall be served on the person to whom the order is addressed in such manner as the judge directs or as may be prescribed by rules of court.
Extension of period for compliance with order
(5) A judge who makes an order under subsection (3) may, on application of the Minister of National Revenue, extend the period within which the order is to be complied with.
Objection to disclosure of information
(6) The Minister of National Revenue or any person specially designated in writing by that Minister for the purposes of this section may object to the disclosure of any information or document in respect of which an order under subsection (3) has been made by certifying orally or in writing that the information or document should not be disclosed on the ground that
(a) the Minister of National Revenue is prohibited from disclosing the information or document by any bilateral or international treaty, convention or other agreement respecting taxation to which the Government of Canada is a signatory;
(b) a privilege is attached by law to the information or document;
(c) the information or document has been placed in a sealed package pursuant to law or an order of a court of competent jurisdiction; or
(d) disclosure of the information or document would not, for any other reason, be in the public interest.
Determination of objection
(7) Where an objection to the disclosure of information or a document is made under subsection (6),

the objection may be determined, on application, in accordance with subsection (8), by the Chief Justice of the Federal Court, or by such other judge of that Court as the Chief Justice may designate to hear such applications.

Judge may examine information

(8) A judge who is to determine an objection pursuant to subsection (7) may, if the judge considers it necessary to determine the objection, examine the information or document in relation to which the objection is made and shall grant the objection and order that disclosure of the information or document be refused where the judge is satisfied of any of the grounds mentioned in subsection (6).

Limitation period

(9) An application under subsection (7) shall be made within ten days after the objection is made or within such greater or lesser period as the Chief Justice of the Federal Court, or such other judge of that Court as the Chief Justice may designate to hear such applications, considers appropriate.

Appeal to Federal Court of Appeal

(10) An appeal lies from a determination under subsection (7) to the Federal Court of Appeal.

Limitation period for appeal

(11) An appeal under subsection (10) shall be brought within ten days from the date of the determination appealed from or within such further time as the Federal Court of Appeal considers appropriate in the circumstances.

Special rules for hearings

(12) An application under subsection (7) or an appeal brought in respect of that application shall
(a) be heard
(b) on the request of the person objecting to the disclosure of information, be heard and determined in the National Capital Region described in the schedule to the
National Capital Act

(13) During the hearing of an application under subsection (7) or an appeal brought in respect of that application, the person who made the objection in respect of which the application was made or the appeal was brought shall, on the request of that person, be given the opportunity to make representations

Copies

(14) When any information or document is examined or provided under subsection (3), the person by whom it is examined or to whom it is provided or any officer of the Canada Revenue Agency may make, or cause to be made, one or more copies of it, and any copy purporting to be certified by the Minister of National Revenue or an authorized person to be a copy made under this subsection is evidence of the nature and content of the original information or document and has the same probative force as the original information or document would have had if it had been proved in the ordinary way.

Further disclosure

(15) No person to whom information or documents have been disclosed or provided pursuant to this subsection or pursuant to an order made under subsection (3) shall further disclose the information or documents except for the purposes of the investigation in relation to which the order was made.

Form

(16) An order made under subsection (3) may be in Form 47.

Definition of
police officer
(17) In this section,
police officer
R.S., 1985, c. 42 (4th Supp.), s. 2;
1994, c. 13, s. 7;
1996, c. 19, s. 70;
1997, c. 23, s. 10;
1999, c. 17, s. 120;
2001, c. 32, s. 26, c. 41, ss. 15, 133;

2005, c. 38, ss. 138, 140;
2010, c. 14, s. 9;
2013, c. 9, s. 15;
2014, c. 17, s. 7.

Specific Rules of Forfeiture

Specific forfeiture provisions unaffected by this Part
462.49 (1) This Part does not affect the operation of any other provision of this or any other Act of Parliament respecting the forfeiture of property.
Priority for restitution to victims of crime
(2) The property of an offender may be used to satisfy the operation of a provision of this or any other Act of Parliament respecting the forfeiture of property only to the extent that it is not required to satisfy the operation of any other provision of this or any other Act of Parliament respecting restitution to or compensation of persons affected by the commission of offences.
R.S., 1985, c. 42 (4th Supp.), s. 2.

Regulations

Regulations
462.5 The Attorney General may make regulations governing the manner of disposing of or otherwise dealing with, in accordance with the law, property forfeited under this Part.
R.S., 1985, c. 42 (4th Supp.), s. 2.

PART XIII

PART XIII
Attempts — Conspiracies — Accessories

Attempts, accessories
463 Except where otherwise expressly provided by law, the following provisions apply in respect of persons who attempt to commit or are accessories after the fact to the commission of offences:
(a) every one who attempts to commit or is an accessory after the fact to the commission of an indictable offence for which, on conviction, an accused is liable to be sentenced to imprisonment for life is guilty of an indictable offence and liable to imprisonment for a term not exceeding fourteen years;
(b) every one who attempts to commit or is an accessory after the fact to the commission of an indictable offence for which, on conviction, an accused is liable to imprisonment for fourteen years or less is guilty of an indictable offence and liable to imprisonment for a term that is one-half of the longest term to which a person who is guilty of that offence is liable;
(c) every one who attempts to commit or is an accessory after the fact to the commission of an offence punishable on summary conviction is guilty of an offence punishable on summary conviction; and
(d) every one who attempts to commit or is an accessory after the fact to the commission of an offence for which the offender may be prosecuted by indictment or for which he is punishable on summary conviction
(i) is guilty of an indictable offence and liable to imprisonment for a term not exceeding a term that is one-half of the longest term to which a person who is guilty of that offence is liable, or
(ii) is guilty of an offence punishable on summary conviction.
R.S., 1985, c. C-46, s. 463;
R.S., 1985, c. 27 (1st Supp.), s. 59;
1998, c. 35, s. 120.

Counselling offence that is not committed
464 Except where otherwise expressly provided by law, the following provisions apply in respect of persons who counsel other persons to commit offences, namely,
(a) every one who counsels another person to commit an indictable offence is, if the offence is not committed, guilty of an indictable offence and liable to the same punishment to which a person who attempts to commit that offence is liable; and
(b) every one who counsels another person to commit an offence punishable on summary conviction is, if the offence is not committed, guilty of an offence punishable on summary conviction.
R.S., 1985, c. C-46, s. 464;
R.S., 1985, c. 27 (1st Supp.), s. 60.

Conspiracy
465 (1) Except where otherwise expressly provided by law, the following provisions apply in respect of conspiracy:
(a) every one who conspires with any one to commit murder or to cause another person to be murdered, whether in Canada or not, is guilty of an indictable offence and liable to a maximum term of imprisonment for life;
(b) every one who conspires with any one to prosecute a person for an alleged offence, knowing that he did not commit that offence, is guilty of an indictable offence and liable
(i) to imprisonment for a term not exceeding ten years, if the alleged offence is one for which, on conviction, that person would be liable to be sentenced to imprisonment for life or for a term not exceeding fourteen years, or
(ii) to imprisonment for a term not exceeding five years, if the alleged offence is one for which, on conviction, that person would be liable to imprisonment for less than fourteen years;
(c) every one who conspires with any one to commit an indictable offence not provided for in paragraph (a) or (b) is guilty of an indictable offence and liable to the same punishment as that to which an accused who is guilty of that offence would, on conviction, be liable; and
(d) every one who conspires with any one to commit an offence punishable on summary conviction is guilty of an offence punishable on summary conviction.

(2) Conspiracy to commit offences
(3) Every one who, while in Canada, conspires with any one to do anything referred to in subsection (1) in a place outside Canada that is an offence under the laws of that place shall be deemed to have conspired to do that thing in Canada.

Idem
(4) Every one who, while in a place outside Canada, conspires with any one to do anything referred to in subsection (1) in Canada shall be deemed to have conspired in Canada to do that thing.

Jurisdiction
(5) Where a person is alleged to have conspired to do anything that is an offence by virtue of subsection (3) or (4), proceedings in respect of that offence may, whether or not that person is in Canada, be commenced in any territorial division in Canada, and the accused may be tried and punished in respect of that offence in the same manner as if the offence had been committed in that territorial division.

Appearance of accused at trial
(6) For greater certainty, the provisions of this Act relating to
(a) requirements that an accused appear at and be present during proceedings, and
(b) the exceptions to those requirements,
apply to proceedings commenced in any territorial division pursuant to subsection (5).

Where previously tried outside Canada
(7) Where a person is alleged to have conspired to do anything that is an offence by virtue of subsection (3) or (4) and that person has been tried and dealt with outside Canada in respect of the offence in such a manner that, if the person had been tried and dealt with in Canada, he would be able to plead
R.S., 1985, c. C-46, s. 465;

R.S., 1985, c. 27 (1st Supp.), s. 61;
1998, c. 35, s. 121.

Conspiracy in restraint of trade

466 (1) A conspiracy in restraint of trade is an agreement between two or more persons to do or to procure to be done any unlawful act in restraint of trade.

Trade union, exception

(2) The purposes of a trade union are not, by reason only that they are in restraint of trade, unlawful within the meaning of subsection (1).

R.S., 1985, c. C-46, s. 466;
1992, c. 1, s. 60(F).

Saving

467 (1) No person shall be convicted of the offence of conspiracy by reason only that he

(a) refuses to work with a workman or for an employer; or

(b) does any act or causes any act to be done for the purpose of a trade combination, unless that act is an offence expressly punishable by law.

Definition of
trade combination

(2) In this section,
trade combination
R.S., c. C-34, s. 425.

Definitions

467.1 (1) The following definitions apply in this Act.
criminal organization

(a) is composed of three or more persons in or outside Canada; and

(b) has as one of its main purposes or main activities the facilitation or commission of one or more serious offences that, if committed, would likely result in the direct or indirect receipt of a material benefit, including a financial benefit, by the group or by any of the persons who constitute the group. It does not include a group of persons that forms randomly for the immediate commission of a single offence.

serious offence

Facilitation

(2) For the purposes of this section, section 467.11 and 467.111, facilitation of an offence does not require knowledge of a particular offence the commission of which is facilitated, or that an offence actually be committed.

Commission of offence

(3) In this section and in sections 467.11 to 467.13, committing an offence means being a party to it or counselling any person to be a party to it.

Regulations

(4) The Governor in Council may make regulations prescribing offences that are included in the definition

1997, c. 23, s. 11;
2001, c. 32, s. 27;
2014, c. 17, s. 8.

Participation in activities of criminal organization

467.11 (1) Every person who, for the purpose of enhancing the ability of a criminal organization to facilitate or commit an indictable offence under this or any other Act of Parliament, knowingly, by act or omission, participates in or contributes to any activity of the criminal organization is guilty of an indictable offence and liable to imprisonment for a term not exceeding five years.

Prosecution

(2) In a prosecution for an offence under subsection (1), it is not necessary for the prosecutor to prove that

(a) the criminal organization actually facilitated or committed an indictable offence;

(b) the participation or contribution of the accused actually enhanced the ability of the criminal organization to facilitate or commit an indictable offence;
(c) the accused knew the specific nature of any indictable offence that may have been facilitated or committed by the criminal organization; or
(d) the accused knew the identity of any of the persons who constitute the criminal organization.

Factors

(3) In determining whether an accused participates in or contributes to any activity of a criminal organization, the Court may consider, among other factors, whether the accused
(a) uses a name, word, symbol or other representation that identifies, or is associated with, the criminal organization;
(b) frequently associates with any of the persons who constitute the criminal organization;
(c) receives any benefit from the criminal organization; or
(d) repeatedly engages in activities at the instruction of any of the persons who constitute the criminal organization.
2001, c. 32, s. 27.

Recruitment of members by a criminal organization

467.111 Every person who, for the purpose of enhancing the ability of a criminal organization to facilitate or commit an indictable offence under this Act or any other Act of Parliament, recruits, solicits, encourages, coerces or invites a person to join the criminal organization, is guilty of an indictable offence and liable,
(a) in the case where the person recruited, solicited, encouraged or invited is under 18 years of age, to imprisonment for a term not exceeding five years, and to a minimum punishment of imprisonment for a term of six months; and
(b) in any other case, to imprisonment for a term not exceeding five years.
2014, c. 17, s. 9.

Commission of offence for criminal organization

467.12 (1) Every person who commits an indictable offence under this or any other Act of Parliament for the benefit of, at the direction of, or in association with, a criminal organization is guilty of an indictable offence and liable to imprisonment for a term not exceeding fourteen years.

Prosecution

(2) In a prosecution for an offence under subsection (1), it is not necessary for the prosecutor to prove that the accused knew the identity of any of the persons who constitute the criminal organization.
2001, c. 32, s. 27.

Instructing commission of offence for criminal organization

467.13 (1) Every person who is one of the persons who constitute a criminal organization and who knowingly instructs, directly or indirectly, any person to commit an offence under this or any other Act of Parliament for the benefit of, at the direction of, or in association with, the criminal organization is guilty of an indictable offence and liable to imprisonment for life.

Prosecution

(2) In a prosecution for an offence under subsection (1), it is not necessary for the prosecutor to prove that
(a) an offence other than the offence under subsection (1) was actually committed;
(b) the accused instructed a particular person to commit an offence; or
(c) the accused knew the identity of all of the persons who constitute the criminal organization.
2001, c. 32, s. 27.

Sentences to be served consecutively

467.14 A sentence imposed on a person for an offence under section 467.11, 467.111, 467.12 or 467.13 shall be served consecutively to any other punishment imposed on the person for an offence arising out of the same event or series of events and to any other sentence to which the person is subject at the time the sentence is imposed on the person for an offence under any of those sections.
2001, c. 32, s. 27;

2014, c. 17, s. 10.
Powers of the Attorney General of Canada
467.2 (1) Notwithstanding the definition of
(a) an offence under section 467.11 or 467.111; or
(b) another criminal organization offence where the alleged offence arises out of conduct that in whole or in part is in relation to an alleged contravention of an Act of Parliament or a regulation made under such an Act, other than this Act or a regulation made under this Act.
For those purposes, the Attorney General of Canada may exercise all the powers and perform all the duties and functions assigned to the Attorney General by or under this Act.
Powers of the Attorney General of a province
(2) Subsection (1) does not affect the authority of the Attorney General of a province to conduct proceedings in respect of an offence referred to in section 467.11, 467.111, 467.12 or 467.13 or to exercise any of the powers or perform any of the duties and functions assigned to the Attorney General by or under this Act.
1997, c. 23, s. 11;
2001, c. 32, s. 28;
2014, c. 17, s. 11.

PART XIV

PART XIV
Jurisdiction

General

Superior court of criminal jurisdiction
468 Every superior court of criminal jurisdiction has jurisdiction to try any indictable offence.
R.S., c. C-34, s. 426.
Court of criminal jurisdiction
469 Every court of criminal jurisdiction has jurisdiction to try an indictable offence other than
(a) an offence under any of the following sections:
(i) section 47 (treason),
(ii) section 49 (alarming Her Majesty),
(iii) section 51 (intimidating Parliament or a legislature),
(iv) section 53 (inciting to mutiny),
(v) section 61 (seditious offences),
(vi) section 74 (piracy),
(vii) section 75 (piratical acts), or
(viii) section 235 (murder);
Accessories
(b) the offence of being an accessory after the fact to high treason or treason or murder;
(c) an offence under section 119 (bribery) by the holder of a judicial office;
Crimes against humanity
(c.1) an offence under any of sections 4 to 7 of the
Crimes Against Humanity and War Crimes Act
Attempts
(d) the offence of attempting to commit any offence mentioned in subparagraphs (a)(i) to (vii); or
Conspiracy
(e) the offence of conspiring to commit any offence mentioned in paragraph (a).
R.S., 1985, c. C-46, s. 469;
R.S., 1985, c. 27 (1st Supp.), s. 62;
2000, c. 24, s. 44.

Jurisdiction over person
470 Subject to this Act, every superior court of criminal jurisdiction and every court of criminal jurisdiction that has power to try an indictable offence is competent to try an accused for that offence
(a) if the accused is found, is arrested or is in custody within the territorial jurisdiction of the court; or
(b) if the accused has been ordered to be tried by
(i) that court, or
(ii) any other court, the jurisdiction of which has by lawful authority been transferred to that court.
R.S., 1985, c. C-46, s. 470;
R.S., 1985, c. 27 (1st Supp.), s. 101.

Trial by jury compulsory
471 Except where otherwise expressly provided by law, every accused who is charged with an indictable offence shall be tried by a court composed of a judge and jury.
R.S., c. C-34, s. 429.

472 Trial without jury
473 (1) Notwithstanding anything in this Act, an accused charged with an offence listed in section 469 may, with the consent of the accused and the Attorney General, be tried without a jury by a judge of a superior court of criminal jurisdiction.

Joinder of other offences
(1.1) Where the consent of the accused and the Attorney General is given in accordance with subsection (1), the judge of the superior court of criminal jurisdiction may order that any offence be tried by that judge in conjunction with the offence listed in section 469.

Withdrawal of consent
(2) Notwithstanding anything in this Act, where the consent of an accused and the Attorney General is given in accordance with subsection (1), that consent shall not be withdrawn unless both the accused and the Attorney General agree to the withdrawal.
R.S., 1985, c. C-46, s. 473;
R.S., 1985, c. 27 (1st Supp.), s. 63;
1994, c. 44, s. 30.

Adjournment when no jury summoned
474 (1) Where the competent authority has determined that a panel of jurors is not to be summoned for a term or sittings of the court for the trial of criminal cases in any territorial division, the clerk of the court may, on the day of the opening of the term or sittings, if a judge is not present to preside over the court, adjourn the court and the business of the court to a subsequent day.

Adjournment on instructions of judge
(2) A clerk of the court for the trial of criminal cases in any territorial division may, at any time, on the instructions of the presiding judge or another judge of the court, adjourn the court and the business of the court to a subsequent day.
R.S., 1985, c. C-46, s. 474;
1994, c. 44, s. 31.

Accused absconding during trial
475 (1) Notwithstanding any other provision of this Act, where an accused, whether or not he is charged jointly with another, absconds during the course of his trial,
(a) he shall be deemed to have waived his right to be present at his trial, and
(b) the court may
(i) continue the trial and proceed to a judgment or verdict and, if it finds the accused guilty, impose a sentence on him in his absence, or
(ii) if a warrant in Form 7 is issued for the arrest of the accused, adjourn the trial to await his appearance,
but where the trial is adjourned pursuant to subparagraph (b)(ii), the court may, at any time, continue the trial if it is satisfied that it is no longer in the interests of justice to await the appearance of the accused.

Adverse inference
(2) Where a court continues a trial pursuant to subsection (1), it may draw an inference adverse to the accused from the fact that he has absconded.

Accused not entitled to re-opening
(3) Where an accused reappears at his trial that is continuing pursuant to subsection (1), he is not entitled to have any part of the proceedings that was conducted in his absence re-opened unless the court is satisfied that because of exceptional circumstances it is in the interests of justice to re-open the proceedings.

Counsel for accused may continue to act
(4) Where an accused has absconded during the course of his trial and the court continues the trial, counsel for the accused is not thereby deprived of any authority he may have to continue to act for the accused in the proceedings.
R.S., 1985, c. C-46, s. 475;
R.S., 1985, c. 27 (1st Supp.), s. 185(F), c. 1 (4th Supp.), s. 18(F).

Special Jurisdiction

Special jurisdictions
476 For the purposes of this Act,
(a) where an offence is committed in or on any water or on a bridge between two or more territorial divisions, the offence shall be deemed to have been committed in any of the territorial divisions;
(b) where an offence is committed on the boundary of two or more territorial divisions or within five hundred metres of any such boundary, or the offence was commenced within one territorial division and completed within another, the offence shall be deemed to have been committed in any of the territorial divisions;
(c) where an offence is committed in or on a vehicle employed in a journey, or on board a vessel employed on a navigable river, canal or inland water, the offence shall be deemed to have been committed in any territorial division through which the vehicle or vessel passed in the course of the journey or voyage on which the offence was committed, and where the center or other part of the road, or navigable river, canal or inland water on which the vehicle or vessel passed in the course of the journey or voyage is the boundary of two or more territorial divisions, the offence shall be deemed to have been committed in any of the territorial divisions;
(d) where an offence is committed in an aircraft in the course of a flight of that aircraft, it shall be deemed to have been committed
(i) in the territorial division in which the flight commenced,
(ii) in any territorial division over which the aircraft passed in the course of the flight, or
(iii) in the territorial division in which the flight ended; and
(e) where an offence is committed in respect of the mail in the course of its door-to-door delivery, the offence shall be deemed to have been committed in any territorial division through which the mail was carried on that delivery.
R.S., 1985, c. C-46, s. 476;
R.S., 1985, c. 27 (1st Supp.), s. 186;
1992, c. 1, s. 58.

Definition of
ship
477 (1) In sections 477.1 to 477.4,
ship

Saving
(2) Nothing in sections 477.1 to 477.4 limits the operation of any other Act of Parliament or the jurisdiction that a court may exercise apart from those sections.
R.S., 1985, c. C-46, s. 477;
1990, c. 44, s. 15;

1996, c. 31, s. 67.
Offences outside of Canada
477.1 Every person who commits an act or omission that, if it occurred in Canada, would be an offence under a federal law, within the meaning of section 2 of the
Oceans Act
(a) in the exclusive economic zone of Canada that
(i) is committed by a person who is in the exclusive economic zone of Canada in connection with exploring or exploiting, conserving or managing the natural resources, whether living or non-living, of the exclusive economic zone of Canada, and
(ii) is committed by or in relation to a person who is a Canadian citizen or a permanent resident within the meaning of subsection 2(1) of the
Immigration and Refugee Protection Act
(b) that is committed in a place in or above the continental shelf of Canada and that is an offence in that place by virtue of section 20 of the
Oceans Act
(c) that is committed outside Canada on board or by means of a ship registered or licensed, or for which an identification number has been issued, pursuant to any Act of Parliament;
(d) that is committed outside Canada in the course of hot pursuit; or
(e) that is committed outside the territory of any state by a Canadian citizen.
1990, c. 44, s. 15;
1996, c. 31, s. 68;
2001, c. 27, s. 247.
Consent of Attorney General of Canada
477.2 (1) No proceedings in respect of an offence committed in or on the territorial sea of Canada shall be continued unless the consent of the Attorney General of Canada is obtained not later than eight days after the proceedings are commenced, if the accused is not a Canadian citizen and the offence is alleged to have been committed on board any ship registered outside Canada.
Exception
(1.1) Subsection (1) does not apply to proceedings by way of summary conviction.
Consent of Attorney General of Canada
(2) No proceedings in respect of which courts have jurisdiction by virtue only of paragraph 477.1(a) or (b) shall be continued unless the consent of the Attorney General of Canada is obtained not later than eight days after the proceedings are commenced, if the accused is not a Canadian citizen and the offence is alleged to have been committed on board any ship registered outside Canada.
Consent of Attorney General of Canada
(3) No proceedings in respect of which courts have jurisdiction by virtue only of paragraph 477.1(d) or (e) shall be continued unless the consent of the Attorney General of Canada is obtained not later than eight days after the proceedings are commenced.
Consent to be filed
(4) The consent of the Attorney General required by subsection (1), (2) or (3) must be filed with the clerk of the court in which the proceedings have been instituted.
1990, c. 44, s. 15;
1994, c. 44, s. 32;
1996, c. 31, s. 69.
Exercising powers of arrest, entry, etc.
477.3 (1) Every power of arrest, entry, search or seizure or other power that could be exercised in Canada in respect of an act or omission referred to in section 477.1 may be exercised, in the circumstances referred to in that section,
(a) at the place or on board the ship or marine installation or structure, within the meaning of section 2 of the
Oceans Act
(b) where hot pursuit has been commenced, at any place on the seas, other than a place that is part of

the territorial sea of any other state.
Arrest, search, seizure, etc.
(2) A justice or judge in any territorial division in Canada has jurisdiction to authorize an arrest, entry, search or seizure or an investigation or other ancillary matter related to an offence
(a) committed in or on the territorial sea of Canada or any area of the sea that forms part of the internal waters of Canada, or
(b) referred to in section 477.1
in the same manner as if the offence had been committed in that territorial division.
Limitation
(3) Where an act or omission that is an offence by virtue only of section 477.1 is alleged to have been committed on board any ship registered outside Canada, the powers referred to in subsection (1) shall not be exercised outside Canada with respect to that act or omission without the consent of the Attorney General of Canada.
1990, c. 44, s. 15;
1996, c. 31, s. 70.
477.4 (1) and (2) Evidence
(3) In proceedings in respect of an offence,
(a) a certificate referred to in subsection 23(1) of the
Oceans Act
(b) a certificate issued by or under the authority of the Minister of Foreign Affairs containing a statement that any geographical location specified in the certificate was, at any time material to the proceedings, in an area of a fishing zone of Canada that is not within the internal waters of Canada or the territorial sea of Canada or outside the territory of any state,
is conclusive proof of the truth of the statement without proof of the signature or official character of the person appearing to have issued the certificate.
Certificate cannot be compelled
(4) A certificate referred to in subsection (3) is admissible in evidence in proceedings referred to in that subsection but its production cannot be compelled.
1990, c. 44, s. 15;
1995, c. 5, s. 25;
1996, c. 31, s. 71.
Offence committed entirely in one province
478 (1) Subject to this Act, a court in a province shall not try an offence committed entirely in another province.
Exception
(2) Every proprietor, publisher, editor or other person charged with the publication of a defamatory libel in a newspaper or with conspiracy to publish a defamatory libel in a newspaper shall be dealt with, indicted, tried and punished in the province where he resides or in which the newspaper is printed.
Idem
(3) An accused who is charged with an offence that is alleged to have been committed in Canada outside the province in which the accused is may, if the offence is not an offence mentioned in section 469 and
(a) in the case of proceedings instituted at the instance of the Government of Canada and conducted by or on behalf of that Government, if the Attorney General of Canada consents, or
(b) in any other case, if the Attorney General of the province where the offence is alleged to have been committed consents,
appear before a court or judge that would have had jurisdiction to try that offence if it had been committed in the province where the accused is, and where the accused consents to plead guilty and pleads guilty to that offence, the court or judge shall determine the accused to be guilty of the offence and impose the punishment warranted by law, but where the accused does not consent to plead guilty and does not plead guilty, the accused shall, if the accused was in custody prior to appearance, be

returned to custody and shall be dealt with according to law.

Where accused ordered to stand trial

(4) Notwithstanding that an accused described in subsection (3) has been ordered to stand trial or that an indictment has been preferred against the accused in respect of the offence to which he desires to plead guilty, the accused shall be deemed simply to stand charged of that offence without a preliminary inquiry having been conducted or an indictment having been preferred with respect thereto.

Definition of
newspaper

(5) In this section,
newspaper

R.S., 1985, c. C-46, s. 478;
R.S., 1985, c. 27 (1st Supp.), ss. 64, 101(E);
1994, c. 44, s. 33(E).

Offence outstanding in same province

479 Where an accused is charged with an offence that is alleged to have been committed in the province in which he is, he may, if the offence is not an offence mentioned in section 469 and

(a) in the case of proceedings instituted at the instance of the Government of Canada and conducted by or on behalf of that Government, the Attorney General of Canada consents, or

(b) in any other case, the Attorney General of the province where the offence is alleged to have been committed consents,

appear before a court or judge that would have had jurisdiction to try that offence if it had been committed in the place where the accused is, and where the accused consents to plead guilty and pleads guilty to that offence, the court or judge shall determine the accused to be guilty of the offence and impose the punishment warranted by law, but where the accused does not consent to plead guilty and does not plead guilty, the accused shall, if the accused was in custody prior to appearance, be returned to custody and shall be dealt with according to law.

R.S., 1985, c. C-46, s. 479;
R.S., 1985, c. 27 (1st Supp.), s. 65;
1994, c. 44, s. 34(E).

Offence in unorganized territory

480 (1) Where an offence is committed in an unorganized tract of country in any province or on a lake, river or other water therein, not included in a territorial division or in a provisional judicial district, proceedings in respect thereof may be commenced and an accused may be charged, tried and punished in respect thereof within any territorial division or provisional judicial district of the province in the same manner as if the offence had been committed within that territorial division or provisional judicial district.

New territorial division

(2) Where a provisional judicial district or a new territorial division is constituted in an unorganized tract referred to in subsection (1), the jurisdiction conferred by that subsection continues until appropriate provision is made by law for the administration of criminal justice within the provisional judicial district or new territorial division.

R.S., c. C-34, s. 436.

Offence not in a province

481 Where an offence is committed in a part of Canada not in a province, proceedings in respect thereof may be commenced and the accused may be charged, tried and punished within any territorial division in any province in the same manner as if that offence had been committed in that territorial division.

R.S., c. C-34, s. 437.

Offence in Canadian waters

481.1 Where an offence is committed in or on the territorial sea of Canada or any area of the sea that forms part of the internal waters of Canada, proceedings in respect thereof may, whether or not the

accused is in Canada, be commenced and an accused may be charged, tried and punished within any territorial division in Canada in the same manner as if the offence had been committed in that territorial division.
1996, c. 31, s. 72.

Offence outside Canada
481.2 Subject to this or any other Act of Parliament, where an act or omission is committed outside Canada and the act or omission is an offence when committed outside Canada under this or any other Act of Parliament, proceedings in respect of the offence may, whether or not the accused is in Canada, be commenced, and an accused may be charged, tried and punished within any territorial division in Canada in the same manner as if the offence had been committed in that territorial division.
1996, c. 31, s. 72;
2008, c. 18, s. 10.

Appearance of accused at trial
481.3 For greater certainty, the provisions of this Act relating to
(a) the requirement of the appearance of an accused at proceedings, and
(b) the exceptions to that requirement
apply to proceedings commenced in any territorial division pursuant to section 481, 481.1 or 481.2.
1996, c. 31, s. 72.

Rules of Court

Power to make rules
482 (1) Every superior court of criminal jurisdiction and every court of appeal may make rules of court not inconsistent with this or any other Act of Parliament, and any rules so made apply to any prosecution, proceeding, action or appeal, as the case may be, within the jurisdiction of that court, instituted in relation to any matter of a criminal nature or arising from or incidental to any such prosecution, proceeding, action or appeal.

Power to make rules
(2) The following courts may, subject to the approval of the lieutenant governor in council of the relevant province, make rules of court not inconsistent with this Act or any other Act of Parliament that are applicable to any prosecution, proceeding, including a preliminary inquiry or proceedings within the meaning of Part XXVII, action or appeal, as the case may be, within the jurisdiction of that court, instituted in relation to any matter of a criminal nature or arising from or incidental to the prosecution, proceeding, action or appeal:
(a) every court of criminal jurisdiction for a province;
(b) every appeal court within the meaning of section 812 that is not a court referred to in subsection (1);
(c) the Ontario Court of Justice;
(d) the Court of Quebec and every municipal court in the Province of Quebec;
(e) the Provincial Court of Nova Scotia;
(f) the Provincial Court of New Brunswick;
(g) the Provincial Court of Manitoba;
(h) the Provincial Court of British Columbia;
(i) the Provincial Court of Prince Edward Island;
(j) the Provincial Court of Saskatchewan;
(k) the Provincial Court of Alberta;
(l) the Provincial Court of Newfoundland and Labrador;
(m) the Territorial Court of Yukon;
(n) the Territorial Court of the Northwest Territories; and
(o) the Nunavut Court of Justice.

Purpose of rules

(3) Rules under subsection (1) or (2) may be made
(a) generally to regulate the duties of the officers of the court and any other matter considered expedient to attain the ends of justice and carry into effect the provisions of the law;
(b) to regulate the sittings of the court or any division thereof, or of any judge of the court sitting in chambers, except in so far as they are regulated by law;
(c) to regulate the pleading, practice and procedure in criminal matters, including pre-hearing conferences held under section 625.1, proceedings with respect to judicial interim release and preliminary inquiries and, in the case of rules under subsection (1), proceedings with respect to
(d) to carry out the provisions of this Act relating to appeals from conviction, acquittal or sentence and, without restricting the generality of this paragraph,
(i) for furnishing necessary forms and instructions in relation to notices of appeal or applications for leave to appeal to officials or other persons requiring or demanding them,
(ii) for ensuring the accuracy of notes taken at a trial and the verification of any copy or transcript,
(iii) for keeping writings, exhibits or other things connected with the proceedings on the trial,
(iv) for securing the safe custody of property during the period in which the operation of an order with respect to that property is suspended under subsection 689(1), and
(v) for providing that the Attorney General and counsel who acted for the Attorney General at the trial be supplied with certified copies of writings, exhibits and things connected with the proceedings that are required for the purposes of their duties.

Publication
(4) Rules of court that are made under the authority of this section shall be published in the Canada Gazette

Regulations to secure uniformity
(5) Notwithstanding anything in this section, the Governor in Council may make such provision as he considers proper to secure uniformity in the rules of court in criminal matters, and all uniform rules made under the authority of this subsection prevail and have effect as if enacted by this Act.
R.S., 1985, c. C-46, s. 482;
R.S., 1985, c. 27 (1st Supp.), s. 66;
1994, c. 44, s. 35;
2002, c. 13, s. 17;
2015, c. 3, s. 50.

Power to make rules respecting case management
482.1 (1) A court referred to in subsection 482(1) or (2) may make rules for case management, including rules
(a) for the determination of any matter that would assist the court in effective and efficient case management;
(b) permitting personnel of the court to deal with administrative matters relating to proceedings out of court if the accused is represented by counsel; and
(c) establishing case management schedules.

Compliance with directions
(2) The parties to a case shall comply with any direction made in accordance with a rule made under subsection (1).

Summons or warrant
(3) If rules are made under subsection (1), a court, justice or judge may issue a summons or warrant to compel the presence of the accused at case management proceedings.

Provisions to apply
(4) Section 512 and subsection 524(1) apply, with any modifications that the circumstances require, to the issuance of a summons or a warrant under subsection (3).

Approval of lieutenant governor in council
(5) Rules made under this section by a court referred to in subsection 482(2) must be approved by the lieutenant governor in council of the relevant province in order to come into force.

Subsections 482(4) and (5) to apply

(6) Subsections 482(4) and (5) apply, with any modifications that the circumstances require, to rules made under subsection (1).
2002, c. 13, s. 18.

PART XV

PART XV
Special Procedure and Powers

General Powers of Certain Officials

Officials with powers of two justices
483 Every judge or provincial court judge authorized by the law of the province in which he is appointed to do anything that is required to be done by two or more justices may do alone anything that this Act or any other Act of Parliament authorizes two or more justices to do.
R.S., 1985, c. C-46, s. 483;
R.S., 1985, c. 27 (1st Supp.), s. 203.

Preserving order in court
484 Every judge or provincial court judge has the same power and authority to preserve order in a court over which he presides as may be exercised by the superior court of criminal jurisdiction of the province during the sittings thereof.
R.S., 1985, c. C-46, s. 484;
R.S., 1985, c. 27 (1st Supp.), s. 203.

Procedural irregularities
485 (1) Jurisdiction over an offence is not lost by reason of the failure of any court, judge, provincial court judge or justice to act in the exercise of that jurisdiction at any particular time, or by reason of a failure to comply with any of the provisions of this Act respecting adjournments or remands.

When accused not present
(1.1) Jurisdiction over an accused is not lost by reason of the failure of the accused to appear personally, so long as subsection 515(2.2), paragraph 537(1)(j), (j.1) or (k), subsection 650(1.1) or (1.2), paragraph 650(2)(b) or 650.01(3)(a), subsection 683(2.1) or 688(2.1) or a rule of court made under section 482 or 482.1 applies.

Summons or warrant
(2) Where jurisdiction over an accused or a defendant is lost and has not been regained, a court, judge, provincial court judge or justice may, within three months after the loss of jurisdiction, issue a summons, or if it or he considers it necessary in the public interest, a warrant for the arrest of the accused or defendant.

Dismissal for want of prosecution
(3) Where no summons or warrant is issued under subsection (2) within the period provided therein, the proceedings shall be deemed to be dismissed for want of prosecution and shall not be recommenced except in accordance with section 485.1.

Adjournment and order
(4) Where, in the opinion of the court, judge, provincial court judge or justice, an accused or a defendant who appears at a proceeding has been misled or prejudiced by reason of any matter referred to in subsection (1), the court, judge, provincial court judge or justice may adjourn the proceeding and may make such order as it or he considers appropriate.

Part XVI to apply
(5) The provisions of Part XVI apply with such modifications as the circumstances require where a summons or warrant is issued under subsection (2).
R.S., 1985, c. C-46, s. 485;
R.S., 1985, c. 27 (1st Supp.), s. 67;
1992, c. 1, s. 60(F);

1997, c. 18, s. 40;
2002, c. 13, s. 19.

Recommencement where dismissal for want of prosecution

485.1 Where an indictment in respect of a transaction is dismissed or deemed by any provision of this Act to be dismissed for want of prosecution, a new information shall not be laid and a new indictment shall not be preferred before any court in respect of the same transaction without
(a) the personal consent in writing of the Attorney General or Deputy Attorney General, in any prosecution conducted by the Attorney General or in which the Attorney General intervenes; or
(b) the written order of a judge of that court, in any prosecution conducted by a prosecutor other than the Attorney General and in which the Attorney General does not intervene.
R.S., 1985, c. 27 (1st Supp.), s. 67.

Exclusion of public

486 (1) Any proceedings against an accused shall be held in open court, but the presiding judge or justice may, on application of the prosecutor or a witness or on his or her own motion, order the exclusion of all or any members of the public from the court room for all or part of the proceedings, or order that the witness testify behind a screen or other device that would allow the witness not to be seen by members of the public, if the judge or justice is of the opinion that such an order is in the interest of public morals, the maintenance of order or the proper administration of justice or is necessary to prevent injury to international relations or national defence or national security.

Application

(1.1) The application may be made, during the proceedings, to the presiding judge or justice or, before the proceedings begin, to the judge or justice who will preside at the proceedings or, if that judge or justice has not been determined, to any judge or justice having jurisdiction in the judicial district where the proceedings will take place.

Factors to be considered

(2) In determining whether the order is in the interest of the proper administration of justice, the judge or justice shall consider
(a) society's interest in encouraging the reporting of offences and the participation of victims and witnesses in the criminal justice process;
(b) the safeguarding of the interests of witnesses under the age of 18 years in all proceedings;
(c) the ability of the witness to give a full and candid account of the acts complained of if the order were not made;
(d) whether the witness needs the order for their security or to protect them from intimidation or retaliation;
(e) the protection of justice system participants who are involved in the proceedings;
(f) whether effective alternatives to the making of the proposed order are available in the circumstances;
(g) the salutary and deleterious effects of the proposed order; and
(h) any other factor that the judge or justice considers relevant.

Reasons to be stated

(3) If an accused is charged with an offence under section 151, 152, 153, 153.1, 155 or 159, subsection 160(2) or (3) or section 163.1, 170, 171, 171.1, 172, 172.1, 172.2, 173, 271, 272, 273, 279.01, 279.011, 279.02, 279.03, 286.1, 286.2 or 286.3 and the prosecutor or the accused applies for an order under subsection (1), the judge or justice shall, if no such order is made, state, by reference to the circumstances of the case, the reason for not making an order.

No adverse inference

(4) No adverse inference may be drawn from the fact that an order is, or is not, made under this section.
R.S., 1985, c. C-46, s. 486;
R.S., 1985, c. 27 (1st Supp.), s. 203, c. 19 (3rd Supp.), s. 14, c. 23 (4th Supp.), s. 1;
1992, c. 1, s. 60(F), c. 21, s. 9;
1993, c. 45, s. 7;

1997, c. 16, s. 6;
1999, c. 25, s. 2(Preamble);
2001, c. 32, s. 29, c. 41, ss. 16, 34, 133;
2002, c. 13, s. 20;
2005, c. 32, s. 15, c. 43, ss. 4, 8;
2010, c. 3, s. 4;
2012, c. 1, s. 28;
2014, c. 25, s. 21;
2015, c. 13, s. 13, c. 20, s. 21.

Support person — witnesses under 18 or who have a disability

486.1 (1) In any proceedings against an accused, the judge or justice shall, on application of the prosecutor in respect of a witness who is under the age of 18 years or who has a mental or physical disability, or on application of such a witness, order that a support person of the witness' choice be permitted to be present and to be close to the witness while the witness testifies, unless the judge or justice is of the opinion that the order would interfere with the proper administration of justice.

Other witnesses

(2) In any proceedings against an accused, the judge or justice may, on application of the prosecutor in respect of a witness, or on application of a witness, order that a support person of the witness' choice be permitted to be present and to be close to the witness while the witness testifies if the judge or justice is of the opinion that the order would facilitate the giving of a full and candid account by the witness of the acts complained of or would otherwise be in the interest of the proper administration of justice.

Application

(2.1) An application referred to in subsection (1) or (2) may be made, during the proceedings, to the presiding judge or justice or, before the proceedings begin, to the judge or justice who will preside at the proceedings or, if that judge or justice has not been determined, to any judge or justice having jurisdiction in the judicial district where the proceedings will take place.

Factors to be considered

(3) In determining whether to make an order under subsection (2), the judge or justice shall consider
(a) the age of the witness;
(b) the witness' mental or physical disabilities, if any;
(c) the nature of the offence;
(d) the nature of any relationship between the witness and the accused;
(e) whether the witness needs the order for their security or to protect them from intimidation or retaliation;
(f) society's interest in encouraging the reporting of offences and the participation of victims and witnesses in the criminal justice process; and
(g) any other factor that the judge or justice considers relevant.

Witness not to be a support person

(4) The judge or justice shall not permit a witness to be a support person unless the judge or justice is of the opinion that doing so is necessary for the proper administration of justice.

No communication while testifying

(5) The judge or justice may order that the support person and the witness not communicate with each other while the witness testifies.

No adverse inference

(6) No adverse inference may be drawn from the fact that an order is, or is not, made under this section.

2005, c. 32, s. 15;
2015, c. 13, s. 14.

Testimony outside court room — witnesses under 18 or who have a disability

486.2 (1) Despite section 650, in any proceedings against an accused, the judge or justice shall, on application of the prosecutor in respect of a witness who is under the age of 18 years or who is able to communicate evidence but may have difficulty doing so by reason of a mental or physical disability, or on application of such a witness, order that the witness testify outside the court room or behind a screen or other device that would allow the witness not to see the accused, unless the judge or justice is of the opinion that the order would interfere with the proper administration of justice.

Other witnesses

(2) Despite section 650, in any proceedings against an accused, the judge or justice may, on application of the prosecutor in respect of a witness, or on application of a witness, order that the witness testify outside the court room or behind a screen or other device that would allow the witness not to see the accused if the judge or justice is of the opinion that the order would facilitate the giving of a full and candid account by the witness of the acts complained of or would otherwise be in the interest of the proper administration of justice.

Application

(2.1) An application referred to in subsection (1) or (2) may be made, during the proceedings, to the presiding judge or justice or, before the proceedings begin, to the judge or justice who will preside at the proceedings or, if that judge or justice has not been determined, to any judge or justice having jurisdiction in the judicial district where the proceedings will take place.

Factors to be considered

(3) In determining whether to make an order under subsection (2), the judge or justice shall consider
(a) the age of the witness;
(b) the witness' mental or physical disabilities, if any;
(c) the nature of the offence;
(d) the nature of any relationship between the witness and the accused;
(e) whether the witness needs the order for their security or to protect them from intimidation or retaliation;
(f) whether the order is needed to protect the identity of a peace officer who has acted, is acting or will be acting in an undercover capacity, or of a person who has acted, is acting or will be acting covertly under the direction of a peace officer;
(f.1) whether the order is needed to protect the witness's identity if they have had, have or will have responsibilities relating to national security or intelligence;
(g) society's interest in encouraging the reporting of offences and the participation of victims and witnesses in the criminal justice process; and
(h) any other factor that the judge or justice considers relevant.

Same procedure for determination

(4) If the judge or justice is of the opinion that it is necessary for a witness to testify in order to determine whether an order under subsection (2) should be made in respect of that witness, the judge or justice shall order that the witness testify in accordance with that subsection.

Conditions of exclusion

(5) A witness shall not testify outside the court room in accordance with an order made under subsection (1) or (2) unless arrangements are made for the accused, the judge or justice and the jury to watch the testimony of the witness by means of closed-circuit television or otherwise and the accused is permitted to communicate with counsel while watching the testimony.

No adverse inference

(6) No adverse inference may be drawn from the fact that an order is, or is not, made under subsection (1) or (2).

2005, c. 32, s. 15;
2014, c. 17, s. 12;
2015, c. 13, s. 15, c. 20, s. 38.

Accused not to cross-examine witness under 18

486.3 (1) In any proceedings against an accused, the judge or justice shall, on application of the prosecutor in respect of a witness who is under the age of 18 years, or on application of such a witness, order that the accused not personally cross-examine the witness, unless the judge or justice is of the opinion that the proper administration of justice requires the accused to personally conduct the cross-examination. If such an order is made, the judge or justice shall appoint counsel to conduct the cross-examination.

Accused not to cross-examine complainant — certain offences

(2) In any proceedings against an accused in respect of an offence under any of sections 264, 271, 272 and 273, the judge or justice shall, on application of the prosecutor in respect of a witness who is a victim, or on application of such a witness, order that the accused not personally cross-examine the witness, unless the judge or justice is of the opinion that the proper administration of justice requires the accused to personally conduct the cross-examination. If such an order is made, the judge or justice shall appoint counsel to conduct the cross-examination.

Other witnesses

(3) In any proceedings against an accused, the judge or justice may, on application of the prosecutor in respect of a witness who is not entitled to make an application under subsection (1) or (2), or on application of such a witness, order that the accused not personally cross-examine the witness if the judge or justice is of the opinion that the order would allow the giving of a full and candid account from the witness of the acts complained of or would otherwise be in the interest of the proper administration of justice. If the order is made, the judge or justice shall appoint counsel to conduct the cross-examination.

Factors to be considered

(4) In determining whether to make an order under subsection (3), the judge or justice shall consider

(a) the age of the witness;
(b) the witness' mental or physical disabilities, if any;
(c) the nature of the offence;
(d) whether the witness needs the order for their security or to protect them from intimidation or retaliation;
(e) the nature of any relationship between the witness and the accused;
(f) society's interest in encouraging the reporting of offences and the participation of victims and witnesses in the criminal justice process; and
(g) any other factor that the judge or justice considers relevant.

Application

(4.1) An application referred to in any of subsections (1) to (3) may be made during the proceedings to the presiding judge or justice or, before the proceedings begin, to the judge or justice who will preside at the proceedings or, if that judge or justice has not been determined, to any judge or justice having jurisdiction in the judicial district where the proceedings will take place.

No adverse inference

(5) No adverse inference may be drawn from the fact that counsel is, or is not, appointed under this section.

2005, c. 32, s. 15;
2015, c. 13, s. 16.

Non-disclosure of witness' identity

486.31 (1) In any proceedings against an accused, the judge or justice may, on application of the prosecutor in respect of a witness, or on application of a witness, make an order directing that any information that could identify the witness not be disclosed in the course of the proceedings if the judge or justice is of the opinion that the order is in the interest of the proper administration of justice.

Hearing may be held

(2) The judge or justice may hold a hearing to determine whether the order should be made, and the hearing may be in private.

Factors to be considered

(3) In determining whether to make the order, the judge or justice shall consider

(a) the right to a fair and public hearing;
(b) the nature of the offence;
(c) whether the witness needs the order for their security or to protect them from intimidation or

retaliation;
(d) whether the order is needed to protect the security of anyone known to the witness;
(e) whether the order is needed to protect the identity of a peace officer who has acted, is acting or will be acting in an undercover capacity, or of a person who has acted, is acting or will be acting covertly under the direction of a peace officer;
(e.1) whether the order is needed to protect the witness's identity if they have had, have or will have responsibilities relating to national security or intelligence;
(f) society's interest in encouraging the reporting of offences and the participation of victims and witnesses in the criminal justice process;
(g) the importance of the witness' testimony to the case;
(h) whether effective alternatives to the making of the proposed order are available in the circumstances;
(i) the salutary and deleterious effects of the proposed order; and
(j) any other factor that the judge or justice considers relevant.

No adverse inference
(4) No adverse inference may be drawn from the fact that an order is, or is not, made under this section.
2015, c. 13, s. 17, c. 20, s. 38.

Order restricting publication — sexual offences
486.4 (1) Subject to subsection (2), the presiding judge or justice may make an order directing that any information that could identify the victim or a witness shall not be published in any document or broadcast or transmitted in any way, in proceedings in respect of
(a) any of the following offences:
(i) an offence under section 151, 152, 153, 153.1, 155, 159, 160, 162, 163.1, 170, 171, 171.1, 172, 172.1, 172.2, 173, 210, 211, 213, 271, 272, 273, 279.01, 279.011, 279.02, 279.03, 280, 281, 286.1, 286.2, 286.3, 346 or 347, or
(ii) any offence under this Act, as it read from time to time before the day on which this subparagraph comes into force, if the conduct alleged would be an offence referred to in subparagraph (i) if it occurred on or after that day; or
(b) two or more offences being dealt with in the same proceeding, at least one of which is an offence referred to in paragraph (a).

Mandatory order on application
(2) In proceedings in respect of the offences referred to in paragraph (1)(a) or (b), the presiding judge or justice shall
(a) at the first reasonable opportunity, inform any witness under the age of eighteen years and the victim of the right to make an application for the order; and
(b) on application made by the victim, the prosecutor or any such witness, make the order.

Victim under 18 — other offences
(2.1) Subject to subsection (2.2), in proceedings in respect of an offence other than an offence referred to in subsection (1), if the victim is under the age of 18 years, the presiding judge or justice may make an order directing that any information that could identify the victim shall not be published in any document or broadcast or transmitted in any way.

Mandatory order on application
(2.2) In proceedings in respect of an offence other than an offence referred to in subsection (1), if the victim is under the age of 18 years, the presiding judge or justice shall
(a) as soon as feasible, inform the victim of their right to make an application for the order; and
(b) on application of the victim or the prosecutor, make the order.

Child pornography
(3) In proceedings in respect of an offence under section 163.1, a judge or justice shall make an order directing that any information that could identify a witness who is under the age of eighteen years, or any person who is the subject of a representation, written material or a recording that constitutes child pornography within the meaning of that section, shall not be published in any document or

broadcast or transmitted in any way.
Limitation
(4) An order made under this section does not apply in respect of the disclosure of information in the course of the administration of justice when it is not the purpose of the disclosure to make the information known in the community.

2005, c. 32, s. 15, c. 43, s. 8;
2010, c. 3, s. 5;
2012, c. 1, s. 29;
2014, c. 25, ss. 22, 48;
2015, c. 13, s. 18.

Order restricting publication — victims and witnesses
486.5 (1) Unless an order is made under section 486.4, on application of the prosecutor in respect of a victim or a witness, or on application of a victim or a witness, a judge or justice may make an order directing that any information that could identify the victim or witness shall not be published in any document or broadcast or transmitted in any way if the judge or justice is of the opinion that the order is in the interest of the proper administration of justice.

Justice system participants
(2) On application of the prosecutor in respect of a justice system participant who is involved in proceedings in respect of an offence referred to in subsection (2.1), or on application of such a justice system participant, a judge or justice may make an order directing that any information that could identify the justice system participant shall not be published in any document or broadcast or transmitted in any way if the judge or justice is of the opinion that the order is in the interest of the proper administration of justice.

Offences
(2.1) The offences for the purposes of subsection (2) are
(a) an offence under section 423.1, 467.11, 467.111, 467.12 or 467.13, or a serious offence committed for the benefit of, at the direction of, or in association with, a criminal organization;
(b) a terrorism offence;
(c) an offence under subsection 16(1) or (2), 17(1), 19(1), 20(1) or 22(1) of the Security of Information Act
(d) an offence under subsection 21(1) or section 23 of the Security of Information Act

Limitation
(3) An order made under this section does not apply in respect of the disclosure of information in the course of the administration of justice if it is not the purpose of the disclosure to make the information known in the community.

Application and notice
(4) An applicant for an order shall
(a) apply in writing to the presiding judge or justice or, if the judge or justice has not been determined, to a judge of a superior court of criminal jurisdiction in the judicial district where the proceedings will take place; and
(b) provide notice of the application to the prosecutor, the accused and any other person affected by the order that the judge or justice specifies.

Grounds
(5) An applicant for an order shall set out the grounds on which the applicant relies to establish that the order is necessary for the proper administration of justice.

Hearing may be held
(6) The judge or justice may hold a hearing to determine whether an order should be made, and the hearing may be in private.

Factors to be considered
(7) In determining whether to make an order, the judge or justice shall consider
(a) the right to a fair and public hearing;

(b) whether there is a real and substantial risk that the victim, witness or justice system participant would suffer harm if their identity were disclosed;
(c) whether the victim, witness or justice system participant needs the order for their security or to protect them from intimidation or retaliation;
(d) society's interest in encouraging the reporting of offences and the participation of victims, witnesses and justice system participants in the criminal justice process;
(e) whether effective alternatives are available to protect the identity of the victim, witness or justice system participant;
(f) the salutary and deleterious effects of the proposed order;
(g) the impact of the proposed order on the freedom of expression of those affected by it; and
(h) any other factor that the judge or justice considers relevant.

Conditions
(8) An order may be subject to any conditions that the judge or justice thinks fit.

Publication prohibited
(9) Unless the judge or justice refuses to make an order, no person shall publish in any document or broadcast or transmit in any way
(a) the contents of an application;
(b) any evidence taken, information given or submissions made at a hearing under subsection (6); or
(c) any other information that could identify the person to whom the application relates as a victim, witness or justice system participant in the proceedings.
2005, c. 32, s. 15;
2015, c. 13, s. 19.

Offence
486.6 (1) Every person who fails to comply with an order made under subsection 486.4(1), (2) or (3) or 486.5(1) or (2) is guilty of an offence punishable on summary conviction.

Application of order
(2) For greater certainty, an order referred to in subsection (1) applies to prohibit, in relation to proceedings taken against any person who fails to comply with the order, the publication in any document or the broadcasting or transmission in any way of information that could identify a victim, witness or justice system participant whose identity is protected by the order.
2005, c. 32, s. 15.

Security of witnesses
486.7 (1) In any proceedings against an accused, the presiding judge or justice may, on application of the prosecutor or a witness or on his or her own motion, make any order, other than one that may be made under any of sections 486 to 486.5, if the judge or justice is of the opinion that the order is necessary to protect the security of any witness and is otherwise in the interest of the proper administration of justice.

Application
(2) The application may be made, during the proceedings, to the presiding judge or justice or, before the proceedings begin, to the judge or justice who will preside at the proceedings or, if that judge or justice has not been determined, to any judge or justice having jurisdiction in the judicial district where the proceedings will take place.

Factors to be considered
(3) In determining whether to make the order, the judge or justice shall consider
(a) the age of the witness;
(b) the witness's mental or physical disabilities, if any;
(c) the right to a fair and public hearing;
(d) the nature of the offence;
(e) whether the witness needs the order to protect them from intimidation or retaliation;
(f) whether the order is needed to protect the security of anyone known to the witness;
(g) society's interest in encouraging the reporting of offences and the participation of victims and witnesses in the criminal justice process;

(h) the importance of the witness's testimony to the case;
(i) whether effective alternatives to the making of the proposed order are available in the circumstances;
(j) the salutary and deleterious effects of the proposed order; and
(k) any other factor that the judge or justice considers relevant.

No adverse inference

(4) No adverse inference may be drawn from the fact that an order is, or is not, made under this section.

2015, c. 20, s. 22.

Information for search warrant

487 (1) A justice who is satisfied by information on oath in Form 1 that there are reasonable grounds to believe that there is in a building, receptacle or place
(a) anything on or in respect of which any offence against this Act or any other Act of Parliament has been or is suspected to have been committed,
(b) anything that there are reasonable grounds to believe will afford evidence with respect to the commission of an offence, or will reveal the whereabouts of a person who is believed to have committed an offence, against this Act or any other Act of Parliament,
(c) anything that there are reasonable grounds to believe is intended to be used for the purpose of committing any offence against the person for which a person may be arrested without warrant, or
(c.1) any offence-related property,
may at any time issue a warrant authorizing a peace officer or a public officer who has been appointed or designated to administer or enforce a federal or provincial law and whose duties include the enforcement of this Act or any other Act of Parliament and who is named in the warrant
(d) to search the building, receptacle or place for any such thing and to seize it, and
(e) subject to any other Act of Parliament, to, as soon as practicable, bring the thing seized before, or make a report in respect thereof to, the justice or some other justice for the same territorial division in accordance with section 489.1.

Endorsement of search warrant

(2) If the building, receptacle or place is in another territorial division, the justice may issue the warrant with any modifications that the circumstances require, and it may be executed in the other territorial division after it has been endorsed, in Form 28, by a justice who has jurisdiction in that territorial division. The endorsement may be made on the original of the warrant or on a copy of the warrant transmitted by any means of telecommunication.

Operation of computer system and copying equipment

(2.1) A person authorized under this section to search a computer system in a building or place for data may
(a) use or cause to be used any computer system at the building or place to search any data contained in or available to the computer system;
(b) reproduce or cause to be reproduced any data in the form of a print-out or other intelligible output;
(c) seize the print-out or other output for examination or copying; and
(d) use or cause to be used any copying equipment at the place to make copies of the data.

Duty of person in possession or control

(2.2) Every person who is in possession or control of any building or place in respect of which a search is carried out under this section shall, on presentation of the warrant, permit the person carrying out the search
(a) to use or cause to be used any computer system at the building or place in order to search any data contained in or available to the computer system for data that the person is authorized by this section to search for;
(b) to obtain a hard copy of the data and to seize it; and
(c) to use or cause to be used any copying equipment at the place to make copies of the data.

Form

(3) A search warrant issued under this section may be in the form set out as Form 5 in Part XXVIII, varied to suit the case.

Effect of endorsement

(4) An endorsement that is made in accordance with subsection (2) is sufficient authority to the peace officers or public officers to whom the warrant was originally directed, and to all peace officers within the jurisdiction of the justice by whom it is endorsed, to execute the warrant and to deal with the things seized in accordance with section 489.1 or as otherwise provided by law.

R.S., 1985, c. C-46, s. 487;
R.S., 1985, c. 27 (1st Supp.), s. 68;
1994, c. 44, s. 36;
1997, c. 18, s. 41, c. 23, s. 12;
1999, c. 5, s. 16;
2008, c. 18, s. 11.

Information for general warrant

487.01 (1) A provincial court judge, a judge of a superior court of criminal jurisdiction or a judge as defined in section 552 may issue a warrant in writing authorizing a peace officer to, subject to this section, use any device or investigative technique or procedure or do any thing described in the warrant that would, if not authorized, constitute an unreasonable search or seizure in respect of a person or a person's property if

(a) the judge is satisfied by information on oath in writing that there are reasonable grounds to believe that an offence against this or any other Act of Parliament has been or will be committed and that information concerning the offence will be obtained through the use of the technique, procedure or device or the doing of the thing;

(b) the judge is satisfied that it is in the best interests of the administration of justice to issue the warrant; and

(c) there is no other provision in this or any other Act of Parliament that would provide for a warrant, authorization or order permitting the technique, procedure or device to be used or the thing to be done.

Limitation

(2) Nothing in subsection (1) shall be construed as to permit interference with the bodily integrity of any person.

Search or seizure to be reasonable

(3) A warrant issued under subsection (1) shall contain such terms and conditions as the judge considers advisable to ensure that any search or seizure authorized by the warrant is reasonable in the circumstances.

Video surveillance

(4) A warrant issued under subsection (1) that authorizes a peace officer to observe, by means of a television camera or other similar electronic device, any person who is engaged in activity in circumstances in which the person has a reasonable expectation of privacy shall contain such terms and conditions as the judge considers advisable to ensure that the privacy of the person or of any other person is respected as much as possible.

Other provisions to apply

(5) The definition

Notice after covert entry

(5.1) A warrant issued under subsection (1) that authorizes a peace officer to enter and search a place covertly shall require, as part of the terms and conditions referred to in subsection (3), that notice of the entry and search be given within any time after the execution of the warrant that the judge considers reasonable in the circumstances.

Extension of period for giving notice

(5.2) Where the judge who issues a warrant under subsection (1) or any other judge having jurisdiction to issue such a warrant is, on the basis of an affidavit submitted in support of an application to vary the period within which the notice referred to in subsection (5.1) is to be given, is

satisfied that the interests of justice warrant the granting of the application, the judge may grant an extension, or a subsequent extension, of the period, but no extension may exceed three years.
Provisions to apply
(6) Subsections 487(2) and (4) apply, with such modifications as the circumstances require, to a warrant issued under subsection (1).
Telewarrant provisions to apply
(7) Where a peace officer believes that it would be impracticable to appear personally before a judge to make an application for a warrant under this section, a warrant may be issued under this section on an information submitted by telephone or other means of telecommunication and, for that purpose, section 487.1 applies, with such modifications as the circumstances require, to the warrant.
1993, c. 40, s. 15;
1997, c. 18, s. 42, c. 23, s. 13.
Definitions
487.011 The following definitions apply in this section and in sections
computer data
data
document
judge
public officer
tracking data
transmission data
(a) relates to the telecommunication functions of dialling, routing, addressing or signalling;
(b) is transmitted to identify, activate or configure a device, including a computer program as defined in subsection 342.1(2), in order to establish or maintain access to a telecommunication service for the purpose of enabling a communication, or is generated during the creation, transmission or reception of a communication and identifies or purports to identify the type, direction, date, time, duration, size, origin, destination or termination of the communication; and
(c) does not reveal the substance, meaning or purpose of the communication.
2004, c. 3, s. 7;
2014, c. 31, s. 20.
Preservation demand
487.012 (1) A peace officer or public officer may make a demand to a person in Form 5.001 requiring them to preserve computer data that is in their possession or control when the demand is made.
Conditions for making demand
(2) The peace officer or public officer may make the demand only if they have reasonable grounds to suspect that
(a) an offence has been or will be committed under this or any other Act of Parliament or has been committed under a law of a foreign state;
(b) in the case of an offence committed under a law of a foreign state, an investigation is being conducted by a person or authority with responsibility in that state for the investigation of such offences; and
(c) the computer data is in the person's possession or control and will assist in the investigation of the offence.
Limitation
(3) A demand may not be made to a person who is under investigation for the offence referred to in paragraph (2)(a).
Expiry and revocation of demand
(4) A peace officer or public officer may revoke the demand by notice given to the person at any time. Unless the demand is revoked earlier, the demand expires
(a) in the case of an offence that has been or will be committed under this or any other Act of Parliament, 21 days after the day on which it is made; and

(b) in the case of an offence committed under a law of a foreign state, 90 days after the day on which it is made.

Conditions in demand

(5) The peace officer or public officer who makes the demand may impose any conditions in the demand that they consider appropriate — including conditions prohibiting the disclosure of its existence or some or all of its contents — and may revoke a condition at any time by notice given to the person.

No further demand

(6) A peace officer or public officer may not make another demand requiring the person to preserve the same computer data in connection with the investigation.

2004, c. 3, s. 7;
2014, c. 31, s. 20.

Preservation order — computer data

487.013 (1) On

Conditions for making order

(2) Before making the order, the justice or judge must be satisfied by information on oath in Form 5.002

(a) that there are reasonable grounds to suspect that an offence has been or will be committed under this or any other Act of Parliament or has been committed under a law of a foreign state, that the computer data is in the person's possession or control and that it will assist in the investigation of the offence; and

(b) that a peace officer or public officer intends to apply or has applied for a warrant or an order in connection with the investigation to obtain a document that contains the computer data.

Offence against law of foreign state

(3) If an offence has been committed under a law of a foreign state, the justice or judge must also be satisfied that a person or authority with responsibility in that state for the investigation of such offences is conducting the investigation.

Form

(4) The order is to be in Form 5.003.

Limitation

(5) A person who is under investigation for an offence referred to in paragraph (2)(a) may not be made subject to an order.

Expiry of order

(6) Unless the order is revoked earlier, it expires 90 days after the day on which it is made.

2004, c. 3, s. 7;
2014, c. 31, s. 20.

General production order

487.014 (1) Subject to sections

Conditions for making order

(2) Before making the order, the justice or judge must be satisfied by information on oath in Form 5.004 that there are reasonable grounds to believe that

(a) an offence has been or will be committed under this or any other Act of Parliament; and

(b) the document or data is in the person's possession or control and will afford evidence respecting the commission of the offence.

Form

(3) The order is to be in Form 5.005.

Limitation

(4) A person who is under investigation for the offence referred to in subsection (2) may not be made subject to an order.

2004, c. 3, s. 7;
2014, c. 31, s. 20.

Production order to trace specified communication

487.015 (1) On
Conditions for making order
(2) Before making the order, the justice or judge must be satisfied by information on oath in Form 5.004 that there are reasonable grounds to suspect that
(a) an offence has been or will be committed under this or any other Act of Parliament;
(b) the identification of a device or person involved in the transmission of a communication will assist in the investigation of the offence; and
(c) transmission data that is in the possession or control of one or more persons whose identity is unknown when the application is made will enable that identification.
Form
(3) The order is to be in Form 5.006.
Service
(4) A peace officer or public officer may serve the order on any person who was involved in the transmission of the communication and whose identity was unknown when the application was made
(a) within 60 days after the day on which the order is made; or
(b) within one year after the day on which the order is made, in the case of an offence under section 467.11, 467.12 or 467.13, an offence committed for the benefit of, at the direction of or in association with a criminal organization, or a terrorism offence.
Limitation
(5) A person who is under investigation for the offence referred to in subsection (2) may not be made subject to an order.
Report
(6) A peace officer or public officer named in the order must provide a written report to the justice or judge who made the order as soon as feasible after the person from whom the communication originated is identified or after the expiry of the period referred to in subsection (4), whichever occurs first. The report must state the name and address of each person on whom the order was served, and the date of service.
2004, c. 3, s. 7;
2014, c. 31, s. 20.
Production order — transmission data
487.016 (1) On
Conditions for making order
(2) Before making the order, the justice or judge must be satisfied by information on oath in Form 5.004 that there are reasonable grounds to suspect that
(a) an offence has been or will be committed under this or any other Act of Parliament; and
(b) the transmission data is in the person's possession or control and will assist in the investigation of the offence.
Form
(3) The order is to be in Form 5.007.
Limitation
(4) A person who is under investigation for the offence referred to in subsection (2) may not be made subject to an order.
2004, c. 3, s. 7;
2014, c. 31, s. 20.
Production order — tracking data
487.017 (1) On
Conditions for making order
(2) Before making the order, the justice or judge must be satisfied by information on oath in Form 5.004 that there are reasonable grounds to suspect that
(a) an offence has been or will be committed under this or any other Act of Parliament; and
(b) the tracking data is in the person's possession or control and will assist in the investigation of the offence.

Form

(3) The order is to be in Form 5.007.

Limitation

(4) A person who is under investigation for the offence referred to in subsection (2) may not be made subject to an order.

2004, c. 3, s. 7;

2014, c. 31, s. 20.

Production order — financial data

487.018 (1) On

Bank Act

Proceeds of Crime (Money Laundering) and Terrorist Financing Act

(a) either the account number of a person named in the order or the name of a person whose account number is specified in the order;

(b) the type of account;

(c) the status of the account; and

(d) the date on which it was opened or closed.

Identification of person

(2) For the purpose of confirming the identity of a person who is named or whose account number is specified in the order, the order may also require the institution, person or entity to prepare and produce a document setting out the following data that is in their possession or control:

(a) the date of birth of a person who is named or whose account number is specified in the order;

(b) that person's current address; and

(c) any previous addresses of that person.

Conditions for making order

(3) Before making the order, the justice or judge must be satisfied by information on oath in Form 5.004 that there are reasonable grounds to suspect that

(a) an offence has been or will be committed under this or any other Act of Parliament; and

(b) the data is in the possession or control of the institution, person or entity and will assist in the investigation of the offence.

Form

(4) The order is to be in Form 5.008.

Limitation

(5) A financial institution, person or entity that is under investigation for the offence referred to in subsection (3) may not be made subject to an order.

2014, c. 31, s. 20.

Conditions in preservation and production orders

487.019 (1) An order made under any of sections

Effect of order

(2) The order has effect throughout Canada and, for greater certainty, no endorsement is needed for the order to be effective in a territorial division that is not the one in which the order is made.

Power to revoke or vary order

(3) On

2014, c. 31, s. 20.

Order prohibiting disclosure

487.0191 (1) On

Conditions for making order

(2) Before making the order, the justice or judge must be satisfied by information on oath in Form 5.009 that there are reasonable grounds to believe that the disclosure during that period would jeopardize the conduct of the investigation of the offence to which the preservation demand or the preservation or production order relates.

Form

(3) The order is to be in Form 5.0091.

Application to revoke or vary order
(4) A peace officer or a public officer or a person, financial institution or entity that is subject to an order made under subsection (1) may apply in writing to the justice or judge who made the order — or to a judge in the judicial district where the order was made — to revoke or vary the order.
2014, c. 31, s. 20.
Particulars — production orders
487.0192 (1) An order made under any of sections
Particulars — production order to trace specified communication
(2) An order made under section
Form of production
(3) For greater certainty, an order under any of sections
Non-application
(4) For greater certainty, sections 489.1 and 490 do not apply to a document that is produced under an order under any of sections
Probative force of copies
(5) Every copy of a document produced under section
Canada Evidence Act
(6) A document that is prepared for the purpose of production is considered to be original for the purposes of the
Canada Evidence Act
2014, c. 31, s. 20.
Application for review of production order
487.0193 (1) Before they are required by an order made under any of sections
Notice required
(2) The person, institution or entity may make the application only if they give notice of their intention to do so to a peace officer or public officer named in the order within 30 days after the day on which the order is made.
No obligation to produce
(3) The person, institution or entity is not required to prepare or produce the document until a final decision is made with respect to the application.
Revocation or variation of order
(4) The justice or judge may revoke or vary the order if satisfied that
(a) it is unreasonable in the circumstances to require the applicant to prepare or produce the document; or
(b) production of the document would disclose information that is privileged or otherwise protected from disclosure by law.
2014, c. 31, s. 20.
Destruction of preserved computer data and documents — preservation demand
487.0194 (1) A person to whom a preservation demand is made under section
Destruction of preserved computer data and documents — preservation order
(2) A person who is subject to a preservation order made under section
Destruction of preserved computer data and documents — production order
(3) A person who is subject to a production order made under any of sections
(a) the day on which the production order is revoked, and
(b) the day on which a document that contains the computer data is produced under the production order.
Destruction of preserved computer data and documents — warrant
(4) Despite subsections (1) to (3), a person who preserved computer data under a preservation demand or order made under section
2014, c. 31, s. 20.
For greater certainty
487.0195 (1) For greater certainty, no preservation demand, preservation order or production order is

necessary for a peace officer or public officer to ask a person to voluntarily preserve data that the person is not prohibited by law from preserving or to voluntarily provide a document to the officer that the person is not prohibited by law from disclosing.
No civil or criminal liability
(2) A person who preserves data or provides a document in those circumstances does not incur any criminal or civil liability for doing so.
2014, c. 31, s. 20.
Self-incrimination
487.0196 No one is excused from complying with an order made under any of sections
2014, c. 31, s. 20.
Offence — preservation demand
487.0197 A person who contravenes a preservation demand made under section
2014, c. 31, s. 20.
Offence — preservation or production order
487.0198 A person, financial institution or entity that contravenes an order made under any of sections
2014, c. 31, s. 20.
Offence — destruction of preserved data
487.0199 A person who contravenes section
2014, c. 31, s. 20.
Assistance order
487.02 If an authorization is given under section 184.2, 184.3, 186 or 188 or a warrant is issued under this Act, the judge or justice who gives the authorization or issues the warrant may order a person to provide assistance, if the person's assistance may reasonably be considered to be required to give effect to the authorization or warrant.
1993, c. 40, s. 15;
1997, c. 18, s. 43;
2014, c. 31, s. 20.
Review
487.021 (1) Within seven years after the coming into force of this section, a comprehensive review of the provisions and operation of sections 487.011 to 487.02 shall be undertaken by such committee of the House of Commons as may be designated or established by the House for that purpose.
Report
(2) The committee referred to in subsection (1) shall, within a year after a review is undertaken pursuant to that subsection or within such further time as the House may authorize, submit a report on the review to the Speaker of the House, including a statement of any changes the committee recommends.
2014, c. 31, s. 20.
Execution in another province
487.03 (1) If a warrant is issued under section 487.01, 487.05 or 492.1 or subsection 492.2(1) in one province, a judge or justice, as the case may be, in another province may, on application, endorse the warrant if it may reasonably be expected that it is to be executed in the other province and that its execution would require entry into or on the property of any person, or would require that an order be made under section 487.02 with respect to any person, in that province.
Endorsement
(1.1) The endorsement may be made on the original of the warrant or on a copy of the warrant that is transmitted by any means of telecommunication and, once endorsed, the warrant has the same force in the other province as though it had originally been issued there.
(2) 1993, c. 40, s. 15;
1995, c. 27, s. 1;
2000, c. 10, s. 13;
2007, c. 22, s. 7;

2008, c. 18, s. 12.

Forensic DNA Analysis

Definitions
487.04 In this section and in sections 487.05 to 487.0911,
adult
Youth Criminal Justice Act
designated offence
DNA
forensic DNA analysis
(a) in relation to a bodily substance that is taken from a person in execution of a warrant under section 487.05, means forensic DNA analysis of the bodily substance and the comparison of the results of that analysis with the results of the analysis of the DNA in the bodily substance referred to in paragraph 487.05(1)(b), and includes any incidental tests associated with that analysis, and
(b) in relation to a bodily substance that is provided voluntarily in the course of an investigation of a designated offence or is taken from a person under an order made under section 487.051 or an authorization granted under section 487.055 or 487.091, or to a bodily substance referred to in paragraph 487.05(1)(b), means forensic DNA analysis of the bodily substance;
primary designated offence
(a) an offence under any of the following provisions, namely,
(i) subsection 7(4.1) (offence in relation to sexual offences against children),
(i.1) section 151 (sexual interference),
(i.2) section 152 (invitation to sexual touching),
(i.3) section 153 (sexual exploitation),
(i.4) section 153.1 (sexual exploitation of person with disability),
(i.5) section 155 (incest),
(i.6) subsection 160(2) (compelling the commission of bestiality),
(i.7) subsection 160(3) (bestiality in presence of or by a child),
(i.8) section 163.1 (child pornography),
(i.9) section 170 (parent or guardian procuring sexual activity),
(i.901) section 171.1 (making sexually explicit material available to child),
(i.91) section 172.1 (luring a child),
(i.911) section 172.2 (agreement or arrangement — sexual offence against child),
(i.92) subsection 173(2) (exposure),
(i.93) to (i.96) (ii) section 235 (murder),
(iii) section 236 (manslaughter),
(iv) section 239 (attempt to commit murder),
(v) section 244 (discharging firearm with intent),
(vi) section 244.1 (causing bodily harm with intent — air gun or pistol),
(vi.1) section 244.2 (discharging firearm — recklessness),
(vii) paragraph 245(a) (administering noxious thing with intent to endanger life or cause bodily harm),
(viii) section 246 (overcoming resistance to commission of offence),
(ix) section 267 (assault with a weapon or causing bodily harm),
(x) section 268 (aggravated assault),
(xi) section 269 (unlawfully causing bodily harm),
(xi.1) section 270.01 (assaulting peace officer with weapon or causing bodily harm),
(xi.2) section 270.02 (aggravated assault of peace officer),
(xi.3) section 271 (sexual assault),
(xii) section 272 (sexual assault with a weapon, threats to a third party or causing bodily harm),
(xiii) section 273 (aggravated sexual assault),

(xiii.1) subsection 273.3(2) (removal of a child from Canada),
(xiv) section 279 (kidnapping),
(xiv.1) section 279.011 (trafficking — person under 18 years),
(xiv.2) subsection 279.02(2) (material benefit — trafficking of person under 18 years),
(xiv.3) subsection 279.03(2) (withholding or destroying documents — trafficking of person under 18 years),
(xiv.4) subsection 286.1(2) (obtaining sexual services for consideration from person under 18 years),
(xiv.5) subsection 286.2(2) (material benefit from sexual services provided by person under 18 years),
(xiv.6) subsection 286.3(2) (procuring — person under 18 years),
(xv) section 344 (robbery), and
(xvi) section 346 (extortion),
(a.1) an offence under any of the following provisions, namely,
(i) section 75 (piratical acts),
(i.01) section 76 (hijacking),
(i.02) section 77 (endangering safety of aircraft or airport),
(i.03) section 78.1 (seizing control of ship or fixed platform),
(i.04) subsection 81(1) (using explosives),
(i.041) section 82.3 (possession, etc., of nuclear material, radioactive material or device),
(i.042) section 82.4 (use or alteration of nuclear material, radioactive material or device),
(i.043) section 82.5 (commission of indictable offence to obtain nuclear material, etc.),
(i.044) section 82.6 (threats),
(i.05) section 83.18 (participation in activity of terrorist group),
(i.051) section 83.181 (leaving Canada to participate in activity of terrorist group),
(i.06) section 83.19 (facilitating terrorist activity),
(i.061) section 83.191 (leaving Canada to facilitate terrorist activity),
(i.07) section 83.2 (commission of offence for terrorist group),
(i.071) section 83.201 (leaving Canada to commit offence for terrorist group,
(i.072) section 83.202 (leaving Canada to commit offence that is terrorist activity),
(i.08) section 83.21 (instructing to carry out activity for terrorist group),
(i.09) section 83.22 (instructing to carry out terrorist activity),
(i.091) subsection 83.221(1) (advocating or promoting commission of terrorism offences),
(i.1) section 83.23 (harbouring or concealing),
(i.11) to (iii.1) (iv) (iv.1) to (iv.5) (v) (v.1) and (v.2) (vi) section 233 (infanticide),
(vii) (vii.1) section 279.01 (trafficking in persons),
(vii.11) subsection 279.02(1) (material benefit — trafficking),
(vii.12) subsection 279.03(1) (withholding or destroying documents — trafficking),
(viii) section 279.1 (hostage taking),
(viii.1) subsection 286.2(1) (material benefit from sexual services),
(viii.2) subsection 286.3(1) (procuring),
(ix) paragraph 348(1)(d) (breaking and entering a dwelling-house),
(x) section 423.1 (intimidation of a justice system participant or journalist),
(xi) section 431 (attack on premises, residence or transport of internationally protected person),
(xii) section 431.1 (attack on premises, accommodation or transport of United Nations or associated personnel),
(xiii) subsection 431.2(2) (explosive or other lethal device),
(xiv) section 467.11 (participation in activities of criminal organization),
(xiv.1) section 467.111 (recruitment of members — criminal organization),
(xv) section 467.12 (commission of offence for criminal organization), and
(xvi) section 467.13 (instructing commission of offence for criminal organization),
(xvi.1) to (xx)
(b) an offence under any of the following provisions of the

Criminal Code
(i) section 144 (rape),
(i.1) section 145 (attempt to commit rape),
(ii) section 146 (sexual intercourse with female under fourteen and between fourteen and sixteen),
(iii) section 148 (sexual intercourse with feeble-minded, etc.),
(iv) section 149 (indecent assault on female),
(v) section 156 (indecent assault on male),
(vi) section 157 (acts of gross indecency), and
(vii) subsection 246(1) (assault with intent) if the intent is to commit an offence referred to in subparagraphs (i) to (vi),
(c) an offence under any of the following provisions of the
Criminal Code
(i) subsection 146(1) (sexual intercourse with a female under age of 14),
(ii) subsection 146(2) (sexual intercourse with a female between ages of 14 and 16),
(iii) section 153 (sexual intercourse with step-daughter),
(iv) section 157 (gross indecency),
(v) section 166 (parent or guardian procuring defilement), and
(vi) section 167 (householder permitting defilement),
(c.01) an offence under any of the following provisions of the
Criminal Code
An Act to amend the Criminal Code in relation to sexual offences and other offences against the person and to amend certain other Acts in relation thereto or in consequence thereof
(i) section 246.1 (sexual assault),
(ii) section 246.2 (sexual assault with a weapon, threats to a third party or causing bodily harm), and
(iii) section 246.3 (aggravated sexual assault),
(c.02) an offence under any of the following provisions of this Act, as they read from time to time before the day on which this paragraph comes into force:
(i) paragraph 212(1)(i) (stupefying or overpowering for the purpose of sexual intercourse),
(ii) subsection 212(2) (living on the avails of prostitution of person under 18 years),
(iii) subsection 212(2.1) (aggravated offence in relation to living on the avails of prostitution of person under 18 years), and
(iv) subsection 212(4) (prostitution of person under 18 years),
(c.03) an offence under any of paragraphs 212(1)(a) to (h) (procuring) of this Act, as they read from time to time before the day on which this paragraph comes into force,
(c.1) an offence under any of the following provisions of the
Security of Information Act
(i) section 6 (approaching, entering, etc., a prohibited place),
(ii) subsection 20(1) (threats or violence), and
(iii) subsection 21(1) (harbouring or concealing), and
(d) an attempt to commit or, other than for the purposes of subsection 487.05(1), a conspiracy to commit an offence referred to in any of paragraphs (a) to (c.03);
provincial court judge
Youth Criminal Justice Act
secondary designated offence
(a) an offence under this Act that may be prosecuted by indictment — or, for section 487.051 to apply, is prosecuted by indictment — for which the maximum punishment is imprisonment for five years or more,
(b) an offence under any of the following provisions of the
Controlled Drugs and Substances Act
(i) section 5 (trafficking in substance and possession for purpose of trafficking),
(ii) section 6 (importing and exporting), and
(iii) section 7 (production of substance),

(c) an offence under any of the following provisions of this Act:
(i) section 145 (escape and being at large without excuse),
(i.1) section 146 (permitting or assisting escape),
(i.2) section 147 (rescue or permitting escape),
(i.3) section 148 (assisting prisoner of war to escape),
(i.4) and (ii) (iii) subsection 173(1) (indecent acts),
(iv) section 252 (failure to stop at scene of accident),
(v) section 264 (criminal harassment),
(vi) section 264.1 (uttering threats),
(vii) section 266 (assault),
(viii) section 270 (assaulting a peace officer),
(viii.1) subsection 286.1(1) (obtaining sexual services for consideration),
(ix) paragraph 348(1)(e) (breaking and entering a place other than a dwelling-house),
(x) section 349 (being unlawfully in dwelling-house), and
(xi) section 423 (intimidation),
(d) an offence under any of the following provisions of the
Criminal Code
(i) section 433 (arson), and
(ii) section 434 (setting fire to other substance), and
(e) an attempt to commit or, other than for the purposes of subsection 487.05(1), a conspiracy to commit
(i) an offence referred to in paragraph (a) or (b) — which, for section 487.051 to apply, is prosecuted by indictment, or
(ii) an offence referred to in paragraph (c) or (d);
Young Offenders Act
Loi sur les jeunes contrevenants
Young Offenders Act
young person
Youth Criminal Justice Act
Young Offenders Act,
1995, c. 27, s. 1;
1998, c. 37, s. 15;
2001, c. 41, s. 17;
2002, c. 1, s. 175;
2005, c. 25, s. 1, c. 43, ss. 5, 9;
2007, c. 22, ss. 2, 8, 47;
2008, c. 6, ss. 35, 63;
2009, c. 22, s. 16;
2010, c. 3, s. 6, c. 17, s. 3;
2012, c. 1, s. 30;
2013, c. 9, s. 16, c. 13, s. 8;
2014, c. 17, s. 13, c. 25, s. 23;
2015, c. 20, s. 23.

Information for warrant to take bodily substances for forensic DNA analysis
487.05 (1) A provincial court judge who on
(a) that a designated offence has been committed,
(b) that a bodily substance has been found or obtained
(i) at the place where the offence was committed,
(ii) on or within the body of the victim of the offence,
(iii) on anything worn or carried by the victim at the time when the offence was committed, or
(iv) on or within the body of any person or thing or at any place associated with the commission of the offence,

(c) that a person was a party to the offence, and

(d) that forensic DNA analysis of a bodily substance from the person will provide evidence about whether the bodily substance referred to in paragraph (b) was from that person

and who is satisfied that it is in the best interests of the administration of justice to do so may issue a warrant in Form 5.02 authorizing the taking, from that person, for the purpose of forensic DNA analysis, of any number of samples of one or more bodily substances that is reasonably required for that purpose, by means of the investigative procedures described in subsection 487.06(1).

Criteria

(2) In considering whether to issue the warrant, the provincial court judge shall have regard to all relevant matters, including

(a) the nature of the designated offence and the circumstances of its commission; and

(b) whether there is

(i) a peace officer who is able, by virtue of training or experience, to take samples of bodily substances from the person, by means of the investigative procedures described in subsection 487.06(1), or

(ii) another person who is able, by virtue of training or experience, to take, under the direction of a peace officer, samples of bodily substances from the person, by means of those investigative procedures.

Telewarrant

(3) Where a peace officer believes that it would be impracticable to appear personally before a judge to make an application for a warrant under this section, a warrant may be issued under this section on an information submitted by telephone or other means of telecommunication and, for that purpose, section 487.1 applies, with such modifications as the circumstances require, to the warrant.

1995, c. 27, s. 1;

1997, c. 18, s. 44;

1998, c. 37, s. 16;

2005, c. 25, s. 2(F).

Order — primary designated offences

487.051 (1) The court shall make an order in Form 5.03 authorizing the taking of the number of samples of bodily substances that is reasonably required for the purpose of forensic DNA analysis from a person who is convicted, discharged under section 730 or found guilty under the

Youth Criminal Justice Act

Young Offenders Act

primary designated offence

Order — primary designated offences

(2) The court shall make such an order in Form 5.03 in relation to a person who is convicted, discharged under section 730 or found guilty under the

Youth Criminal Justice Act

Young Offenders Act

primary designated offence

Order — persons found not criminally responsible and secondary designated offences

(3) The court may, on application by the prosecutor and if it is satisfied that it is in the best interests of the administration of justice to do so, make such an order in Form 5.04 in relation to

(a) a person who is found not criminally responsible on account of mental disorder for an offence committed at any time, including before June 30, 2000, if that offence is a designated offence when the finding is made; or

(b) a person who is convicted, discharged under section 730 or found guilty under the

Youth Criminal Justice Act

Young Offenders Act

In deciding whether to make the order, the court shall consider the person's criminal record, whether they were previously found not criminally responsible on account of mental disorder for a designated offence, the nature of the offence, the circumstances surrounding its commission and the impact such

an order would have on the person's privacy and security of the person and shall give reasons for its decision.
Order to offender
(4) When the court makes an order authorizing the taking of samples of bodily substances, it may make an order in Form 5.041 to require the person to report at the place, day and time set out in the order and submit to the taking of the samples.
1998, c. 37, s. 17;
2002, c. 1, s. 176;
2005, c. 25, s. 3;
2007, c. 22, ss. 9, 47;
2014, c. 25, s. 24.
487.052 Timing of order
487.053 (1) The court may make an order under section 487.051 authorizing the taking of samples of bodily substances when it imposes a sentence on a person, finds the person not criminally responsible on account of mental disorder or directs that they be discharged under section 730.
Hearing
(2) If the court does not consider the matter at that time, it
(a) shall, within 90 days after the day on which it imposes the sentence, makes the finding or directs that the person be discharged, set a date for a hearing to do so;
(b) retains jurisdiction over the matter; and
(c) may require the person to appear by closed-circuit television or any other means that allows the court and the person to engage in simultaneous visual and oral communication, as long as the person is given the opportunity to communicate privately with counsel if they are represented by counsel.
1998, c. 37, s. 17;
2000, c. 10, s. 14;
2005, c. 25, s. 4;
2007, c. 22, s. 3.
Appeal
487.054 The offender or the prosecutor may appeal from a decision of the court under any of subsections 487.051(1) to (3).
1998, c. 37, s. 17;
2007, c. 22, s. 10.
Offenders serving sentences
487.055 (1) A provincial court judge may, on
(a) had been declared a dangerous offender under Part XXIV;
(b) had been declared a dangerous offender or a dangerous sexual offender under Part XXI of the Criminal Code
(c) had been convicted of murder;
(c.1) had been convicted of attempted murder or conspiracy to commit murder or to cause another person to be murdered and, on the date of the application, is serving a sentence of imprisonment for that offence;
(d) had been convicted of a sexual offence within the meaning of subsection (3) and, on the date of the application, is serving a sentence of imprisonment for that offence; or
(e) had been convicted of manslaughter and, on the date of the application, is serving a sentence of imprisonment for that offence.
Certificate
(2) The application shall be accompanied by a certificate referred to in paragraph 667(1)(a) that establishes that the person is a person referred to in subsection (1). The certificate may be received in evidence without giving the notice referred to in subsection 667(4).
Definition of
sexual offence
(3) For the purposes of subsection (1),

sexual offence
(a) an offence under any of the following provisions, namely,
(i) section 151 (sexual interference),
(ii) section 152 (invitation to sexual touching),
(iii) section 153 (sexual exploitation),
(iv) section 155 (incest),
(v) subsection 212(4) (offence in relation to juvenile prostitution),
(vi) section 271 (sexual assault),
(vii) section 272 (sexual assault with a weapon, threats to a third party or causing bodily harm), and
(viii) section 273 (aggravated sexual assault);
(a.1) an offence under subsection 348(1) if the indictable offence referred to in that subsection is a sexual offence within the meaning of paragraph (a), (b), (c) or (d);
(b) an offence under any of the following provisions of the
Criminal Code
(i) section 144 (rape),
(ii) section 146 (sexual intercourse with female under fourteen or between fourteen and sixteen),
(iii) section 148 (sexual intercourse with feeble-minded, etc.),
(iv) section 149 (indecent assault on female),
(v) section 156 (indecent assault on male), or
(vi) section 157 (acts of gross indecency);
(c) an offence under paragraph 153(1)(a) (sexual intercourse with step-daughter, etc.) of the
Criminal Code
(d) an attempt to commit an offence referred to in any of paragraphs (a) to (c).

Manner of appearance
(3.01) The court may require a person who is given notice of an application under subsection (1) and who wishes to appear at the hearing to appear by closed-circuit television or any other means that allows the court and the person to engage in simultaneous visual and oral communication, as long as the person is given the opportunity to communicate privately with counsel if they are represented by counsel.

Criteria
(3.1) In deciding whether to grant an authorization under subsection (1), the court shall consider the person's criminal record, the nature of the offence and the circumstances surrounding its commission and the impact such an authorization would have on the privacy and security of the person and shall give reasons for its decision.

Order
(3.11) If the court authorizes the taking of samples of bodily substances from a person who is on conditional release and who has appeared at the hearing, it shall make an order in Form 5.041 to require the person to report at the place, day and time set out in the order and submit to the taking of the samples.

Summons
(4) However, if a person who is on conditional release has not appeared at the hearing, a summons in Form 5.061 setting out the information referred to in paragraphs 487.07(1)(b) to (d) shall be directed to them requiring them to report at the place, day and time set out in the summons and submit to the taking of the samples.

Service on individual
(5) The summons shall be accompanied by a copy of the authorization referred to in subsection (1) and be served by a peace officer who shall either deliver it personally to the person to whom it is directed or, if that person cannot conveniently be found, leave it for the person at their latest or usual place of residence with any person found there who appears to be at least sixteen years of age.
(6) (7) to (10)
1998, c. 37, s. 17;
2000, c. 10, s. 15;

2005, c. 25, s. 5;
2007, c. 22, s. 11;
2008, c. 18, s. 13.

Failure to appear

487.0551 (1) If a person fails to appear at the place, day and time set out in an order made under subsection 487.051(4) or 487.055(3.11) or in a summons referred to in subsection 487.055(4) or 487.091(3), a justice of the peace may issue a warrant for their arrest in Form 5.062 to allow samples of bodily substances to be taken.

Execution of warrant

(2) The warrant may be executed anywhere in Canada by a peace officer who has jurisdiction in that place or over the person. The warrant remains in force until it is executed.

2007, c. 22, s. 12.

Failure to comply with order or summons

487.0552 (1) Every person who, without reasonable excuse, fails to comply with an order made under subsection 487.051(4) or 487.055(3.11) of this Act or under subsection 196.14(4) or 196.24(4) of the
National Defence Act
(a) an indictable offence and liable to imprisonment for a term of not more than two years; or
(b) an offence punishable on summary conviction.

For greater certainty

(2) For greater certainty, a lawful command that prevents a person from complying with an order or summons is a reasonable excuse if, at the time, the person is subject to the Code of Service Discipline within the meaning of subsection 2(1) of the
National Defence Act
2007, c. 22, s. 12.

When collection to take place

487.056 (1) Samples of bodily substances shall be taken as authorized under section 487.051
(a) at the place, day and time set out in an order made under subsection 487.051(4) or as soon as feasible afterwards; or
(b) in any other case, on the day on which the order authorizing the taking of the samples is made or as soon as feasible afterwards.

When collection to take place

(2) Samples of bodily substances shall be taken as authorized under section 487.055 or 487.091
(a) at the place, day and time set out in an order made under subsection 487.055(3.11) or a summons referred to in subsection 487.055(4) or 487.091(3) or as soon as feasible afterwards; or
(b) in any other case, as soon as feasible after the authorization is granted.

When collection to take place

(3) If a person fails to appear as required by an order made under subsection 487.051(4) or 487.055(3.11) or a summons referred to in subsection 487.055(4) or 487.091(3), samples of bodily substances shall be taken
(a) when the person is arrested under a warrant issued under subsection 487.0551(1) or as soon as feasible afterwards; or
(b) as soon as feasible after the person appears at the place set out in the order or summons if no warrant is issued.

Appeal

(4) Subsections (1) to (3) apply even if the order or authorization to take the samples of bodily substances is appealed.

Collection of samples

(5) A peace officer who is authorized under section 487.051, 487.055 or 487.091 to take samples of bodily substances may cause the samples to be taken in any place in Canada in which the person who is subject to the order or authorization is located.

Who collects samples

(6) The samples shall be taken by a peace officer who has jurisdiction over the person or in the place in which the samples are taken — or a person acting under their direction — who is able, by virtue of training or experience, to take them.

1998, c. 37, s. 17;
2000, c. 10, s. 16;
2002, c. 1, s. 179(E);
2005, c. 25, s. 6;
2007, c. 22, s. 13.

Report of peace officer

487.057 (1) A peace officer who takes samples of bodily substances from a person or who causes a person who is not a peace officer to take samples under their direction shall, as soon as feasible after the samples are taken, make a written report in Form 5.07 and cause the report to be filed with
(a) the provincial court judge who issued the warrant under section 487.05 or granted the authorization under section 487.055 or 487.091 or another judge of that provincial court; or
(b) the court that made the order under section 487.051.

Contents of report

(2) The report shall include
(a) a statement of the time and date the samples were taken; and
(b) a description of the bodily substances that were taken.

Copy of report

(3) A peace officer who takes the samples or causes the samples to be taken under their direction at the request of another peace officer shall send a copy of the report to the other peace officer unless that other peace officer had jurisdiction to take the samples.

1998, c. 37, s. 17;
2000, c. 10, s. 17;
2007, c. 22, s. 14.

No criminal or civil liability

487.058 No peace officer, and no person acting under a peace officer's direction, incurs any criminal or civil liability for anything necessarily done with reasonable care and skill in the taking of samples of bodily substances from a person under a warrant issued under section 487.05, an order made under section 487.051 or an authorization granted under section 487.055 or 487.091.

1998, c. 37, s. 17;
2000, c. 10, s. 18;
2007, c. 22, s. 15.

Investigative procedures

487.06 (1) A peace officer or a person acting under a peace officer's direction is authorized by a warrant issued under section 487.05, an order made under section 487.051 or an authorization granted under section 487.055 or 487.091 to take samples of bodily substances by any of the following means:
(a) the plucking of individual hairs from the person, including the root sheath;
(b) the taking of buccal swabs by swabbing the lips, tongue and inside cheeks of the mouth to collect epithelial cells; or
(c) the taking of blood by pricking the skin surface with a sterile lancet.

Terms and conditions

(2) The warrant, order or authorization shall include any terms and conditions that the provincial court judge or court, as the case may be, considers advisable to ensure that the taking of the samples authorized by the warrant, order or authorization is reasonable in the circumstances.

Fingerprints

(3) A peace officer who is authorized to take samples of bodily substances from a person by an order made under section 487.051 or an authorization granted under section 487.055 or 487.091, or a person acting under their direction, may take fingerprints from the person for the purpose of the DNA Identification Act

1995, c. 27, s. 1;
1998, c. 37, s. 18;
2000, c. 10, s. 19;
2007, c. 22, s. 16.

Duty to inform

487.07 (1) Before taking samples of bodily substances from a person, or causing samples to be taken under their direction, in execution of a warrant issued under section 487.05 or an order made under section 487.051 or under an authorization granted under section 487.055 or 487.091, a peace officer shall inform the person of

(a) the contents of the warrant, order or authorization;

(b) the nature of the investigative procedures by means of which the samples are to be taken;

(c) the purpose of taking the samples;

(d) the authority of the peace officer and any other person under the direction of the peace officer to use as much force as is necessary for the purpose of taking the samples; and

(d.1) (e) in the case of samples of bodily substances taken in execution of a warrant,

(i) the possibility that the results of forensic DNA analysis may be used in evidence, and

(ii) if the sample is taken from a young person, the rights of the young person under subsection (4).

Detention of person

(2) A person from whom samples of bodily substances are to be taken may

(a) be detained for that purpose for a period that is reasonable in the circumstances; and

(b) be required to accompany a peace officer for that purpose.

Respect of privacy

(3) A peace officer who takes samples of bodily substances from a person, or a person who takes such samples under the direction of a peace officer, shall ensure that the person's privacy is respected in a manner that is reasonable in the circumstances.

Execution of warrant against young person

(4) A young person against whom a warrant is executed has, in addition to any other rights arising from his or her detention under the warrant,

(a) the right to a reasonable opportunity to consult with, and

(b) the right to have the warrant executed in the presence of

counsel and a parent or, in the absence of a parent, an adult relative or, in the absence of a parent and an adult relative, any other appropriate adult chosen by the young person.

Waiver of rights of young person

(5) A young person may waive his or her rights under subsection (4) but any such waiver

(a) must be recorded on audio tape or video tape or otherwise; or

(b) must be made in writing and contain a statement signed by the young person that he or she has been informed of the right being waived.

1995, c. 27, ss. 1, 3;
1998, c. 37, s. 19;
2000, c. 10, s. 20;
2007, c. 22, s. 17.

Verification

487.071 (1) Before taking samples of bodily substances from a person under an order made under section 487.051 or an authorization granted under section 487.055 or 487.091, a peace officer, or a person acting under their direction, shall verify whether the convicted offenders index of the national DNA data bank, established under the
DNA Identification Act

DNA profile in data bank

(2) If the person's DNA profile is in the convicted offenders index of the national DNA data bank, the peace officer or person acting under their direction shall not take any bodily substances from the person but shall

(a) confirm in writing on the order or authorization that he or she has been advised that the person's

DNA profile is in the DNA data bank; and

(b) transmit a copy of the order or authorization containing that confirmation and any other information prescribed by regulations made under the

DNA Identification Act

DNA profile not in data bank

(3) If the person's DNA profile is not in the convicted offenders index of the national DNA data bank, the peace officer or person acting under their direction shall execute the order or authorization and transmit to the Commissioner of the Royal Canadian Mounted Police

(a) any bodily substances taken; and

(b) a copy of the order or authorization and any other information prescribed by regulations made under the

DNA Identification Act

1998, c. 37, s. 20;

2000, c. 10, s. 21;

2005, c. 25, s. 8;

2007, c. 22, s. 18.

Use of bodily substances — warrant

487.08 (1) No person shall use bodily substances that are taken in execution of a warrant under section 487.05 or under section 196.12 of the

National Defence Act

Use of bodily substances — order, authorization

(1.1) No person shall use bodily substances that are taken in execution of an order made under section 487.051 of this Act or section 196.14 of the

National Defence Act

DNA Identification Act

Use of results — warrant

(2) No person shall use the results of forensic DNA analysis of bodily substances that are taken in execution of a warrant under section 487.05 or under section 196.12 of the

National Defence Act

(a) in the course of an investigation of the designated offence or any other designated offence in respect of which a warrant was issued or a bodily substance was found in the circumstances described in paragraph 487.05(1)(b) or in paragraph 196.12(1)(b) of the

National Defence Act

(b) in any proceeding for such an offence.

(2.1) Offence

(3) Every person who contravenes subsection (1) or (2) is guilty of an offence punishable on summary conviction.

Offence

(4) Every person who contravenes subsection (1.1)

(a) is guilty of an indictable offence and liable to imprisonment for a term not exceeding two years; or

(b) is guilty of an offence punishable on summary conviction and liable to a fine not exceeding $2,000 or to imprisonment for a term not exceeding six months, or to both.

1995, c. 27, s. 1;

1998, c. 37, s. 21;

2000, c. 10, s. 22;

2005, c. 25, s. 9;

2007, c. 22, s. 19.

Destruction of bodily substances, etc. — warrant

487.09 (1) Subject to subsection (2), bodily substances that are taken from a person in execution of a warrant under section 487.05 and the results of forensic DNA analysis shall be destroyed or, in the case of results in electronic form, access to those results shall be permanently removed, without delay after

(a) the results of that analysis establish that the bodily substance referred to in paragraph 487.05(1)
(b) was not from that person;

(b) the person is finally acquitted of the designated offence and any other offence in respect of the same transaction; or

(c) the expiration of one year after

(i) the person is discharged after a preliminary inquiry into the designated offence or any other offence in respect of the same transaction,

(ii) the dismissal, for any reason other than acquittal, or the withdrawal of any information charging the person with the designated offence or any other offence in respect of the same transaction, or

(iii) any proceeding against the person for the offence or any other offence in respect of the same transaction is stayed under section 579 or under that section as applied by section 572 or 795, unless during that year a new information is laid or an indictment is preferred charging the person with the designated offence or any other offence in respect of the same transaction or the proceeding is recommenced.

Exception

(2) A provincial court judge may order that the bodily substances that are taken from a person and the results of forensic DNA analysis not be destroyed during any period that the provincial court judge considers appropriate if the provincial court judge is satisfied that the bodily substances or results might reasonably be required in an investigation or prosecution of the person for another designated offence or of another person for the designated offence or any other offence in respect of the same transaction.

Destruction of bodily substances, etc., voluntarily given

(3) Bodily substances that are provided voluntarily by a person and the results of forensic DNA analysis shall be destroyed or, in the case of results in electronic form, access to those results shall be permanently removed, without delay after the results of that analysis establish that the bodily substance referred to in paragraph 487.05(1)(b) was not from that person.

1995, c. 27, s. 1;

1998, c. 37, s. 22.

Collection of additional bodily substances

487.091 (1) A provincial court judge may, on

(a) a DNA profile cannot be derived from the bodily substances that were taken from that person under an order made under section 487.051 or an authorization granted under section 487.055; or

(b) the information or bodily substances required by regulations made under the

DNA Identification Act

Reasons

(2) The application shall state the reasons why a DNA profile cannot be derived from the bodily substances or why the information or bodily substances were not transmitted in accordance with the regulations or were lost.

Persons not in custody

(3) If the court authorizes the taking of samples of bodily substances from a person who is not in custody, a summons in Form 5.061 setting out the information referred to in paragraphs 487.07(1)(b) to (d) shall be directed to the person requiring them to report at the place, day and time set out in the summons and submit to the taking of the samples. Subsections 487.055(5) and (6) apply, with any modifications that the circumstances require.

1998, c. 37, s. 23;

2000, c. 10, s. 23;

2005, c. 25, s. 10;

2007, c. 22, s. 20.

Review by Attorney General

487.0911 (1) On receipt of a notice from the Commissioner of the Royal Canadian Mounted Police under subsection 5.2(1) of the

DNA Identification Act
Clerical error
(2) If the Attorney General is of the opinion that the defect is due to a clerical error, the Attorney General shall
(a) apply,
(b) transmit a copy of the corrected order or authorization, if any, to the Commissioner.
Substantive defect
(3) If the Attorney General is of the opinion that the offence referred to in the order or authorization is not a designated offence, the Attorney General shall inform the Commissioner of that opinion.
No defect
(4) If the Attorney General is of the opinion that the offence referred to in the order or authorization is a designated offence, the Attorney General shall transmit that opinion, with written reasons, to the Commissioner.
2005, c. 25, s. 11;
2007, c. 22, s. 21.
Information for impression warrant
487.092 (1) A justice may issue a warrant in writing authorizing a peace officer to do any thing, or cause any thing to be done under the direction of the peace officer, described in the warrant in order to obtain any handprint, fingerprint, footprint, foot impression, teeth impression or other print or impression of the body or any part of the body in respect of a person if the justice is satisfied
(a) by information on oath in writing that there are reasonable grounds to believe that an offence against this or any other Act of Parliament has been committed and that information concerning the offence will be obtained by the print or impression; and
(b) that it is in the best interests of the administration of justice to issue the warrant.
Search or seizure to be reasonable
(2) A warrant issued under subsection (1) shall contain such terms and conditions as the justice considers advisable to ensure that any search or seizure authorized by the warrant is reasonable in the circumstances.
Provisions to apply
(3) Subsections 487(2) and (4) apply, with such modifications as the circumstances require, to a warrant issued under subsection (1).
Telewarrant
(4) Where a peace officer believes that it would be impracticable to appear personally before a justice to make an application for a warrant under this section, a warrant may be issued under this section on an information submitted by telephone or other means of telecommunication and, for that purpose, section 487.1 applies, with such modifications as the circumstances require, to the warrant.
1997, c. 18, s. 45;
1998, c. 37, s. 23.

Other Provisions Respecting Search Warrants, Preservation Orders and Production Orders

Telewarrants
487.1 (1) Where a peace officer believes that an indictable offence has been committed and that it would be impracticable to appear personally before a justice to make application for a warrant in accordance with section 256 or 487, the peace officer may submit an information on oath by telephone or other means of telecommunication to a justice designated for the purpose by the chief judge of the provincial court having jurisdiction in the matter.
Information submitted by telephone
(2) An information submitted by telephone or other means of telecommunication, other than a means of telecommunication that produces a writing, shall be on oath and shall be recorded verbatim by the justice, who shall, as soon as practicable, cause to be filed, with the clerk of the court for the

territorial division in which the warrant is intended for execution, the record or a transcription of it, certified by the justice as to time, date and contents.
Information submitted by other means of telecommunication
(2.1) The justice who receives an information submitted by a means of telecommunication that produces a writing shall, as soon as practicable, cause to be filed, with the clerk of the court for the territorial division in which the warrant is intended for execution, the information certified by the justice as to time and date of receipt.
Administration of oath
(3) For the purposes of subsection (2), an oath may be administered by telephone or other means of telecommunication.
Alternative to oath
(3.1) A peace officer who uses a means of telecommunication referred to in subsection (2.1) may, instead of swearing an oath, make a statement in writing stating that all matters contained in the information are true to his or her knowledge and belief and such a statement is deemed to be a statement made under oath.
Contents of information
(4) An information submitted by telephone or other means of telecommunication shall include
(a) a statement of the circumstances that make it impracticable for the peace officer to appear personally before a justice;
(b) a statement of the indictable offence alleged, the place or premises to be searched and the items alleged to be liable to seizure;
(c) a statement of the peace officer's grounds for believing that items liable to seizure in respect of the offence alleged will be found in the place or premises to be searched; and
(d) a statement as to any prior application for a warrant under this section or any other search warrant, in respect of the same matter, of which the peace officer has knowledge.
Issuing warrant
(5) A justice referred to in subsection (1) who is satisfied that an information submitted by telephone or other means of telecommunication
(a) is in respect of an indictable offence and conforms to the requirements of subsection (4),
(b) discloses reasonable grounds for dispensing with an information presented personally and in writing, and
(c) discloses reasonable grounds, in accordance with subsection 256(1) or paragraph 487(1)(a), (b) or (c), as the case may be, for the issuance of a warrant in respect of an indictable offence,
may issue a warrant to a peace officer conferring the same authority respecting search and seizure as may be conferred by a warrant issued by a justice before whom the peace officer appears personally pursuant to subsection 256(1) or 487(1), as the case may be, and may require that the warrant be executed within such time period as the justice may order.
Formalities respecting warrant and facsimiles
(6) Where a justice issues a warrant by telephone or other means of telecommunication, other than a means of telecommunication that produces a writing,
(a) the justice shall complete and sign the warrant in Form 5.1, noting on its face the time, date and place of issuance;
(b) the peace officer, on the direction of the justice, shall complete, in duplicate, a facsimile of the warrant in Form 5.1, noting on its face the name of the issuing justice and the time, date and place of issuance; and
(c) the justice shall, as soon as practicable after the warrant has been issued, cause the warrant to be filed with the clerk of the court for the territorial division in which the warrant is intended for execution.
Issuance of warrant where telecommunication produces writing
(6.1) Where a justice issues a warrant by a means of telecommunication that produces a writing,
(a) the justice shall complete and sign the warrant in Form 5.1, noting on its face the time, date and place of issuance;

(b) the justice shall transmit the warrant by the means of telecommunication to the peace officer who submitted the information and the copy of the warrant received by the peace officer is deemed to be a facsimile within the meaning of paragraph (6)(b);

(c) the peace officer shall procure another facsimile of the warrant; and

(d) the justice shall, as soon as practicable after the warrant has been issued, cause the warrant to be filed with the clerk of the court for the territorial division in which the warrant is intended for execution.

Providing facsimile

(7) A peace officer who executes a warrant issued by telephone or other means of telecommunication, other than a warrant issued pursuant to subsection 256(1), shall, before entering the place or premises to be searched or as soon as practicable thereafter, give a facsimile of the warrant to any person present and ostensibly in control of the place or premises.

Affixing facsimile

(8) A peace officer who, in any unoccupied place or premises, executes a warrant issued by telephone or other means of telecommunication, other than a warrant issued pursuant to subsection 256(1), shall, on entering the place or premises or as soon as practicable thereafter, cause a facsimile of the warrant to be suitably affixed in a prominent place within the place or premises.

Report of peace officer

(9) A peace officer to whom a warrant is issued by telephone or other means of telecommunication shall file a written report with the clerk of the court for the territorial division in which the warrant was intended for execution as soon as practicable but within a period not exceeding seven days after the warrant has been executed, which report shall include

(a) a statement of the time and date the warrant was executed or, if the warrant was not executed, a statement of the reasons why it was not executed;

(b) a statement of the things, if any, that were seized pursuant to the warrant and the location where they are being held; and

(c) a statement of the things, if any, that were seized in addition to the things mentioned in the warrant and the location where they are being held, together with a statement of the peace officer's grounds for believing that those additional things had been obtained by, or used in, the commission of an offence.

Bringing before justice

(10) The clerk of the court shall, as soon as practicable, cause the report, together with the information and the warrant to which it pertains, to be brought before a justice to be dealt with, in respect of the things seized referred to in the report, in the same manner as if the things were seized pursuant to a warrant issued, on an information presented personally by a peace officer, by that justice or another justice for the same territorial division.

Proof of authorization

(11) In any proceeding in which it is material for a court to be satisfied that a search or seizure was authorized by a warrant issued by telephone or other means of telecommunication, the absence of the information or warrant, signed by the justice and carrying on its face a notation of the time, date and place of issuance, is, in the absence of evidence to the contrary, proof that the search or seizure was not authorized by a warrant issued by telephone or other means of telecommunication.

Duplicates and facsimiles acceptable

(12) A duplicate or a facsimile of an information or a warrant has the same probative force as the original for the purposes of subsection (11).

R.S., 1985, c. 27 (1st Supp.), s. 69;

1992, c. 1, ss. 58, 59(E), 60(F);

1994, c. 44, s. 37.

Where warrant not necessary

487.11 A peace officer, or a public officer who has been appointed or designated to administer or enforce any federal or provincial law and whose duties include the enforcement of this or any other Act of Parliament, may, in the course of his or her duties, exercise any of the powers described in

subsection 487(1) or 492.1(1) without a warrant if the conditions for obtaining a warrant exist but by reason of exigent circumstances it would be impracticable to obtain a warrant.
1997, c. 18, s. 46.

Restriction on publication
487.2 If a search warrant is issued under section 487 or 487.1 or a search is made under such a warrant, every one who publishes in any document, or broadcasts or transmits in any way, any information with respect to
(a) the location of the place searched or to be searched, or
(b) the identity of any person who is or appears to occupy or be in possession or control of that place or who is suspected of being involved in any offence in relation to which the warrant was issued, without the consent of every person referred to in paragraph (b) is, unless a charge has been laid in respect of any offence in relation to which the warrant was issued, guilty of an offence punishable on summary conviction.
R.S., 1985, c. 27 (1st Supp.), s. 69;
2005, c. 32, s. 16.

Order denying access to information
487.3 (1) On application made at the time an application is made for a warrant under this or any other Act of Parliament, an order under any of sections
(a) the ends of justice would be subverted by the disclosure for one of the reasons referred to in subsection (2) or the information might be used for an improper purpose; and
(b) the reason referred to in paragraph (a) outweighs in importance the access to the information.

Reasons
(2) For the purposes of paragraph (1)(a), an order may be made under subsection (1) on the ground that the ends of justice would be subverted by the disclosure
(a) if disclosure of the information would
(i) compromise the identity of a confidential informant,
(ii) compromise the nature and extent of an ongoing investigation,
(iii) endanger a person engaged in particular intelligence-gathering techniques and thereby prejudice future investigations in which similar techniques would be used, or
(iv) prejudice the interests of an innocent person; and
(b) for any other sufficient reason.

Procedure
(3) Where an order is made under subsection (1), all documents relating to the application shall, subject to any terms and conditions that the justice or judge considers desirable in the circumstances, including, without limiting the generality of the foregoing, any term or condition concerning the duration of the prohibition, partial disclosure of a document, deletion of any information or the occurrence of a condition, be placed in a packet and sealed by the justice or judge immediately on determination of the application, and that packet shall be kept in the custody of the court in a place to which the public has no access or in any other place that the justice or judge may authorize and shall not be dealt with except in accordance with the terms and conditions specified in the order or as varied under subsection (4).

Application for variance of order
(4) An application to terminate the order or vary any of its terms and conditions may be made to the justice or judge who made the order or a judge of the court before which any proceedings arising out of the investigation in relation to which the warrant or production order was obtained may be held.
1997, c. 23, s. 14, c. 39, s. 1;
2004, c. 3, s. 8;
2014, c. 31, s. 22.

Execution of search warrant
488 A warrant issued under section 487 or 487.1 shall be executed by day, unless
(a) the justice is satisfied that there are reasonable grounds for it to be executed by night;
(b) the reasonable grounds are included in the information; and

(c) the warrant authorizes that it be executed by night.
R.S., 1985, c. C-46, s. 488;
R.S., 1985, c. 27 (1st Supp.), s. 70;
1997, c. 18, s. 47.

Definitions

488.01 (1) The following definitions apply in this section and in section 488.02.

data
document
journalist
Canada Evidence Act
journalistic source
Canada Evidence Act
officer

Warrant, authorization and order

(2) Despite any other provision of this Act, if an applicant for a warrant under section 487.01, 487.1, 492.1 or 492.2, a search warrant under this Act, notably under section 487, an authorization under section 184.2, 184.3, 186 or 188, or an order under any of sections 487.014 to 487.017 knows that the application relates to a journalist's communications or an object, document or data relating to or in the possession of a journalist, they shall make an application to a judge of a superior court of criminal jurisdiction or to a judge as defined in section 552. That judge has exclusive jurisdiction to dispose of the application.

Warrant, authorization and order

(3) A judge may issue a warrant, authorization or order under subsection (2) only if, in addition to the conditions required for the issue of the warrant, authorization or order, he or she is satisfied that
(a) there is no other way by which the information can reasonably be obtained; and
(b) the public interest in the investigation and prosecution of a criminal offence outweighs the journalist's right to privacy in gathering and disseminating information.

Special Advocate

(4) The judge to whom the application for the warrant, authorization or order is made may, in his or her discretion, request that a special advocate present observations in the interests of freedom of the press concerning the conditions set out in subsection (3).

Offence by journalist — exception

(5) Subsections (3) and (4) do not apply in respect of an application for a warrant, authorization or order that is made in relation to the commission of an offence by a journalist.

Offence by journalist — order

(6) If a warrant, authorization or order referred to in subsection (2) is sought in relation to the commission of an offence by a journalist and the judge considers it necessary to protect the confidentiality of journalistic sources, the judge may order that some or all documents obtained pursuant to the warrant, authorization or order are to be dealt with in accordance with section 488.02.

Conditions

(7) The warrant, authorization or order referred to in subsection (2) may contain any conditions that the judge considers appropriate to protect the confidentiality of journalistic sources and to limit the disruption of journalistic activities.

Powers

(8) The judge who rules on the application for the warrant, authorization or order referred to in subsection (2) has the same powers, with the necessary adaptations, as the authority who may issue the warrant, authorization or order.

Discovery of relation to journalist

(9) If an officer, acting under a warrant, authorization or order referred to in subsection (2) for which an application was not made in accordance with that subsection, becomes aware that the warrant, authorization or order relates to a journalist's communications or an object, document or data relating to or in the possession of a journalist, the officer shall, as soon as possible, make an

(a) refrain from examining or reproducing, in whole or in part, any document obtained pursuant to the warrant, authorization or order; and
(b) place any document obtained pursuant to the warrant, authorization or order in a sealed packet and keep it in a place to which the public has no access.

Powers of judge

(10) On an application under subsection (9), the judge may
(a) confirm the warrant, authorization or order if the judge is of the opinion that no additional conditions to protect the confidentiality of journalistic sources and to limit the disruption of journalistic activities should be imposed;
(b) vary the warrant, authorization or order to impose any conditions that the judge considers appropriate to protect the confidentiality of journalistic sources and to limit the disruption of journalistic activities;
(c) if the judge considers it necessary to protect the confidentiality of journalistic sources, order that some or all documents that were or will be obtained pursuant to the warrant, authorization or order are to be dealt with in accordance with section 488.02; or
(d) revoke the warrant, authorization or order if the judge is of the opinion that the applicant knew or ought reasonably to have known that the application for the warrant, authorization or order related to a journalist's communications or an object, document or data relating to or in the possession of a journalist.
2017, c. 22, s. 3.

Documents

488.02 (1) Any document obtained pursuant to a warrant, authorization or order issued in accordance with subsection 488.01(3), or that is the subject of an order made under subsection 488.01(6) or paragraph 488.01(10)(c), is to be placed in a packet and sealed by the court that issued the warrant, authorization or order and is to be kept in the custody of the court in a place to which the public has no access or in such other place as the judge may authorize and is not to be dealt with except in accordance with this section.

Notice

(2) No officer is to examine or reproduce, in whole or in part, a document referred to in subsection (1) without giving the journalist and relevant media outlet notice of his or her intention to examine or reproduce the document.

Application

(3) The journalist or relevant media outlet may, within 10 days of receiving the notice referred to in subsection (2), apply to a judge of the court that issued the warrant, authorization or order to issue an order that the document is not to be disclosed to an officer on the grounds that the document identifies or is likely to identity a journalistic source.

Disclosure: prohibition

(4) A document that is subject to an application under subsection (3) is to be disclosed to an officer only following a disclosure order in accordance with paragraph (7)(b).

Disclosure order

(5) The judge may order the disclosure of a document only if he or she is satisfied that
(a) there is no other way by which the information can reasonably be obtained; and
(b) the public interest in the investigation and prosecution of a criminal offence outweighs the journalist's right to privacy in gathering and disseminating information.

Examination

(6) The judge may, if he or she considers it necessary, examine a document to determine whether it should be disclosed.

Order

(7) The judge must,
(a) if he or she is of the opinion that the document should not be disclosed, order that it be returned to the journalist or the media outlet, as the case may be; or
(b) if he or she is of the opinion that the document should be disclosed, order that it be delivered to

the officer who gave the notice under subsection (2), subject to such restrictions and conditions as the judge deems appropriate.
2017, c. 22, s. 3.

Definitions
488.1 (1) In this section,
custodian
document
judge
lawyer
officer

Examination or seizure of certain documents where privilege claimed
(2) Where an officer acting under the authority of this or any other Act of Parliament is about to examine, copy or seize a document in the possession of a lawyer who claims that a named client of his has a solicitor-client privilege in respect of that document, the officer shall, without examining or making copies of the document,
(a) seize the document and place it in a package and suitably seal and identify the package; and
(b) place the package in the custody of the sheriff of the district or county in which the seizure was made or, if there is agreement in writing that a specified person act as custodian, in the custody of that person.

Application to judge
(3) Where a document has been seized and placed in custody under subsection (2), the Attorney General or the client or the lawyer on behalf of the client, may
(a) within fourteen days from the day the document was so placed in custody, apply, on two days notice of motion to all other persons entitled to make application, to a judge for an order
(i) appointing a place and a day, not later than twenty-one days after the date of the order, for the determination of the question whether the document should be disclosed, and
(ii) requiring the custodian to produce the document to the judge at that time and place;
(b) serve a copy of the order on all other persons entitled to make application and on the custodian within six days of the date on which it was made; and
(c) if he has proceeded as authorized by paragraph (b), apply, at the appointed time and place, for an order determining the question.

Disposition of application
(4) On an application under paragraph (3)(c), the judge
(a) may, if the judge considers it necessary to determine the question whether the document should be disclosed, inspect the document;
(b) where the judge is of the opinion that it would materially assist him in deciding whether or not the document is privileged, may allow the Attorney General to inspect the document;
(c) shall allow the Attorney General and the person who objects to the disclosure of the document to make representations; and
(d) shall determine the question summarily and,
(i) if the judge is of the opinion that the document should not be disclosed, ensure that it is repackaged and resealed and order the custodian to deliver the document to the lawyer who claimed the solicitor-client privilege or to the client, or
(ii) if the judge is of the opinion that the document should be disclosed, order the custodian to deliver the document to the officer who seized the document or some other person designated by the Attorney General, subject to such restrictions or conditions as the judge deems appropriate,
and shall, at the same time, deliver concise reasons for the determination in which the nature of the document is described without divulging the details thereof.

Privilege continues
(5) Where the judge determines pursuant to paragraph (4)(d) that a solicitor-client privilege exists in respect of a document, whether or not the judge has, pursuant to paragraph (4)(b), allowed the Attorney General to inspect the document, the document remains privileged and inadmissible as

evidence unless the client consents to its admission in evidence or the privilege is otherwise lost.
Order to custodian to deliver
(6) Where a document has been seized and placed in custody under subsection (2) and a judge, on the application of the Attorney General, is satisfied that no application has been made under paragraph (3)(a) or that following such an application no further application has been made under paragraph (3)(c), the judge shall order the custodian to deliver the document to the officer who seized the document or to some other person designated by the Attorney General.
Application to another judge
(7) Where the judge to whom an application has been made under paragraph (3)(c) cannot act or continue to act under this section for any reason, subsequent applications under that paragraph may be made to another judge.
Prohibition
(8) No officer shall examine, make copies of or seize any document without affording a reasonable opportunity for a claim of solicitor-client privilege to be made under subsection (2).
Authority to make copies
(9) At any time while a document is in the custody of a custodian under this section, a judge may, on an
Hearing in private
(10) An application under paragraph (3)(c) shall be heard in private.
Exception
(11) This section does not apply in circumstances where a claim of solicitor-client privilege may be made under the
Income Tax Act
Proceeds of Crime (Money Laundering) and Terrorist Financing Act
R.S., 1985, c. 27 (1st Supp.), s. 71;
2000, c. 17, s. 89;
2001, c. 41, s. 80.
Seizure of things not specified
489 (1) Every person who executes a warrant may seize, in addition to the things mentioned in the warrant, any thing that the person believes on reasonable grounds
(a) has been obtained by the commission of an offence against this or any other Act of Parliament;
(b) has been used in the commission of an offence against this or any other Act of Parliament; or
(c) will afford evidence in respect of an offence against this or any other Act of Parliament.
Seizure without warrant
(2) Every peace officer, and every public officer who has been appointed or designated to administer or enforce any federal or provincial law and whose duties include the enforcement of this or any other Act of Parliament, who is lawfully present in a place pursuant to a warrant or otherwise in the execution of duties may, without a warrant, seize any thing that the officer believes on reasonable grounds
(a) has been obtained by the commission of an offence against this or any other Act of Parliament;
(b) has been used in the commission of an offence against this or any other Act of Parliament; or
(c) will afford evidence in respect of an offence against this or any other Act of Parliament.
R.S., 1985, c. C-46, s. 489;
R.S., 1985, c. 27 (1st Supp.), s. 72, c. 42 (4th Supp.), s. 3;
1993, c. 40, s. 16;
1997, c. 18, s. 48.
Restitution of property or report by peace officer
489.1 (1) Subject to this or any other Act of Parliament, where a peace officer has seized anything under a warrant issued under this Act or under section 487.11 or 489 or otherwise in the execution of duties under this or any other Act of Parliament, the peace officer shall, as soon as is practicable,
(a) where the peace officer is satisfied,
(i) that there is no dispute as to who is lawfully entitled to possession of the thing seized, and

(ii) that the continued detention of the thing seized is not required for the purposes of any investigation or a preliminary inquiry, trial or other proceeding,

return the thing seized, on being issued a receipt therefor, to the person lawfully entitled to its possession and report to the justice who issued the warrant or some other justice for the same territorial division or, if no warrant was issued, a justice having jurisdiction in respect of the matter, that he has done so; or

(b) where the peace officer is not satisfied as described in subparagraphs (a)(i) and (ii),

(i) bring the thing seized before the justice referred to in paragraph (a), or

(ii) report to the justice that he has seized the thing and is detaining it or causing it to be detained

to be dealt with by the justice in accordance with subsection 490(1).

Restitution of property or report by peace officer

(2) Subject to this or any other Act of Parliament, where a person, other than a peace officer, has seized anything under a warrant issued under this Act or under section 487.11 or 489 or otherwise in the execution of duties under this or any other Act of Parliament, that person shall, as soon as is practicable,

(a) bring the thing seized before the justice who issued the warrant or some other justice for the same territorial division or, if no warrant was issued, before a justice having jurisdiction in respect of the matter, or

(b) report to the justice referred to in paragraph (a) that he has seized the thing and is detaining it or causing it to be detained,

to be dealt with by the justice in accordance with subsection 490(1).

Form

(3) A report to a justice under this section shall be in the form set out as Form 5.2 in Part XXVIII, varied to suit the case and shall include, in the case of a report in respect of a warrant issued by telephone or other means of telecommunication, the statements referred to in subsection 487.1(9).

R.S., 1985, c. 27 (1st Supp.), s. 72;

1993, c. 40, s. 17;

1997, c. 18, s. 49.

Detention of things seized

490 (1) Subject to this or any other Act of Parliament, where, pursuant to paragraph 489.1(1)(b) or subsection 489.1(2), anything that has been seized is brought before a justice or a report in respect of anything seized is made to a justice, the justice shall,

(a) where the lawful owner or person who is lawfully entitled to possession of the thing seized is known, order it to be returned to that owner or person, unless the prosecutor, or the peace officer or other person having custody of the thing seized, satisfies the justice that the detention of the thing seized is required for the purposes of any investigation or a preliminary inquiry, trial or other proceeding; or

(b) where the prosecutor, or the peace officer or other person having custody of the thing seized, satisfies the justice that the thing seized should be detained for a reason set out in paragraph (a), detain the thing seized or order that it be detained, taking reasonable care to ensure that it is preserved until the conclusion of any investigation or until it is required to be produced for the purposes of a preliminary inquiry, trial or other proceeding.

Further detention

(2) Nothing shall be detained under the authority of paragraph (1)(b) for a period of more than three months after the day of the seizure, or any longer period that ends when an application made under paragraph (a) is decided, unless

(a) a justice, on the making of a summary application to him after three clear days notice thereof to the person from whom the thing detained was seized, is satisfied that, having regard to the nature of the investigation, its further detention for a specified period is warranted and the justice so orders; or

(b) proceedings are instituted in which the thing detained may be required.

Idem

(3) More than one order for further detention may be made under paragraph (2)(a) but the cumulative

period of detention shall not exceed one year from the day of the seizure, or any longer period that ends when an application made under paragraph (a) is decided, unless

(a) a judge of a superior court of criminal jurisdiction or a judge as defined in section 552, on the making of a summary application to him after three clear days notice thereof to the person from whom the thing detained was seized, is satisfied, having regard to the complex nature of the investigation, that the further detention of the thing seized is warranted for a specified period and subject to such other conditions as the judge considers just, and the judge so orders; or

(b) proceedings are instituted in which the thing detained may be required.

Detention without application where consent

(3.1) A thing may be detained under paragraph (1)(b) for any period, whether or not an application for an order under subsection (2) or (3) is made, if the lawful owner or person who is lawfully entitled to possession of the thing seized consents in writing to its detention for that period.

When accused ordered to stand trial

(4) When an accused has been ordered to stand trial, the justice shall forward anything detained pursuant to subsections (1) to (3) to the clerk of the court to which the accused has been ordered to stand trial to be detained by the clerk of the court and disposed of as the court directs.

Where continued detention no longer required

(5) Where at any time before the expiration of the periods of detention provided for or ordered under subsections (1) to (3) in respect of anything seized, the prosecutor, or the peace officer or other person having custody of the thing seized, determines that the continued detention of the thing seized is no longer required for any purpose mentioned in subsection (1) or (4), the prosecutor, peace officer or other person shall apply to

(a) a judge of a superior court of criminal jurisdiction or a judge as defined in section 552, where a judge ordered its detention under subsection (3), or

(b) a justice, in any other case,

who shall, after affording the person from whom the thing was seized or the person who claims to be the lawful owner thereof or person entitled to its possession, if known, an opportunity to establish that he is lawfully entitled to the possession thereof, make an order in respect of the property under subsection (9).

Idem

(6) Where the periods of detention provided for or ordered under subsections (1) to (3) in respect of anything seized have expired and proceedings have not been instituted in which the thing detained may be required, the prosecutor, peace officer or other person shall apply to a judge or justice referred to in paragraph (5)(a) or (b) in the circumstances set out in that paragraph, for an order in respect of the property under subsection (9) or (9.1).

Application for order of return

(7) A person from whom anything has been seized may, after the expiration of the periods of detention provided for or ordered under subsections (1) to (3) and on three clear days notice to the Attorney General, apply summarily to

(a) a judge of a superior court of criminal jurisdiction or a judge as defined in section 552, where a judge ordered the detention of the thing seized under subsection (3), or

(b) a justice, in any other case,

for an order under paragraph (9)(c) that the thing seized be returned to the applicant.

Exception

(8) A judge of a superior court of criminal jurisdiction or a judge as defined in section 552, where a judge ordered the detention of the thing seized under subsection (3), or a justice, in any other case, may allow an application to be made under subsection (7) prior to the expiration of the periods referred to therein where he is satisfied that hardship will result unless the application is so allowed.

Disposal of things seized

(9) Subject to this or any other Act of Parliament, if

(a) a judge referred to in subsection (7), where a judge ordered the detention of anything seized under subsection (3), or

(b) a justice, in any other case,
is satisfied that the periods of detention provided for or ordered under subsections (1) to (3) in respect of anything seized have expired and proceedings have not been instituted in which the thing detained may be required or, where those periods have not expired, that the continued detention of the thing seized will not be required for any purpose mentioned in subsection (1) or (4), he shall
(c) if possession of it by the person from whom it was seized is lawful, order it to be returned to that person, or
(d) if possession of it by the person from whom it was seized is unlawful and the lawful owner or person who is lawfully entitled to its possession is known, order it to be returned to the lawful owner or to the person who is lawfully entitled to its possession,
and may, if possession of it by the person from whom it was seized is unlawful, or if it was seized when it was not in the possession of any person, and the lawful owner or person who is lawfully entitled to its possession is not known, order it to be forfeited to Her Majesty, to be disposed of as the Attorney General directs, or otherwise dealt with in accordance with the law.

Exception
(9.1) Notwithstanding subsection (9), a judge or justice referred to in paragraph (9)(a) or (b) may, if the periods of detention provided for or ordered under subsections (1) to (3) in respect of a thing seized have expired but proceedings have not been instituted in which the thing may be required, order that the thing continue to be detained for such period as the judge or justice considers necessary if the judge or justice is satisfied
(a) that the continued detention of the thing might reasonably be required for a purpose mentioned in subsection (1) or (4); and
(b) that it is in the interests of justice to do so.

Application by lawful owner
(10) Subject to this or any other Act of Parliament, a person, other than a person who may make an application under subsection (7), who claims to be the lawful owner or person lawfully entitled to possession of anything seized and brought before or reported to a justice under section 489.1 may, at any time, on three clear days notice to the Attorney General and the person from whom the thing was seized, apply summarily to
(a) a judge referred to in subsection (7), where a judge ordered the detention of the thing seized under subsection (3), or
(b) a justice, in any other case,
for an order that the thing detained be returned to the applicant.

Order
(11) Subject to this or any other Act of Parliament, on an application under subsection (10), where a judge or justice is satisfied that
(a) the applicant is the lawful owner or lawfully entitled to possession of the thing seized, and
(b) the periods of detention provided for or ordered under subsections (1) to (3) in respect of the thing seized have expired and proceedings have not been instituted in which the thing detained may be required or, where such periods have not expired, that the continued detention of the thing seized will not be required for any purpose mentioned in subsection (1) or (4),
the judge or justice shall order that
(c) the thing seized be returned to the applicant, or
(d) except as otherwise provided by law, where, pursuant to subsection (9), the thing seized was forfeited, sold or otherwise dealt with in such a manner that it cannot be returned to the applicant, the applicant be paid the proceeds of sale or the value of the thing seized.

Detention pending appeal, etc.
(12) Notwithstanding anything in this section, nothing shall be returned, forfeited or disposed of under this section pending any application made, or appeal taken, thereunder in respect of the thing or proceeding in which the right of seizure thereof is questioned or within thirty days after an order in respect of the thing is made under this section.

Copies of documents returned

(13) The Attorney General, the prosecutor or the peace officer or other person having custody of a document seized may, before bringing it before a justice or complying with an order that the document be returned, forfeited or otherwise dealt with under subsection (1), (9) or (11), make or cause to be made, and may retain, a copy of the document.
Probative force
(14) Every copy made under subsection (13) that is certified as a true copy by the Attorney General, the person who made the copy or the person in whose presence the copy was made is admissible in evidence and, in the absence of evidence to the contrary, has the same probative force as the original document would have if it had been proved in the ordinary way.
Access to anything seized
(15) Where anything is detained pursuant to subsections (1) to (3.1), a judge of a superior court of criminal jurisdiction, a judge as defined in section 552 or a provincial court judge may, on summary application on behalf of a person who has an interest in what is detained, after three clear days notice to the Attorney General, order that the person by or on whose behalf the application is made be permitted to examine anything so detained.
Conditions
(16) An order that is made under subsection (15) shall be made on such terms as appear to the judge to be necessary or desirable to ensure that anything in respect of which the order is made is safeguarded and preserved for any purpose for which it may subsequently be required.
Appeal
(17) A person who feels aggrieved by an order made under subsection (8), (9), (9.1) or (11) may appeal from the order
(a) to the court of appeal as defined in section 673 if the order was made by a judge of a superior court of criminal jurisdiction, in which case sections 678 to 689 apply with any modifications that the circumstances require; or
(b) to the appeal court as defined in section 812 in any other case, in which case sections 813 to 828 apply with any modifications that the circumstances require.
Waiver of notice
(18) Any person to whom three days notice must be given under paragraph (2)(a) or (3)(a) or subsection (7), (10) or (15) may agree that the application for which the notice is given be made before the expiration of the three days.
R.S., 1985, c. C-46, s. 490;
R.S., 1985, c. 27 (1st Supp.), s. 73;
1994, c. 44, s. 38;
1997, c. 18, s. 50;
2008, c. 18, s. 14;
2017, c. 7, s. 63(F).
Perishable things
490.01 Where any thing seized pursuant to this Act is perishable or likely to depreciate rapidly, the person who seized the thing or any other person having custody of the thing
(a) may return it to its lawful owner or the person who is lawfully entitled to possession of it; or
(b) where, on
(i) dispose of it and give the proceeds of disposition to the lawful owner of the thing seized, if the lawful owner was not a party to an offence in relation to the thing or, if the identity of that lawful owner cannot be reasonably ascertained, the proceeds of disposition are forfeited to Her Majesty, or
(ii) destroy it.
1997, c. 18, s. 51;
1999, c. 5, s. 17.

Sex Offender Information

Interpretation

Definitions
490.011 (1) The following definitions apply in this section and in sections 490.012 to 490.032.
crime of a sexual nature
Sex Offender Information Registration Act
database
Sex Offender Information Registration Act
designated offence
(a) an offence under any of the following provisions:
(i) subsection 7(4.1) (offence in relation to sexual offences against children),
(ii) section 151 (sexual interference),
(iii) section 152 (invitation to sexual touching),
(iv) section 153 (sexual exploitation),
(v) section 153.1 (sexual exploitation of person with disability),
(vi) section 155 (incest),
(vi.1) subsection 160(2) (compelling the commission of bestiality),
(vii) subsection 160(3) (bestiality in presence of or by a child),
(viii) section 163.1 (child pornography),
(ix) section 170 (parent or guardian procuring sexual activity),
(ix.1) section 171.1 (making sexually explicit material available to child),
(x) section 172.1 (luring a child),
(x.1) section 172.2 (agreement or arrangement — sexual offence against child),
(xi) subsection 173(2) (exposure),
(xii) to (xv) (xvi) section 271 (sexual assault),
(xvii) section 272 (sexual assault with a weapon, threats to a third party or causing bodily harm),
(xviii) paragraph 273(2)(a) (aggravated sexual assault — use of a restricted firearm or prohibited firearm or any firearm in connection with criminal organization),
(xviii.1) paragraph 273(2)(a.1) (aggravated sexual assault — use of a firearm),
(xix) paragraph 273(2)(b) (aggravated sexual assault),
(xx) subsection 273.3(2) (removal of a child from Canada),
(xxi) section 279.011 (trafficking — person under 18 years),
(xxii) subsection 279.02(2) (material benefit — trafficking of person under 18 years),
(xxiii) subsection 279.03(2) (withholding or destroying documents — trafficking of person under 18 years),
(xxiv) subsection 286.1(2) (obtaining sexual services for consideration from person under 18 years),
(xxv) subsection 286.2(2) (material benefit from sexual services provided by person under 18 years), and
(xxvi) subsection 286.3(2) (procuring — person under 18 years);
(b) an offence under any of the following provisions:
(i) section 162 (voyeurism),
(i.1) subsection 173(1) (indecent acts),
(ii) section 177 (trespassing at night),
(iii) section 230 (murder in commission of offences),
(iii.1) section 231 (murder),
(iv) section 234 (manslaughter),
(v) paragraph 246(b) (overcoming resistance to commission of offence),
(vi) section 264 (criminal harassment),
(vii) section 279 (kidnapping),
(vii.1) section 279.01 (trafficking in persons),
(vii.11) subsection 279.02(1) (material benefit — trafficking),
(vii.12) subsection 279.03(1) (withholding or destroying documents — trafficking),

(viii) section 280 (abduction of a person under age of sixteen),
(ix) section 281 (abduction of a person under age of fourteen),
(ix.1) subsection 286.1(1) (obtaining sexual services for consideration),
(ix.2) subsection 286.2(1) (material benefit from sexual services),
(ix.3) subsection 286.3(1) (procuring),
(x) paragraph 348(1)(d) (breaking and entering a dwelling house with intent to commit an indictable offence),
(xi) paragraph 348(1)(d) (breaking and entering a dwelling house and committing an indictable offence),
(xii) paragraph 348(1)(e) (breaking and entering a place other than a dwelling house with intent to commit an indictable offence), and
(xiii) paragraph 348(1)(e) (breaking and entering a place other than a dwelling house and committing an indictable offence);
(c) an offence under any of the following provisions of the
Criminal Code
(i) section 144 (rape),
(ii) section 145 (attempt to commit rape),
(iii) section 149 (indecent assault on female),
(iv) section 156 (indecent assault on male), and
(v) subsection 246(1) (assault with intent) if the intent is to commit an offence referred to in any of subparagraphs (i) to (iv);
(c.1) an offence under any of the following provisions of the
Criminal Code
An Act to amend the Criminal Code in relation to sexual offences and other offences against the person and to amend certain other Acts in relation thereto or in consequence thereof
(i) section 246.1 (sexual assault),
(ii) section 246.2 (sexual assault with a weapon, threats to a third party or causing bodily harm), and
(iii) section 246.3 (aggravated sexual assault);
(d) an offence under any of the following provisions of the
Criminal Code
(i) subsection 146(1) (sexual intercourse with a female under age of fourteen),
(ii) subsection 146(2) (sexual intercourse with a female between ages of fourteen and sixteen),
(iii) section 153 (sexual intercourse with step-daughter),
(iv) section 157 (gross indecency),
(v) section 166 (parent or guardian procuring defilement), and
(vi) section 167 (householder permitting defilement);
(d.1) an offence under any of the following provisions of this Act, as they read from time to time before the day on which this paragraph comes into force:
(i) paragraph 212(1)(i) (stupefying or overpowering for the purpose of sexual intercourse),
(ii) subsection 212(2) (living on the avails of prostitution of person under 18 years),
(iii) subsection 212(2.1) (aggravated offence in relation to living on the avails of prostitution of person under 18 years), and
(iv) subsection 212(4) (prostitution of person under 18 years);
(e) an attempt or conspiracy to commit an offence referred to in any of paragraphs (a), (c), (c.1), (d) and (d.1); or
(f) an attempt or conspiracy to commit an offence referred to in paragraph (b).
Ontario Act
Christopher's Law (Sex Offender Registry), 2000
pardon
record suspension
Criminal Records Act
registration centre

Sex Offender Information Registration Act
Review Board
verdict of not criminally responsible on account of mental disorder
National Defence Act

Interpretation

(2) For the purpose of this section and sections 490.012 to 490.032, a person who is convicted of, or found not criminally responsible on account of mental disorder for, a designated offence does not include a young person
(a) within the meaning of subsection 2(1) of the
Youth Criminal Justice Act
(b) within the meaning of subsection 2(1) of the
Young Offenders Act
2004, c. 10, s. 20;
2005, c. 43, s. 6;
2007, c. 5, s. 11;
2008, c. 6, s. 36;
2010, c. 3, s. 7, c. 17, s. 4;
2012, c. 1, ss. 31, 141;
2014, c. 25, s. 25.

Order to Comply with the

Sex Offender Information Registration Act
Order
490.012 (1) When a court imposes a sentence on a person for an offence referred to in paragraph (a), (c), (c.1), (d), (d.1) or (e) of the definition
designated offence
Sex Offender Information Registration Act
Order — if intent established
(2) When a court imposes a sentence on a person for an offence referred to in paragraph (b) or (f) of the definition
designated offence
Sex Offender Information Registration Act
Order — if previous offence established
(3) When a court imposes a sentence on a person for a designated offence in connection with which an order may be made under subsection (1) or (2) or renders a verdict of not criminally responsible on account of mental disorder for such an offence, it shall, on application of the prosecutor, make an order in Form 52 requiring the person to comply with the
Sex Offender Information Registration Act
(a) the person was, before or after the coming into force of this paragraph, previously convicted of, or found not criminally responsible on account of mental disorder for, an offence referred to in paragraph (a), (c), (c.1), (d), (d.1) or (e) of the definition
designated offence
National Defence Act
(b) the person was not served with a notice under section 490.021 or 490.02903 or under section 227.08 of the
National Defence Act
(c) no order was made under subsection (1) or under subsection 227.01(1) of the
National Defence Act
Failure to make order
(4) If the court does not consider the matter under subsection (1) or (3) at that time, the court
(a) shall, within 90 days after the day on which it imposes the sentence or renders the verdict, set a

date for a hearing to do so;
(b) retains jurisdiction over the matter; and
(c) may require the person to appear by closed-circuit television or any other means that allows the court and the person to engage in simultaneous visual and oral communication, as long as the person is given the opportunity to communicate privately with counsel if they are represented by counsel.
2004, c. 10, s. 20;
2007, c. 5, s. 13;
2010, c. 17, s. 5;
2014, c. 25, s. 26.

Date order begins
490.013 (1) An order made under section 490.012 begins on the day on which it is made.

Duration of order
(2) An order made under subsection 490.012(1) or (2)
(a) ends 10 years after it was made if the offence in connection with which it was made was prosecuted summarily or if the maximum term of imprisonment for the offence is two or five years;
(b) ends 20 years after it was made if the maximum term of imprisonment for the offence is 10 or 14 years; and
(c) applies for life if the maximum term of imprisonment for the offence is life.

Duration of order
(2.1) An order made under subsection 490.012(1) applies for life if the person is convicted of, or found not criminally responsible on account of mental disorder for, more than one offence referred to in paragraph (a), (c), (c.1), (d), (d.1) or (e) of the definition
designated offence

Duration of order
(3) An order made under subsection 490.012(1) or (2) applies for life if the person is, or was at any time, subject to an obligation under section 490.019 or 490.02901, under section 227.06 of the National Defence Act
International Transfer of Offenders Act

Duration of order
(4) An order made under subsection 490.012(1) or (2) applies for life if the person is, or was at any time, subject to an order made previously under section 490.012 of this Act or section 227.01 of the National Defence Act

Duration of order
(5) An order made under subsection 490.012(3) applies for life.
2004, c. 10, s. 20;
2007, c. 5, s. 14;
2010, c. 17, s. 6;
2014, c. 25, s. 27.

Appeal
490.014 The prosecutor, or a person who is subject to an order under subsection 490.012(2), may appeal from a decision of the court under that subsection on any ground of appeal that raises a question of law or of mixed law and fact. The appeal court may dismiss the appeal, or allow it and order a new hearing, quash the order or make an order that may be made under that subsection.
2004, c. 10, s. 20;
2010, c. 17, s. 7.

Application for termination order
490.015 (1) A person who is subject to an order may apply for a termination order
(a) if five years have elapsed since the order was made, in the case of an order referred to in paragraph 490.013(2)(a);
(b) if 10 years have elapsed since the order was made, in the case of an order referred to in paragraph 490.013(2)(b); or
(c) if 20 years have elapsed since the order was made, in the case of an order referred to in paragraph

490.013(2)(c) or subsection 490.013(2.1), (3) or (5).

Multiple orders

(2) A person who is subject to more than one order made under section 490.012 of this Act, or under that section and section 227.01 of the

National Defence Act

Pardon or record suspension

(3) Despite subsections (1) and (2), a person may apply for a termination order once they receive a pardon or once a record suspension is ordered.

Scope of application

(4) The application shall be in relation to every order that is in effect. If a person is subject to an obligation under section 490.019 or 490.02901, under section 227.06 of the

National Defence Act

International Transfer of Offenders Act

Re-application

(5) A person whose application is refused may re-apply if five years have elapsed since they made the previous application. They may also re-apply once they receive a pardon or once a record suspension is ordered. However, they may not re-apply under this subsection if an order is made with respect to them under section 490.012 of this Act or section 227.01 of the

National Defence Act

Jurisdiction

(6) The application shall be made to

(a) a superior court of criminal jurisdiction if

(i) one or more of the orders to which it relates were made by such a court under section 490.012, or

(ii) one or more of the orders to which it relates were made under section 227.01 of the

National Defence Act

(b) a court of criminal jurisdiction, in any other case in which the application relates to one or more orders made under section 490.012.

2004, c. 10, s. 20;

2007, c. 5, s. 15;

2010, c. 17, s. 8;

2012, c. 1, s. 142.

Termination order

490.016 (1) The court shall make a termination order if it is satisfied that the person has established that the impact on them of continuing an order or an obligation, including on their privacy or liberty, would be grossly disproportionate to the public interest in protecting society through the effective prevention or investigation of crimes of a sexual nature, to be achieved by the registration of information relating to sex offenders under the

Sex Offender Information Registration Act

Reasons for decision

(2) The court shall give reasons for its decision.

Requirements relating to notice

(3) If the court makes a termination order, it shall cause the Commissioner of the Royal Canadian Mounted Police and the Attorney General of the province, or the minister of justice of the territory, to be notified of the decision.

2004, c. 10, s. 20;

2007, c. 5, s. 16;

2010, c. 17, s. 9.

Appeal

490.017 (1) The prosecutor or the person who applied for a termination order may appeal from a decision made under subsection 490.016(1) on any ground of appeal that raises a question of law or of mixed law and fact. The appeal court may dismiss the appeal, or allow it and order a new hearing, quash the termination order or make an order that may be made under that subsection.

Requirements relating to notice
(2) If the appeal court makes an order that may be made under subsection 490.016(1), it shall cause the Commissioner of the Royal Canadian Mounted Police and the Attorney General of the province, or the minister of justice of the territory, in which the application for the order was made to be notified of the decision.
2004, c. 10, s. 20;
2007, c. 5, s. 17;
2010, c. 17, s. 10.

Requirements relating to notice
490.018 (1) When a court or appeal court makes an order under section 490.012, it shall cause
(a) the order to be read by or to the person who is subject to it;
(b) a copy of the order to be given to that person;
(c) that person to be informed of sections 4 to 7.1 of the
Sex Offender Information Registration Act
National Defence Act
(d) a copy of the order to be sent to
(i) the Review Board that is responsible for making a disposition with respect to that person, if applicable,
(ii) the person in charge of the place in which that person is to serve the custodial portion of a sentence or is to be detained in custody as part of a disposition under Part XX.1, if applicable,
(iii) the police service whose member charged that person with the offence in connection with which the order is made, and
(iv) the Commissioner of the Royal Canadian Mounted Police.

Endorsement
(2) After paragraphs (1)(a) to (c) have been complied with, the person who is subject to the order shall endorse the order.

Notice on disposition by Review Board
(3) A Review Board shall cause a copy of the order to be given to the person who is subject to it when it directs
(a) under paragraph 672.54(a), that the person be discharged absolutely; or
(b) under paragraph 672.54(b), that the person be discharged subject to conditions, unless the conditions restrict the person's liberty in a manner and to an extent that prevent them from complying with sections 4, 4.1, 4.3 and 6 of the
Sex Offender Information Registration Act

Notice before release
(4) The person in charge of the place in which the person is serving the custodial portion of a sentence, or is detained in custody, before their release or discharge shall give the person a copy of the order not earlier than 10 days before their release or discharge.
2004, c. 10, s. 20;
2007, c. 5, s. 18;
2010, c. 17, s. 11.

Notice and Obligation to Comply with the

Sex Offender Information Registration Act
Obligation to comply
490.019 A person who is served with a notice in Form 53 shall comply with the
Sex Offender Information Registration Act
2004, c. 10, s. 20.

Persons who may be served
490.02 (1) The Attorney General of a province or minister of justice of a territory may serve a person with a notice only if the person was convicted of, or found not criminally responsible on account of

mental disorder for, an offence referred to in paragraph (a), (c), (c.1), (d) or (e) of the definition designated offence
(a) on the day on which the
Sex Offender Information Registration Act
(b) in any other case,
(i) their name appears in connection with the offence, immediately before the
Sex Offender Information Registration Act
(ii) they either were a resident of Ontario at any time between April 23, 2001 and the day on which the
Sex Offender Information Registration Act

Exception
(2) A notice shall not be served on a person
(a) if they have been finally acquitted of, or have received a free pardon granted under Her Majesty's royal prerogative of mercy or under section 748 for, every offence in connection with which a notice may be served on them under section 490.021 of this Act or section 227.08 of the
National Defence Act
(b) if an application has been made for an order under subsection 490.012(3) of this Act or subsection 227.01(3) of the
National Defence Act
(c) who is referred to in paragraph (1)(b) if they have provided proof of a pardon in accordance with subsection 9(1) of the Ontario Act.
2004, c. 10, s. 20;
2007, c. 5, s. 20.

Period for and method of service
490.021 (1) The notice shall be personally served within one year after the day on which the
Sex Offender Information Registration Act

Exception
(2) If a person referred to in paragraph 490.02(1)(a) is unlawfully at large or is in breach of any terms of their sentence or discharge, or of any conditions set under this Act or under Part III of the
National Defence Act

Exception
(3) If a person referred to in paragraph 490.02(1)(b) is not in compliance with section 3 of the Ontario Act on the day on which the
Sex Offender Information Registration Act

Exception
(4) If a person referred to in paragraph 490.02(1)(b) is in compliance with section 3 and subsection 7(2) of the Ontario Act on the day on which the
Sex Offender Information Registration Act

Proof of service
(5) An affidavit of the person who served the notice, sworn before a commissioner or other person authorized to take affidavits, is evidence of the service and the notice if it sets out that
(a) the person who served the notice has charge of the appropriate records and has knowledge of the facts in the particular case;
(b) the notice was personally served on, or mailed to, the person to whom it was directed on a named day; and
(c) the person who served the notice identifies a true copy of the notice as an exhibit attached to the affidavit.

Requirements relating to notice
(6) The person who served the notice shall, without delay, send a copy of the affidavit and the notice to the Attorney General of the province, or the minister of justice of the territory, in which the person was served.
2004, c. 10, s. 20;

2007, c. 5, s. 21.
Date obligation begins
490.022 (1) The obligation under section 490.019 begins
(a) either one year after the day on which the person is served with the notice or when an exemption order is refused under subsection 490.023(2), whichever is later; or
(b) when an exemption order is quashed.
Date obligation ends
(2) The obligation ends on the earliest of
(a) the day on which an exemption order is made on an appeal from a decision made under subsection 490.023(2),
(b) the day on which the obligation of a person referred to in paragraph 490.02(1)(b) to comply with section 3 of the Ontario Act ends under paragraph 7(1)(a) of that Act, or
(c) the day on which a person referred to in paragraph 490.02(1)(b) provides satisfactory proof of a pardon or record suspension to a person who collects information, as defined in subsection 3(1) of the
Sex Offender Information Registration Act
Duration of obligation
(3) If none of paragraphs (2)(a) to (c) applies earlier, the obligation
(a) ends 10 years after the person was sentenced, or found not criminally responsible on account of mental disorder, for the offence listed in the notice if the offence was prosecuted summarily or if the maximum term of imprisonment for the offence is two or five years;
(b) ends 20 years after the person was sentenced, or found not criminally responsible on account of mental disorder, for the offence listed in the notice if the maximum term of imprisonment for the offence is 10 or 14 years;
(c) applies for life if the maximum term of imprisonment for the offence listed in the notice is life; or
(d) applies for life if, at any time, the person was convicted of, or found not criminally responsible on account of mental disorder for, more than one offence that is referred to in paragraph (a), (c), (c.1), (d) or (e) of the definition
designated offence
National Defence Act
2004, c. 10, s. 20;
2007, c. 5, s. 22;
2012, c. 1, s. 143.
Application for exemption order
490.023 (1) A person who is not subject to an order under section 490.012 of this Act or section 227.01 of the
National Defence Act
Jurisdiction
(1.1) The application shall be made to a court of criminal jurisdiction if
(a) it relates to an obligation under section 490.019 of this Act; or
(b) it relates to an obligation under section 227.06 of the
National Defence Act
Exemption order
(2) The court shall make an exemption order if it is satisfied that the person has established that the impact of the obligation on them, including on their privacy or liberty, would be grossly disproportionate to the public interest in protecting society through the effective prevention or investigation of crimes of a sexual nature, to be achieved by the registration of information relating to sex offenders under the
Sex Offender Information Registration Act
Reasons for decision
(3) The court shall give reasons for its decision.
Removal of information from database

(4) If the court makes an exemption order, it shall also make an order requiring the Royal Canadian Mounted Police to permanently remove from the database all information that relates to the person that was registered in the database on receipt of the copy of the notice.
2004, c. 10, s. 20;
2007, c. 5, s. 23;
2010, c. 17, s. 13.

Appeal
490.024 (1) The Attorney General or the person who applied for an exemption order may appeal from a decision of the court under subsection 490.023(2) on any ground of appeal that raises a question of law or of mixed law and fact. The appeal court may dismiss the appeal, or allow it and order a new hearing, quash the exemption order or make an order that may be made under that subsection.

Removal of information from database
(2) If the appeal court makes an exemption order, it shall also make an order requiring the Royal Canadian Mounted Police to permanently remove from the database all information that relates to the person that was registered in the database on receipt of the copy of the notice.
2004, c. 10, s. 20;
2010, c. 17, s. 14.

Requirements relating to notice
490.025 If a court refuses to make an exemption order or an appeal court dismisses an appeal from such a decision or quashes an exemption order, it shall cause the Commissioner of the Royal Canadian Mounted Police and the Attorney General of the province, or the minister of justice of the territory, in which the application for the order was made to be notified of the decision and shall cause the person who applied for the order to be informed of sections 4 to 7.1 of the
Sex Offender Information Registration Act
National Defence Act
2004, c. 10, s. 20;
2007, c. 5, s. 24;
2010, c. 17, s. 15.

Application for termination order
490.026 (1) A person who is subject to an obligation under section 490.019 may apply for a termination order unless they are also subject to an obligation under section 490.02901, under section 227.06 of the
National Defence Act
International Transfer of Offenders Act
National Defence Act

Time for application
(2) A person may apply for a termination order if the following period has elapsed since they were sentenced, or found not criminally responsible on account of mental disorder, for an offence referred to in paragraph (a), (c), (c.1), (d) or (e) of the definition
designated offence
National Defence Act
(a) five years if the offence was prosecuted summarily or if the maximum term of imprisonment for the offence is two or five years;
(b) 10 years if the maximum term of imprisonment for the offence is 10 or 14 years; or
(c) 20 years if the maximum term of imprisonment for the offence is life.

More than one offence
(3) If more than one offence is listed in the notice served under section 490.021, the person may apply for a termination order if 20 years have elapsed since they were sentenced, or found not criminally responsible on account of mental disorder, for the most recent offence referred to in paragraph (a), (c), (c.1), (d) or (e) of the definition
designated offence

National Defence Act
Pardon or record suspension
(4) Despite subsections (2) and (3), a person may apply for a termination order once they receive a pardon or once a record suspension is ordered.
Re-application
(5) A person whose application is refused may apply again if five years have elapsed since they made the previous application. They may also apply again once they receive a pardon or once a record suspension is ordered. However, they may not apply again if, after the previous application was made, they become subject to an obligation under section 490.02901, under section 227.06 of the National Defence Act
International Transfer of Offenders Act
National Defence Act
Jurisdiction
(6) The application shall be made to a court of criminal jurisdiction if
(a) it relates to an obligation under section 490.019 of this Act; or
(b) it relates to an obligation under section 227.06 of the
National Defence Act
2004, c. 10, s. 20;
2007, c. 5, s. 24;
2010, c. 17, s. 16;
2012, c. 1, s. 144.
Termination order
490.027 (1) The court shall make an order terminating the obligation if it is satisfied that the person has established that the impact on them of continuing the obligation, including on their privacy or liberty, would be grossly disproportionate to the public interest in protecting society through the effective prevention or investigation of crimes of a sexual nature, to be achieved by the registration of information relating to sex offenders under the
Sex Offender Information Registration Act
Reasons for decision
(2) The court shall give reasons for its decision.
Requirements relating to notice
(3) If the court makes a termination order, it shall cause the Commissioner of the Royal Canadian Mounted Police and the Attorney General of the province, or the minister of justice of the territory, to be notified of the decision.
2004, c. 10, s. 20;
2007, c. 5, s. 25;
2010, c. 17, s. 17.
Deemed application
490.028 If a person is eligible to apply for both an exemption order under section 490.023 and a termination order under section 490.026 within one year after they are served with a notice under section 490.021 of this Act or section 227.08 of the
National Defence Act
2004, c. 10, s. 20;
2007, c. 5, s. 26.
Appeal
490.029 (1) The Attorney General or the person who applied for a termination order may appeal from a decision of the court made under subsection 490.027(1) on any ground of appeal that raises a question of law or of mixed law and fact. The appeal court may dismiss the appeal, or allow it and order a new hearing, quash the termination order or make an order that may be made under that subsection.
Requirements relating to notice
(2) If the appeal court makes an order that may be made under subsection 490.027(1), it shall cause

the Commissioner of the Royal Canadian Mounted Police and the Attorney General of the province, or the minister of justice of the territory, in which the application for the order was made to be notified of the decision.
2004, c. 10, s. 20;
2007, c. 5, s. 26;
2010, c. 17, s. 18.

Notice and Obligation to Comply with the

Sex Offender Information Registration Act
Obligation
490.02901 A person who is served with a notice in Form 54 shall comply with the
Sex Offender Information Registration Act
2010, c. 17, s. 19.
Persons who may be served
490.02902 (1) The Attorney General of a province, or the minister of justice of a territory, may serve a person with a notice in Form 54 only if the person arrived in Canada after the coming into force of this subsection and they were convicted of or found not criminally responsible on account of mental disorder for an offence outside Canada — other than a service offence as defined in subsection 2(1) of the
National Defence Act
designated offence
Exception
(2) The notice shall not be served on a person who has been acquitted of every offence in connection with which a notice may be served on them under section 490.02903.
2010, c. 17, s. 19.
Period for and method of service
490.02903 (1) A notice in Form 54 shall be personally served.
Proof of service
(2) An affidavit of the person who served the notice, sworn before a commissioner or other person authorized to take affidavits, is evidence of the service and the notice if it sets out that
(a) the person who served the notice has charge of the appropriate records and has knowledge of the facts in the particular case;
(b) the notice was personally served on the person to whom it was directed on a named day; and
(c) the person who served the notice identifies a true copy of the notice as an exhibit attached to the affidavit.
Requirements relating to notice
(3) The person who served the notice shall, without delay, send a copy of the affidavit and the notice to the Attorney General of the province, or the minister of justice of the territory, in which the person was served.
2010, c. 17, s. 19.
When obligation begins
490.02904 (1) The obligation under section 490.02901 begins on the day on which the person is served with the notice.
When obligation ends
(2) The obligation ends on the day on which an exemption order is made.
Duration of obligation
(3) If subsection (2) does not apply, the obligation
(a) ends 10 years after the person was sentenced or found not criminally responsible on account of mental disorder if the maximum term of imprisonment provided for in Canadian law for the equivalent offence is two or five years;
(b) ends 20 years after the person was sentenced or found not criminally responsible on account of

mental disorder if the maximum term of imprisonment provided for in Canadian law for the equivalent offence is 10 or 14 years;

(c) applies for life if the maximum term of imprisonment provided for in Canadian law for the equivalent offence is life; or

(d) applies for life if, before or after the coming into force of this paragraph, the person was convicted of, or found not criminally responsible on account of mental disorder for, more than one offence referred to in paragraph (a), (c), (c.1), (d), (d.1) or (e) of the definition
designated offence
National Defence Act
2010, c. 17, s. 19;
2014, c. 25, s. 28.

Application for exemption order

490.02905 (1) A person who is served with a notice in Form 54 under section 490.02903 may apply to a court of criminal jurisdiction for an order exempting them from the obligation within one year after they are served.

Exemption order

(2) The court

(a) shall make an exemption order if it is satisfied that the person has established that

(i) they were not convicted of or found not criminally responsible on account of mental disorder for or were acquitted of the offence in question, or

(ii) the offence in question is not equivalent to an offence referred to in paragraph (a) of the definition
designated offence

(b) shall order that the notice be corrected if it is satisfied that the offence in question is not equivalent to the offence referred to in the notice but is equivalent to another offence referred to in paragraph (a) of the definition
designated offence

Reasons for decision

(3) The court shall give reasons for its decision.

Removal of information from database

(4) If the court makes an exemption order, it shall also make an order requiring the Royal Canadian Mounted Police to permanently remove from the database all information that relates to the person that was registered in the database on receipt of the copy of the notice.

Notification

(5) If the court makes an order referred to in paragraph (2)(b), it shall cause the Commissioner of the Royal Canadian Mounted Police and the Attorney General of the province, or the minister of justice of the territory, in which the application for the order was made to be notified of the decision.
2010, c. 17, s. 19.

Appeal

490.02906 (1) The Attorney General or the person who applied for an exemption order may appeal from a decision under subsection 490.02905(2) on any ground of appeal that raises a question of law or of mixed law and fact. The appeal court may

(a) dismiss the appeal;

(b) allow the appeal and order a new hearing;

(c) quash the exemption order; or

(d) make an order that may be made under that subsection.

Removal of information from database

(2) If an appeal court makes an exemption order, it shall also make an order requiring the Royal Canadian Mounted Police to permanently remove from the database all information that relates to the person that was registered in the database on receipt of the copy of the notice.
2010, c. 17, s. 19.

Requirements relating to notice

490.02907 If an appeal court quashes an exemption order, it shall cause the Commissioner of the Royal Canadian Mounted Police and the Attorney General of the province, or the minister of justice of the territory, in which the application for the order was made to be notified of the decision and shall cause the person who applied for the order to be informed of sections 4 to 7.1 of the Sex Offender Information Registration Act
National Defence Act
2010, c. 17, s. 19.

Application for termination order

490.02908 (1) A person who is subject to an obligation under section 490.02901 may apply to a court of criminal jurisdiction for a termination order unless they are also subject to another obligation under that section — or to an obligation under section 490.019, under section 227.06 of the
National Defence Act
International Transfer of Offenders Act
National Defence Act

Time for application — one offence

(2) The person may apply for a termination order if the following period has elapsed since the sentence was imposed or the verdict of not criminally responsible on account of mental disorder was rendered:

(a) five years if the maximum term of imprisonment provided for in Canadian law for the equivalent offence is two or five years;

(b) 10 years if the maximum term of imprisonment provided for in Canadian law for the equivalent offence is 10 or 14 years; or

(c) 20 years if the maximum term of imprisonment provided for in Canadian law for the equivalent offence is life.

Time for application — more than one offence

(3) If more than one offence is listed in the notice served under section 490.02903, the person may apply for a termination order if 20 years have elapsed since the sentence was imposed, or the verdict of not criminally responsible on account of mental disorder was rendered, for the most recent offence.

Re-application

(4) A person whose application is refused may apply again if five years have elapsed since the application was made.

2010, c. 17, s. 19.

Termination order

490.02909 (1) The court shall make an order terminating the obligation if it is satisfied that the person has established that the impact on them of continuing the obligation, including on their privacy or liberty, would be grossly disproportionate to the public interest in protecting society through the effective prevention or investigation of crimes of a sexual nature to be achieved by the registration of information relating to sex offenders under the
Sex Offender Information Registration Act

Reasons for decision

(2) The court shall give reasons for its decision.

Requirements relating to notice

(3) If the court makes a termination order, it shall cause the Commissioner of the Royal Canadian Mounted Police and the Attorney General of the province, or the minister of justice of the territory, to be notified of the decision.

2010, c. 17, s. 19.

Appeal

490.0291 (1) The Attorney General or the person who applied for a termination order may appeal from a decision under subsection 490.02909(1) on any ground of appeal that raises a question of law or of mixed law and fact. The appeal court may dismiss the appeal, allow the appeal and order a new hearing, quash the termination order or make an order that may be made under that subsection.

Requirements relating to notice
(2) If the appeal court makes an order that may be made under subsection 490.02909(1), it shall cause the Commissioner of the Royal Canadian Mounted Police and the Attorney General of the province, or the minister of justice of the territory, in which the application for the order was made to be notified of the decision.
2010, c. 17, s. 19.
Obligation to advise police service
490.02911 (1) A person who was convicted of or found not criminally responsible on account of mental disorder for an offence outside Canada shall, if the offence is equivalent to one referred to in paragraph (a) of the definition
designated offence
Change in address
(2) The person shall, if they are in Canada, advise a police service of a change in address within seven days after the day on which the change is made.
Information to be provided to Attorney General
(3) The police service shall cause the Attorney General of the province, or the minister of justice of the territory, in which it is located to be provided with the information.
Obligation ends
(4) A person's obligation under subsection (2) ends when they are served under section 490.02902 or, if it is earlier, one year after the day on which they advise the police service under subsection (1).
2010, c. 17, s. 19.
International Transfer of Offenders Act
Application for termination order
490.02912 (1) A person who is subject to an obligation under section 36.1 of the
International Transfer of Offenders Act
National Defence Act
Time for application — one offence
(2) The person may apply for a termination order if the following period has elapsed since the sentence was imposed or the verdict of not criminally responsible on account of mental disorder was rendered:
(a) five years if the maximum term of imprisonment provided for in Canadian law for the equivalent offence is two or five years;
(b) 10 years if the maximum term of imprisonment provided for in Canadian law for the equivalent offence is 10 or 14 years; or
(c) 20 years if the maximum term of imprisonment provided for in Canadian law for the equivalent offence is life.
More than one offence
(3) If more than one offence is listed in the copy of the Form 1 that was delivered under subparagraph 8(4)(a)(ii) of the
International Transfer of Offenders Act
Re-application
(4) A person whose application is refused may apply again if five years have elapsed since the application was made.
2010, c. 17, s. 19.
Termination order
490.02913 (1) The court shall make an order terminating the obligation if it is satisfied that the person has established that the impact on them of continuing the obligation, including on their privacy or liberty, would be grossly disproportionate to the public interest in protecting society through the effective prevention or investigation of crimes of a sexual nature to be achieved by the registration of information relating to sex offenders under the
Sex Offender Information Registration Act
Reasons for decision

(2) The court shall give reasons for its decision.
Requirements relating to notice
(3) If the court makes a termination order, it shall cause the Commissioner of the Royal Canadian Mounted Police and the Attorney General of the province, or the minister of justice of the territory, to be notified of the decision.
2010, c. 17, s. 19.
Appeal
490.02914 (1) The Attorney General or the person who applied for a termination order may appeal from a decision under subsection 490.02913(1) on any ground of appeal that raises a question of law or of mixed law and fact. The appeal court may dismiss the appeal, allow the appeal and order a new hearing, quash the termination order or make an order that may be made under that subsection.
Requirements relating to notice
(2) If the appeal court makes an order that may be made under subsection 490.02913(1), it shall cause the Commissioner of the Royal Canadian Mounted Police and the Attorney General of the province, or the minister of justice of the territory, in which the application for the order was made to be notified of the decision.
2010, c. 17, s. 19.
Notice before release
490.02915 (1) The person in charge of the place in which a person who is subject to an obligation under section 36.1 of the
International Transfer of Offenders Act
Notice on disposition by Review Board
(2) A Review Board shall cause a copy of the Form 1 to be given to the person when it directs
(a) under paragraph 672.54(a), that the person be discharged absolutely; or
(b) under paragraph 672.54(b), that the person be discharged subject to conditions unless the conditions restrict the person's liberty in a manner and to an extent that prevent them from complying with sections 4, 4.1, 4.3 and 6 of the
Sex Offender Information Registration Act
2010, c. 17, s. 19.

Disclosure of Information

Disclosure
490.03 (1) The Commissioner of the Royal Canadian Mounted Police or a person authorized by the Commissioner shall, on request, disclose information that is registered in the database or the fact that such information is registered in the database
(a) to the prosecutor if the disclosure is necessary for the purpose of a proceeding under section 490.012; or
(b) to the Attorney General if the disclosure is necessary for the purpose of a proceeding under subsection 490.016(1), 490.023(2), 490.027(1), 490.02905(2), 490.02909(1) or 490.02913(1) or for the purpose of an appeal from a decision made in any of those proceedings or in a proceeding under subsection 490.012(2).
Disclosure in connection with proceedings
(2) The Commissioner or that person shall, on request, disclose to the prosecutor or Attorney General the information that is registered in the database relating to a person if the person discloses, in connection with a proceeding or appeal other than one referred to in subsection (1), the fact that information relating to them is registered in the database.
Disclosure in proceedings
(3) The prosecutor or the Attorney General may, if the information is relevant to the proceeding, appeal or any subsequent appeal, disclose it to the presiding court.
(4) 2004, c. 10, s. 20;
2007, c. 5, s. 27;

2010, c. 17, s. 20.

Offences

Offence

490.031 (1) Every person who, without reasonable excuse, fails to comply with an order made under section 490.012 or under section 227.01 of the
National Defence Act
International Transfer of Offenders Act
(a) on conviction on indictment, to a fine of not more than $10,000 or to imprisonment for a term of not more than two years, or to both; or
(b) on summary conviction, to a fine of not more than $10,000 or to imprisonment for a term of not more than six months, or to both.

Reasonable excuse

(2) For greater certainty, a lawful command that prevents a person from complying with an order or obligation is a reasonable excuse if, at the time, the person is subject to the Code of Service Discipline within the meaning of subsection 2(1) of the
National Defence Act

Proof of certain facts by certificate

(3) In proceedings under subsection (1), a certificate of a person referred to in paragraph 16(2)(b) of the
Sex Offender Information Registration Act

Attendance and cross-examination

(4) The sex offender named in the certificate may, with the leave of the court, require the attendance of the person who signed it for the purpose of cross-examination.

Notice of intention to produce

(5) A certificate is not to be received in evidence unless, before the commencement of the trial, the party who intends to produce it gives the sex offender a copy of it and reasonable notice of their intention to produce it.

2004, c. 10, s. 20;
2007, c. 5, s. 28;
2010, c. 17, s. 21.

Offence

490.0311 Every person who knowingly provides false or misleading information under subsection 5(1) or 6(1) of the
Sex Offender Information Registration Act
(a) on conviction on indictment, to a fine of not more than $10,000 or to imprisonment for a term of not more than two years, or to both; or
(b) on summary conviction, to a fine of not more than $10,000 or to imprisonment for a term of not more than six months, or to both.

2007, c. 5, s. 29;
2010, c. 17, s. 22.

Offence

490.0312 Every person who, without reasonable excuse, fails to comply with an obligation under subsection 490.02911(1) or (2) is guilty of an offence punishable on summary conviction.
2010, c. 17, s. 23.

Regulations

Regulations

490.032 The Governor in Council may make regulations
(a) requiring that additional information be contained in a notice under Form 53 or Form 54; and

(b) prescribing, for one or more provinces, the form and content of that information.
2004, c. 10, s. 20;
2010, c. 17, s. 24.

Forfeiture of Offence-related Property

Order of forfeiture of property on conviction
490.1 (1) Subject to sections 490.3 to 490.41, if a person is convicted of an indictable offence under this Act or the
Corruption of Foreign Public Officials Act
(a) where the prosecution of the offence was commenced at the instance of the government of a province and conducted by or on behalf of that government, order that the property be forfeited to Her Majesty in right of that province and disposed of by the Attorney General or Solicitor General of that province in accordance with the law; and
(b) in any other case, order that the property be forfeited to Her Majesty in right of Canada and disposed of by the member of the Queen's Privy Council for Canada that may be designated for the purpose of this paragraph in accordance with the law.
(1.1) Property related to other offences
(2) Subject to sections 490.3 to 490.41, if the evidence does not establish to the satisfaction of the court that the indictable offence under this Act or the
Corruption of Foreign Public Officials Act
Property outside Canada
(2.1) An order may be issued under this section in respect of property situated outside Canada, with any modifications that the circumstances require.
Appeal
(3) A person who has been convicted of an indictable offence under this Act or the
Corruption of Foreign Public Officials Act
1997, c. 23, s. 15;
2001, c. 32, s. 30, c. 41, ss. 18, 130;
2007, c. 13, s. 8.
Application for
490.2 (1) If an information has been laid in respect of an indictable offence under this Act or the
Corruption of Foreign Public Officials Act
Order of forfeiture of property
(2) Subject to sections 490.3 to 490.41, the judge to whom an application is made under subsection (1) shall order that the property that is subject to the application be forfeited and disposed of in accordance with subsection (4) if the judge is satisfied
(a) beyond a reasonable doubt that the property is offence-related property;
(b) that proceedings in respect of an indictable offence under this Act or the
Corruption of Foreign Public Officials Act
(c) that the accused charged with the offence has died or absconded.
Accused deemed absconded
(3) For the purpose of subsection (2), an accused is deemed to have absconded in connection with the indictable offence if
(a) an information has been laid alleging the commission of the offence by the accused,
(b) a warrant for the arrest of the accused has been issued in relation to that information, and
(c) reasonable attempts to arrest the accused under the warrant have been unsuccessful during a period of six months beginning on the day on which the warrant was issued,
and the accused is deemed to have so absconded on the last day of that six month period.
Who may dispose of forfeited property
(4) For the purpose of subsection (2), the judge shall
(a) where the prosecution of the offence was commenced at the instance of the government of a

province and conducted by or on behalf of that government, order that the property be forfeited to Her Majesty in right of that province and disposed of by the Attorney General or Solicitor General of that province in accordance with the law; and

(b) in any other case, order that the property be forfeited to Her Majesty in right of Canada and disposed of by the member of the Queen's Privy Council for Canada that may be designated for the purpose of this paragraph in accordance with the law.

Property outside Canada

(4.1) An order may be issued under this section in respect of property situated outside Canada, with any modifications that the circumstances require.

Definition of

judge

(5) In this section and sections 490.5 and 490.8,

judge

1997, c. 23, s. 15;
2001, c. 32, s. 31;
2007, c. 13, s. 9.

Voidable transfers

490.3 A court may, before ordering that offence-related property be forfeited under subsection 490.1(1) or 490.2(2), set aside any conveyance or transfer of the property that occurred after the seizure of the property, or the making of a restraint order in respect of the property, unless the conveyance or transfer was for valuable consideration to a person acting in good faith.

1997, c. 23, s. 15.

Notice

490.4 (1) Before making an order under subsection 490.1(1) or 490.2(2) in relation to any property, a court shall require notice in accordance with subsection (2) to be given to, and may hear, any person who, in the opinion of the court, appears to have a valid interest in the property.

Manner of giving notice

(2) A notice given under subsection (1) shall

(a) be given or served in the manner that the court directs or that may be specified in the rules of the court;

(b) be of any duration that the court considers reasonable or that may be specified in the rules of the court; and

(c) set out the offence charged and a description of the property.

Order of restoration of property

(3) A court may order that all or part of the property that would otherwise be forfeited under subsection 490.1(1) or 490.2(2) be returned to a person — other than a person who was charged with an indictable offence under this Act or the

Corruption of Foreign Public Officials Act

1997, c. 23, s. 15;
2001, c. 32, s. 32;
2007, c. 13, s. 10.

Notice

490.41 (1) If all or part of offence-related property that would otherwise be forfeited under subsection 490.1(1) or 490.2(2) is a dwelling-house, before making an order of forfeiture, a court shall require that notice in accordance with subsection (2) be given to, and may hear, any person who resides in the dwelling-house and is a member of the immediate family of the person charged with or convicted of the indictable offence under this Act or the

Corruption of Foreign Public Officials Act

Manner of giving notice

(2) A notice shall

(a) be given or served in the manner that the court directs or that may be specified in the rules of the court;

(b) be of any duration that the court considers reasonable or that may be specified in the rules of the court; and

(c) set out the offence charged and a description of the property.

Non-forfeiture of property

(3) Subject to an order made under subsection 490.4(3), if a court is satisfied that the impact of an order of forfeiture made under subsection 490.1(1) or 490.2(2) would be disproportionate to the nature and gravity of the offence, the circumstances surrounding the commission of the offence and the criminal record, if any, of the person charged with or convicted of the offence, as the case may be, it may decide not to order the forfeiture of the property or part of the property and may revoke any restraint order made in respect of that property or part.

Factors in relation to dwelling-house

(4) Where all or part of the property that would otherwise be forfeited under subsection 490.1(1) or 490.2(2) is a dwelling-house, when making a decision under subsection (3), the court shall also consider

(a) the impact of an order of forfeiture on any member of the immediate family of the person charged with or convicted of the offence, if the dwelling-house was the member's principal residence at the time the charge was laid and continues to be the member's principal residence; and

(b) whether the member referred to in paragraph (a) appears innocent of any complicity in the offence or of any collusion in relation to the offence.

2001, c. 32, s. 33;

2007, c. 13, s. 11.

Application

490.5 (1) Where any offence-related property is forfeited to Her Majesty pursuant to an order made under subsection 490.1(1) or 490.2(2), any person who claims an interest in the property, other than

(a) in the case of property forfeited pursuant to an order made under subsection 490.1(1), a person who was convicted of the indictable offence in relation to which the property was forfeited,

(b) in the case of property forfeited pursuant to an order made under subsection 490.2(2), a person who was charged with the indictable offence in relation to which the property was forfeited, or

(c) a person who acquired title to or a right of possession of the property from a person referred to in paragraph (a) or (b) under circumstances that give rise to a reasonable inference that the title or right was transferred from that person for the purpose of avoiding the forfeiture of the property,

may, within thirty days after the forfeiture, apply by notice in writing to a judge for an order under subsection (4).

Fixing day for hearing

(2) The judge to whom an application is made under subsection (1) shall fix a day not less than thirty days after the date of the filing of the application for the hearing of the application.

Notice

(3) An applicant shall serve a notice of the application made under subsection (1) and of the hearing of it on the Attorney General at least fifteen days before the day fixed for the hearing.

Order declaring interest not affected by forfeiture

(4) Where, on the hearing of an application made under subsection (1), the judge is satisfied that the applicant

(a) is not a person referred to in paragraph (1)(a), (b) or (c) and appears innocent of any complicity in any indictable offence that resulted in the forfeiture of the property or of any collusion in relation to such an offence, and

(b) exercised all reasonable care to be satisfied that the property was not likely to have been used in connection with the commission of an unlawful act by the person who was permitted by the applicant to obtain possession of the property or from whom the applicant obtained possession or, where the applicant is a mortgagee or lienholder, by the mortgagor or lien-giver,

the judge may make an order declaring that the interest of the applicant is not affected by the forfeiture and declaring the nature and the extent or value of the interest.

Appeal from order made under subsection (4)

(5) An applicant or the Attorney General may appeal to the court of appeal from an order made under subsection (4), and the provisions of Part XXI with respect to procedure on appeals apply, with any modifications that the circumstances require, in respect of appeals under this subsection.

Return of property

(6) The Attorney General shall, on application made to the Attorney General by any person in respect of whom a judge has made an order under subsection (4), and where the periods with respect to the taking of appeals from that order have expired and any appeal from that order taken under subsection (5) has been determined, direct that

(a) the property, or the part of it to which the interest of the applicant relates, be returned to the applicant; or

(b) an amount equal to the value of the interest of the applicant, as declared in the order, be paid to the applicant.

1997, c. 23, s. 15;
2001, c. 32, s. 34.

Appeals from orders under subsection 490.2(2)

490.6 Any person who, in their opinion, is aggrieved by an order made under subsection 490.2(2) may appeal from the order as if the order were an appeal against conviction or against a judgment or verdict of acquittal, as the case may be, under Part XXI, and that Part applies, with any modifications that the circumstances require, in respect of such an appeal.

1997, c. 23, s. 15.

Suspension of order pending appeal

490.7 Notwithstanding anything in this Act, the operation of an order made in respect of property under subsection 490.1(1), 490.2(2) or 490.5(4) is suspended pending

(a) any application made in respect of the property under any of those provisions or any other provision of this or any other Act of Parliament that provides for restoration or forfeiture of the property, or

(b) any appeal taken from an order of forfeiture or restoration in respect of the property,

and the property shall not be disposed of or otherwise dealt with until thirty days have expired after an order is made under any of those provisions.

1997, c. 23, s. 15.

Application for restraint order

490.8 (1) The Attorney General may make an application in accordance with this section for a restraint order under this section in respect of any offence-related property.

Procedure

(2) An application made under subsection (1) for a restraint order in respect of any offence-related property may be made

(a) the indictable offence to which the offence-related property relates;

(b) the person who is believed to be in possession of the offence-related property; and

(c) a description of the offence-related property.

Restraint order

(3) Where an application for a restraint order is made to a judge under subsection (1), the judge may, if satisfied that there are reasonable grounds to believe that the property is offence-related property, make a restraint order prohibiting any person from disposing of, or otherwise dealing with any interest in, the offence-related property specified in the order otherwise than in the manner that may be specified in the order.

Property outside Canada

(3.1) A restraint order may be issued under this section in respect of property situated outside Canada, with any modifications that the circumstances require.

Conditions

(4) A restraint order made by a judge under this section may be subject to any reasonable conditions that the judge thinks fit.

Order in writing

(5) A restraint order made under this section shall be made in writing.
Service of order
(6) A copy of a restraint order made under this section shall be served on the person to whom the order is addressed in any manner that the judge making the order directs or in accordance with the rules of the court.
Registration of order
(7) A copy of a restraint order made under this section shall be registered against any property in accordance with the laws of the province in which the property is situated.
Order continues in force
(8) A restraint order made under this section remains in effect until

(a) an order is made under subsection 490(9) or (11), 490.4(3) or 490.41(3) in relation to the property; or

(b) an order of forfeiture of the property is made under section 490 or subsection 490.1(1) or 490.2(2).

Offence
(9) Any person on whom a restraint order made under this section is served in accordance with this section and who, while the order is in force, acts in contravention of or fails to comply with the order is guilty of an indictable offence or an offence punishable on summary conviction.

1997, c. 23, s. 15;
2001, c. 32, s. 35.

Management order
490.81 (1) With respect to offence-related property other than a controlled substance within the meaning of the

Controlled Drugs and Substances Act

(a) appoint a person to take control of and to manage or otherwise deal with all or part of the property in accordance with the directions of the judge or justice; and

(b) require any person having possession of that property to give possession of the property to the person appointed under paragraph (a).

Appointment of Minister of Public Works and Government Services
(2) When the Attorney General of Canada so requests, a judge or justice appointing a person under subsection (1) shall appoint the Minister of Public Works and Government Services.

Power to manage
(3) The power to manage or otherwise deal with property under subsection (1) includes

(a) in the case of perishable or rapidly depreciating property, the power to make an interlocutory sale of that property; and

(b) in the case of property that has little or no value, the power to destroy that property.

Application for destruction order
(4) Before a person appointed to manage property destroys property that has little or no value, he or she shall apply to a court for a destruction order.

Notice
(5) Before making a destruction order in relation to any property, a court shall require notice in accordance with subsection (6) to be given to, and may hear, any person who, in the opinion of the court, appears to have a valid interest in the property.

Manner of giving notice
(6) A notice shall

(a) be given or served in the manner that the court directs or that may be specified in the rules of the court; and

(b) be of any duration that the court considers reasonable or that may be specified in the rules of the court.

Order
(7) A court may order that the property be destroyed if it is satisfied that the property has little or no value, whether financial or other.

When management order ceases to have effect
(8) A management order ceases to have effect when the property that is the subject of the management order is returned in accordance with the law to an applicant or forfeited to Her Majesty.
Application to vary conditions
(9) The Attorney General may at any time apply to the judge or justice to cancel or vary any condition to which a management order is subject, but may not apply to vary an appointment made under subsection (2).
2001, c. 32, s. 36.
Sections 489.1 and 490 applicable
490.9 (1) Subject to sections 490.1 to 490.7, sections 489.1 and 490 apply, with any modifications that the circumstances require, to any offence-related property that is the subject of a restraint order made under section 490.8.
Recognizance
(2) Where, pursuant to subsection (1), an order is made under paragraph 490(9)(c) for the return of any offence-related property that is the subject of a restraint order under section 490.8, the judge or justice making the order may require the applicant for the order to enter into a recognizance before the judge or justice, with or without sureties, in any amount and with any conditions that the judge or justice directs and, where the judge or justice considers it appropriate, require the applicant to deposit with the judge or justice any sum of money or other valuable security that the judge or justice directs.
1997, c. 23, s. 15.
Forfeiture of weapons and ammunition
491 (1) Subject to subsection (2), where it is determined by a court that
(a) a weapon, an imitation firearm, a prohibited device, any ammunition, any prohibited ammunition or an explosive substance was used in the commission of an offence and that thing has been seized and detained, or
(b) that a person has committed an offence that involves, or the subject-matter of which is, a firearm, a cross-bow, a prohibited weapon, a restricted weapon, a prohibited device, ammunition, prohibited ammunition or an explosive substance and any such thing has been seized and detained,
the thing so seized and detained is forfeited to Her Majesty and shall be disposed of as the Attorney General directs.
Return to lawful owner
(2) If the court by which a determination referred to in subsection (1) is made is satisfied that the lawful owner of any thing that is or may be forfeited to Her Majesty under subsection (1) was not a party to the offence and had no reasonable grounds to believe that the thing would or might be used in the commission of an offence, the court shall order that the thing be returned to that lawful owner, that the proceeds of any sale of the thing be paid to that lawful owner or, if the thing was destroyed, that an amount equal to the value of the thing be paid to the owner.
Application of proceeds
(3) Where any thing in respect of which this section applies is sold, the proceeds of the sale shall be paid to the Attorney General or, where an order is made under subsection (2), to the person who was, immediately prior to the sale, the lawful owner of the thing.
R.S., 1985, c. C-46, s. 491;
1991, c. 40, s. 30;
1995, c. 39, s. 152.
Order for restitution or forfeiture of property obtained by crime
491.1 (1) Where an accused or defendant is tried for an offence and the court determines that an offence has been committed, whether or not the accused has been convicted or discharged under section 730 of the offence, and at the time of the trial any property obtained by the commission of the offence
(a) is before the court or has been detained so that it can be immediately dealt with, and
(b) will not be required as evidence in any other proceedings,
section 490 does not apply in respect of the property and the court shall make an order under

subsection (2) in respect of the property.
Idem
(2) In the circumstances referred to in subsection (1), the court shall order, in respect of any property,
(a) if the lawful owner or person lawfully entitled to possession of the property is known, that it be returned to that person; and
(b) if the lawful owner or person lawfully entitled to possession of the property is not known, that it be forfeited to Her Majesty, to be disposed of as the Attorney General directs or otherwise dealt with in accordance with the law.
When certain orders not to be made
(3) An order shall not be made under subsection (2)
(a) in the case of proceedings against a trustee, banker, merchant, attorney, factor, broker or other agent entrusted with the possession of goods or documents of title to goods, for an offence under section 330, 331, 332 or 336; or
(b) in respect of
(i) property to which a person acting in good faith and without notice has acquired lawful title for valuable consideration,
(ii) a valuable security that has been paid or discharged in good faith by a person who was liable to pay or discharge it,
(iii) a negotiable instrument that has, in good faith, been taken or received by transfer or delivery for valuable consideration by a person who had no notice and no reasonable cause to suspect that an offence had been committed, or
(iv) property in respect of which there is a dispute as to ownership or right of possession by claimants other than the accused or defendant.
By whom order executed
(4) An order made under this section shall, on the direction of the court, be executed by the peace officers by whom the process of the court is ordinarily executed.
R.S., 1985, c. 27 (1st Supp.), s. 74, c. 1 (4th Supp.), s. 18(F);
1995, c. 22, s. 18;
2017, c. 7, s. 69(F).
Photographic evidence
491.2 (1) Before any property that would otherwise be required to be produced for the purposes of a preliminary inquiry, trial or other proceeding in respect of an offence under section 334, 344, 348, 354, 355.2, 355.4, 362 or 380 is returned or ordered to be returned, forfeited or otherwise dealt with under section 489.1 or 490 or is otherwise returned, a peace officer or any person under the direction of a peace officer may take and retain a photograph of the property.
Certified photograph admissible in evidence
(2) Every photograph of property taken under subsection (1), accompanied by a certificate of a person containing the statements referred to in subsection (3), shall be admissible in evidence and, in the absence of evidence to the contrary, shall have the same probative force as the property would have had if it had been proved in the ordinary way.
Statements made in certificate
(3) For the purposes of subsection (2), a certificate of a person stating that
(a) the person took the photograph under the authority of subsection (1),
(b) the person is a peace officer or took the photograph under the direction of a peace officer, and
(c) the photograph is a true photograph
shall be admissible in evidence and, in the absence of evidence to the contrary, is evidence of the statements contained in the certificate without proof of the signature of the person appearing to have signed the certificate.
Secondary evidence of peace officer
(4) An affidavit or solemn declaration of a peace officer or other person stating that the person has seized property and detained it or caused it to be detained from the time that person took possession of the property until a photograph of the property was taken under subsection (1) and that the

property was not altered in any manner before the photograph was taken shall be admissible in evidence and, in the absence of evidence to the contrary, is evidence of the statements contained in the affidavit or solemn declaration without proof of the signature or official character of the person appearing to have signed the affidavit or solemn declaration.

Notice of intention to produce certified photograph

(5) Unless the court orders otherwise, no photograph, certificate, affidavit or solemn declaration shall be received in evidence at a trial or other proceeding pursuant to subsection (2), (3) or (4) unless the prosecutor has, before the trial or other proceeding, given to the accused a copy thereof and reasonable notice of intention to produce it in evidence.

Attendance for examination

(6) Notwithstanding subsection (3) or (4), the court may require the person who appears to have signed a certificate, an affidavit or a solemn declaration referred to in that subsection to appear before it for examination or cross-examination in respect of the issue of proof of any of the facts contained in the certificate, affidavit or solemn declaration.

Production of property in court

(7) A court may order any property seized and returned pursuant to section 489.1 or 490 to be produced in court or made available for examination by all parties to a proceeding at a reasonable time and place, notwithstanding that a photograph of the property has been received in evidence pursuant to subsection (2), where the court is satisfied that the interests of justice so require and that it is possible and practicable to do so in the circumstances.

Definition of
photograph

(8) In this section,
photograph

R.S., 1985, c. 23 (4th Supp.), s. 2;
1992, c. 1, s. 58;
2010, c. 14, s. 10.

Seizure of explosives

492 (1) Every person who executes a warrant issued under section 487 or 487.1 may seize any explosive substance that he suspects is intended to be used for an unlawful purpose, and shall, as soon as possible, remove to a place of safety anything that he seizes by virtue of this section and detain it until he is ordered by a judge of a superior court to deliver it to some other person or an order is made pursuant to subsection (2).

Forfeiture

(2) Where an accused is convicted of an offence in respect of anything seized by virtue of subsection (1), it is forfeited and shall be dealt with as the court that makes the conviction may direct.

Application of proceeds

(3) Where anything to which this section applies is sold, the proceeds of the sale shall be paid to the Attorney General.

R.S., 1985, c. C-46, s. 492;
R.S., 1985, c. 27 (1st Supp.), s. 70.

Warrant for tracking device — transactions and things

492.1 (1) A justice or judge who is satisfied by information on oath that there are reasonable grounds to suspect that an offence has been or will be committed under this or any other Act of Parliament and that tracking the location of one or more transactions or the location or movement of a thing, including a vehicle, will assist in the investigation of the offence may issue a warrant authorizing a peace officer or a public officer to obtain that tracking data by means of a tracking device.

Warrant for tracking device — individuals

(2) A justice or judge who is satisfied by information on oath that there are reasonable grounds to believe that an offence has been or will be committed under this or any other Act of Parliament and that tracking an individual's movement by identifying the location of a thing that is usually carried or worn by the individual will assist in the investigation of the offence may issue a warrant authorizing

a peace officer or a public officer to obtain that tracking data by means of a tracking device.
Scope of warrant
(3) The warrant authorizes the peace officer or public officer, or a person acting under their direction, to install, activate, use, maintain, monitor and remove the tracking device, including covertly.
Conditions
(4) A warrant may contain any conditions that the justice or judge considers appropriate, including conditions to protect a person's interests.
Period of validity
(5) Subject to subsection (6), a warrant is valid for the period specified in it as long as that period ends no more than 60 days after the day on which the warrant is issued.
Period of validity — organized crime and terrorism offence
(6) A warrant is valid for the period specified in it as long as that period ends no more than one year after the day on which the warrant is issued, if the warrant relates to
(a) an offence under any of sections 467.11 to 467.13;
(b) an offence committed for the benefit of, at the direction of, or in association with a criminal organization; or
(c) a terrorism offence.
Removal after expiry of warrant
(7) On
Definitions
(8) The following definitions apply in this section.
data
judge
public officer
tracking data
tracking device
1993, c. 40, s. 18;
1999, c. 5, s. 18;
2014, c. 31, s. 23.
Warrant for transmission data recorder
492.2 (1) A justice or judge who is satisfied by information on oath that there are reasonable grounds to suspect that an offence has been or will be committed against this or any other Act of Parliament and that transmission data will assist in the investigation of the offence may issue a warrant authorizing a peace officer or a public officer to obtain the transmission data by means of a transmission data recorder.
Scope of warrant
(2) The warrant authorizes the peace officer or public officer, or a person acting under their direction, to install, activate, use, maintain, monitor and remove the transmission data recorder, including covertly.
Limitation
(3) No warrant shall be issued under this section for the purpose of obtaining tracking data.
Period of validity
(4) Subject to subsection (5), a warrant is valid for the period specified in it as long as that period ends no more than 60 days after the day on which the warrant is issued.
Period of validity — organized crime or terrorism offence
(5) The warrant is valid for the period specified in it as long as that period ends no more than one year after the day on which the warrant is issued, if the warrant relates to
(a) an offence under any of sections 467.11 to 467.13;
(b) an offence committed for the benefit of, at the direction of, or in association with a criminal organization; or
(c) a terrorism offence.
Definitions

(6) The following definitions apply in this section.
data
judge
public officer
transmission data
(a) relates to the telecommunication functions of dialling, routing, addressing or signalling;
(b) is transmitted to identify, activate or configure a device, including a computer program as defined in subsection 342.1(2), in order to establish or maintain access to a telecommunication service for the purpose of enabling a communication, or is generated during the creation, transmission or reception of a communication and identifies or purports to identify the type, direction, date, time, duration, size, origin, destination or termination of the communication; and
(c) does not reveal the substance, meaning or purpose of the communication.
transmission data recorder
1993, c. 40, s. 18;
1999, c. 5, s. 19;
2014, c. 31, s. 23.

PART XVI

PART XVI
Compelling Appearance of Accused Before a Justice and Interim Release

Interpretation

Definitions
493 In this Part,
accused
(a) a person to whom a peace officer has issued an appearance notice under section 496, and
(b) a person arrested for a criminal offence;
appearance notice
judge
(a) in the Province of Ontario, a judge of the superior court of criminal jurisdiction of the Province,
(b) in the Province of Quebec, a judge of the superior court of criminal jurisdiction of the province or three judges of the Court of Quebec,
(c) (d) in the Provinces of Nova Scotia, New Brunswick, Manitoba, British Columbia, Prince Edward Island, Saskatchewan, Alberta and Newfoundland and Labrador, a judge of the superior court of criminal jurisdiction of the Province,
(e) in Yukon and the Northwest Territories, a judge of the Supreme Court, and
(f) in Nunavut, a judge of the Nunavut Court of Justice;
officer in charge
promise to appear
recognizance
summons
undertaking
warrant
R.S., 1985, c. C-46, s. 493;
R.S., 1985, c. 11 (1st Supp.), s. 2, c. 27 (2nd Supp.), s. 10, c. 40 (4th Supp.), s. 2;
1990, c. 16, s. 5, c. 17, s. 12;
1992, c. 51, s. 37;
1994, c. 44, s. 39;
1999, c. 3, s. 30;
2002, c. 7, s. 143;

2015, c. 3, s. 51.

Arrest without Warrant and Release from Custody

Arrest without warrant by any person
494 (1) Any one may arrest without warrant
(a) a person whom he finds committing an indictable offence; or
(b) a person who, on reasonable grounds, he believes
(i) has committed a criminal offence, and
(ii) is escaping from and freshly pursued by persons who have lawful authority to arrest that person.

Arrest by owner, etc., of property
(2) The owner or a person in lawful possession of property, or a person authorized by the owner or by a person in lawful possession of property, may arrest a person without a warrant if they find them committing a criminal offence on or in relation to that property and
(a) they make the arrest at that time; or
(b) they make the arrest within a reasonable time after the offence is committed and they believe on reasonable grounds that it is not feasible in the circumstances for a peace officer to make the arrest.

Delivery to peace officer
(3) Any one other than a peace officer who arrests a person without warrant shall forthwith deliver the person to a peace officer.

For greater certainty
(4) For greater certainty, a person who is authorized to make an arrest under this section is a person who is authorized by law to do so for the purposes of section 25.
R.S., 1985, c. C-46, s. 494;
2012, c. 9, s. 3.

Arrest without warrant by peace officer
495 (1) A peace officer may arrest without warrant
(a) a person who has committed an indictable offence or who, on reasonable grounds, he believes has committed or is about to commit an indictable offence;
(b) a person whom he finds committing a criminal offence; or
(c) a person in respect of whom he has reasonable grounds to believe that a warrant of arrest or committal, in any form set out in Part XXVIII in relation thereto, is in force within the territorial jurisdiction in which the person is found.

Limitation
(2) A peace officer shall not arrest a person without warrant for
(a) an indictable offence mentioned in section 553,
(b) an offence for which the person may be prosecuted by indictment or for which he is punishable on summary conviction, or
(c) an offence punishable on summary conviction,
in any case where
(d) he believes on reasonable grounds that the public interest, having regard to all the circumstances including the need to
(i) establish the identity of the person,
(ii) secure or preserve evidence of or relating to the offence, or
(iii) prevent the continuation or repetition of the offence or the commission of another offence,
may be satisfied without so arresting the person, and
(e) he has no reasonable grounds to believe that, if he does not so arrest the person, the person will fail to attend court in order to be dealt with according to law.

Consequences of arrest without warrant
(3) Notwithstanding subsection (2), a peace officer acting under subsection (1) is deemed to be acting lawfully and in the execution of his duty for the purposes of
(a) any proceedings under this or any other Act of Parliament; and

(b) any other proceedings, unless in any such proceedings it is alleged and established by the person making the allegation that the peace officer did not comply with the requirements of subsection (2).
R.S., 1985, c. C-46, s. 495;
R.S., 1985, c. 27 (1st Supp.), s. 75.

Issue of appearance notice by peace officer

496 Where, by virtue of subsection 495(2), a peace officer does not arrest a person, he may issue an appearance notice to the person if the offence is
(a) an indictable offence mentioned in section 553;
(b) an offence for which the person may be prosecuted by indictment or for which he is punishable on summary conviction; or
(c) an offence punishable on summary conviction.
R.S., c. C-34, s. 451;
R.S., c. 2(2nd Supp.), s. 5.

Release from custody by peace officer

497 (1) Subject to subsection (1.1), if a peace officer arrests a person without warrant for an offence described in paragraph 496(a), (b) or (c), the peace officer shall, as soon as practicable,
(a) release the person from custody with the intention of compelling their appearance by way of summons; or
(b) issue an appearance notice to the person and then release them.

Exception

(1.1) A peace officer shall not release a person under subsection (1) if the peace officer believes, on reasonable grounds,
(a) that it is necessary in the public interest that the person be detained in custody or that the matter of their release from custody be dealt with under another provision of this Part, having regard to all the circumstances including the need to
(i) establish the identity of the person,
(ii) secure or preserve evidence of or relating to the offence,
(iii) prevent the continuation or repetition of the offence or the commission of another offence, or
(iv) ensure the safety and security of any victim of or witness to the offence; or
(b) that if the person is released from custody, the person will fail to attend court in order to be dealt with according to law.

Where subsection (1) does not apply

(2) Subsection (1) does not apply in respect of a person who has been arrested without warrant by a peace officer for an offence described in subsection 503(3).

Consequences of non-release

(3) A peace officer who has arrested a person without warrant for an offence described in subsection (1) and who does not release the person from custody as soon as practicable in the manner described in that subsection shall be deemed to be acting lawfully and in the execution of the peace officer's duty for the purposes of
(a) any proceedings under this or any other Act of Parliament; and
(b) any other proceedings, unless in any such proceedings it is alleged and established by the person making the allegation that the peace officer did not comply with the requirements of subsection (1).
R.S., 1985, c. C-46, s. 497;
1999, c. 25, s. 3(Preamble).

Release from custody by officer in charge

498 (1) Subject to subsection (1.1), if a person who has been arrested without warrant by a peace officer is taken into custody, or if a person who has been arrested without warrant and delivered to a peace officer under subsection 494(3) or placed in the custody of a peace officer under subsection 163.5(3) of the
Customs Act
(a) release the person with the intention of compelling their appearance by way of summons;
(b) release the person on their giving a promise to appear;

(c) release the person on the person's entering into a recognizance before the officer in charge or another peace officer without sureties in an amount not exceeding $500 that the officer directs, but without deposit of money or other valuable security; or

(d) if the person is not ordinarily resident in the province in which the person is in custody or does not ordinarily reside within 200 kilometres of the place in which the person is in custody, release the person on the person's entering into a recognizance before the officer in charge or another peace officer without sureties in an amount not exceeding $500 that the officer directs and, if the officer so directs, on depositing with the officer a sum of money or other valuable security not exceeding in amount or value $500, that the officer directs.

Exception

(1.1) The officer in charge or the peace officer shall not release a person under subsection (1) if the officer in charge or peace officer believes, on reasonable grounds,

(a) that it is necessary in the public interest that the person be detained in custody or that the matter of their release from custody be dealt with under another provision of this Part, having regard to all the circumstances including the need to

(i) establish the identity of the person,

(ii) secure or preserve evidence of or relating to the offence,

(iii) prevent the continuation or repetition of the offence or the commission of another offence, or

(iv) ensure the safety and security of any victim of or witness to the offence; or

(b) that, if the person is released from custody, the person will fail to attend court in order to be dealt with according to law.

Where subsection (1) does not apply

(2) Subsection (1) does not apply in respect of a person who has been arrested without warrant by a peace officer for an offence described in subsection 503(3).

Consequences of non-release

(3) An officer in charge or another peace officer who has the custody of a person taken into or detained in custody for an offence described in subsection (1) and who does not release the person from custody as soon as practicable in the manner described in that subsection shall be deemed to be acting lawfully and in the execution of the officer's duty for the purposes of

(a) any proceedings under this or any other Act of Parliament; or

(b) any other proceedings, unless in any such proceedings it is alleged and established by the person making the allegation that the officer in charge or other peace officer did not comply with the requirements of subsection (1).

R.S., 1985, c. C-46, s. 498;

R.S., 1985, c. 27 (1st Supp.), s. 186;

1997, c. 18, s. 52;

1998, c. 7, s. 2;

1999, c. 25, ss. 4, 30(Preamble).

Release from custody by officer in charge where arrest made with warrant

499 (1) Where a person who has been arrested with a warrant by a peace officer is taken into custody for an offence other than one mentioned in section 522, the officer in charge may, if the warrant has been endorsed by a justice under subsection 507(6),

(a) release the person on the person's giving a promise to appear;

(b) release the person on the person's entering into a recognizance before the officer in charge without sureties in the amount not exceeding five hundred dollars that the officer in charge directs, but without deposit of money or other valuable security; or

(c) if the person is not ordinarily resident in the province in which the person is in custody or does not ordinarily reside within two hundred kilometres of the place in which the person is in custody, release the person on the person's entering into a recognizance before the officer in charge without sureties in the amount not exceeding five hundred dollars that the officer in charge directs and, if the officer in charge so directs, on depositing with the officer in charge such sum of money or other valuable security not exceeding in amount or value five hundred dollars, as the officer in charge directs.

Additional conditions

(2) In addition to the conditions for release set out in paragraphs (1)(a), (b) and (c), the officer in charge may also require the person to enter into an undertaking in Form 11.1 in which the person, in order to be released, undertakes to do one or more of the following things:

(a) to remain within a territorial jurisdiction specified in the undertaking;

(b) to notify a peace officer or another person mentioned in the undertaking of any change in his or her address, employment or occupation;

(c) to abstain from communicating, directly or indirectly, with any victim, witness or other person identified in the undertaking, or from going to a place specified in the undertaking, except in accordance with the conditions specified in the undertaking;

(d) to deposit the person's passport with the peace officer or other person mentioned in the undertaking;

(e) to abstain from possessing a firearm and to surrender any firearm in the possession of the person and any authorization, licence or registration certificate or other document enabling that person to acquire or possess a firearm;

(f) to report at the times specified in the undertaking to a peace officer or other person designated in the undertaking;

(g) to abstain from

(i) the consumption of alcohol or other intoxicating substances, or

(ii) the consumption of drugs except in accordance with a medical prescription; and

(h) to comply with any other condition specified in the undertaking that the officer in charge considers necessary to ensure the safety and security of any victim of or witness to the offence.

Application to justice

(3) A person who has entered into an undertaking under subsection (2) may, at any time before or at his or her appearance pursuant to a promise to appear or recognizance, apply to a justice for an order under subsection 515(1) to replace his or her undertaking, and section 515 applies, with such modifications as the circumstances require, to such a person.

Application by prosecutor

(4) Where a person has entered into an undertaking under subsection (2), the prosecutor may

(a) at any time before the appearance of the person pursuant to a promise to appear or recognizance, after three days notice has been given to that person, or

(b) at the appearance,

apply to a justice for an order under subsection 515(2) to replace the undertaking, and section 515 applies, with such modifications as the circumstances require, to such a person.

R.S., 1985, c. C-46, s. 499;

R.S., 1985, c. 27 (1st Supp.), s. 186;

1994, c. 44, s. 40;

1997, c. 18, s. 53;

1999, c. 25, s. 5(Preamble).

Money or other valuable security to be deposited with justice

500 If a person has, under paragraph 498(1)(d) or 499(1)(c), deposited any sum of money or other valuable security with the officer in charge, the officer in charge shall, without delay after the deposit, cause the money or valuable security to be delivered to a justice for deposit with the justice.

R.S., 1985, c. C-46, s. 500;

1999, c. 5, s. 20, c. 25, s. 6(Preamble).

Contents of appearance notice, promise to appear and recognizance

501 (1) An appearance notice issued by a peace officer or a promise to appear given to, or a recognizance entered into before, an officer in charge or another peace officer shall

(a) set out the name of the accused;

(b) set out the substance of the offence that the accused is alleged to have committed; and

(c) require the accused to attend court at a time and place to be stated therein and to attend thereafter

as required by the court in order to be dealt with according to law.
Idem
(2) An appearance notice issued by a peace officer or a promise to appear given to, or a recognizance entered into before, an officer in charge or another peace officer shall set out the text of subsections 145(5) and (6) and section 502.
Attendance for purposes of
Identification of Criminals Act
(3) An appearance notice issued by a peace officer or a promise to appear given to, or a recognizance entered into before, an officer in charge or another peace officer may require the accused to appear at a time and place stated in it for the purposes of the
Identification of Criminals Act
Contraventions Act
Signature of accused
(4) An accused shall be requested to sign in duplicate his appearance notice, promise to appear or recognizance and, whether or not he complies with that request, one of the duplicates shall be given to the accused, but if the accused fails or refuses to sign, the lack of his signature does not invalidate the appearance notice, promise to appear or recognizance, as the case may be.
(5) R.S., 1985, c. C-46, s. 501;
R.S., 1985, c. 27 (1st Supp.), s. 76;
1992, c. 47, s. 69;
1994, c. 44, ss. 41, 94;
1996, c. 7, s. 38;
2008, c. 18, s. 15.
Failure to appear
502 Where an accused who is required by an appearance notice or promise to appear or by a recognizance entered into before an officer in charge or another peace officer to appear at a time and place stated therein for the purposes of the
Identification of Criminals Act
R.S., 1985, c. C-46, s. 502;
1992, c. 47, s. 70;
1996, c. 7, s. 38;
1997, c. 18, s. 54.

Appearance of Accused before Justice

Taking before justice
503 (1) A peace officer who arrests a person with or without warrant or to whom a person is delivered under subsection 494(3) or into whose custody a person is placed under subsection 163.5(3) of the
Customs Act
(a) where a justice is available within a period of twenty-four hours after the person has been arrested by or delivered to the peace officer, the person shall be taken before a justice without unreasonable delay and in any event within that period, and
(b) where a justice is not available within a period of twenty-four hours after the person has been arrested by or delivered to the peace officer, the person shall be taken before a justice as soon as possible,
unless, at any time before the expiration of the time prescribed in paragraph (a) or (b) for taking the person before a justice,
(c) the peace officer or officer in charge releases the person under any other provision of this Part, or
(d) the peace officer or officer in charge is satisfied that the person should be released from custody, whether unconditionally under subsection (4) or otherwise conditionally or unconditionally, and so releases him.

Conditional release
(2) If a peace officer or an officer in charge is satisfied that a person described in subsection (1) should be released from custody conditionally, the officer may, unless the person is detained in custody for an offence mentioned in section 522, release that person on the person's giving a promise to appear or entering into a recognizance in accordance with paragraphs 498(1)(b) to (d) and subsection (2.1).

Undertaking
(2.1) In addition to the conditions referred to in subsection (2), the peace officer or officer in charge may, in order to release the person, require the person to enter into an undertaking in Form 11.1 in which the person undertakes to do one or more of the following things:
(a) to remain within a territorial jurisdiction specified in the undertaking;
(b) to notify the peace officer or another person mentioned in the undertaking of any change in his or her address, employment or occupation;
(c) to abstain from communicating, directly or indirectly, with any victim, witness or other person identified in the undertaking, or from going to a place specified in the undertaking, except in accordance with the conditions specified in the undertaking;
(d) to deposit the person's passport with the peace officer or other person mentioned in the undertaking;
(e) to abstain from possessing a firearm and to surrender any firearm in the possession of the person and any authorization, licence or registration certificate or other document enabling that person to acquire or possess a firearm;
(f) to report at the times specified in the undertaking to a peace officer or other person designated in the undertaking;
(g) to abstain from
(i) the consumption of alcohol or other intoxicating substances, or
(ii) the consumption of drugs except in accordance with a medical prescription; or
(h) to comply with any other condition specified in the undertaking that the peace officer or officer in charge considers necessary to ensure the safety and security of any victim of or witness to the offence.

Application to justice
(2.2) A person who has entered into an undertaking under subsection (2.1) may, at any time before or at his or her appearance pursuant to a promise to appear or recognizance, apply to a justice for an order under subsection 515(1) to replace his or her undertaking, and section 515 applies, with such modifications as the circumstances require, to such a person.

Application by prosecutor
(2.3) Where a person has entered into an undertaking under subsection (2.1), the prosecutor may
(a) at any time before the appearance of the person pursuant to a promise to appear or recognizance, after three days notice has been given to that person, or
(b) at the appearance,
apply to a justice for an order under subsection 515(2) to replace the undertaking, and section 515 applies, with such modifications as the circumstances require, to such a person.

Remand in custody for return to jurisdiction where offence alleged to have been committed
(3) Where a person has been arrested without warrant for an indictable offence alleged to have been committed in Canada outside the territorial division where the arrest took place, the person shall, within the time prescribed in paragraph (1)(a) or (b), be taken before a justice within whose jurisdiction the person was arrested unless, where the offence was alleged to have been committed within the province in which the person was arrested, the person was taken before a justice within whose jurisdiction the offence was alleged to have been committed, and the justice within whose jurisdiction the person was arrested
(a) if the justice is not satisfied that there are reasonable grounds to believe that the person arrested is the person alleged to have committed the offence, shall release that person; or
(b) if the justice is satisfied that there are reasonable grounds to believe that the person arrested is the

person alleged to have committed the offence, may
(i) remand the person to the custody of a peace officer to await execution of a warrant for his or her arrest in accordance with section 528, but if no warrant is so executed within a period of six days after the time he or she is remanded to such custody, the person in whose custody he or she then is shall release him or her, or
(ii) where the offence was alleged to have been committed within the province in which the person was arrested, order the person to be taken before a justice having jurisdiction with respect to the offence.

Interim release
(3.1) Notwithstanding paragraph (3)(b), a justice may, with the consent of the prosecutor, order that the person referred to in subsection (3), pending the execution of a warrant for the arrest of that person, be released
(a) unconditionally; or
(b) on any of the following terms to which the prosecutor consents, namely,
(i) giving an undertaking, including an undertaking to appear at a specified time before the court that has jurisdiction with respect to the indictable offence that the person is alleged to have committed, or
(ii) entering into a recognizance described in any of paragraphs 515(2)(a) to (e)
with such conditions described in subsection 515(4) as the justice considers desirable and to which the prosecutor consents.

Release of person about to commit indictable offence
(4) A peace officer or an officer in charge having the custody of a person who has been arrested without warrant as a person about to commit an indictable offence shall release that person unconditionally as soon as practicable after he is satisfied that the continued detention of that person in custody is no longer necessary in order to prevent the commission by him of an indictable offence.

Consequences of non-release
(5) Notwithstanding subsection (4), a peace officer or an officer in charge having the custody of a person referred to in that subsection who does not release the person before the expiration of the time prescribed in paragraph (1)(a) or (b) for taking the person before the justice shall be deemed to be acting lawfully and in the execution of his duty for the purposes of
(a) any proceedings under this or any other Act of Parliament; or
(b) any other proceedings, unless in such proceedings it is alleged and established by the person making the allegation that the peace officer or officer in charge did not comply with the requirements of subsection (4).
R.S., 1985, c. C-46, s. 503;
R.S., 1985, c. 27 (1st Supp.), s. 77;
1994, c. 44, s. 42;
1997, c. 18, s. 55;
1998, c. 7, s. 3;
1999, c. 25, s. 7(Preamble).

Information, Summons and Warrant

In what cases justice may receive information
504 Any one who, on reasonable grounds, believes that a person has committed an indictable offence may lay an information in writing and under oath before a justice, and the justice shall receive the information, where it is alleged
(a) that the person has committed, anywhere, an indictable offence that may be tried in the province in which the justice resides, and that the person
(i) is or is believed to be, or
(ii) resides or is believed to reside,
within the territorial jurisdiction of the justice;
(b) that the person, wherever he may be, has committed an indictable offence within the territorial

jurisdiction of the justice;
(c) that the person has, anywhere, unlawfully received property that was unlawfully obtained within the territorial jurisdiction of the justice; or
(d) that the person has in his possession stolen property within the territorial jurisdiction of the justice.
R.S., c. C-34, s. 455;
R.S., c. 2(2nd Supp.), s. 5.

Time within which information to be laid in certain cases
505 Where
(a) an appearance notice has been issued to an accused under section 496, or
(b) an accused has been released from custody under section 497 or 498,
an information relating to the offence alleged to have been committed by the accused or relating to an included or other offence alleged to have been committed by him shall be laid before a justice as soon as practicable thereafter and in any event before the time stated in the appearance notice, promise to appear or recognizance issued to or given or entered into by the accused for his attendance in court.
R.S., c. 2(2nd Supp.), s. 5.

Form
506 An information laid under section 504 or 505 may be in Form 2.
R.S., c. 2(2nd Supp.), s. 5.

Justice to hear informant and witnesses — public prosecutions
507 (1) Subject to subsection 523(1.1), a justice who receives an information laid under section 504 by a peace officer, a public officer, the Attorney General or the Attorney General's agent, other than an information laid before the justice under section 505, shall, except if an accused has already been arrested with or without a warrant,
(a) hear and consider,
(i) the allegations of the informant, and
(ii) the evidence of witnesses, where he considers it desirable or necessary to do so; and
(b) where he considers that a case for so doing is made out, issue, in accordance with this section, either a summons or a warrant for the arrest of the accused to compel the accused to attend before him or some other justice for the same territorial division to answer to a charge of an offence.

Process compulsory
(2) No justice shall refuse to issue a summons or warrant by reason only that the alleged offence is one for which a person may be arrested without warrant.

Procedure when witnesses attend
(3) A justice who hears the evidence of a witness pursuant to subsection (1) shall
(a) take the evidence on oath; and
(b) cause the evidence to be taken in accordance with section 540 in so far as that section is capable of being applied.

Summons to be issued except in certain cases
(4) Where a justice considers that a case is made out for compelling an accused to attend before him to answer to a charge of an offence, he shall issue a summons to the accused unless the allegations of the informant or the evidence of any witness or witnesses taken in accordance with subsection (3) discloses reasonable grounds to believe that it is necessary in the public interest to issue a warrant for the arrest of the accused.

No process in blank
(5) A justice shall not sign a summons or warrant in blank.

Endorsement of warrant by justice
(6) A justice who issues a warrant under this section or section 508 or 512 may, unless the offence is one mentioned in section 522, authorize the release of the accused pursuant to section 499 by making an endorsement on the warrant in Form 29.

Promise to appear or recognizance deemed to have been confirmed

(7) Where, pursuant to subsection (6), a justice authorizes the release of an accused pursuant to section 499, a promise to appear given by the accused or a recognizance entered into by the accused pursuant to that section shall be deemed, for the purposes of subsection 145(5), to have been confirmed by a justice under section 508.

Issue of summons or warrant

(8) Where, on an appeal from or review of any decision or matter of jurisdiction, a new trial or hearing or a continuance or renewal of a trial or hearing is ordered, a justice may issue either a summons or a warrant for the arrest of the accused in order to compel the accused to attend at the new or continued or renewed trial or hearing.

R.S., 1985, c. C-46, s. 507;
R.S., 1985, c. 27 (1st Supp.), s. 78;
1994, c. 44, s. 43;
2002, c. 13, s. 21.

Referral when private prosecution

507.1 (1) A justice who receives an information laid under section 504, other than an information referred to in subsection 507(1), shall refer it to a provincial court judge or, in Quebec, a judge of the Court of Quebec, or to a designated justice, to consider whether to compel the appearance of the accused on the information.

Summons or warrant

(2) A judge or designated justice to whom an information is referred under subsection (1) and who considers that a case for doing so is made out shall issue either a summons or warrant for the arrest of the accused to compel him or her to attend before a justice to answer to a charge of the offence charged in the information.

Conditions for issuance

(3) The judge or designated justice may issue a summons or warrant only if he or she
(a) has heard and considered the allegations of the informant and the evidence of witnesses;
(b) is satisfied that the Attorney General has received a copy of the information;
(c) is satisfied that the Attorney General has received reasonable notice of the hearing under paragraph (a); and
(d) has given the Attorney General an opportunity to attend the hearing under paragraph (a) and to cross-examine and call witnesses and to present any relevant evidence at the hearing.

Appearance of Attorney General

(4) The Attorney General may appear at the hearing held under paragraph (3)(a) without being deemed to intervene in the proceeding.

Information deemed not to have been laid

(5) If the judge or designated justice does not issue a summons or warrant under subsection (2), he or she shall endorse the information with a statement to that effect. Unless the informant, not later than six months after the endorsement, commences proceedings to compel the judge or designated justice to issue a summons or warrant, the information is deemed never to have been laid.

Information deemed not to have been laid — proceedings commenced

(6) If proceedings are commenced under subsection (5) and a summons or warrant is not issued as a result of those proceedings, the information is deemed never to have been laid.

New evidence required for new hearing

(7) If a hearing in respect of an offence has been held under paragraph (3)(a) and the judge or designated justice has not issued a summons or a warrant, no other hearings may be held under that paragraph with respect to the offence or an included offence unless there is new evidence in support of the allegation in respect of which the hearing is sought to be held.

Subsections 507(2) to (8) to apply

(8) Subsections 507(2) to (8) apply to proceedings under this section.

Non-application — informations laid under sections 810 and 810.1

(9) Subsections (1) to (8) do not apply in respect of an information laid under section 810 or 810.1.

Definition of

(10) In this section,
designated justice
Meaning of
(11) In this section,
Attorney General
2002, c. 13, s. 22;
2008, c. 18, s. 16.
Justice to hear informant and witnesses
508 (1) A justice who receives an information laid before him under section 505 shall
(a) hear and consider,
(i) the allegations of the informant, and
(ii) the evidence of witnesses, where he considers it desirable or necessary to do so;
(b) where he considers that a case for so doing is made out, whether the information relates to the offence alleged in the appearance notice, promise to appear or recognizance or to an included or other offence,
(i) confirm the appearance notice, promise to appear or recognizance, as the case may be, and endorse the information accordingly, or
(ii) cancel the appearance notice, promise to appear or recognizance, as the case may be, and issue, in accordance with section 507, either a summons or a warrant for the arrest of the accused to compel the accused to attend before him or some other justice for the same territorial division to answer to a charge of an offence and endorse on the summons or warrant that the appearance notice, promise to appear or recognizance, as the case may be, has been cancelled; and
(c) where he considers that a case is not made out for the purposes of paragraph (b), cancel the appearance notice, promise to appear or recognizance, as the case may be, and cause the accused to be notified forthwith of the cancellation.
Procedure when witnesses attend
(2) A justice who hears the evidence of a witness pursuant to subsection (1) shall
(a) take the evidence on oath; and
(b) cause the evidence to be taken in accordance with section 540 in so far as that section is capable of being applied.
R.S., 1985, c. C-46, s. 508;
R.S., 1985, c. 27 (1st Supp.), s. 79.
Information laid otherwise than in person
508.1 (1) For the purposes of sections 504 to 508, a peace officer may lay an information by any means of telecommunication that produces a writing.
Alternative to oath
(2) A peace officer who uses a means of telecommunication referred to in subsection (1) shall, instead of swearing an oath, make a statement in writing stating that all matters contained in the information are true to the officer's knowledge and belief, and such a statement is deemed to be a statement made under oath.
1997, c. 18, s. 56.
Summons
509 (1) A summons issued under this Part shall
(a) be directed to the accused;
(b) set out briefly the offence in respect of which the accused is charged; and
(c) require the accused to attend court at a time and place to be stated therein and to attend thereafter as required by the court in order to be dealt with according to law.
Service on individual
(2) A summons shall be served by a peace officer who shall deliver it personally to the person to whom it is directed or, if that person cannot conveniently be found, shall leave it for him at his latest or usual place of abode with an inmate thereof who appears to be at least sixteen years of age.
(3) Content of summons

(4) There shall be set out in every summons the text of subsection 145(4) and section 510.
Attendance for purposes of
Identification of Criminals Act
(5) A summons may require the accused to appear at a time and place stated in it for the purposes of the
Identification of Criminals Act
Contraventions Act
R.S., 1985, c. C-46, s. 509;
R.S., 1985, c. 27 (1st Supp.), s. 80;
1992, c. 47, s. 71;
1996, c. 7, s. 38;
2008, c. 18, s. 17.
Failure to appear
510 Where an accused who is required by a summons to appear at a time and place stated in it for the purposes of the
Identification of Criminals Act
Contraventions Act,
R.S., 1985, c. C-46, s. 510;
1992, c. 47, s. 72;
1996, c. 7, s. 38.
Contents of warrant to arrest
511 (1) A warrant issued under this Part shall
(a) name or describe the accused;
(b) set out briefly the offence in respect of which the accused is charged; and
(c) order that the accused be forthwith arrested and brought before the judge or justice who issued the warrant or before some other judge or justice having jurisdiction in the same territorial division, to be dealt with according to law.
No return day
(2) A warrant issued under this Part remains in force until it is executed and need not be made returnable at any particular time.
Discretion to postpone execution
(3) Notwithstanding paragraph (1)(c), a judge or justice who issues a warrant may specify in the warrant the period before which the warrant shall not be executed, to allow the accused to appear voluntarily before a judge or justice having jurisdiction in the territorial division in which the warrant was issued.
Deemed execution of warrant
(4) Where the accused appears voluntarily for the offence in respect of which the accused is charged, the warrant is deemed to be executed.
R.S., 1985, c. C-46, s. 511;
R.S., 1985, c. 27 (1st Supp.), s. 81;
1997, c. 18, s. 57.
Certain actions not to preclude issue of warrant
512 (1) A justice may, where the justice has reasonable and probable grounds to believe that it is necessary in the public interest to issue a summons or a warrant for the arrest of the accused, issue a summons or warrant, notwithstanding that
(a) an appearance notice or a promise to appear or a recognizance entered into before an officer in charge or another peace officer has been confirmed or cancelled under subsection 508(1);
(b) a summons has previously been issued under subsection 507(4); or
(c) the accused has been released unconditionally or with the intention of compelling his appearance by way of summons.
Warrant in default of appearance
(2) Where

(a) service of a summons is proved and the accused fails to attend court in accordance with the summons,
(b) an appearance notice or a promise to appear or a recognizance entered into before an officer in charge or another peace officer has been confirmed under subsection 508(1) and the accused fails to attend court in accordance therewith in order to be dealt with according to law, or
(c) it appears that a summons cannot be served because the accused is evading service,
a justice may issue a warrant for the arrest of the accused.
R.S., 1985, c. C-46, s. 512;
R.S., 1985, c. 27 (1st Supp.), s. 82;
1997, c. 18, s. 58.

Formalities of warrant
513 A warrant in accordance with this Part shall be directed to the peace officers within the territorial jurisdiction of the justice, judge or court by whom or by which it is issued.
R.S., c. 2(2nd Supp.), s. 5.

Execution of warrant
514 (1) A warrant in accordance with this Part may be executed by arresting the accused
(a) wherever he is found within the territorial jurisdiction of the justice, judge or court by whom or by which the warrant was issued; or
(b) wherever he is found in Canada, in the case of fresh pursuit.

By whom warrant may be executed
(2) A warrant in accordance with this Part may be executed by a person who is one of the peace officers to whom it is directed, whether or not the place in which the warrant is to be executed is within the territory for which the person is a peace officer.
R.S., c. 2(2nd Supp.), s. 5.

Judicial Interim Release

Order of release
515 (1) Subject to this section, where an accused who is charged with an offence other than an offence listed in section 469 is taken before a justice, the justice shall, unless a plea of guilty by the accused is accepted, order, in respect of that offence, that the accused be released on his giving an undertaking without conditions, unless the prosecutor, having been given a reasonable opportunity to do so, shows cause, in respect of that offence, why the detention of the accused in custody is justified or why an order under any other provision of this section should be made and where the justice makes an order under any other provision of this section, the order shall refer only to the particular offence for which the accused was taken before the justice.

Release on undertaking with conditions, etc.
(2) Where the justice does not make an order under subsection (1), he shall, unless the prosecutor shows cause why the detention of the accused is justified, order that the accused be released
(a) on his giving an undertaking with such conditions as the justice directs;
(b) on his entering into a recognizance before the justice, without sureties, in such amount and with such conditions, if any, as the justice directs but without deposit of money or other valuable security;
(c) on his entering into a recognizance before the justice with sureties in such amount and with such conditions, if any, as the justice directs but without deposit of money or other valuable security;
(d) with the consent of the prosecutor, on his entering into a recognizance before the justice, without sureties, in such amount and with such conditions, if any, as the justice directs and on his depositing with the justice such sum of money or other valuable security as the justice directs; or
(e) if the accused is not ordinarily resident in the province in which the accused is in custody or does not ordinarily reside within two hundred kilometres of the place in which he is in custody, on his entering into a recognizance before the justice with or without sureties in such amount and with such conditions, if any, as the justice directs, and on his depositing with the justice such sum of money or other valuable security as the justice directs.

Power of justice to name sureties in order
(2.1) Where, pursuant to subsection (2) or any other provision of this Act, a justice, judge or court orders that an accused be released on his entering into a recognizance with sureties, the justice, judge or court may, in the order, name particular persons as sureties.

Alternative to physical presence
(2.2) Where, by this Act, the appearance of an accused is required for the purposes of judicial interim release, the appearance shall be by actual physical attendance of the accused but the justice may, subject to subsection (2.3), allow the accused to appear by means of any suitable telecommunication device, including telephone, that is satisfactory to the justice.

Where consent required
(2.3) The consent of the prosecutor and the accused is required for the purposes of an appearance if the evidence of a witness is to be taken at the appearance and the accused cannot appear by closed-circuit television or any other means that allow the court and the accused to engage in simultaneous visual and oral communication.

Idem
(3) The justice shall not make an order under any of paragraphs (2)(b) to (e) unless the prosecution shows cause why an order under the immediately preceding paragraph should not be made.

Conditions authorized
(4) The justice may direct as conditions under subsection (2) that the accused shall do any one or more of the following things as specified in the order:
(a) report at times to be stated in the order to a peace officer or other person designated in the order;
(b) remain within a territorial jurisdiction specified in the order;
(c) notify the peace officer or other person designated under paragraph (a) of any change in his address or his employment or occupation;
(d) abstain from communicating, directly or indirectly, with any victim, witness or other person identified in the order, or refrain from going to any place specified in the order, except in accordance with the conditions specified in the order that the justice considers necessary;
(e) where the accused is the holder of a passport, deposit his passport as specified in the order;
(e.1) comply with any other condition specified in the order that the justice considers necessary to ensure the safety and security of any victim of or witness to the offence; and
(f) comply with such other reasonable conditions specified in the order as the justice considers desirable.

Condition prohibiting possession of firearms, etc.
(4.1) When making an order under subsection (2), in the case of an accused who is charged with
(a) an offence in the commission of which violence against a person was used, threatened or attempted,
(a.1) a terrorism offence,
(b) an offence under section 264 (criminal harassment),
(b.1) an offence under section 423.1 (intimidation of a justice system participant),
(c) an offence relating to the contravention of any of sections 5 to 7 of the
Controlled Drugs and Substances Act
(d) an offence that involves, or the subject-matter of which is, a firearm, a cross-bow, a prohibited weapon, a restricted weapon, a prohibited device, ammunition, prohibited ammunition or an explosive substance, or
(e) an offence under subsection 20(1) of the
Security of Information Act
the justice shall add to the order a condition prohibiting the accused from possessing a firearm, cross-bow, prohibited weapon, restricted weapon, prohibited device, ammunition, prohibited ammunition or explosive substance, or all those things, until the accused is dealt with according to law unless the justice considers that such a condition is not required in the interests of the safety of the accused or the safety and security of a victim of the offence or of any other person.

Surrender, etc.

(4.11) Where the justice adds a condition described in subsection (4.1) to an order made under subsection (2), the justice shall specify in the order the manner and method by which
(a) the things referred to in subsection (4.1) that are in the possession of the accused shall be surrendered, disposed of, detained, stored or dealt with; and
(b) the authorizations, licences and registration certificates held by the person shall be surrendered.

Reasons
(4.12) Where the justice does not add a condition described in subsection (4.1) to an order made under subsection (2), the justice shall include in the record a statement of the reasons for not adding the condition.

Additional conditions
(4.2) Before making an order under subsection (2), in the case of an accused who is charged with an offence referred to in subsection (4.3), the justice shall consider whether it is desirable, in the interests of the safety and security of any person, particularly a victim of or witness to the offence or a justice system participant, to include as a condition of the order
(a) that the accused abstain from communicating, directly or indirectly, with any victim, witness or other person identified in the order, or refrain from going to any place specified in the order; or
(b) that the accused comply with any other condition specified in the order that the justice considers necessary to ensure the safety and security of those persons.

Offences
(4.3) The offences for the purposes of subsection (4.2) are
(a) a terrorism offence;
(b) an offence described in section 264 or 423.1;
(c) an offence in the commission of which violence against a person was used, threatened or attempted; and
(d) an offence under subsection 20(1) of the
Security of Information Act

Detention in custody
(5) Where the prosecutor shows cause why the detention of the accused in custody is justified, the justice shall order that the accused be detained in custody until he is dealt with according to law and shall include in the record a statement of his reasons for making the order.

Order of detention
(6) Unless the accused, having been given a reasonable opportunity to do so, shows cause why the accused's detention in custody is not justified, the justice shall order, despite any provision of this section, that the accused be detained in custody until the accused is dealt with according to law, if the accused is charged
(a) with an indictable offence, other than an offence listed in section 469,
(i) that is alleged to have been committed while at large after being released in respect of another indictable offence pursuant to the provisions of this Part or section 679 or 680,
(ii) that is an offence under section 467.11, 467.111, 467.12 or 467.13, or a serious offence alleged to have been committed for the benefit of, at the direction of, or in association with, a criminal organization,
(iii) that is an offence under any of sections 83.02 to 83.04 and 83.18 to 83.23 or otherwise is alleged to be a terrorism offence,
(iv) an offence under subsection 16(1) or (2), 17(1), 19(1), 20(1) or 22(1) of the
Security of Information Act
(v) an offence under subsection 21(1) or 22(1) or section 23 of the
Security of Information Act
(vi) that is an offence under section 99, 100 or 103,
(vii) that is an offence under section 244 or 244.2, or an offence under section 239, 272 or 273, subsection 279(1) or section 279.1, 344 or 346 that is alleged to have been committed with a firearm, or
(viii) that is alleged to involve, or whose subject-matter is alleged to be, a firearm, a cross-bow, a

prohibited weapon, a restricted weapon, a prohibited device, any ammunition or prohibited ammunition or an explosive substance, and that is alleged to have been committed while the accused was under a prohibition order within the meaning of subsection 84(1);

(b) with an indictable offence, other than an offence listed in section 469 and is not ordinarily resident in Canada,

(c) with an offence under any of subsections 145(2) to (5) that is alleged to have been committed while he was at large after being released in respect of another offence pursuant to the provisions of this Part or section 679, 680 or 816, or

(d) with having committed an offence punishable by imprisonment for life under any of sections 5 to 7 of the
Controlled Drugs and Substances Act

Reasons

(6.1) If the justice orders that an accused to whom subsection (6) applies be released, the justice shall include in the record a statement of the justice's reasons for making the order.

Order of release

(7) Where an accused to whom paragraph 6(a), (c) or (d) applies shows cause why the accused's detention in custody is not justified, the justice shall order that the accused be released on giving an undertaking or entering into a recognizance described in any of paragraphs (2)(a) to (e) with the conditions described in subsections (4) to (4.2) or, where the accused was at large on an undertaking or recognizance with conditions, the additional conditions described in subsections (4) to (4.2), that the justice considers desirable, unless the accused, having been given a reasonable opportunity to do so, shows cause why the conditions or additional conditions should not be imposed.

Idem

(8) Where an accused to whom paragraph (6)(b) applies shows cause why the accused's detention in custody is not justified, the justice shall order that the accused be released on giving an undertaking or entering into a recognizance described in any of paragraphs (2)(a) to (e) with the conditions, described in subsections (4) to (4.2), that the justice considers desirable.

Sufficiency of record

(9) For the purposes of subsections (5) and (6), it is sufficient if a record is made of the reasons in accordance with the provisions of Part XVIII relating to the taking of evidence at preliminary inquiries.

Written reasons

(9.1) Despite subsection (9), if the justice orders that the accused be detained in custody primarily because of a previous conviction of the accused, the justice shall state that reason, in writing, in the record.

Justification for detention in custody

(10) For the purposes of this section, the detention of an accused in custody is justified only on one or more of the following grounds:

(a) where the detention is necessary to ensure his or her attendance in court in order to be dealt with according to law;

(b) where the detention is necessary for the protection or safety of the   public,   including any victim of or witness to the offence, or any person under the age of 18 years, having regard to all the circumstances including any substantial likelihood that the accused will, if released from custody, commit a criminal offence or interfere with the administration of justice; and

(c) if the detention is necessary to maintain confidence in the administration of justice, having regard to all the circumstances, including

(i) the apparent strength of the prosecution's case,

(ii) the gravity of the offence,

(iii) the circumstances surrounding the commission of the offence, including whether a firearm was used, and

(iv) the fact that the accused is liable, on conviction, for a potentially lengthy term of imprisonment or, in the case of an offence that involves, or whose subject-matter is, a firearm, a minimum

punishment of imprisonment for a term of three years or more.
Detention in custody for offence listed in section 469
(11) Where an accused who is charged with an offence mentioned in section 469 is taken before a justice, the justice shall order that the accused be detained in custody until he is dealt with according to law and shall issue a warrant in Form 8 for the committal of the accused.
Order re no communication
(12) A justice who orders that an accused be detained in custody under this section may include in the order a direction that the accused abstain from communicating, directly or indirectly, with any victim, witness or other person identified in the order, except in accordance with such conditions specified in the order as the justice considers necessary.
Consideration of victim's safety and security
(13) A justice who makes an order under this section shall include in the record of the proceedings a statement that he or she considered the safety and security of every victim of the offence when making the order.
Copy to victim
(14) If an order is made under this section, the justice shall, on request by a victim of the offence, cause a copy of the order to be given to the victim.
R.S., 1985, c. C-46, s. 515;
R.S., 1985, c. 27 (1st Supp.), ss. 83, 186;
1991, c. 40, s. 31;
1993, c. 45, s. 8;
1994, c. 44, s. 44;
1995, c. 39, s. 153;
1996, c. 19, ss. 71, 93.3;
1997, c. 18, s. 59, c. 23, s. 16;
1999, c. 5, s. 21, c. 25, s. 8(Preamble);
2001, c. 32, s. 37, c. 41, ss. 19, 133;
2008, c. 6, s. 37;
2009, c. 22, s. 17, c. 29, s. 2;
2010, c. 20, s. 1;
2012, c. 1, s. 32;
2014, c. 17, s. 14;
2015, c. 13, s. 20.
Variation of undertaking or recognizance
515.1 An undertaking or recognizance pursuant to which the accused was released that has been entered into under section 499, 503 or 515 may, with the written consent of the prosecutor, be varied, and where so varied, is deemed to have been entered into pursuant to section 515.
1997, c. 18, s. 60.
Remand in custody
516 (1) A justice may, before or at any time during the course of any proceedings under section 515, on application by the prosecutor or the accused, adjourn the proceedings and remand the accused to custody in prison by warrant in Form 19, but no adjournment shall be for more than three clear days except with the consent of the accused.
Detention pending bail hearing
(2) A justice who remands an accused to custody under subsection (1) or subsection 515(11) may order that the accused abstain from communicating, directly or indirectly, with any victim, witness or other person identified in the order, except in accordance with any conditions specified in the order that the justice considers necessary.
R.S., 1985, c. C-46, s. 516;
1999, c. 5, s. 22, c. 25, s. 31(Preamble).
Order directing matters not to be published for specified period
517 (1) If the prosecutor or the accused intends to show cause under section 515, he or she shall so

state to the justice and the justice may, and shall on application by the accused, before or at any time during the course of the proceedings under that section, make an order directing that the evidence taken, the information given or the representations made and the reasons, if any, given or to be given by the justice shall not be published in any document, or broadcast or transmitted in any way before such time as
(a) if a preliminary inquiry is held, the accused in respect of whom the proceedings are held is discharged; or
(b) if the accused in respect of whom the proceedings are held is tried or ordered to stand trial, the trial is ended.
Failure to comply
(2) Every one who fails without lawful excuse, the proof of which lies on him, to comply with an order made under subsection (1) is guilty of an offence punishable on summary conviction.
(3) R.S., 1985, c. C-46, s. 517;
R.S., 1985, c. 27 (1st Supp.), s. 101(E);
2005, c. 32, s. 17.
Inquiries to be made by justice and evidence
518 (1) In any proceedings under section 515,
(a) the justice may, subject to paragraph (b), make such inquiries, on oath or otherwise, of and concerning the accused as he considers desirable;
(b) the accused shall not be examined by the justice or any other person except counsel for the accused respecting the offence with which the accused is charged, and no inquiry shall be made of the accused respecting that offence by way of cross-examination unless the accused has testified respecting the offence;
(c) the prosecutor may, in addition to any other relevant evidence, lead evidence
(i) to prove that the accused has previously been convicted of a criminal offence,
(ii) to prove that the accused has been charged with and is awaiting trial for another criminal offence,
(iii) to prove that the accused has previously committed an offence under section 145, or
(iv) to show the circumstances of the alleged offence, particularly as they relate to the probability of conviction of the accused;
(d) the justice may take into consideration any relevant matters agreed on by the prosecutor and the accused or his counsel;
(d.1) the justice may receive evidence obtained as a result of an interception of a private communication under and within the meaning of Part VI, in writing, orally or in the form of a recording and, for the purposes of this section, subsection 189(5) does not apply to that evidence;
(d.2) the justice shall take into consideration any evidence submitted regarding the need to ensure the safety or security of any victim of or witness to an offence; and
(e) the justice may receive and base his decision on evidence considered credible or trustworthy by him in the circumstances of each case.
Release pending sentence
(2) Where, before or at any time during the course of any proceedings under section 515, the accused pleads guilty and that plea is accepted, the justice may make any order provided for in this Part for the release of the accused until the accused is sentenced.
R.S., 1985, c. C-46, s. 518;
R.S., 1985, c. 27 (1st Supp.), ss. 84, 185(F);
1994, c. 44, s. 45;
1999, c. 25, s. 9(Preamble).
Release of accused
519 (1) Where a justice makes an order under subsection 515(1), (2), (7) or (8),
(a) if the accused thereupon complies with the order, the justice shall direct that the accused be released
(i) forthwith, if the accused is not required to be detained in custody in respect of any other matter, or
(ii) as soon thereafter as the accused is no longer required to be detained in custody in respect of any

other matter; and

(b) if the accused does not thereupon comply with the order, the justice who made the order or another justice having jurisdiction shall issue a warrant for the committal of the accused and may endorse thereon an authorization to the person having the custody of the accused to release the accused when the accused complies with the order

(i) forthwith after the compliance, if the accused is not required to be detained in custody in respect of any other matter, or

(ii) as soon thereafter as the accused is no longer required to be detained in custody in respect of any other matter

and if the justice so endorses the warrant, he shall attach to it a copy of the order.

Discharge from custody

(2) Where the accused complies with an order referred to in paragraph (1)(b) and is not required to be detained in custody in respect of any other matter, the justice who made the order or another justice having jurisdiction shall, unless the accused has been or will be released pursuant to an authorization referred to in that paragraph, issue an order for discharge in Form 39.

Warrant for committal

(3) Where the justice makes an order under subsection 515(5) or (6) for the detention of the accused, he shall issue a warrant for the committal of the accused.

R.S., 1985, c. C-46, s. 519;

R.S., 1985, c. 27 (1st Supp.), s. 85.

Review of order

520 (1) If a justice, or a judge of the Nunavut Court of Justice, makes an order under subsection 515(2), (5), (6), (7), (8) or (12) or makes or vacates any order under paragraph 523(2)(b), the accused may, at any time before the trial of the charge, apply to a judge for a review of the order.

Notice to prosecutor

(2) An application under this section shall not, unless the prosecutor otherwise consents, be heard by a judge unless the accused has given to the prosecutor at least two clear days notice in writing of the application.

Accused to be present

(3) If the judge so orders or the prosecutor or the accused or his counsel so requests, the accused shall be present at the hearing of an application under this section and, where the accused is in custody, the judge may order, in writing, the person having the custody of the accused to bring him before the court.

Adjournment of proceedings

(4) A judge may, before or at any time during the hearing of an application under this section, on application by the prosecutor or the accused, adjourn the proceedings, but if the accused is in custody no adjournment shall be for more than three clear days except with the consent of the accused.

Failure of accused to attend

(5) Where an accused, other than an accused who is in custody, has been ordered by a judge to be present at the hearing of an application under this section and does not attend the hearing, the judge may issue a warrant for the arrest of the accused.

Execution

(6) A warrant issued under subsection (5) may be executed anywhere in Canada.

Evidence and powers of judge on review

(7) On the hearing of an application under this section, the judge may consider

(a) the transcript, if any, of the proceedings heard by the justice and by any judge who previously reviewed the order made by the justice,

(b) the exhibits, if any, filed in the proceedings before the justice, and

(c) such additional evidence or exhibits as may be tendered by the accused or the prosecutor, and shall either

(d) dismiss the application, or

(e) if the accused shows cause, allow the application, vacate the order previously made by the justice

and make any other order provided for in section 515 that he considers is warranted.
Limitation of further applications
(8) Where an application under this section or section 521 has been heard, a further or other application under this section or section 521 shall not be made with respect to that same accused, except with leave of a judge, prior to the expiration of thirty days from the date of the decision of the judge who heard the previous application.
Application of sections 517, 518 and 519
(9) The provisions of sections 517, 518 and 519 apply with such modifications as the circumstances require in respect of an application under this section.
R.S., 1985, c. C-46, s. 520;
R.S., 1985, c. 27 (1st Supp.), s. 86;
1994, c. 44, s. 46;
1999, c. 3, s. 31.
Review of order
521 (1) If a justice, or a judge of the Nunavut Court of Justice, makes an order under subsection 515(1), (2), (7), (8) or (12) or makes or vacates any order under paragraph 523(2)(b), the prosecutor may, at any time before the trial of the charge, apply to a judge for a review of the order.
Notice to accused
(2) An application under this section shall not be heard by a judge unless the prosecutor has given to the accused at least two clear days notice in writing of the application.
Accused to be present
(3) If the judge so orders or the prosecutor or the accused or his counsel so requests, the accused shall be present at the hearing of an application under this section and, where the accused is in custody, the judge may order, in writing, the person having the custody of the accused to bring him before the court.
Adjournment of proceedings
(4) A judge may, before or at any time during the hearing of an application under this section, on application of the prosecutor or the accused, adjourn the proceedings, but if the accused is in custody no adjournment shall be for more than three clear days except with the consent of the accused.
Failure of accused to attend
(5) Where an accused, other than an accused who is in custody, has been ordered by a judge to be present at the hearing of an application under this section and does not attend the hearing, the judge may issue a warrant for the arrest of the accused.
Warrant for detention
(6) Where, pursuant to paragraph (8)(e), the judge makes an order that the accused be detained in custody until he is dealt with according to law, he shall, if the accused is not in custody, issue a warrant for the committal of the accused.
Execution
(7) A warrant issued under subsection (5) or (6) may be executed anywhere in Canada.
Evidence and powers of judge on review
(8) On the hearing of an application under this section, the judge may consider
(a) the transcript, if any, of the proceedings heard by the justice and by any judge who previously reviewed the order made by the justice,
(b) the exhibits, if any, filed in the proceedings before the justice, and
(c) such additional evidence or exhibits as may be tendered by the prosecutor or the accused,
and shall either
(d) dismiss the application, or
(e) if the prosecutor shows cause, allow the application, vacate the order previously made by the justice and make any other order provided for in section 515 that he considers to be warranted.
Limitation of further applications
(9) Where an application under this section or section 520 has been heard, a further or other application under this section or section 520 shall not be made with respect to the same accused,

except with leave of a judge, prior to the expiration of thirty days from the date of the decision of the judge who heard the previous application.

Application of sections 517, 518 and 519

(10) The provisions of sections 517, 518 and 519 apply with such modifications as the circumstances require in respect of an application under this section.

R.S., 1985, c. C-46, s. 521;
R.S., 1985, c. 27 (1st Supp.), s. 87;
1994, c. 44, s. 47;
1999, c. 3, s. 32.

Interim release by judge only

522 (1) Where an accused is charged with an offence listed in section 469, no court, judge or justice, other than a judge of or a judge presiding in a superior court of criminal jurisdiction for the province in which the accused is so charged, may release the accused before or after the accused has been ordered to stand trial.

Idem

(2) Where an accused is charged with an offence listed in section 469, a judge of or a judge presiding in a superior court of criminal jurisdiction for the province in which the accused is charged shall order that the accused be detained in custody unless the accused, having been given a reasonable opportunity to do so, shows cause why his detention in custody is not justified within the meaning of subsection 515(10).

Order re no communication

(2.1) A judge referred to in subsection (2) who orders that an accused be detained in custody under this section may include in the order a direction that the accused abstain from communicating, directly or indirectly, with any victim, witness or other person identified in the order except in accordance with such conditions specified in the order as the judge considers necessary.

Release of accused

(3) If the judge does not order that the accused be detained in custody under subsection (2), the judge may order that the accused be released on giving an undertaking or entering into a recognizance described in any of paragraphs 515(2)(a) to (e) with such conditions described in subsections 515(4), (4.1) and (4.2) as the judge considers desirable.

Order not reviewable except under section 680

(4) An order made under this section is not subject to review, except as provided in section 680.

Application of sections 517, 518 and 519

(5) The provisions of sections 517, 518 except subsection (2) thereof, and 519 apply with such modifications as the circumstances require in respect of an application for an order under subsection (2).

Other offences

(6) Where an accused is charged with an offence mentioned in section 469 and with any other offence, a judge acting under this section may apply the provisions of this Part respecting judicial interim release to that other offence.

R.S., 1985, c. C-46, s. 522;
R.S., 1985, c. 27 (1st Supp.), s. 88;
1991, c. 40, s. 32;
1994, c. 44, s. 48;
1999, c. 25, s. 10(Preamble).

Period for which appearance notice, etc., continues in force

523 (1) Where an accused, in respect of an offence with which he is charged, has not been taken into custody or has been released from custody under or by virtue of any provision of this Part, the appearance notice, promise to appear, summons, undertaking or recognizance issued to, given or entered into by the accused continues in force, subject to its terms, and applies in respect of any new information charging the same offence or an included offence that was received after the appearance notice, promise to appear, summons, undertaking or recognizance was issued, given or entered into,

(a) where the accused was released from custody pursuant to an order of a judge made under subsection 522(3), until his trial is completed; or
(b) in any other case,
(i) until his trial is completed, and
(ii) where the accused is, at his trial, determined to be guilty of the offence, until a sentence within the meaning of section 673 is imposed on the accused unless, at the time the accused is determined to be guilty, the court, judge or justice orders that the accused be taken into custody pending such sentence.

Where new information charging same offence
(1.1) Where an accused, in respect of an offence with which he is charged, has not been taken into custody or is being detained or has been released from custody under or by virtue of any provision of this Part and after the order for interim release or detention has been made, or the appearance notice, promise to appear, summons, undertaking or recognizance has been issued, given or entered into, a new information, charging the same offence or an included offence, is received, section 507 or 508, as the case may be, does not apply in respect of the new information and the order for interim release or detention of the accused and the appearance notice, promise to appear, summons, undertaking or recognizance, if any, applies in respect of the new information.

When direct indictment is preferred charging same offence
(1.2) When an accused, in respect of an offence with which the accused is charged, has not been taken into custody or is being detained or has been released from custody under or by virtue of any provision of this Part and after the order for interim release or detention has been made, or the appearance notice, promise to appear, summons, undertaking or recognizance has been issued, given or entered into, and an indictment is preferred under section 577 charging the same offence or an included offence, the order for interim release or detention of the accused and the appearance notice, promise to appear, summons, undertaking or recognizance, if any, applies in respect of the indictment.

Order vacating previous order for release or detention
(2) Despite subsections (1) to (1.2),
(a) the court, judge or justice before which or whom an accused is being tried, at any time,
(b) the justice, on completion of the preliminary inquiry in relation to an offence for which an accused is ordered to stand trial, other than an offence listed in section 469, or
(c) with the consent of the prosecutor and the accused or, where the accused or the prosecutor applies to vacate an order that would otherwise apply pursuant to subsection (1.1), without such consent, at any time
(i) where the accused is charged with an offence other than an offence listed in section 469, the justice by whom an order was made under this Part or any other justice,
(ii) where the accused is charged with an offence listed in section 469, a judge of or a judge presiding in a superior court of criminal jurisdiction for the province, or
(iii) the court, judge or justice before which or whom an accused is to be tried,
may, on cause being shown, vacate any order previously made under this Part for the interim release or detention of the accused and make any other order provided for in this Part for the detention or release of the accused until his trial is completed that the court, judge or justice considers to be warranted.

Provisions applicable to proceedings under subsection (2)
(3) The provisions of sections 517, 518 and 519 apply, with such modifications as the circumstances require, in respect of any proceedings under subsection (2), except that subsection 518(2) does not apply in respect of an accused who is charged with an offence listed in section 469.
R.S., 1985, c. C-46, s. 523;
R.S., 1985, c. 27 (1st Supp.), s. 89;
2011, c. 16, s. 2.

Arrest of Accused on Interim Release

Issue of warrant for arrest of accused
524 (1) Where a justice is satisfied that there are reasonable grounds to believe that an accused
(a) has contravened or is about to contravene any summons, appearance notice, promise to appear, undertaking or recognizance that was issued or given to him or entered into by him, or
(b) has committed an indictable offence after any summons, appearance notice, promise to appear, undertaking or recognizance was issued or given to him or entered into by him,
he may issue a warrant for the arrest of the accused.

Arrest of accused without warrant
(2) Notwithstanding anything in this Act, a peace officer who believes on reasonable grounds that an accused
(a) has contravened or is about to contravene any summons, appearance notice, promise to appear, undertaking or recognizance that was issued or given to him or entered into by him, or
(b) has committed an indictable offence after any summons, appearance notice, promise to appear, undertaking or recognizance was issued or given to him or entered into by him,
may arrest the accused without warrant.

Hearing
(3) Where an accused who has been arrested with a warrant issued under subsection (1), or who has been arrested under subsection (2), is taken before a justice, the justice shall
(a) where the accused was released from custody pursuant to an order made under subsection 522(3) by a judge of the superior court of criminal jurisdiction of any province, order that the accused be taken before a judge of that court; or
(b) in any other case, hear the prosecutor and his witnesses, if any, and the accused and his witnesses, if any.

Retention of accused
(4) Where an accused described in paragraph (3)(a) is taken before a judge and the judge finds
(a) that the accused has contravened or had been about to contravene his summons, appearance notice, promise to appear, undertaking or recognizance, or
(b) that there are reasonable grounds to believe that the accused has committed an indictable offence after any summons, appearance notice, promise to appear, undertaking or recognizance was issued or given to him or entered into by him,
he shall cancel the summons, appearance notice, promise to appear, undertaking or recognizance and order that the accused be detained in custody unless the accused, having been given a reasonable opportunity to do so, shows cause why his detention in custody is not justified within the meaning of subsection 515(10).

Release of accused
(5) Where the judge does not order that the accused be detained in custody pursuant to subsection (4), he may order that the accused be released on his giving an undertaking or entering into a recognizance described in any of paragraphs 515(2)(a) to (e) with such conditions described in subsection 515(4) or, where the accused was at large on an undertaking or a recognizance with conditions, such additional conditions, described in subsection 515(4), as the judge considers desirable.

Order not reviewable
(6) Any order made under subsection (4) or (5) is not subject to review, except as provided in section 680.

Release of accused
(7) Where the judge does not make a finding under paragraph (4)(a) or (b), he shall order that the accused be released from custody.

Powers of justice after hearing
(8) Where an accused described in subsection (3), other than an accused to whom paragraph (a) of that subsection applies, is taken before the justice and the justice finds

(a) that the accused has contravened or had been about to contravene his summons, appearance notice, promise to appear, undertaking or recognizance, or
(b) that there are reasonable grounds to believe that the accused has committed an indictable offence after any summons, appearance notice, promise to appear, undertaking or recognizance was issued or given to him or entered into by him,
he shall cancel the summons, appearance notice, promise to appear, undertaking or recognizance and order that the accused be detained in custody unless the accused, having been given a reasonable opportunity to do so, shows cause why his detention in custody is not justified within the meaning of subsection 515(10).

Release of accused
(9) Where an accused shows cause why his detention in custody is not justified within the meaning of subsection 515(10), the justice shall order that the accused be released on his giving an undertaking or entering into a recognizance described in any of paragraphs 515(2)(a) to (e) with such conditions, described in subsection 515(4), as the justice considers desirable.

Reasons
(10) Where the justice makes an order under subsection (9), he shall include in the record a statement of his reasons for making the order, and subsection 515(9) is applicable with such modifications as the circumstances require in respect thereof.

Where justice to order that accused be released
(11) Where the justice does not make a finding under paragraph (8)(a) or (b), he shall order that the accused be released from custody.

Provisions applicable to proceedings under this section
(12) The provisions of sections 517, 518 and 519 apply with such modifications as the circumstances require in respect of any proceedings under this section, except that subsection 518(2) does not apply in respect of an accused who is charged with an offence mentioned in section 522.

Certain provisions applicable to order under this section
(13) Section 520 applies in respect of any order made under subsection (8) or (9) as though the order were an order made by a justice or a judge of the Nunavut Court of Justice under subsection 515(2) or (5), and section 521 applies in respect of any order made under subsection (9) as though the order were an order made by a justice or a judge of the Nunavut Court of Justice under subsection 515(2).
R.S., 1985, c. C-46, s. 524;
1999, c. 3, s. 33.

Review of Detention where Trial Delayed

Time for application to judge
525 (1) Where an accused who has been charged with an offence other than an offence listed in section 469 and who is not required to be detained in custody in respect of any other matter is being detained in custody pending his trial for that offence and the trial has not commenced
(a) in the case of an indictable offence, within ninety days from
(i) the day on which the accused was taken before a justice under section 503, or
(ii) where an order that the accused be detained in custody has been made under section 521 or 524, or a decision has been made with respect to a review under section 520, the later of the day on which the accused was taken into custody under that order and the day of the decision, or
(b) in the case of an offence for which the accused is being prosecuted in proceedings by way of summary conviction, within thirty days from
(i) the day on which the accused was taken before a justice under subsection 503(1), or
(ii) where an order that the accused be detained in custody has been made under section 521 or 524, or a decision has been made with respect to a review under section 520, the later of the day on which the accused was taken into custody under that order and the day of the decision,
the person having the custody of the accused shall, forthwith on the expiration of those ninety or thirty days, as the case may be, apply to a judge having jurisdiction in the place in which the accused

is in custody to fix a date for a hearing to determine whether or not the accused should be released from custody.

Notice of hearing

(2) On receiving an application under subsection (1), the judge shall

(a) fix a date for the hearing described in subsection (1) to be held in the jurisdiction

(i) where the accused is in custody, or

(ii) where the trial is to take place; and

(b) direct that notice of the hearing be given to such persons, including the prosecutor and the accused, and in such manner as the judge may specify.

Matters to be considered on hearing

(3) On the hearing described in subsection (1), the judge may, in deciding whether or not the accused should be released from custody, take into consideration whether the prosecutor or the accused has been responsible for any unreasonable delay in the trial of the charge.

Order

(4) If, following the hearing described in subsection (1), the judge is not satisfied that the continued detention of the accused in custody is justified within the meaning of subsection 515(10), the judge shall order that the accused be released from custody pending the trial of the charge on his giving an undertaking or entering into a recognizance described in any of paragraphs 515(2)(a) to (e) with such conditions described in subsection 515(4) as the judge considers desirable.

Warrant of judge for arrest

(5) Where a judge having jurisdiction in the province where an order under subsection (4) for the release of an accused has been made is satisfied that there are reasonable grounds to believe that the accused

(a) has contravened or is about to contravene the undertaking or recognizance on which he has been released, or

(b) has, after his release from custody on his undertaking or recognizance, committed an indictable offence,

he may issue a warrant for the arrest of the accused.

Arrest without warrant by peace officer

(6) Notwithstanding anything in this Act, a peace officer who believes on reasonable grounds that an accused who has been released from custody under subsection (4)

(a) has contravened or is about to contravene the undertaking or recognizance on which he has been released, or

(b) has, after his release from custody on his undertaking or recognizance, committed an indictable offence,

may arrest the accused without warrant and take him or cause him to be taken before a judge having jurisdiction in the province where the order for his release was made.

Hearing and order

(7) A judge before whom an accused is taken pursuant to a warrant issued under subsection (5) or pursuant to subsection (6) may, where the accused shows cause why his detention in custody is not justified within the meaning of subsection 515(10), order that the accused be released on his giving an undertaking or entering into a recognizance described in any of paragraphs 515(2)(a) to (e) with such conditions, described in subsection 515(4), as the judge considers desirable.

Provisions applicable to proceedings

(8) The provisions of sections 517, 518 and 519 apply with such modifications as the circumstances require in respect of any proceedings under this section.

Directions for expediting trial

(9) Where an accused is before a judge under any of the provisions of this section, the judge may give directions for expediting the trial of the accused.

R.S., 1985, c. C-46, s. 525;

R.S., 1985, c. 27 (1st Supp.), s. 90;

1994, c. 44, s. 49;

1997, c. 18, s. 61.
Directions for expediting proceedings
526 Subject to subsection 525(9), a court, judge or justice before which or whom an accused appears pursuant to this Part may give directions for expediting any proceedings in respect of the accused.
R.S., 1985, c. C-46, s. 526;
R.S., 1985, c. 27 (1st Supp.), s. 91.

Procedure to Procure Attendance of a Prisoner

Procuring attendance
527 (1) A judge of a superior court of criminal jurisdiction may order in writing that a person who is confined in a prison be brought before the court, judge, justice or provincial court judge before whom the prisoner is required to attend, from day to day as may be necessary, if
(a) the applicant for the order sets out the facts of the case in an affidavit and produces the warrant, if any; and
(b) the judge is satisfied that the ends of justice require that an order be made.
Provincial court judge's order
(2) A provincial court judge has the same powers for the purposes of subsection (1) or (7) as a judge has under that subsection where the person whose attendance is required is within the province in which the provincial court judge has jurisdiction.
Conveyance of prisoner
(3) An order that is made under subsection (1) or (2) shall be addressed to the person who has custody of the prisoner, and on receipt thereof that person shall
(a) deliver the prisoner to any person who is named in the order to receive him; or
(b) bring the prisoner before the court, judge, justice or provincial court judge, as the case may be, on payment of his reasonable charges in respect thereof.
Detention of prisoner required as witness
(4) Where a prisoner is required as a witness, the judge or provincial court judge shall direct, in the order, the manner in which the prisoner shall be kept in custody and returned to the prison from which he is brought.
Detention in other cases
(5) Where the appearance of a prisoner is required for the purposes of paragraph (1)(a) or (b), the judge or provincial court judge shall give appropriate directions in the order with respect to the manner in which the prisoner is
(a) to be kept in custody, if he is ordered to stand trial; or
(b) to be returned, if he is discharged on a preliminary inquiry or if he is acquitted of the charge against him.
Application of sections respecting sentence
(6) Sections 718.3 and 743.1 apply where a prisoner to whom this section applies is convicted and sentenced to imprisonment by the court, judge, justice or provincial court judge.
Transfer of prisoner
(7) On application by the prosecutor, a judge of a superior court of criminal jurisdiction may, if a prisoner or a person in the custody of a peace officer consents in writing, order the transfer of the prisoner or other person to the custody of a peace officer named in the order for a period specified in the order, where the judge is satisfied that the transfer is required for the purpose of assisting a peace officer acting in the execution of his or her duties.
Conveyance of prisoner
(8) An order under subsection (7) shall be addressed to the person who has custody of the prisoner and on receipt thereof that person shall deliver the prisoner to the peace officer who is named in the order to receive him.
Return
(9) When the purposes of any order made under this section have been carried out, the prisoner shall

be returned to the place where he was confined at the time the order was made.
R.S., 1985, c. C-46, s. 527;
R.S., 1985, c. 27 (1st Supp.), ss. 92, 101(E), 203;
1994, c. 44, s. 50;
1995, c. 22, s. 10;
1997, c. 18, s. 62;
2015, c. 3, s. 52(F).

Endorsement of Warrant

Endorsing warrant
528 (1) Where a warrant for the arrest or committal of an accused, in any form set out in Part XXVIII in relation thereto, cannot be executed in accordance with section 514 or 703, a justice within whose jurisdiction the accused is or is believed to be shall, on application and proof on oath or by affidavit of the signature of the justice who issued the warrant, authorize the arrest of the accused within his jurisdiction by making an endorsement, which may be in Form 28, on the warrant.
Copy of affidavit or warrant
(1.1) A copy of an affidavit or warrant submitted by a means of telecommunication that produces a writing has the same probative force as the original for the purposes of subsection (1).
Effect of endorsement
(2) An endorsement that is made on a warrant pursuant to subsection (1) is sufficient authority to the peace officers to whom it was originally directed, and to all peace officers within the territorial jurisdiction of the justice by whom it is endorsed, to execute the warrant and to take the accused before the justice who issued the warrant or before any other justice for the same territorial division.
R.S., 1985, c. C-46, s. 528;
R.S., 1985, c. 27 (1st Supp.), s. 93;
1994, c. 44, s. 51.

Powers to Enter Dwelling-houses to Carry out Arrests

Including authorization to enter in warrant of arrest
529 (1) A warrant to arrest or apprehend a person issued by a judge or justice under this or any other Act of Parliament may authorize a peace officer, subject to subsection (2), to enter a dwelling-house described in the warrant for the purpose of arresting or apprehending the person if the judge or justice is satisfied by information on oath in writing that there are reasonable grounds to believe that the person is or will be present in the dwelling-house.
Execution
(2) An authorization to enter a dwelling-house granted under subsection (1) is subject to the condition that the peace officer may not enter the dwelling-house unless the peace officer has, immediately before entering the dwelling-house, reasonable grounds to believe that the person to be arrested or apprehended is present in the dwelling-house.
R.S., 1985, c. C-46, s. 529;
1994, c. 44, s. 52;
1997, c. 39, s. 2.
Warrant to enter dwelling-house
529.1 A judge or justice may issue a warrant in Form 7.1 authorizing a peace officer to enter a dwelling-house described in the warrant for the purpose of arresting or apprehending a person identified or identifiable by the warrant if the judge or justice is satisfied by information on oath that there are reasonable grounds to believe that the person is or will be present in the dwelling-house and that
(a) a warrant referred to in this or any other Act of Parliament to arrest or apprehend the person is in force anywhere in Canada;

(b) grounds exist to arrest the person without warrant under paragraph 495(1)(a) or (b) or section 672.91; or

(c) grounds exist to arrest or apprehend without warrant the person under an Act of Parliament, other than this Act.

1997, c. 39, s. 2;
2002, c. 13, s. 23.

Reasonable terms and conditions

529.2 Subject to section 529.4, the judge or justice shall include in a warrant referred to in section 529 or 529.1 any terms and conditions that the judge or justice considers advisable to ensure that the entry into the dwelling-house is reasonable in the circumstances.

1997, c. 39, s. 2.

Authority to enter dwelling without warrant

529.3 (1) Without limiting or restricting any power a peace officer may have to enter a dwelling-house under this or any other Act or law, the peace officer may enter the dwelling-house for the purpose of arresting or apprehending a person, without a warrant referred to in section 529 or 529.1 authorizing the entry, if the peace officer has reasonable grounds to believe that the person is present in the dwelling-house, and the conditions for obtaining a warrant under section 529.1 exist but by reason of exigent circumstances it would be impracticable to obtain a warrant.

Exigent circumstances

(2) For the purposes of subsection (1), exigent circumstances include circumstances in which the peace officer

(a) has reasonable grounds to suspect that entry into the dwelling-house is necessary to prevent imminent bodily harm or death to any person; or

(b) has reasonable grounds to believe that evidence relating to the commission of an indictable offence is present in the dwelling-house and that entry into the dwelling-house is necessary to prevent the imminent loss or imminent destruction of the evidence.

1997, c. 39, s. 2.

Omitting announcement before entry

529.4 (1) A judge or justice who authorizes a peace officer to enter a dwelling-house under section 529 or 529.1, or any other judge or justice, may authorize the peace officer to enter the dwelling-house without prior announcement if the judge or justice is satisfied by information on oath that there are reasonable grounds to believe that prior announcement of the entry would

(a) expose the peace officer or any other person to imminent bodily harm or death; or

(b) result in the imminent loss or imminent destruction of evidence relating to the commission of an indictable offence.

Execution of authorization

(2) An authorization under this section is subject to the condition that the peace officer may not enter the dwelling-house without prior announcement despite being authorized to do so unless the peace officer has, immediately before entering the dwelling-house,

(a) reasonable grounds to suspect that prior announcement of the entry would expose the peace officer or any other person to imminent bodily harm or death; or

(b) reasonable grounds to believe that prior announcement of the entry would result in the imminent loss or imminent destruction of evidence relating to the commission of an indictable offence.

Exception

(3) A peace officer who enters a dwelling-house without a warrant under section 529.3 may not enter the dwelling-house without prior announcement unless the peace officer has, immediately before entering the dwelling-house,

(a) reasonable grounds to suspect that prior announcement of the entry would expose the peace officer or any other person to imminent bodily harm or death; or

(b) reasonable grounds to believe that prior announcement of the entry would result in the imminent loss or imminent destruction of evidence relating to the commission of an indictable offence.

1997, c. 39, s. 2.

Telewarrant
529.5 If a peace officer believes that it would be impracticable in the circumstances to appear personally before a judge or justice to make an application for a warrant under section 529.1 or an authorization under section 529 or 529.4, the warrant or authorization may be issued on an information submitted by telephone or other means of telecommunication and, for that purpose, section 487.1 applies, with any modifications that the circumstances require, to the warrant or authorization.
1997, c. 39, s. 2.

PART XVII

PART XVII
Language of Accused

Language of accused
530 (1) On application by an accused whose language is one of the official languages of Canada, made not later than
(a) the time of the appearance of the accused at which his trial date is set, if
(i) he is accused of an offence mentioned in section 553 or punishable on summary conviction, or
(ii) the accused is to be tried on an indictment preferred under section 577,
(b) the time of the accused's election, if the accused elects under section 536 to be tried by a provincial court judge or under section 536.1 to be tried by a judge without a jury and without having a preliminary inquiry, or
(c) the time when the accused is ordered to stand trial, if the accused
(i) is charged with an offence listed in section 469,
(ii) has elected to be tried by a court composed of a judge or a judge and jury, or
(iii) is deemed to have elected to be tried by a court composed of a judge and jury,
a justice of the peace, provincial court judge or judge of the Nunavut Court of Justice shall grant an order directing that the accused be tried before a justice of the peace, provincial court judge, judge or judge and jury, as the case may be, who speak the official language of Canada that is the language of the accused or, if the circumstances warrant, who speak both official languages of Canada.
Idem
(2) On application by an accused whose language is not one of the official languages of Canada, made not later than whichever of the times referred to in paragraphs (1)(a) to (c) is applicable, a justice of the peace or provincial court judge may grant an order directing that the accused be tried before a justice of the peace, provincial court judge, judge or judge and jury, as the case may be, who speak the official language of Canada in which the accused, in the opinion of the justice or provincial court judge, can best give testimony or, if the circumstances warrant, who speak both official languages of Canada.
Accused to be advised of right
(3) The justice of the peace or provincial court judge before whom an accused first appears shall ensure that they are advised of their right to apply for an order under subsection (1) or (2) and of the time before which such an application must be made.
Remand
(4) Where an accused fails to apply for an order under subsection (1) or (2) and the justice of the peace, provincial court judge or judge before whom the accused is to be tried, in this Part referred to as "the court", is satisfied that it is in the best interests of justice that the accused be tried before a justice of the peace, provincial court judge, judge or judge and jury who speak the official language of Canada that is the language of the accused or, if the language of the accused is not one of the official languages of Canada, the official language of Canada in which the accused, in the opinion of the court, can best give testimony, the court may, if it does not speak that language, by order remand the accused to be tried by a justice of the peace, provincial court judge, judge or judge and jury, as

the case may be, who speak that language or, if the circumstances warrant, who speak both official languages of Canada.

Variation of order

(5) An order under this section that a trial be held in one of the official languages of Canada may, if the circumstances warrant, be varied by the court to require that it be held in both official languages of Canada, and vice versa.

Circumstances warranting order directing trial in both official languages

(6) The facts that two or more accused who are to be tried together are each entitled to be tried before a justice of the peace, provincial court judge, judge or judge and jury who speak one of the official languages of Canada and that those official languages are different may constitute circumstances that warrant that an order be granted directing that they be tried before a justice of the peace, provincial court judge, judge or judge and jury who speak both official languages of Canada.

R.S., 1985, c. C-46, s. 530;
R.S., 1985, c. 27 (1st Supp.), ss. 94, 203;
1999, c. 3, s. 34;
2008, c. 18, s. 18.

Translation of documents

530.01 (1) If an order is granted under section 530, a prosecutor — other than a private prosecutor — shall, on application by the accused,

(a) cause the portions of an information or indictment against the accused that are in an official language that is not that of the accused or that in which the accused can best give testimony to be translated into the other official language; and

(b) provide the accused with a written copy of the translated text at the earliest possible time.

Original version prevails

(2) In the case of a discrepancy between the original version of a document and the translated text, the original version shall prevail.

2008, c. 18, s. 19.

If order granted

530.1 If an order is granted under section 530,

(a) the accused and his counsel have the right to use either official language for all purposes during the preliminary inquiry and trial of the accused;

(b) the accused and his counsel may use either official language in written pleadings or other documents used in any proceedings relating to the preliminary inquiry or trial of the accused;

(c) any witness may give evidence in either official language during the preliminary inquiry or trial;

(c.1) the presiding justice or judge may, if the circumstances warrant, authorize the prosecutor to examine or cross-examine a witness in the official language of the witness even though it is not that of the accused or that in which the accused can best give testimony;

(d) the accused has a right to have a justice presiding over the preliminary inquiry who speaks the official language of the accused or both official languages, as the case may be;

(e) the accused has a right to have a prosecutor — other than a private prosecutor — who speaks the official language of the accused or both official languages, as the case may be;

(f) the court shall make interpreters available to assist the accused, his counsel or any witness during the preliminary inquiry or trial;

(g) the record of proceedings during the preliminary inquiry or trial shall include

(i) a transcript of everything that was said during those proceedings in the official language in which it was said,

(ii) a transcript of any interpretation into the other official language of what was said, and

(iii) any documentary evidence that was tendered during those proceedings in the official language in which it was tendered; and

(h) any trial judgment, including any reasons given therefor, issued in writing in either official language, shall be made available by the court in the official language that is the language of the accused.

R.S., 1985, c. 31 (4th Supp.), s. 94;
2008, c. 18, s. 20.
Language used in proceeding
530.2 (1) If an order is granted directing that an accused be tried before a justice of the peace, provincial court judge, judge or judge and jury who speak both official languages, the justice or judge presiding over a preliminary inquiry or trial may, at the start of the proceeding, make an order setting out the circumstances in which, and the extent to which, the prosecutor and the justice or judge may use each official language.
Right of the accused
(2) Any order granted under this section shall, to the extent possible, respect the right of the accused to be tried in his or her official language.
2008, c. 18, s. 21.
Change of venue
531 Despite any other provision of this Act but subject to any regulations made under section 533, if an order made under section 530 cannot be conveniently complied with in the territorial division in which the offence would otherwise be tried, the court shall, except if that territorial division is in the Province of New Brunswick, order that the trial of the accused be held in another territorial division in the same province.
R.S., 1985, c. C-46, s. 531;
R.S., 1985, c. 27 (1st Supp.), s. 203;
2008, c. 18, s. 21.
Saving
532 Nothing in this Part or the
Official Languages Act
1977-78, c. 36, s. 1.
Regulations
533 The Lieutenant Governor in Council of a province may make regulations generally for carrying into effect the purposes and provisions of this Part in the province and the Commissioner of Yukon, the Commissioner of the Northwest Territories and the Commissioner of Nunavut may make regulations generally for carrying into effect the purposes and provisions of this Part in Yukon, the Northwest Territories and Nunavut, respectively.
R.S., 1985, c. C-46, s. 533;
1993, c. 28, s. 78;
2002, c. 7, s. 144.
Review
533.1 (1) Within three years after this section comes into force, a comprehensive review of the provisions and operation of this Part shall be undertaken by any committee of the Senate, of the House of Commons or of both Houses of Parliament that may be designated or established by the Senate or the House of Commons, or by both Houses of Parliament, as the case may be, for that purpose.
Report
(2) The committee referred to in subsection (1) shall, within a year after a review is undertaken under that subsection or within any further time that may be authorized by the Senate, the House of Commons or both Houses of Parliament, as the case may be, submit a report on the review to Parliament, including a statement of any changes that the committee recommends.
2008, c. 18, s. 21.1.
534
PART XVIII

PART XVIII
Procedure on Preliminary Inquiry

Jurisdiction

Inquiry by justice
535 If an accused who is charged with an indictable offence is before a justice and a request has been made for a preliminary inquiry under subsection 536(4) or 536.1(3), the justice shall, in accordance with this Part, inquire into the charge and any other indictable offence, in respect of the same transaction, founded on the facts that are disclosed by the evidence taken in accordance with this Part.
R.S., 1985, c. C-46, s. 535;
R.S., 1985, c. 27 (1st Supp.), s. 96;
2002, c. 13, s. 24.

Remand by justice to provincial court judge in certain cases
536 (1) Where an accused is before a justice other than a provincial court judge charged with an offence over which a provincial court judge has absolute jurisdiction under section 553, the justice shall remand the accused to appear before a provincial court judge having jurisdiction in the territorial division in which the offence is alleged to have been committed.

Election before justice in certain cases
(2) If an accused is before a justice charged with an indictable offence, other than an offence listed in section 469, and the offence is not one over which a provincial court judge has absolute jurisdiction under section 553, the justice shall, after the information has been read to the accused, put the accused to an election in the following words:

Procedure where accused elects trial by provincial court judge
(3) Where an accused elects to be tried by a provincial court judge, the justice shall endorse on the information a record of the election and shall
(a) where the justice is not a provincial court judge, remand the accused to appear and plead to the charge before a provincial court judge having jurisdiction in the territorial division in which the offence is alleged to have been committed; or
(b) where the justice is a provincial court judge, call on the accused to plead to the charge and if the accused does not plead guilty, proceed with the trial or fix a time for the trial.

Request for preliminary inquiry
(4) If an accused elects to be tried by a judge without a jury or by a court composed of a judge and jury or does not elect when put to the election or is deemed under paragraph 565(1)(b) to have elected to be tried by a court composed of a judge and jury or is charged with an offence listed in section 469, the justice shall, subject to section 577, on the request of the accused or the prosecutor made at that time or within the period fixed by rules of court made under section 482 or 482.1 or, if there are no such rules, by the justice, hold a preliminary inquiry into the charge.

Endorsement on the information
(4.1) If an accused elects to be tried by a judge without a jury or by a court composed of a judge and jury or does not elect when put to the election or is deemed under paragraph 565(1)(b) to have elected to be tried by a court composed of a judge and jury or is charged with an offence listed in section 469, the justice shall endorse on the information and, if the accused is in custody, on the warrant of remand, a statement showing
(a) the nature of the election or deemed election of the accused or that the accused did not elect, as the case may be; and
(b) whether the accused or the prosecutor has requested that a preliminary inquiry be held.

Preliminary inquiry if two or more accused
(4.2) If two or more persons are jointly charged in an information and one or more of them make a request for a preliminary inquiry under subsection (4), a preliminary inquiry must be held with respect to all of them.

When no request for preliminary inquiry
(4.3) If no request for a preliminary inquiry is made under subsection (4), the justice shall fix the date for the trial or the date on which the accused must appear in the trial court to have the date fixed.

Jurisdiction
(5) Where a justice before whom a preliminary inquiry is being or is to be held has not commenced to take evidence, any justice having jurisdiction in the province where the offence with which the accused is charged is alleged to have been committed has jurisdiction for the purposes of subsection (4).
R.S., 1985, c. C-46, s. 536;
R.S., 1985, c. 27 (1st Supp.), s. 96;
2002, c. 13, s. 25;
2004, c. 12, s. 9.

Remand by justice — Nunavut
536.1 (1) If an accused is before a justice of the peace charged with an indictable offence mentioned in section 553, the justice of the peace shall remand the accused to appear before a judge.

Election before justice in certain cases — Nunavut
(2) If an accused is before a justice of the peace or a judge charged with an indictable offence, other than an offence mentioned in section 469 or 553, the justice of the peace or judge shall, after the information has been read to the accused, put the accused to an election in the following words:

Request for preliminary inquiry — Nunavut
(3) If an accused elects to be tried by a judge without a jury or by a court composed of a judge and jury or does not elect when put to the election or is deemed under paragraph 565(1)(b) to have elected to be tried by a court composed of a judge and jury or is charged with an offence listed in section 469, the justice or judge shall, subject to section 577, on the request of the accused or the prosecutor made at that time or within the period fixed by rules of court made under section 482 or 482.1 or, if there are no such rules, by the judge or justice, hold a preliminary inquiry into the charge.

Endorsement on the information
(4) If an accused elects to be tried by a judge without a jury or by a court composed of a judge and jury or does not elect when put to the election or is deemed under paragraph 565(1)(b) to have elected to be tried by a court composed of a judge and jury or is charged with an offence listed in section 469, the justice or judge shall endorse on the information and, if the accused is in custody, on the warrant of remand, a statement showing
(a) the nature of the election or deemed election of the accused or that the accused did not elect, as the case may be; and
(b) whether the accused or the prosecutor has requested that a preliminary inquiry be held.

Preliminary inquiry if two or more accused
(4.1) If two or more persons are jointly charged in an information and one or more of them make a request for a preliminary inquiry under subsection (3), a preliminary inquiry must be held with respect to all of them.

Procedure if accused elects trial by judge — Nunavut
(4.2) If no request for a preliminary inquiry is made under subsection (3),
(a) if the accused is before a justice of the peace, the justice of the peace shall remand the accused to appear and plead to the charge before a judge; or
(b) if the accused is before a judge, the judge shall
(i) if the accused elects to be tried by a judge without a jury, call on the accused to plead to the charge and if the accused does not plead guilty, proceed with the trial or fix a time for the trial, or
(ii) if the accused elects or is deemed to have elected to be tried by a court composed of a judge and jury, fix a time for the trial.

Jurisdiction — Nunavut
(5) If a justice of the peace before whom a preliminary inquiry is being or is to be held has not commenced to take evidence, any justice of the peace having jurisdiction in Nunavut has jurisdiction for the purpose of subsection (3).

Application to Nunavut
(6) This section, and not section 536, applies in respect of criminal proceedings in Nunavut.
1999, c. 3, s. 35;

2002, c. 13, s. 26;
2004, c. 12, s. 10.
Elections and re-elections in writing
536.2 An election or a re-election by an accused in respect of a mode of trial may be made by submission of a document in writing without the personal appearance of the accused.
2002, c. 13, s. 27.

Procedures before Preliminary Inquiry

Statement of issues and witnesses
536.3 If a request for a preliminary inquiry is made, the prosecutor or, if the request was made by the accused, counsel for the accused shall, within the period fixed by rules of court made under section 482 or 482.1 or, if there are no such rules, by the justice, provide the court and the other party with a statement that identifies
(a) the issues on which the requesting party wants evidence to be given at the inquiry; and
(b) the witnesses that the requesting party wants to hear at the inquiry.
2002, c. 13, s. 27;
2011, c. 16, s. 3(F).
Order for hearing
536.4 (1) The justice before whom a preliminary inquiry is to be held may order, on application of the prosecutor or the accused or on the justice's own motion, that a hearing be held, within the period fixed by rules of court made under section 482 or 482.1 or, if there are no such rules, by the justice, to
(a) assist the parties to identify the issues on which evidence will be given at the inquiry;
(b) assist the parties to identify the witnesses to be heard at the inquiry, taking into account the witnesses' needs and circumstances; and
(c) encourage the parties to consider any other matters that would promote a fair and expeditious inquiry.
Agreement to be recorded
(2) When the hearing is completed, the justice shall record any admissions of fact agreed to by the parties and any agreement reached by the parties.
2002, c. 13, s. 27.
Agreement to limit scope of preliminary inquiry
536.5 Whether or not a hearing is held under section 536.4 in respect of a preliminary inquiry, the prosecutor and the accused may agree to limit the scope of the preliminary inquiry to specific issues. An agreement shall be filed with the court or recorded under subsection 536.4(2), as the case may be.
2002, c. 13, s. 27.

Powers of Justice

Powers of justice
537 (1) A justice acting under this Part may
(a) adjourn an inquiry from time to time and change the place of hearing, where it appears to be desirable to do so by reason of the absence of a witness, the inability of a witness who is ill to attend at the place where the justice usually sits or for any other sufficient reason;
(b) remand the accused to custody for the purposes of the
Identification of Criminals Act
(c) except where the accused is authorized pursuant to Part XVI to be at large, remand the accused to custody in a prison by warrant in Form 19;
(d) resume an inquiry before the expiration of a period for which it has been adjourned with the consent of the prosecutor and the accused or his counsel;
(e) order in writing, in Form 30, that the accused be brought before him, or any other justice for the

same territorial division, at any time before the expiration of the time for which the accused has been remanded;
(f) grant or refuse permission to the prosecutor or his counsel to address him in support of the charge, by way of opening or summing up or by way of reply on any evidence that is given on behalf of the accused;
(g) receive evidence on the part of the prosecutor or the accused, as the case may be, after hearing any evidence that has been given on behalf of either of them;
(h) order that no person other than the prosecutor, the accused and their counsel shall have access to or remain in the room in which the inquiry is held, where it appears to him that the ends of justice will be best served by so doing;
(i) regulate the course of the inquiry in any way that appears to the justice to be consistent with this Act and that, unless the justice is satisfied that to do so would be contrary to the best interests of the administration of justice, is in accordance with any admission of fact or agreement recorded under subsection 536.4(2) or agreement made under section 536.5;
(j) where the prosecutor and the accused so agree, permit the accused to appear by counsel or by closed-circuit television or any other means that allow the court and the accused to engage in simultaneous visual and oral communication, for any part of the inquiry other than a part in which the evidence of a witness is taken;
(j.1) permit, on the request of the accused, that the accused be out of court during the whole or any part of the inquiry on any conditions that the justice considers appropriate; and
(k) for any part of the inquiry other than a part in which the evidence of a witness is taken, require an accused who is confined in prison to appear by closed-circuit television or any other means that allow the court and the accused to engage in simultaneous visual and oral communication, if the accused is given the opportunity to communicate privately with counsel, in a case in which the accused is represented by counsel.

Section 715
(1.01) Where a justice grants a request under paragraph (1)(j.1), the Court must inform the accused that the evidence taken during his or her absence could still be admissible under section 715.

Inappropriate questioning
(1.1) A justice acting under this Part shall order the immediate cessation of any part of an examination or cross-examination of a witness that is, in the opinion of the justice, abusive, too repetitive or otherwise inappropriate.

Change of venue
(2) Where a justice changes the place of hearing under paragraph (1)(a) to a place in the same province, other than a place in a territorial division in which the justice has jurisdiction, any justice who has jurisdiction in the place to which the hearing is changed may continue the hearing.
(3) and (4) R.S., 1985, c. C-46, s. 537;
1991, c. 43, s. 9;
1994, c. 44, s. 53;
1997, c. 18, s. 64;
2002, c. 13, s. 28;
2008, c. 18, s. 22.

Organization
538 Where an accused is an organization, subsections 556(1) and (2) apply with such modifications as the circumstances require.
R.S., 1985, c. C-46, s. 538;
2003, c. 21, s. 8.

Taking Evidence of Witnesses

Order restricting publication of evidence taken at preliminary inquiry
539 (1) Prior to the commencement of the taking of evidence at a preliminary inquiry, the justice

holding the inquiry
(a) may, if application therefor is made by the prosecutor, and
(b) shall, if application therefor is made by any of the accused,
make an order directing that the evidence taken at the inquiry shall not be published in any document or broadcast or transmitted in any way before such time as, in respect of each of the accused,
(c) he or she is discharged, or
(d) if he or she is ordered to stand trial, the trial is ended.

Accused to be informed of right to apply for order
(2) Where an accused is not represented by counsel at a preliminary inquiry, the justice holding the inquiry shall, prior to the commencement of the taking of evidence at the inquiry, inform the accused of his right to make application under subsection (1).

Failure to comply with order
(3) Every one who fails to comply with an order made pursuant to subsection (1) is guilty of an offence punishable on summary conviction.
(4) R.S., 1985, c. C-46, s. 539;
R.S., 1985, c. 27 (1st Supp.), s. 97;
2005, c. 32, s. 18.

Taking evidence
540 (1) Where an accused is before a justice holding a preliminary inquiry, the justice shall
(a) take the evidence under oath of the witnesses called on the part of the prosecution and allow the accused or counsel for the accused to cross-examine them; and
(b) cause a record of the evidence of each witness to be taken
(i) in legible writing in the form of a deposition, in Form 31, or by a stenographer appointed by him or pursuant to law, or
(ii) in a province where a sound recording apparatus is authorized by or under provincial legislation for use in civil cases, by the type of apparatus so authorized and in accordance with the requirements of the provincial legislation.

Reading and signing depositions
(2) Where a deposition is taken down in writing, the justice shall, in the presence of the accused, before asking the accused if he wishes to call witnesses,
(a) cause the deposition to be read to the witness;
(b) cause the deposition to be signed by the witness; and
(c) sign the deposition himself.

Authentication by justice
(3) Where depositions are taken down in writing, the justice may sign
(a) at the end of each deposition; or
(b) at the end of several or of all the depositions in a manner that will indicate that his signature is intended to authenticate each deposition.

Stenographer to be sworn
(4) Where the stenographer appointed to take down the evidence is not a duly sworn court stenographer, he shall make oath that he will truly and faithfully report the evidence.

Authentication of transcript
(5) Where the evidence is taken down by a stenographer appointed by the justice or pursuant to law, it need not be read to or signed by the witnesses, but, on request of the justice or of one of the parties, shall be transcribed, in whole or in part, by the stenographer and the transcript shall be accompanied by
(a) an affidavit of the stenographer that it is a true report of the evidence; or
(b) a certificate that it is a true report of the evidence if the stenographer is a duly sworn court stenographer.

Transcription of record taken by sound recording apparatus
(6) Where, in accordance with this Act, a record is taken in any proceedings under this Act by a sound recording apparatus, the record so taken shall, on request of the justice or of one of the parties,

be dealt with and transcribed, in whole or in part, and the transcription certified and used in accordance with the provincial legislation, with such modifications as the circumstances require mentioned in subsection (1).

Evidence

(7) A justice acting under this Part may receive as evidence any information that would not otherwise be admissible but that the justice considers credible or trustworthy in the circumstances of the case, including a statement that is made by a witness in writing or otherwise recorded.

Notice of intention to tender

(8) Unless the justice orders otherwise, no information may be received as evidence under subsection (7) unless the party has given to each of the other parties reasonable notice of his or her intention to tender it, together with a copy of the statement, if any, referred to in that subsection.

Appearance for examination

(9) The justice shall, on application of a party, require any person whom the justice considers appropriate to appear for examination or cross-examination with respect to information intended to be tendered as evidence under subsection (7).

R.S., 1985, c. C-46, s. 540;
R.S., 1985, c. 27 (1st Supp.), s. 98;
1997, c. 18, s. 65;
2002, c. 13, s. 29.

Hearing of witnesses

541 (1) When the evidence of the witnesses called on the part of the prosecution has been taken down and, where required by this Part, has been read, the justice shall, subject to this section, hear the witnesses called by the accused.

Contents of address to accused

(2) Before hearing any witness called by an accused who is not represented by counsel, the justice shall address the accused as follows or to the like effect:

Statement of accused

(3) Where the accused who is not represented by counsel says anything in answer to the address made by the justice pursuant to subsection (2), the answer shall be taken down in writing and shall be signed by the justice and kept with the evidence of the witnesses and dealt with in accordance with this Part.

Witnesses for accused

(4) Where an accused is not represented by counsel, the justice shall ask the accused if he or she wishes to call any witnesses after subsections (2) and (3) have been complied with.

Depositions of such witnesses

(5) The justice shall hear each witness called by the accused who testifies to any matter relevant to the inquiry, and for the purposes of this subsection, section 540 applies with such modifications as the circumstances require.

R.S., 1985, c. C-46, s. 541;
R.S., 1985, c. 27 (1st Supp.), s. 99;
1994, c. 44, s. 54.

Confession or admission of accused

542 (1) Nothing in this Act prevents a prosecutor giving in evidence at a preliminary inquiry any admission, confession or statement made at any time by the accused that by law is admissible against him.

Restriction of publication of reports of preliminary inquiry

(2) Every one who publishes in any document, or broadcasts or transmits in any way, a report that any admission or confession was tendered in evidence at a preliminary inquiry or a report of the nature of such admission or confession so tendered in evidence unless

(a) the accused has been discharged, or

(b) if the accused has been ordered to stand trial, the trial has ended,

is guilty of an offence punishable on summary conviction.

(3) R.S., 1985, c. C-46, s. 542;
R.S., 1985, c. 27 (1st Supp.), s. 101(E);
2005, c. 32, s. 19.

Remand Where Offence Committed in Another Jurisdiction

Order that accused appear or be taken before justice where offence committed
543 (1) Where an accused is charged with an offence alleged to have been committed out of the limits of the jurisdiction in which he has been charged, the justice before whom he appears or is brought may, at any stage of the inquiry after hearing both parties,
(a) order the accused to appear, or
(b) if the accused is in custody, issue a warrant in Form 15 to convey the accused
before a justice having jurisdiction in the place where the offence is alleged to have been committed, who shall continue and complete the inquiry.

Transmission of transcript and documents and effect of order or warrant
(2) Where a justice makes an order or issues a warrant pursuant to subsection (1), he shall cause the transcript of any evidence given before him in the inquiry and all documents that were then before him and that are relevant to the inquiry to be transmitted to a justice having jurisdiction in the place where the offence is alleged to have been committed and
(a) any evidence the transcript of which is so transmitted shall be deemed to have been taken by the justice to whom it is transmitted; and
(b) any appearance notice, promise to appear, undertaking or recognizance issued to or given or entered into by the accused under Part XVI shall be deemed to have been issued, given or entered into in the jurisdiction where the offence is alleged to have been committed and to require the accused to appear before the justice to whom the transcript and documents are transmitted at the time provided in the order made in respect of the accused under paragraph (1)(a).
R.S., c. C-34, s. 471;
R.S., c. 2(2nd Supp.), s. 7.

Absconding Accused

Accused absconding during inquiry
544 (1) Notwithstanding any other provision of this Act, where an accused, whether or not he is charged jointly with another, absconds during the course of a preliminary inquiry into an offence with which he is charged,
(a) he shall be deemed to have waived his right to be present at the inquiry, and
(b) the justice
(i) may continue the inquiry and, when all the evidence has been taken, shall dispose of the inquiry in accordance with section 548, or
(ii) if a warrant is issued for the arrest of the accused, may adjourn the inquiry to await his appearance,
but where the inquiry is adjourned pursuant to subparagraph (b)(ii), the justice may continue it at any time pursuant to subparagraph (b)(i) if he is satisfied that it would no longer be in the interests of justice to await the appearance of the accused.

Adverse inference
(2) Where the justice continues a preliminary inquiry pursuant to subsection (1), he may draw an inference adverse to the accused from the fact that he has absconded.

Accused not entitled to re-opening
(3) Where an accused reappears at a preliminary inquiry that is continuing pursuant to subsection (1), he is not entitled to have any part of the proceedings that was conducted in his absence re-opened unless the justice is satisfied that because of exceptional circumstances it is in the interests of justice to re-open the inquiry.

Counsel for accused may continue to act
(4) Where an accused has absconded during the course of a preliminary inquiry and the justice continues the inquiry, counsel for the accused is not thereby deprived of any authority he may have to continue to act for the accused in the proceedings.
Accused calling witnesses
(5) Where, at the conclusion of the evidence on the part of the prosecution at a preliminary inquiry that has been continued pursuant to subsection (1), the accused is absent but counsel for the accused is present, he or she shall be given an opportunity to call witnesses on behalf of the accused and subsection 541(5) applies with such modifications as the circumstances require.
R.S., 1985, c. C-46, s. 544;
1994, c. 44, s. 55.

Procedure where Witness Refuses to Testify

Witness refusing to be examined
545 (1) Where a person, being present at a preliminary inquiry and being required by the justice to give evidence,
(a) refuses to be sworn,
(b) having been sworn, refuses to answer the questions that are put to him,
(c) fails to produce any writings that he is required to produce, or
(d) refuses to sign his deposition,
without offering a reasonable excuse for his failure or refusal, the justice may adjourn the inquiry and may, by warrant in Form 20, commit the person to prison for a period not exceeding eight clear days or for the period during which the inquiry is adjourned, whichever is the lesser period.
Further commitment
(2) Where a person to whom subsection (1) applies is brought before the justice on the resumption of the adjourned inquiry and again refuses to do what is required of him, the justice may again adjourn the inquiry for a period not exceeding eight clear days and commit him to prison for the period of adjournment or any part thereof, and may adjourn the inquiry and commit the person to prison from time to time until the person consents to do what is required of him.
Saving
(3) Nothing in this section shall be deemed to prevent the justice from sending the case for trial on any other sufficient evidence taken by him.
R.S., c. C-34, s. 472.

Remedial Provisions

Irregularity or variance not to affect validity
546 The validity of any proceeding at or subsequent to a preliminary inquiry is not affected by
(a) any irregularity or defect in the substance or form of the summons or warrant;
(b) any variance between the charge set out in the summons or warrant and the charge set out in the information; or
(c) any variance between the charge set out in the summons, warrant or information and the evidence adduced by the prosecution at the inquiry.
R.S., c. C-34, s. 473.
Adjournment if accused misled
547 Where it appears to the justice that the accused has been deceived or misled by any irregularity, defect or variance mentioned in section 546, he may adjourn the inquiry and may remand the accused or grant him interim release in accordance with Part XVI.
R.S., c. C-34, s. 474;
1974-75-76, c. 93, s. 59.1.
Inability of justice to continue

547.1 Where a justice acting under this Part has commenced to take evidence and dies or is unable to continue for any reason, another justice may
(a) continue taking the evidence at the point at which the interruption in the taking of the evidence occurred, where the evidence was recorded pursuant to section 540 and is available; or
(b) commence taking the evidence as if no evidence had been taken, where no evidence was recorded pursuant to section 540 or where the evidence is not available.
R.S., 1985, c. 27 (1st Supp.), s. 100.

Adjudication and Recognizances

Order to stand trial or discharge
548 (1) When all the evidence has been taken by the justice, he shall
(a) if in his opinion there is sufficient evidence to put the accused on trial for the offence charged or any other indictable offence in respect of the same transaction, order the accused to stand trial; or
(b) discharge the accused, if in his opinion on the whole of the evidence no sufficient case is made out to put the accused on trial for the offence charged or any other indictable offence in respect of the same transaction.

Endorsing charge
(2) Where the justice orders the accused to stand trial for an indictable offence, other than or in addition to the one with which the accused was charged, the justice shall endorse on the information the charges on which he orders the accused to stand trial.

Where accused ordered to stand trial
(2.1) A justice who orders that an accused is to stand trial has the power to fix the date for the trial or the date on which the accused must appear in the trial court to have that date fixed.

Defect not to affect validity
(3) The validity of an order to stand trial is not affected by any defect apparent on the face of the information in respect of which the preliminary inquiry is held or in respect of any charge on which the accused is ordered to stand trial unless, in the opinion of the court before which an objection to the information or charge is taken, the accused has been misled or prejudiced in his defence by reason of that defect.
R.S., 1985, c. C-46, s. 548;
R.S., 1985, c. 27 (1st Supp.), s. 101;
1994, c. 44, s. 56.

Order to stand trial at any stage of inquiry with consent
549 (1) Notwithstanding any other provision of this Act, the justice may, at any stage of a preliminary inquiry, with the consent of the accused and the prosecutor, order the accused to stand trial in the court having criminal jurisdiction, without taking or recording any evidence or further evidence.

Limited preliminary inquiry
(1.1) If the prosecutor and the accused agree under section 536.5 to limit the scope of a preliminary inquiry to specific issues, the justice, without recording evidence on any other issues, may order the accused to stand trial in the court having criminal jurisdiction.

Procedure
(2) If an accused is ordered to stand trial under this section, the justice shall endorse on the information a statement of the consent of the accused and the prosecutor, and the accused shall after that be dealt with in all respects as if ordered to stand trial under section 548.
R.S., 1985, c. C-46, s. 549;
R.S., 1985, c. 27 (1st Supp.), s. 101;
2002, c. 13, s. 30.

Recognizance of witness
550 (1) Where an accused is ordered to stand trial, the justice who held the preliminary inquiry may require any witness whose evidence is, in his opinion, material to enter into a recognizance to give

evidence at the trial of the accused and to comply with such reasonable conditions prescribed in the recognizance as the justice considers desirable for securing the attendance of the witness to give evidence at the trial of the accused.

Form

(2) A recognizance entered into pursuant to this section may be in Form 32, and may be set out at the end of a deposition or be separate therefrom.

Sureties or deposit for appearance of witness

(3) A justice may, for any reason satisfactory to him, require any witness entering into a recognizance pursuant to this section

(a) to produce one or more sureties in such amount as he may direct; or

(b) to deposit with him a sum of money sufficient in his opinion to ensure that the witness will appear and give evidence.

Witness refusing to be bound

(4) Where a witness does not comply with subsection (1) or (3) when required to do so by a justice, he may be committed by the justice, by warrant in Form 24, to a prison in the territorial division where the trial is to be held, there to be kept until he does what is required of him or until the trial is concluded.

Discharge

(5) Where a witness has been committed to prison pursuant to subsection (4), the court before which the witness appears or a justice having jurisdiction in the territorial division where the prison is situated may, by order in Form 39, discharge the witness from custody when the trial is concluded.
R.S., 1985, c. C-46, s. 550;
R.S., 1985, c. 27 (1st Supp.), s. 101.

Transmission of Record

Transmitting record

551 Where a justice orders an accused to stand trial, the justice shall forthwith send to the clerk or other proper officer of the court by which the accused is to be tried, the information, the evidence, the exhibits, the statement if any of the accused taken down in writing under section 541, any promise to appear, undertaking or recognizance given or entered into in accordance with Part XVI, or any evidence taken before a coroner, that is in the possession of the justice.
R.S., 1985, c. C-46, s. 551;
R.S., 1985, c. 27 (1st Supp.), s. 102.

PART XVIII.1

PART XVIII.1
Case Management Judge

Appointment

551.1 (1) On application by the prosecutor or the accused or on his or her own motion, the Chief Justice or the Chief Judge of the court before which a trial is to be or is being held or the judge that the Chief Justice or the Chief Judge designates may, if he or she is of the opinion that it is necessary for the proper administration of justice, appoint a judge as the case management judge for that trial at any time before the jury selection, if the trial is before a judge and jury, or before the stage at which the evidence on the merits is presented, if the trial is being heard by a judge without a jury or a provincial court judge.

Conference or hearing

(2) The Chief Justice or the Chief Judge or his or her designate may order that a conference between the prosecutor and the accused or counsel for the accused or a hearing be held for the purpose of deciding if it is necessary for the proper administration of justice to proceed with the appointment.

Timing of application or appointment
(3) In the case of a trial for an indictable offence, other than a trial before a provincial court judge, the application or appointment may only be made after the prosecution prefers the indictment.
Same judge
(4) The appointment of a judge as the case management judge does not prevent him or her from becoming the judge who hears the evidence on the merits.
2011, c. 16, s. 4.
Role
551.2 The case management judge shall assist in promoting a fair and efficient trial, including by ensuring that the evidence on the merits is presented, to the extent possible, without interruption.
2011, c. 16, s. 4.
Powers before evidence on merits presented
551.3 (1) In performing his or her duties before the stage of the presentation of the evidence on the merits, the case management judge, as a trial judge, may exercise the powers that a trial judge has before that stage, including
(a) assisting the parties to identify the witnesses to be heard, taking into account the witnesses' needs and circumstances;
(b) encouraging the parties to make admissions and reach agreements;
(c) encouraging the parties to consider any other matters that would promote a fair and efficient trial;
(d) establishing schedules and imposing deadlines on the parties;
(e) hearing guilty pleas and imposing sentences;
(f) assisting the parties to identify the issues that are to be dealt with at the stage at which the evidence on the merits is presented; and
(g) subject to section 551.7, adjudicating any issues that can be decided before that stage, including those related to
(i) the disclosure of evidence,
(ii) the admissibility of evidence,
(iii) the
Canadian Charter of Rights and Freedoms
(iv) expert witnesses,
(v) the severance of counts, and
(vi) the separation of trials on one or more counts when there is more than one accused.
Hearing
(2) The case management judge shall order that a hearing be held for the purpose of exercising the power referred to in paragraph (1)(g).
Power exercised at trial
(3) When the case management judge exercises the power referred to in paragraph (1)(g), he or she is doing so at trial.
Decision binding
(4) A decision that results from the exercise of the power referred to in paragraph (1)(g) is binding on the parties for the remainder of the trial — even if the judge who hears the evidence on the merits is not the same as the case management judge — unless the court is satisfied that it would not be in the interests of justice because, among other considerations, fresh evidence has been adduced.
2011, c. 16, s. 4.
Information relevant to presentation of evidence on merits to be part of court record
551.4 (1) When the case management judge is of the opinion that the measures to promote a fair and efficient trial that can be taken before the stage of the presentation of the evidence on the merits have been taken — including adjudicating the issues that can be decided — he or she shall ensure that the court record includes information that, in his or her opinion, may be relevant at the stage of the presentation of the evidence on the merits, including
(a) the names of the witnesses to be heard that have been identified by the parties;
(b) any admissions made and agreements reached by the parties;

(c) the estimated time required to conclude the trial;
(d) any orders and decisions; and
(e) any issues identified by the parties that are to be dealt with at the stage of the presentation of the evidence on the merits.

Exception

(2) This section does not apply to a case management judge who also hears the evidence on the merits.

2011, c. 16, s. 4.

Trial continuous

551.5 Even if the judge who hears the evidence on the merits is not the same as the case management judge, the trial of an accused shall proceed continuously, subject to adjournment by the court.

2011, c. 16, s. 4.

Issues referred to case management judge

551.6 (1) During the presentation of the evidence on the merits, the case management judge shall adjudicate any issue referred to him or her by the judge hearing the evidence on the merits.

Powers at stage of presentation of evidence on merits

(2) For the purposes of adjudicating an issue, the case management judge may exercise the powers of a trial judge.

2011, c. 16, s. 4.

Decision whether to hold joint hearing

551.7 (1) If an issue referred to in any of subparagraphs 551.3(1)(g)(i) to (iii) is to be adjudicated in related trials that are to be or are being held in the same province before a court of the same jurisdiction, the Chief Justice or the Chief Judge of that court or his or her designate may, on application by the prosecutor or the accused or on his or her own motion, determine if it is in the interests of justice, including ensuring consistent decisions, to adjudicate that issue at a joint hearing for some or all of those trials.

Considerations

(2) To make the determination, the Chief Justice or the Chief Judge or his or her designate
(a) shall take into account, among other considerations, the degree to which the evidence relating to the issue is similar in the related trials; and
(b) may order that a conference between the prosecutor and the accused or counsel for the accused or a hearing be held.

Order for joint hearing

(3) If the Chief Justice or the Chief Judge or his or her designate determines that it is in the interests of justice to adjudicate the issue at a joint hearing for some or all of the related trials, he or she shall issue an order
(a) declaring that a joint hearing be held to adjudicate the issue in the related trials that he or she specifies;
(b) naming the parties who are to appear at the hearing;
(c) appointing a judge to adjudicate the issue; and
(d) designating the territorial division in which the hearing is to be held, if the trials are being held in different territorial divisions.

Limitation — indictable offence

(4) However, the order may only be made in respect of a trial for an indictable offence, other than a trial before a provincial court judge, if the indictment has been preferred.

Order in court record and transmission to parties

(5) The Chief Justice or the Chief Judge or his or her designate shall cause a copy of the order to be included in the court record of each of the trials specified in the order and to be provided to each of the parties named in it.

Transmission of court record

(6) If one of the specified trials is being held in a territorial division other than the one in which the joint hearing will be held, the officer in that territorial division who has custody of the indictment or

information and the writings relating to the trial shall, when he or she receives the order, transmit the indictment or information and the writings without delay to the clerk of the court before which the joint hearing is to be held.

Order to appear at joint hearing

(7) The judge appointed under the order shall require the parties who are named in it to appear at the joint hearing.

Removal of prisoner

(8) The order made under subsection (2) or (3) is sufficient warrant, justification and authority to all sheriffs, keepers of prisons and peace officers for an accused's removal, disposal and reception in accordance with the terms of the order, and the sheriff may appoint and authorize any peace officer to convey the accused to a prison for the territorial division in which the hearing, as the case may be, is to be held.

Powers of judge

(9) The judge appointed under the order may, as a trial judge and for the purpose of adjudicating the issue at the joint hearing, exercise the powers of a trial judge.

Adjudication at trial

(10) When the judge adjudicates the issue, he or she is doing so at trial.

Decision in court records and return of documents

(11) Once the judge has adjudicated the issue, he or she shall cause his or her decision, with reasons, to be included in the court record of each of the related trials in respect of which the joint hearing was held and, in the case of a trial for which an indictment, information or writings were transmitted by an officer under subsection (6), the judge shall have the documents returned to the officer.
2011, c. 16, s. 4.

PART XIX

PART XIX
Indictable Offences — Trial Without Jury

Interpretation

Definitions
552 In this Part,
judge
(a) in the Province of Ontario, a judge of the superior court of criminal jurisdiction of the Province,
(b) in the Province of Quebec, a judge of the Court of Quebec,
(c) in the Province of Nova Scotia, a judge of the superior court of criminal jurisdiction of the Province,
(d) in the Province of New Brunswick, a judge of the Court of Queen's Bench,
(e) in the Province of British Columbia, the Chief Justice or a puisne judge of the Supreme Court,
(f) in the Province of Prince Edward Island, a judge of the Supreme Court,
(g) in the Province of Manitoba, the Chief Justice or a puisne judge of the Court of Queen's Bench,
(h) in the Provinces of Saskatchewan and Alberta, a judge of the superior court of criminal jurisdiction of the province,
(h.1) in the Province of Newfoundland and Labrador, a judge of the Trial Division of the Supreme Court,
(i) in Yukon and the Northwest Territories, a judge of the Supreme Court, and
(j) in Nunavut, a judge of the Nunavut Court of Justice.
magistrate
R.S., 1985, c. C-46, s. 552;
R.S., 1985, c. 11 (1st Supp.), s. 2, c. 27 (1st Supp.), s. 103, c. 27 (2nd Supp.), s. 10, c. 40 (4th Supp.), s. 2;

1990, c. 16, s. 6, c. 17, s. 13;
1992, c. 51, s. 38;
1999, c. 3, s. 36;
2002, c. 7, s. 145;
2015, c. 3, s. 53.

Jurisdiction of Provincial Court Judges

Absolute Jurisdiction

Absolute jurisdiction
553 The jurisdiction of a provincial court judge, or in Nunavut, of a judge of the Nunavut Court of Justice, to try an accused is absolute and does not depend on the consent of the accused where the accused is charged in an information
(a) with
(i) theft, other than theft of cattle,
(ii) obtaining money or property by false pretences,
(iii) unlawfully having in his possession any property or thing or any proceeds of any property or thing knowing that all or a part of the property or thing or of the proceeds was obtained by or derived directly or indirectly from the commission in Canada of an offence punishable by indictment or an act or omission anywhere that, if it had occurred in Canada, would have constituted an offence punishable by indictment,
(iv) having, by deceit, falsehood or other fraudulent means, defrauded the public or any person, whether ascertained or not, of any property, money or valuable security, or
(v) mischief under subsection 430(4),
where the subject-matter of the offence is not a testamentary instrument and the alleged value of the subject-matter of the offence does not exceed five thousand dollars;
(b) with counselling or with a conspiracy or attempt to commit or with being an accessory after the fact to the commission of
(i) any offence referred to in paragraph (a) in respect of the subject-matter and value thereof referred to in that paragraph, or
(ii) any offence referred to in paragraph (c); or
(c) with an offence under
(i) section 201 (keeping gaming or betting house),
(ii) section 202 (betting, pool-selling, book-making, etc.),
(iii) section 203 (placing bets),
(iv) section 206 (lotteries and games of chance),
(v) section 209 (cheating at play),
(vi) section 210 (keeping common bawdy-house),
(vii) (viii) section 393 (fraud in relation to fares),
(viii.01) section 490.031 (failure to comply with order or obligation),
(viii.02) section 490.0311 (providing false or misleading information),
(viii.1) section 811 (breach of recognizance),
(ix) subsection 733.1(1) (failure to comply with probation order),
(x) paragraph 4(4)(a) of the
Controlled Drugs and Substances Act
(xi) paragraph 5(3)(a.1) of the
Controlled Drugs and Substances Act
R.S., 1985, c. C-46, s. 553;
R.S., 1985, c. 27 (1st Supp.), s. 104;
1992, c. 1, s. 58;
1994, c. 44, s. 57;

1995, c. 22, s. 2;
1996, c. 19, s. 72;
1997, c. 18, s. 66;
1999, c. 3, s. 37;
2000, c. 25, s. 4;
2010, c. 17, s. 25;
2012, c. 1, s. 33.

Provincial Court Judge's Jurisdiction with Consent

Trial by provincial court judge with consent

554 (1) Subject to subsection (2), if an accused is charged in an information with an indictable offence other than an offence that is mentioned in section 469, and the offence is not one over which a provincial court judge has absolute jurisdiction under section 553, a provincial court judge may try the accused if the accused elects to be tried by a provincial court judge.

Nunavut

(2) With respect to criminal proceedings in Nunavut, if an accused is charged in an information with an indictable offence other than an offence that is mentioned in section 469 and the offence is not one over which a judge of the Nunavut Court of Justice has absolute jurisdiction under section 553, a judge of the Nunavut Court of Justice may try the accused if the accused elects to be tried by a judge without a jury.

R.S., 1985, c. C-46, s. 554;
R.S., 1985, c. 27 (1st Supp.), ss. 105, 203;
1999, c. 3, s. 38;
2002, c. 13, s. 31.

Provincial court judge may decide to hold preliminary inquiry

555 (1) Where in any proceedings under this Part an accused is before a provincial court judge and it appears to the provincial court judge that for any reason the charge should be prosecuted by indictment, he may, at any time before the accused has entered on his defence, decide not to adjudicate and shall thereupon inform the accused of his decision and continue the proceedings as a preliminary inquiry.

Where subject-matter is a testamentary instrument or exceeds $5,000 in value

(2) Where an accused is before a provincial court judge charged with an offence mentioned in paragraph 553(a) or subparagraph 553(b)(i), and, at any time before the provincial court judge makes an adjudication, the evidence establishes that the subject-matter of the offence is a testamentary instrument or that its value exceeds five thousand dollars, the provincial court judge shall put the accused to his or her election in accordance with subsection 536(2).

Continuing proceedings

(3) Where an accused is put to his election pursuant to subsection (2), the following provisions apply, namely,

(a) if the accused elects to be tried by a judge without a jury or a court composed of a judge and jury or does not elect when put to his or her election, the provincial court judge shall continue the proceedings as a preliminary inquiry under Part XVIII and, if the provincial court judge orders the accused to stand trial, he or she shall endorse on the information a record of the election; and

(b) if the accused elects to be tried by a provincial court judge, the provincial court judge shall endorse on the information a record of the election and continue with the trial.

R.S., 1985, c. C-46, s. 555;
R.S., 1985, c. 27 (1st Supp.), ss. 106, 203;
1994, c. 44, s. 58;
2002, c. 13, s. 32.

Decision to hold preliminary inquiry — Nunavut

555.1 (1) If in any criminal proceedings under this Part an accused is before a judge of the Nunavut

Court of Justice and it appears to the judge that for any reason the charge should be prosecuted by indictment, the judge may, at any time before the accused has entered a defence, decide not to adjudicate and shall then inform the accused of the decision and continue the proceedings as a preliminary inquiry.

If subject-matter is a testamentary instrument or exceeds $5,000 in value — Nunavut
(2) If an accused is before a judge of the Nunavut Court of Justice charged with an indictable offence mentioned in paragraph 553(a) or subparagraph 553(b)(i), and, at any time before the judge makes an adjudication, the evidence establishes that the subject-matter of the offence is a testamentary instrument or that its value exceeds five thousand dollars, the judge shall put the accused to an election in accordance with subsection 536.1(2).

Continuation as preliminary inquiry — Nunavut
(3) A judge shall continue the proceedings as a preliminary inquiry under Part XVIII if the accused is put to an election under subsection (2) and elects to be tried by a judge without a jury and requests a preliminary inquiry under subsection 536.1(3) or elects to be tried by a court composed of a judge and jury or does not elect when put to the election.

Continuing proceedings — Nunavut
(4) If an accused is put to an election under subsection (2) and elects to be tried by a judge without a jury and does not request a preliminary inquiry under subsection 536.1(3), the judge shall endorse on the information a record of the election and continue with the trial.

Application to Nunavut
(5) This section, and not section 555, applies in respect of criminal proceedings in Nunavut.
1999, c. 3, s. 39;
2002, c. 13, s. 33.

Organization
556 (1) An accused organization shall appear by counsel or agent.

Non-appearance
(2) Where an accused organization does not appear pursuant to a summons and service of the summons on the organization is proved, the provincial court judge or, in Nunavut, the judge of the Nunavut Court of Justice
(a) may, if the charge is one over which the judge has absolute jurisdiction, proceed with the trial of the charge in the absence of the accused organization; and
(b) shall, if the charge is not one over which the judge has absolute jurisdiction, fix the date for the trial or the date on which the accused organization must appear in the trial court to have that date fixed.

Preliminary inquiry not requested
(3) If an accused organization appears and a preliminary inquiry is not requested under subsection 536(4), the provincial court judge shall fix the date for the trial or the date on which the organization must appear in the trial court to have that date fixed.

Preliminary inquiry not requested — Nunavut
(4) If an accused organization appears and a preliminary inquiry is not requested under subsection 536.1(3), the justice of the peace or the judge of the Nunavut Court of Justice shall fix the date for the trial or the date on which the organization must appear in the trial court to have that date fixed.
R.S., 1985, c. C-46, s. 556;
R.S., 1985, c. 27 (1st Supp.), s. 107;
1999, c. 3, s. 40;
2002, c. 13, s. 34;
2003, c. 21, ss. 9, 22.

Taking evidence
557 If an accused is tried by a provincial court judge or a judge of the Nunavut Court of Justice in accordance with this Part, the evidence of witnesses for the prosecutor and the accused must be taken in accordance with the provisions of Part XVIII, other than subsections 540(7) to (9), relating to preliminary inquiries.

R.S., 1985, c. C-46, s. 557;
R.S., 1985, c. 27 (1st Supp.), s. 203;
1999, c. 3, s. 41;
2002, c. 13, s. 35.

Jurisdiction of Judges

Judge's Jurisdiction with Consent

Trial by judge without a jury
558 If an accused who is charged with an indictable offence, other than an offence mentioned in section 469, elects under section 536 or 536.1 or re-elects under section 561 or 561.1 to be tried by a judge without a jury, the accused shall, subject to this Part, be tried by a judge without a jury.
R.S., 1985, c. C-46, s. 558;
R.S., 1985, c. 27 (1st Supp.), s. 108;
1999, c. 3, s. 41.
Court of record
559 (1) A judge who holds a trial under this Part shall, for all purposes thereof and proceedings connected therewith or relating thereto, be a court of record.
Custody of records
(2) The record of a trial that a judge holds under this Part shall be kept in the court over which the judge presides.
R.S., c. C-34, s. 489.

Election

Duty of judge
560 (1) If an accused elects, under section 536 or 536.1, to be tried by a judge without a jury, a judge having jurisdiction shall
(a) on receiving a written notice from the sheriff or other person having custody of the accused stating that the accused is in custody and setting out the nature of the charge against him, or
(b) on being notified by the clerk of the court that the accused is not in custody and of the nature of the charge against him,
fix a time and place for the trial of the accused.
Notice by sheriff, when given
(2) The sheriff or other person having custody of the accused shall give the notice mentioned in paragraph (1)(a) within twenty-four hours after the accused is ordered to stand trial, if the accused is in custody pursuant to that order or if, at the time of the order, he is in custody for any other reason.
Duty of sheriff when date set for trial
(3) Where, pursuant to subsection (1), a time and place is fixed for the trial of an accused who is in custody, the accused
(a) shall be notified forthwith by the sheriff or other person having custody of the accused of the time and place so fixed; and
(b) shall be produced at the time and place so fixed.
Duty of accused when not in custody
(4) Where an accused is not in custody, the duty of ascertaining from the clerk of the court the time and place fixed for the trial, pursuant to subsection (1), is on the accused, and he shall attend for his trial at the time and place so fixed.
(5) R.S., 1985, c. C-46, s. 560;
R.S., 1985, c. 27 (1st Supp.), ss. 101(E), 109;
1999, c. 3, s. 42;
2002, c. 13, s. 36.

Right to re-elect
561 (1) An accused who elects or is deemed to have elected a mode of trial other than trial by a provincial court judge may re-elect
(a) at any time before or after the completion of the preliminary inquiry, with the written consent of the prosecutor, to be tried by a provincial court judge;
(b) at any time before the completion of the preliminary inquiry or before the fifteenth day following the completion of the preliminary inquiry, as of right, another mode of trial other than trial by a provincial court judge; and
(c) on or after the fifteenth day following the completion of the preliminary inquiry, any mode of trial with the written consent of the prosecutor.
Right to re-elect
(2) An accused who elects to be tried by a provincial court judge or who does not request a preliminary inquiry under subsection 536(4) may, not later than 14 days before the day first appointed for the trial, re-elect as of right another mode of trial, and may do so after that time with the written consent of the prosecutor.
Notice
(3) Where an accused wishes to re-elect under subsection (1) before the completion of the preliminary inquiry, the accused shall give notice in writing that he wishes to re-elect, together with the written consent of the prosecutor, where that consent is required, to the justice presiding at the preliminary inquiry who shall on receipt of the notice,
(a) in the case of a re-election under paragraph (1)(b), put the accused to his re-election in the manner set out in subsection (7); or
(b) where the accused wishes to re-elect under paragraph (1)(a) and the justice is not a provincial court judge, notify a provincial court judge or clerk of the court of the accused's intention to re-elect and send to the provincial court judge or clerk the information and any promise to appear, undertaking or recognizance given or entered into in accordance with Part XVI, or any evidence taken before a coroner, that is in the possession of the justice.
Idem
(4) Where an accused wishes to re-elect under subsection (2), the accused shall give notice in writing that he wishes to re-elect together with the written consent of the prosecutor, where that consent is required, to the provincial court judge before whom the accused appeared and pleaded or to a clerk of the court.
Notice and transmitting record
(5) Where an accused wishes to re-elect under subsection (1) after the completion of the preliminary inquiry, the accused shall give notice in writing that he wishes to re-elect, together with the written consent of the prosecutor, where that consent is required, to a judge or clerk of the court of his original election who shall, on receipt of the notice, notify the judge or provincial court judge or clerk of the court by which the accused wishes to be tried of the accused's intention to re-elect and send to that judge or provincial court judge or clerk the information, the evidence, the exhibits and the statement, if any, of the accused taken down in writing under section 541 and any promise to appear, undertaking or recognizance given or entered into in accordance with Part XVI, or any evidence taken before a coroner, that is in the possession of the first-mentioned judge or clerk.
Time and place for re-election
(6) Where a provincial court judge or judge or clerk of the court is notified under paragraph (3)(b) or subsection (4) or (5) that the accused wishes to re-elect, the provincial court judge or judge shall forthwith appoint a time and place for the accused to re-elect and shall cause notice thereof to be given to the accused and the prosecutor.
Proceedings on re-election
(7) The accused shall attend or, if he is in custody, shall be produced at the time and place appointed under subsection (6) and shall, after
(a) the charge on which he has been ordered to stand trial or the indictment, where an indictment has been preferred pursuant to section 566, 574 or 577 or is filed with the court before which the

indictment is to be preferred pursuant to section 577, or

(b) in the case of a re-election under subsection (1) before the completion of the preliminary inquiry or under subsection (2), the information

has been read to the accused, be put to his re-election in the following words or in words to the like effect:

R.S., 1985, c. C-46, s. 561;

R.S., 1985, c. 27 (1st Supp.), s. 110;

2002, c. 13, s. 37.

Right to re-elect with consent — Nunavut

561.1 (1) An accused who has elected or is deemed to have elected a mode of trial may re-elect any other mode of trial at any time with the written consent of the prosecutor.

Right to re-elect before trial — Nunavut

(2) An accused who has elected or is deemed to have elected a mode of trial but has not requested a preliminary inquiry under subsection 536.1(3) may, as of right, re-elect to be tried by any other mode of trial at any time up to 14 days before the day first appointed for the trial.

Right to re-elect at preliminary inquiry — Nunavut

(3) An accused who has elected or is deemed to have elected a mode of trial and has requested a preliminary inquiry under subsection 536.1(3) may, as of right, re-elect to be tried by the other mode of trial at any time before the completion of the preliminary inquiry or before the 15th day after its completion.

Notice of re-election under subsection (1) or (3) — Nunavut

(4) If an accused wishes to re-elect under subsection (1) or (3), before the completion of the preliminary inquiry, the accused shall give notice in writing of the wish to re-elect, together with the written consent of the prosecutor, if that consent is required, to the justice of the peace or judge presiding at the preliminary inquiry who shall on receipt of the notice put the accused to a re-election in the manner set out in subsection (9).

Notice at preliminary inquiry — Nunavut

(5) If at a preliminary inquiry an accused wishes to re-elect under subsection (1) or (3) to be tried by a judge without a jury but does not wish to request a preliminary inquiry under subsection 536.1(3), the presiding justice of the peace shall notify a judge or a clerk of the Nunavut Court of Justice of the accused's intention to re-elect and send to the judge or clerk the information and any promise to appear, undertaking or recognizance given or entered into in accordance with Part XVI, or any evidence taken before a coroner, that is in the possession of the justice of the peace.

Notice when no preliminary inquiry or preliminary inquiry completed — Nunavut

(6) If an accused who has not requested a preliminary inquiry under subsection 536.1(3) or who has had one wishes to re-elect under this section, the accused shall give notice in writing of the wish to re-elect together with the written consent of the prosecutor, if that consent is required, to the judge before whom the accused appeared and pleaded or to a clerk of the Nunavut Court of Justice.

(7) Time and place for re-election — Nunavut

(8) On receipt of a notice given under any of subsections (4) to (7) that the accused wishes to re-elect, a judge shall immediately appoint a time and place for the accused to re-elect and shall cause notice of the time and place to be given to the accused and the prosecutor.

Proceedings on re-election — Nunavut

(9) The accused shall attend or, if in custody, shall be produced at the time and place appointed under subsection (8) and shall, after

(a) the charge on which the accused has been ordered to stand trial or the indictment, if an indictment has been preferred pursuant to section 566, 574 or 577 or is filed with the court before which the indictment is to be preferred pursuant to section 577, or

(b) in the case of a re-election under subsection (1) or (3), before the completion of the preliminary inquiry or under subsection (2), the information

has been read to the accused, be put to a re-election in the following words or in words to the like effect:

Application to Nunavut
(10) This section, and not section 561, applies in respect of criminal proceedings in Nunavut.
1999, c. 3, s. 43;
2002, c. 13, s. 38.

Proceedings following re-election
562 (1) Where the accused re-elects under paragraph 561(1)(a) before the completion of the preliminary inquiry or under subsection 561(1) after the completion of the preliminary inquiry, the provincial court judge or judge, as the case may be, shall proceed with the trial or appoint a time and place for the trial.

Idem
(2) Where the accused re-elects under paragraph 561(1)(b) before the completion of the preliminary inquiry or under subsection 561(2), the justice shall proceed with the preliminary inquiry.
R.S., 1985, c. C-46, s. 562;
R.S., 1985, c. 27 (1st Supp.), s. 110.

Proceedings following re-election — Nunavut
562.1 (1) If the accused re-elects under subsection 561.1(1) to be tried by a judge without a jury and does not request a preliminary inquiry under subsection 536.1(3), the judge shall proceed with the trial or appoint a time and place for the trial.

Proceedings following re-election — Nunavut
(2) If the accused re-elects under section 561.1 before the completion of the preliminary inquiry to be tried by a judge without a jury or by a court composed of a judge and jury, and requests a preliminary inquiry under subsection 536.1(3), the justice of the peace or judge shall proceed with the preliminary inquiry.

Application to Nunavut
(3) This section, and not section 562, applies in respect of criminal proceedings in Nunavut.
1999, c. 3, s. 44;
2002, c. 13, s. 39.

Proceedings on re-election to be tried by provincial court judge without jury
563 Where an accused re-elects under section 561 to be tried by a provincial court judge,
(a) the accused shall be tried on the information that was before the justice at the preliminary inquiry, subject to any amendments thereto that may be allowed by the provincial court judge by whom the accused is tried; and
(b) the provincial court judge before whom the re-election is made shall endorse on the information a record of the re-election.
R.S., 1985, c. C-46, s. 563;
R.S., 1985, c. 27 (1st Supp.), s. 110.

Proceedings on re-election to be tried by judge without jury — Nunavut
563.1 (1) If an accused re-elects under section 561.1 to be tried by a judge without a jury and does not request a preliminary inquiry under subsection 536.1(3),
(a) the accused shall be tried on the information that was before the justice of the peace or judge at the preliminary inquiry, subject to any amendments that may be allowed by the judge by whom the accused is tried; and
(b) the judge before whom the re-election is made shall endorse on the information a record of the re-election.

Application to Nunavut
(2) This section, and not section 563, applies in respect of criminal proceedings in Nunavut.
1999, c. 3, s. 45;
2002, c. 13, s. 40.

564 Election deemed to have been made
565 (1) Subject to subsection (1.1), if an accused is ordered to stand trial for an offence that, under this Part, may be tried by a judge without a jury, the accused shall, for the purposes of the provisions of this Part relating to election and re-election, be deemed to have elected to be tried by a court

composed of a judge and jury if

(a) the accused was ordered to stand trial by a provincial court judge who, pursuant to subsection 555(1), continued the proceedings before him as a preliminary inquiry;

(b) the justice, provincial court judge or judge, as the case may be, declined pursuant to section 567 to record the election or re-election of the accused; or

(c) the accused does not elect when put to an election under section 536.

Nunavut

(1.1) With respect to criminal proceedings in Nunavut, if an accused is ordered to stand trial for an offence that, under this Part, may be tried by a judge without a jury, the accused shall, for the purposes of the provisions of this Part relating to election and re-election, be deemed to have elected to be tried by a court composed of a judge and jury if

(a) the accused was ordered to stand trial by a judge who, under subsection 555.1(1), continued the proceedings as a preliminary inquiry;

(b) the justice of the peace or judge, as the case may be, declined pursuant to subsection 567.1(1) to record the election or re-election of the accused; or

(c) the accused did not elect when put to an election under section 536.1.

When direct indictment preferred

(2) If an accused is to be tried after an indictment has been preferred against the accused pursuant to a consent or order given under section 577, the accused is, for the purposes of the provisions of this Part relating to election and re-election, deemed both to have elected to be tried by a court composed of a judge and jury and not to have requested a preliminary inquiry under subsection 536(4) or 536.1(3) and may re-elect to be tried by a judge without a jury without a preliminary inquiry.

Notice of re-election

(3) Where an accused wishes to re-elect under subsection (2), the accused shall give notice in writing that he wishes to re-elect to a judge or clerk of the court where the indictment has been filed or preferred who shall, on receipt of the notice, notify a judge having jurisdiction or clerk of the court by which the accused wishes to be tried of the accused's intention to re-elect and send to that judge or clerk the indictment and any promise to appear, undertaking or recognizance given or entered into in accordance with Part XVI, any summons or warrant issued under section 578, or any evidence taken before a coroner, that is in the possession of the first-mentioned judge or clerk.

Application

(4) Subsections 561(6) and (7), or subsections 561.1(8) and (9), as the case may be, apply to a re-election made under subsection (3).

R.S., 1985, c. C-46, s. 565;
R.S., 1985, c. 27 (1st Supp.), s. 111;
1999, c. 3, s. 46;
2002, c. 13, s. 41;
2008, c. 18, s. 23.

Trial

Indictment

566 (1) The trial of an accused for an indictable offence, other than a trial before a provincial court judge, shall be on an indictment in writing setting forth the offence with which he is charged.

Preferring indictment

(2) Where an accused elects under section 536 or re-elects under section 561 to be tried by a judge without a jury, an indictment in Form 4 may be preferred.

What counts may be included and who may prefer indictment

(3) Section 574 and subsection 576(1) apply, with such modifications as the circumstances require, to the preferring of an indictment pursuant to subsection (2).

R.S., 1985, c. C-46, s. 566;
R.S., 1985, c. 27 (1st Supp.), s. 111;

1997, c. 18, s. 67.

Indictment — Nunavut

566.1 (1) The trial of an accused for an indictable offence, other than an indictable offence referred to in section 553 or an offence in respect of which the accused has elected or re-elected to be tried by a judge without a jury and in respect of which no party has requested a preliminary inquiry under subsection 536.1(3), must be on an indictment in writing setting out the offence with which the accused is charged.

Preferring indictment — Nunavut

(2) If an accused elects under section 536.1 or re-elects under section 561.1 to be tried by a judge without a jury and one of the parties requests a preliminary inquiry under subsection 536.1(3), an indictment in Form 4 may be preferred.

What counts may be included and who may prefer indictment — Nunavut

(3) Section 574 and subsection 576(1) apply, with any modifications that the circumstances require, to the preferring of an indictment under subsection (2).

Application to Nunavut

(4) This section, and not section 566, applies in respect of criminal proceedings in Nunavut.

1999, c. 3, s. 47;
2002, c. 13, s. 42.

General

Mode of trial when two or more accused

567 Despite any other provision of this Part, if two or more persons are jointly charged in an information, unless all of them elect or re-elect or are deemed to have elected the same mode of trial, the justice, provincial court judge or judge may decline to record any election, re-election or deemed election for trial by a provincial court judge or a judge without a jury.

R.S., 1985, c. C-46, s. 567;
R.S., 1985, c. 27 (1st Supp.), s. 111;
2002, c. 13, s. 43.

Mode of trial if two or more accused — Nunavut

567.1 (1) Despite any other provision of this Part, if two or more persons are jointly charged in an information, unless all of them elect or re-elect or are deemed to have elected the same mode of trial, the justice of the peace or judge may decline to record any election, re-election or deemed election for trial by a judge without a jury.

Application to Nunavut

(2) This section, and not section 567, applies in respect of criminal proceedings in Nunavut.

1999, c. 3, s. 48;
2002, c. 13, s. 43.

Attorney General may require trial by jury

568 Even if an accused elects under section 536 or re-elects under section 561 or subsection 565(2) to be tried by a judge or provincial court judge, as the case may be, the Attorney General may require the accused to be tried by a court composed of a judge and jury unless the alleged offence is one that is punishable with imprisonment for five years or less. If the Attorney General so requires, a judge or provincial court judge has no jurisdiction to try the accused under this Part and a preliminary inquiry must be held if requested under subsection 536(4), unless one has already been held or the re-election was made under subsection 565(2).

R.S., 1985, c. C-46, s. 568;
R.S., 1985, c. 27 (1st Supp.), s. 111;
2002, c. 13, s. 43;
2008, c. 18, s. 24.

Attorney General may require trial by jury — Nunavut

569 (1) Even if an accused elects under section 536.1 or re-elects under section 561.1 or subsection

565(2) to be tried by a judge without a jury, the Attorney General may require the accused to be tried by a court composed of a judge and jury unless the alleged offence is one that is punishable with imprisonment for five years or less. If the Attorney General so requires, a judge has no jurisdiction to try the accused under this Part and a preliminary inquiry must be held if requested under subsection 536.1(3), unless one has already been held or the re-election was made under subsection 565(2).

Application to Nunavut

(2) This section, and not section 568, applies in respect of criminal proceedings in Nunavut.

R.S., 1985, c. C-46, s. 569;

R.S., 1985, c. 27 (1st Supp.), s. 111;

1999, c. 3, s. 49;

2002, c. 13, s. 44;

2008, c. 18, s. 24.1.

Record of conviction or order

570 (1) Where an accused who is tried under this Part is determined by a judge or provincial court judge to be guilty of an offence on acceptance of a plea of guilty or on a finding of guilt, the judge or provincial court judge, as the case may be, shall endorse the information accordingly and shall sentence the accused or otherwise deal with the accused in the manner authorized by law and, on request by the accused, the prosecutor, a peace officer or any other person, shall cause a conviction in Form 35 and a certified copy of it, or an order in Form 36 and a certified copy of it, to be drawn up and shall deliver the certified copy to the person making the request.

Acquittal and record of acquittal

(2) Where an accused who is tried under this Part is found not guilty of an offence with which the accused is charged, the judge or provincial court judge, as the case may be, shall immediately acquit the accused in respect of that offence and shall cause an order in Form 37 to be drawn up, and on request shall make out and deliver to the accused a certified copy of the order.

Transmission of record

(3) Where an accused elects to be tried by a provincial court judge under this Part, the provincial court judge shall transmit the written charge, the memorandum of adjudication and the conviction, if any, into such custody as the Attorney General may direct.

Proof of conviction, order or acquittal

(4) A copy of a conviction in Form 35 or of an order in Form 36 or 37, certified by the judge or by the clerk or other proper officer of the court, or by the provincial court judge, as the case may be, or proved to be a true copy, is, on proof of the identity of the person to whom the conviction or order relates, sufficient evidence in any legal proceedings to prove the conviction of that person or the making of the order against that person or his acquittal, as the case may be, for the offence mentioned in the copy of the conviction or order.

Warrant of committal

(5) Where an accused other than an organization is convicted, the judge or provincial court judge, as the case may be, shall issue or cause to be issued a warrant of committal in Form 21, and section 528 applies in respect of a warrant of committal issued under this subsection.

Admissibility of certified copy

(6) Where a warrant of committal is issued by a clerk of a court, a copy of the warrant of committal, certified by the clerk, is admissible in evidence in any proceeding.

R.S., 1985, c. C-46, s. 570;

R.S., 1985, c. 27 (1st Supp.), ss. 112, 203, c. 1 (4th Supp.), s. 18(F);

1994, c. 44, s. 59;

2003, c. 21, s. 10.

Adjournment

571 A judge or provincial court judge acting under this Part may from time to time adjourn a trial until it is finally terminated.

R.S., 1985, c. C-46, s. 571;

R.S., 1985, c. 27 (1st Supp.), s. 203.

Application of Parts XVI, XVIII, XX and XXIII
572 The provisions of Part XVI, the provisions of Part XVIII relating to transmission of the record by a provincial court judge where he holds a preliminary inquiry, and the provisions of Parts XX and XXIII, in so far as they are not inconsistent with this Part, apply, with such modifications as the circumstances require, to proceedings under this Part.
R.S., 1985, c. C-46, s. 572;
R.S., 1985, c. 27 (1st Supp.), s. 203.

PART XIX.1

PART XIX.1
Nunavut Court of Justice

Nunavut Court of Justice
573 (1) The powers to be exercised and the duties and functions to be performed under this Act by a court of criminal jurisdiction, a summary conviction court, a judge, a provincial court judge, a justice or a justice of the peace may be exercised or performed by a judge of the Nunavut Court of Justice.
Status when exercising power
(2) A power exercised or a duty or function performed by a judge of the Nunavut Court of Justice under subsection (1) is exercised or performed by that judge as a judge of a superior court.
Interpretation
(3) Subsection (2) does not authorize a judge of the Nunavut Court of Justice who is presiding at a preliminary inquiry to grant a remedy under section 24 of the
Canadian Charter of Rights and Freedoms
R.S., 1985, c. C-46, s. 573;
R.S., 1985, c. 27 (1st Supp.), s. 113;
1999, c. 3, s. 50.
Application for review — Nunavut
573.1 (1) An application for review may be made by the Attorney General or the accused, or by any person directly affected by the decision or order, to a judge of the Court of Appeal of Nunavut in respect of a decision or order of a judge of the Nunavut Court of Justice
(a) relating to a warrant or summons;
(b) relating to the conduct of a preliminary inquiry, including an order under subsection 548(1);
(c) relating to a subpoena;
(d) relating to the publication or broadcasting of information or access to the court room for all or part of the proceedings;
(e) to refuse to quash an information or indictment; or
(f) relating to the detention, disposal or forfeiture of any thing seized under a warrant or order.
Limitation
(2) A decision or order may not be reviewed under this section if
(a) the decision or order is of a kind that could only be made in a province or a territory other than Nunavut by a superior court of criminal jurisdiction or a judge as defined in section 552; or
(b) another statutory right of review is available.
Grounds of review
(3) The judge of the Court of Appeal of Nunavut may grant relief under subsection (4) only if the judge is satisfied that
(a) in the case of any decision or order mentioned in subsection (1),
(i) the judge of the Nunavut Court of Justice failed to observe a principle of natural justice or failed or refused to exercise the judge's jurisdiction, or
(ii) the decision or order was made as a result of an irrelevant consideration or for an improper purpose;
(b) in the case of a decision or order mentioned in paragraph (1)(a), that

(i) the judge failed to comply with a statutory requirement for the making of the decision or order,
(ii) the decision or order was made in the absence of any evidence that a statutory requirement for the making of the decision or order was met,
(iii) the decision or order was made as a result of reckless disregard for the truth, fraud, intentional misrepresentation of material facts or intentional omission to state material facts,
(iv) the warrant is so vague or lacking in particularity that it authorizes an unreasonable search, or
(v) the warrant lacks a material term or condition that is required by law;
(c) in the case of a decision or order mentioned in paragraph (1)(b), that the judge of the Nunavut Court of Justice
(i) failed to follow a mandatory provision of this Act relating to the conduct of a preliminary inquiry,
(ii) ordered the accused to stand trial when there was no evidence adduced on which a properly instructed jury acting reasonably could convict, or
(iii) discharged the accused when there was some evidence adduced on which a properly instructed jury acting reasonably could convict;
(d) in the case of a decision or order mentioned in paragraph (1)(c) or (d), that the judge of the Nunavut Court of Justice erred in law;
(e) in the case of a decision or order mentioned in paragraph (1)(e), that
(i) the information or indictment failed to give the accused notice of the charge,
(ii) the judge of the Nunavut Court of Justice did not have jurisdiction to try the offence, or
(iii) the provision creating the offence alleged to have been committed by the accused is unconstitutional; or
(f) in the case of a decision or order mentioned in paragraph (1)(f), that
(i) the judge failed to comply with a statutory requirement for the making of the decision or order,
(ii) the decision or order was made in the absence of any evidence that a statutory requirement for the making of the decision or order was met, or
(iii) the decision or order was made as a result of reckless disregard for the truth, fraud, intentional misrepresentation of material facts or intentional omission to state material facts.

Powers of judge
(4) On the hearing of the application for review, the judge of the Court of Appeal of Nunavut may do one or more of the following:
(a) order a judge of the Nunavut Court of Justice to do any act or thing that the judge or any other judge of that court failed or refused to do or has delayed in doing;
(b) prohibit or restrain a decision, order or proceeding of a judge of the Nunavut Court of Justice;
(c) declare invalid or unlawful, quash or set aside, in whole or in part, a decision, order or proceeding of a judge of the Nunavut Court of Justice;
(d) refer back for determination in accordance with any directions that the judge considers to be appropriate, a decision, order or proceeding of a judge of the Nunavut Court of Justice;
(e) grant any remedy under subsection 24(1) of the
Canadian Charter of Rights and Freedoms
(f) refuse to grant any relief if the judge is of the opinion that no substantial wrong or miscarriage of justice has occurred or that the subject-matter of the application should be determined at trial or on appeal; and
(g) dismiss the application.

Interim orders
(5) If an application for review is made, a judge of the Court of Appeal of Nunavut may make any interim order that the judge considers appropriate pending the final disposition of the application for review.

Rules
(6) A person who proposes to make an application for review shall do so in the manner and within the period that may be directed by rules of court, except that a judge of the Court of Appeal of Nunavut may at any time extend any period specified in the rules.

Appeal

(7) An appeal lies to the Court of Appeal of Nunavut against a decision or order made under subsection (4). The provisions of Part XXI apply, with any modifications that the circumstances require, to the appeal.
1999, c. 3, s. 50.
573.2 (1) (a) the order or warrant is of a kind that could only be made or issued in a province or a territory other than Nunavut by a superior court of criminal jurisdiction or a judge as defined in section 552; or
(b) another statutory right of review or appeal is available.
Exception
(2) Despite subsection (1),
Provisions apply
(3) Subsections 784(2) to (6) apply in respect of any proceedings brought under subsection (1) or (2).
1999, c. 3, s. 50.

PART XX

PART XX
Procedure in Jury Trials and General Provisions

Preferring Indictment

Prosecutor may prefer indictment
574 (1) Subject to subsection (3), the prosecutor may, whether the charges were included in one information or not, prefer an indictment against any person who has been ordered to stand trial in respect of
(a) any charge on which that person was ordered to stand trial; or
(b) any charge founded on the facts disclosed by the evidence taken on the preliminary inquiry, in addition to or in substitution for any charge on which that person was ordered to stand trial.
Preferring indictment when no preliminary inquiry requested
(1.1) If a person has not requested a preliminary inquiry under subsection 536(4) or 536.1(3) into the charge, the prosecutor may, subject to subsection (3), prefer an indictment against a person in respect of a charge set out in an information or informations, or any included charge, at any time after the person has made an election, re-election or deemed election on the information or informations.
Preferring single indictment
(1.2) If indictments may be preferred under both subsections (1) and (1.1), the prosecutor may prefer a single indictment in respect of one or more charges referred to in subsection (1) combined with one or more charges or included charges referred to in subsection (1.1).
Consent to inclusion of other charges
(2) An indictment preferred under any of subsections (1) to (1.2) may, if the accused consents, include a charge that is not referred to in those subsections, and the offence charged may be dealt with, tried and determined and punished in all respects as if it were an offence in respect of which the accused had been ordered to stand trial. However, if the offence was committed wholly in a province other than that in which the accused is before the court, subsection 478(3) applies.
Private prosecutor requires consent
(3) In a prosecution conducted by a prosecutor other than the Attorney General and in which the Attorney General does not intervene, an indictment may not be preferred under any of subsections (1) to (1.2) before a court without the written order of a judge of that court.
R.S., 1985, c. C-46, s. 574;
R.S., 1985, c. 27 (1st Supp.), s. 113;
2002, c. 13, s. 45.
575 Indictment
576 (1) Except as provided in this Act, no indictment shall be preferred.

Criminal information and bill of indictment
(2) No criminal information shall be laid or granted and no bill of indictment shall be preferred before a grand jury.
Coroner's inquisition
(3) No person shall be tried on a coroner's inquisition.

R.S., 1985, c. C-46, s. 576;
R.S., 1985, c. 27 (1st Supp.), s. 114.
Direct indictments
577 Despite section 574, an indictment may be preferred even if the accused has not been given the opportunity to request a preliminary inquiry, a preliminary inquiry has been commenced but not concluded or a preliminary inquiry has been held and the accused has been discharged, if
(a) in the case of a prosecution conducted by the Attorney General or one in which the Attorney General intervenes, the personal consent in writing of the Attorney General or Deputy Attorney General is filed in court; or
(b) in any other case, a judge of the court so orders.

R.S., 1985, c. C-46, s. 577;
R.S., 1985, c. 27 (1st Supp.), s. 115, c. 1 (4th Supp.), s. 18(F);
2002, c. 13, s. 46.
Summons or warrant
578 (1) Where notice of the recommencement of proceedings has been given pursuant to subsection 579(2) or an indictment has been filed with the court before which the proceedings are to commence or recommence, the court, if it considers it necessary, may issue
(a) a summons addressed to, or
(b) a warrant for the arrest of,
the accused or defendant, as the case may be, to compel him to attend before the court to answer the charge described in the indictment.
Part XVI to apply
(2) The provisions of Part XVI apply with such modifications as the circumstances require where a summons or warrant is issued under subsection (1).

R.S., 1985, c. C-46, s. 578;
R.S., 1985, c. 27 (1st Supp.), s. 116.
Attorney General may direct stay
579 (1) The Attorney General or counsel instructed by him for that purpose may, at any time after any proceedings in relation to an accused or a defendant are commenced and before judgment, direct the clerk or other proper officer of the court to make an entry on the record that the proceedings are stayed by his direction, and such entry shall be made forthwith thereafter, whereupon the proceedings shall be stayed accordingly and any recognizance relating to the proceedings is vacated.
Recommencement of proceedings
(2) Proceedings stayed in accordance with subsection (1) may be recommenced, without laying a new information or preferring a new indictment, as the case may be, by the Attorney General or counsel instructed by him for that purpose giving notice of the recommencement to the clerk of the court in which the stay of the proceedings was entered, but where no such notice is given within one year after the entry of the stay of proceedings, or before the expiration of the time within which the proceedings could have been commenced, whichever is the earlier, the proceedings shall be deemed never to have been commenced.

R.S., 1985, c. C-46, s. 579;
R.S., 1985, c. 27 (1st Supp.), s. 117.
When Attorney General does not stay proceedings
579.01 If the Attorney General intervenes in proceedings and does not stay them under section 579, he or she may, without conducting the proceedings, call witnesses, examine and cross-examine witnesses, present evidence and make submissions.

2002, c. 13, s. 47.

Intervention by Attorney General of Canada
579.1 (1) The Attorney General of Canada or counsel instructed by him or her for that purpose may intervene in proceedings in the following circumstances:
(a) the proceedings are in respect of a contravention of, a conspiracy or attempt to contravene or counselling the contravention of an Act of Parliament or a regulation made under that Act, other than this Act or a regulation made under this Act;
(b) the proceedings have not been instituted by an Attorney General;
(c) judgment has not been rendered; and
(d) the Attorney General of the province in which the proceedings are taken has not intervened.
Section 579 to apply
(2) Section 579 applies, with such modifications as the circumstances require, to proceedings in which the Attorney General of Canada intervenes pursuant to this section.
1994, c. 44, s. 60.
Form of indictment
580 An indictment is sufficient if it is on paper and is in Form 4.
R.S., 1985, c. C-46, s. 580;
R.S., 1985, c. 27 (1st Supp.), s. 117.

General Provisions respecting Counts

Substance of offence
581 (1) Each count in an indictment shall in general apply to a single transaction and shall contain in substance a statement that the accused or defendant committed an offence therein specified.
Form of statement
(2) The statement referred to in subsection (1) may be
(a) in popular language without technical averments or allegations of matters that are not essential to be proved;
(b) in the words of the enactment that describes the offence or declares the matters charged to be an indictable offence; or
(c) in words that are sufficient to give to the accused notice of the offence with which he is charged.
Details of circumstances
(3) A count shall contain sufficient detail of the circumstances of the alleged offence to give to the accused reasonable information with respect to the act or omission to be proved against him and to identify the transaction referred to, but otherwise the absence or insufficiency of details does not vitiate the count.
Indictment for treason
(4) Where an accused is charged with an offence under section 47 or sections 49 to 53, every overt act that is to be relied on shall be stated in the indictment.
Reference to section
(5) A count may refer to any section, subsection, paragraph or subparagraph of the enactment that creates the offence charged, and for the purpose of determining whether a count is sufficient, consideration shall be given to any such reference.
General provisions not restricted
(6) Nothing in this Part relating to matters that do not render a count insufficient shall be deemed to restrict or limit the application of this section.
R.S., 1985, c. C-46, s. 581;
R.S., 1985, c. 27 (1st Supp.), s. 118.
High treason and first degree murder
582 No person shall be convicted for the offence of high treason or first degree murder unless in the indictment charging the offence he is specifically charged with that offence.
R.S., c. C-34, s. 511;
1973-74, c. 38, s. 4;

1974-75-76, c. 105, s. 6.

Certain omissions not grounds for objection
583 No count in an indictment is insufficient by reason of the absence of details where, in the opinion of the court, the count otherwise fulfils the requirements of section 581 and, without restricting the generality of the foregoing, no count in an indictment is insufficient by reason only that
(a) it does not name the person injured or intended or attempted to be injured;
(b) it does not name the person who owns or has a special property or interest in property mentioned in the count;
(c) it charges an intent to defraud without naming or describing the person whom it was intended to defraud;
(d) it does not set out any writing that is the subject of the charge;
(e) it does not set out the words used where words that are alleged to have been used are the subject of the charge;
(f) it does not specify the means by which the alleged offence was committed;
(g) it does not name or describe with precision any person, place or thing; or
(h) it does not, where the consent of a person, official or authority is required before proceedings may be instituted for an offence, state that the consent has been obtained.
R.S., c. C-34, s. 512.

Special Provisions respecting Counts

Sufficiency of count charging libel
584 (1) No count for publishing a blasphemous, seditious or defamatory libel, or for selling or exhibiting an obscene book, pamphlet, newspaper or other written matter, is insufficient by reason only that it does not set out the words that are alleged to be libellous or the writing that is alleged to be obscene.

Specifying sense
(2) A count for publishing a libel may charge that the published matter was written in a sense that by innuendo made the publication thereof criminal, and may specify that sense without any introductory assertion to show how the matter was written in that sense.

Proof
(3) It is sufficient, on the trial of a count for publishing a libel, to prove that the matter published was libellous, with or without innuendo.
R.S., c. C-34, s. 513.

Sufficiency of count charging perjury, etc.
585 No count that charges
(a) perjury,
(b) the making of a false oath or a false statement,
(c) fabricating evidence, or
(d) procuring the commission of an offence mentioned in paragraph (a), (b) or (c),

is insufficient by reason only that it does not state the nature of the authority of the tribunal before which the oath or statement was taken or made, or the subject of the inquiry, or the words used or the evidence fabricated, or that it does not expressly negative the truth of the words used.
R.S., 1985, c. C-46, s. 585;
1992, c. 1, s. 60(F).

Sufficiency of count relating to fraud
586 No count that alleges false pretences, fraud or any attempt or conspiracy by fraudulent means is insufficient by reason only that it does not set out in detail the nature of the false pretence, fraud or fraudulent means.
R.S., c. C-34, s. 515.

Particulars

What may be ordered
587 (1) A court may, where it is satisfied that it is necessary for a fair trial, order the prosecutor to furnish particulars and, without restricting the generality of the foregoing, may order the prosecutor to furnish particulars
(a) of what is relied on in support of a charge of perjury, the making of a false oath or a false statement, fabricating evidence or counselling the commission of any of those offences;
(b) of any false pretence or fraud that is alleged;
(c) of any alleged attempt or conspiracy by fraudulent means;
(d) setting out the passages in a book, pamphlet, newspaper or other printing or writing that are relied on in support of a charge of selling or exhibiting an obscene book, pamphlet, newspaper, printing or writing;
(e) further describing any writing or words that are the subject of a charge;
(f) further describing the means by which an offence is alleged to have been committed; or
(g) further describing a person, place or thing referred to in an indictment.

Regard to evidence
(2) For the purpose of determining whether or not a particular is required, the court may give consideration to any evidence that has been taken.

Particular
(3) Where a particular is delivered pursuant to this section,
(a) a copy shall be given without charge to the accused or his counsel;
(b) the particular shall be entered in the record; and
(c) the trial shall proceed in all respects as if the indictment had been amended to conform with the particular.
R.S., 1985, c. C-46, s. 587;
R.S., 1985, c. 27 (1st Supp.), s. 7.

Ownership of Property

Ownership
588 The real and personal property of which a person has, by law, the management, control or custody shall, for the purposes of an indictment or proceeding against any other person for an offence committed on or in respect of the property, be deemed to be the property of the person who has the management, control or custody of it.
R.S., c. C-34, s. 517.

Joinder or Severance of Counts

Count for murder
589 No count that charges an indictable offence other than murder shall be joined in an indictment to a count that charges murder unless
(a) the count that charges the offence other than murder arises out of the same transaction as a count that charges murder; or
(b) the accused signifies consent to the joinder of the counts.
R.S., 1985, c. C-46, s. 589;
1991, c. 4, s. 2.

Offences may be charged in the alternative
590 (1) A count is not objectionable by reason only that
(a) it charges in the alternative several different matters, acts or omissions that are stated in the alternative in an enactment that describes as an indictable offence the matters, acts or omissions charged in the count; or

(b) it is double or multifarious.
Application to amend or divide counts
(2) An accused may at any stage of his trial apply to the court to amend or to divide a count that
(a) charges in the alternative different matters, acts or omissions that are stated in the alternative in the enactment that describes the offence or declares that the matters, acts or omissions charged are an indictable offence, or
(b) is double or multifarious,
on the ground that, as framed, it embarrasses him in his defence.
Order
(3) The court may, where it is satisfied that the ends of justice require it, order that a count be amended or divided into two or more counts, and thereupon a formal commencement may be inserted before each of the counts into which it is divided.
R.S., c. C-34, s. 519.
Joinder of counts
591 (1) Subject to section 589, any number of counts for any number of offences may be joined in the same indictment, but the counts shall be distinguished in the manner shown in Form 4.
Each count separate
(2) Where there is more than one count in an indictment, each count may be treated as a separate indictment.
Severance of accused and counts
(3) The court may, where it is satisfied that the interests of justice so require, order
(a) that the accused or defendant be tried separately on one or more of the counts; and
(b) where there is more than one accused or defendant, that one or more of them be tried separately on one or more of the counts.
Order for severance
(4) An order under subsection (3) may be made before or during the trial but, if the order is made during the trial, the jury shall be discharged from giving a verdict on the counts
(a) on which the trial does not proceed; or
(b) in respect of the accused or defendant who has been granted a separate trial.
Delayed enforcement
(4.1) The court may make an order under subsection (3) that takes effect either at a specified later date or on the occurrence of a specified event if, taking into account, among other considerations, the need to ensure consistent decisions, it is satisfied that it is in the interests of justice to do so.
Decisions binding on parties
(4.2) Unless the court is satisfied that it would not be in the interests of justice, the decisions relating to the disclosure or admissibility of evidence or the
Canadian Charter of Rights and Freedoms
Subsequent procedure
(5) The counts in respect of which a jury is discharged pursuant to paragraph (4)(a) may subsequently be proceeded on in all respects as if they were contained in a separate indictment.
Idem
(6) Where an order is made in respect of an accused or defendant under paragraph (3)(b), the accused or defendant may be tried separately on the counts in relation to which the order was made as if they were contained in a separate indictment.
R.S., 1985, c. C-46, s. 591;
R.S., 1985, c. 27 (1st Supp.), s. 119;
2011, c. 16, s. 5.

Joinder of Accused in Certain Cases

Accessories after the fact
592 Any one who is charged with being an accessory after the fact to any offence may be indicted,

whether or not the principal or any other party to the offence has been indicted or convicted or is or is not amenable to justice.
R.S., c. C-34, s. 521.

Trial of persons jointly

593 (1) Any number of persons may be charged in the same indictment with an offence under section 354 or 355.4 or paragraph 356(1)(b), even though
(a) the property was had in possession at different times; or
(b) the person by whom the property was obtained
(i) is not indicted with them, or
(ii) is not in custody or is not amenable to justice.

Conviction of one or more

(2) Where, pursuant to subsection (1), two or more persons are charged in the same indictment with an offence referred to in that subsection, any one or more of those persons who separately committed the offence in respect of the property or any part of it may be convicted.
R.S., 1985, c. C-46, s. 593;
2010, c. 14, s. 11.
594 to 596

Proceedings when Person Indicted is at Large

Bench warrant

597 (1) Where an indictment has been preferred against a person who is at large, and that person does not appear or remain in attendance for his trial, the court before which the accused should have appeared or remained in attendance may issue a warrant in Form 7 for his arrest.

Execution

(2) A warrant issued under subsection (1) may be executed anywhere in Canada.

Interim release

(3) Where an accused is arrested under a warrant issued under subsection (1), a judge of the court that issued the warrant may order that the accused be released on his giving an undertaking that he will do any one or more of the following things as specified in the order, namely,
(a) report at times to be stated in the order to a peace officer or other person designated in the order;
(b) remain within a territorial jurisdiction specified in the order;
(c) notify the peace officer or other person designated under paragraph (a) of any change in his address or his employment or occupation;
(d) abstain from communicating with any witness or other person expressly named in the order except in accordance with such conditions specified in the order as the judge deems necessary;
(e) where the accused is the holder of a passport, deposit his passport as specified in the order; and
(f) comply with such other reasonable conditions specified in the order as the judge considers desirable.

Discretion to postpone execution

(4) A judge who issues a warrant may specify in the warrant the period before which the warrant shall not be executed, to allow the accused to appear voluntarily before a judge having jurisdiction in the territorial division in which the warrant was issued.

Deemed execution of warrant

(5) Where the accused appears voluntarily for the offence in respect of which the accused is charged, the warrant is deemed to be executed.
R.S., 1985, c. C-46, s. 597;
R.S., 1985, c. 27 (1st Supp.), s. 121;
1997, c. 18, s. 68.

Election deemed to be waived

598 (1) Notwithstanding anything in this Act, where a person to whom subsection 597(1) applies has elected or is deemed to have elected to be tried by a court composed of a judge and jury and, at the time he failed to appear or to remain in attendance for his trial, he had not re-elected to be tried by a

court composed of a judge without a jury or a provincial court judge without a jury, he shall not be tried by a court composed of a judge and jury unless

(a) he establishes to the satisfaction of a judge of the court in which he is indicted that there was a legitimate excuse for his failure to appear or remain in attendance for his trial; or

(b) the Attorney General requires pursuant to section 568 or 569 that the accused be tried by a court composed of a judge and jury.

Election deemed to be waived

(2) An accused who, under subsection (1), may not be tried by a court composed of a judge and jury is deemed to have elected under section 536 or 536.1 to be tried without a jury by a judge of the court where the accused was indicted and section 561 or 561.1, as the case may be, does not apply in respect of the accused.

R.S., 1985, c. C-46, s. 598;
R.S., 1985, c. 27 (1st Supp.), ss. 122, 185(F), 203(E);
1999, c. 3, s. 51;
2002, c. 13, s. 48(E).

Change of Venue

Reasons for change of venue

599 (1) A court before which an accused is or may be indicted, at any term or sittings thereof, or a judge who may hold or sit in that court, may at any time before or after an indictment is found, on the application of the prosecutor or the accused, order the trial to be held in a territorial division in the same province other than that in which the offence would otherwise be tried if

(a) it appears expedient to the ends of justice; or

(b) a competent authority has directed that a jury is not to be summoned at the time appointed in a territorial division where the trial would otherwise by law be held.

(2) Conditions respecting expense

(3) The court or judge may, in an order made on an application by the prosecutor under subsection (1), prescribe conditions that he thinks proper with respect to the payment of additional expenses caused to the accused as a result of the change of venue.

Transmission of record

(4) Where an order is made under subsection (1), the officer who has custody of the indictment, if any, and the writings and exhibits relating to the prosecution, shall transmit them forthwith to the clerk of the court before which the trial is ordered to be held, and all proceedings in the case shall be held or, if previously commenced, shall be continued in that court.

Idem

(5) Where the writings and exhibits referred to in subsection (4) have not been returned to the court in which the trial was to be held at the time an order is made to change the place of trial, the person who obtains the order shall serve a true copy thereof on the person in whose custody they are and that person shall thereupon transmit them to the clerk of the court before which the trial is to be held.

R.S., 1985, c. C-46, s. 599;
R.S., 1985, c. 1 (4th Supp.), s. 16.

Order is authority to remove prisoner

600 An order that is made under section 599 is sufficient warrant, justification and authority to all sheriffs, keepers of prisons and peace officers for the removal, disposal and reception of an accused in accordance with the terms of the order, and the sheriff may appoint and authorize any peace officer to convey the accused to a prison in the territorial division in which the trial is ordered to be held.

R.S., c. C-34, s. 528.

Amendment

Particulars

What may be ordered
587 (1) A court may, where it is satisfied that it is necessary for a fair trial, order the prosecutor to furnish particulars and, without restricting the generality of the foregoing, may order the prosecutor to furnish particulars
(a) of what is relied on in support of a charge of perjury, the making of a false oath or a false statement, fabricating evidence or counselling the commission of any of those offences;
(b) of any false pretence or fraud that is alleged;
(c) of any alleged attempt or conspiracy by fraudulent means;
(d) setting out the passages in a book, pamphlet, newspaper or other printing or writing that are relied on in support of a charge of selling or exhibiting an obscene book, pamphlet, newspaper, printing or writing;
(e) further describing any writing or words that are the subject of a charge;
(f) further describing the means by which an offence is alleged to have been committed; or
(g) further describing a person, place or thing referred to in an indictment.

Regard to evidence
(2) For the purpose of determining whether or not a particular is required, the court may give consideration to any evidence that has been taken.

Particular
(3) Where a particular is delivered pursuant to this section,
(a) a copy shall be given without charge to the accused or his counsel;
(b) the particular shall be entered in the record; and
(c) the trial shall proceed in all respects as if the indictment had been amended to conform with the particular.
R.S., 1985, c. C-46, s. 587;
R.S., 1985, c. 27 (1st Supp.), s. 7.

Ownership of Property

Ownership
588 The real and personal property of which a person has, by law, the management, control or custody shall, for the purposes of an indictment or proceeding against any other person for an offence committed on or in respect of the property, be deemed to be the property of the person who has the management, control or custody of it.
R.S., c. C-34, s. 517.

Joinder or Severance of Counts

Count for murder
589 No count that charges an indictable offence other than murder shall be joined in an indictment to a count that charges murder unless
(a) the count that charges the offence other than murder arises out of the same transaction as a count that charges murder; or
(b) the accused signifies consent to the joinder of the counts.
R.S., 1985, c. C-46, s. 589;
1991, c. 4, s. 2.

Offences may be charged in the alternative
590 (1) A count is not objectionable by reason only that
(a) it charges in the alternative several different matters, acts or omissions that are stated in the alternative in an enactment that describes as an indictable offence the matters, acts or omissions charged in the count; or

(b) it is double or multifarious.
Application to amend or divide counts
(2) An accused may at any stage of his trial apply to the court to amend or to divide a count that
(a) charges in the alternative different matters, acts or omissions that are stated in the alternative in the enactment that describes the offence or declares that the matters, acts or omissions charged are an indictable offence, or
(b) is double or multifarious,
on the ground that, as framed, it embarrasses him in his defence.
Order
(3) The court may, where it is satisfied that the ends of justice require it, order that a count be amended or divided into two or more counts, and thereupon a formal commencement may be inserted before each of the counts into which it is divided.
R.S., c. C-34, s. 519.
Joinder of counts
591 (1) Subject to section 589, any number of counts for any number of offences may be joined in the same indictment, but the counts shall be distinguished in the manner shown in Form 4.
Each count separate
(2) Where there is more than one count in an indictment, each count may be treated as a separate indictment.
Severance of accused and counts
(3) The court may, where it is satisfied that the interests of justice so require, order
(a) that the accused or defendant be tried separately on one or more of the counts; and
(b) where there is more than one accused or defendant, that one or more of them be tried separately on one or more of the counts.
Order for severance
(4) An order under subsection (3) may be made before or during the trial but, if the order is made during the trial, the jury shall be discharged from giving a verdict on the counts
(a) on which the trial does not proceed; or
(b) in respect of the accused or defendant who has been granted a separate trial.
Delayed enforcement
(4.1) The court may make an order under subsection (3) that takes effect either at a specified later date or on the occurrence of a specified event if, taking into account, among other considerations, the need to ensure consistent decisions, it is satisfied that it is in the interests of justice to do so.
Decisions binding on parties
(4.2) Unless the court is satisfied that it would not be in the interests of justice, the decisions relating to the disclosure or admissibility of evidence or the
Canadian Charter of Rights and Freedoms
Subsequent procedure
(5) The counts in respect of which a jury is discharged pursuant to paragraph (4)(a) may subsequently be proceeded on in all respects as if they were contained in a separate indictment.
Idem
(6) Where an order is made in respect of an accused or defendant under paragraph (3)(b), the accused or defendant may be tried separately on the counts in relation to which the order was made as if they were contained in a separate indictment.
R.S., 1985, c. C-46, s. 591;
R.S., 1985, c. 27 (1st Supp.), s. 119;
2011, c. 16, s. 5.

Joinder of Accused in Certain Cases

Accessories after the fact
592 Any one who is charged with being an accessory after the fact to any offence may be indicted,

Amending defective indictment or count
601 (1) An objection to an indictment preferred under this Part or to a count in an indictment, for a defect apparent on its face, shall be taken by motion to quash the indictment or count before the accused enters a plea, and, after the accused has entered a plea, only by leave of the court before which the proceedings take place. The court before which an objection is taken under this section may, if it considers it necessary, order the indictment or count to be amended to cure the defect.

Amendment where variance
(2) Subject to this section, a court may, on the trial of an indictment, amend the indictment or a count therein or a particular that is furnished under section 587, to make the indictment, count or particular conform to the evidence, where there is a variance between the evidence and
(a) a count in the indictment as preferred; or
(b) a count in the indictment
(i) as amended, or
(ii) as it would have been if it had been amended in conformity with any particular that has been furnished pursuant to section 587.

Amending indictment
(3) Subject to this section, a court shall, at any stage of the proceedings, amend the indictment or a count therein as may be necessary where it appears
(a) that the indictment has been preferred under a particular Act of Parliament instead of another Act of Parliament;
(b) that the indictment or a count thereof
(i) fails to state or states defectively anything that is requisite to constitute the offence,
(ii) does not negative an exception that should be negatived,
(iii) is in any way defective in substance,
and the matters to be alleged in the proposed amendment are disclosed by the evidence taken on the preliminary inquiry or on the trial; or
(c) that the indictment or a count thereof is in any way defective in form.

Matters to be considered by the court
(4) The court shall, in considering whether or not an amendment should be made to the indictment or a count in it, consider
(a) the matters disclosed by the evidence taken on the preliminary inquiry;
(b) the evidence taken on the trial, if any;
(c) the circumstances of the case;
(d) whether the accused has been misled or prejudiced in his defence by any variance, error or omission mentioned in subsection (2) or (3); and
(e) whether, having regard to the merits of the case, the proposed amendment can be made without injustice being done.

Variance not material
(4.1) A variance between the indictment or a count therein and the evidence taken is not material with respect to
(a) the time when the offence is alleged to have been committed, if it is proved that the indictment was preferred within the prescribed period of limitation, if any; or
(b) the place where the subject-matter of the proceedings is alleged to have arisen, if it is proved that it arose within the territorial jurisdiction of the court.

Adjournment if accused prejudiced
(5) Where, in the opinion of the court, the accused has been misled or prejudiced in his defence by a variance, error or omission in an indictment or a count therein, the court may, if it is of the opinion that the misleading or prejudice may be removed by an adjournment, adjourn the proceedings to a specified day or sittings of the court and may make such an order with respect to the payment of costs resulting from the necessity for amendment as it considers desirable.

Question of law
(6) The question whether an order to amend an indictment or a count thereof should be granted or

refused is a question of law.
Endorsing indictment
(7) An order to amend an indictment or a count therein shall be endorsed on the indictment as part of the record and the proceedings shall continue as if the indictment or count had been originally preferred as amended.
Mistakes not material
(8) A mistake in the heading of an indictment shall be corrected as soon as it is discovered but, whether corrected or not, is not material.
Limitation
(9) The authority of a court to amend indictments does not authorize the court to add to the overt acts stated in an indictment for high treason or treason or for an offence against any provision in sections 49, 50, 51 and 53.
Definition of
court
(10) In this section,
court
Application
(11) This section applies to all proceedings, including preliminary inquiries, with such modifications as the circumstances require.
R.S., 1985, c. C-46, s. 601;
R.S., 1985, c. 27 (1st Supp.), s. 123;
1999, c. 5, s. 23(E);
2011, c. 16, s. 6.
602

Inspection and Copies of Documents

Right of accused
603 An accused is entitled, after he has been ordered to stand trial or at his trial,
(a) to inspect without charge the indictment, his own statement, the evidence and the exhibits, if any; and
(b) to receive, on payment of a reasonable fee determined in accordance with a tariff of fees fixed or approved by the Attorney General of the province, a copy
(i) of the evidence,
(ii) of his own statement, if any, and
(iii) of the indictment;
but the trial shall not be postponed to enable the accused to secure copies unless the court is satisfied that the failure of the accused to secure them before the trial is not attributable to lack of diligence on the part of the accused.
R.S., 1985, c. C-46, s. 603;
R.S., 1985, c. 27 (1st Supp.), s. 101(E).
604 Release of exhibits for testing
605 (1) A judge of a superior court of criminal jurisdiction or a court of criminal jurisdiction may, on summary application on behalf of the accused or the prosecutor, after three days notice to the accused or prosecutor, as the case may be, order the release of any exhibit for the purpose of a scientific or other test or examination, subject to such terms as appear to be necessary or desirable to ensure the safeguarding of the exhibit and its preservation for use at the trial.
Disobeying orders
(2) Every one who fails to comply with the terms of an order made under subsection (1) is guilty of contempt of court and may be dealt with summarily by the judge or provincial court judge who made the order or before whom the trial of the accused takes place.
R.S., 1985, c. C-46, s. 605;
R.S., 1985, c. 27 (1st Supp.), s. 203.

Pleas

Pleas permitted
606 (1) An accused who is called on to plead may plead guilty or not guilty, or the special pleas authorized by this Part and no others.
Conditions for accepting guilty plea
(1.1) A court may accept a plea of guilty only if it is satisfied that the accused
(a) is making the plea voluntarily; and
(b) understands
(i) that the plea is an admission of the essential elements of the offence,
(ii) the nature and consequences of the plea, and
(iii) that the court is not bound by any agreement made between the accused and the prosecutor.
Validity of plea
(1.2) The failure of the court to fully inquire whether the conditions set out in subsection (1.1) are met does not affect the validity of the plea.
Refusal to plead
(2) Where an accused refuses to plead or does not answer directly, the court shall order the clerk of the court to enter a plea of not guilty.
Allowing time
(3) An accused is not entitled as of right to have his trial postponed but the court may, if it considers that the accused should be allowed further time to plead, move to quash or prepare for his defence or for any other reason, adjourn the trial to a later time in the session or sittings of the court, or to the next of any subsequent session or sittings of the court, on such terms as the court considers proper.
Included or other offence
(4) Notwithstanding any other provision of this Act, where an accused or defendant pleads not guilty of the offence charged but guilty of any other offence arising out of the same transaction, whether or not it is an included offence, the court may, with the consent of the prosecutor, accept that plea of guilty and, if the plea is accepted, the court shall find the accused or defendant not guilty of the offence charged and find him guilty of the offence in respect of which the plea of guilty was accepted and enter those findings in the record of the court.
Inquiry of court — murder and serious personal injury offences
(4.1) If the accused is charged with a serious personal injury offence, as that expression is defined in section 752, or with the offence of murder, and the accused and the prosecutor have entered into an agreement under which the accused will enter a plea of guilty of the offence charged — or a plea of not guilty of the offence charged but guilty of any other offence arising out of the same transaction, whether or not it is an included offence — the court shall, after accepting the plea of guilty, inquire of the prosecutor if reasonable steps were taken to inform the victims of the agreement.
Inquiry of court — certain indictable offences
(4.2) If the accused is charged with an offence, as defined in section 2 of the
Canadian Victims Bill of Rights
Duty to inform
(4.3) If subsection (4.1) or (4.2) applies, and any victim was not informed of the agreement before the plea of guilty was accepted, the prosecutor shall, as soon as feasible, take reasonable steps to inform the victim of the agreement and the acceptance of the plea.
Validity of plea
(4.4) Neither the failure of the court to inquire of the prosecutor, nor the failure of the prosecutor to take reasonable steps to inform the victims of the agreement, affects the validity of the plea.
Video links
(5) For greater certainty, subsections 650(1.1) and (1.2) apply, with any modifications that the circumstances require, to pleas under this section if the accused has agreed to use a means referred to in those subsections.

R.S., 1985, c. C-46, s. 606;
R.S., 1985, c. 27 (1st Supp.), s. 125;
2002, c. 13, s. 49;
2015, c. 13, s. 21.
Special pleas
607 (1) An accused may plead the special pleas of
(a) (b) (c) pardon.
In case of libel
(2) An accused who is charged with defamatory libel may plead in accordance with sections 611 and 612.
Disposal
(3) The pleas of
Pleading over
(4) When the pleas referred to in subsection (3) are disposed of against the accused, he may plead guilty or not guilty.
Statement sufficient
(5) Where an accused pleads
(a) states that he has been lawfully acquitted, convicted or discharged under subsection 730(1), as the case may be, of the offence charged in the count to which the plea relates; and
(b) indicates the time and place of the acquittal, conviction or discharge under subsection 730(1).
Exception — foreign trials
(6) A person who is alleged to have committed an act or omission outside Canada that is an offence in Canada by virtue of any of subsections 7(2) to (3.1) or (3.7), or an offence under the
Crimes Against Humanity and War Crimes Act
(a) at the trial outside Canada the person was not present and was not represented by counsel acting under the person's instructions, and
(b) the person was not punished in accordance with the sentence imposed on conviction in respect of the act or omission,
notwithstanding that the person is deemed by virtue of subsection 7(6), or subsection 12(1) of the Crimes Against Humanity and War Crimes Act
R.S., 1985, c. C-46, s. 607;
R.S., 1985, c. 27 (1st Supp.), s. 126, c. 30 (3rd Supp.), s. 2, c. 1 (4th Supp.), s. 18(F);
1992, c. 1, s. 60(F);
1995, c. 22, s. 10;
2000, c. 24, s. 45;
2013, c. 13, s. 9.
Evidence of identity of charges
608 Where an issue on a plea of
R.S., c. C-34, s. 536.
What determines identity
609 (1) Where an issue on a plea of
(a) that the matter on which the accused was given in charge on the former trial is the same in whole or in part as that on which it is proposed to give him in charge, and
(b) that on the former trial, if all proper amendments had been made that might then have been made, he might have been convicted of all the offences of which he may be convicted on the count to which the plea of
the judge shall give judgment discharging the accused in respect of that count.
Allowance of special plea in part
(2) The following provisions apply where an issue on a plea of
(a) where it appears that the accused might on the former trial have been convicted of an offence of which he may be convicted on the count in issue, the judge shall direct that the accused shall not be found guilty of any offence of which he might have been convicted on the former trial; and

(b) where it appears that the accused may be convicted on the count in issue of an offence of which he could not have been convicted on the former trial, the accused shall plead guilty or not guilty with respect to that offence.
R.S., c. C-34, s. 537.

Circumstances of aggravation

610 (1) Where an indictment charges substantially the same offence as that charged in an indictment on which an accused was previously convicted or acquitted, but adds a statement of intention or circumstances of aggravation tending, if proved, to increase the punishment, the previous conviction or acquittal bars the subsequent indictment.

Effect of previous charge of murder or manslaughter

(2) A conviction or an acquittal on an indictment for murder bars a subsequent indictment for the same homicide charging it as manslaughter or infanticide, and a conviction or acquittal on an indictment for manslaughter or infanticide bars a subsequent indictment for the same homicide charging it as murder.

Previous charges of first degree murder

(3) A conviction or an acquittal on an indictment for first degree murder bars a subsequent indictment for the same homicide charging it as second degree murder, and a conviction or acquittal on an indictment for second degree murder bars a subsequent indictment for the same homicide charging it as first degree murder.

Effect of previous charge of infanticide or manslaughter

(4) A conviction or an acquittal on an indictment for infanticide bars a subsequent indictment for the same homicide charging it as manslaughter, and a conviction or acquittal on an indictment for manslaughter bars a subsequent indictment for the same homicide charging it as infanticide.
R.S., c. C-34, s. 538;
1973-74, c. 38, s. 5;
1974-75-76, c. 105, s. 9.

Libel, plea of justification

611 (1) An accused who is charged with publishing a defamatory libel may plead that the defamatory matter published by him was true, and that it was for the public benefit that the matter should have been published in the manner in which and at the time when it was published.

Where more than one sense alleged

(2) A plea that is made under subsection (1) may justify the defamatory matter in any sense in which it is specified in the count, or in the sense that the defamatory matter bears without being specified, or separate pleas justifying the defamatory matter in each sense may be pleaded separately to each count as if two libels had been charged in separate counts.

Plea in writing

(3) A plea that is made under subsection (1) shall be in writing and shall set out the particular facts by reason of which it is alleged to have been for the public good that the matter should have been published.

Reply

(4) The prosecutor may in his reply deny generally the truth of a plea that is made under this section.
R.S., c. C-34, s. 539.

Plea of justification necessary

612 (1) The truth of the matters charged in an alleged libel shall not be inquired into in the absence of a plea of justification under section 611 unless the accused is charged with publishing the libel knowing it to be false, in which case evidence of the truth may be given to negative the allegation that the accused knew that the libel was false.

Not guilty, in addition

(2) The accused may, in addition to a plea that is made under section 611, plead not guilty and the pleas shall be inquired into together.

Effect of plea on punishment

(3) Where a plea of justification is pleaded and the accused is convicted, the court may, in

pronouncing sentence, consider whether the guilt of the accused is aggravated or mitigated by the plea.
R.S., c. C-34, s. 540.
Plea of not guilty
613 Any ground of defence for which a special plea is not provided by this Act may be relied on under the plea of not guilty.
R.S., c. C-34, s. 541.
614 to 619

Organizations

Appearance by attorney
620 Every organization against which an indictment is filed shall appear and plead by counsel or agent.
R.S., 1985, c. C-46, s. 620;
1997, c. 18, s. 70;
2003, c. 21, s. 11.
Notice to organization
621 (1) The clerk of the court or the prosecutor may, where an indictment is filed against an organization, cause a notice of the indictment to be served on the organization.
Contents of notice
(2) A notice of an indictment referred to in subsection (1) shall set out the nature and purport of the indictment and advise that, unless the organization appears on the date set out in the notice or the date fixed under subsection 548(2.1), and enters a plea, a plea of not guilty will be entered for the accused by the court, and that the trial of the indictment will be proceeded with as though the organization had appeared and pleaded.
R.S., 1985, c. C-46, s. 621;
1997, c. 18, s. 71;
2003, c. 21, s. 11.
Procedure on default of appearance
622 Where an organization does not appear in accordance with the notice referred to in section 621, the presiding judge may, on proof of service of the notice, order the clerk of the court to enter a plea of not guilty on behalf of the organization, and the plea has the same force and effect as if the organization had appeared by its counsel or agent and pleaded that plea.
R.S., 1985, c. C-46, s. 622;
1997, c. 18, s. 72;
2003, c. 21, s. 11.
Trial of organization
623 Where an organization appears and pleads to an indictment or a plea of not guilty is entered by order of the court under section 622, the court shall proceed with the trial of the indictment and, where the organization is convicted, section 735 applies.
R.S., 1985, c. C-46, s. 623;
1995, c. 22, s. 10;
2003, c. 21, s. 11.

Record of Proceedings

How recorded
624 (1) It is sufficient, in making up the record of a conviction or acquittal on an indictment, to copy the indictment and the plea that was pleaded, without a formal caption or heading.
Record of proceedings
(2) The court shall keep a record of every arraignment and of proceedings subsequent to arraignment.
R.S., c. C-34, s. 552.

Form of record in case of amendment
625 Where it is necessary to draw up a formal record in proceedings in which the indictment has been amended, the record shall be drawn up in the form in which the indictment remained after the amendment, without reference to the fact that the indictment was amended.
R.S., c. C-34, s. 553.

Pre-hearing Conference

Pre-hearing conference
625.1 (1) Subject to subsection (2), on application by the prosecutor or the accused or on its own motion, the court, or a judge of the court, before which, or the judge, provincial court judge or justice before whom, any proceedings are to be held may order that a conference between the prosecutor and the accused or counsel for the accused, to be presided over by the court, judge, provincial court judge or justice, be held prior to the proceedings to consider the matters that, to promote a fair and expeditious hearing, would be better decided before the start of the proceedings, and other similar matters, and to make arrangements for decisions on those matters.
Mandatory pre-trial hearing for jury trials
(2) In any case to be tried with a jury, a judge of the court before which the accused is to be tried shall, before the trial, order that a conference between the prosecutor and the accused or counsel for the accused, to be presided over by a judge of that court, be held in accordance with the rules of court made under sections 482 and 482.1 to consider any matters that would promote a fair and expeditious trial.
R.S., 1985, c. 27 (1st Supp.), s. 127, c. 1 (4th Supp.), s. 45(F);
1997, c. 18, s. 73;
2002, c. 13, s. 50.

Juries

Qualification of jurors
626 (1) A person who is qualified as a juror according to, and summoned as a juror in accordance with, the laws of a province is qualified to serve as a juror in criminal proceedings in that province.
No disqualification based on sex
(2) Notwithstanding any law of a province referred to in subsection (1), no person may be disqualified, exempted or excused from serving as a juror in criminal proceedings on the grounds of his or her sex.
R.S., 1985, c. C-46, s. 626;
R.S., 1985, c. 27 (1st Supp.), s. 128.
Presiding judge
626.1 The judge before whom an accused is tried may be either the judge who presided over matters pertaining to the selection of a jury before the commencement of a trial or another judge of the same court.
2002, c. 13, s. 51.
Support for juror with physical disability
627 The judge may permit a juror with a physical disability who is otherwise qualified to serve as a juror to have technical, personal, interpretative or other support services.
R.S., 1985, c. C-46, s. 627;
R.S., 1985, c. 2 (1st Supp.), s. 1;
1998, c. 9, s. 4.

Challenging the Array

628 Challenging the jury panel

629 (1) The accused or the prosecutor may challenge the jury panel only on the ground of partiality, fraud or wilful misconduct on the part of the sheriff or other officer by whom the panel was returned.
In writing
(2) A challenge under subsection (1) shall be in writing and shall state that the person who returned the panel was partial or fraudulent or that he wilfully misconducted himself, as the case may be.
Form
(3) A challenge under this section may be in Form 40.
R.S., 1985, c. C-46, s. 629;
R.S., 1985, c. 27 (1st Supp.), s. 130.
Trying ground of challenge
630 Where a challenge is made under section 629, the judge shall determine whether the alleged ground of challenge is true or not, and where he is satisfied that the alleged ground of challenge is true, he shall direct a new panel to be returned.
R.S., c. C-34, s. 559.

Empanelling Jury

Names of jurors on cards
631 (1) The name of each juror on a panel of jurors that has been returned, his number on the panel and his address shall be written on a separate card, and all the cards shall, as far as possible, be of equal size.
To be placed in box
(2) The sheriff or other officer who returns the panel shall deliver the cards referred to in subsection (1) to the clerk of the court who shall cause them to be placed together in a box to be provided for the purpose and to be thoroughly shaken together.
Alternate jurors
(2.1) If the judge considers it advisable in the interests of justice to have one or two alternate jurors, the judge shall so order before the clerk of the court draws out the cards under subsection (3) or (3.1).
Additional jurors
(2.2) If the judge considers it advisable in the interests of justice, he or she may order that 13 or 14 jurors, instead of 12, be sworn in accordance with this Part before the clerk of the court draws out the cards under subsection (3) or (3.1).
Cards to be drawn by clerk of court
(3) If the array of jurors is not challenged or the array of jurors is challenged but the judge does not direct a new panel to be returned, the clerk of the court shall, in open court, draw out one after another the cards referred to in subsection (1), call out the number on each card as it is drawn and confirm with the person who responds that he or she is the person whose name appears on the card drawn, until the number of persons who have answered is, in the opinion of the judge, sufficient to provide a full jury and any alternate jurors ordered by the judge after allowing for orders to excuse, challenges and directions to stand by.
Exception
(3.1) The court, or a judge of the court, before which the jury trial is to be held may, if the court or judge is satisfied that it is necessary for the proper administration of justice, order the clerk of the court to call out the name and the number on each card.
Juror and other persons to be sworn
(4) The clerk of the court shall swear each member of the jury, and any alternate jurors, in the order in which his or her card was drawn and shall swear any other person providing technical, personal, interpretative or other support services to a juror with a physical disability.
Drawing additional cards if necessary
(5) If the number of persons who answer under subsection (3) or (3.1) is not sufficient to provide a full jury and the number of alternate jurors ordered by the judge, the clerk of the court shall proceed

in accordance with subsections (3), (3.1) and (4) until 12 jurors — or 13 or 14 jurors, as the case may be, if the judge makes an order under subsection (2.2) — and any alternate jurors are sworn.

Ban on publication, limitation to access or use of information

(6) On application by the prosecutor or on its own motion, the court or judge before which a jury trial is to be held may, if the court or judge is satisfied that such an order is necessary for the proper administration of justice, make an order

(a) directing that the identity of a juror or any information that could disclose their identity shall not be published in any document or broadcast or transmitted in any way; or

(b) limiting access to or the use of that information.

R.S., 1985, c. C-46, s. 631;
R.S., 1985, c. 27 (1st Supp.), s. 131;
1992, c. 41, s. 1;
1998, c. 9, s. 5;
2001, c. 32, ss. 38, 82;
2002, c. 13, s. 52;
2005, c. 32, s. 20;
2011, c. 16, s. 7.

Excusing jurors

632 The judge may, at any time before the commencement of a trial, order that any juror be excused from jury service, whether or not the juror has been called pursuant to subsection 631(3) or (3.1) or any challenge has been made in relation to the juror, for reasons of

(a) personal interest in the matter to be tried;

(b) relationship with the judge presiding over the jury selection process, the judge before whom the accused is to be tried, the prosecutor, the accused, the counsel for the accused or a prospective witness; or

(c) personal hardship or any other reasonable cause that, in the opinion of the judge, warrants that the juror be excused.

R.S., 1985, c. C-46, s. 632;
1992, c. 41, s. 2;
2001, c. 32, s. 39;
2002, c. 13, s. 53.

Stand by

633 The judge may direct a juror who has been called pursuant to subsection 631(3) or (3.1) to stand by for reasons of personal hardship or any other reasonable cause.

R.S., 1985, c. C-46, s. 633;
R.S., 1985, c. 27 (1st Supp.), s. 185(F);
1992, c. 41, s. 2;
2001, c. 32, s. 40.

Peremptory challenges

634 (1) A juror may be challenged peremptorily whether or not the juror has been challenged for cause pursuant to section 638.

Maximum number

(2) Subject to subsections (2.1) to (4), the prosecutor and the accused are each entitled to

(a) twenty peremptory challenges, where the accused is charged with high treason or first degree murder;

(b) twelve peremptory challenges, where the accused is charged with an offence, other than an offence mentioned in paragraph (a), for which the accused may be sentenced to imprisonment for a term exceeding five years; or

(c) four peremptory challenges, where the accused is charged with an offence that is not referred to in paragraph (a) or (b).

If 13 or 14 jurors

(2.01) If the judge orders under subsection 631(2.2) that 13 or 14 jurors be sworn in accordance with this Part, the total number of peremptory challenges that the prosecutor and the accused are each entitled to is increased by one in the case of 13 jurors or two in the case of 14 jurors.

If alternate jurors

(2.1) If the judge makes an order for alternate jurors, the total number of peremptory challenges that the prosecutor and the accused are each entitled to is increased by one for each alternate juror.

Supplemental peremptory challenges

(2.2) For the purposes of replacing jurors under subsection 644(1.1), the prosecutor and the accused are each entitled to one peremptory challenge for each juror to be replaced.

Where there are multiple counts

(3) Where two or more counts in an indictment are to be tried together, the prosecutor and the accused are each entitled only to the number of peremptory challenges provided in respect of the count for which the greatest number of peremptory challenges is available.

Where there are joint trials

(4) Where two or more accused are to be tried together,

(a) each accused is entitled to the number of peremptory challenges to which the accused would be entitled if tried alone; and

(b) the prosecutor is entitled to the total number of peremptory challenges available to all the accused.

R.S., 1985, c. C-46, s. 634;

1992, c. 41, s. 2;

2002, c. 13, s. 54;

2008, c. 18, s. 25;

2011, c. 16, s. 8.

Order of challenges

635 (1) The accused shall be called on before the prosecutor is called on to declare whether the accused challenges the first juror, for cause or peremptorily, and thereafter the prosecutor and the accused shall be called on alternately, in respect of each of the remaining jurors, to first make such a declaration.

Where there are joint trials

(2) Subsection (1) applies where two or more accused are to be tried together, but all of the accused shall exercise the challenges of the defence in turn, in the order in which their names appear in the indictment or in any other order agreed on by them,

(a) in respect of the first juror, before the prosecutor; and

(b) in respect of each of the remaining jurors, either before or after the prosecutor, in accordance with subsection (1).

R.S., 1985, c. C-46, s. 635;

R.S., 1985, c. 2 (1st Supp.), s. 2;

1992, c. 41, s. 2.

636 and 637 Challenge for cause

638 (1) A prosecutor or an accused is entitled to any number of challenges on the ground that

(a) the name of a juror does not appear on the panel, but no misnomer or misdescription is a ground of challenge where it appears to the court that the description given on the panel sufficiently designates the person referred to;

(b) a juror is not indifferent between the Queen and the accused;

(c) a juror has been convicted of an offence for which he was sentenced to death or to a term of imprisonment exceeding twelve months;

(d) a juror is an alien;

(e) a juror, even with the aid of technical, personal, interpretative or other support services provided to the juror under section 627, is physically unable to perform properly the duties of a juror; or

(f) a juror does not speak the official language of Canada that is the language of the accused or the official language of Canada in which the accused can best give testimony or both official languages of Canada, where the accused is required by reason of an order under section 530 to be tried before a judge and jury who speak the official language of Canada that is the language of the accused or the official language of Canada in which the accused can best give testimony or who speak both official languages of Canada, as the case may be.

No other ground

(2) No challenge for cause shall be allowed on a ground not mentioned in subsection (1).

(3) and (4) (5) R.S., 1985, c. C-46, s. 638;

R.S., 1985, c. 27 (1st Supp.), s. 132, c. 31 (4th Supp.), s. 96;

1997, c. 18, s. 74;

1998, c. 9, s. 6.

Challenge in writing

639 (1) Where a challenge is made on a ground mentioned in section 638, the court may, in its discretion, require the party that challenges to put the challenge in writing.

Form

(2) A challenge may be in Form 41.

Denial

(3) A challenge may be denied by the other party to the proceedings on the ground that it is not true. R.S., c. C-34, s. 568.

Objection that name not on panel

640 (1) Where the ground of a challenge is that the name of a juror does not appear on the panel, the issue shall be tried by the judge on the

Other grounds

(2) If the ground of a challenge is one that is not mentioned in subsection (1) and no order has been made under subsection (2.1), the two jurors who were last sworn — or, if no jurors have been sworn, two persons present who are appointed by the court for the purpose — shall be sworn to determine whether the ground of challenge is true.

Challenge for cause

(2.1) If the challenge is for cause and if the ground of the challenge is one that is not mentioned in subsection (1), on the application of the accused, the court may order the exclusion of all jurors — sworn and unsworn — from the court room until it is determined whether the ground of challenge is true, if the court is of the opinion that such an order is necessary to preserve the impartiality of the jurors.

Exclusion order

(2.2) If an order is made under subsection (2.1), two unsworn jurors, who are then exempt from the order, or two persons present who are appointed by the court for that purpose, shall be sworn to determine whether the ground of challenge is true. Those persons so appointed shall exercise their duties until 12 jurors — or 13 or 14 jurors, as the case may be, if the judge makes an order under subsection 631(2.2) — and any alternate jurors are sworn.

If challenge not sustained, or if sustained

(3) Where the finding, pursuant to subsection (1), (2) or (2.2) is that the ground of challenge is not true, the juror shall be sworn, but if the finding is that the ground of challenge is true, the juror shall not be sworn.

Disagreement of triers

(4) Where, after what the court considers to be a reasonable time, the two persons who are sworn to determine whether the ground of challenge is true are unable to agree, the court may discharge them from giving a verdict and may direct two other persons to be sworn to determine whether the ground of challenge is true.

R.S., 1985, c. C-46, s. 640;

2008, c. 18, s. 26;

2011, c. 16, s. 9.

Calling persons who have stood by

641 (1) If a full jury and any alternate jurors have not been sworn and no cards remain to be drawn, the persons who have been directed to stand by shall be called again in the order in which their cards

were drawn and shall be sworn, unless excused by the judge or challenged by the accused or the prosecutor.

Other persons becoming available

(2) If, before a person is sworn as a juror under subsection (1), other persons in the panel become available, the prosecutor may require the cards of those persons to be put into and drawn from the box in accordance with section 631, and those persons shall be challenged, directed to stand by, excused or sworn, as the case may be, before the persons who were originally directed to stand by are called again.

R.S., 1985, c. C-46, s. 641;
1992, c. 41, s. 3;
2001, c. 32, s. 41;
2002, c. 13, s. 55;
2011, c. 16, s. 10.

Summoning other jurors when panel exhausted

642 (1) If a full jury and any alternate jurors considered advisable cannot be provided notwithstanding that the relevant provisions of this Part have been complied with, the court may, at the request of the prosecutor, order the sheriff or other proper officer to summon without delay as many persons, whether qualified jurors or not, as the court directs for the purpose of providing a full jury and alternate jurors.

Orally

(2) Jurors may be summoned under subsection (1) by word of mouth, if necessary.

Adding names to panel

(3) The names of the persons who are summoned under this section shall be added to the general panel for the purposes of the trial, and the same proceedings shall be taken with respect to calling and challenging those persons, excusing them and directing them to stand by as are provided in this Part with respect to the persons named in the original panel.

R.S., 1985, c. C-46, s. 642;
1992, c. 41, s. 4;
2002, c. 13, s. 56.

Substitution of alternate jurors

642.1 (1) Alternate jurors shall attend at the commencement of the presentation of the evidence on the merits and, if there is not a full jury present, shall replace any absent juror, in the order in which their cards were drawn under subsection 631(3).

Excusing of alternate jurors

(2) An alternate juror who is not required as a substitute shall be excused.

2002, c. 13, s. 57;
2011, c. 16, s. 11.

Who shall be the jury

643 (1) The 12, 13 or 14 jurors who are sworn in accordance with this Part and present at the commencement of the presentation of the evidence on the merits shall be the jury to hear the evidence on the merits.

Names of jurors

(1.1) The name of each juror, including alternate jurors, who is sworn shall be kept apart until the juror is excused or the jury gives its verdict or is discharged, at which time the name shall be returned to the box as often as occasion arises, as long as an issue remains to be tried before a jury.

Same jury may try another issue by consent

(2) The court may try an issue with the same jury in whole or in part that previously tried or was drawn to try another issue, without the jurors being sworn again, but if the prosecutor or the accused objects to any of the jurors or the court excuses any of the jurors, the court shall order those persons to withdraw and shall direct that the required number of cards to make up a full jury be drawn and, subject to the provisions of this Part relating to challenges, orders to excuse and directions to stand by, the persons whose cards are drawn shall be sworn.

Sections directory
(3) Failure to comply with the directions of this section or section 631, 635 or 641 does not affect the validity of a proceeding.
R.S., 1985, c. C-46, s. 643;
1992, c. 41, s. 5;
2001, c. 32, s. 42;
2002, c. 13, s. 58;
2011, c. 16, s. 12.

Discharge of juror
644 (1) Where in the course of a trial the judge is satisfied that a juror should not, by reason of illness or other reasonable cause, continue to act, the judge may discharge the juror.

Replacement of juror
(1.1) A judge may select another juror to take the place of a juror who by reason of illness or other reasonable cause cannot continue to act, if the jury has not yet begun to hear evidence, either by drawing a name from a panel of persons who were summoned to act as jurors and who are available at the court at the time of replacing the juror or by using the procedure referred to in section 642.

Trial may continue
(2) Where in the course of a trial a member of the jury dies or is discharged pursuant to subsection (1), the jury shall, unless the judge otherwise directs and if the number of jurors is not reduced below ten, be deemed to remain properly constituted for all purposes of the trial and the trial shall proceed and a verdict may be given accordingly.
R.S., 1985, c. C-46, s. 644;
1992, c. 41, s. 6;
1997, c. 18, s. 75.

Trial

Trial continuous
645 (1) The trial of an accused shall proceed continuously subject to adjournment by the court.

Adjournment
(2) A judge may adjourn a trial from time to time in the same sittings.

Formal adjournment unnecessary
(3) For the purpose of subsection (2), no formal adjournment of trial or entry thereof is required.

Questions reserved for decision
(4) A judge, in any case tried without a jury, may reserve final decision on any question raised at the trial, or any matter raised further to a pre-hearing conference, and the decision, when given, shall be deemed to have been given at the trial.

Questions reserved for decision in a trial with a jury
(5) In any case to be tried with a jury, the judge before whom an accused is or is to be tried has jurisdiction, before any juror on a panel of jurors is called pursuant to subsection 631(3) or (3.1) and in the absence of any such juror, to deal with any matter that would ordinarily or necessarily be dealt with in the absence of the jury after it has been sworn.
R.S., 1985, c. C-46, s. 645;
R.S., 1985, c. 27 (1st Supp.), s. 133;
1997, c. 18, s. 76;
2001, c. 32, s. 43.

Taking evidence
646 On the trial of an accused for an indictable offence, the evidence of the witnesses for the prosecutor and the accused and the addresses of the prosecutor and the accused or counsel for the accused by way of summing up shall be taken in accordance with the provisions of Part XVIII, other than subsections 540(7) to (9), relating to the taking of evidence at preliminary inquiries.
R.S., 1985, c. C-46, s. 646;

2002, c. 13, s. 59.
Separation of jurors
647 (1) The judge may, at any time before the jury retires to consider its verdict, permit the members of the jury to separate.
Keeping in charge
(2) Where permission to separate under subsection (1) cannot be given or is not given, the jury shall be kept under the charge of an officer of the court as the judge directs, and that officer shall prevent the jurors from communicating with anyone other than himself or another member of the jury without leave of the judge.
Non-compliance with subsection (2)
(3) Failure to comply with subsection (2) does not affect the validity of the proceedings.
Empanelling new jury in certain cases
(4) Where the fact that there has been a failure to comply with this section or section 648 is discovered before the verdict of the jury is returned, the judge may, if he considers that the failure to comply might lead to a miscarriage of justice, discharge the jury and
(a) direct that the accused be tried with a new jury during the same session or sittings of the court; or
(b) postpone the trial on such terms as justice may require.
Refreshment and accommodation
(5) The judge shall direct the sheriff to provide the jurors who are sworn with suitable and sufficient refreshment, food and lodging while they are together until they have given their verdict.
R.S., c. C-34, s. 576;
1972, c. 13, s. 48.
Restriction on publication
648 (1) After permission to separate is given to members of a jury under subsection 647(1), no information regarding any portion of the trial at which the jury is not present shall be published in any document or broadcast or transmitted in any way before the jury retires to consider its verdict.
Offence
(2) Every one who fails to comply with subsection (1) is guilty of an offence punishable on summary conviction.
(3) R.S., 1985, c. C-46, s. 648;
2005, c. 32, s. 21.
Disclosure of jury proceedings
649 Every member of a jury, and every person providing technical, personal, interpretative or other support services to a juror with a physical disability, who, except for the purposes of
(a) an investigation of an alleged offence under subsection 139(2) in relation to a juror, or
(b) giving evidence in criminal proceedings in relation to such an offence,
discloses any information relating to the proceedings of the jury when it was absent from the courtroom that was not subsequently disclosed in open court is guilty of an offence punishable on summary conviction.
R.S., 1985, c. C-46, s. 649;
1998, c. 9, s. 7.
Accused to be present
650 (1) Subject to subsections (1.1) to (2) and section 650.01, an accused, other than an organization, shall be present in court during the whole of his or her trial.
Video links
(1.1) Where the court so orders, and where the prosecutor and the accused so agree, the accused may appear by counsel or by closed-circuit television or any other means that allow the court and the accused to engage in simultaneous visual and oral communication, for any part of the trial other than a part in which the evidence of a witness is taken.
Video links
(1.2) Where the court so orders, an accused who is confined in prison may appear by closed-circuit television or any other means that allow the court and the accused to engage in simultaneous visual

and oral communication, for any part of the trial other than a part in which the evidence of a witness is taken, if the accused is given the opportunity to communicate privately with counsel, in a case in which the accused is represented by counsel.

Exceptions

(2) The court may

(a) cause the accused to be removed and to be kept out of court, where he misconducts himself by interrupting the proceedings so that to continue the proceedings in his presence would not be feasible;

(b) permit the accused to be out of court during the whole or any part of his trial on such conditions as the court considers proper; or

(c) cause the accused to be removed and to be kept out of court during the trial of an issue as to whether the accused is unfit to stand trial, where it is satisfied that failure to do so might have an adverse effect on the mental condition of the accused.

To make defence

(3) An accused is entitled, after the close of the case for the prosecution, to make full answer and defence personally or by counsel.

R.S., 1985, c. C-46, s. 650;
1991, c. 43, s. 9;
1994, c. 44, s. 61;
1997, c. 18, s. 77;
2002, c. 13, s. 60;
2003, c. 21, s. 12.

Designation of counsel of record

650.01 (1) An accused may appoint counsel to represent the accused for any proceedings under this Act by filing a designation with the court.

Contents of designation

(2) The designation must contain the name and address of the counsel and be signed by the accused and the designated counsel.

Effect of designation

(3) If a designation is filed,

(a) the accused may appear by the designated counsel without being present for any part of the proceedings, other than

(i) a part during which oral evidence of a witness is taken,

(ii) a part during which jurors are being selected, and

(iii) an application for a writ of

(b) an appearance by the designated counsel is equivalent to the accused's being present, unless the court orders otherwise; and

(c) a plea of guilty may be made, and a sentence may be pronounced, only if the accused is present, unless the court orders otherwise.

When court orders presence of accused

(4) If the court orders the accused to be present otherwise than by appearance by the designated counsel, the court may

(a) issue a summons to compel the presence of the accused and order that it be served by leaving a copy at the address contained in the designation; or

(b) issue a warrant to compel the presence of the accused.

2002, c. 13, s. 61.

Technological appearance

650.02 The prosecutor or the counsel designated under section 650.01 may appear before the court by any technological means satisfactory to the court that permits the court and all counsel to communicate simultaneously.

2002, c. 13, s. 61.

Pre-charge conference

650.1 A judge in a jury trial may, before the charge to the jury, confer with the accused or counsel for the accused and the prosecutor with respect to the matters that should be explained to the jury and with respect to the choice of instructions to the jury.
1997, c. 18, s. 78.

Summing up by prosecutor

651 (1) Where an accused, or any one of several accused being tried together, is defended by counsel, the counsel shall, at the end of the case for the prosecution, declare whether or not he intends to adduce evidence on behalf of the accused for whom he appears and if he does not announce his intention to adduce evidence, the prosecutor may address the jury by way of summing up.

Summing up by accused

(2) Counsel for the accused or the accused, where he is not defended by counsel, is entitled, if he thinks fit, to open the case for the defence, and after the conclusion of that opening to examine such witnesses as he thinks fit, and when all the evidence is concluded to sum up the evidence.

Accused's right of reply

(3) Where no witnesses are examined for an accused, he or his counsel is entitled to address the jury last, but otherwise counsel for the prosecution is entitled to address the jury last.

Prosecutor's right of reply where more than one accused

(4) Where two or more accused are tried jointly and witnesses are examined for any of them, all the accused or their respective counsel are required to address the jury before it is addressed by the prosecutor.
R.S., c. C-34, s. 578.

View

652 (1) The judge may, where it appears to be in the interests of justice, at any time after the jury has been sworn and before it gives its verdict, direct the jury to have a view of any place, thing or person, and shall give directions respecting the manner in which, and the persons by whom, the place, thing or person shall be shown to the jury, and may for that purpose adjourn the trial.

Directions to prevent communication

(2) Where a view is ordered under subsection (1), the judge shall give any directions that he considers necessary for the purpose of preventing undue communication by any person with members of the jury, but failure to comply with any directions given under this subsection does not affect the validity of the proceedings.

Who shall attend

(3) Where a view is ordered under subsection (1), the accused and the judge shall attend.
R.S., c. C-34, s. 579.

Trying of issues of indictment by jury

652.1 (1) After the charge to the jury, the jury shall retire to try the issues of the indictment.

Reduction of number of jurors to 12

(2) However, if there are more than 12 jurors remaining, the judge shall identify the 12 jurors who are to retire to consider the verdict by having the number of each juror written on a card that is of equal size, by causing the cards to be placed together in a box that is to be thoroughly shaken together and by drawing one card if 13 jurors remain or two cards if 14 jurors remain. The judge shall then discharge any juror whose number is drawn.
2011, c. 16, s. 13.

Disagreement of jury

653 (1) Where the judge is satisfied that the jury is unable to agree on its verdict and that further detention of the jury would be useless, he may in his discretion discharge that jury and direct a new jury to be empanelled during the sittings of the court, or may adjourn the trial on such terms as justice may require.

Discretion not reviewable

(2) A discretion that is exercised under subsection (1) by a judge is not reviewable.
R.S., c. C-34, s. 580.

Mistrial — rulings binding at new trial
653.1 In the case of a mistrial, unless the court is satisfied that it would not be in the interests of justice, rulings relating to the disclosure or admissibility of evidence or the
Canadian Charter of Rights and Freedoms
2011, c. 16, s. 14.
Proceeding on Sunday, etc., not invalid
654 The taking of the verdict of a jury and any proceeding incidental thereto is not invalid by reason only that it is done on Sunday or on a holiday.
R.S., c. C-34, s. 581.

Evidence on Trial

Admissions at trial
655 Where an accused is on trial for an indictable offence, he or his counsel may admit any fact alleged against him for the purpose of dispensing with proof thereof.
R.S., c. C-34, s. 582.
Presumption — valuable minerals
656 In any proceeding in relation to theft or possession of a valuable mineral that is unrefined, partly refined, uncut or otherwise unprocessed by any person actively engaged in or on a mine, if it is established that the person possesses the valuable mineral, the person is presumed, in the absence of evidence raising a reasonable doubt to the contrary, to have stolen or unlawfully possessed the valuable mineral.
R.S., 1985, c. C-46, s. 656;
1999, c. 5, s. 24.
Use in evidence of statement by accused
657 A statement made by an accused under subsection 541(3) and purporting to be signed by the justice before whom it was made may be given in evidence against the accused at his or her trial without proof of the signature of the justice, unless it is proved that the justice by whom the statement purports to be signed did not sign it.
R.S., 1985, c. C-46, s. 657;
1994, c. 44, s. 62.
Proof of ownership and value of property
657.1 (1) In any proceedings, an affidavit or a solemn declaration of a person who claims to be the lawful owner of, or the person lawfully entitled to possession of, property that was the subject-matter of the offence, or any other person who has specialized knowledge of the property or of that type of property, containing the statements referred to in subsection (2), shall be admissible in evidence and, in the absence of evidence to the contrary, is evidence of the statements contained in the affidavit or solemn declaration without proof of the signature of the person appearing to have signed the affidavit or solemn declaration.
Statements to be made
(2) For the purposes of subsection (1), a person shall state in an affidavit or a solemn declaration
(a) that the person is the lawful owner of, or is lawfully entitled to possession of, the property, or otherwise has specialized knowledge of the property or of property of the same type as that property;
(b) the value of the property;
(c) in the case of a person who is the lawful owner of or is lawfully entitled to possession of the property, that the person has been deprived of the property by fraudulent means or otherwise without the lawful consent of the person;
(c.1) in the case of proceedings in respect of an offence under section 342, that the credit card had been revoked or cancelled, is a false document within the meaning of section 321 or that no credit card that meets the exact description of that credit card was ever issued; and
(d) any facts within the personal knowledge of the person relied on to justify the statements referred to in paragraphs (a) to (c.1).

Notice of intention to produce affidavit or solemn declaration
(3) Unless the court orders otherwise, no affidavit or solemn declaration shall be received in evidence pursuant to subsection (1) unless the prosecutor has, before the trial or other proceeding, given to the accused a copy of the affidavit or solemn declaration and reasonable notice of intention to produce it in evidence.

Attendance for examination
(4) Notwithstanding subsection (1), the court may require the person who appears to have signed an affidavit or solemn declaration referred to in that subsection to appear before it for examination or cross-examination in respect of the issue of proof of any of the statements contained in the affidavit or solemn declaration.

R.S., 1985, c. 23 (4th Supp.), s. 3;

1994, c. 44, s. 63;

1997, c. 18, s. 79.

Theft and possession
657.2 (1) Where an accused is charged with possession of any property obtained by the commission of an offence, evidence of the conviction or discharge of another person of theft of the property is admissible against the accused, and in the absence of evidence to the contrary is proof that the property was stolen.

Accessory after the fact
(2) Where an accused is charged with being an accessory after the fact to the commission of an offence, evidence of the conviction or discharge of another person of the offence is admissible against the accused, and in the absence of evidence to the contrary is proof that the offence was committed.

1997, c. 18, s. 80.

Expert testimony
657.3 (1) In any proceedings, the evidence of a person as an expert may be given by means of a report accompanied by the affidavit or solemn declaration of the person, setting out, in particular, the qualifications of the person as an expert if

(a) the court recognizes that person as an expert; and

(b) the party intending to produce the report in evidence has, before the proceeding, given to the other party a copy of the affidavit or solemn declaration and the report and reasonable notice of the intention to produce it in evidence.

Attendance for examination
(2) Notwithstanding subsection (1), the court may require the person who appears to have signed an affidavit or solemn declaration referred to in that subsection to appear before it for examination or cross-examination in respect of the issue of proof of any of the statements contained in the affidavit or solemn declaration or report.

Notice for expert testimony
(3) For the purpose of promoting the fair, orderly and efficient presentation of the testimony of witnesses,

(a) a party who intends to call a person as an expert witness shall, at least thirty days before the commencement of the trial or within any other period fixed by the justice or judge, give notice to the other party or parties of his or her intention to do so, accompanied by

(i) the name of the proposed witness,

(ii) a description of the area of expertise of the proposed witness that is sufficient to permit the other parties to inform themselves about that area of expertise, and

(iii) a statement of the qualifications of the proposed witness as an expert;

(b) in addition to complying with paragraph (a), a prosecutor who intends to call a person as an expert witness shall, within a reasonable period before trial, provide to the other party or parties

(i) a copy of the report, if any, prepared by the proposed witness for the case, and

(ii) if no report is prepared, a summary of the opinion anticipated to be given by the proposed witness and the grounds on which it is based; and

(c) in addition to complying with paragraph (a), an accused, or his or her counsel, who intends to call a person as an expert witness shall, not later than the close of the case for the prosecution, provide to the other party or parties the material referred to in paragraph (b).

If notices not given

(4) If a party calls a person as an expert witness without complying with subsection (3), the court shall, at the request of any other party,

(a) grant an adjournment of the proceedings to the party who requests it to allow him or her to prepare for cross-examination of the expert witness;

(b) order the party who called the expert witness to provide that other party and any other party with the material referred to in paragraph (3)(b); and

(c) order the calling or recalling of any witness for the purpose of giving testimony on matters related to those raised in the expert witness's testimony, unless the court considers it inappropriate to do so.

Additional court orders

(5) If, in the opinion of the court, a party who has received the notice and material referred to in subsection (3) has not been able to prepare for the evidence of the proposed witness, the court may do one or more of the following:

(a) adjourn the proceedings;

(b) order that further particulars be given of the evidence of the proposed witness; and

(c) order the calling or recalling of any witness for the purpose of giving testimony on matters related to those raised in the expert witness's testimony.

Use of material by prosecution

(6) If the proposed witness does not testify, the prosecutor may not produce material provided to him or her under paragraph (3)(c) in evidence without the consent of the accused.

No further disclosure

(7) Unless otherwise ordered by a court, information disclosed under this section in relation to a proceeding may only be used for the purpose of that proceeding.

1997, c. 18, s. 80;
2002, c. 13, s. 62.

Children and Young Persons

Testimony as to date of birth

658 (1) In any proceedings to which this Act applies, the testimony of a person as to the date of his or her birth is admissible as evidence of that date.

Testimony of a parent

(2) In any proceedings to which this Act applies, the testimony of a parent as to the age of a person of whom he or she is a parent is admissible as evidence of the age of that person.

Proof of age

(3) In any proceedings to which this Act applies,

(a) a birth or baptismal certificate or a copy of such a certificate purporting to be certified under the hand of the person in whose custody the certificate is held is evidence of the age of that person; and

(b) an entry or record of an incorporated society or its officers who have had the control or care of a child or young person at or about the time the child or young person was brought to Canada is evidence of the age of the child or young person if the entry or record was made before the time when the offence is alleged to have been committed.

Other evidence

(4) In the absence of any certificate, copy, entry or record mentioned in subsection (3), or in corroboration of any such certificate, copy, entry or record, a jury, judge, justice or provincial court judge, as the case may be, may receive and act on any other information relating to age that they consider reliable.

Inference from appearance

(5) In the absence of other evidence, or by way of corroboration of other evidence, a jury, judge,

justice or provincial court judge, as the case may be, may infer the age of a child or young person from his or her appearance.
R.S., 1985, c. C-46, s. 658;
1994, c. 44, s. 64.

Corroboration

Children's evidence
659 Any requirement whereby it is mandatory for a court to give the jury a warning about convicting an accused on the evidence of a child is abrogated.
R.S., 1985, c. C-46, s. 659;
R.S., 1985, c. 19 (3rd Supp.), s. 15;
1993, c. 45, s. 9.

Verdicts

Full offence charged, attempt proved
660 Where the complete commission of an offence charged is not proved but the evidence establishes an attempt to commit the offence, the accused may be convicted of the attempt.
R.S., c. C-34, s. 587.
Attempt charged, full offence proved
661 (1) Where an attempt to commit an offence is charged but the evidence establishes the commission of the complete offence, the accused is not entitled to be acquitted, but the jury may convict him of the attempt unless the judge presiding at the trial, in his discretion, discharges the jury from giving a verdict and directs that the accused be indicted for the complete offence.
Conviction a bar
(2) An accused who is convicted under this section is not liable to be tried again for the offence that he was charged with attempting to commit.
R.S., c. C-34, s. 588.
Offence charged, part only proved
662 (1) A count in an indictment is divisible and where the commission of the offence charged, as described in the enactment creating it or as charged in the count, includes the commission of another offence, whether punishable by indictment or on summary conviction, the accused may be convicted
(a) of an offence so included that is proved, notwithstanding that the whole offence that is charged is not proved; or
(b) of an attempt to commit an offence so included.
First degree murder charged
(2) For greater certainty and without limiting the generality of subsection (1), where a count charges first degree murder and the evidence does not prove first degree murder but proves second degree murder or an attempt to commit second degree murder, the jury may find the accused not guilty of first degree murder but guilty of second degree murder or an attempt to commit second degree murder, as the case may be.
Conviction for infanticide or manslaughter on charge of murder
(3) Subject to subsection (4), where a count charges murder and the evidence proves manslaughter or infanticide but does not prove murder, the jury may find the accused not guilty of murder but guilty of manslaughter or infanticide, but shall not on that count find the accused guilty of any other offence.
Conviction for concealing body of child where murder or infanticide charged
(4) Where a count charges the murder of a child or infanticide and the evidence proves the commission of an offence under section 243 but does not prove murder or infanticide, the jury may find the accused not guilty of murder or infanticide, as the case may be, but guilty of an offence under section 243.

Conviction for dangerous driving where manslaughter charged
(5) For greater certainty, where a count charges an offence under section 220, 221 or 236 arising out of the operation of a motor vehicle or the navigation or operation of a vessel or aircraft, and the evidence does not prove such offence but does prove an offence under section 249 or subsection 249.1(3), the accused may be convicted of an offence under section 249 or subsection 249.1(3), as the case may be.
Conviction for break and enter with intent
(6) Where a count charges an offence under paragraph 98(1)(b) or 348(1)(b) and the evidence does not prove that offence but does prove an offence under, respectively, paragraph 98(1)(a) or 348(1)(a), the accused may be convicted of an offence under that latter paragraph.
R.S., 1985, c. C-46, s. 662;
R.S., 1985, c. 27 (1st Supp.), s. 134;
2000, c. 2, s. 3;
2008, c. 6, s. 38.
No acquittal unless act or omission not wilful
663 Where a female person is charged with infanticide and the evidence establishes that she caused the death of her child but does not establish that, at the time of the act or omission by which she caused the death of the child,
(a) she was not fully recovered from the effects of giving birth to the child or from the effect of lactation consequent on the birth of the child, and
(b) the balance of her mind was, at that time, disturbed by reason of the effect of giving birth to the child or of the effect of lactation consequent on the birth of the child,
she may be convicted unless the evidence establishes that the act or omission was not wilful.
R.S., c. C-34, s. 590.

Previous Convictions

No reference to previous conviction
664 No indictment in respect of an offence for which, by reason of previous convictions, a greater punishment may be imposed shall contain any reference to previous convictions.
R.S., c. C-34, s. 591.
665 Evidence of character
666 Where, at a trial, the accused adduces evidence of his good character, the prosecutor may, in answer thereto, before a verdict is returned, adduce evidence of the previous conviction of the accused for any offences, including any previous conviction by reason of which a greater punishment may be imposed.
R.S., c. C-34, s. 593.
Proof of previous conviction
667 (1) In any proceedings,
(a) a certificate setting out with reasonable particularity the conviction or discharge under section 730, the finding of guilt under the
Young Offenders Act
Youth Criminal Justice Act
(i) the person who made the conviction, order for the discharge or finding of guilt,
(ii) the clerk of the court in which the conviction, order for the discharge or finding of guilt was made, or
(iii) a fingerprint examiner;
(b) evidence that the fingerprints of the accused or defendant are the same as the fingerprints of the offender whose fingerprints are reproduced in or attached to a certificate issued under subparagraph (a)(iii) is, in the absence of evidence to the contrary, proof that the accused or defendant is the offender referred to in that certificate;
(c) a certificate of a fingerprint examiner stating that he has compared the fingerprints reproduced in

or attached to that certificate with the fingerprints reproduced in or attached to a certificate issued under subparagraph (a)(iii) and that they are those of the same person is evidence of the statements contained in the certificate without proof of the signature or the official character of the person appearing to have signed the certificate; and

(d) a certificate under subparagraph (a)(iii) may be in Form 44, and a certificate under paragraph (c) may be in Form 45.

Idem

(2) In any proceedings, a copy of the summary conviction or discharge under section 730 in Canada of an offender, signed by the person who made the conviction or order for the discharge or by the clerk of the court in which the conviction or order for the discharge was made, is, on proof that the accused or defendant is the offender referred to in the copy of the summary conviction, evidence of the conviction or discharge under section 730 of the accused or defendant, without proof of the signature or the official character of the person appearing to have signed it.

Proof of identity

(2.1) In any summary conviction proceedings, where the name of a defendant is similar to the name of an offender referred to in a certificate made under subparagraph (1)(a)(i) or (ii) in respect of a summary conviction or referred to in a copy of a summary conviction mentioned in subsection (2), that similarity of name is, in the absence of evidence to the contrary, evidence that the defendant is the offender referred to in the certificate or the copy of the summary conviction.

Attendance and right to cross-examine

(3) An accused against whom a certificate issued under subparagraph (1)(a)(iii) or paragraph (1)(c) is produced may, with leave of the court, require the attendance of the person who signed the certificate for the purposes of cross-examination.

Notice of intention to produce certificate

(4) No certificate issued under subparagraph (1)(a)(iii) or paragraph (1)(c) shall be received in evidence unless the party intending to produce it has given to the accused reasonable notice of his intention together with a copy of the certificate.

Definition of
fingerprint examiner
(5) In this section,
fingerprint examiner
R.S., 1985, c. C-46, s. 667;
R.S., 1985, c. 27 (1st Supp.), s. 136, c. 1 (4th Supp.), s. 18(F);
1995, c. 22, s. 10;
2002, c. 1, s. 181;
2005, c. 10, s. 34;
2008, c. 18, s. 27(F);
2012, c. 1, s. 200.
668 and 669

Jurisdiction

Jurisdiction

669.1 (1) Where any judge, court or provincial court judge by whom or which the plea of the accused or defendant to an offence was taken has not commenced to hear evidence, any judge, court or provincial court judge having jurisdiction to try the accused or defendant has jurisdiction for the purpose of the hearing and adjudication.

Adjournment

(2) Any court, judge or provincial court judge having jurisdiction to try an accused or a defendant, or any clerk or other proper officer of the court, or in the case of an offence punishable on summary conviction, any justice, may, at any time before or after the plea of the accused or defendant is taken, adjourn the proceedings.
R.S., 1985, c. 27 (1st Supp.), s. 137.

Continuation of proceedings
669.2 (1) Subject to this section, where an accused or a defendant is being tried by
(a) a judge or provincial court judge,
(b) a justice or other person who is, or is a member of, a summary conviction court, or
(c) a court composed of a judge and jury,
as the case may be, and the judge, provincial court judge, justice or other person dies or is for any reason unable to continue, the proceedings may be continued before another judge, provincial court judge, justice or other person, as the case may be, who has jurisdiction to try the accused or defendant.

Where adjudication is made
(2) Where a verdict was rendered by a jury or an adjudication was made by a judge, provincial court judge, justice or other person before whom the trial was commenced, the judge, provincial court judge, justice or other person before whom the proceedings are continued shall, without further election by an accused, impose the punishment or make the order that is authorized by law in the circumstances.

If no adjudication made
(3) Subject to subsections (4) and (5), if the trial was commenced but no adjudication was made or verdict rendered, the judge, provincial court judge, justice or other person before whom the proceedings are continued shall, without further election by an accused, commence the trial again as if no evidence on the merits had been taken.

If no adjudication made — jury trials
(4) If a trial that is before a court composed of a judge and a jury was commenced but no adjudication was made or verdict rendered, the judge before whom the proceedings are continued may, without further election by an accused, continue the trial or commence the trial again as if no evidence on the merits had been taken.

Where trial continued
(5) Where a trial is continued under paragraph (4)(a), any evidence that was adduced before a judge referred to in paragraph (1)(c) is deemed to have been adduced before the judge before whom the trial is continued but, where the prosecutor and the accused so agree, any part of that evidence may be adduced again before the judge before whom the trial is continued.
R.S., 1985, c. 27 (1st Supp.), s. 137;
1994, c. 44, s. 65;
2011, c. 16, s. 15.

Jurisdiction when appointment to another court
669.3 Where a court composed of a judge and a jury, a judge or a provincial court judge is conducting a trial and the judge or provincial court judge is appointed to another court, he or she continues to have jurisdiction in respect of the trial until its completion.
1994, c. 44, s. 66.

Formal Defects in Jury Process

Judgment not to be stayed on certain grounds
670 Judgment shall not be stayed or reversed after verdict on an indictment
(a) by reason of any irregularity in the summoning or empanelling of the jury; or
(b) for the reason that a person who served on the jury was not returned as a juror by a sheriff or other officer.
R.S., c. C-34, s. 598.

Directions respecting jury or jurors directory
671 No omission to observe the directions contained in any Act with respect to the qualification, selection, balloting or distribution of jurors, the preparation of the jurors' book, the selecting of jury lists or the drafting of panels from the jury lists is a ground for impeaching or quashing a verdict rendered in criminal proceedings.

R.S., c. C-34, s. 599.
Saving powers of court
672 Nothing in this Act alters, abridges or affects any power or authority that a court or judge had immediately before April 1, 1955, or any practice or form that existed immediately before April 1, 1955, with respect to trials by jury, jury process, juries or jurors, except where the power or authority, practice or form is expressly altered by or is inconsistent with this Act.
R.S., c. C-34, s. 600.

PART XX.1

PART XX.1
Mental Disorder

Interpretation

Definitions
672.1 (1) In this Part,
accused
assessment
chairperson
court
disposition
dual status offender
high-risk accused
hospital
medical practitioner
party
(a) the accused,
(b) the person in charge of the hospital where the accused is detained or is to attend pursuant to an assessment order or a disposition,
(c) an Attorney General designated by the court or Review Board under subsection 672.5(3),
(d) any interested person designated by the court or Review Board under subsection 672.5(4), or
(e) where the disposition is to be made by a court, the prosecutor of the charge against the accused;
placement decision
prescribed
Review Board
verdict of not criminally responsible on account of mental disorder
Reference
(2) For the purposes of subsections 672.5(3) and (5), paragraph 672.86(1)(b) and subsections 672.86(2) and (2.1), 672.88(2) and 672.89(2), in respect of a territory or proceedings commenced at the instance of the Government of Canada and conducted by or on behalf of that Government, a reference to the Attorney General of a province shall be read as a reference to the Attorney General of Canada.
1991, c. 43, s. 4;
2005, c. 22, s. 1;
2014, c. 6, s. 2.

Assessment Orders

Assessment order
672.11 A court having jurisdiction over an accused in respect of an offence may order an assessment of the mental condition of the accused, if it has reasonable grounds to believe that such evidence is

necessary to determine

(a) whether the accused is unfit to stand trial;

(b) whether the accused was, at the time of the commission of the alleged offence, suffering from a mental disorder so as to be exempt from criminal responsibility by virtue of subsection 16(1);

(c) whether the balance of the mind of the accused was disturbed at the time of commission of the alleged offence, where the accused is a female person charged with an offence arising out of the death of her newly-born child;

(d) the appropriate disposition to be made, where a verdict of not criminally responsible on account of mental disorder or unfit to stand trial has been rendered in respect of the accused;

(d.1) whether a finding that the accused is a high-risk accused should be revoked under subsection 672.84(3); or

(e) whether an order should be made under section 672.851 for a stay of proceedings, where a verdict of unfit to stand trial has been rendered against the accused.

1991, c. 43, s. 4;
1995, c. 22, s. 10;
2005, c. 22, s. 2;
2014, c. 6, s. 3.

Where court may order assessment

672.12 (1) The court may make an assessment order at any stage of proceedings against the accused of its own motion, on application of the accused or, subject to subsections (2) and (3), on application of the prosecutor.

Limitation on prosecutor's application for assessment of fitness

(2) Where the prosecutor applies for an assessment in order to determine whether the accused is unfit to stand trial for an offence that is prosecuted by way of summary conviction, the court may only order the assessment if

(a) the accused raised the issue of fitness; or

(b) the prosecutor satisfies the court that there are reasonable grounds to doubt that the accused is fit to stand trial.

Limitation on prosecutor's application for assessment

(3) Where the prosecutor applies for an assessment in order to determine whether the accused was suffering from a mental disorder at the time of the offence so as to be exempt from criminal responsibility, the court may only order the assessment if

(a) the accused puts his or her mental capacity for criminal intent into issue; or

(b) the prosecutor satisfies the court that there are reasonable grounds to doubt that the accused is criminally responsible for the alleged offence, on account of mental disorder.

1991, c. 43, s. 4.

Review Board may order assessment

672.121 The Review Board that has jurisdiction over an accused found not criminally responsible on account of mental disorder or unfit to stand trial may order an assessment of the mental condition of the accused of its own motion or on application of the prosecutor or the accused, if it has reasonable grounds to believe that such evidence is necessary to

(a) make a recommendation to the court under subsection 672.851(1);

(b) make a disposition under section 672.54 in one of the following circumstances:

(i) no assessment report on the mental condition of the accused is available,

(ii) no assessment of the mental condition of the accused has been conducted in the last twelve months, or

(iii) the accused has been transferred from another province under section 672.86; or

(c) determine whether to refer to the court for review under subsection 672.84(1) a finding that an accused is a high-risk accused.

2005, c. 22, s. 3;
2014, c. 6, s. 4.

Contents of assessment order

672.13 (1) An assessment order must specify
(a) the service that or the person who is to make the assessment, or the hospital where it is to be made;
(b) whether the accused is to be detained in custody while the order is in force; and
(c) the period that the order is to be in force, including the time required for the assessment and for the accused to travel to and from the place where the assessment is to be made.
Form
(2) An assessment order may be in Form 48 or 48.1.
1991, c. 43, s. 4;
2005, c. 22, s. 4.
General rule for period
672.14 (1) An assessment order shall not be in force for more than thirty days.
Exception in fitness cases
(2) No assessment order to determine whether the accused is unfit to stand trial shall be in force for more than five days, excluding holidays and the time required for the accused to travel to and from the place where the assessment is to be made, unless the accused and the prosecutor agree to a longer period not exceeding thirty days.
Exception for compelling circumstances
(3) Despite subsections (1) and (2), a court or Review Board may make an assessment order that remains in force for sixty days if the court or Review Board is satisfied that compelling circumstances exist that warrant it.
1991, c. 43, s. 4;
2005, c. 22, s. 5.
Extension
672.15 (1) Subject to subsection (2), a court or Review Board may extend an assessment order, of its own motion or on the application of the accused or the prosecutor made during or at the end of the period during which the order is in force, for any further period that is required, in its opinion, to complete the assessment of the accused.
Maximum duration of extensions
(2) No extension of an assessment order shall exceed thirty days, and the period of the initial order together with all extensions shall not exceed sixty days.
1991, c. 43, s. 4;
2005, c. 22, s. 6.
Presumption against custody
672.16 (1) Subject to subsection (3), an accused shall not be detained in custody under an assessment order of a court unless
(a) the court is satisfied that on the evidence custody is necessary to assess the accused, or that on the evidence of a medical practitioner custody is desirable to assess the accused and the accused consents to custody;
(b) custody of the accused is required in respect of any other matter or by virtue of any other provision of this Act; or
(c) the prosecutor, having been given a reasonable opportunity to do so, shows that detention of the accused in custody is justified on either of the grounds set out in subsection 515(10).
Presumption against custody — Review Board
(1.1) If the Review Board makes an order for an assessment of an accused under section 672.121, the accused shall not be detained in custody under the order unless
(a) the accused is currently subject to a disposition made under paragraph 672.54(c);
(b) the Review Board is satisfied on the evidence that custody is necessary to assess the accused, or that on the evidence of a medical practitioner custody is desirable to assess the accused and the accused consents to custody; or
(c) custody of the accused is required in respect of any other matter or by virtue of any other provision of this Act.

Residency as a condition of disposition
(1.2) Subject to paragraphs (1.1)(b) and (c), if the accused is subject to a disposition made under paragraph 672.54(b) that requires the accused to reside at a specified place, an assessment ordered under section 672.121 shall require the accused to reside at the same place.
Report of medical practitioner
(2) For the purposes of paragraphs (1)(a) and (1.1)(b), if the prosecutor and the accused agree, the evidence of a medical practitioner may be received in the form of a report in writing.
Presumption of custody in certain circumstances
(3) An assessment order made in respect of an accused who is detained under subsection 515(6) or 522(2) shall order that the accused be detained in custody under the same circumstances referred to in that subsection, unless the accused shows that custody is not justified under the terms of that subsection.
1991, c. 43, s. 4;
2005, c. 22, s. 7.
Assessment order takes precedence over bail hearing
672.17 During the period that an assessment order made by a court in respect of an accused charged with an offence is in force, no order for the interim release or detention of the accused may be made by virtue of Part XVI or section 679 in respect of that offence or an included offence.
1991, c. 43, s. 4;
2005, c. 22, s. 8.
Application to vary assessment order
672.18 Where at any time while an assessment order made by a court is in force the prosecutor or an accused shows cause, the court may vary the terms of the order respecting the interim release or detention of the accused in such manner as it considers appropriate in the circumstances.
1991, c. 43, s. 4;
2005, c. 22, s. 9(F).
No treatment order on assessment
672.19 No assessment order may direct that psychiatric or any other treatment of the accused be carried out, or direct the accused to submit to such treatment.
1991, c. 43, s. 4.
When assessment completed
672.191 An accused in respect of whom an assessment order is made shall appear before the court or Review Board that made the order as soon as practicable after the assessment is completed and not later than the last day of the period that the order is to be in force.
1997, c. 18, s. 81;
2005, c. 22, s. 10.

Assessment Reports

Assessment report
672.2 (1) An assessment order may require the person who makes the assessment to submit in writing an assessment report on the mental condition of the accused.
Assessment report to be filed
(2) An assessment report shall be filed with the court or Review Board that ordered it, within the period fixed by the court or Review Board, as the case may be.
Court to send assessment report to Review Board
(3) The court shall send to the Review Board without delay a copy of any report filed with it pursuant to subsection (2), to assist in determining the appropriate disposition to be made in respect of the accused.
Copies of reports to accused and prosecutor
(4) Subject to subsection 672.51(3), copies of any report filed with a court or Review Board under subsection (2) shall be provided without delay to the prosecutor, the accused and any counsel

representing the accused.
1991, c. 43, s. 4;
2005, c. 22, s. 11.

Protected Statements

Definition of
672.21 (1) In this section,
protected statement
Protected statements not admissible against accused
(2) No protected statement or reference to a protected statement made by an accused is admissible in evidence, without the consent of the accused, in any proceeding before a court, tribunal, body or person with jurisdiction to compel the production of evidence.
Exceptions
(3) Notwithstanding subsection (2), evidence of a protected statement is admissible for the purpose of
(a) determining whether the accused is unfit to stand trial;
(b) making a disposition or placement decision respecting the accused;
(c) determining, under section 672.84, whether to refer to the court for review a finding that an accused is a high-risk accused or whether to revoke such a finding;
(d) determining whether the balance of the mind of the accused was disturbed at the time of commission of the alleged offence, where the accused is a female person charged with an offence arising out of the death of her newly-born child;
(e) determining whether the accused was, at the time of the commission of an alleged offence, suffering from automatism or a mental disorder so as to be exempt from criminal responsibility by virtue of subsection 16(1), if the accused puts his or her mental capacity for criminal intent into issue, or if the prosecutor raises the issue after verdict;
(f) challenging the credibility of an accused in any proceeding where the testimony of the accused is inconsistent in a material particular with a protected statement that the accused made previously; or
(g) establishing the perjury of an accused who is charged with perjury in respect of a statement made in any proceeding.
1991, c. 43, s. 4;
2005, c. 22, s. 12;
2014, c. 6, s. 5.

Fitness to Stand Trial

Presumption of fitness
672.22 An accused is presumed fit to stand trial unless the court is satisfied on the balance of probabilities that the accused is unfit to stand trial.
1991, c. 43, s. 4.
Court may direct issue to be tried
672.23 (1) Where the court has reasonable grounds, at any stage of the proceedings before a verdict is rendered, to believe that the accused is unfit to stand trial, the court may direct, of its own motion or on application of the accused or the prosecutor, that the issue of fitness of the accused be tried.
Burden of proof
(2) An accused or a prosecutor who makes an application under subsection (1) has the burden of proof that the accused is unfit to stand trial.
1991, c. 43, s. 4.
Counsel
672.24 (1) Where the court has reasonable grounds to believe that an accused is unfit to stand trial and the accused is not represented by counsel, the court shall order that the accused be represented

by counsel.
Counsel fees and disbursements
(2) Where counsel is assigned pursuant to subsection (1) and legal aid is not granted to the accused pursuant to a provincial legal aid program, the fees and disbursements of counsel shall be paid by the Attorney General to the extent that the accused is unable to pay them.
Taxation of fees and disbursements
(3) Where counsel and the Attorney General cannot agree on the fees or disbursements of counsel, the Attorney General or the counsel may apply to the registrar of the court and the registrar may tax the disputed fees and disbursements.
1991, c. 43, s. 4;
1997, c. 18, s. 82.
Postponing trial of issue
672.25 (1) The court shall postpone directing the trial of the issue of fitness of an accused in proceedings for an offence for which the accused may be prosecuted by indictment or that is punishable on summary conviction, until the prosecutor has elected to proceed by way of indictment or summary conviction.
Idem
(2) The court may postpone directing the trial of the issue of fitness of an accused
(a) where the issue arises before the close of the case for the prosecution at a preliminary inquiry, until a time that is not later than the time the accused is called on to answer to the charge; or
(b) where the issue arises before the close of the case for the prosecution at trial, until a time not later than the opening of the case for the defence or, on motion of the accused, any later time that the court may direct.
1991, c. 43, s. 4.
Trial of issue by judge and jury
672.26 Where an accused is tried or is to be tried before a court composed of a judge and jury,
(a) if the judge directs that the issue of fitness of the accused be tried before the accused is given in charge to a jury for trial on the indictment, a jury composed of the number of jurors required in respect of the indictment in the province where the trial is to be held shall be sworn to try that issue and, with the consent of the accused, the issues to be tried on the indictment; and
(b) if the judge directs that the issue of fitness of the accused be tried after the accused has been given in charge to a jury for trial on the indictment, the jury shall be sworn to try that issue in addition to the issues in respect of which it is already sworn.
1991, c. 43, s. 4.
Trial of issue by court
672.27 The court shall try the issue of fitness of an accused and render a verdict where the issue arises
(a) in respect of an accused who is tried or is to be tried before a court other than a court composed of a judge and jury; or
(b) before a court at a preliminary inquiry or at any other stage of the proceedings.
1991, c. 43, s. 4.
Proceeding continues where accused is fit
672.28 Where the verdict on trial of the issue is that an accused is fit to stand trial, the arraignment, preliminary inquiry, trial or other stage of the proceeding shall continue as if the issue of fitness of the accused had never arisen.
1991, c. 43, s. 4.
Where continued detention in custody
672.29 Where an accused is detained in custody on delivery of a verdict that the accused is fit to stand trial, the court may order the accused to be detained in a hospital until the completion of the trial, if the court has reasonable grounds to believe that the accused would become unfit to stand trial if released.
1991, c. 43, s. 4.

Acquittal

672.3 Where the court has postponed directing the trial of the issue of fitness of an accused pursuant to subsection 672.25(2) and the accused is discharged or acquitted before the issue is tried, it shall not be tried.

1991, c. 43, s. 4.

Verdict of unfit to stand trial

672.31 Where the verdict on trial of the issue is that an accused is unfit to stand trial, any plea that has been made shall be set aside and any jury shall be discharged.

1991, c. 43, s. 4.

Subsequent proceedings

672.32 (1) A verdict of unfit to stand trial shall not prevent the accused from being tried subsequently where the accused becomes fit to stand trial.

Burden of proof

(2) The burden of proof that the accused has subsequently become fit to stand trial is on the party who asserts it, and is discharged by proof on the balance of probabilities.

1991, c. 43, s. 4.

672.33 (1) The court that has jurisdiction in respect of the offence charged against an accused who is found unfit to stand trial shall hold an inquiry, not later than two years after the verdict is rendered and every two years thereafter until the accused is acquitted pursuant to subsection (6) or tried, to decide whether sufficient evidence can be adduced at that time to put the accused on trial.

Extension of time for holding inquiry

(1.1) Despite subsection (1), the court may extend the period for holding an inquiry where it is satisfied on the basis of an application by the prosecutor or the accused that the extension is necessary for the proper administration of justice.

Court may order inquiry to be held

(2) On application of the accused, the court may order an inquiry under this section to be held at any time if it is satisfied, on the basis of the application and any written material submitted by the accused, that there is reason to doubt that there is a

Burden of proof

(3) At an inquiry under this section, the burden of proof that sufficient evidence can be adduced to put the accused on trial is on the prosecutor.

Admissible evidence at an inquiry

(4) In an inquiry under this section, the court shall admit as evidence

(a) any affidavit containing evidence that would be admissible if given by the person making the affidavit as a witness in court; or

(b) any certified copy of the oral testimony given at a previous inquiry or hearing held before a court in respect of the offence with which the accused is charged.

Conduct of inquiry

(5) The court may determine the manner in which an inquiry under this section is conducted and may follow the practices and procedures in respect of a preliminary inquiry under Part XVIII where it concludes that the interests of justice so require.

Where

(6) Where, on the completion of an inquiry under this section, the court is satisfied that sufficient evidence cannot be adduced to put the accused on trial, the court shall acquit the accused.

1991, c. 43, s. 4;
2005, c. 22, ss. 13, 42(F).

Verdict of Not Criminally Responsible on Account of Mental Disorder

Verdict of not criminally responsible on account of mental disorder

672.34 Where the jury, or the judge or provincial court judge where there is no jury, finds that an accused committed the act or made the omission that formed the basis of the offence charged, but

was at the time suffering from mental disorder so as to be exempt from criminal responsibility by virtue of subsection 16(1), the jury or the judge shall render a verdict that the accused committed the act or made the omission but is not criminally responsible on account of mental disorder.
1991, c. 43, s. 4.

Effect of verdict of not criminally responsible on account of mental disorder
672.35 Where a verdict of not criminally responsible on account of mental disorder is rendered, the accused shall not be found guilty or convicted of the offence, but
(a) the accused may plead
(b) any court may take the verdict into account in considering an application for judicial interim release or in considering what dispositions to make or sentence to impose for any other offence; and
(c) the Parole Board of Canada or any provincial parole board may take the verdict into account in considering an application by the accused for parole or for a record suspension under the Criminal Records Act
1991, c. 43, s. 4;
2012, c. 1, ss. 145, 160.

Verdict not a previous conviction
672.36 A verdict of not criminally responsible on account of mental disorder is not a previous conviction for the purposes of any offence under any Act of Parliament for which a greater punishment is provided by reason of previous convictions.
1991, c. 43, s. 4.

Definition of
672.37 (1) In this section,
application for federal employment
(a) employment in any department, as defined in section 2 of the
Financial Administration Act
(b) employment by any Crown corporation as defined in subsection 83(1) of the
Financial Administration Act
(c) enrolment in the Canadian Forces; or
(d) employment in connection with the operation of any work, undertaking or business that is within the legislative authority of Parliament.

Application for federal employment
(2) No application for federal employment shall contain any question that requires the applicant to disclose any charge or finding that the applicant committed an offence that resulted in a finding or a verdict of not criminally responsible on account of mental disorder if the applicant was discharged absolutely or is no longer subject to any disposition in respect of that offence.

Punishment
(3) Any person who uses or authorizes the use of an application for federal employment that contravenes subsection (2) is guilty of an offence punishable on summary conviction.
1991, c. 43, s. 4.

Review Boards

Review Boards to be established
672.38 (1) A Review Board shall be established or designated for each province to make or review dispositions concerning any accused in respect of whom a verdict of not criminally responsible by reason of mental disorder or unfit to stand trial is rendered, and shall consist of not fewer than five members appointed by the lieutenant governor in council of the province.

Treated as provincial Board
(2) A Review Board shall be treated as having been established under the laws of the province.

Personal liability
(3) No member of a Review Board is personally liable for any act done in good faith in the exercise of the member's powers or the performance of the member's duties and functions or for any default

or neglect in good faith in the exercise of those powers or the performance of those duties and functions.
1991, c. 43, s. 4;
1997, c. 18, s. 83.
Members of Review Board
672.39 A Review Board must have at least one member who is entitled under the laws of a province to practise psychiatry and, where only one member is so entitled, at least one other member must have training and experience in the field of mental health, and be entitled under the laws of a province to practise medicine or psychology.
1991, c. 43, s. 4.
Chairperson of a Review Board
672.4 (1) Subject to subsection (2), the chairperson of a Review Board shall be a judge of the Federal Court or of a superior, district or county court of a province, or a person who is qualified for appointment to, or has retired from, such a judicial office.
Transitional
(2) Where the chairperson of a Review Board that was established before the coming into force of subsection (1) is not a judge or other person referred to therein, the chairperson may continue to act until the expiration of his or her term of office if at least one other member of the Review Board is a judge or other person referred to in subsection (1) or is a member of the bar of the province.
1991, c. 43, s. 4.
Quorum of Review Board
672.41 (1) Subject to subsection (2), the quorum of a Review Board is constituted by the chairperson, a member who is entitled under the laws of a province to practise psychiatry, and any other member.
Transitional
(2) Where the chairperson of a Review Board that was established before the coming into force of this section is not a judge or other person referred to in subsection 672.4(1), the quorum of the Review Board is constituted by the chairperson, a member who is entitled under the laws of a province to practise psychiatry, and a member who is a person referred to in that subsection or a member of the bar of the province.
1991, c. 43, s. 4.
Majority vote
672.42 A decision of a majority of the members present and voting is the decision of a Review Board.
1991, c. 43, s. 4.
Powers of Review Boards
672.43 At a hearing held by a Review Board to make a disposition or review a disposition in respect of an accused, the chairperson has all the powers that are conferred by sections 4 and 5 of the Inquiries Act
1991, c. 43, s. 4;
2005, c. 22, s. 42(F).
Rules of Review Board
672.44 (1) A Review Board may, subject to the approval of the lieutenant governor in council of the province, make rules providing for the practice and procedure before the Review Board.
Application and publication of rules
(2) The rules made by a Review Board under subsection (1) apply to any proceeding within its jurisdiction, and shall be published in the
Canada Gazette
Regulations
(3) Notwithstanding anything in this section, the Governor in Council may make regulations to provide for the practice and procedure before Review Boards, in particular to make the rules of Review Boards uniform, and all regulations made under this subsection prevail over any rules made

under subsection (1).
1991, c. 43, s. 4.

Disposition Hearings

Hearing to be held by a court
672.45 (1) Where a verdict of not criminally responsible on account of mental disorder or unfit to stand trial is rendered in respect of an accused, the court may of its own motion, and shall on application by the accused or the prosecutor, hold a disposition hearing.
Transmittal of transcript to Review Board
(1.1) If the court does not hold a hearing under subsection (1), it shall send without delay, following the verdict, in original or copied form, any transcript of the court proceedings in respect of the accused, any other document or information related to the proceedings, and all exhibits filed with it, to the Review Board that has jurisdiction in respect of the matter, if the transcript, document, information or exhibits are in its possession.
Disposition to be made
(2) At a disposition hearing, the court shall make a disposition in respect of the accused, if it is satisfied that it can readily do so and that a disposition should be made without delay.
1991, c. 43, s. 4;
2005, c. 22, ss. 14, 42(F).
Status quo pending Review Board hearing
672.46 (1) Where the court does not make a disposition in respect of the accused at a disposition hearing, any order for the interim release or detention of the accused or any appearance notice, promise to appear, summons, undertaking or recognizance in respect of the accused that is in force at the time the verdict of not criminally responsible on account of mental disorder or unfit to stand trial is rendered continues in force, subject to its terms, until the Review Board makes a disposition.
Variation of order
(2) Notwithstanding subsection (1), a court may, on cause being shown, vacate any order, appearance notice, promise to appear, summons, undertaking or recognizance referred to in that subsection and make any other order for the interim release or detention of the accused that the court considers to be appropriate in the circumstances, including an order directing that the accused be detained in custody in a hospital pending a disposition by the Review Board in respect of the accused.
1991, c. 43, s. 4;
2005, c. 22, s. 42(F).
Review Board to make disposition where court does not
672.47 (1) Where a verdict of not criminally responsible on account of mental disorder or unfit to stand trial is rendered and the court makes no disposition in respect of an accused, the Review Board shall, as soon as is practicable but not later than forty-five days after the verdict was rendered, hold a hearing and make a disposition.
Extension of time for hearing
(2) Where the court is satisfied that there are exceptional circumstances that warrant it, the court may extend the time for holding a hearing under subsection (1) to a maximum of ninety days after the verdict was rendered.
Disposition made by court
(3) Where a court makes a disposition under section 672.54 other than an absolute discharge in respect of an accused, the Review Board shall, not later than ninety days after the disposition was made, hold a hearing and make a disposition in respect of the accused.
Exception — high-risk accused
(4) Despite subsections (1) to (3), if the court makes a disposition under subsection 672.64(3), the Review Board shall, not later than 45 days after the day on which the disposition is made, hold a hearing and make a disposition under paragraph 672.54(c), subject to the restrictions set out in that subsection.

Extension of time for hearing
(5) If the court is satisfied that there are exceptional circumstances that warrant it, the court may extend the time for holding a hearing under subsection (4) to a maximum of 90 days after the day on which the disposition is made.
1991, c. 43, s. 4;
2005, c. 22, ss. 15, 42(F);
2014, c. 6, s. 6.

Review Board to determine fitness
672.48 (1) Where a Review Board holds a hearing to make or review a disposition in respect of an accused who has been found unfit to stand trial, it shall determine whether in its opinion the accused is fit to stand trial at the time of the hearing.

Review Board shall send accused to court
(2) If a Review Board determines that the accused is fit to stand trial, it shall order that the accused be sent back to court, and the court shall try the issue and render a verdict.

Chairperson may send accused to court
(3) The chairperson of a Review Board may, with the consent of the accused and the person in charge of the hospital where an accused is being detained, order that the accused be sent back to court for trial of the issue of whether the accused is unfit to stand trial, where the chairperson is of the opinion that
(a) the accused is fit to stand trial; and
(b) the Review Board will not hold a hearing to make or review a disposition in respect of the accused within a reasonable period.
1991, c. 43, s. 4;
2005, c. 22, s. 42(F).

Continued detention in hospital
672.49 (1) In a disposition made pursuant to section 672.47 the Review Board or chairperson may require the accused to continue to be detained in a hospital until the court determines whether the accused is fit to stand trial, if the Review Board or chairperson has reasonable grounds to believe that the accused would become unfit to stand trial if released.

Copy of disposition to be sent to court
(2) The Review Board or chairperson shall send a copy of a disposition made pursuant to section 672.47 without delay to the court having jurisdiction over the accused and to the Attorney General of the province where the accused is to be tried.
1991, c. 43, s. 4.

Procedure at disposition hearing
672.5 (1) A hearing held by a court or Review Board to make or review a disposition in respect of an accused, including a hearing referred to in subsection 672.84(1) or (3), shall be held in accordance with this section.

Hearing to be informal
(2) The hearing may be conducted in as informal a manner as is appropriate in the circumstances.

Attorneys General may be parties
(3) On application, the court or Review Board shall designate as a party the Attorney General of the province where the disposition is to be made and, where an accused is transferred from another province, the Attorney General of the province from which the accused is transferred.

Interested person may be a party
(4) The court or Review Board may designate as a party any person who has a substantial interest in protecting the interests of the accused, if the court or Review Board is of the opinion that it is just to do so.

Notice of hearing
(5) Notice of the hearing shall be given to the parties, the Attorney General of the province where the disposition is to be made and, where the accused is transferred to another province, the Attorney General of the province from which the accused is transferred, within the time and in the manner

prescribed, or within the time and in the manner fixed by the rules of the court or Review Board.
Notice
(5.1) At the victim's request, notice of the hearing and of the relevant provisions of the Act shall be given to the victim within the time and in the manner fixed by the rules of the court or Review Board.
Notice of discharge and intended place of residence
(5.2) If the accused is discharged absolutely under paragraph 672.54(a) or conditionally under paragraph 672.54(b), a notice of the discharge and accused's intended place of residence shall, at the victim's request, be given to the victim within the time and in the manner fixed by the rules of the court or Review Board.
Order excluding the public
(6) Where the court or Review Board considers it to be in the best interests of the accused and not contrary to the public interest, the court or Review Board may order the public or any members of the public to be excluded from the hearing or any part of the hearing.
Right to counsel
(7) The accused or any other party has the right to be represented by counsel.
Assigning counsel
(8) If an accused is not represented by counsel, the court or Review Board shall, either before or at the time of the hearing, assign counsel to act for any accused
(a) who has been found unfit to stand trial; or
(b) wherever the interests of justice so require.
Counsel fees and disbursements
(8.1) Where counsel is assigned pursuant to subsection (8) and legal aid is not granted to the accused pursuant to a provincial legal aid program, the fees and disbursements of counsel shall be paid by the Attorney General to the extent that the accused is unable to pay them.
Taxation of fees and disbursements
(8.2) Where counsel and the Attorney General cannot agree on the fees or disbursements of counsel, the Attorney General or the counsel may apply to the registrar of the court and the registrar may tax the disputed fees and disbursements.
Right of accused to be present
(9) Subject to subsection (10), the accused has the right to be present during the whole of the hearing.
Removal or absence of accused
(10) The court or the chairperson of the Review Board may
(a) permit the accused to be absent during the whole or any part of the hearing on such conditions as the court or chairperson considers proper; or
(b) cause the accused to be removed and barred from re-entry for the whole or any part of the hearing
(i) where the accused interrupts the hearing so that to continue in the presence of the accused would not be feasible,
(ii) on being satisfied that failure to do so would likely endanger the life or safety of another person or would seriously impair the treatment or recovery of the accused, or
(iii) in order to hear, in the absence of the accused, evidence, oral or written submissions, or the cross-examination of any witness concerning whether grounds exist for removing the accused pursuant to subparagraph (ii).
Rights of parties at hearing
(11) Any party may adduce evidence, make oral or written submissions, call witnesses and cross-examine any witness called by any other party and, on application, cross-examine any person who made an assessment report that was submitted to the court or Review Board in writing.
Request to compel attendance of witnesses
(12) A party may not compel the attendance of witnesses, but may request the court or the chairperson of the Review Board to do so.
Video links
(13) Where the accused so agrees, the court or the chairperson of the Review Board may permit the

accused to appear by closed-circuit television or any other means that allow the court or Review Board and the accused to engage in simultaneous visual and oral communication, for any part of the hearing.

Adjournment

(13.1) The Review Board may adjourn the hearing for a period not exceeding thirty days if necessary for the purpose of ensuring that relevant information is available to permit it to make or review a disposition or for any other sufficient reason.

Determination of mental condition of the accused

(13.2) On receiving an assessment report, the court or Review Board shall determine whether, since the last time the disposition in respect of the accused was made or reviewed there has been any change in the mental condition of the accused that may provide grounds for the discharge of the accused under paragraph 672.54(a) or (b) and, if there has been such a change, the court or Review Board shall notify every victim of the offence that they are entitled to file a statement in accordance with subsection (14).

Notice to victims — referral of finding to court

(13.3) If the Review Board refers to the court for review under subsection 672.84(1) a finding that an accused is a high-risk accused, it shall notify every victim of the offence that they are entitled to file a statement with the court in accordance with subsection (14).

Victim impact statement

(14) A victim of the offence may prepare and file with the court or Review Board a written statement describing the physical or emotional harm, property damage or economic loss suffered by the victim as the result of the commission of the offence and the impact of the offence on the victim. Form 48.2 in Part XXVIII, or a form approved by the lieutenant governor in council of the province in which the court or Review Board is exercising its jurisdiction, must be used for this purpose.

Copy of statement

(15) The court or Review Board shall ensure that a copy of any statement filed in accordance with subsection (14) is provided to the accused or counsel for the accused, and the prosecutor, as soon as practicable after a verdict of not criminally responsible on account of mental disorder is rendered in respect of the offence.

Presentation of victim statement

(15.1) The court or Review Board shall, at the request of a victim, permit the victim to read a statement prepared and filed in accordance with subsection (14), or to present the statement in any other manner that the court or Review Board considers appropriate, unless the court or Review Board is of the opinion that the reading or presentation of the statement would interfere with the proper administration of justice.

Inquiry by court or Review Board

(15.2) The court or Review Board shall, as soon as practicable after a verdict of not criminally responsible on account of mental disorder is rendered in respect of an offence and before making a disposition under section 672.45, 672.47 or 672.64, inquire of the prosecutor or a victim of the offence, or any person representing a victim of the offence, whether the victim has been advised of the opportunity to prepare a statement referred to in subsection (14).

Adjournment

(15.3) On application of the prosecutor or a victim or of its own motion, the court or Review Board may adjourn the hearing held under section 672.45, 672.47 or 672.64 to permit the victim to prepare a statement referred to in subsection (14) if the court or Review Board is satisfied that the adjournment would not interfere with the proper administration of justice.

(16) 1991, c. 43, s. 4;
1997, c. 18, s. 84;
1999, c. 25, s. 11(Preamble);
2005, c. 22, ss. 16, 42(F);
2014, c. 6, s. 7;
2015, c. 13, s. 22.

Order restricting publication — sexual offences
672.501 (1) Where a Review Board holds a hearing referred to in section 672.5 in respect of an accused who has been declared not criminally responsible on account of mental disorder or unfit to stand trial for an offence referred to in subsection 486.4(1), the Review Board shall make an order directing that any information that could identify a victim, or a witness who is under the age of eighteen years, shall not be published in any document or broadcast or transmitted in any way.

Order restricting publication — child pornography
(2) Where a Review Board holds a hearing referred to in section 672.5 in respect of an accused who has been declared not criminally responsible on account of mental disorder or unfit to stand trial for an offence referred to in section 163.1, a Review Board shall make an order directing that any information that could identify a witness who is under the age of eighteen years, or any person who is the subject of a representation, written material or a recording that constitutes child pornography within the meaning of section 163.1, shall not be published in any document or broadcast or transmitted in any way.

Order restricting publication — other offences
(3) Where a Review Board holds a hearing referred to in section 672.5 in respect of an accused who has been declared not criminally responsible on account of mental disorder or unfit to stand trial for an offence other than the offences referred to in subsection (1) or (2), on application of the prosecutor, a victim or a witness, the Review Board may make an order directing that any information that could identify the victim or witness shall not be published in any document or broadcast or transmitted in any way if the Review Board is satisfied that the order is necessary for the proper administration of justice.

Order restricting publication
(4) An order made under any of subsections (1) to (3) does not apply in respect of the disclosure of information in the course of the administration of justice if it is not the purpose of the disclosure to make the information known in the community.

Application and notice
(5) An applicant for an order under subsection (3) shall
(a) apply in writing to the Review Board; and
(b) provide notice of the application to the prosecutor, the accused and any other person affected by the order that the Review Board specifies.

Grounds
(6) An applicant for an order under subsection (3) shall set out the grounds on which the applicant relies to establish that the order is necessary for the proper administration of justice.

Hearing may be held
(7) The Review Board may hold a hearing to determine whether an order under subsection (3) should be made, and the hearing may be in private.

Factors to be considered
(8) In determining whether to make an order under subsection (3), the Review Board shall consider
(a) the right to a fair and public hearing;
(b) whether there is a real and substantial risk that the victim or witness would suffer significant harm if their identity were disclosed;
(c) whether the victim or witness needs the order for their security or to protect them from intimidation or retaliation;
(d) society's interest in encouraging the reporting of offences and the participation of victims and witnesses in the criminal justice process;
(e) whether effective alternatives are available to protect the identity of the victim or witness;
(f) the salutary and deleterious effects of the proposed order;
(g) the impact of the proposed order on the freedom of expression of those affected by it; and
(h) any other factor that the Review Board considers relevant.

Conditions
(9) An order made under subsection (3) may be subject to any conditions that the Review Board

thinks fit.
Publication of application prohibited
(10) Unless the Review Board refuses to make an order under subsection (3), no person shall publish in any document or broadcast or transmit in any way
(a) the contents of an application;
(b) any evidence taken, information given or submissions made at a hearing under subsection (7); or
(c) any other information that could identify the person to whom the application relates as a victim or witness in the proceedings.
Offence
(11) Every person who fails to comply with an order made under any of subsections (1) to (3) is guilty of an offence punishable on summary conviction.
Application of order
(12) For greater certainty, an order referred to in subsection (11) also prohibits, in relation to proceedings taken against any person who fails to comply with the order, the publication in any document or the broadcasting or transmission in any way of information that could identify a victim or witness whose identity is protected by the order.
2005, c. 22, ss. 17, 64.
Definition of
disposition information
672.51 (1) In this section,
disposition information
Disposition information to be made available to parties
(2) Subject to this section, all disposition information shall be made available for inspection by, and the court or Review Board shall provide a copy of it to, each party and any counsel representing the accused.
Exception where disclosure dangerous to any person
(3) The court or Review Board shall withhold some or all of the disposition information from an accused where it is satisfied, on the basis of that information and the evidence or report of the medical practitioner responsible for the assessment or treatment of the accused, that disclosure of the information would be likely to endanger the life or safety of another person or would seriously impair the treatment or recovery of the accused.
Idem
(4) Notwithstanding subsection (3), the court or Review Board may release some or all of the disposition information to an accused where the interests of justice make disclosure essential in its opinion.
Exception where disclosure unnecessary or prejudicial
(5) The court or Review Board shall withhold disposition information from a party other than the accused or an Attorney General, where disclosure to that party, in the opinion of the court or Review Board, is not necessary to the proceeding and may be prejudicial to the accused.
Exclusion of certain persons from hearing
(6) A court or Review Board that withholds disposition information from the accused or any other party pursuant to subsection (3) or (5) shall exclude the accused or the other party, as the case may be, from the hearing during
(a) the oral presentation of that disposition information; or
(b) the questioning by the court or Review Board or the cross-examination of any person concerning that disposition information.
Prohibition of disclosure in certain cases
(7) No disposition information shall be made available for inspection or disclosed to any person who is not a party to the proceedings
(a) where the disposition information has been withheld from the accused or any other party pursuant to subsection (3) or (5); or
(b) where the court or Review Board is of the opinion that disclosure of the disposition information

would be seriously prejudicial to the accused and that, in the circumstances, protection of the accused takes precedence over the public interest in disclosure.

Idem

(8) No part of the record of the proceedings in respect of which the accused was excluded pursuant to subparagraph 672.5(10)(b)(ii) or (iii) shall be made available for inspection to the accused or to any person who is not a party to the proceedings.

Information to be made available to specified persons

(9) Notwithstanding subsections (7) and (8), the court or Review Board may make any disposition information, or a copy of it, available on request to any person or member of a class of persons

(a) that has a valid interest in the information for research or statistical purposes, where the court or Review Board is satisfied that disclosure is in the public interest;

(b) that has a valid interest in the information for the purposes of the proper administration of justice; or

(c) that the accused requests or authorizes in writing to inspect it, where the court or Review Board is satisfied that the person will not disclose or give to the accused a copy of any disposition information withheld from the accused pursuant to subsection (3), or of any part of the record of proceedings referred to in subsection (8), or that the reasons for withholding that information from the accused no longer exist.

Disclosure for research or statistical purposes

(10) A person to whom the court or Review Board makes disposition information available under paragraph (9)(a) may disclose it for research or statistical purposes, but not in any form or manner that could reasonably be expected to identify any person to whom it relates.

Prohibition on publication

(11) No person shall publish in any document or broadcast or transmit in any way

(a) any disposition information that is prohibited from being disclosed pursuant to subsection (7); or

(b) any part of the record of the proceedings in respect of which the accused was excluded pursuant to subparagraph 672.5(10)(b)(ii) or (iii).

Powers of courts not limited

(12) Except as otherwise provided in this section, nothing in this section limits the powers that a court may exercise apart from this section.

1991, c. 43, s. 4;
1997, c. 18, s. 85;
2005, c. 22, ss. 18, 42(F), c. 32, s. 22;
2014, c. 6, s. 8.

Record of proceedings

672.52 (1) The court or Review Board shall cause a record of the proceedings of its disposition hearings to be kept, and include in the record any assessment report submitted.

Transmittal of transcript to Review Board

(2) If a court holds a disposition hearing under subsection 672.45(1), whether or not it makes a disposition, it shall send without delay to the Review Board that has jurisdiction in respect of the matter, in original or copied form, a transcript of the hearing, any other document or information related to the hearing, and all exhibits filed with it, if the transcript, document, information or exhibits are in its possession.

Reasons for disposition and copies to be provided

(3) The court or Review Board shall state its reasons for making a disposition in the record of the proceedings, and shall provide every party with a copy of the disposition and those reasons.

1991, c. 43, s. 4;
2005, c. 22, ss. 19, 42(F).

Proceedings not invalid

672.53 Any procedural irregularity in relation to a disposition hearing does not affect the validity of the hearing unless it causes the accused substantial prejudice.

1991, c. 43, s. 4.

Dispositions by a Court or Review Board

Terms of Dispositions

Dispositions that may be made

672.54 When a court or Review Board makes a disposition under subsection 672.45(2), section 672.47, subsection 672.64(3) or section 672.83 or 672.84, it shall, taking into account the safety of the public, which is the paramount consideration, the mental condition of the accused, the reintegration of the accused into society and the other needs of the accused, make one of the following dispositions that is necessary and appropriate in the circumstances:

(a) where a verdict of not criminally responsible on account of mental disorder has been rendered in respect of the accused and, in the opinion of the court or Review Board, the accused is not a significant threat to the safety of the public, by order, direct that the accused be discharged absolutely;

(b) by order, direct that the accused be discharged subject to such conditions as the court or Review Board considers appropriate; or

(c) by order, direct that the accused be detained in custody in a hospital, subject to such conditions as the court or Review Board considers appropriate.

1991, c. 43, s. 4;
2005, c. 22, s. 20;
2014, c. 6, s. 9.

Significant threat to safety of public

672.5401 For the purposes of section 672.54, a significant threat to the safety of the public means a risk of serious physical or psychological harm to members of the public — including any victim of or witness to the offence, or any person under the age of 18 years — resulting from conduct that is criminal in nature but not necessarily violent.

2014, c. 6, s. 10.

Victim impact statement

672.541 If a verdict of not criminally responsible on account of mental disorder has been rendered in respect of an accused, the court or Review Board shall

(a) at a hearing held under section 672.45, 672.47, 672.64, 672.81 or 672.82 or subsection 672.84(5), take into consideration any statement filed by a victim in accordance with subsection 672.5(14) in determining the appropriate disposition or conditions under section 672.54, to the extent that the statement is relevant to its consideration of the criteria set out in section 672.54;

(b) at a hearing held under section 672.64 or subsection 672.84(3), take into consideration any statement filed by a victim in accordance with subsection 672.5(14), to the extent that the statement is relevant to its consideration of the criteria set out in subsection 672.64(1) or 672.84(3), as the case may be, in deciding whether to find that the accused is a high-risk accused, or to revoke such a finding; and

(c) at a hearing held under section 672.81 or 672.82 in respect of a high-risk accused, take into consideration any statement filed by a victim in accordance with subsection 672.5(14) in determining whether to refer to the court for review the finding that the accused is a high-risk accused, to the extent that the statement is relevant to its consideration of the criteria set out in subsection 672.84(1).

1999, c. 25, s. 12(Preamble);
2005, c. 22, s. 21;
2014, c. 6, s. 10.

Additional conditions — safety and security

672.542 When a court or Review Board holds a hearing referred to in section 672.5, the court or Review Board shall consider whether it is desirable, in the interests of the safety and security of any person, particularly a victim of or witness to the offence or a justice system participant, to include as a condition of the disposition that the accused

(a) abstain from communicating, directly or indirectly, with any victim, witness or other person identified in the disposition, or refrain from going to any place specified in the disposition; or
(b) comply with any other condition specified in the disposition that the court or Review Board considers necessary to ensure the safety and security of those persons.
2014, c. 6, s. 10.

Treatment not a condition

672.55 (1) No disposition made under section 672.54 shall direct that any psychiatric or other treatment of the accused be carried out or that the accused submit to such treatment except that the disposition may include a condition regarding psychiatric or other treatment where the accused has consented to the condition and the court or Review Board considers the condition to be reasonable and necessary in the interests of the accused.

(2) 1991, c. 43, s. 4;

1997, c. 18, s. 86;

2005, c. 22, s. 22.

Delegated authority to vary restrictions on liberty of accused

672.56 (1) A Review Board that makes a disposition in respect of an accused under paragraph 672.54(b) or (c) may delegate to the person in charge of the hospital authority to direct that the restrictions on the liberty of the accused be increased or decreased within any limits and subject to any conditions set out in that disposition, and any direction so made is deemed for the purposes of this Act to be a disposition made by the Review Board.

Exception — high-risk accused

(1.1) If the accused is a high-risk accused, any direction is subject to the restrictions set out in subsection 672.64(3).

Notice to accused and Review Board of increase in restrictions

(2) A person who increases the restrictions on the liberty of the accused significantly pursuant to authority delegated to the person by a Review Board shall
(a) make a record of the increased restrictions on the file of the accused; and
(b) give notice of the increase as soon as is practicable to the accused and, if the increased restrictions remain in force for a period exceeding seven days, to the Review Board.
1991, c. 43, s. 4;
2014, c. 6, s. 11.

Warrant of committal

672.57 Where the court or Review Board makes a disposition under paragraph 672.54(c), it shall issue a warrant of committal of the accused, which may be in Form 49.
1991, c. 43, s. 4.

Treatment disposition

672.58 Where a verdict of unfit to stand trial is rendered and the court has not made a disposition under section 672.54 in respect of an accused, the court may, on application by the prosecutor, by order, direct that treatment of the accused be carried out for a specified period not exceeding sixty days, subject to such conditions as the court considers appropriate and, where the accused is not detained in custody, direct that the accused submit to that treatment by the person or at the hospital specified.
1991, c. 43, s. 4.

Criteria for disposition

672.59 (1) No disposition may be made under section 672.58 unless the court is satisfied, on the basis of the testimony of a medical practitioner, that a specific treatment should be administered to the accused for the purpose of making the accused fit to stand trial.

Evidence required

(2) The testimony required by the court for the purposes of subsection (1) shall include a statement that the medical practitioner has made an assessment of the accused and is of the opinion, based on the grounds specified, that
(a) the accused, at the time of the assessment, was unfit to stand trial;

(b) the psychiatric treatment and any other related medical treatment specified by the medical practitioner will likely make the accused fit to stand trial within a period not exceeding sixty days and that without that treatment the accused is likely to remain unfit to stand trial;
(c) the risk of harm to the accused from the psychiatric and other related medical treatment specified is not disproportionate to the benefit anticipated to be derived from it; and
(d) the psychiatric and other related medical treatment specified is the least restrictive and least intrusive treatment that could, in the circumstances, be specified for the purpose referred to in subsection (1), considering the opinions referred to in paragraphs (b) and (c).
1991, c. 43, s. 4.

Notice required

672.6 (1) The court shall not make a disposition under section 672.58 unless the prosecutor notifies the accused, in writing and as soon as practicable, of the application.

Challenge by accused

(2) On receiving the notice referred to in subsection (1), the accused may challenge the application and adduce evidence for that purpose.
1991, c. 43, s. 4;
1997, c. 18, s. 87.

Exception

672.61 (1) The court shall not direct, and no disposition made under section 672.58 shall include, the performance of psychosurgery or electro-convulsive therapy or any other prohibited treatment that is prescribed.

Definitions

(2) In this section,
electro-convulsive therapy
psychosurgery
1991, c. 43, s. 4.

Consent of hospital required for treatment

672.62 (1) No court shall make a disposition under section 672.58 without the consent of
(a) the person in charge of the hospital where the accused is to be treated; or
(b) the person to whom responsibility for the treatment of the accused is assigned by the court.

Consent of accused not required for treatment

(2) The court may direct that treatment of an accused be carried out pursuant to a disposition made under section 672.58 without the consent of the accused or a person who, according to the laws of the province where the disposition is made, is authorized to consent for the accused.
1991, c. 43, s. 4.

Effective date of disposition

672.63 A disposition shall come into force on the day on which it is made or on any later day that the court or Review Board specifies in it, and shall remain in force until the Review Board holds a hearing to review the disposition and makes another disposition.
1991, c. 43, s. 4;
2005, c. 22, s. 23.

High-Risk Accused

Finding

672.64 (1) On application made by the prosecutor before any disposition to discharge an accused absolutely, the court may, at the conclusion of a hearing, find the accused to be a high-risk accused if the accused has been found not criminally responsible on account of mental disorder for a serious personal injury offence, as defined in subsection 672.81(1.3), the accused was 18 years of age or more at the time of the commission of the offence and
(a) the court is satisfied that there is a substantial likelihood that the accused will use violence that could endanger the life or safety of another person; or

(b) the court is of the opinion that the acts that constitute the offence were of such a brutal nature as to indicate a risk of grave physical or psychological harm to another person.

Factors to consider

(2) In deciding whether to find that the accused is a high-risk accused, the court shall consider all relevant evidence, including

(a) the nature and circumstances of the offence;

(b) any pattern of repetitive behaviour of which the offence forms a part;

(c) the accused's current mental condition;

(d) the past and expected course of the accused's treatment, including the accused's willingness to follow treatment; and

(e) the opinions of experts who have examined the accused.

Detention of high-risk accused

(3) If the court finds the accused to be a high-risk accused, the court shall make a disposition under paragraph 672.54(c), but the accused's detention must not be subject to any condition that would permit the accused to be absent from the hospital unless

(a) it is appropriate, in the opinion of the person in charge of the hospital, for the accused to be absent from the hospital for medical reasons or for any purpose that is necessary for the accused's treatment, if the accused is escorted by a person who is authorized by the person in charge of the hospital; and

(b) a structured plan has been prepared to address any risk related to the accused's absence and, as a result, that absence will not present an undue risk to the public.

Appeal

(4) A decision not to find an accused to be a high-risk accused is deemed to be a disposition for the purpose of sections 672.72 to 672.78.

For greater certainty

(5) For greater certainty, a finding that an accused is a high-risk accused is a disposition and sections 672.72 to 672.78 apply to it.

1991, c. 43, s. 4;
2005, c. 22, s. 24;
2014, c. 6, s. 12.
672.65 and 672.66 [No sections 672.65 and 672.66]

Dual Status Offenders

Where court imposes a sentence

672.67 (1) Where a court imposes a sentence of imprisonment on an offender who is, or thereby becomes, a dual status offender, that sentence takes precedence over any prior custodial disposition, pending any placement decision by the Review Board.

Custodial disposition by court

(2) Where a court imposes a custodial disposition on an accused who is, or thereby becomes, a dual status offender, the disposition takes precedence over any prior sentence of imprisonment pending any placement decision by the Review Board.

1991, c. 43, s. 4;
1995, c. 22, s. 10;
2005, c. 22, s. 25.

Definition of
Minister

672.68 (1) In this section and in sections 672.69 and 672.7,
Minister

Placement decision by Review Board

(2) On application by the Minister or of its own motion, where the Review Board is of the opinion that the place of custody of a dual status offender pursuant to a sentence or custodial disposition

made by the court is inappropriate to meet the mental health needs of the offender or to safeguard the well-being of other persons, the Review Board shall, after giving the offender and the Minister reasonable notice, decide whether to place the offender in custody in a hospital or in a prison.

Idem

(3) In making a placement decision, the Review Board shall take into consideration
(a) the need to protect the public from dangerous persons;
(b) the treatment needs of the offender and the availability of suitable treatment resources to address those needs;
(c) whether the offender would consent to or is a suitable candidate for treatment;
(d) any submissions made to the Review Board by the offender or any other party to the proceedings and any assessment report submitted in writing to the Review Board; and
(e) any other factors that the Review Board considers relevant.

Time for making placement decision

(4) The Review Board shall make its placement decision as soon as practicable but not later than thirty days after receiving an application from, or giving notice to, the Minister under subsection (2), unless the Review Board and the Minister agree to a longer period not exceeding sixty days.

Effects of placement decision

(5) Where the offender is detained in a prison pursuant to the placement decision of the Review Board, the Minister is responsible for the supervision and control of the offender.

1991, c. 43, s. 4;
2005, c. 10, s. 34.

Minister and Review Board entitled to access

672.69 (1) The Minister and the Review Board are entitled to have access to any dual status offender in respect of whom a placement decision has been made, for the purpose of conducting a review of the sentence or disposition imposed.

Review of placement decisions

(2) The Review Board shall hold a hearing as soon as is practicable to review a placement decision, on application by the Minister or the dual status offender who is the subject of the decision, where the Review Board is satisfied that a significant change in circumstances requires it.

Idem

(3) The Review Board may of its own motion hold a hearing to review a placement decision after giving the Minister and the dual status offender who is subject to it reasonable notice.

Minister shall be a party

(4) The Minister shall be a party in any proceedings relating to the placement of a dual status offender.

1991, c. 43, s. 4;
2005, c. 22, s. 42(F).

Notice of discharge

672.7 (1) Where the Minister or the Review Board intends to discharge a dual status offender from custody, each shall give written notice to the other indicating the time, place and conditions of the discharge.

Warrant of committal

(2) A Review Board that makes a placement decision shall issue a warrant of committal of the accused, which may be in Form 50.

1991, c. 43, s. 4.

Detention to count as service of term

672.71 (1) Each day of detention of a dual status offender pursuant to a placement decision or a custodial disposition shall be treated as a day of service of the term of imprisonment, and the accused shall be deemed, for all purposes, to be lawfully confined in a prison.

Disposition takes precedence over probation orders

(2) When a dual status offender is convicted or discharged on the conditions set out in a probation order made under section 730 in respect of an offence but is not sentenced to a term of imprisonment,

the custodial disposition in respect of the accused comes into force and, notwithstanding subsection 732.2(1), takes precedence over any probation order made in respect of the offence.
1991, c. 43, s. 4;
1995, c. 22, s. 10.

Appeals

Grounds for appeal
672.72 (1) Any party may appeal against a disposition made by a court or a Review Board, or a placement decision made by a Review Board, to the court of appeal of the province where the disposition or placement decision was made on any ground of appeal that raises a question of law or fact alone or of mixed law and fact.

Limitation period for appeal
(2) An appellant shall give notice of an appeal against a disposition or placement decision in the manner directed by the applicable rules of court within fifteen days after the day on which the appellant receives a copy of the placement decision or disposition and the reasons for it or within any further time that the court of appeal, or a judge of that court, may direct.

Appeal to be heard expeditiously
(3) The court of appeal shall hear an appeal against a disposition or placement decision in or out of the regular sessions of the court, as soon as practicable after the day on which the notice of appeal is given, within any period that may be fixed by the court of appeal, a judge of the court of appeal, or the rules of that court.
1991, c. 43, s. 4;
1997, c. 18, s. 88.

Appeal on the transcript
672.73 (1) An appeal against a disposition by a court or Review Board or placement decision by a Review Board shall be based on a transcript of the proceedings and any other evidence that the court of appeal finds necessary to admit in the interests of justice.

Additional evidence
(2) For the purpose of admitting additional evidence under this section, subsections 683(1) and (2) apply, with such modifications as the circumstances require.
1991, c. 43, s. 4.

Notice of appeal to be given to court or Review Board
672.74 (1) The clerk of the court of appeal, on receiving notice of an appeal against a disposition or placement decision, shall notify the court or Review Board that made the disposition.

Transmission of records to court of appeal
(2) On receipt of notification under subsection (1), the court or Review Board shall transmit to the court of appeal, before the time that the appeal is to be heard or within any time that the court of appeal or a judge of that court may direct,
(a) a copy of the disposition or placement decision;
(b) all exhibits filed with the court or Review Board or a copy of them; and
(c) all other material in its possession respecting the hearing.

Record to be kept by court of appeal
(3) The clerk of the court of appeal shall keep the material referred to in subsection (2) with the records of the court of appeal.

Appellant to provide transcript of evidence
(4) Unless it is contrary to an order of the court of appeal or any applicable rules of court, the appellant shall provide the court of appeal and the respondent with a transcript of any evidence taken before a court or Review Board by a stenographer or a sound recording apparatus, certified by the stenographer or in accordance with subsection 540(6), as the case may be.

Saving
(5) An appeal shall not be dismissed by the court of appeal by reason only that a person other than

the appellant failed to comply with this section.
1991, c. 43, s. 4;
2005, c. 22, s. 42(F).

Automatic suspension of certain dispositions

672.75 The filing of a notice of appeal against a disposition made under section 672.58 suspends the application of the disposition pending the determination of the appeal.
1991, c. 43, s. 4;
2014, c. 6, s. 13.

Application respecting dispositions under appeal

672.76 (1) Any party who gives notice to each of the other parties, within the time and in the manner prescribed, may apply to a judge of the court of appeal for an order under this section respecting a disposition or placement decision that is under appeal.

Discretionary powers respecting suspension of dispositions

(2) On receipt of an application made pursuant to subsection (1) a judge of the court of appeal may, if satisfied that the mental condition of the accused justifies it,

(a) by order, direct that a disposition made under section 672.58 be carried out pending the determination of the appeal, despite section 672.75;

(a.1) by order, direct that a disposition made under paragraph 672.54(a) be suspended pending the determination of the appeal;

(b) by order, direct that the application of a placement decision or a disposition made under paragraph 672.54(b) or (c) be suspended pending the determination of the appeal;

(c) where the application of a disposition is suspended pursuant to section 672.75 or paragraph (b), make any other disposition in respect of the accused that is appropriate in the circumstances, other than a disposition under paragraph 672.54(a) or section 672.58, pending the determination of the appeal;

(d) where the application of a placement decision is suspended pursuant to an order made under paragraph (b), make any other placement decision that is appropriate in the circumstances, pending the determination of the appeal; and

(e) give any directions that the judge considers necessary for expediting the appeal.

Copy of order to parties

(3) A judge of the court of appeal who makes an order under this section shall send a copy of the order to each of the parties without delay.
1991, c. 43, s. 4;
2014, c. 6, s. 14.

Effect of suspension of disposition

672.77 Where the application of a disposition or placement decision appealed from is suspended, a disposition, or in the absence of a disposition any order for the interim release or detention of the accused, that was in effect immediately before the disposition or placement decision appealed from took effect, shall be in force pending the determination of the appeal, subject to any disposition made under paragraph 672.76(2)(c).
1991, c. 43, s. 4.

Powers of court of appeal

672.78 (1) The court of appeal may allow an appeal against a disposition or placement decision and set aside an order made by the court or Review Board, where the court of appeal is of the opinion that

(a) it is unreasonable or cannot be supported by the evidence;

(b) it is based on a wrong decision on a question of law; or

(c) there was a miscarriage of justice.

Idem

(2) The court of appeal may dismiss an appeal against a disposition or placement decision where the court is of the opinion

(a) that paragraphs (1)(a), (b) and (c) do not apply; or

(b) that paragraph (1)(b) may apply, but the court finds that no substantial wrong or miscarriage of justice has occurred.
Orders that the court may make
(3) Where the court of appeal allows an appeal against a disposition or placement decision, it may
(a) make any disposition under section 672.54 or any placement decision that the Review Board could have made;
(b) refer the matter back to the court or Review Board for re-hearing, in whole or in part, in accordance with any directions that the court of appeal considers appropriate; or
(c) make any other order that justice requires.
1991, c. 43, s. 4;
1997, c. 18, s. 89.
672.79 672.8

Review of Dispositions

Mandatory review of dispositions
672.81 (1) A Review Board shall hold a hearing not later than twelve months after making a disposition and every twelve months thereafter for as long as the disposition remains in force, to review any disposition that it has made in respect of an accused, other than an absolute discharge under paragraph 672.54(a).
Extension on consent
(1.1) Despite subsection (1), the Review Board may extend the time for holding a hearing to a maximum of twenty-four months after the making or reviewing of a disposition if the accused is represented by counsel and the accused and the Attorney General consent to the extension.
Extension for serious personal violence offence
(1.2) Despite subsection (1), at the conclusion of a hearing under this section the Review Board may, after making a disposition, extend the time for holding a subsequent hearing under this section to a maximum of twenty-four months if
(a) the accused has been found not criminally responsible for a serious personal injury offence;
(b) the accused is subject to a disposition made under paragraph 672.54(c); and
(c) the Review Board is satisfied on the basis of any relevant information, including disposition information within the meaning of subsection 672.51(1) and an assessment report made under an assessment ordered under paragraph 672.121(a), that the condition of the accused is not likely to improve and that detention remains necessary for the period of the extension.
Definition of
serious personal injury offence
(1.3) For the purposes of subsection (1.2),
serious personal injury offence
(a) an indictable offence involving
(i) the use or attempted use of violence against another person, or
(ii) conduct endangering or likely to endanger the life or safety of another person or inflicting or likely to inflict severe psychological damage upon another person; or
(b) an indictable offence referred to in section 151, 152, 153, 153.1, 155, 160, 170, 171, 172, 271, 272 or 273 or an attempt to commit such an offence.
Extension on consent — high-risk accused
(1.31) Despite subsections (1) to (1.2), the Review Board may extend the time for holding a hearing in respect of a high-risk accused to a maximum of 36 months after making or reviewing a disposition if the accused is represented by counsel and the accused and the Attorney General consent to the extension.
Extension — no likely improvement
(1.32) Despite subsections (1) to (1.2), at the conclusion of a hearing under subsection 672.47(4) or this section in respect of a high-risk accused, the Review Board may, after making a disposition, extend the time for holding a subsequent hearing under this section to a maximum of 36 months if

the Review Board is satisfied on the basis of any relevant information, including disposition information as defined in subsection 672.51(1) and an assessment report made under an assessment ordered under paragraph 672.121(c), that the accused's condition is not likely to improve and that detention remains necessary for the period of the extension.

Notice

(1.4) If the Review Board extends the time for holding a hearing under subsection (1.2) or (1.32), it shall provide notice of the extension to the accused, the prosecutor and the person in charge of the hospital where the accused is detained.

Appeal

(1.5) A decision by the Review Board to extend the time for holding a hearing under subsection (1.2) or (1.32) is deemed to be a disposition for the purpose of sections 672.72 to 672.78.

Additional mandatory reviews in custody cases

(2) The Review Board shall hold a hearing to review any disposition made under paragraph 672.54(b) or (c) as soon as practicable after receiving notice that the person in charge of the place where the accused is detained or directed to attend requests the review.

Review in case of increase on restrictions on liberty

(2.1) The Review Board shall hold a hearing to review a decision to significantly increase the restrictions on the liberty of the accused, as soon as practicable after receiving the notice referred to in subsection 672.56(2).

Idem

(3) Where an accused is detained in custody pursuant to a disposition made under paragraph 672.54(c) and a sentence of imprisonment is subsequently imposed on the accused in respect of another offence, the Review Board shall hold a hearing to review the disposition as soon as is practicable after receiving notice of that sentence.

1991, c. 43, s. 4;
2005, c. 22, ss. 27, 42(F);
2014, c. 6, s. 15.

Discretionary review

672.82 (1) A Review Board may hold a hearing to review any of its dispositions at any time, of its own motion or at the request of the accused or any other party.

Review Board to provide notice

(1.1) Where a Review Board holds a hearing under subsection (1) of its own motion, it shall provide notice to the prosecutor, the accused and any other party.

Review cancels appeal

(2) Where a party requests a review of a disposition under this section, the party is deemed to abandon any appeal against the disposition taken under section 672.72.

1991, c. 43, s. 4;
2005, c. 22, s. 28.

Disposition by Review Board

672.83 (1) At a hearing held pursuant to section 672.81 or 672.82, the Review Board shall, except where a determination is made under subsection 672.48(1) that the accused is fit to stand trial, review the disposition made in respect of the accused and make any other disposition that the Review Board considers to be appropriate in the circumstances.

(2) 1991, c. 43, s. 4;
1997, c. 18, s. 90;
2005, c. 22, ss. 29, 42(F).

Review of finding — high-risk accused

672.84 (1) If a Review Board holds a hearing under section 672.81 or 672.82 in respect of a high-risk accused, it shall, on the basis of any relevant information, including disposition information as defined in subsection 672.51(1) and an assessment report made under an assessment ordered under paragraph 672.121(c), if it is satisfied that there is not a substantial likelihood that the accused — whether found to be a high-risk accused under paragraph 672.64(1)(a) or (b) — will use violence that could endanger the life or safety of another person, refer the finding for review to the superior court of criminal jurisdiction.

Review of conditions
(2) If the Review Board is not so satisfied, it shall review the conditions of detention imposed under paragraph 672.54(c), subject to the restrictions set out in subsection 672.64(3).

Review of finding by court
(3) If the Review Board refers the finding to the superior court of criminal jurisdiction for review, the court shall, at the conclusion of a hearing, revoke the finding if the court is satisfied that there is not a substantial likelihood that the accused will use violence that could endanger the life or safety of another person, in which case the court or the Review Board shall make a disposition under any of paragraphs 672.54(a) to (c).

Hearing and disposition
(4) Any disposition referred to in subsection (3) is subject to sections 672.45 to 672.47 as if the revocation is a verdict.

Review of conditions
(5) If the court does not revoke the finding, it shall immediately send to the Review Board, in original or copied form, a transcript of the hearing, any other document or information related to the hearing, and all exhibits filed with it, if the transcript, document, information or exhibits are in its possession. The Review Board shall, as soon as practicable but not later than 45 days after the day on which the court decides not to revoke the finding, hold a hearing and review the conditions of detention imposed under paragraph 672.54(c), subject to the restrictions set out in subsection 672.64(3).

Appeal
(6) A decision under subsection (1) about referring the finding to the court for review and a decision under subsection (3) about revoking the finding are deemed to be dispositions for the purpose of sections 672.72 to 672.78.

1991, c. 43, s. 4;
2005, c. 22, s. 30;
2014, c. 6, s. 16.

Power to Compel Appearance

Bringing accused before Review Board
672.85 For the purpose of bringing the accused in respect of whom a hearing is to be held before the Review Board, including in circumstances in which the accused did not attend a previous hearing in contravention of a summons or warrant, the chairperson
(a) shall order the person having custody of the accused to bring the accused to the hearing at the time and place fixed for it; or
(b) may, if the accused is not in custody, issue a summons or warrant to compel the accused to appear at the hearing at the time and place fixed for it.

1991, c. 43, s. 4;
2005, c. 22, ss. 32, 42(F).

Stay of Proceedings

Recommendation by Review Board
672.851 (1) The Review Board may, of its own motion, make a recommendation to the court that has jurisdiction in respect of the offence charged against an accused found unfit to stand trial to hold an inquiry to determine whether a stay of proceedings should be ordered if
(a) the Review Board has held a hearing under section 672.81 or 672.82 in respect of the accused; and
(b) on the basis of any relevant information, including disposition information within the meaning of

subsection 672.51(1) and an assessment report made under an assessment ordered under paragraph 672.121(a), the Review Board is of the opinion that
(i) the accused remains unfit to stand trial and is not likely to ever become fit to stand trial, and
(ii) the accused does not pose a significant threat to the safety of the public.
Notice
(2) If the Review Board makes a recommendation to the court to hold an inquiry, the Review Board shall provide notice to the accused, the prosecutor and any party who, in the opinion of the Review Board, has a substantial interest in protecting the interests of the accused.
Inquiry
(3) As soon as practicable after receiving the recommendation referred to in subsection (1), the court may hold an inquiry to determine whether a stay of proceedings should be ordered.
Court may act on own motion
(4) A court may, of its own motion, conduct an inquiry to determine whether a stay of proceedings should be ordered if the court is of the opinion, on the basis of any relevant information, that
(a) the accused remains unfit to stand trial and is not likely to ever become fit to stand trial; and
(b) the accused does not pose a significant threat to the safety of the public.
Assessment order
(5) If the court holds an inquiry under subsection (3) or (4), it shall order an assessment of the accused.
Application
(6) Section 672.51 applies to an inquiry of the court under this section.
Stay
(7) The court may, on completion of an inquiry under this section, order a stay of proceedings if it is satisfied
(a) on the basis of clear information, that the accused remains unfit to stand trial and is not likely to ever become fit to stand trial;
(b) that the accused does not pose a significant threat to the safety of the public; and
(c) that a stay is in the interests of the proper administration of justice.
Proper administration of justice
(8) In order to determine whether a stay of proceedings is in the interests of the proper administration of justice, the court shall consider any submissions of the prosecutor, the accused and all other parties and the following factors:
(a) the nature and seriousness of the alleged offence;
(b) the salutary and deleterious effects of the order for a stay of proceedings, including any effect on public confidence in the administration of justice;
(c) the time that has elapsed since the commission of the alleged offence and whether an inquiry has been held under section 672.33 to decide whether sufficient evidence can be adduced to put the accused on trial; and
(d) any other factor that the court considers relevant.
Effect of stay
(9) If a stay of proceedings is ordered by the court, any disposition made in respect of the accused ceases to have effect. If a stay of proceedings is not ordered, the finding of unfit to stand trial and any disposition made in respect of the accused remain in force, until the Review Board holds a disposition hearing and makes a disposition in respect of the accused under section 672.83.
2005, c. 22, s. 33.
Appeal
672.852 (1) The Court of Appeal may allow an appeal against an order made under subsection 672.851(7) for a stay of proceedings, if the Court of Appeal is of the opinion that the order is unreasonable or cannot be supported by the evidence.
Effect
(2) If the Court of Appeal allows the appeal, it may set aside the order for a stay of proceedings and restore the finding that the accused is unfit to stand trial and the disposition made in respect of the

accused.
2005, c. 22, s. 33.

Interprovincial Transfers

Interprovincial transfers
672.86 (1) An accused who is detained in custody or directed to attend at a hospital pursuant to a disposition made by a court or Review Board under paragraph 672.54(c) or a court under section 672.58 may be transferred to any other place in Canada where
(a) the Review Board of the province where the accused is detained or directed to attend recommends a transfer for the purpose of the reintegration of the accused into society or the recovery, treatment or custody of the accused; and
(b) the Attorney General of the province to which the accused is being transferred, or an officer authorized by that Attorney General, and the Attorney General of the province from which the accused is being transferred, or an officer authorized by that Attorney General, give their consent.
Transfer where accused in custody
(2) Where an accused who is detained in custody is to be transferred, an officer authorized by the Attorney General of the province where the accused is being detained shall sign a warrant specifying the place in Canada to which the accused is to be transferred.
Transfer if accused not in custody
(2.1) An accused who is not detained in custody may be transferred to any other place in Canada where
(a) the Review Board of the province from which the accused is being transferred recommends a transfer for the purpose of the reintegration of the accused into society or the recovery or treatment of the accused; and
(b) the Attorney General of the province to which the accused is being transferred, or an officer authorized by that Attorney General, and the Attorney General of the province from which the accused is being transferred, or an officer authorized by that Attorney General, give their consent.
Order
(3) Where an accused is being transferred in accordance with subsection (2.1), the Review Board of the province from which the accused is being transferred shall, by order,
(a) direct that the accused be taken into custody and transferred pursuant to a warrant under subsection (2); or
(b) direct that the accused attend at a specified place in Canada, subject to any conditions that the Review Board of the province to or from which the accused is being transferred considers appropriate.
1991, c. 43, s. 4;
2005, c. 22, s. 34.
Delivery and detention of accused
672.87 A warrant described in subsection 672.86(2) is sufficient authority
(a) for any person who is responsible for the custody of an accused to have the accused taken into custody and conveyed to the person in charge of the place specified in the warrant; and
(b) for the person specified in the warrant to detain the accused in accordance with any disposition made in respect of the accused under paragraph 672.54(c).
1991, c. 43, s. 4.
Review Board of receiving province
672.88 (1) The Review Board of the prov-ince to which an accused is transferred under section 672.86 has exclusive jurisdiction over the accused, and may exercise the powers and shall perform the duties mentioned in sections 672.5 and 672.81 to 672.84 as if that Review Board had made the disposition in respect of the accused.
Agreement
(2) Notwithstanding subsection (1), the Attorney General of the province to which an accused is

transferred may enter into an agreement subject to this Act with the Attorney General of the province from which the accused is transferred, enabling the Review Board of that province to exercise the powers and perform the duties referred to in subsection (1) in respect of the accused, in the circumstances and subject to the terms and conditions set out in the agreement.
1991, c. 43, s. 4;
2014, c. 6, s. 17.

Other interprovincial transfers

672.89 (1) If an accused who is detained in custody under a disposition made by a Review Board is transferred to another province otherwise than under section 672.86, the Review Board of the province from which the accused is transferred has exclusive jurisdiction over the accused and may continue to exercise the powers and shall continue to perform the duties mentioned in sections 672.5 and 672.81 to 672.84.

Agreement

(2) Notwithstanding subsection (1), the Attorneys General of the provinces to and from which the accused is to be transferred as described in that subsection may, after the transfer is made, enter into an agreement subject to this Act, enabling the Review Board of the province to which an accused is transferred to exercise the powers and perform the duties referred to in subsection (1) in respect of the accused, subject to the terms and conditions and in the circumstances set out in the agreement.
1991, c. 43, s. 4;
2014, c. 6, s. 18.

Enforcement of Orders and Regulations

Execution of warrant anywhere in Canada

672.9 Any warrant or process issued in relation to an assessment order or disposition made in respect of an accused may be executed or served in any place in Canada outside the province where the order or disposition was made as if it had been issued in that province.
1991, c. 43, s. 4;
1997, c. 18, s. 91;
2005, c. 22, s. 35(F).

Arrest without warrant for contravention of disposition

672.91 A peace officer may arrest an accused without a warrant at any place in Canada if the peace officer has reasonable grounds to believe that the accused has contravened or wilfully failed to comply with the assessment order or disposition or any condition of it, or is about to do so.
1991, c. 43, s. 4;
2005, c. 22, s. 36.

Release or delivery of accused subject to paragraph 672.54(b) disposition order

672.92 (1) If a peace officer arrests an accused under section 672.91 who is subject to a disposition made under paragraph 672.54(b) or an assessment order, the peace officer, as soon as practicable, may release the accused from custody and

(a) issue a summons or appearance notice compelling the accused's appearance before a justice; and

(b) deliver the accused to the place specified in the disposition or assessment order.

No release

(2) A peace officer shall not release an accused under subsection (1) if the peace officer believes, on reasonable grounds,

(a) that it is necessary in the public interest that the accused be detained in custody having regard to all the circumstances, including the need to

(i) establish the identity of the accused,

(ii) establish the terms and conditions of a disposition made under section 672.54 or of an assessment order,

(iii) prevent the commission of an offence, or

(iv) prevent the accused from contravening or failing to comply with the disposition or assessment

order;
(b) that the accused is subject to a disposition or an assessment order of a court, or Review Board, of another province; or
(c) that, if the accused is released from custody, the accused will fail to attend, as required, before a justice.

Accused to be brought before justice
(3) If a peace officer does not release the accused, the accused shall be taken before a justice having jurisdiction in the territorial division in which the accused is arrested, without unreasonable delay and in any event within twenty-four hours after the arrest.

Accused subject to paragraph 672.54(c) disposition order
(4) If a peace officer arrests an accused under section 672.91 who is subject to a disposition under paragraph 672.54(c), the accused shall be taken before a justice having jurisdiction in the territorial division in which the accused is arrested without unreasonable delay and, in any event, within twenty-four hours.

Justice not available
(5) If a justice described in subsection (3) or (4) is not available within twenty-four hours after the arrest, the accused shall be taken before a justice as soon as practicable.
1991, c. 43, s. 4;
2005, c. 22, s. 36.

Where justice to release accused
672.93 (1) A justice shall release an accused who is brought before the justice under section 672.92 unless the justice is satisfied that there are reasonable grounds to believe that the accused has contravened or failed to comply with a disposition or an assessment order.

Notice
(1.1) If the justice releases the accused, notice shall be given to the court or Review Board, as the case may be, that made the disposition or assessment order.

Order of justice pending decision of Review Board
(2) If the justice is satisfied that there are reasonable grounds to believe that the accused has contravened or failed to comply with a disposition or an assessment order, the justice, pending a hearing of a Review Board with respect to the disposition or a hearing of a court or Review Board with respect to the assessment order, may make an order that is appropriate in the circumstances in relation to the accused, including an order that the accused be returned to a place that is specified in the disposition or assessment order. If the justice makes an order under this subsection, notice shall be given to the court or Review Board, as the case may be, that made the disposition or assessment order.
1991, c. 43, s. 4;
2005, c. 22, s. 36.

Powers of Review Board
672.94 Where a Review Board receives a notice given under subsection 672.93(1.1) or (2), it may exercise the powers and shall perform the duties mentioned in sections 672.5 and 672.81 to 672.83 as if the Review Board were reviewing a disposition.
1991, c. 43, s. 4;
2005, c. 22, s. 36.

Regulations
672.95 The Governor in Council may make regulations
(a) prescribing anything that may be prescribed under this Part; and
(b) generally to carry out the purposes and provisions of this Part.
1991, c. 43, s. 4.

PART XXI

PART XXI

Appeals — Indictable Offences

Interpretation

Definitions
673 In this Part,
court of appeal
indictment
registrar
sentence
(a) a declaration made under subsection 199(3),
(b) an order made under subsection 109(1) or 110(1), section 161, subsection 164.2(1) or 194(1), section 259, 261 or 462.37, subsection 491.1(2), 730(1) or 737(3) or section 738, 739, 742.1, 742.3, 743.6, 745.4 or 745.5,
(c) a disposition made under section 731 or 732 or subsection 732.2(3) or (5), 742.4(3) or 742.6(9), and
(d) an order made under subsection 16(1) of the
Controlled Drugs and Substances Act
trial court
R.S., 1985, c. C-46, s. 673;
R.S., 1985, c. 27 (1st Supp.), ss. 138, 203, c. 23 (4th Supp.), s. 4, c. 42 (4th Supp.), s. 4;
1992, c. 1, s. 58;
1993, c. 45, s. 10;
1995, c. 22, s. 5, c. 39, ss. 155, 190;
1996, c. 19, s. 74;
1999, c. 5, ss. 25, 51, c. 25, ss. 13, 31(Preamble);
2002, c. 13, s. 63;
2005, c. 22, ss. 38, 45;
2006, c. 14, s. 6;
2013, c. 11, s. 2.

Right of Appeal

Procedure abolished
674 No proceedings other than those authorized by this Part and Part XXVI shall be taken by way of appeal in proceedings in respect of indictable offences.
R.S., c. C-34, s. 602.

Right of appeal of person convicted
675 (1) A person who is convicted by a trial court in proceedings by indictment may appeal to the court of appeal
(a) against his conviction
(i) on any ground of appeal that involves a question of law alone,
(ii) on any ground of appeal that involves a question of fact or a question of mixed law and fact, with leave of the court of appeal or a judge thereof or on the certificate of the trial judge that the case is a proper case for appeal, or
(iii) on any ground of appeal not mentioned in subparagraph (i) or (ii) that appears to the court of appeal to be a sufficient ground of appeal, with leave of the court of appeal; or
(b) against the sentence passed by the trial court, with leave of the court of appeal or a judge thereof unless that sentence is one fixed by law.

Summary conviction appeals
(1.1) A person may appeal, pursuant to subsection (1), with leave of the court of appeal or a judge of that court, to that court in respect of a summary conviction or a sentence passed with respect to a

summary conviction as if the summary conviction had been a conviction in proceedings by indictment if
(a) there has not been an appeal with respect to the summary conviction;
(b) the summary conviction offence was tried with an indictable offence; and
(c) there is an appeal in respect of the indictable offence.

Appeal against absolute term in excess of 10 years
(2) A person who has been convicted of second degree murder and sentenced to imprisonment for life without eligibility for parole for a specified number of years in excess of ten may appeal to the court of appeal against the number of years in excess of ten of his imprisonment without eligibility for parole.

Appeal against section 743.6 order
(2.1) A person against whom an order under section 743.6 has been made may appeal to the court of appeal against the order.

Persons under eighteen
(2.2) A person who was under the age of eighteen at the time of the commission of the offence for which the person was convicted of first degree murder or second degree murder and sentenced to imprisonment for life without eligibility for parole until the person has served the period specified by the judge presiding at the trial may appeal to the court of appeal against the number of years in excess of the minimum number of years of imprisonment without eligibility for parole that are required to be served in respect of that person's case.

Appeal against s. 745.51(1) order
(2.3) A person against whom an order under subsection 745.51(1) has been made may appeal to the court of appeal against the order.

Appeals against verdicts based on mental disorder
(3) Where a verdict of not criminally responsible on account of mental disorder or unfit to stand trial is rendered in respect of a person, that person may appeal to the court of appeal against that verdict on any ground of appeal mentioned in subparagraph (1)(a)(i), (ii) or (iii) and subject to the conditions described therein.

Where application for leave to appeal refused by judge
(4) Where a judge of the court of appeal refuses leave to appeal under this section otherwise than under paragraph (1)(b), the appellant may, by filing notice in writing with the court of appeal within seven days after the refusal, have the application for leave to appeal determined by the court of appeal.

R.S., 1985, c. C-46, s. 675;
1991, c. 43, s. 9;
1995, c. 42, s. 73;
1997, c. 18, s. 92;
1999, c. 31, s. 68;
2002, c. 13, s. 64;
2011, c. 5, s. 2.

Right of Attorney General to appeal
676 (1) The Attorney General or counsel instructed by him for the purpose may appeal to the court of appeal
(a) against a judgment or verdict of acquittal or a verdict of not criminally responsible on account of mental disorder of a trial court in proceedings by indictment on any ground of appeal that involves a question of law alone;
(b) against an order of a superior court of criminal jurisdiction that quashes an indictment or in any manner refuses or fails to exercise jurisdiction on an indictment;
(c) against an order of a trial court that stays proceedings on an indictment or quashes an indictment; or
(d) with leave of the court of appeal or a judge thereof, against the sentence passed by a trial court in proceedings by indictment, unless that sentence is one fixed by law.

Summary conviction appeals
(1.1) The Attorney General or counsel instructed by the Attorney General may appeal, pursuant to subsection (1), with leave of the court of appeal or a judge of that court, to that court in respect of a verdict of acquittal in a summary offence proceeding or a sentence passed with respect to a summary conviction as if the summary offence proceeding was a proceeding by indictment if
(a) there has not been an appeal with respect to the summary conviction;
(b) the summary conviction offence was tried with an indictable offence; and
(c) there is an appeal in respect of the indictable offence.
Acquittal
(2) For the purposes of this section, a judgment or verdict of acquittal includes an acquittal in respect of an offence specifically charged where the accused has, on the trial thereof, been convicted or discharged under section 730 of any other offence.
Appeal against verdict of unfit to stand trial
(3) The Attorney General or counsel instructed by the Attorney General for the purpose may appeal to the court of appeal against a verdict that an accused is unfit to stand trial, on any ground of appeal that involves a question of law alone.
Appeal against ineligible parole period
(4) The Attorney General or counsel instructed by him for the purpose may appeal to the court of appeal in respect of a conviction for second degree murder, against the number of years of imprisonment without eligibility for parole, being less than twenty-five, that has been imposed as a result of that conviction.
Appeal against decision not to make section 743.6 order
(5) The Attorney General or counsel instructed by the Attorney General for the purpose may appeal to the court of appeal against the decision of the court not to make an order under section 743.6.
Appeal against decision not to make s. 745.51(1) order
(6) The Attorney General or counsel instructed by the Attorney General for the purpose may appeal to the court of appeal against the decision of the court not to make an order under subsection 745.51(1).
R.S., 1985, c. C-46, s. 676;
R.S., 1985, c. 27 (1st Supp.), s. 139, c. 1 (4th Supp.), s. 18(F);
1991, c. 43, s. 9;
1995, c. 22, s. 10, c. 42, s. 74;
1997, c. 18, s. 93;
2002, c. 13, s. 65;
2008, c. 18, s. 28;
2011, c. 5, s. 3.
Appeal re costs
676.1 A party who is ordered to pay costs may, with leave of the court of appeal or a judge of a court of appeal, appeal the order or the amount of costs ordered.
1997, c. 18, s. 94.
Specifying grounds of dissent
677 Where a judge of the court of appeal expresses an opinion dissenting from the judgment of the court, the judgment of the court shall specify any grounds in law on which the dissent, in whole or in part, is based.
R.S., 1985, c. C-46, s. 677;
1994, c. 44, s. 67.

Procedure on Appeals

Notice of appeal
678 (1) An appellant who proposes to appeal to the court of appeal or to obtain the leave of that court to appeal shall give notice of appeal or notice of his application for leave to appeal in such manner

and within such period as may be directed by rules of court.
Extension of time
(2) The court of appeal or a judge thereof may at any time extend the time within which notice of appeal or notice of an application for leave to appeal may be given.

R.S., c. C-34, s. 607;
1972, c. 13, s. 53;
1974-75-76, c. 105, s. 16.

Service where respondent cannot be found
678.1 Where a respondent cannot be found after reasonable efforts have been made to serve the respondent with a notice of appeal or notice of an application for leave to appeal, service of the notice of appeal or the notice of the application for leave to appeal may be effected substitutionally in the manner and within the period directed by a judge of the court of appeal.

R.S., 1985, c. 27 (1st Supp.), s. 140;
1992, c. 1, s. 60(F).

Release pending determination of appeal
679 (1) A judge of the court of appeal may, in accordance with this section, release an appellant from custody pending the determination of his appeal if,
(a) in the case of an appeal to the court of appeal against conviction, the appellant has given notice of appeal or, where leave is required, notice of his application for leave to appeal pursuant to section 678;
(b) in the case of an appeal to the court of appeal against sentence only, the appellant has been granted leave to appeal; or
(c) in the case of an appeal or an application for leave to appeal to the Supreme Court of Canada, the appellant has filed and served his notice of appeal or, where leave is required, his application for leave to appeal.

Notice of application for release
(2) Where an appellant applies to a judge of the court of appeal to be released pending the determination of his appeal, he shall give written notice of the application to the prosecutor or to such other person as a judge of the court of appeal directs.

Circumstances in which appellant may be released
(3) In the case of an appeal referred to in paragraph (1)(a) or (c), the judge of the court of appeal may order that the appellant be released pending the determination of his appeal if the appellant establishes that
(a) the appeal or application for leave to appeal is not frivolous;
(b) he will surrender himself into custody in accordance with the terms of the order; and
(c) his detention is not necessary in the public interest.

Idem
(4) In the case of an appeal referred to in paragraph (1)(b), the judge of the court of appeal may order that the appellant be released pending the determination of his appeal or until otherwise ordered by a judge of the court of appeal if the appellant establishes that
(a) the appeal has sufficient merit that, in the circumstances, it would cause unnecessary hardship if he were detained in custody;
(b) he will surrender himself into custody in accordance with the terms of the order; and
(c) his detention is not necessary in the public interest.

Conditions of order
(5) Where the judge of the court of appeal does not refuse the application of the appellant, he shall order that the appellant be released
(a) on his giving an undertaking to the judge, without conditions or with such conditions as the judge directs, to surrender himself into custody in accordance with the order, or
(b) on his entering into a recognizance
(i) with one or more sureties,
(ii) with deposit of money or other valuable security,

(iii) with both sureties and deposit, or
(iv) with neither sureties nor deposit,
in such amount, subject to such conditions, if any, and before such justice as the judge directs,
(c) and the person having the custody of the appellant shall, where the appellant complies with the order, forthwith release the appellant.
Conditions
(5.1) The judge may direct that the undertaking or recognizance referred to in subsection (5) include the conditions described in subsections 515(4), (4.1) and (4.2) that the judge considers desirable.
Application of certain provisions of section 525
(6) The provisions of subsections 525(5), (6) and (7) apply with such modifications as the circumstances require in respect of a person who has been released from custody under subsection (5) of this section.
Release or detention pending hearing of reference
(7) If, with respect to any person, the Minister of Justice gives a direction or makes a reference under section 696.3, this section applies to the release or detention of that person pending the hearing and determination of the reference as though that person were an appellant in an appeal described in paragraph (1)(a).
Release or detention pending new trial or new hearing
(7.1) Where, with respect to any person, the court of appeal or the Supreme Court of Canada orders a new trial, section 515 or 522, as the case may be, applies to the release or detention of that person pending the new trial or new hearing as though that person were charged with the offence for the first time, except that the powers of a justice under section 515 or of a judge under section 522 are exercised by a judge of the court of appeal.
Application to appeals on summary conviction proceedings
(8) This section applies to applications for leave to appeal and appeals to the Supreme Court of Canada in summary conviction proceedings.
Form of undertaking or recognizance
(9) An undertaking under this section may be in Form 12 and a recognizance under this section may be in Form 32.
Directions for expediting appeal, new trial, etc.
(10) A judge of the court of appeal, where on the application of an appellant he does not make an order under subsection (5) or where he cancels an order previously made under this section, or a judge of the Supreme Court of Canada on application by an appellant in the case of an appeal to that Court, may give such directions as he thinks necessary for expediting the hearing of the appellant's appeal or for expediting the new trial or new hearing or the hearing of the reference, as the case may be.
R.S., 1985, c. C-46, s. 679;
R.S., 1985, c. 27 (1st Supp.), s. 141;
1997, c. 18, s. 95;
1999, c. 25, s. 14(Preamble);
2002, c. 13, s. 66.
Review by court of appeal
680 (1) A decision made by a judge under section 522 or subsection 524(4) or (5) or a decision made by a judge of the court of appeal under section 261 or 679 may, on the direction of the chief justice or acting chief justice of the court of appeal, be reviewed by that court and that court may, if it does not confirm the decision,
(a) vary the decision; or
(b) substitute such other decision as, in its opinion, should have been made.
Single judge acting
(2) On consent of the parties, the powers of the court of appeal under subsection (1) may be exercised by a judge of that court.
Enforcement of decision

(3) A decision as varied or substituted under this section shall have effect and may be enforced in all respects as though it were the decision originally made.
R.S., 1985, c. C-46, s. 680;
R.S., 1985, c. 27 (1st Supp.), s. 142;
1994, c. 44, s. 68.

681 Report by judge
682 (1) Where, under this Part, an appeal is taken or an application for leave to appeal is made, the judge or provincial court judge who presided at the trial shall, at the request of the court of appeal or a judge thereof, in accordance with rules of court, furnish it or him with a report on the case or on any matter relating to the case that is specified in the request.

Transcript of evidence
(2) A copy or transcript of
(a) the evidence taken at the trial,
(b) any charge to the jury and any objections that were made to a charge to the jury,
(c) the reasons for judgment, if any, and
(d) the addresses of the prosecutor and the accused, if a ground for the appeal is based on either of the addresses,
shall be furnished to the court of appeal, except in so far as it is dispensed with by order of a judge of that court.

(3) Copies to interested parties
(4) A party to an appeal is entitled to receive, on payment of any charges that are fixed by rules of court, a copy or transcript of any material that is prepared under subsections (1) and (2).

Copy for Minister of Justice
(5) The Minister of Justice is entitled, on request, to receive a copy or transcript of any material that is prepared under subsections (1) and (2).
R.S., 1985, c. C-46, s. 682;
R.S., 1985, c. 27 (1st Supp.), ss. 143, 203;
1997, c. 18, s. 96.

Powers of court of appeal
683 (1) For the purposes of an appeal under this Part, the court of appeal may, where it considers it in the interests of justice,
(a) order the production of any writing, exhibit or other thing connected with the proceedings;
(b) order any witness who would have been a compellable witness at the trial, whether or not he was called at the trial,
(i) to attend and be examined before the court of appeal, or
(ii) to be examined in the manner provided by rules of court before a judge of the court of appeal, or before any officer of the court of appeal or justice of the peace or other person appointed by the court of appeal for the purpose;
(c) admit, as evidence, an examination that is taken under subparagraph (b)(ii);
(d) receive the evidence, if tendered, of any witness, including the appellant, who is a competent but not compellable witness;
(e) order that any question arising on the appeal that
(i) involves prolonged examination of writings or accounts, or scientific or local investigation, and
(ii) cannot in the opinion of the court of appeal conveniently be inquired into before the court of appeal,
be referred for inquiry and report, in the manner provided by rules of court, to a special commissioner appointed by the court of appeal;
(f) act on the report of a commissioner who is appointed under paragraph (e) in so far as the court of appeal thinks fit to do so; and
(g) amend the indictment, unless it is of the opinion that the accused has been misled or prejudiced in his defence or appeal.

Parties entitled to adduce evidence and be heard

(2) In proceedings under this section, the parties or their counsel are entitled to examine or cross-examine witnesses and, in an inquiry under paragraph (1)(e), are entitled to be present during the inquiry, to adduce evidence and to be heard.

Virtual presence of parties

(2.1) In proceedings under this section, the court of appeal may order that the presence of a party may be by any technological means satisfactory to the court that permits the court and the other party or parties to communicate simultaneously.

Virtual presence of witnesses

(2.2) Sections 714.1 to 714.8 apply, with any modifications that the circumstances require, to examinations and cross-examinations of witnesses under this section.

Other powers

(3) A court of appeal may exercise, in relation to proceedings in the court, any powers not mentioned in subsection (1) that may be exercised by the court on appeals in civil matters, and may issue any process that is necessary to enforce the orders or sentences of the court, but no costs shall be allowed to the appellant or respondent on the hearing and determination of an appeal or on any proceedings preliminary or incidental thereto.

Execution of process

(4) Any process that is issued by the court of appeal under this section may be executed anywhere in Canada.

Power to order suspension

(5) If an appeal or an application for leave to appeal has been filed in the court of appeal, that court, or a judge of that court, may, when the court, or the judge, considers it to be in the interests of justice, order that any of the following be suspended until the appeal has been determined:

(a) an obligation to pay a fine;

(b) an order of forfeiture or disposition of forfeited property;

(c) an order to make restitution under section 738 or 739;

(d) an obligation to pay a victim surcharge under section 737;

(e) a probation order under section 731; and

(f) a conditional sentence order under section 742.1.

Undertaking or recognizance

(5.1) Before making an order under paragraph (5)(e) or (f), the court of appeal, or a judge of that court, may order the offender to enter into an undertaking or recognizance.

Revocation of suspension order

(6) The court of appeal may revoke any order it makes under subsection (5) where it considers the revocation to be in the interests of justice.

Undertaking or recognizance to be taken into account

(7) If the offender has been ordered to enter into an undertaking or recognizance under subsection (5.1), the court of appeal shall, in determining whether to vary the sentence of the offender, take into account the conditions of that undertaking or recognizance and the period during which they were imposed.

R.S., 1985, c. C-46, s. 683;

R.S., 1985, c. 27 (1st Supp.), s. 144, c. 23 (4th Supp.), s. 5;

1995, c. 22, s. 10;

1997, c. 18, ss. 97, 141;

1999, c. 25, s. 15(Preamble);

2002, c. 13, s. 67;

2008, c. 18, s. 29.

Legal assistance for appellant

684 (1) A court of appeal or a judge of that court may, at any time, assign counsel to act on behalf of an accused who is a party to an appeal or to proceedings preliminary or incidental to an appeal where, in the opinion of the court or judge, it appears desirable in the interests of justice that the accused should have legal assistance and where it appears that the accused has not sufficient means

to obtain that assistance.
Counsel fees and disbursements
(2) Where counsel is assigned pursuant to subsection (1) and legal aid is not granted to the accused pursuant to a provincial legal aid program, the fees and disbursements of counsel shall be paid by the Attorney General who is the appellant or respondent, as the case may be, in the appeal.
Taxation of fees and disbursements
(3) Where subsection (2) applies and counsel and the Attorney General cannot agree on fees or disbursements of counsel, the Attorney General or the counsel may apply to the registrar of the court of appeal and the registrar may tax the disputed fees and disbursements.
R.S., 1985, c. C-46, s. 684;
R.S., 1985, c. 34 (3rd Supp.), s. 9.
Summary determination of frivolous appeals
685 (1) Where it appears to the registrar that a notice of appeal, which purports to be on a ground of appeal that involves a question of law alone, does not show a substantial ground of appeal, the registrar may refer the appeal to the court of appeal for summary determination, and, where an appeal is referred under this section, the court of appeal may, if it considers that the appeal is frivolous or vexatious and can be determined without being adjourned for a full hearing, dismiss the appeal summarily, without calling on any person to attend the hearing or to appear for the respondent on the hearing.
Summary determination of appeals filed in error
(2) If it appears to the registrar that a notice of appeal should have been filed with another court, the registrar may refer the appeal to a judge of the court of appeal for summary determination, and the judge may dismiss the appeal summarily without calling on any person to attend the hearing or to appear for the respondent on the hearing.
R.S., 1985, c. C-46, s. 685;
2008, c. 18, s. 30.

Powers of the Court of Appeal

Powers
686 (1) On the hearing of an appeal against a conviction or against a verdict that the appellant is unfit to stand trial or not criminally responsible on account of mental disorder, the court of appeal
(a) may allow the appeal where it is of the opinion that
(i) the verdict should be set aside on the ground that it is unreasonable or cannot be supported by the evidence,
(ii) the judgment of the trial court should be set aside on the ground of a wrong decision on a question of law, or
(iii) on any ground there was a miscarriage of justice;
(b) may dismiss the appeal where
(i) the court is of the opinion that the appellant, although he was not properly convicted on a count or part of the indictment, was properly convicted on another count or part of the indictment,
(ii) the appeal is not decided in favour of the appellant on any ground mentioned in paragraph (a),
(iii) notwithstanding that the court is of the opinion that on any ground mentioned in subparagraph (a)(ii) the appeal might be decided in favour of the appellant, it is of the opinion that no substantial wrong or miscarriage of justice has occurred, or
(iv) notwithstanding any procedural irregularity at trial, the trial court had jurisdiction over the class of offence of which the appellant was convicted and the court of appeal is of the opinion that the appellant suffered no prejudice thereby;
(c) may refuse to allow the appeal where it is of the opinion that the trial court arrived at a wrong conclusion respecting the effect of a special verdict, may order the conclusion to be recorded that appears to the court to be required by the verdict and may pass a sentence that is warranted in law in substitution for the sentence passed by the trial court; or

(d) may set aside a conviction and find the appellant unfit to stand trial or not criminally responsible on account of mental disorder and may exercise any of the powers of the trial court conferred by or referred to in section 672.45 in any manner deemed appropriate to the court of appeal in the circumstances.

(e) Order to be made
(2) Where a court of appeal allows an appeal under paragraph (1)(a), it shall quash the conviction and
(a) direct a judgment or verdict of acquittal to be entered; or
(b) order a new trial.

Substituting verdict
(3) Where a court of appeal dismisses an appeal under subparagraph (1)(b)(i), it may substitute the verdict that in its opinion should have been found and
(a) affirm the sentence passed by the trial court; or
(b) impose a sentence that is warranted in law or remit the matter to the trial court and direct the trial court to impose a sentence that is warranted in law.

Appeal from acquittal
(4) If an appeal is from an acquittal or verdict that the appellant or respondent was unfit to stand trial or not criminally responsible on account of mental disorder, the court of appeal may
(a) dismiss the appeal; or
(b) allow the appeal, set aside the verdict and
(i) order a new trial, or
(ii) except where the verdict is that of a court composed of a judge and jury, enter a verdict of guilty with respect to the offence of which, in its opinion, the accused should have been found guilty but for the error in law, and pass a sentence that is warranted in law, or remit the matter to the trial court and direct the trial court to impose a sentence that is warranted in law.

New trial under Part XIX
(5) Subject to subsection (5.01), if an appeal is taken in respect of proceedings under Part XIX and the court of appeal orders a new trial under this Part, the following provisions apply:
(a) if the accused, in his notice of appeal or notice of application for leave to appeal, requested that the new trial, if ordered, should be held before a court composed of a judge and jury, the new trial shall be held accordingly;
(b) if the accused, in his notice of appeal or notice of application for leave to appeal, did not request that the new trial, if ordered, should be held before a court composed of a judge and jury, the new trial shall, without further election by the accused, be held before a judge or provincial court judge, as the case may be, acting under Part XIX, other than a judge or provincial court judge who tried the accused in the first instance, unless the court of appeal directs that the new trial be held before the judge or provincial court judge who tried the accused in the first instance;
(c) if the court of appeal orders that the new trial shall be held before a court composed of a judge and jury, the new trial shall be commenced by an indictment in writing setting forth the offence in respect of which the new trial was ordered; and
(d) notwithstanding paragraph (a), if the conviction against which the accused appealed was for an offence mentioned in section 553 and was made by a provincial court judge, the new trial shall be held before a provincial court judge acting under Part XIX, other than the provincial court judge who tried the accused in the first instance, unless the court of appeal directs that the new trial be held before the provincial court judge who tried the accused in the first instance.

New trial under Part XIX — Nunavut
(5.01) If an appeal is taken in respect of proceedings under Part XIX and the Court of Appeal of Nunavut orders a new trial under Part XXI, the following provisions apply:
(a) if the accused, in the notice of appeal or notice of application for leave to appeal, requested that the new trial, if ordered, should be held before a court composed of a judge and jury, the new trial shall be held accordingly;
(b) if the accused, in the notice of appeal or notice of application for leave to appeal, did not request

that the new trial, if ordered, should be held before a court composed of a judge and jury, the new trial shall, without further election by the accused, and without a further preliminary inquiry, be held before a judge, acting under Part XIX, other than a judge who tried the accused in the first instance, unless the Court of Appeal of Nunavut directs that the new trial be held before the judge who tried the accused in the first instance;

(c) if the Court of Appeal of Nunavut orders that the new trial shall be held before a court composed of a judge and jury, the new trial shall be commenced by an indictment in writing setting forth the offence in respect of which the new trial was ordered; and

(d) despite paragraph (a), if the conviction against which the accused appealed was for an indictable offence mentioned in section 553, the new trial shall be held before a judge acting under Part XIX, other than the judge who tried the accused in the first instance, unless the Court of Appeal of Nunavut directs that the new trial be held before the judge who tried the accused in the first instance.

Election if new trial a jury trial

(5.1) Subject to subsection (5.2), if a new trial ordered by the court of appeal is to be held before a court composed of a judge and jury,

(a) the accused may, with the consent of the prosecutor, elect to have the trial heard before a judge without a jury or a provincial court judge;

(b) the election shall be deemed to be a re-election within the meaning of subsection 561(5); and

(c) subsection 561(5) applies, with such modifications as the circumstances require, to the election.

Election if new trial a jury trial — Nunavut

(5.2) If a new trial ordered by the Court of Appeal of Nunavut is to be held before a court composed of a judge and jury, the accused may, with the consent of the prosecutor, elect to have the trial heard before a judge without a jury. The election shall be deemed to be a re-election within the meaning of subsection 561.1(1), and subsection 561.1(6) applies, with any modifications that the circumstances require, to the election.

Where appeal allowed against verdict of unfit to stand trial

(6) Where a court of appeal allows an appeal against a verdict that the accused is unfit to stand trial, it shall, subject to subsection (7), order a new trial.

Appeal court may set aside verdict of unfit to stand trial

(7) Where the verdict that the accused is unfit to stand trial was returned after the close of the case for the prosecution, the court of appeal may, notwithstanding that the verdict is proper, if it is of the opinion that the accused should have been acquitted at the close of the case for the prosecution, allow the appeal, set aside the verdict and direct a judgment or verdict of acquittal to be entered.

Additional powers

(8) Where a court of appeal exercises any of the powers conferred by subsection (2), (4), (6) or (7), it may make any order, in addition, that justice requires.

R.S., 1985, c. C-46, s. 686;
R.S., 1985, c. 27 (1st Supp.), ss. 145, 203;
1991, c. 43, s. 9;
1997, c. 18, s. 98;
1999, c. 3, s. 52, c. 5, s. 26;
2015, c. 3, s. 54(F).

Powers of court on appeal against sentence

687 (1) Where an appeal is taken against sentence, the court of appeal shall, unless the sentence is one fixed by law, consider the fitness of the sentence appealed against, and may on such evidence, if any, as it thinks fit to require or to receive,

(a) vary the sentence within the limits prescribed by law for the offence of which the accused was convicted; or

(b) dismiss the appeal.

Effect of judgment

(2) A judgment of a court of appeal that varies the sentence of an accused who was convicted has the same force and effect as if it were a sentence passed by the trial court.

R.S., c. C-34, s. 614.
Right of appellant to attend
688 (1) Subject to subsection (2), an appellant who is in custody is entitled, if he desires, to be present at the hearing of the appeal.
Appellant represented by counsel
(2) An appellant who is in custody and who is represented by counsel is not entitled to be present
(a) at the hearing of the appeal, where the appeal is on a ground involving a question of law alone,
(b) on an application for leave to appeal, or
(c) on any proceedings that are preliminary or incidental to an appeal,
unless rules of court provide that he is entitled to be present or the court of appeal or a judge thereof gives him leave to be present.
Manner of appearance
(2.1) In the case of an appellant who is in custody and who is entitled to be present at any proceedings on an appeal, the court may order that, instead of the appellant personally appearing,
(a) at an application for leave to appeal or at any proceedings that are preliminary or incidental to an appeal, the appellant appear by means of any suitable telecommunication device, including telephone, that is satisfactory to the court; and
(b) at the hearing of the appeal, if the appellant has access to legal advice, he or she appear by means of closed-circuit television or any other means that permits the court and all parties to engage in simultaneous visual and oral communication.
Argument may be oral or in writing
(3) An appellant may present his case on appeal and his argument in writing instead of orally, and the court of appeal shall consider any case of argument so presented.
Sentence in absence of appellant
(4) A court of appeal may exercise its power to impose sentence notwithstanding that the appellant is not present.
R.S., 1985, c. C-46, s. 688;
2002, c. 13, s. 68.
Restitution or forfeiture of property
689 (1) If the trial court makes an order for compensation or for the restitution of property under section 738 or 739 or an order of forfeiture of property under subsection 164.2(1) or 462.37(1) or (2.01), the operation of the order is suspended
(a) until the expiration of the period prescribed by rules of court for the giving of notice of appeal or of notice of application for leave to appeal, unless the accused waives an appeal; and
(b) until the appeal or application for leave to appeal has been determined, where an appeal is taken or application for leave to appeal is made.
Annulling or varying order
(2) The court of appeal may by order annul or vary an order made by the trial court with respect to compensation or the restitution of property within the limits prescribed by the provision under which the order was made by the trial court, whether or not the conviction is quashed.
R.S., 1985, c. C-46, s. 689;
R.S., 1985, c. 42 (4th Supp.), s. 5;
1995, c. 22, s. 10;
2002, c. 13, s. 69;
2005, c. 44, s. 12.
690
Appeals to the Supreme Court of Canada

Appeal from conviction
691 (1) A person who is convicted of an indictable offence and whose conviction is affirmed by the court of appeal may appeal to the Supreme Court of Canada
(a) on any question of law on which a judge of the court of appeal dissents; or

(b) on any question of law, if leave to appeal is granted by the Supreme Court of Canada.
Appeal where acquittal set aside
(2) A person who is acquitted of an indictable offence other than by reason of a verdict of not criminally responsible on account of mental disorder and whose acquittal is set aside by the court of appeal may appeal to the Supreme Court of Canada
(a) on any question of law on which a judge of the court of appeal dissents;
(b) on any question of law, if the Court of Appeal enters a verdict of guilty against the person; or
(c) on any question of law, if leave to appeal is granted by the Supreme Court of Canada.
R.S., 1985, c. C-46, s. 691;
R.S., 1985, c. 34 (3rd Supp.), s. 10;
1991, c. 43, s. 9;
1997, c. 18, s. 99.
Appeal against affirmation of verdict of not criminally responsible on account of mental disorder
692 (1) A person who has been found not criminally responsible on account of mental disorder and
(a) whose verdict is affirmed on that ground by the court of appeal, or
(b) against whom a verdict of guilty is entered by the court of appeal under subparagraph 686(4)(b)(ii),
may appeal to the Supreme Court of Canada.
Appeal against affirmation of verdict of unfit to stand trial
(2) A person who is found unfit to stand trial and against whom that verdict is affirmed by the court of appeal may appeal to the Supreme Court of Canada.
Grounds of appeal
(3) An appeal under subsection (1) or (2) may be
(a) on any question of law on which a judge of the court of appeal dissents; or
(b) on any question of law, if leave to appeal is granted by the Supreme Court of Canada.
R.S., 1985, c. C-46, s. 692;
R.S., 1985, c. 34 (3rd Supp.), s. 11;
1991, c. 43, s. 9.
Appeal by Attorney General
693 (1) Where a judgment of a court of appeal sets aside a conviction pursuant to an appeal taken under section 675 or dismisses an appeal taken pursuant to paragraph 676(1)(a), (b) or (c) or subsection 676(3), the Attorney General may appeal to the Supreme Court of Canada
(a) on any question of law on which a judge of the court of appeal dissents; or
(b) on any question of law, if leave to appeal is granted by the Supreme Court of Canada.
Terms
(2) Where leave to appeal is granted under paragraph (1)(b), the Supreme Court of Canada may impose such terms as it sees fit.
R.S., 1985, c. C-46, s. 693;
R.S., 1985, c. 27 (1st Supp.), s. 146, c. 34 (3rd Supp.), s. 12.
Notice of appeal
694 No appeal lies to the Supreme Court of Canada unless notice of appeal in writing is served by the appellant on the respondent in accordance with the
Supreme Court Act
R.S., 1985, c. C-46, s. 694;
R.S., 1985, c. 34 (3rd Supp.), s. 13.
Legal assistance for accused
694.1 (1) The Supreme Court of Canada or a judge thereof may, at any time, assign counsel to act on behalf of an accused who is a party to an appeal to the Court or to proceedings preliminary or incidental to an appeal to the Court where, in the opinion of the Court or judge, it appears desirable in the interests of justice that the accused should have legal assistance and where it appears that the accused has not sufficient means to obtain that assistance.

Counsel fees and disbursements
(2) Where counsel is assigned pursuant to subsection (1) and legal aid is not granted to the accused pursuant to a provincial legal aid program, the fees and disbursements of counsel shall be paid by the Attorney General who is the appellant or respondent, as the case may be, in the appeal.

Taxation of fees and disbursements
(3) Where subsection (2) applies and counsel and the Attorney General cannot agree on fees or disbursements of counsel, the Attorney General or the counsel may apply to the Registrar of the Supreme Court of Canada, and the Registrar may tax the disputed fees and disbursements.
R.S., 1985, c. 34 (3rd Supp.), s. 13;
1992, c. 1, s. 60(F).

Right of appellant to attend
694.2 (1) Subject to subsection (2), an appellant who is in custody and who desires to be present at the hearing of the appeal before the Supreme Court of Canada is entitled to be present at it.

Appellant represented by counsel
(2) An appellant who is in custody and who is represented by counsel is not entitled to be present before the Supreme Court of Canada
(a) on an application for leave to appeal,
(b) on any proceedings that are preliminary or incidental to an appeal, or
(c) at the hearing of the appeal,
unless rules of court provide that entitlement or the Supreme Court of Canada or a judge thereof gives the appellant leave to be present.
R.S., 1985, c. 34 (3rd Supp.), s. 13.

Order of Supreme Court of Canada
695 (1) The Supreme Court of Canada may, on an appeal under this Part, make any order that the court of appeal might have made and may make any rule or order that is necessary to give effect to its judgment.

Election if new trial
(2) Subject to subsection (3), if a new trial ordered by the Supreme Court of Canada is to be held before a court composed of a judge and jury, the accused may, with the consent of the prosecutor, elect to have the trial heard before a judge without a jury or a provincial court judge. The election is deemed to be a re-election within the meaning of subsection 561(5) and subsections 561(5) to (7) apply to it with any modifications that the circumstances require.

Nunavut
(3) If a new trial ordered by the Supreme Court of Canada is to be held before a court composed of a judge and jury in Nunavut, the accused may, with the consent of the prosecutor, elect to have the trial heard before a judge without a jury. The election is deemed to be a re-election within the meaning of subsection 561.1(6) and subsections 561.1(6) to (9) apply to it with any modifications that the circumstances require.
R.S., 1985, c. C-46, s. 695;
1999, c. 5, s. 27;
2008, c. 18, s. 31.

Appeals by Attorney General of Canada

Right of Attorney General of Canada to appeal
696 The Attorney General of Canada has the same rights of appeal in proceedings instituted at the instance of the Government of Canada and conducted by or on behalf of that Government as the Attorney General of a province has under this Part.
R.S., c. C-34, s. 624.

PART XXI.1

PART XXI.1
Applications for Ministerial Review — Miscarriages of Justice

Application
696.1 (1) An application for ministerial review on the grounds of miscarriage of justice may be made to the Minister of Justice by or on behalf of a person who has been convicted of an offence under an Act of Parliament or a regulation made under an Act of Parliament or has been found to be a dangerous offender or a long-term offender under Part XXIV and whose rights of judicial review or appeal with respect to the conviction or finding have been exhausted.

Form of application
(2) The application must be in the form, contain the information and be accompanied by any documents prescribed by the regulations.
2002, c. 13, s. 71.

Review of applications
696.2 (1) On receipt of an application under this Part, the Minister of Justice shall review it in accordance with the regulations.

Powers of investigation
(2) For the purpose of any investigation in relation to an application under this Part, the Minister of Justice has and may exercise the powers of a commissioner under Part I of the
Inquiries Act

Delegation
(3) Despite subsection 11(3) of the
Inquiries Act
2002, c. 13, s. 71.

Definition of
696.3 (1) In this section,
the court of appeal

Power to refer
(2) The Minister of Justice may, at any time, refer to the court of appeal, for its opinion, any question in relation to an application under this Part on which the Minister desires the assistance of that court, and the court shall furnish its opinion accordingly.

Powers of Minister of Justice
(3) On an application under this Part, the Minister of Justice may
(a) if the Minister is satisfied that there is a reasonable basis to conclude that a miscarriage of justice likely occurred,
(i) direct, by order in writing, a new trial before any court that the Minister thinks proper or, in the case of a person found to be a dangerous offender or a long-term offender under Part XXIV, a new hearing under that Part, or
(ii) refer the matter at any time to the court of appeal for hearing and determination by that court as if it were an appeal by the convicted person or the person found to be a dangerous offender or a long-term offender under Part XXIV, as the case may be; or
(b) dismiss the application.

No appeal
(4) A decision of the Minister of Justice made under subsection (3) is final and is not subject to appeal.
2002, c. 13, s. 71.

Considerations
696.4 In making a decision under subsection 696.3(3), the Minister of Justice shall take into account all matters that the Minister considers relevant, including
(a) whether the application is supported by new matters of significance that were not considered by the courts or previously considered by the Minister in an application in relation to the same conviction or finding under Part XXIV;

(b) the relevance and reliability of information that is presented in connection with the application; and

(c) the fact that an application under this Part is not intended to serve as a further appeal and any remedy available on such an application is an extraordinary remedy.

2002, c. 13, s. 71.

Annual report

696.5 The Minister of Justice shall within six months after the end of each financial year submit an annual report to Parliament in relation to applications under this Part.

2002, c. 13, s. 71.

Regulations

696.6 The Governor in Council may make regulations

(a) prescribing the form of, the information required to be contained in and any documents that must accompany an application under this Part;

(b) prescribing the process of review in relation to applications under this Part, which may include the following stages, namely, preliminary assessment, investigation, reporting on investigation and decision; and

(c) respecting the form and content of the annual report under section 696.5.

2002, c. 13, s. 71.

PART XXII

PART XXII
Procuring Attendance

Application

Application

697 Except where section 527 applies, this Part applies where a person is required to attend to give evidence in a proceeding to which this Act applies.

R.S., c. C-34, s. 625.

Process

Subpoena

698 (1) Where a person is likely to give material evidence in a proceeding to which this Act applies, a subpoena may be issued in accordance with this Part requiring that person to attend to give evidence.

Warrant in Form 17

(2) Where it is made to appear that a person who is likely to give material evidence

(a) will not attend in response to a subpoena if a subpoena is issued, or

(b) is evading service of a subpoena,

a court, justice or provincial court judge having power to issue a subpoena to require the attendance of that person to give evidence may issue a warrant in Form 17 to cause that person to be arrested and to be brought to give evidence.

Subpoena issued first

(3) Except where paragraph (2)(a) applies, a warrant in Form 17 shall not be issued unless a subpoena has first been issued.

R.S., 1985, c. C-46, s. 698;

R.S., 1985, c. 27 (1st Supp.), s. 203.

Who may issue

699 (1) If a person is required to attend to give evidence before a superior court of criminal jurisdiction, a court of appeal, an appeal court or a court of criminal jurisdiction other than a

provincial court judge acting under Part XIX, a subpoena directed to that person shall be issued out of the court before which the attendance of that person is required.
Order of judge
(2) If a person is required to attend to give evidence before a provincial court judge acting under Part XIX or a summary conviction court under Part XXVII or in proceedings over which a justice has jurisdiction, a subpoena directed to the person shall be issued
(a) by a provincial court judge or a justice, where the person whose attendance is required is within the province in which the proceedings were instituted; or
(b) by a provincial court judge or out of a superior court of criminal jurisdiction of the province in which the proceedings were instituted, where the person whose attendance is required is not within the province.
Order of judge
(3) A subpoena shall not be issued out of a superior court of criminal jurisdiction pursuant to paragraph (2)(b), except pursuant to an order of a judge of the court made on application by a party to the proceedings.
Seal
(4) A subpoena or warrant that is issued by a court under this Part shall be under the seal of the court and shall be signed by a judge of the court or by the clerk of the court.
Signature
(5) A subpoena or warrant that is issued by a justice or provincial court judge under this Part shall be signed by the justice or provincial court judge.
Sexual offences
(5.1) Notwithstanding anything in subsections (1) to (5), in the case of an offence referred to in subsection 278.2(1), a subpoena requiring a witness to bring to the court a record, the production of which is governed by sections 278.1 to 278.91, must be issued and signed by a judge.
Form of subpoena
(6) Subject to subsection (7), a subpoena issued under this Part may be in Form 16.
Form of subpoena in sexual offences
(7) In the case of an offence referred to in subsection 278.2(1), a subpoena requiring a witness to bring anything to the court shall be in Form 16.1.
R.S., 1985, c. C-46, s. 699;
R.S., 1985, c. 27 (1st Supp.), s. 203;
1994, c. 44, s. 69;
1997, c. 30, s. 2;
1999, c. 5, s. 28.
Contents of subpoena
700 (1) A subpoena shall require the person to whom it is directed to attend, at a time and place to be stated in the subpoena, to give evidence and, if required, to bring with him anything that he has in his possession or under his control relating to the subject-matter of the proceedings.
Witness to appear and remain
(2) A person who is served with a subpoena issued under this Part shall attend and shall remain in attendance throughout the proceedings unless he is excused by the presiding judge, justice or provincial court judge.
R.S., 1985, c. C-46, s. 700;
R.S., 1985, c. 27 (1st Supp.), ss. 148, 203.
Video links, etc.
700.1 (1) If a person is to give evidence under section 714.1 or 714.3 or under subsection 46(2) of the
Canada Evidence Act
Mutual Legal Assistance in Criminal Matters Act
Sections of
Criminal Code

(2) Sections 699, 700 and 701 to 703.2 apply, with any modifications that the circumstances require, to a subpoena issued under this section.
1999, c. 18, s. 94.

Execution or Service of Process

Service
701 (1) Subject to subsection (2), a subpoena shall be served in a province by a peace officer or any other person who is qualified in that province to serve civil process, in accordance with subsection 509(2), with such modifications as the circumstances require.

Personal service
(2) A subpoena that is issued pursuant to paragraph 699(2)(b) shall be served personally on the person to whom it is directed.
(3) R.S., 1985, c. C-46, s. 701;
1994, c. 44, s. 70;
2008, c. 18, s. 32.

Service in accordance with provincial laws
701.1 Despite section 701, in any province, service of a document may be made in accordance with the laws of the province relating to offences created by the laws of that province.
1997, c. 18, s. 100;
2008, c. 18, s. 33.

Subpoena effective throughout Canada
702 (1) A subpoena that is issued by a provincial court judge or out of a superior court of criminal jurisdiction, a court of appeal, an appeal court or a court of criminal jurisdiction has effect anywhere in Canada according to its terms.

Subpoena effective throughout province
(2) A subpoena that is issued by a justice has effect anywhere in the province in which it is issued.
R.S., 1985, c. C-46, s. 702;
1994, c. 44, s. 71.

Warrant effective throughout Canada
703 (1) Notwithstanding any other provision of this Act, a warrant of arrest or committal that is issued out of a superior court of criminal jurisdiction, a court of appeal, an appeal court within the meaning of section 812 or a court of criminal jurisdiction other than a provincial court judge acting under Part XIX may be executed anywhere in Canada.

Warrant effective in a province
(2) Despite any other provision of this Act but subject to subsections 487.0551(2) and 705(3), a warrant of arrest or committal that is issued by a justice or provincial court judge may be executed anywhere in the province in which it is issued.
R.S., 1985, c. C-46, s. 703;
R.S., 1985, c. 27 (1st Supp.), s. 149;
2007, c. 22, s. 22.

Summons effective throughout Canada
703.1 A summons may be served anywhere in Canada and, if served, is effective notwithstanding the territorial jurisdiction of the authority that issued the summons.
R.S., 1985, c. 27 (1st Supp.), s. 149.

Service of process on an organization
703.2 Where any summons, notice or other process is required to be or may be served on an organization, and no other method of service is provided, service may be effected by delivery
(a) in the case of a municipality, to the mayor, warden, reeve or other chief officer of the municipality, or to the secretary, treasurer or clerk of the municipality; and
(b) in the case of any other organization, to the manager, secretary or other senior officer of the organization or one of its branches.

R.S., 1985, c. 27 (1st Supp.), s. 149;
2003, c. 21, s. 13.

Defaulting or Absconding Witness

Warrant for absconding witness
704 (1) Where a person is bound by recognizance to give evidence in any proceedings, a justice who is satisfied on information being made before him in writing and under oath that the person is about to abscond or has absconded may issue his warrant in Form 18 directing a peace officer to arrest that person and to bring him before the court, judge, justice or provincial court judge before whom he is bound to appear.
Endorsement of warrant
(2) Section 528 applies, with such modifications as the circumstances require, to a warrant issued under this section.
Copy of information
(3) A person who is arrested under this section is entitled, on request, to receive a copy of the information on which the warrant for his arrest was issued.
R.S., 1985, c. C-46, s. 704;
R.S., 1985, c. 27 (1st Supp.), s. 203.
Warrant when witness does not attend
705 (1) Where a person who has been served with a subpoena to give evidence in a proceeding does not attend or remain in attendance, the court, judge, justice or provincial court judge before whom that person was required to attend may, if it is established
(a) that the subpoena has been served in accordance with this Part, and
(b) that the person is likely to give material evidence,
issue or cause to be issued a warrant in Form 17 for the arrest of that person.
Warrant where witness bound by recognizance
(2) Where a person who has been bound by a recognizance to attend to give evidence in any proceeding does not attend or does not remain in attendance, the court, judge, justice or provincial court judge before whom that person was bound to attend may issue or cause to be issued a warrant in Form 17 for the arrest of that person.
Warrant effective throughout Canada
(3) A warrant that is issued by a justice or provincial court judge pursuant to subsection (1) or (2) may be executed anywhere in Canada.
R.S., 1985, c. C-46, s. 705;
R.S., 1985, c. 27 (1st Supp.), s. 203.
Order where witness arrested under warrant
706 Where a person is brought before a court, judge, justice or provincial court judge under a warrant issued pursuant to subsection 698(2) or section 704 or 705, the court, judge, justice or provincial court judge may order that the person
(a) be detained in custody, or
(b) be released on recognizance in Form 32, with or without sureties,
to appear and give evidence when required.
R.S., 1985, c. C-46, s. 706;
R.S., 1985, c. 27 (1st Supp.), s. 203.
Maximum period for detention of witness
707 (1) No person shall be detained in custody under the authority of any provision of this Act, for the purpose only of appearing and giving evidence when required as a witness, for any period exceeding thirty days unless prior to the expiration of those thirty days he has been brought before a judge of a superior court of criminal jurisdiction in the province in which he is being detained.
Application by witness to judge
(2) Where at any time prior to the expiration of the thirty days referred to in subsection (1), a witness

being detained in custody as described in that subsection applies to be brought before a judge of a court described therein, the judge before whom the application is brought shall fix a time prior to the expiration of those thirty days for the hearing of the application and shall cause notice of the time so fixed to be given to the witness, the person having custody of the witness and such other persons as the judge may specify, and at the time so fixed for the hearing of the application the person having custody of the witness shall cause the witness to be brought before a judge of the court for that purpose.

Review of detention

(3) If the judge before whom a witness is brought under this section is not satisfied that the continued detention of the witness is justified, he shall order him to be discharged, or to be released on recognizance in Form 32, with or without sureties, to appear and to give evidence when required, but if the judge is satisfied that the continued detention of the witness is justified, he may order his continued detention until the witness does what is required of him pursuant to section 550 or the trial is concluded, or until the witness appears and gives evidence when required, as the case may be, except that the total period of detention of the witness from the time he was first detained in custody shall not in any case exceed ninety days.

R.S., c. C-34, s. 635.

Contempt

708 (1) A person who, being required by law to attend or remain in attendance for the purpose of giving evidence, fails, without lawful excuse, to attend or remain in attendance accordingly is guilty of contempt of court.

Punishment

(2) A court, judge, justice or provincial court judge may deal summarily with a person who is guilty of contempt of court under this section and that person is liable to a fine not exceeding one hundred dollars or to imprisonment for a term not exceeding ninety days or to both, and may be ordered to pay the costs that are incident to the service of any process under this Part and to his detention, if any.

Form

(3) A conviction under this section may be in Form 38 and a warrant of committal in respect of a conviction under this section may be in Form 25.

R.S., 1985, c. C-46, s. 708;
R.S., 1985, c. 27 (1st Supp.), s. 203.

Electronically Transmitted Copies

Electronically transmitted copies

708.1 A copy of a summons, warrant or subpoena transmitted by a means of telecommunication that produces a writing has the same probative force as the original for the purposes of this Act.

1997, c. 18, s. 101.

Evidence on Commission

Order appointing commissioner

709 (1) A party to proceedings by way of indictment or summary conviction may apply for an order appointing a commissioner to take the evidence of a witness who
(a) is, by reason of
(i) physical disability arising out of illness, or
(ii) any other good and sufficient cause,
not likely to be able to attend at the time the trial is held; or
(b) is out of Canada.

Idem

(2) A decision under subsection (1) is deemed to have been made at the trial held in relation to the

proceedings mentioned in that subsection.
R.S., 1985, c. C-46, s. 709;
R.S., 1985, c. 27 (1st Supp.), s. 150;
1994, c. 44, s. 72.
Application where witness is ill
710 (1) An application under paragraph 709(1)(a) shall be made
(a) to a judge of a superior court of the province in which the proceedings are taken;
(b) to a judge of a county or district court in the territorial division in which the proceedings are taken; or
(c) to a provincial court judge, where
(i) at the time the application is made, the accused is before a provincial court judge presiding over a preliminary inquiry under Part XVIII, or
(ii) the accused or defendant is to be tried by a provincial court judge acting under Part XIX or XXVII.
Evidence of medical practitioner
(2) An application under subparagraph 709(1)(a)(i) may be granted on the evidence of a registered medical practitioner.
R.S., 1985, c. C-46, s. 710;
R.S., 1985, c. 27 (1st Supp.), s. 151;
1994, c. 44, s. 73.
Admitting evidence of witness who is ill
711 Where the evidence of a witness mentioned in paragraph 709(1)(a) is taken by a commissioner appointed under section 710, it may be admitted in evidence in the proceedings if
(a) it is proved by oral evidence or by affidavit that the witness is unable to attend by reason of death or physical disability arising out of illness or some other good and sufficient cause;
(b) the transcript of the evidence is signed by the commissioner by or before whom it purports to have been taken; and
(c) it is proved to the satisfaction of the court that reasonable notice of the time for taking the evidence was given to the other party, and that the accused or his counsel, or the prosecutor or his counsel, as the case may be, had or might have had full opportunity to cross-examine the witness.
R.S., 1985, c. C-46, s. 711;
R.S., 1985, c. 27 (1st Supp.), s. 152;
1994, c. 44, s. 74;
1997, c. 18, s. 102.
Application for order when witness out of Canada
712 (1) An application that is made under paragraph 709(1)(b) shall be made
(a) to a judge of a superior court of criminal jurisdiction or of a court of criminal jurisdiction before which the accused is to be tried; or
(b) to a provincial court judge, where the accused or defendant is to be tried by a provincial court judge acting under Part XIX or XXVII.
Admitting evidence of witness out of Canada
(2) Where the evidence of a witness is taken by a commissioner appointed under this section, it may be admitted in evidence in the proceedings.
(3) R.S., 1985, c. C-46, s. 712;
R.S., 1985, c. 27 (1st Supp.), s. 153;
1994, c. 44, s. 75;
1997, c. 18, s. 103.
Providing for presence of accused counsel
713 (1) A judge or provincial court judge who appoints a commissioner may make provision in the order to enable an accused to be present or represented by counsel when the evidence is taken, but failure of the accused to be present or to be represented by counsel in accordance with the order does not prevent the admission of the evidence in the proceedings if the evidence has otherwise been

taken in accordance with the order and with this Part.
Return of evidence
(2) An order for the taking of evidence by commission shall indicate the officer of the court to whom the evidence that is taken under the order shall be returned.
R.S., 1985, c. C-46, s. 713;
R.S., 1985, c. 27 (1st Supp.), s. 203;
1997, c. 18, s. 104.
Evidence not excluded
713.1 Evidence taken by a commissioner appointed under section 712 shall not be excluded by reason only that it would have been taken differently in Canada, provided that the process used to take the evidence is consistent with the law of the country where it was taken and that the process used to take the evidence was not contrary to the principles of fundamental justice.
1994, c. 44, s. 76.
Rules and practice same as in civil cases
714 Except where otherwise provided by this Part or by rules of court, the practice and procedure in connection with the appointment of commissioners under this Part, the taking of evidence by commissioners, the certifying and return thereof and the use of the evidence in the proceedings shall, as far as possible, be the same as those that govern like matters in civil proceedings in the superior court of the province in which the proceedings are taken.
R.S., c. C-34, s. 642.

Video and Audio Evidence

Video links, etc. — witness in Canada
714.1 A court may order that a witness in Canada give evidence by means of technology that permits the witness to testify elsewhere in Canada in the virtual presence of the parties and the court, if the court is of the opinion that it would be appropriate in all the circumstances, including
(a) the location and personal circumstances of the witness;
(b) the costs that would be incurred if the witness had to be physically present; and
(c) the nature of the witness' anticipated evidence.
1999, c. 18, s. 95.
Video links, etc. — witness outside Canada
714.2 (1) A court shall receive evidence given by a witness outside Canada by means of technology that permits the witness to testify in the virtual presence of the parties and the court unless one of the parties satisfies the court that the reception of such testimony would be contrary to the principles of fundamental justice.
Notice
(2) A party who wishes to call a witness to give evidence under subsection (1) shall give notice to the court before which the evidence is to be given and the other parties of their intention to do so not less than ten days before the witness is scheduled to testify.
1999, c. 18, s. 95.
Audio evidence — witness in Canada
714.3 The court may order that a witness in Canada give evidence by means of technology that permits the parties and the court to hear and examine the witness elsewhere in Canada, if the court is of the opinion that it would be appropriate, considering all the circumstances including
(a) the location and personal circumstances of the witness;
(b) the costs that would be incurred if the witness had to be physically present;
(c) the nature of the witness' anticipated evidence; and
(d) any potential prejudice to either of the parties caused by the fact that the witness would not be seen by them.
1999, c. 18, s. 95.
Audio evidence — witness outside Canada

714.4 The court may receive evidence given by a witness outside Canada by means of technology that permits the parties and the court in Canada to hear and examine the witness, if the court is of the opinion that it would be appropriate, considering all the circumstances including
(a) the nature of the witness' anticipated evidence; and
(b) any potential prejudice to either of the parties caused by the fact that the witness would not be seen by them.
1999, c. 18, s. 95.

Oath or affirmation
714.5 The evidence given under section 714.2 or 714.4 shall be given
(a) under oath or affirmation in accordance with Canadian law;
(b) under oath or affirmation in accordance with the law in the place in which the witness is physically present; or
(c) in any other manner that demonstrates that the witness understands that they must tell the truth.
1999, c. 18, s. 95.

Other laws about witnesses to apply
714.6 When a witness who is outside Canada gives evidence under section 714.2 or 714.4, the evidence is deemed to be given in Canada, and given under oath or affirmation in accordance with Canadian law, for the purposes of the laws relating to evidence, procedure, perjury and contempt of court.
1999, c. 18, s. 95.

Costs of technology
714.7 A party who wishes to call a witness to give evidence by means of the technology referred to in section 714.1, 714.2, 714.3 or 714.4 shall pay any costs associated with the use of the technology.
1999, c. 18, s. 95.

Consent
714.8 Nothing in sections 714.1 to 714.7 is to be construed as preventing a court from receiving evidence by means of the technology referred to in sections 714.1 to 714.4 if the parties so consent.
1999, c. 18, s. 95.

Evidence Previously Taken

Evidence at preliminary inquiry may be read at trial in certain cases
715 (1) Where, at the trial of an accused, a person whose evidence was given at a previous trial on the same charge, or whose evidence was taken in the investigation of the charge against the accused or on the preliminary inquiry into the charge, refuses to be sworn or to give evidence, or if facts are proved on oath from which it can be inferred reasonably that the person
(a) is dead,
(b) has since become and is insane,
(c) is so ill that he is unable to travel or testify, or
(d) is absent from Canada,
and where it is proved that the evidence was taken in the presence of the accused, it may be admitted as evidence in the proceedings without further proof, unless the accused proves that the accused did not have full opportunity to cross-examine the witness.

Admission of evidence
(2) Evidence that has been taken on the preliminary inquiry or other investigation of a charge against an accused may be admitted as evidence in the prosecution of the accused for any other offence on the same proof and in the same manner in all respects, as it might, according to law, be admitted as evidence in the prosecution of the offence with which the accused was charged when the evidence was taken.

Admission of evidence
(2.1) Despite subsections (1) and (2), evidence that has been taken at a preliminary inquiry in the absence of the accused may be admitted as evidence for the purposes referred to in those subsections

if the accused was absent further to the permission of a justice granted under paragraph 537(1)(j.1).
Absconding accused deemed present
(3) For the purposes of this section, where evidence was taken at a previous trial or preliminary hearing or other proceeding in respect of an accused in the absence of the accused, who was absent by reason of having absconded, the accused is deemed to have been present during the taking of the evidence and to have had full opportunity to cross-examine the witness.
Exception
(4) Subsections (1) to (3) do not apply in respect of evidence received under subsection 540(7).
R.S., 1985, c. C-46, s. 715;
1994, c. 44, s. 77;
1997, c. 18, s. 105;
2002, c. 13, s. 72;
2008, c. 18, s. 34.

Video-recorded Evidence

Evidence of victim or witness under 18
715.1 (1) In any proceeding against an accused in which a victim or other witness was under the age of eighteen years at the time the offence is alleged to have been committed, a video recording made within a reasonable time after the alleged offence, in which the victim or witness describes the acts complained of, is admissible in evidence if the victim or witness, while testifying, adopts the contents of the video recording, unless the presiding judge or justice is of the opinion that admission of the video recording in evidence would interfere with the proper administration of justice.
Order prohibiting use
(2) The presiding judge or justice may prohibit any other use of a video recording referred to in subsection (1).
R.S., 1985, c. 19 (3rd Supp.), s. 16;
1997, c. 16, s. 7;
2005, c. 32, s. 23.
Evidence of victim or witness who has a disability
715.2 (1) In any proceeding against an accused in which a victim or other witness is able to communicate evidence but may have difficulty doing so by reason of a mental or physical disability, a video recording made within a reasonable time after the alleged offence, in which the victim or witness describes the acts complained of, is admissible in evidence if the victim or witness, while testifying, adopts the contents of the video recording, unless the presiding judge or justice is of the opinion that admission of the video recording in evidence would interfere with the proper administration of justice.
Order prohibiting use
(2) The presiding judge or justice may prohibit any other use of a video recording referred to in subsection (1).
1998, c. 9, s. 8;
2005, c. 32, s. 23.

PART XXIII

PART XXIII
Sentencing

Interpretation

Definitions
716 In this Part,

accused
alternative measures
court
(a) a superior court of criminal jurisdiction,
(b) a court of criminal jurisdiction,
(c) a justice or provincial court judge acting as a summary conviction court under Part XXVII, or
(d) a court that hears an appeal;
fine
R.S., 1985, c. C-46, s. 716;
R.S., 1985, c. 27 (1st Supp.), s. 154;
1995, c. 22, s. 6;
1999, c. 5, s. 29(E).

Alternative Measures

When alternative measures may be used
717 (1) Alternative measures may be used to deal with a person alleged to have committed an offence only if it is not inconsistent with the protection of society and the following conditions are met:
(a) the measures are part of a program of alternative measures authorized by the Attorney General or the Attorney General's delegate or authorized by a person, or a person within a class of persons, designated by the lieutenant governor in council of a province;
(b) the person who is considering whether to use the measures is satisfied that they would be appropriate, having regard to the needs of the person alleged to have committed the offence and the interests of society and of the victim;
(c) the person, having been informed of the alternative measures, fully and freely consents to participate therein;
(d) the person has, before consenting to participate in the alternative measures, been advised of the right to be represented by counsel;
(e) the person accepts responsibility for the act or omission that forms the basis of the offence that the person is alleged to have committed;
(f) there is, in the opinion of the Attorney General or the Attorney General's agent, sufficient evidence to proceed with the prosecution of the offence; and
(g) the prosecution of the offence is not in any way barred at law.
Restriction on use
(2) Alternative measures shall not be used to deal with a person alleged to have committed an offence if the person
(a) denies participation or involvement in the commission of the offence; or
(b) expresses the wish to have any charge against the person dealt with by the court.
Admissions not admissible in evidence
(3) No admission, confession or statement accepting responsibility for a given act or omission made by a person alleged to have committed an offence as a condition of the person being dealt with by alternative measures is admissible in evidence against that person in any civil or criminal proceedings.
No bar to proceedings
(4) The use of alternative measures in respect of a person alleged to have committed an offence is not a bar to proceedings against the person under this Act, but, if a charge is laid against that person in respect of that offence,
(a) where the court is satisfied on a balance of probabilities that the person has totally complied with the terms and conditions of the alternative measures, the court shall dismiss the charge; and
(b) where the court is satisfied on a balance of probabilities that the person has partially complied with the terms and conditions of the alternative measures, the court may dismiss the charge if, in the

opinion of the court, the prosecution of the charge would be unfair, having regard to the circumstances and that person's performance with respect to the alternative measures.

Laying of information, etc.

(5) Subject to subsection (4), nothing in this section shall be construed as preventing any person from laying an information, obtaining the issue or confirmation of any process, or proceeding with the prosecution of any offence, in accordance with law.

R.S., 1985, c. C-46, s. 717;
1995, c. 22, s. 6.

Records of persons dealt with

717.1 Sections 717.2 to 717.4 apply only in respect of persons who have been dealt with by alternative measures, regardless of the degree of their compliance with the terms and conditions of the alternative measures.

1995, c. 22, s. 6.

Police records

717.2 (1) A record relating to any offence alleged to have been committed by a person, including the original or a copy of any fingerprints or photographs of the person, may be kept by any police force responsible for, or participating in, the investigation of the offence.

Disclosure by peace officer

(2) A peace officer may disclose to any person any information in a record kept pursuant to this section that it is necessary to disclose in the conduct of the investigation of an offence.

Idem

(3) A peace officer may disclose to an insurance company any information in a record kept pursuant to this section for the purpose of investigating any claim arising out of an offence committed or alleged to have been committed by the person to whom the record relates.

1995, c. 22, s. 6.

Government records

717.3 (1) A department or agency of any government in Canada may keep records containing information obtained by the department or agency

(a) for the purposes of an investigation of an offence alleged to have been committed by a person;
(b) for use in proceedings against a person under this Act; or
(c) as a result of the use of alternative measures to deal with a person.

Private records

(2) Any person or organization may keep records containing information obtained by the person or organization as a result of the use of alternative measures to deal with a person alleged to have committed an offence.

1995, c. 22, s. 6.

Disclosure of records

717.4 (1) Any record that is kept pursuant to section 717.2 or 717.3 may be made available to
(a) any judge or court for any purpose relating to proceedings relating to offences committed or alleged to have been committed by the person to whom the record relates;
(b) any peace officer
(i) for the purpose of investigating any offence that the person is suspected on reasonable grounds of having committed, or in respect of which the person has been arrested or charged, or
(ii) for any purpose related to the administration of the case to which the record relates;
(c) any member of a department or agency of a government in Canada, or any agent thereof, that is
(i) engaged in the administration of alternative measures in respect of the person, or
(ii) preparing a report in respect of the person pursuant to this Act; or
(d) any other person who is deemed, or any person within a class of persons that is deemed, by a judge of a court to have a valid interest in the record, to the extent directed by the judge, if the judge is satisfied that the disclosure is
(i) desirable in the public interest for research or statistical purposes, or
(ii) desirable in the interest of the proper administration of justice.

Subsequent disclosure
(2) Where a record is made available for inspection to any person under subparagraph (1)(d)(i), that person may subsequently disclose information contained in the record, but may not disclose the information in any form that would reasonably be expected to identify the person to whom it relates.

Information, copies
(3) Any person to whom a record is authorized to be made available under this section may be given any information contained in the record and may be given a copy of any part of the record.

Evidence
(4) Nothing in this section authorizes the introduction into evidence of any part of a record that would not otherwise be admissible in evidence.

Idem
(5) A record kept pursuant to section 717.2 or 717.3 may not be introduced into evidence, except for the purposes set out in paragraph 721(3)(c), more than two years after the end of the period for which the person agreed to participate in the alternative measures.
1995, c. 22, s. 6.

Purpose and Principles of Sentencing

Purpose
718 The fundamental purpose of sentencing is to protect society and to contribute, along with crime prevention initiatives, to respect for the law and the maintenance of a just, peaceful and safe society by imposing just sanctions that have one or more of the following objectives:
(a) to denounce unlawful conduct and the harm done to victims or to the community that is caused by unlawful conduct;
(b) to deter the offender and other persons from committing offences;
(c) to separate offenders from society, where necessary;
(d) to assist in rehabilitating offenders;
(e) to provide reparations for harm done to victims or to the community; and
(f) to promote a sense of responsibility in offenders, and acknowledgment of the harm done to victims or to the community.
R.S., 1985, c. C-46, s. 718;
R.S., 1985, c. 27 (1st Supp.), s. 155;
1995, c. 22, s. 6;
2015, c. 13, s. 23.

Objectives — offences against children
718.01 When a court imposes a sentence for an offence that involved the abuse of a person under the age of eighteen years, it shall give primary consideration to the objectives of denunciation and deterrence of such conduct.
2005, c. 32, s. 24.

Objectives — offence against peace officer or other justice system participant
718.02 When a court imposes a sentence for an offence under subsection 270(1), section 270.01 or 270.02 or paragraph 423.1(1)(b), the court shall give primary consideration to the objectives of denunciation and deterrence of the conduct that forms the basis of the offence.
2009, c. 22, s. 18.

Objectives — offence against certain animals
718.03 When a court imposes a sentence for an offence under subsection 445.01(1), the court shall give primary consideration to the objectives of denunciation and deterrence of the conduct that forms the basis of the offence.
2015, c. 34, s. 4.

Fundamental principle
718.1 A sentence must be proportionate to the gravity of the offence and the degree of responsibility of the offender.

R.S., 1985, c. 27 (1st Supp.), s. 156;
1995, c. 22, s. 6.

Other sentencing principles

718.2 A court that imposes a sentence shall also take into consideration the following principles:
(a) a sentence should be increased or reduced to account for any relevant aggravating or mitigating circumstances relating to the offence or the offender, and, without limiting the generality of the foregoing,
(i) evidence that the offence was motivated by bias, prejudice or hate based on race, national or ethnic origin, language, colour, religion, sex, age, mental or physical disability, sexual orientation, or gender identity or expression, or on any other similar factor,
(ii) evidence that the offender, in committing the offence, abused the offender's spouse or common-law partner,
(ii.1) evidence that the offender, in committing the offence, abused a person under the age of eighteen years,
(iii) evidence that the offender, in committing the offence, abused a position of trust or authority in relation to the victim,
(iii.1) evidence that the offence had a significant impact on the victim, considering their age and other personal circumstances, including their health and financial situation,
(iv) evidence that the offence was committed for the benefit of, at the direction of or in association with a criminal organization,
(v) evidence that the offence was a terrorism offence, or
(vi) evidence that the offence was committed while the offender was subject to a conditional sentence order made under section 742.1 or released on parole, statutory release or unescorted temporary absence under the
Corrections and Conditional Release Act
shall be deemed to be aggravating circumstances;
(b) a sentence should be similar to sentences imposed on similar offenders for similar offences committed in similar circumstances;
(c) where consecutive sentences are imposed, the combined sentence should not be unduly long or harsh;
(d) an offender should not be deprived of liberty, if less restrictive sanctions may be appropriate in the circumstances; and
(e) all available sanctions, other than imprisonment, that are reasonable in the circumstances and consistent with the harm done to victims or to the community should be considered for all offenders, with particular attention to the circumstances of Aboriginal offenders.
1995, c. 22, s. 6;
1997, c. 23, s. 17;
2000, c. 12, s. 95;
2001, c. 32, s. 44(F), c. 41, s. 20;
2005, c. 32, s. 25;
2012, c. 29, s. 2;
2015, c. 13, s. 24, c. 23, s. 16;
2017, c. 13, s. 4.

Organizations

Additional factors

718.21 A court that imposes a sentence on an organization shall also take into consideration the following factors:
(a) any advantage realized by the organization as a result of the offence;
(b) the degree of planning involved in carrying out the offence and the duration and complexity of the offence;

(c) whether the organization has attempted to conceal its assets, or convert them, in order to show that it is not able to pay a fine or make restitution;
(d) the impact that the sentence would have on the economic viability of the organization and the continued employment of its employees;
(e) the cost to public authorities of the investigation and prosecution of the offence;
(f) any regulatory penalty imposed on the organization or one of its representatives in respect of the conduct that formed the basis of the offence;
(g) whether the organization was — or any of its representatives who were involved in the commission of the offence were — convicted of a similar offence or sanctioned by a regulatory body for similar conduct;
(h) any penalty imposed by the organization on a representative for their role in the commission of the offence;
(i) any restitution that the organization is ordered to make or any amount that the organization has paid to a victim of the offence; and
(j) any measures that the organization has taken to reduce the likelihood of it committing a subsequent offence.
2003, c. 21, s. 14.

Punishment Generally

Degrees of punishment
718.3 (1) Where an enactment prescribes different degrees or kinds of punishment in respect of an offence, the punishment to be imposed is, subject to the limitations prescribed in the enactment, in the discretion of the court that convicts a person who commits the offence.
Discretion respecting punishment
(2) Where an enactment prescribes a punishment in respect of an offence, the punishment to be imposed is, subject to the limitations prescribed in the enactment, in the discretion of the court that convicts a person who commits the offence, but no punishment is a minimum punishment unless it is declared to be a minimum punishment.
Imprisonment in default where term not specified
(3) Where an accused is convicted of an offence punishable with both fine and imprisonment and a term of imprisonment in default of payment of the fine is not specified in the enactment that prescribes the punishment to be imposed, the imprisonment that may be imposed in default of payment shall not exceed the term of imprisonment that is prescribed in respect of the offence.
Cumulative punishments
(4) The court that sentences an accused shall consider directing
(a) that the term of imprisonment that it imposes be served consecutively to a sentence of imprisonment to which the accused is subject at the time of sentencing; and
(b) that the terms of imprisonment that it imposes at the same time for more than one offence be served consecutively, including when
(i) the offences do not arise out of the same event or series of events,
(ii) one of the offences was committed while the accused was on judicial interim release, including pending the determination of an appeal, or
(iii) one of the offences was committed while the accused was fleeing from a peace officer.
Cumulative punishments — fines
(5) For the purposes of subsection (4), a term of imprisonment includes imprisonment that results from the operation of subsection 734(4).
Cumulative punishments — youth
(6) For the purposes of subsection (4), a sentence of imprisonment includes
(a) a disposition made under paragraph 20(1)(k) or (k.1) of the
Young Offenders Act
(b) a youth sentence imposed under paragraph 42(2)(n), (o), (q) or (r) of the

Youth Criminal Justice Act

(c) a sentence that results from the operation of subsection 743.5(1) or (2).

Cumulative punishments — sexual offences against children

(7) When a court sentences an accused at the same time for more than one sexual offence committed against a child, the court shall direct

(a) that a sentence of imprisonment it imposes for an offence under section 163.1 be served consecutively to a sentence of imprisonment it imposes for a sexual offence under another section of this Act committed against a child; and

(b) that a sentence of imprisonment it imposes for a sexual offence committed against a child, other than an offence under section 163.1, be served consecutively to a sentence of imprisonment it imposes for a sexual offence committed against another child other than an offence under section 163.1.

1995, c. 22, s. 6;
1997, c. 18, s. 141;
2002, c. 1, s. 182;
2015, c. 23, s. 17.

Commencement of sentence

719 (1) A sentence commences when it is imposed, except where a relevant enactment otherwise provides.

Time at large excluded from term of imprisonment

(2) Any time during which a convicted person is unlawfully at large or is lawfully at large on interim release granted pursuant to any provision of this Act does not count as part of any term of imprisonment imposed on the person.

Determination of sentence

(3) In determining the sentence to be imposed on a person convicted of an offence, a court may take into account any time spent in custody by the person as a result of the offence but the court shall limit any credit for that time to a maximum of one day for each day spent in custody.

Exception

(3.1) Despite subsection (3), if the circumstances justify it, the maximum is one and one-half days for each day spent in custody unless the reason for detaining the person in custody was stated in the record under subsection 515(9.1) or the person was detained in custody under subsection 524(4) or (8).

Reasons

(3.2) The court shall give reasons for any credit granted and shall cause those reasons to be stated in the record.

Record of proceedings

(3.3) The court shall cause to be stated in the record and on the warrant of committal the offence, the amount of time spent in custody, the term of imprisonment that would have been imposed before any credit was granted, the amount of time credited, if any, and the sentence imposed.

Validity not affected

(3.4) Failure to comply with subsection (3.2) or (3.3) does not affect the validity of the sentence imposed by the court.

When time begins to run

(4) Notwithstanding subsection (1), a term of imprisonment, whether imposed by a trial court or the court appealed to, commences or shall be deemed to be resumed, as the case may be, on the day on which the convicted person is arrested and taken into custody under the sentence.

When fine imposed

(5) Notwithstanding subsection (1), where the sentence that is imposed is a fine with a term of imprisonment in default of payment, no time prior to the day of execution of the warrant of committal counts as part of the term of imprisonment.

Application for leave to appeal

(6) An application for leave to appeal is an appeal for the purposes of this section.

R.S., 1985, c. C-46, s. 719;
R.S., 1985, c. 27 (1st Supp.), s. 157;
1995, c. 22, s. 6;
2009, c. 29, s. 3.

Procedure and Evidence

Sentencing proceedings
720 (1) A court shall, as soon as practicable after an offender has been found guilty, conduct proceedings to determine the appropriate sentence to be imposed.
Court-supervised programs
(2) The court may, with the consent of the Attorney General and the offender and after considering the interests of justice and of any victim of the offence, delay sentencing to enable the offender to attend a treatment program approved by the province under the supervision of the court, such as an addiction treatment program or a domestic violence counselling program.
R.S., 1985, c. C-46, s. 720;
1995, c. 22, s. 6;
2008, c. 18, s. 35.
Report by probation officer
721 (1) Subject to regulations made under subsection (2), where an accused, other than an organization, pleads guilty to or is found guilty of an offence, a probation officer shall, if required to do so by a court, prepare and file with the court a report in writing relating to the accused for the purpose of assisting the court in imposing a sentence or in determining whether the accused should be discharged under section 730.
Provincial regulations
(2) The lieutenant governor in council of a province may make regulations respecting the types of offences for which a court may require a report, and respecting the content and form of the report.
Content of report
(3) Unless otherwise specified by the court, the report must, wherever possible, contain information on the following matters:
(a) the offender's age, maturity, character, behaviour, attitude and willingness to make amends;
(b) subject to subsection 119(2) of the

Youth Criminal Justice Act
Young Offenders Act
Youth Criminal Justice Act
(c) the history of any alternative measures used to deal with the offender, and the offender's response to those measures; and
(d) any matter required, by any regulation made under subsection (2), to be included in the report.
Idem
(4) The report must also contain information on any other matter required by the court, after hearing argument from the prosecutor and the offender, to be included in the report, subject to any contrary regulation made under subsection (2).
Copy of report
(5) The clerk of the court shall provide a copy of the report, as soon as practicable after filing, to the offender or counsel for the offender, as directed by the court, and to the prosecutor.
R.S., 1985, c. C-46, s. 721;
R.S., 1985, c. 27 (1st Supp.), s. 203;
1995, c. 22, s. 6;
1999, c. 25, s. 16(Preamble);
2002, c. 1, s. 183;
2003, c. 21, s. 15.

Victim impact statement

722 (1) When determining the sentence to be imposed on an offender or determining whether the offender should be discharged under section 730 in respect of any offence, the court shall consider any statement of a victim prepared in accordance with this section and filed with the court describing the physical or emotional harm, property damage or economic loss suffered by the victim as the result of the commission of the offence and the impact of the offence on the victim.

Inquiry by court

(2) As soon as feasible after a finding of guilt and in any event before imposing sentence, the court shall inquire of the prosecutor if reasonable steps have been taken to provide the victim with an opportunity to prepare a statement referred to in subsection (1).

Adjournment

(3) On application of the prosecutor or a victim or on its own motion, the court may adjourn the proceedings to permit the victim to prepare a statement referred to in subsection (1) or to present evidence in accordance with subsection (9), if the court is satisfied that the adjournment would not interfere with the proper administration of justice.

Form

(4) The statement must be prepared in writing, using Form 34.2 in Part XXVIII, in accordance with the procedures established by a program designated for that purpose by the lieutenant governor in council of the province in which the court is exercising its jurisdiction.

Presentation of statement

(5) The court shall, on the request of a victim, permit the victim to present the statement by
(a) reading it;
(b) reading it in the presence and close proximity of any support person of the victim's choice;
(c) reading it outside the court room or behind a screen or other device that would allow the victim not to see the offender; or
(d) presenting it in any other manner that the court considers appropriate.

Photograph

(6) During the presentation
(a) the victim may have with them a photograph of themselves taken before the commission of the offence if it would not, in the opinion of the court, disrupt the proceedings; or
(b) if the statement is presented by someone acting on the victim's behalf, that individual may have with them a photograph of the victim taken before the commission of the offence if it would not, in the opinion of the court, disrupt the proceedings.

Conditions of exclusion

(7) The victim shall not present the statement outside the court room unless arrangements are made for the offender and the judge or justice to watch the presentation by means of closed-circuit television or otherwise and the offender is permitted to communicate with counsel while watching the presentation.

Consideration of statement

(8) In considering the statement, the court shall take into account the portions of the statement that it considers relevant to the determination referred to in subsection (1) and disregard any other portion.

Evidence concerning victim admissible

(9) Whether or not a statement has been prepared and filed in accordance with this section, the court may consider any other evidence concerning any victim of the offence for the purpose of determining the sentence to be imposed on the offender or whether the offender should be discharged under section 730.

R.S., 1985, c. C-46, s. 722;
1995, c. 22, s. 6;
1999, c. 25, s. 17(Preamble);
2000, c. 12, s. 95;
2015, c. 13, s. 25.

Copy of statement

722.1 The clerk of the court shall provide a copy of a statement referred to in subsection 722(1), as soon as practicable after a finding of guilt, to the offender or counsel for the offender, and to the prosecutor.
1995, c. 22, s. 6;
1999, c. 25, s. 18(Preamble).

Community impact statement
722.2 (1) When determining the sentence to be imposed on an offender or determining whether the offender should be discharged under section 730 in respect of any offence, the court shall consider any statement made by an individual on a community's behalf that was prepared in accordance with this section and filed with the court describing the harm or loss suffered by the community as the result of the commission of the offence and the impact of the offence on the community.

Form
(2) The statement must be prepared in writing, using Form 34.3 in Part XXVIII, in accordance with the procedures established by a program designated for that purpose by the lieutenant governor in council of the province in which the court is exercising its jurisdiction.

Presentation of statement
(3) The court shall, on the request of the individual making the statement, permit the individual to present the statement by
(a) reading it;
(b) reading it in the presence and close proximity of any support person of the individual's choice;
(c) reading it outside the court room or behind a screen or other device that would allow the individual not to see the offender; or
(d) presenting it in any other manner that the court considers appropriate.

Conditions of exclusion
(4) The individual making the statement shall not present it outside the court room unless arrangements are made for the offender and the judge or justice to watch the presentation by means of closed-circuit television or otherwise and the offender is permitted to communicate with counsel while watching the presentation.

Copy of statement
(5) The clerk of the court shall, as soon as feasible after a finding of guilt, provide a copy of the statement to the offender or counsel for the offender, and to the prosecutor.
1999, c. 25, s. 18(Preamble);
2015, c. 13, s. 26.

Submissions on facts
723 (1) Before determining the sentence, a court shall give the prosecutor and the offender an opportunity to make submissions with respect to any facts relevant to the sentence to be imposed.

Submission of evidence
(2) The court shall hear any relevant evidence presented by the prosecutor or the offender.

Production of evidence
(3) The court may, on its own motion, after hearing argument from the prosecutor and the offender, require the production of evidence that would assist it in determining the appropriate sentence.

Compel appearance
(4) Where it is necessary in the interests of justice, the court may, after consulting the parties, compel the appearance of any person who is a compellable witness to assist the court in determining the appropriate sentence.

Hearsay evidence
(5) Hearsay evidence is admissible at sentencing proceedings, but the court may, if the court considers it to be in the interests of justice, compel a person to testify where the person
(a) has personal knowledge of the matter;
(b) is reasonably available; and
(c) is a compellable witness.
R.S., 1985, c. C-46, s. 723;

1995, c. 22, s. 6.
Information accepted
724 (1) In determining a sentence, a court may accept as proved any information disclosed at the trial or at the sentencing proceedings and any facts agreed on by the prosecutor and the offender.
Jury
(2) Where the court is composed of a judge and jury, the court
(a) shall accept as proven all facts, express or implied, that are essential to the jury's verdict of guilty; and
(b) may find any other relevant fact that was disclosed by evidence at the trial to be proven, or hear evidence presented by either party with respect to that fact.
Disputed facts
(3) Where there is a dispute with respect to any fact that is relevant to the determination of a sentence,
(a) the court shall request that evidence be adduced as to the existence of the fact unless the court is satisfied that sufficient evidence was adduced at the trial;
(b) the party wishing to rely on a relevant fact, including a fact contained in a presentence report, has the burden of proving it;
(c) either party may cross-examine any witness called by the other party;
(d) subject to paragraph (e), the court must be satisfied on a balance of probabilities of the existence of the disputed fact before relying on it in determining the sentence; and
(e) the prosecutor must establish, by proof beyond a reasonable doubt, the existence of any aggravating fact or any previous conviction by the offender.
R.S., 1985, c. C-46, s. 724;
1995, c. 22, s. 6.
Other offences
725 (1) In determining the sentence, a court
(a) shall consider, if it is possible and appropriate to do so, any other offences of which the offender was found guilty by the same court, and shall determine the sentence to be imposed for each of those offences;
(b) shall consider, if the Attorney General and the offender consent, any outstanding charges against the offender to which the offender consents to plead guilty and pleads guilty, if the court has jurisdiction to try those charges, and shall determine the sentence to be imposed for each charge unless the court is of the opinion that a separate prosecution for the other offence is necessary in the public interest;
(b.1) shall consider any outstanding charges against the offender, unless the court is of the opinion that a separate prosecution for one or more of the other offences is necessary in the public interest, subject to the following conditions:
(i) the Attorney General and the offender consent,
(ii) the court has jurisdiction to try each charge,
(iii) each charge has been described in open court,
(iv) the offender has agreed with the facts asserted in the description of each charge, and
(v) the offender has acknowledged having committed the offence described in each charge; and
(c) may consider any facts forming part of the circumstances of the offence that could constitute the basis for a separate charge.
Attorney General's consent
(1.1) For the purpose of paragraphs (1)(b) and (b.1), the Attorney General shall take the public interest into account before consenting.
No further proceedings
(2) The court shall, on the information or indictment, note
(a) any outstanding charges considered in determining the sentence under paragraph (1)(b.1), and
(b) any facts considered in determining the sentence under paragraph (1)(c),
and no further proceedings may be taken with respect to any offence described in those charges or

disclosed by those facts unless the conviction for the offence of which the offender has been found guilty is set aside or quashed on appeal.

R.S., 1985, c. C-46, s. 725;
R.S., 1985, c. 27 (1st Supp.), s. 158, c. 1 (4th Supp.), s. 18(F);
1995, c. 22, s. 6;
1999, c. 5, s. 31.

Offender may speak to sentence

726 Before determining the sentence to be imposed, the court shall ask whether the offender, if present, has anything to say.

R.S., 1985, c. C-46, s. 726;
R.S., 1985, c. 27 (1st Supp.), s. 159, c. 1 (4th Supp.), s. 18(F);
1995, c. 22, s. 6.

Relevant information

726.1 In determining the sentence, a court shall consider any relevant information placed before it, including any representations or submissions made by or on behalf of the prosecutor or the offender.

1995, c. 22, s. 6.

Reasons for sentence

726.2 When imposing a sentence, a court shall state the terms of the sentence imposed, and the reasons for it, and enter those terms and reasons into the record of the proceedings.

1995, c. 22, s. 6.

Previous conviction

727 (1) Subject to subsections (3) and (4), where an offender is convicted of an offence for which a greater punishment may be imposed by reason of previous convictions, no greater punishment shall be imposed on the offender by reason thereof unless the prosecutor satisfies the court that the offender, before making a plea, was notified that a greater punishment would be sought by reason thereof.

Procedure

(2) Where an offender is convicted of an offence for which a greater punishment may be imposed by reason of previous convictions, the court shall, on application by the prosecutor and on being satisfied that the offender was notified in accordance with subsection (1), ask whether the offender was previously convicted and, if the offender does not admit to any previous convictions, evidence of previous convictions may be adduced.

Where hearing

(3) Where a summary conviction court holds a trial pursuant to subsection 803(2) and convicts the offender, the court may, whether or not the offender was notified that a greater punishment would be sought by reason of a previous conviction, make inquiries and hear evidence with respect to previous convictions of the offender and, if any such conviction is proved, may impose a greater punishment by reason thereof.

Organizations

(4) If, under section 623, the court proceeds with the trial of an organization that has not appeared and pleaded and convicts the organization, the court may, whether or not the organization was notified that a greater punishment would be sought by reason of a previous conviction, make inquiries and hear evidence with respect to previous convictions of the organization and, if any such conviction is proved, may impose a greater punishment by reason of that conviction.

Section does not apply

(5) This section does not apply to a person referred to in paragraph 745(b).

R.S., 1985, c. C-46, s. 727;
R.S., 1985, c. 27 (1st Supp.), s. 160;
1995, c. 22, s. 6;
2003, c. 21, s. 16.

Sentence justified by any count

728 Where one sentence is passed on a verdict of guilty on two or more counts of an indictment, the

sentence is good if any of the counts would have justified the sentence.
R.S., 1985, c. C-46, s. 728;
1995, c. 22, s. 6.

Proof of certificate of analyst

729 (1) In

(a) a prosecution for failure to comply with a condition in a probation order that the accused not have in possession or use drugs, or

(b) a hearing to determine whether the offender breached a condition of a conditional sentence order that the offender not have in possession or use drugs,

a certificate purporting to be signed by an analyst stating that the analyst has analyzed or examined a substance and stating the result of the analysis or examination is admissible in evidence and, in the absence of evidence to the contrary, is proof of the statements contained in the certificate without proof of the signature or official character of the person appearing to have signed the certificate.

Definition of
analyst

(2) In this section,
analyst
Controlled Drugs and Substances Act

Notice of intention to produce certificate

(3) No certificate shall be admitted in evidence unless the party intending to produce it has, before the trial or hearing, as the case may be, given reasonable notice and a copy of the certificate to the party against whom it is to be produced.

(4) and (5) Requiring attendance of analyst

(6) The party against whom a certificate of an analyst is produced may, with leave of the court, require the attendance of the analyst for cross-examination.

R.S., 1985, c. C-46, s. 729;
1995, c. 22, s. 6;
1999, c. 31, s. 69;
2004, c. 12, s. 11(E);
2008, c. 18, s. 36.

Proof of certificate of analyst — bodily substance

729.1 (1) In a prosecution for failure to comply with a condition in a probation order that the accused not consume drugs, alcohol or any other intoxicating substance, or in a hearing to determine whether the offender breached such a condition of a conditional sentence order, a certificate purporting to be signed by an analyst that states that the analyst has analyzed a sample of a bodily substance and that states the result of the analysis is admissible in evidence and, in the absence of evidence to the contrary, is proof of the statements contained in the certificate without proof of the signature or official character of the person who appears to have signed the certificate.

Definition of
analyst

(2) In this section,
analyst

Notice of intention to produce certificate

(3) No certificate shall be admitted in evidence unless the party intending to produce it has, before the trial or hearing, as the case may be, given reasonable notice and a copy of the certificate to the party against whom it is to be produced.

Requiring attendance of analyst

(4) The party against whom a certificate of an analyst is produced may, with leave of the court, require the attendance of the analyst for cross-examination.

2011, c. 7, s. 2.

Absolute and Conditional Discharges

Conditional and absolute discharge
730 (1) Where an accused, other than an organization, pleads guilty to or is found guilty of an offence, other than an offence for which a minimum punishment is prescribed by law or an offence punishable by imprisonment for fourteen years or for life, the court before which the accused appears may, if it considers it to be in the best interests of the accused and not contrary to the public interest, instead of convicting the accused, by order direct that the accused be discharged absolutely or on the conditions prescribed in a probation order made under subsection 731(2).

Period for which appearance notice, etc., continues in force
(2) Subject to Part XVI, where an accused who has not been taken into custody or who has been released from custody under or by virtue of any provision of Part XVI pleads guilty of or is found guilty of an offence but is not convicted, the appearance notice, promise to appear, summons, undertaking or recognizance issued to or given or entered into by the accused continues in force, subject to its terms, until a disposition in respect of the accused is made under subsection (1) unless, at the time the accused pleads guilty or is found guilty, the court, judge or justice orders that the accused be taken into custody pending such a disposition.

Effect of discharge
(3) Where a court directs under subsection (1) that an offender be discharged of an offence, the offender shall be deemed not to have been convicted of the offence except that
(a) the offender may appeal from the determination of guilt as if it were a conviction in respect of the offence;
(b) the Attorney General and, in the case of summary conviction proceedings, the informant or the informant's agent may appeal from the decision of the court not to convict the offender of the offence as if that decision were a judgment or verdict of acquittal of the offence or a dismissal of the information against the offender; and
(c) the offender may plead

Where person bound by probation order convicted of offence
(4) Where an offender who is bound by the conditions of a probation order made at a time when the offender was directed to be discharged under this section is convicted of an offence, including an offence under section 733.1, the court that made the probation order may, in addition to or in lieu of exercising its authority under subsection 732.2(5), at any time when it may take action under that subsection, revoke the discharge, convict the offender of the offence to which the discharge relates and impose any sentence that could have been imposed if the offender had been convicted at the time of discharge, and no appeal lies from a conviction under this subsection where an appeal was taken from the order directing that the offender be discharged.

R.S., 1985, c. C-46, s. 730;
1995, c. 22, s. 6;
1997, c. 18, s. 141;
2003, c. 21, s. 17.

Probation

Making of probation order
731 (1) Where a person is convicted of an offence, a court may, having regard to the age and character of the offender, the nature of the offence and the circumstances surrounding its commission,
(a) if no minimum punishment is prescribed by law, suspend the passing of sentence and direct that the offender be released on the conditions prescribed in a probation order; or
(b) in addition to fining or sentencing the offender to imprisonment for a term not exceeding two years, direct that the offender comply with the conditions prescribed in a probation order.

Idem

(2) A court may also make a probation order where it discharges an accused under subsection 730(1).
(3.1) R.S., 1985, c. C-46, s. 731;
1992, c. 1, s. 58, c. 20, s. 200;
1995, c. 22, s. 6;
1997, c. 17, s. 1.

Firearm, etc., prohibitions

731.1 (1) Before making a probation order, the court shall consider whether section 109 or 110 is applicable.

Application of section 109 or 110

(2) For greater certainty, a condition of a probation order referred to in paragraph 732.1(3)(d) does not affect the operation of section 109 or 110.
1992, c. 20, s. 201;
1995, c. 22, s. 6;
2002, c. 13, s. 73.

Intermittent sentence

732 (1) Where the court imposes a sentence of imprisonment of ninety days or less on an offender convicted of an offence, whether in default of payment of a fine or otherwise, the court may, having regard to the age and character of the offender, the nature of the offence and the circumstances surrounding its commission, and the availability of appropriate accommodation to ensure compliance with the sentence, order
(a) that the sentence be served intermittently at such times as are specified in the order; and
(b) that the offender comply with the conditions prescribed in a probation order when not in confinement during the period that the sentence is being served and, if the court so orders, on release from prison after completing the intermittent sentence.

Application to vary intermittent sentence

(2) An offender who is ordered to serve a sentence of imprisonment intermittently may, on giving notice to the prosecutor, apply to the court that imposed the sentence to allow it to be served on consecutive days.

Court may vary intermittent sentence if subsequent offence

(3) Where a court imposes a sentence of imprisonment on a person who is subject to an intermittent sentence in respect of another offence, the unexpired portion of the intermittent sentence shall be served on consecutive days unless the court otherwise orders.
R.S., 1985, c. C-46, s. 732;
1995, c. 22, s. 6.

Definitions

732.1 (1) In this section and section 732.2,
change
optional conditions

Compulsory conditions of probation order

(2) The court shall prescribe, as conditions of a probation order, that the offender do all of the following:
(a) keep the peace and be of good behaviour;
(a.1) abstain from communicating, directly or indirectly, with any victim, witness or other person identified in the order, or refrain from going to any place specified in the order, except in accordance with the conditions specified in the order that the court considers necessary, unless
(i) the victim, witness or other person gives their consent or, if the victim, witness or other person is a minor, the parent or guardian, or any other person who has the lawful care or charge of them, gives their consent, or
(ii) the court decides that, because of exceptional circumstances, it is not appropriate to impose the condition;
(b) appear before the court when required to do so by the court; and
(c) notify the court or the probation officer in advance of any change of name or address, and

promptly notify the court or the probation officer of any change of employment or occupation.
Consent
(2.1) For the purposes of subparagraph (2)(a.1)(i), the consent is valid only if it is given in writing or in the manner specified in the order.
Reasons
(2.2) If the court makes the decision described in subparagraph (2)(a.1)(ii), it shall state the reasons for the decision in the record.
Optional conditions of probation order
(3) The court may prescribe, as additional conditions of a probation order, that the offender do one or more of the following:
(a) report to a probation officer
(i) within two working days, or such longer period as the court directs, after the making of the probation order, and
(ii) thereafter, when required by the probation officer and in the manner directed by the probation officer;
(b) remain within the jurisdiction of the court unless written permission to go outside that jurisdiction is obtained from the court or the probation officer;
(c) abstain from the consumption of drugs except in accordance with a medical prescription, of alcohol or of any other intoxicating substance;
(c.1) provide, for the purpose of analysis, a sample of a bodily substance prescribed by regulation on the demand of a peace officer, a probation officer or someone designated under subsection (9) to make a demand, at the place and time and on the day specified by the person making the demand, if that person has reasonable grounds to believe that the offender has breached a condition of the order that requires them to abstain from the consumption of drugs, alcohol or any other intoxicating substance;
(c.2) provide, for the purpose of analysis, a sample of a bodily substance prescribed by regulation at regular intervals that are specified by a probation officer in a notice in Form 51 served on the offender, if a condition of the order requires the offender to abstain from the consumption of drugs, alcohol or any other intoxicating substance;
(d) abstain from owning, possessing or carrying a weapon;
(e) provide for the support or care of dependants;
(f) perform up to 240 hours of community service over a period not exceeding eighteen months;
(g) if the offender agrees, and subject to the program director's acceptance of the offender, participate actively in a treatment program approved by the province;
(g.1) where the lieutenant governor in council of the province in which the probation order is made has established a program for curative treatment in relation to the consumption of alcohol or drugs, attend at a treatment facility, designated by the lieutenant governor in council of the province, for assessment and curative treatment in relation to the consumption by the offender of alcohol or drugs that is recommended pursuant to the program;
(g.2) where the lieutenant governor in council of the province in which the probation order is made has established a program governing the use of an alcohol ignition interlock device by an offender and if the offender agrees to participate in the program, comply with the program; and
(h) comply with such other reasonable conditions as the court considers desirable, subject to any regulations made under subsection 738(2), for protecting society and for facilitating the offender's successful reintegration into the community.
Optional conditions — organization
(3.1) The court may prescribe, as additional conditions of a probation order made in respect of an organization, that the offender do one or more of the following:
(a) make restitution to a person for any loss or damage that they suffered as a result of the offence;
(b) establish policies, standards and procedures to reduce the likelihood of the organization committing a subsequent offence;
(c) communicate those policies, standards and procedures to its representatives;

(d) report to the court on the implementation of those policies, standards and procedures;
(e) identify the senior officer who is responsible for compliance with those policies, standards and procedures;
(f) provide, in the manner specified by the court, the following information to the public, namely,
(i) the offence of which the organization was convicted,
(ii) the sentence imposed by the court, and
(iii) any measures that the organization is taking — including any policies, standards and procedures established under paragraph (b) — to reduce the likelihood of it committing a subsequent offence; and
(g) comply with any other reasonable conditions that the court considers desirable to prevent the organization from committing subsequent offences or to remedy the harm caused by the offence.

Consideration — organizations
(3.2) Before making an order under paragraph (3.1)(b), a court shall consider whether it would be more appropriate for another regulatory body to supervise the development or implementation of the policies, standards and procedures referred to in that paragraph.

Form and period of order
(4) A probation order may be in Form 46, and the court that makes the probation order shall specify therein the period for which it is to remain in force.

Obligations of court
(5) The court that makes a probation order shall
(a) cause a copy of the order to be given to the offender and, on request, to the victim;
(b) explain the conditions of the order set under subsections (2) to (3.1) and the substance of section 733.1 to the offender;
(c) cause an explanation to be given to the offender of the procedure for applying under subsection 732.2(3) for a change to the optional conditions and of the substance of subsections 732.2(3) and (5); and
(d) take reasonable measures to ensure that the offender understands the order and the explanations.

For greater certainty
(6) For greater certainty, a failure to comply with subsection (5) does not affect the validity of the probation order.

Notice — samples at regular intervals
(7) The notice referred to in paragraph (3)(c.2) must specify the places and times at which and the days on which the offender must provide samples of a bodily substance under a condition described in that paragraph. The first sample may not be taken earlier than 24 hours after the offender is served with the notice, and subsequent samples must be taken at regular intervals of at least seven days.

Designations and specifications
(8) For the purposes of paragraphs (3)(c.1) and (c.2) and subject to the regulations, the Attorney General of a province or the minister of justice of a territory shall, with respect to the province or territory,
(a) designate the persons or classes of persons that may take samples of bodily substances;
(b) designate the places or classes of places at which the samples are to be taken;
(c) specify the manner in which the samples are to be taken;
(d) specify the manner in which the samples are to be analyzed;
(e) specify the manner in which the samples are to be stored, handled and destroyed;
(f) specify the manner in which the records of the results of the analysis of the samples are to be protected and destroyed;
(g) designate the persons or classes of persons that may destroy the samples; and
(h) designate the persons or classes of persons that may destroy the records of the results of the analysis of the samples.

Further designations
(9) For the purpose of paragraph (3)(c.1) and subject to the regulations, the Attorney General of a province or the minister of justice of a territory may, with respect to the province or territory,

designate persons or classes of persons to make a demand for a sample of a bodily substance.
Restriction
(10) Samples of bodily substances referred to in paragraphs (3)(c.1) and (c.2) may not be taken, analyzed, stored, handled or destroyed, and the records of the results of the analysis of the samples may not be protected or destroyed, except in accordance with the designations and specifications made under subsection (8).
Destruction of samples
(11) The Attorney General of a province or the minister of justice of a territory, or a person authorized by the Attorney General or minister, shall cause all samples of bodily substances provided under a probation order to be destroyed within the periods prescribed by regulation unless the samples are reasonably expected to be used as evidence in a proceeding for an offence under section 733.1.
Regulations
(12) The Governor in Council may make regulations
(a) prescribing bodily substances for the purposes of paragraphs (3)(c.1) and (c.2);
(b) respecting the designations and specifications referred to in subsections (8) and (9);
(c) prescribing the periods within which samples of bodily substances are to be destroyed under subsection (11); and
(d) respecting any other matters relating to the samples of bodily substances.
1995, c. 22, s. 6;
1999, c. 32, s. 6(Preamble);
2003, c. 21, s. 18;
2008, c. 18, s. 37;
2011, c. 7, s. 3;
2014, c. 21, s. 2;
2015, c. 13, s. 27.
Prohibition on use of bodily substance
732.11 (1) No person shall use a bodily substance provided under a probation order except for the purpose of determining whether an offender is complying with a condition of the order that they abstain from the consumption of drugs, alcohol or any other intoxicating substance.
Prohibition on use or disclosure of result
(2) Subject to subsection (3), no person shall use, disclose or allow the disclosure of the results of the analysis of a bodily substance provided under a probation order.
Exception
(3) The results of the analysis of a bodily substance provided under a probation order may be disclosed to the offender to whom they relate, and may also be used or disclosed in the course of an investigation of, or in a proceeding for, an offence under section 733.1 or, if the results are made anonymous, for statistical or other research purposes.
Offence
(4) Every person who contravenes subsection (1) or (2) is guilty of an offence punishable on summary conviction.
2011, c. 7, s. 4.
Coming into force of order
732.2 (1) A probation order comes into force
(a) on the date on which the order is made;
(b) where the offender is sentenced to imprisonment under paragraph 731(1)(b) or was previously sentenced to imprisonment for another offence, as soon as the offender is released from prison or, if released from prison on conditional release, at the expiration of the sentence of imprisonment; or
(c) where the offender is under a conditional sentence order, at the expiration of the conditional sentence order.
Duration of order and limit on term of order
(2) Subject to subsection (5),

(a) where an offender who is bound by a probation order is convicted of an offence, including an offence under section 733.1, or is imprisoned under paragraph 731(1)(b) in default of payment of a fine, the order continues in force except in so far as the sentence renders it impossible for the offender for the time being to comply with the order; and

(b) no probation order shall continue in force for more than three years after the date on which the order came into force.

Changes to probation order

(3) A court that makes a probation order may at any time, on application by the offender, the probation officer or the prosecutor, require the offender to appear before it and, after hearing the offender and one or both of the probation officer and the prosecutor,

(a) make any changes to the optional conditions that in the opinion of the court are rendered desirable by a change in the circumstances since those conditions were prescribed,

(b) relieve the offender, either absolutely or on such terms or for such period as the court deems desirable, of compliance with any optional condition, or

(c) decrease the period for which the probation order is to remain in force,

and the court shall thereupon endorse the probation order accordingly and, if it changes the optional conditions, inform the offender of its action and give the offender a copy of the order so endorsed.

Judge may act in chambers

(4) All the functions of the court under subsection (3) may be exercised in chambers.

Where person convicted of offence

(5) Where an offender who is bound by a probation order is convicted of an offence, including an offence under section 733.1, and

(a) the time within which an appeal may be taken against that conviction has expired and the offender has not taken an appeal,

(b) the offender has taken an appeal against that conviction and the appeal has been dismissed, or

(c) the offender has given written notice to the court that convicted the offender that the offender elects not to appeal the conviction or has abandoned the appeal, as the case may be,

in addition to any punishment that may be imposed for that offence, the court that made the probation order may, on application by the prosecutor, require the offender to appear before it and, after hearing the prosecutor and the offender,

(d) where the probation order was made under paragraph 731(1)(a), revoke the order and impose any sentence that could have been imposed if the passing of sentence had not been suspended, or

(e) make such changes to the optional conditions as the court deems desirable, or extend the period for which the order is to remain in force for such period, not exceeding one year, as the court deems desirable,

and the court shall thereupon endorse the probation order accordingly and, if it changes the optional conditions or extends the period for which the order is to remain in force, inform the offender of its action and give the offender a copy of the order so endorsed.

Compelling appearance of person bound

(6) The provisions of Parts XVI and XVIII with respect to compelling the appearance of an accused before a justice apply, with such modifications as the circumstances require, to proceedings under subsections (3) and (5).

1995, c. 22, s. 6;
2004, c. 12, s. 12(E).

Transfer of order

733 (1) Where an offender who is bound by a probation order becomes a resident of, or is convicted or discharged under section 730 of an offence including an offence under section 733.1 in, a territorial division other than the territorial division where the order was made, on the application of a probation officer, the court that made the order may, subject to subsection (1.1), transfer the order to a court in that other territorial division that would, having regard to the mode of trial of the offender, have had jurisdiction to make the order in that other territorial division if the offender had been tried and convicted there of the offence in respect of which the order was made, and the order

may thereafter be dealt with and enforced by the court to which it is so transferred in all respects as if that court had made the order.
Attorney General's consent
(1.1) The transfer may be granted only with
(a) the consent of the Attorney General of the province in which the probation order was made, if the two territorial divisions are not in the same province; or
(b) the consent of the Attorney General of Canada, if the proceedings that led to the issuance of the probation order were instituted by or on behalf of the Attorney General of Canada.
Where court unable to act
(2) Where a court that has made a probation order or to which a probation order has been transferred pursuant to subsection (1) is for any reason unable to act, the powers of that court in relation to the probation order may be exercised by any other court that has equivalent jurisdiction in the same province.
R.S., 1985, c. C-46, s. 733;
R.S., 1985, c. 24 (2nd Supp.), s. 46;
1995, c. 22, s. 6;
1999, c. 5, s. 32.
Failure to comply with probation order
733.1 (1) An offender who is bound by a probation order and who, without reasonable excuse, fails or refuses to comply with that order is guilty of
(a) an indictable offence and is liable to imprisonment for a term of not more than four years; or
(b) an offence punishable on summary conviction and is liable to imprisonment for a term of not more than 18 months, or to a fine of not more than $5000, or to both.
Where accused may be tried and punished
(2) An accused who is charged with an offence under subsection (1) may be tried and punished by any court having jurisdiction to try that offence in the place where the offence is alleged to have been committed or in the place where the accused is found, is arrested or is in custody, but where the place where the accused is found, is arrested or is in custody is outside the province in which the offence is alleged to have been committed, no proceedings in respect of that offence shall be instituted in that place without the consent of the Attorney General of that province.
1995, c. 22, s. 6;
2015, c. 23, s. 18.

Fines and Forfeiture

Power of court to impose fine
734 (1) Subject to subsection (2), a court that convicts a person, other than an organization, of an offence may fine the offender by making an order under section 734.1
(a) if the punishment for the offence does not include a minimum term of imprisonment, in addition to or in lieu of any other sanction that the court is authorized to impose; or
(b) if the punishment for the offence includes a minimum term of imprisonment, in addition to any other sanction that the court is required or authorized to impose.
Offender's ability to pay
(2) Except when the punishment for an offence includes a minimum fine or a fine is imposed in lieu of a forfeiture order, a court may fine an offender under this section only if the court is satisfied that the offender is able to pay the fine or discharge it under section 736.
Meaning of default of payment
(3) For the purposes of this section and sections 734.1 to 737, a person is in default of payment of a fine if the fine has not been paid in full by the time set out in the order made under section 734.1.
Imprisonment in default of payment
(4) Where an offender is fined under this section, a term of imprisonment, determined in accordance with subsection (5), shall be deemed to be imposed in default of payment of the fine.

Determination of term
(5) The term of imprisonment referred to in subsection (4) is the lesser of
(a) the number of days that corresponds to a fraction, rounded down to the nearest whole number, of which
(i) the numerator is the unpaid amount of the fine plus the costs and charges of committing and conveying the defaulter to prison, calculated in accordance with regulations made under subsection (7), and
(ii) the denominator is equal to eight times the provincial minimum hourly wage, at the time of default, in the province in which the fine was imposed, and
(b) the maximum term of imprisonment that the court could itself impose on conviction or, if the punishment for the offence does not include a term of imprisonment, five years in the case of an indictable offence or six months in the case of a summary conviction offence.

Moneys found on offender
(6) All or any part of a fine imposed under this section may be taken out of moneys found in the possession of the offender at the time of the arrest of the offender if the court making the order, on being satisfied that ownership of or right to possession of those moneys is not disputed by claimants other than the offender, so directs.

Provincial regulations
(7) The lieutenant governor in council of a province may make regulations respecting the calculation of the costs and charges referred to in subparagraph (5)(a)(i) and in paragraph 734.8(1)(b).

Application to other law
(8) This section and sections 734.1 to 734.8 and 736 apply to a fine imposed under any Act of Parliament, except that subsections (4) and (5) do not apply if the term of imprisonment in default of payment of the fine provided for in that Act or regulation is
(a) calculated by a different method; or
(b) specified, either as a minimum or a maximum.

R.S., 1985, c. C-46, s. 734;
R.S., 1985, c. 27 (1st Supp.), s. 161;
1995, c. 22, s. 6;
1999, c. 5, s. 33;
2003, c. 21, s. 19;
2008, c. 18, s. 38.

Terms of order imposing fine
734.1 A court that fines an offender under section 734 shall do so by making an order that clearly sets out
(a) the amount of the fine;
(b) the manner in which the fine is to be paid;
(c) the time or times by which the fine, or any portion thereof, must be paid; and
(d) such other terms respecting the payment of the fine as the court deems appropriate.

1995, c. 22, s. 6.

Obligations of court
734.2 (1) A court that makes an order under section 734.1 shall
(a) cause a copy of the order to be given to the offender;
(b) explain the substance of sections 734 to 734.8 and 736 to the offender;
(c) cause an explanation to be given to the offender of the procedure for applying under section 734.3 for a change to the optional conditions and of any available fine option programs referred to in section 736 as well as the procedure to apply for admission to them; and
(d) take reasonable measures to ensure that the offender understands the order and the explanations.

For greater certainty
(2) For greater certainty, a failure to comply with subsection (1) does not affect the validity of the order.

1995, c. 22, s. 6;

2008, c. 18, s. 39.
Change in terms of order
734.3 A court that makes an order under section 734.1, or a person designated either by name or by title of office by that court, may, on application by or on behalf of the offender, subject to any rules made by the court under section 482 or 482.1, change any term of the order except the amount of the fine, and any reference in this section and sections 734, 734.1, 734.2 and 734.6 to an order shall be read as including a reference to the order as changed under this section.

1995, c. 22, s. 6;
2002, c. 13, s. 74.
Proceeds to go to provincial treasurer
734.4 (1) Where a fine or forfeiture is imposed or a recognizance is forfeited and no provision, other than this section, is made by law for the application of the proceeds thereof, the proceeds belong to Her Majesty in right of the province in which the fine or forfeiture was imposed or the recognizance was forfeited, and shall be paid by the person who receives them to the treasurer of that province.
Proceeds to go to Receiver General for Canada
(2) Where
(a) a fine or forfeiture is imposed
(i) in respect of a contravention of a revenue law of Canada,
(ii) in respect of a breach of duty or malfeasance in office by an officer or employee of the Government of Canada, or
(iii) in respect of any proceedings instituted at the instance of the Government of Canada in which that government bears the costs of prosecution, or
(b) a recognizance in connection with proceedings mentioned in paragraph (a) is forfeited,
the proceeds of the fine, forfeiture or recognizance belong to Her Majesty in right of Canada and shall be paid by the person who receives them to the Receiver General.
Direction for payment to municipality
(3) Where a provincial, municipal or local authority bears, in whole or in part, the expense of administering the law under which a fine or forfeiture is imposed or under which proceedings are taken in which a recognizance is forfeited,
(a) the lieutenant governor in council of a province may direct that the proceeds of a fine, forfeiture or recognizance that belongs to Her Majesty in right of the province shall be paid to that authority; and
(b) the Governor in Council may direct that the proceeds of a fine, forfeiture or recognizance that belongs to Her Majesty in right of Canada shall be paid to that authority.

1995, c. 22, s. 6.
Licences, permits, etc.
734.5 If an offender is in default of payment of a fine,
(a) where the proceeds of the fine belong to Her Majesty in right of a province by virtue of subsection 734.4(1), the person responsible, by or under an Act of the legislature of the province, for issuing, renewing or suspending a licence, permit or other similar instrument in relation to the offender may refuse to issue or renew or may suspend the licence, permit or other instrument until the fine is paid in full, proof of which lies on the offender; or
(b) where the proceeds of the fine belong to Her Majesty in right of Canada by virtue of subsection 734.4(2), the person responsible, by or under an Act of Parliament, for issuing or renewing a licence, permit or other similar instrument in relation to the offender may refuse to issue or renew or may suspend the licence, permit or other instrument until the fine is paid in full, proof of which lies on the offender.

1995, c. 22, s. 6;
1999, c. 5, s. 34.
Civil enforcement of fines, forfeiture
734.6 (1) Where
(a) an offender is in default of payment of a fine, or

(b) a forfeiture imposed by law is not paid as required by the order imposing it,

then, in addition to any other method provided by law for recovering the fine or forfeiture,

(c) the Attorney General of the province to whom the proceeds of the fine or forfeiture belong, or

(d) the Attorney General of Canada, where the proceeds of the fine or forfeiture belong to Her Majesty in right of Canada,

may, by filing the order, enter as a judgment the amount of the fine or forfeiture, and costs, if any, in any civil court in Canada that has jurisdiction to enter a judgment for that amount.

Effect of filing order

(2) An order that is entered as a judgment under this section is enforceable in the same manner as if it were a judgment obtained by the Attorney General of the province or the Attorney General of Canada, as the case may be, in civil proceedings.

1995, c. 22, s. 6.

Warrant of committal

734.7 (1) Where time has been allowed for payment of a fine, the court shall not issue a warrant of committal in default of payment of the fine

(a) until the expiration of the time allowed for payment of the fine in full; and

(b) unless the court is satisfied

(i) that the mechanisms provided by sections 734.5 and 734.6 are not appropriate in the circumstances, or

(ii) that the offender has, without reasonable excuse, refused to pay the fine or discharge it under section 736.

Reasons for committal

(2) Where no time has been allowed for payment of a fine and a warrant committing the offender to prison for default of payment of the fine is issued, the court shall state in the warrant the reason for immediate committal.

Period of imprisonment

(2.1) The period of imprisonment in default of payment of the fine shall be specified in a warrant of committal referred to in subsection (1) or (2).

Compelling appearance of person bound

(3) The provisions of Parts XVI and XVIII with respect to compelling the appearance of an accused before a justice apply, with such modifications as the circumstances require, to proceedings under paragraph (1)(b).

Effect of imprisonment

(4) The imprisonment of an offender for default of payment of a fine terminates the operation of sections 734.5 and 734.6 in relation to that fine.

1995, c. 22, s. 6;

1999, c. 5, s. 35.

Definition of

penalty

734.8 (1) In this section,

penalty

(a) the fine, and

(b) the costs and charges of committing and conveying the defaulter to prison, calculated in accordance with regulations made under subsection 734(7).

Reduction of imprisonment on part payment

(2) The term of imprisonment in default of payment of a fine shall, on payment of a part of the penalty, whether the payment was made before or after the execution of a warrant of committal, be reduced by the number of days that bears the same proportion to the number of days in the term as the part paid bears to the total penalty.

Minimum that can be accepted

(3) No amount offered in part payment of a penalty shall be accepted after the execution of a warrant of committal unless it is sufficient to secure a reduction of sentence of one day, or a whole number

multiple of one day, and no part payment shall be accepted until any fee that is payable in respect of the warrant or its execution has been paid.

To whom payment made

(4) Payment may be made under this section to the person that the Attorney General directs or, if the offender is imprisoned, to the person who has lawful custody of the prisoner or to any other person that the Attorney General directs.

Application of money paid

(5) A payment under this section shall be applied firstly to the payment in full of costs and charges, secondly to the payment in full of any victim surcharge imposed under section 737, and then to payment of any part of the fine that remains unpaid.

1995, c. 22, s. 6;
1999, c. 5, s. 36, c. 25, s. 19(Preamble).

Fines on organizations

735 (1) An organization that is convicted of an offence is liable, in lieu of any imprisonment that is prescribed as punishment for that offence, to be fined in an amount, except where otherwise provided by law,

(a) that is in the discretion of the court, where the offence is an indictable offence; or

(b) not exceeding one hundred thousand dollars, where the offence is a summary conviction offence.

Application of certain provisions — fines

(1.1) A court that imposes a fine under subsection (1) or under any other Act of Parliament shall make an order that clearly sets out

(a) the amount of the fine;

(b) the manner in which the fine is to be paid;

(c) the time or times by which the fine, or any portion of it, must be paid; and

(d) any other terms respecting the payment of the fine that the court deems appropriate.

Effect of filing order

(2) Section 734.6 applies, with any modifications that are required, when an organization fails to pay the fine in accordance with the terms of the order.

R.S., 1985, c. C-46, s. 735;
R.S., 1985, c. 1 (4th Supp.), s. 18(F), c. 23 (4th Supp.), s. 7;
1995, c. 22, s. 6;
1999, c. 5, s. 37;
2003, c. 21, s. 20.

Fine option program

736 (1) An offender who is fined under section 734 may, whether or not the offender is serving a term of imprisonment imposed in default of payment of the fine, discharge the fine in whole or in part by earning credits for work performed during a period not greater than two years in a program established for that purpose by the lieutenant governor in council

(a) of the province in which the fine was imposed, or

(b) of the province in which the offender resides, where an appropriate agreement is in effect between the government of that province and the government of the province in which the fine was imposed,

if the offender is admissible to such a program.

Credits and other matters

(2) A program referred to in subsection (1) shall determine the rate at which credits are earned and may provide for the manner of crediting any amounts earned against the fine and any other matters necessary for or incidental to carrying out the program.

Deemed payment

(3) Credits earned for work performed as provided by subsection (1) shall, for the purposes of this Act, be deemed to be payment in respect of a fine.

Federal-provincial agreement

(4) Where, by virtue of subsection 734.4(2), the proceeds of a fine belong to Her Majesty in right of

Canada, an offender may discharge the fine in whole or in part in a fine option program of a province pursuant to subsection (1), where an appropriate agreement is in effect between the government of the province and the Government of Canada.

R.S., 1985, c. C-46, s. 736;

R.S., 1985, c. 27 (1st Supp.), s. 162, c. 1 (4th Supp.), s. 18(F);

1992, c. 1, s. 60(F);

1995, c. 22, s. 6.

Victim surcharge

737 (1) An offender who is convicted, or discharged under section 730, of an offence under this Act or the

Controlled Drugs and Substances Act

Amount of surcharge

(2) Subject to subsection (3), the amount of the victim surcharge in respect of an offence is

(a) 30 per cent of any fine that is imposed on the offender for the offence; or

(b) if no fine is imposed on the offender for the offence,

(i) $100 in the case of an offence punishable by summary conviction, and

(ii) $200 in the case of an offence punishable by indictment.

Increase in surcharge

(3) The court may order an offender to pay a victim surcharge in an amount exceeding that set out in subsection (2) if the court considers it appropriate in the circumstances and is satisfied that the offender is able to pay the higher amount.

Time for payment

(4) The victim surcharge imposed in respect of an offence is payable within the time established by the lieutenant governor in council of the province in which the surcharge is imposed. If no time has been so established, the surcharge is payable within a reasonable time after its imposition.

(5) and (6) Amounts applied to aid victims

(7) A victim surcharge imposed under subsection (1) shall be applied for the purposes of providing such assistance to victims of offences as the lieutenant governor in council of the province in which the surcharge is imposed may direct from time to time.

Notice

(8) The court shall cause to be given to the offender a written notice setting out

(a) the amount of the victim surcharge;

(b) the manner in which the victim surcharge is to be paid;

(c) the time by which the victim surcharge must be paid; and

(d) the procedure for applying for a change in any terms referred to in paragraphs (b) and (c) in accordance with section 734.3.

Enforcement

(9) Subsections 734(3) to (7) and sections 734.3, 734.5, 734.7, 734.8 and 736 apply, with any modifications that the circumstances require, in respect of a victim surcharge imposed under subsection (1) and, in particular,

(a) a reference in any of those provisions to "fine", other than in subsection 734.8(5), must be read as if it were a reference to "victim surcharge"; and

(b) the notice provided under subsection (8) is deemed to be an order made under section 734.1.

(10) R.S., 1985, c. C-46, s. 737;

1995, c. 22, ss. 6, 18;

1996, c. 19, s. 75;

1999, c. 5, s. 38, c. 25, s. 20(Preamble);

2013, c. 11, s. 3;

2015, c. 13, s. 28.

Restitution

Court to consider restitution order
737.1 (1) If an offender is convicted or is discharged under section 730 of an offence, the court that sentences or discharges the offender, in addition to any other measure imposed on the offender, shall consider making a restitution order under section 738 or 739.
Inquiry by court
(2) As soon as feasible after a finding of guilt and in any event before imposing the sentence, the court shall inquire of the prosecutor if reasonable steps have been taken to provide the victims with an opportunity to indicate whether they are seeking restitution for their losses and damages, the amount of which must be readily ascertainable.
Adjournment
(3) On application of the prosecutor or on its own motion, the court may adjourn the proceedings to permit the victims to indicate whether they are seeking restitution or to establish their losses and damages, if the court is satisfied that the adjournment would not interfere with the proper administration of justice.
Form
(4) Victims and other persons may indicate whether they are seeking restitution by completing Form 34.1 in Part XXVIII or a form approved for that purpose by the lieutenant governor in council of the province in which the court is exercising its jurisdiction or by using any other method approved by the court, and, if they are seeking restitution, shall establish their losses and damages, the amount of which must be readily ascertainable, in the same manner.
Reasons
(5) If a victim seeks restitution and the court does not make a restitution order, it shall include in the record a statement of the court's reasons for not doing so.
2015, c. 13, s. 29.
Restitution to victims of offences
738 (1) Where an offender is convicted or discharged under section 730 of an offence, the court imposing sentence on or discharging the offender may, on application of the Attorney General or on its own motion, in addition to any other measure imposed on the offender, order that the offender make restitution to another person as follows:
(a) in the case of damage to, or the loss or destruction of, the property of any person as a result of the commission of the offence or the arrest or attempted arrest of the offender, by paying to the person an amount not exceeding the replacement value of the property as of the date the order is imposed, less the value of any part of the property that is returned to that person as of the date it is returned, where the amount is readily ascertainable;
(b) in the case of bodily or psychological harm to any person as a result of the commission of the offence or the arrest or attempted arrest of the offender, by paying to the person an amount not exceeding all pecuniary damages incurred as a result of the harm, including loss of income or support, if the amount is readily ascertainable;
(c) in the case of bodily harm or threat of bodily harm to the offender's spouse or common-law partner or child, or any other person, as a result of the commission of the offence or the arrest or attempted arrest of the offender, where the spouse or common-law partner, child or other person was a member of the offender's household at the relevant time, by paying to the person in question, independently of any amount ordered to be paid under paragraphs (a) and (b), an amount not exceeding actual and reasonable expenses incurred by that person, as a result of moving out of the offender's household, for temporary housing, food, child care and transportation, where the amount is readily ascertainable;
(d) in the case of an offence under section 402.2 or 403, by paying to a person who, as a result of the offence, incurs expenses to re-establish their identity, including expenses to replace their identity documents and to correct their credit history and credit rating, an amount that is not more than the amount of those expenses, to the extent that they are reasonable, if the amount is readily ascertainable; and
(e) in the case of an offence under subsection 162.1(1), by paying to a person who, as a result of the

offence, incurs expenses to remove the intimate image from the Internet or other digital network, an amount that is not more than the amount of those expenses, to the extent that they are reasonable, if the amount is readily ascertainable.

Regulations

(2) The lieutenant governor in council of a province may make regulations precluding the inclusion of provisions on enforcement of restitution orders as an optional condition of a probation order or of a conditional sentence order.

R.S., 1985, c. C-46, s. 738;
1995, c. 22, s. 6;
2000, c. 12, s. 95;
2005, c. 43, s. 7;
2009, c. 28, s. 11;
2014, c. 31, s. 24.

Restitution to persons acting in good faith

739 Where an offender is convicted or discharged under section 730 of an offence and
(a) any property obtained as a result of the commission of the offence has been conveyed or transferred for valuable consideration to a person acting in good faith and without notice, or
(b) the offender has borrowed money on the security of that property from a person acting in good faith and without notice,
the court may, where that property has been returned to the lawful owner or the person who had lawful possession of that property at the time the offence was committed, order the offender to pay as restitution to the person referred to in paragraph (a) or (b) an amount not exceeding the amount of consideration for that property or the total amount outstanding in respect of the loan, as the case may be.

R.S., 1985, c. C-46, s. 739;
R.S., 1985, c. 27 (1st Supp.), s. 163, c. 1 (4th Supp.), s. 18(F);
1995, c. 22, s. 6.

Ability to pay

739.1 The offender's financial means or ability to pay does not prevent the court from making an order under section 738 or 739.

2015, c. 13, s. 30.

Payment under order

739.2 In making an order under section 738 or 739, the court shall require the offender to pay the full amount specified in the order by the day specified in the order, unless the court is of the opinion that the amount should be paid in instalments, in which case the court shall set out a periodic payment scheme in the order.

2015, c. 13, s. 30.

More than one person

739.3 An order under section 738 or 739 may be made in respect of more than one person, in which case the order must specify the amount that is payable to each person. The order may also specify the order of priority in which those persons are to be paid.

2015, c. 13, s. 30.

Public authority

739.4 (1) On the request of a person in whose favour an order under section 738 or 739 would be made, the court may make the order in favour of a public authority, designated by the regulations, who is to be responsible for enforcing the order and remitting to the person making the request all amounts received under it.

Orders

(2) The lieutenant governor in council of a province may, by order, designate any person or body as a public authority for the purpose of subsection (1).

2015, c. 13, s. 30.

Priority to restitution

740 Where the court finds it applicable and appropriate in the circumstances of a case to make, in relation to an offender, an order of restitution under section 738 or 739, and
(a) an order of forfeiture under this or any other Act of Parliament may be made in respect of property that is the same as property in respect of which the order of restitution may be made, or
(b) the court is considering ordering the offender to pay a fine and it appears to the court that the offender would not have the means or ability to comply with both the order of restitution and the order to pay the fine,
the court shall first make the order of restitution and shall then consider whether and to what extent an order of forfeiture or an order to pay a fine is appropriate in the circumstances.
R.S., 1985, c. C-46, s. 740;
1995, c. 22, s. 6.

Enforcing restitution order

741 (1) An offender who fails to pay all of the amount that is ordered to be paid under section 732.1, 738, 739 or 742.3 by the day specified in the order or who fails to make a periodic payment required under the order is in default of the order and the person to whom the amount, or the periodic payment, as the case may be, was to be made may, by filing the order, enter as a judgment any amount ordered to be paid that remains unpaid under the order in any civil court in Canada that has jurisdiction to enter a judgment for that amount, and that judgment is enforceable against the offender in the same manner as if it were a judgment rendered against the offender in that court in civil proceedings.

Moneys found on offender

(2) All or any part of an amount that is ordered to be paid under section 738 or 739 may be taken out of moneys found in the possession of the offender at the time of the arrest of the offender if the court making the order, on being satisfied that ownership of or right to possession of those moneys is not disputed by claimants other than the offender, so directs.
R.S., 1985, c. C-46, s. 741;
R.S., 1985, c. 27 (1st Supp.), s. 164;
1995, c. 22, s. 6;
2004, c. 12, s. 13;
2015, c. 13, s. 31.

Notice of orders of restitution

741.1 If a court makes an order of restitution under section 738 or 739, it shall cause notice of the content of the order, or a copy of the order, to be given to the person to whom the restitution is ordered to be paid, and if it is to be paid to a public authority designated by regulations made under subsection 739.4(2), to the public authority and the person to whom the public authority is to remit amounts received under the order.
R.S., 1985, c. 24 (2nd Supp.), s. 47;
1992, c. 11, s. 14, c. 20, s. 202;
1995, c. 19, s. 37, c. 22, s. 6;
2015, c. 13, s. 32.

Civil remedy not affected

741.2 A civil remedy for an act or omission is not affected by reason only that an order for restitution under section 738 or 739 has been made in respect of that act or omission.
1992, c. 20, s. 203;
1995, c. 22, s. 6, c. 42, s. 75.

Conditional Sentence of Imprisonment

Definitions

742 In sections 742.1 to 742.7,
change
optional conditions

supervisor
R.S., 1985, c. C-46, s. 742;
R.S., 1985, c. 27 (1st Supp.), s. 165;
1992, c. 11, s. 15;
1995, c. 22, s. 6.

Imposing of conditional sentence

742.1 If a person is convicted of an offence and the court imposes a sentence of imprisonment of less than two years, the court may, for the purpose of supervising the offender's behaviour in the community, order that the offender serve the sentence in the community, subject to the conditions imposed under section 742.3, if

(a) the court is satisfied that the service of the sentence in the community would not endanger the safety of the community and would be consistent with the fundamental purpose and principles of sentencing set out in sections 718 to 718.2;

(b) the offence is not an offence punishable by a minimum term of imprisonment;

(c) the offence is not an offence, prosecuted by way of indictment, for which the maximum term of imprisonment is 14 years or life;

(d) the offence is not a terrorism offence, or a criminal organization offence, prosecuted by way of indictment, for which the maximum term of imprisonment is 10 years or more;

(e) the offence is not an offence, prosecuted by way of indictment, for which the maximum term of imprisonment is 10 years, that

(i) resulted in bodily harm,

(ii) involved the import, export, trafficking or production of drugs, or

(iii) involved the use of a weapon; and

(f) the offence is not an offence, prosecuted by way of indictment, under any of the following provisions:

(i) section 144 (prison breach),

(ii) section 264 (criminal harassment),

(iii) section 271 (sexual assault),

(iv) section 279 (kidnapping),

(v) section 279.02 (trafficking in persons — material benefit),

(vi) section 281 (abduction of person under fourteen),

(vii) section 333.1 (motor vehicle theft),

(viii) paragraph 334(a) (theft over $5000),

(ix) paragraph 348(1)(e) (breaking and entering a place other than a dwelling-house),

(x) section 349 (being unlawfully in a dwelling-house), and

(xi) section 435 (arson for fraudulent purpose).

1992, c. 11, s. 16;
1995, c. 19, s. 38, c. 22, s. 6;
1997, c. 18, s. 107.1;
2007, c. 12, s. 1;
2012, c. 1, s. 34.

Firearm, etc., prohibitions

742.2 (1) Before imposing a conditional sentence under section 742.1, the court shall consider whether section 109 or 110 is applicable.

Application of section 109 or 110

(2) For greater certainty, a condition of a conditional sentence order referred to in paragraph 742.3(2)(b) does not affect the operation of section 109 or 110.

1995, c. 22, s. 6;
2002, c. 13, s. 75;
2004, c. 12, s. 14(E).

Compulsory conditions of conditional sentence order

742.3 (1) The court shall prescribe, as conditions of a conditional sentence order, that the offender do

all of the following:
(a) keep the peace and be of good behaviour;
(b) appear before the court when required to do so by the court;
(c) report to a supervisor
(i) within two working days, or such longer period as the court directs, after the making of the conditional sentence order, and
(ii) thereafter, when required by the supervisor and in the manner directed by the supervisor;
(d) remain within the jurisdiction of the court unless written permission to go outside that jurisdiction is obtained from the court or the supervisor; and
(e) notify the court or the supervisor in advance of any change of name or address, and promptly notify the court or the supervisor of any change of employment or occupation.

Abstain from communicating

(1.1) The court shall prescribe, as a condition of a conditional sentence order, that the offender abstain from communicating, directly or indirectly, with any victim, witness or other person identified in the order, or refrain from going to any place specified in the order, except in accordance with the conditions specified in the order that the court considers necessary, unless
(a) the victim, witness or other person gives their consent or, if the victim, witness or other person is a minor, the parent or guardian, or any other person who has the lawful care or charge of them, gives their consent; or
(b) the court decides that, because of exceptional circumstances, it is not appropriate to impose the condition.

Consent

(1.2) For the purposes of paragraph (1.1)(a), the consent is valid only if it is given in writing or in the manner specified in the order.

Reasons

(1.3) If the court makes the decision described in paragraph (1.1)(b), it shall state the reasons for the decision in the record.

Optional conditions of conditional sentence order

(2) The court may prescribe, as additional conditions of a conditional sentence order, that the offender do one or more of the following:
(a) abstain from the consumption of drugs except in accordance with a medical prescription, of alcohol or of any other intoxicating substance;
(a.1) provide, for the purpose of analysis, a sample of a bodily substance prescribed by regulation on the demand of a peace officer, the supervisor or someone designated under subsection (7) to make a demand, at the place and time and on the day specified by the person making the demand, if that person has reasonable grounds to suspect that the offender has breached a condition of the order that requires them to abstain from the consumption of drugs, alcohol or any other intoxicating substance;
(a.2) provide, for the purpose of analysis, a sample of a bodily substance prescribed by regulation at regular intervals that are specified by the supervisor in a notice in Form 51 served on the offender, if a condition of the order requires the offender to abstain from the consumption of drugs, alcohol or any other intoxicating substance;
(b) abstain from owning, possessing or carrying a weapon;
(c) provide for the support or care of dependants;
(d) perform up to 240 hours of community service over a period not exceeding eighteen months;
(e) attend a treatment program approved by the province; and
(f) comply with such other reasonable conditions as the court considers desirable, subject to any regulations made under subsection 738(2), for securing the good conduct of the offender and for preventing a repetition by the offender of the same offence or the commission of other offences.

Obligations of court

(3) A court that makes an order under this section shall
(a) cause a copy of the order to be given to the offender and, on request, to the victim;
(b) explain the substance of subsection (1) and sections 742.4 and 742.6 to the offender;

(c) cause an explanation to be given to the offender of the procedure for applying under section 742.4 for a change to the optional conditions; and
(d) take reasonable measures to ensure that the offender understands the order and the explanations.

For greater certainty

(4) For greater certainty, a failure to comply with subsection (3) does not affect the validity of the order.

Notice — samples at regular intervals

(5) The notice referred to in paragraph (2)(a.2) must specify the places and times at which and the days on which the offender must provide samples of a bodily substance under a condition described in that paragraph. The first sample may not be taken earlier than 24 hours after the offender is served with the notice, and subsequent samples must be taken at regular intervals of at least seven days.

Designations and specifications

(6) For the purposes of paragraphs (2)(a.1) and (a.2) and subject to the regulations, the Attorney General of a province or the minister of justice of a territory shall, with respect to the province or territory,
(a) designate the persons or classes of persons that may take samples of bodily substances;
(b) designate the places or classes of places at which the samples are to be taken;
(c) specify the manner in which the samples are to be taken;
(d) specify the manner in which the samples are to be analyzed;
(e) specify the manner in which the samples are to be stored, handled and destroyed;
(f) specify the manner in which the records of the results of the analysis of the samples are to be protected and destroyed;
(g) designate the persons or classes of persons that may destroy the samples; and
(h) designate the persons or classes of persons that may destroy the records of the results of the analysis of the samples.

Further designations

(7) For the purpose of paragraph (2)(a.1) and subject to the regulations, the Attorney General of a province or the minister of justice of a territory may, with respect to the province or territory, designate persons or classes of persons to make a demand for a sample of a bodily substance.

Restriction

(8) Samples of bodily substances referred to in paragraphs (2)(a.1) and (a.2) may not be taken, analyzed, stored, handled or destroyed, and the records of the results of the analysis of the samples may not be protected or destroyed, except in accordance with the designations and specifications made under subsection (6).

Destruction of samples

(9) The Attorney General of a province or the minister of justice of a territory, or a person authorized by the Attorney General or minister, shall cause all samples of bodily substances provided under a conditional sentence order to be destroyed within the periods prescribed by regulation, unless the samples are reasonably expected to be used as evidence in proceedings under section 742.6.

Regulations

(10) The Governor in Council may make regulations
(a) prescribing bodily substances for the purposes of paragraphs (2)(a.1) and (a.2);
(b) respecting the designations and specifications referred to in subsections (6) and (7);
(c) prescribing the periods within which samples of bodily substances are to be destroyed under subsection (9); and
(d) respecting any other matters relating to the samples of bodily substances.

1995, c. 22, s. 6;
2008, c. 18, s. 40;
2011, c. 7, s. 5;
2014, c. 21, s. 3;
2015, c. 13, s. 33.

Prohibition on use of bodily substance

742.31 (1) No person shall use a bodily substance provided under a conditional sentence order except for the purpose of determining whether an offender is complying with a condition of the order that they abstain from the consumption of drugs, alcohol or any other intoxicating substance.

Prohibition on use or disclosure of result

(2) Subject to subsection (3), no person shall use, disclose or allow the disclosure of the results of the analysis of a bodily substance provided under a conditional sentence order.

Exception

(3) The results of the analysis of a bodily substance provided under a conditional sentence order may be disclosed to the offender to whom they relate, and may also be used or disclosed in the course of proceedings under section 742.6 or, if the results are made anonymous, for statistical or other research purposes.

Offence

(4) Every person who contravenes subsection (1) or (2) is guilty of an offence punishable on summary conviction.

2011, c. 7, s. 6.

Supervisor may propose changes to optional conditions

742.4 (1) Where an offender's supervisor is of the opinion that a change in circumstances makes a change to the optional conditions desirable, the supervisor shall give written notification of the proposed change, and the reasons for it, to the offender, to the prosecutor and to the court.

Hearing

(2) Within seven days after receiving a notification referred to in subsection (1),

(a) the offender or the prosecutor may request the court to hold a hearing to consider the proposed change, or

(b) the court may, of its own initiative, order that a hearing be held to consider the proposed change, and a hearing so requested or ordered shall be held within thirty days after the receipt by the court of the notification referred to in subsection (1).

Decision at hearing

(3) At a hearing held pursuant to subsection (2), the court

(a) shall approve or refuse to approve the proposed change; and

(b) may make any other change to the optional conditions that the court deems appropriate.

Where no hearing requested or ordered

(4) Where no request or order for a hearing is made within the time period stipulated in subsection (2), the proposed change takes effect fourteen days after the receipt by the court of the notification referred to in subsection (1), and the supervisor shall so notify the offender and file proof of that notification with the court.

Changes proposed by offender or prosecutor

(5) Subsections (1) and (3) apply, with such modifications as the circumstances require, in respect of a change proposed by the offender or the prosecutor to the optional conditions, and in all such cases a hearing must be held, and must be held within thirty days after the receipt by the court of the notification referred to in subsection (1).

Judge may act in chambers

(6) All the functions of the court under this section may be exercised in chambers.

1995, c. 22, s. 6;

1999, c. 5, s. 39.

Transfer of order

742.5 (1) Where an offender who is bound by a conditional sentence order becomes a resident of a territorial division, other than the territorial division where the order was made, on the application of a supervisor, the court that made the order may, subject to subsection (1.1), transfer the order to a court in that other territorial division that would, having regard to the mode of trial of the offender, have had jurisdiction to make the order in that other territorial division if the offender had been tried and convicted there of the offence in respect of which the order was made, and the order may thereafter be dealt with and enforced by the court to which it is so transferred in all respects as if that

court had made the order.
Attorney General's consent
(1.1) The transfer may be granted only with
(a) the consent of the Attorney General of the province in which the conditional sentence order was made, if the two territorial divisions are not in the same province; or
(b) the consent of the Attorney General of Canada, if the proceedings that led to the issuance of the conditional sentence order were instituted by or on behalf of the Attorney General of Canada.
Where court unable to act
(2) Where a court that has made a conditional sentence order or to which a conditional sentence order has been transferred pursuant to subsection (1) is for any reason unable to act, the powers of that court in relation to the conditional sentence order may be exercised by any other court that has equivalent jurisdiction in the same province.
1995, c. 22, s. 6;
1999, c. 5, s. 40.
Procedure on breach of condition
742.6 (1) For the purpose of proceedings under this section,
(a) the provisions of Parts XVI and XVIII with respect to compelling the appearance of an accused before a justice apply, with any modifications that the circumstances require, and any reference in those Parts to committing an offence shall be read as a reference to breaching a condition of a conditional sentence order;
(b) the powers of arrest for breach of a condition are those that apply to an indictable offence, with any modifications that the circumstances require, and subsection 495(2) does not apply;
(c) despite paragraph (a), if an allegation of breach of condition is made, the proceeding is commenced by
(i) the issuance of a warrant for the arrest of the offender for the alleged breach,
(ii) the arrest without warrant of the offender for the alleged breach, or
(iii) the compelling of the offender's appearance in accordance with paragraph (d);
(d) if the offender is already detained or before a court, the offender's appearance may be compelled under the provisions referred to in paragraph (a);
(e) if an offender is arrested for the alleged breach, the peace officer who makes the arrest, the officer in charge or a judge or justice may release the offender and the offender's appearance may be compelled under the provisions referred to in paragraph (a); and
(f) any judge of a superior court of criminal jurisdiction or of a court of criminal jurisdiction or any justice of the peace may issue a warrant to arrest no matter which court, judge or justice sentenced the offender, and the provisions that apply to the issuance of telewarrants apply, with any modifications that the circumstances require, as if a breach of condition were an indictable offence.
Interim release
(2) For the purpose of the application of section 515, the release from custody of an offender who is detained on the basis of an alleged breach of a condition of a conditional sentence order shall be governed by subsection 515(6).
Hearing
(3) The hearing of an allegation of a breach of condition shall be commenced within thirty days, or as soon thereafter as is practicable, after
(a) the offender's arrest; or
(b) the compelling of the offender's appearance in accordance with paragraph (1)(d).
Place
(3.1) The allegation may be heard by any court having jurisdiction to hear that allegation in the place where the breach is alleged to have been committed or the offender is found, arrested or in custody.
Attorney General's consent
(3.2) If the place where the offender is found, arrested or in custody is outside the province in which the breach is alleged to have been committed, no proceedings in respect of that breach shall be instituted in that place without

(a) the consent of the Attorney General of the province in which the breach is alleged to have been committed; or
(b) the consent of the Attorney General of Canada, if the proceedings that led to the issuance of the conditional sentence order were instituted by or on behalf of the Attorney General of Canada.

Adjournment
(3.3) A judge may, at any time during a hearing of an allegation of breach of condition, adjourn the hearing for a reasonable period.

Report of supervisor
(4) An allegation of a breach of condition must be supported by a written report of the supervisor, which report must include, where appropriate, signed statements of witnesses.

Admission of report on notice of intent
(5) The report is admissible in evidence if the party intending to produce it has, before the hearing, given the offender reasonable notice and a copy of the report.

(6) and (7) Requiring attendance of supervisor or witness
(8) The offender may, with leave of the court, require the attendance, for cross-examination, of the supervisor or of any witness whose signed statement is included in the report.

Powers of court
(9) Where the court is satisfied, on a balance of probabilities, that the offender has without reasonable excuse, the proof of which lies on the offender, breached a condition of the conditional sentence order, the court may
(a) take no action;
(b) change the optional conditions;
(c) suspend the conditional sentence order and direct
(i) that the offender serve in custody a portion of the unexpired sentence, and
(ii) that the conditional sentence order resume on the offender's release from custody, either with or without changes to the optional conditions; or
(d) terminate the conditional sentence order and direct that the offender be committed to custody until the expiration of the sentence.

Warrant or arrest — suspension of running of conditional sentence order
(10) The running of a conditional sentence order imposed on an offender is suspended during the period that ends with the determination of whether a breach of condition had occurred and begins with the earliest of
(a) the issuance of a warrant for the arrest of the offender for the alleged breach,
(b) the arrest without warrant of the offender for the alleged breach, and
(c) the compelling of the offender's appearance in accordance with paragraph (1)(d).

Conditions continue
(11) If the offender is not detained in custody during any period referred to in subsection (10), the conditions of the order continue to apply, with any changes made to them under section 742.4, and any subsequent breach of those conditions may be dealt with in accordance with this section.

Detention under s. 515(6)
(12) A conditional sentence order referred to in subsection (10) starts running again on the making of an order to detain the offender in custody under subsection 515(6) and, unless section 742.7 applies, continues running while the offender is detained under the order.

Earned remission does not apply
(13) Section 6 of the
Prisons and Reformatories Act

Unreasonable delay in execution
(14) Despite subsection (10), if there was unreasonable delay in the execution of a warrant, the court may, at any time, order that any period between the issuance and execution of the warrant that it considers appropriate in the interests of justice is deemed to be time served under the conditional sentence order unless the period has been so deemed under subsection (15).

Allegation dismissed or reasonable excuse

(15) If the allegation is withdrawn or dismissed or the offender is found to have had a reasonable excuse for the breach, the sum of the following periods is deemed to be time served under the conditional sentence order:
(a) any period for which the running of the conditional sentence order was suspended; and
(b) if subsection (12) applies, a period equal to one half of the period that the conditional sentence order runs while the offender is detained under an order referred to in that subsection.

Powers of court
(16) If a court is satisfied, on a balance of probabilities, that the offender has without reasonable excuse, the proof of which lies on the offender, breached a condition of the conditional sentence order, the court may, in exceptional cases and in the interests of justice, order that some or all of the period of suspension referred to in subsection (10) is deemed to be time served under the conditional sentence order.

Considerations
(17) In exercising its discretion under subsection (16), a court shall consider
(a) the circumstances and seriousness of the breach;
(b) whether not making the order would cause the offender undue hardship based on the offender's individual circumstances; and
(c) the period for which the offender was subject to conditions while the running of the conditional sentence order was suspended and whether the offender complied with those conditions during that period.
1995, c. 22, s. 6;
1999, c. 5, s. 41;
2004, c. 12, s. 15(E);
2008, c. 18, s. 41.

If person imprisoned for new offence
742.7 (1) If an offender who is subject to a conditional sentence order is imprisoned as a result of a sentence imposed for another offence, whenever committed, the running of the conditional sentence order is suspended during the period of imprisonment for that other offence.

Breach of condition
(2) If an order is made under paragraph 742.6(9)(c) or (d) to commit an offender to custody, the custodial period ordered shall, unless the court considers that it would not be in the interests of justice, be served consecutively to any other period of imprisonment that the offender is serving when that order is made.

Multiple sentences
(3) If an offender is serving both a custodial period referred to in subsection (2) and any other period of imprisonment, the periods shall, for the purpose of section 743.1 and section 139 of the Corrections and Conditional Release Act

Conditional sentence order resumes
(4) The running of any period of the conditional sentence order that is to be served in the community resumes upon the release of the offender from prison on parole, on statutory release, on earned remission, or at the expiration of the sentence.
1995, c. 22, s. 6;
1999, c. 5, s. 42;
2004, c. 12, s. 16(E).

Imprisonment

Imprisonment when no other provision
743 Every one who is convicted of an indictable offence for which no punishment is specially provided is liable to imprisonment for a term not exceeding five years.
R.S., 1985, c. C-46, s. 743;
1992, c. 11, s. 16;

1995, c. 22, s. 6.
Imprisonment for life or more than two years
743.1 (1) Except where otherwise provided, a person who is sentenced to imprisonment for
(a) life,
(b) a term of two years or more, or
(c) two or more terms of less than two years each that are to be served one after the other and that, in the aggregate, amount to two years or more,
shall be sentenced to imprisonment in a penitentiary.
Subsequent term less than two years
(2) Where a person who is sentenced to imprisonment in a penitentiary is, before the expiration of that sentence, sentenced to imprisonment for a term of less than two years, the person shall serve that term in a penitentiary, but if the previous sentence of imprisonment in a penitentiary is set aside, that person shall serve that term in accordance with subsection (3).
Imprisonment for term less than two years
(3) A person who is sentenced to imprisonment and who is not required to be sentenced as provided in subsection (1) or (2) shall, unless a special prison is prescribed by law, be sentenced to imprisonment in a prison or other place of confinement, other than a penitentiary, within the province in which the person is convicted, in which the sentence of imprisonment may be lawfully executed.
Long-term supervision
(3.1) Despite subsection (3), an offender who is subject to long-term supervision under Part XXIV and is sentenced for another offence during the period of the supervision shall be sentenced to imprisonment in a penitentiary.
Sentence to penitentiary of person serving sentence elsewhere
(4) Where a person is sentenced to imprisonment in a penitentiary while the person is lawfully imprisoned in a place other than a penitentiary, that person shall, except where otherwise provided, be sent immediately to the penitentiary, and shall serve in the penitentiary the unexpired portion of the term of imprisonment that that person was serving when sentenced to the penitentiary as well as the term of imprisonment for which that person was sentenced to the penitentiary.
Transfer to penitentiary
(5) Where, at any time, a person who is imprisoned in a prison or place of confinement other than a penitentiary is subject to two or more terms of imprisonment, each of which is for less than two years, that are to be served one after the other, and the aggregate of the unexpired portions of those terms at that time amounts to two years or more, the person shall be transferred to a penitentiary to serve those terms, but if any one or more of such terms is set aside or reduced and the unexpired portions of the remaining term or terms on the day on which that person was transferred under this section amounted to less than two years, that person shall serve that term or terms in accordance with subsection (3).
Newfoundland
(6) For the purposes of subsection (3), "penitentiary" does not, until a day to be fixed by order of the Governor in Council, include the facility mentioned in subsection 15(2) of the
Corrections and Conditional Release Act
1992, c. 11, s. 16;
1995, c. 19, s. 39, c. 22, s. 6;
1997, c. 17, s. 1;
2008, c. 6, s. 39.
Report by court to Correctional Service
743.2 A court that sentences or commits a person to penitentiary shall forward to the Correctional Service of Canada its reasons and recommendation relating to the sentence or committal, any relevant reports that were submitted to the court, and any other information relevant to administering the sentence or committal.
1995, c. 22, s. 6.
Non-communication order

743.21 (1) The sentencing judge may issue an order prohibiting the offender from communicating, directly or indirectly, with any victim, witness or other person identified in the order during the custodial period of the sentence, except in accordance with any conditions specified in the order that the sentencing judge considers necessary.
Failure to comply with order
(2) Every person who fails, without lawful excuse, the proof of which lies on that person, to comply with the order
(a) is guilty of an indictable offence and liable to imprisonment for a term not exceeding two years; or
(b) is guilty of an offence punishable on summary conviction and liable to imprisonment for a term not exceeding eighteen months.
2008, c. 18, s. 42.
Sentence served according to regulations
743.3 A sentence of imprisonment shall be served in accordance with the enactments and rules that govern the institution to which the prisoner is sentenced.
1995, c. 22, s. 6.
743.4 Transfer of jurisdiction when person already sentenced under
Youth Criminal Justice Act
743.5 (1) If a young person or an adult is or has been sentenced to a term of imprisonment for an offence while subject to a disposition made under paragraph 20(1)(k) or (k.1) of the
Young Offenders Act
Youth Criminal Justice Act
Transfer of jurisdiction when youth sentence imposed under
Youth Criminal Justice Act
(2) If a disposition is made under paragraph 20(1)(k) or (k.1) of the
Young Offenders Act
Youth Criminal Justice Act
Sentences deemed to constitute one sentence — section 743.1
(3) For greater certainty, the following are deemed to constitute one sentence of imprisonment for the purposes of section 139 of the
Corrections and Conditional Release Act
(a) for the purposes of subsection (1), the remainder of the youth sentence or disposition and the subsequent term of imprisonment; and
(b) for the purposes of subsection (2), the term of imprisonment and the subsequent youth sentence or disposition.
1995, c. 22, ss. 6, 19, 20;
2002, c. 1, s. 184;
2008, c. 18, s. 43.

Eligibility for Parole

Power of court to delay parole
743.6 (1) Notwithstanding subsection 120(1) of the
Corrections and Conditional Release Act
Power of court to delay parole
(1.1) Notwithstanding section 120 of the
Corrections and Conditional Release Act
Power of court to delay parole
(1.2) Notwithstanding section 120 of the
Corrections and Conditional Release Act
Principles that are to guide the court
(2) For greater certainty, the paramount principles which are to guide the court under this section are

denunciation and specific or general deterrence, with rehabilitation of the offender, in all cases, being subordinate to these paramount principles.
1995, c. 22, s. 6, c. 42, s. 86;
1997, c. 23, s. 18;
2001, c. 32, s. 45, c. 41, ss. 21, 133;
2014, c. 17, ss. 15, 16.

Delivery of Offender to Keeper of Prison

Execution of warrant of committal
744 A peace officer or other person to whom a warrant of committal authorized by this or any other Act of Parliament is directed shall arrest the person named or described therein, if it is necessary to do so in order to take that person into custody, convey that person to the prison mentioned in the warrant and deliver that person, together with the warrant, to the keeper of the prison who shall thereupon give to the peace officer or other person who delivers the prisoner a receipt in Form 43 setting out the state and condition of the prisoner when delivered into custody.
R.S., 1985, c. C-46, s. 744;
R.S., 1985, c. 27 (1st Supp.), s. 166, c. 1 (4th Supp.), s. 18(F);
1992, c. 11, s. 16;
1995, c. 22, s. 6.

Imprisonment for Life

Sentence of life imprisonment
745 Subject to section 745.1, the sentence to be pronounced against a person who is to be sentenced to imprisonment for life shall be
(a) in respect of a person who has been convicted of high treason or first degree murder, that the person be sentenced to imprisonment for life without eligibility for parole until the person has served twenty-five years of the sentence;
(b) in respect of a person who has been convicted of second degree murder where that person has previously been convicted of culpable homicide that is murder, however described in this Act, that that person be sentenced to imprisonment for life without eligibility for parole until the person has served twenty-five years of the sentence;
(b.1) in respect of a person who has been convicted of second degree murder where that person has previously been convicted of an offence under section 4 or 6 of the
Crimes Against Humanity and War Crimes Act
(c) in respect of a person who has been convicted of second degree murder, that the person be sentenced to imprisonment for life without eligibility for parole until the person has served at least ten years of the sentence or such greater number of years, not being more than twenty-five years, as has been substituted therefor pursuant to section 745.4; and
(d) in respect of a person who has been convicted of any other offence, that the person be sentenced to imprisonment for life with normal eligibility for parole.
R.S., 1985, c. C-46, s. 745;
R.S., 1985, c. 27 (2nd Supp.), s. 10;
1990, c. 17, s. 14;
1992, c. 51, s. 39;
1995, c. 22, s. 6;
2000, c. 24, s. 46.
Information in respect of parole
745.01 (1) Except where subsection 745.6(2) applies, at the time of sentencing under paragraph 745(a), (b) or (c), the judge who presided at the trial of the offender shall state the following, for the record:

The offender has been found guilty of (
Criminal Code
Corrections and Conditional Release Act
Exception
(2) Subsection (1) does not apply if the offender is convicted of an offence committed on or after the day on which this subsection comes into force.
1999, c. 25, s. 21(Preamble);
2011, c. 2, s. 2.
Persons under eighteen
745.1 The sentence to be pronounced against a person who was under the age of eighteen at the time of the commission of the offence for which the person was convicted of first degree murder or second degree murder and who is to be sentenced to imprisonment for life shall be that the person be sentenced to imprisonment for life without eligibility for parole until the person has served
(a) such period between five and seven years of the sentence as is specified by the judge presiding at the trial, or if no period is specified by the judge presiding at the trial, five years, in the case of a person who was under the age of sixteen at the time of the commission of the offence;
(b) ten years, in the case of a person convicted of first degree murder who was sixteen or seventeen years of age at the time of the commission of the offence; and
(c) seven years, in the case of a person convicted of second degree murder who was sixteen or seventeen years of age at the time of the commission of the offence.
1995, c. 22, ss. 6, 21.
Recommendation by jury
745.2 Subject to section 745.3, where a jury finds an accused guilty of second degree murder, the judge presiding at the trial shall, before discharging the jury, put to them the following question:
1995, c. 22, s. 6.
Recommendation by jury — multiple murders
745.21 (1) Where a jury finds an accused guilty of murder and that accused has previously been convicted of murder, the judge presiding at the trial shall, before discharging the jury, put to them the following question:
Application
(2) Subsection (1) applies to an offender who is convicted of murders committed on a day after the day on which this section comes into force and for which the offender is sentenced under this Act, the
National Defence Act
Crimes Against Humanity and War Crimes Act
2011, c. 5, s. 4.
Persons under sixteen
745.3 Where a jury finds an accused guilty of first degree murder or second degree murder and the accused was under the age of sixteen at the time of the commission of the offence, the judge presiding at the trial shall, before discharging the jury, put to them the following question:
1995, c. 22, ss. 6, 22.
Ineligibility for parole
745.4 Subject to section 745.5, at the time of the sentencing under section 745 of an offender who is convicted of second degree murder, the judge who presided at the trial of the offender or, if that judge is unable to do so, any judge of the same court may, having regard to the character of the offender, the nature of the offence and the circumstances surrounding its commission, and to the recommendation, if any, made pursuant to section 745.2, by order, substitute for ten years a number of years of imprisonment (being more than ten but not more than twenty-five) without eligibility for parole, as the judge deems fit in the circumstances.
1995, c. 22, s. 6.
Idem
745.5 At the time of the sentencing under section 745.1 of an offender who is convicted of first

degree murder or second degree murder and who was under the age of sixteen at the time of the commission of the offence, the judge who presided at the trial of the offender or, if that judge is unable to do so, any judge of the same court, may, having regard to the age and character of the offender, the nature of the offence and the circumstances surrounding its commission, and to the recommendation, if any, made pursuant to section 745.3, by order, decide the period of imprisonment the offender is to serve that is between five years and seven years without eligibility for parole, as the judge deems fit in the circumstances.
1995, c. 22, ss. 6, 23.

Ineligibility for parole — multiple murders

745.51 (1) At the time of the sentencing under section 745 of an offender who is convicted of murder and who has already been convicted of one or more other murders, the judge who presided at the trial of the offender or, if that judge is unable to do so, any judge of the same court may, having regard to the character of the offender, the nature of the offence and the circumstances surrounding its commission, and the recommendation, if any, made pursuant to section 745.21, by order, decide that the periods without eligibility for parole for each murder conviction are to be served consecutively.

Reasons

(2) The judge shall give, either orally or in writing, reasons for the decision to make or not to make an order under subsection (1).

Application

(3) Subsections (1) and (2) apply to an offender who is convicted of murders committed on a day after the day on which this section comes into force and for which the offender is sentenced under this Act, the
National Defence Act
Crimes Against Humanity and War Crimes Act
2011, c. 5, s. 5.

Application for judicial review

745.6 (1) Subject to subsections (2) to (2.6), a person may apply, in writing, to the appropriate Chief Justice in the province in which their conviction took place for a reduction in the number of years of imprisonment without eligibility for parole if the person
(a) has been convicted of murder or high treason;
(a.1) committed the murder or high treason before the day on which this paragraph comes into force;
(b) has been sentenced to imprisonment for life without eligibility for parole until more than fifteen years of their sentence has been served; and
(c) has served at least fifteen years of their sentence.

Exception — multiple murderers

(2) A person who has been convicted of more than one murder may not make an application under subsection (1), whether or not proceedings were commenced in respect of any of the murders before another murder was committed.

Less than 15 years of sentence served

(2.1) A person who is convicted of murder or high treason and who has served less than 15 years of their sentence on the day on which this subsection comes into force may, within 90 days after the day on which they have served 15 years of their sentence, make an application under subsection (1).

At least 15 years of sentence served

(2.2) A person who is convicted of murder or high treason and who has served at least 15 years of their sentence on the day on which this subsection comes into force may make an application under subsection (1) within 90 days after
(a) the end of five years after the day on which the person was the subject of a determination made under subsection 745.61(4) or a determination or conclusion to which subsection 745.63(8) applies; or
(b) the day on which this subsection comes into force, if the person has not made an application under subsection (1).

Non-application of subsection (2.2)

(2.3) Subsection (2.2) has no effect on a determination or decision made under subsection 745.61(3) or (5) or 745.63(3), (5) or (6) as it read immediately before the day on which this subsection comes into force. A person in respect of whom a time is set under paragraph 745.61(3)(a) or 745.63(6)(a) as it read immediately before that day may make an application under subsection (1) within 90 days after the end of that time.

Further five-year period if no application made

(2.4) If the person does not make an application in accordance with subsection (2.1), (2.2) or (2.3), as the case may be, they may make an application within 90 days after the day on which they have served a further five years of their sentence following the 90-day period referred to in that subsection, as the case may be.

Subsequent applications

(2.5) A person who makes an application in accordance with subsection (2.1), (2.2) or (2.3), as the case may be, may make another application under subsection (1) within 90 days after

(a) the end of the time set under paragraph 745.61(3)(a) or 745.63(6)(a), if a time is set under that paragraph; or

(b) the end of five years after the day on which the person is the subject of a determination made under subsection 745.61(4) or a determination or conclusion to which subsection 745.63(8) applies, if the person is the subject of such a determination or conclusion.

Subsequent applications

(2.6) A person who had made an application under subsection (1) as it read immediately before the day on which this subsection comes into force, whose application was finally disposed of on or after that day and who has then made a subsequent application may make a further application in accordance with subsection (2.5), if either paragraph (2.5)(a) or (b) is applicable.

(2.7) The 90-day time limits for the making of any application referred to in subsections (2.1) to (2.5) may be extended by the appropriate Chief Justice, or his or her designate, to a maximum of 180 days if the person, due to circumstances beyond their control, is unable to make an application within the 90-day time limit.

(2.8) If a person convicted of murder does not make an application under subsection (1) within the maximum time period allowed by this section, the Commissioner of Correctional Service Canada, or his or her designate, shall immediately notify in writing a parent, child, spouse or common-law partner of the victim that the convicted person did not make an application. If it is not possible to notify one of the aforementioned relatives, then the notification shall be given to another relative of the victim. The notification shall specify the next date on which the convicted person will be eligible to make an application under subsection (1).

Definition of
appropriate Chief Justice

(3) For the purposes of this section and sections 745.61 to 745.64, the appropriate Chief Justice

(a) in relation to the Province of Ontario, the Chief Justice of the Ontario Court;

(b) in relation to the Province of Quebec, the Chief Justice of the Superior Court;

(c) in relation to the Province of Newfoundland and Labrador, the Chief Justice of the Supreme Court, Trial Division;

(d) in relation to the Provinces of New Brunswick, Manitoba, Saskatchewan and Alberta, the Chief Justice of the Court of Queen's Bench;

(e) in relation to the Provinces of Nova Scotia, British Columbia and Prince Edward Island, the Chief Justice of the Supreme Court; and

(f) in relation to Yukon, the Northwest Territories and Nunavut, the Chief Justice of the Court of Appeal.

1993, c. 28, s. 78;
1995, c. 22, s. 6;
1996, c. 34, s. 2;
1998, c. 15, s. 20;

2002, c. 7, s. 146;
2011, c. 2, s. 3;
2015, c. 3, s. 55.
Judicial screening
745.61 (1) On receipt of an application under subsection 745.6(1), the appropriate Chief Justice shall determine, or shall designate a judge of the superior court of criminal jurisdiction to determine, on the basis of the following written material, whether the applicant has shown, on a balance of probabilities, that there is a substantial likelihood that the application will succeed:
(a) the application;
(b) any report provided by the Correctional Service of Canada or other correctional authorities; and
(c) any other written evidence presented to the Chief Justice or judge by the applicant or the Attorney General.
Criteria
(2) In determining whether the applicant has shown that there is a substantial likelihood that the application will succeed, the Chief Justice or judge shall consider the criteria set out in paragraphs 745.63(1)(a) to (e), with any modifications that the circumstances require.
Decision re new application
(3) If the Chief Justice or judge determines that the applicant has not shown that there is a substantial likelihood that the application will succeed, the Chief Justice or judge may
(a) set a time, no earlier than five years after the date of the determination, at or after which the applicant may make another application under subsection 745.6(1); or
(b) decide that the applicant may not make another application under that subsection.
If no decision re new application
(4) If the Chief Justice or judge determines that the applicant has not shown that there is a substantial likelihood that the application will succeed but does not set a time for another application or decide that such an application may not be made, the applicant may make another application no earlier than five years after the date of the determination.
Designation of judge to empanel jury
(5) If the Chief Justice or judge determines that the applicant has shown that there is a substantial likelihood that the application will succeed, the Chief Justice shall designate a judge of the superior court of criminal jurisdiction to empanel a jury to hear the application.
1996, c. 34, s. 2;
2011, c. 2, s. 4.
Appeal
745.62 (1) The applicant or the Attorney General may appeal to the Court of Appeal from a determination or a decision made under section 745.61 on any question of law or fact or mixed law and fact.
Documents to be considered
(2) The appeal shall be determined on the basis of the documents presented to the Chief Justice or judge who made the determination or decision, any reasons for the determination or decision and any other documents that the Court of Appeal requires.
Sections to apply
(3) Sections 673 to 696 apply, with such modifications as the circumstances require.
1996, c. 34, s. 2.
Hearing of application
745.63 (1) The jury empanelled under subsection 745.61(5) to hear the application shall consider the following criteria and determine whether the applicant's number of years of imprisonment without eligibility for parole ought to be reduced:
(a) the character of the applicant;
(b) the applicant's conduct while serving the sentence;
(c) the nature of the offence for which the applicant was convicted;
(d) any information provided by a victim at the time of the imposition of the sentence or at the time

of the hearing under this section; and

(e) any other matters that the judge considers relevant in the circumstances.

Information provided by victim

(1.1) Information provided by a victim referred to in paragraph (1)(d) may be provided either orally or in writing, at the discretion of the victim, or in any other manner that the judge considers appropriate.

(2) Reduction

(3) The jury hearing an application under subsection (1) may determine that the applicant's number of years of imprisonment without eligibility for parole ought to be reduced. The determination to reduce the number of years must be by unanimous vote.

No reduction

(4) The applicant's number of years of imprisonment without eligibility for parole is not reduced if

(a) the jury hearing an application under subsection (1) determines that the number of years ought not to be reduced;

(b) the jury hearing an application under subsection (1) concludes that it cannot unanimously determine that the number of years ought to be reduced; or

(c) the presiding judge, after the jury has deliberated for a reasonable period, concludes that the jury is unable to unanimously determine that the number of years ought to be reduced.

Where determination to reduce number of years

(5) If the jury determines that the number of years of imprisonment without eligibility for parole ought to be reduced, the jury may, by a vote of not less than two thirds of the members of the jury,

(a) substitute a lesser number of years of imprisonment without eligibility for parole than that then applicable; or

(b) terminate the ineligibility for parole.

Decision re new application

(6) If the applicant's number of years of imprisonment without eligibility for parole is not reduced, the jury may

(a) set a time, no earlier than five years after the date of the determination or conclusion under subsection (4), at or after which the applicant may make another application under subsection 745.6(1); or

(b) decide that the applicant may not make another application under that subsection.

Two-thirds decision

(7) The decision of the jury under paragraph (6)(a) or (b) must be made by not less than two thirds of its members.

If no decision re new application

(8) If the jury does not set a date on or after which another application may be made or decide that such an application may not be made, the applicant may make another application no earlier than five years after the date of the determination or conclusion under subsection (4).

1996, c. 34, s. 2;

1999, c. 25, s. 22(Preamble);

2011, c. 2, s. 5;

2015, c. 13, s. 34.

Rules

745.64 (1) The appropriate Chief Justice in each province or territory may make such rules as are required for the purposes of sections 745.6 to 745.63.

Territories

(2) When the appropriate Chief Justice is designating a judge of the superior court of criminal jurisdiction, for the purpose of a judicial screening under subsection 745.61(1) or to empanel a jury to hear an application under subsection 745.61(5), in respect of a conviction that took place in Yukon, the Northwest Territories or Nunavut, the appropriate Chief Justice may designate the judge from the Court of Appeal of Yukon, the Northwest Territories or Nunavut, or the Supreme Court of Yukon or the Northwest Territories or the Nunavut Court of Justice, as the case may be.

1996, c. 34, s. 2;
1999, c. 3, s. 53;
2002, c. 7, s. 147(E).

Time spent in custody

746 In calculating the period of imprisonment served for the purposes of section 745, 745.1, 745.4, 745.5 or 745.6, there shall be included any time spent in custody between

(a) in the case of a sentence of imprisonment for life after July 25, 1976, the day on which the person was arrested and taken into custody in respect of the offence for which that person was sentenced to imprisonment for life and the day the sentence was imposed; or

(b) in the case of a sentence of death that has been or is deemed to have been commuted to a sentence of imprisonment for life, the day on which the person was arrested and taken into custody in respect of the offence for which that person was sentenced to death and the day the sentence was commuted or deemed to have been commuted to a sentence of imprisonment for life.

R.S., 1985, c. C-46, s. 746;
1995, c. 19, s. 41, c. 22, ss. 6, 24.

Parole prohibited

746.1 (1) Unless Parliament otherwise provides by an enactment making express reference to this section, a person who has been sentenced to imprisonment for life without eligibility for parole for a specified number of years pursuant to this Act shall not be considered for parole or released pursuant to a grant of parole under the

Corrections and Conditional Release Act

Absence with or without escort and day parole

(2) Subject to subsection (3), in respect of a person sentenced to imprisonment for life without eligibility for parole for a specified number of years pursuant to this Act, until the expiration of all but three years of the specified number of years of imprisonment,

(a) no day parole may be granted under the

Corrections and Conditional Release Act

(b) no absence without escort may be authorized under that Act or the

Prisons and Reformatories Act

(c) except with the approval of the Parole Board of Canada, no absence with escort otherwise than for medical reasons or in order to attend judicial proceedings or a coroner's inquest may be authorized under either of those Acts.

Young offenders

(3) In the case of any person convicted of first degree murder or second degree murder who was under the age of eighteen at the time of the commission of the offence and who is sentenced to imprisonment for life without eligibility for parole for a specified number of years pursuant to this Act, until the expiration of all but one fifth of the period of imprisonment the person is to serve without eligibility for parole,

(a) no day parole may be granted under the

Corrections and Conditional Release Act

(b) no absence without escort may be authorized under that Act or the

Prisons and Reformatories Act

(c) except with the approval of the Parole Board of Canada, no absence with escort otherwise than for medical reasons or in order to attend judicial proceedings or a coroner's inquest may be authorized under either of those Acts.

1995, c. 22, s. 6, c. 42, s. 87;
1997, c. 17, s. 2;
2012, c. 1, ss. 160, 201.

747

Pardons and Remissions

To whom pardon may be granted

748 (1) Her Majesty may extend the royal mercy to a person who is sentenced to imprisonment under the authority of an Act of Parliament, even if the person is imprisoned for failure to pay money to another person.

Free or conditional pardon

(2) The Governor in Council may grant a free pardon or a conditional pardon to any person who has been convicted of an offence.

Effect of free pardon

(3) Where the Governor in Council grants a free pardon to a person, that person shall be deemed thereafter never to have committed the offence in respect of which the pardon is granted.

Punishment for subsequent offence not affected

(4) No free pardon or conditional pardon prevents or mitigates the punishment to which the person might otherwise be lawfully sentenced on a subsequent conviction for an offence other than that for which the pardon was granted.

R.S., 1985, c. C-46, s. 748;
1992, c. 22, s. 12;
1995, c. 22, s. 6.

Remission by Governor in Council

748.1 (1) The Governor in Council may order the remission, in whole or in part, of a fine or forfeiture imposed under an Act of Parliament, whoever the person may be to whom it is payable or however it may be recoverable.

Terms of remission

(2) An order for remission under subsection (1) may include the remission of costs incurred in the proceedings, but no costs to which a private prosecutor is entitled shall be remitted.
1995, c. 22, s. 6.

Royal prerogative

749 Nothing in this Act in any manner limits or affects Her Majesty's royal prerogative of mercy.
R.S., 1985, c. C-46, s. 749;
1995, c. 22, s. 6.

Disabilities

Public office vacated for conviction

750 (1) Where a person is convicted of an indictable offence for which the person is sentenced to imprisonment for two years or more and holds, at the time that person is convicted, an office under the Crown or other public employment, the office or employment forthwith becomes vacant.

When disability ceases

(2) A person to whom subsection (1) applies is, until undergoing the punishment imposed on the person or the punishment substituted therefor by competent authority or receives a free pardon from Her Majesty, incapable of holding any office under the Crown or other public employment, or of being elected or sitting or voting as a member of Parliament or of a legislature or of exercising any right of suffrage.

Disability to contract

(3) No person who is convicted of
(a) an offence under section 121, 124 or 418,
(b) an offence under section 380 committed against Her Majesty, or
(c) an offence under paragraph 80(1)(d), subsection 80(2) or section 154.01 of the Financial Administration Act
has, after that conviction, capacity to contract with Her Majesty or to receive any benefit under a contract between Her Majesty and any other person or to hold office under Her Majesty.

Application for restoration of privileges

(4) A person to whom subsection (3) applies may, at any time before a record suspension for which he or she has applied is ordered under the

Criminal Records Act
Order of restoration
(5) Where an application is made under subsection (4), the Governor in Council may order that the capacities lost by the applicant by virtue of subsection (3) be restored to that applicant in whole or in part and subject to such conditions as the Governor in Council considers desirable in the public interest.
Removal of disability
(6) Where a conviction is set aside by competent authority, any disability imposed by this section is removed.
R.S., 1985, c. C-46, s. 750;
1995, c. 22, s. 6;
2000, c. 1, s. 9;
2006, c. 9, s. 246;
2012, c. 1, s. 146.

Miscellaneous Provisions

Costs to successful party in case of libel
751 The person in whose favour judgment is given in proceedings by indictment for defamatory libel is entitled to recover from the opposite party costs in a reasonable amount to be fixed by order of the court.
R.S., 1985, c. C-46, s. 751;
1995, c. 22, s. 6.
How recovered
751.1 Where costs that are fixed under section 751 are not paid forthwith, the party in whose favour judgment is given may enter judgment for the amount of the costs by filing the order in any civil court of the province in which the trial was held that has jurisdiction to enter a judgment for that amount, and that judgment is enforceable against the opposite party in the same manner as if it were a judgment rendered against that opposite party in that court in civil proceedings.
1995, c. 22, s. 6.

PART XXIV

PART XXIV
Dangerous Offenders and Long-term Offenders

Interpretation

Definitions
752 In this Part,
court
designated offence
(a) a primary designated offence,
(b) an offence under any of the following provisions:
(i) paragraph 81(1)(a) (using explosives),
(ii) paragraph 81(1)(b) (using explosives),
(iii) section 85 (using firearm or imitation firearm in commission of offence),
(iv) section 87 (pointing firearm),
(iv.1) section 98 (breaking and entering to steal firearm),
(iv.2) section 98.1 (robbery to steal firearm),
(v) section 153.1 (sexual exploitation of person with disability),
(vi) section 163.1 (child pornography),

(vii) section 170 (parent or guardian procuring sexual activity),
(viii) section 171 (householder permitting sexual activity by or in presence of child),
(ix) section 172.1 (luring child),
(ix.1) section 172.2 (agreement or arrangement — sexual offence against child),
(x) to (xii) (xiii) section 245 (administering noxious thing),
(xiv) section 266 (assault),
(xv) section 269 (unlawfully causing bodily harm),
(xvi) section 269.1 (torture),
(xvii) paragraph 270(1)(a) (assaulting peace officer),
(xviii) section 273.3 (removal of child from Canada),
(xix) subsection 279(2) (forcible confinement),
(xx) section 279.01 (trafficking in persons),
(xx.1) section 279.011 (trafficking of a person under the age of eighteen years),
(xx.2) section 279.02 (material benefit — trafficking),
(xx.3) section 279.03 (withholding or destroying documents — trafficking),
(xxi) section 279.1 (hostage taking),
(xxii) section 280 (abduction of person under age of 16),
(xxiii) section 281 (abduction of person under age of 14),
(xxiii.1) subsection 286.1(2) (obtaining sexual services for consideration from person under 18 years),
(xxiii.2) section 286.2 (material benefit from sexual services),
(xxiii.3) section 286.3 (procuring),
(xxiv) section 344 (robbery), and
(xxv) section 348 (breaking and entering with intent, committing offence or breaking out),
(c) an offence under any of the following provisions of the
Criminal Code
(i) subsection 146(2) (sexual intercourse with female between ages of 14 and 16),
(ii) section 148 (sexual intercourse with feeble-minded),
(iii) section 166 (parent or guardian procuring defilement), and
(iv) section 167 (householder permitting defilement),
(c.1) an offence under any of the following provisions of this Act, as they read from time to time before the day on which this paragraph comes into force:
(i) subsection 212(1) (procuring),
(ii) subsection 212(2) (living on the avails of prostitution of person under 18 years),
(iii) subsection 212(2.1) (aggravated offence in relation to living on the avails of prostitution of person under 18 years), and
(iv) subsection 212(4) (prostitution of person under 18 years); or
(d) an attempt or conspiracy to commit an offence referred to in paragraph (b), (c) or (c.1);
long-term supervision
primary designated offence
(a) an offence under any of the following provisions:
(i) section 151 (sexual interference),
(ii) section 152 (invitation to sexual touching),
(iii) section 153 (sexual exploitation),
(iv) section 155 (incest),
(v) section 239 (attempt to commit murder),
(vi) section 244 (discharging firearm with intent),
(vii) section 267 (assault with weapon or causing bodily harm),
(viii) section 268 (aggravated assault),
(ix) section 271 (sexual assault),
(x) section 272 (sexual assault with weapon, threats to third party or causing bodily harm),
(xi) section 273 (aggravated sexual assault), and

(xii) subsection 279(1) (kidnapping),
(b) an offence under any of the following provisions of the
Criminal Code
(i) section 144 (rape),
(ii) section 145 (attempt to commit rape),
(iii) section 149 (indecent assault on female),
(iv) section 156 (indecent assault on male),
(v) subsection 245(2) (assault causing bodily harm), and
(vi) subsection 246(1) (assault with intent) if the intent is to commit an offence referred to in any of subparagraphs (i) to (v) of this paragraph,
(c) an offence under any of the following provisions of the
Criminal Code
An Act to amend the Criminal Code in relation to sexual offences and other offences against the person and to amend certain other Acts in relation thereto or in consequence thereof
(i) section 246.1 (sexual assault),
(ii) section 246.2 (sexual assault with weapon, threats to third party or causing bodily harm), and
(iii) section 246.3 (aggravated sexual assault),
(d) an offence under any of the following provisions of the
Criminal Code
(i) subsection 146(1) (sexual intercourse with female under age of 14), and
(ii) paragraph 153(1)(a) (sexual intercourse with step-daughter), or
(e) an attempt or conspiracy to commit an offence referred to in any of paragraphs (a) to (d);
serious personal injury offence
(a) an indictable offence, other than high treason, treason, first degree murder or second degree murder, involving
(i) the use or attempted use of violence against another person, or
(ii) conduct endangering or likely to endanger the life or safety of another person or inflicting or likely to inflict severe psychological damage on another person,
and for which the offender may be sentenced to imprisonment for ten years or more, or
(b) an offence or attempt to commit an offence mentioned in section 271 (sexual assault), 272 (sexual assault with a weapon, threats to a third party or causing bodily harm) or 273 (aggravated sexual assault).
R.S., 1985, c. C-46, s. 752;
2008, c. 6, ss. 40, 61;
2010, c. 3, s. 8;
2012, c. 1, s. 35;
2014, c. 25, s. 29.

Dangerous Offenders and Long-Term Offenders

Prosecutor's duty to advise court
752.01 If the prosecutor is of the opinion that an offence for which an offender is convicted is a serious personal injury offence that is a designated offence and that the offender was convicted previously at least twice of a designated offence and was sentenced to at least two years of imprisonment for each of those convictions, the prosecutor shall advise the court, as soon as feasible after the finding of guilt and in any event before sentence is imposed, whether the prosecutor intends to make an application under subsection 752.1(1).
2008, c. 6, s. 41.
Application for remand for assessment
752.1 (1) On application by the prosecutor, if the court is of the opinion that there are reasonable grounds to believe that an offender who is convicted of a serious personal injury offence or an offence referred to in paragraph 753.1(2)(a) might be found to be a dangerous offender under section

753 or a long-term offender under section 753.1, the court shall, by order in writing, before sentence is imposed, remand the offender, for a period not exceeding 60 days, to the custody of a person designated by the court who can perform an assessment or have an assessment performed by experts for use as evidence in an application under section 753 or 753.1.

Report

(2) The person to whom the offender is remanded shall file a report of the assessment with the court not later than 30 days after the end of the assessment period and make copies of it available to the prosecutor and counsel for the offender.

Extension of time

(3) On application by the prosecutor, the court may extend the period within which the report must be filed by a maximum of 30 days if the court is satisfied that there are reasonable grounds to do so.
1997, c. 17, s. 4;
2008, c. 6, s. 41.

Application for finding that an offender is a dangerous offender

753 (1) On application made under this Part after an assessment report is filed under subsection 752.1(2), the court shall find the offender to be a dangerous offender if it is satisfied

(a) that the offence for which the offender has been convicted is a serious personal injury offence described in paragraph (a) of the definition of that expression in section 752 and the offender constitutes a threat to the life, safety or physical or mental well-being of other persons on the basis of evidence establishing

(i) a pattern of repetitive behaviour by the offender, of which the offence for which he or she has been convicted forms a part, showing a failure to restrain his or her behaviour and a likelihood of causing death or injury to other persons, or inflicting severe psychological damage on other persons, through failure in the future to restrain his or her behaviour,

(ii) a pattern of persistent aggressive behaviour by the offender, of which the offence for which he or she has been convicted forms a part, showing a substantial degree of indifference on the part of the offender respecting the reasonably foreseeable consequences to other persons of his or her behaviour, or

(iii) any behaviour by the offender, associated with the offence for which he or she has been convicted, that is of such a brutal nature as to compel the conclusion that the offender's behaviour in the future is unlikely to be inhibited by normal standards of behavioural restraint; or

(b) that the offence for which the offender has been convicted is a serious personal injury offence described in paragraph (b) of the definition of that expression in section 752 and the offender, by his or her conduct in any sexual matter including that involved in the commission of the offence for which he or she has been convicted, has shown a failure to control his or her sexual impulses and a likelihood of causing injury, pain or other evil to other persons through failure in the future to control his or her sexual impulses.

Presumption

(1.1) If the court is satisfied that the offence for which the offender is convicted is a primary designated offence for which it would be appropriate to impose a sentence of imprisonment of two years or more and that the offender was convicted previously at least twice of a primary designated offence and was sentenced to at least two years of imprisonment for each of those convictions, the conditions in paragraph (1)(a) or (b), as the case may be, are presumed to have been met unless the contrary is proved on a balance of probabilities.

Time for making application

(2) An application under subsection (1) must be made before sentence is imposed on the offender unless

(a) before the imposition of sentence, the prosecutor gives notice to the offender of a possible intention to make an application under section 752.1 and an application under subsection (1) not later than six months after that imposition; and

(b) at the time of the application under subsection (1) that is not later than six months after the imposition of sentence, it is shown that relevant evidence that was not reasonably available to the prosecutor at the time of the imposition of sentence became available in the interim.

Application for remand for assessment after imposition of sentence

(3) Notwithstanding subsection 752.1(1), an application under that subsection may be made after the imposition of sentence or after an offender begins to serve the sentence in a case to which paragraphs (2)(a) and (b) apply.

Sentence for dangerous offender

(4) If the court finds an offender to be a dangerous offender, it shall
(a) impose a sentence of detention in a penitentiary for an indeterminate period;
(b) impose a sentence for the offence for which the offender has been convicted — which must be a minimum punishment of imprisonment for a term of two years — and order that the offender be subject to long-term supervision for a period that does not exceed 10 years; or
(c) impose a sentence for the offence for which the offender has been convicted.

Sentence of indeterminate detention

(4.1) The court shall impose a sentence of detention in a penitentiary for an indeterminate period unless it is satisfied by the evidence adduced during the hearing of the application that there is a reasonable expectation that a lesser measure under paragraph (4)(b) or (c) will adequately protect the public against the commission by the offender of murder or a serious personal injury offence.

If application made after sentencing

(4.2) If the application is made after the offender begins to serve the sentence in a case to which paragraphs (2)(a) and (b) apply, a sentence imposed under paragraph (4)(a), or a sentence imposed and an order made under paragraph 4(b), replaces the sentence that was imposed for the offence for which the offender was convicted.

If offender not found to be dangerous offender

(5) If the court does not find an offender to be a dangerous offender,
(a) the court may treat the application as an application to find the offender to be a long-term offender, section 753.1 applies to the application and the court may either find that the offender is a long-term offender or hold another hearing for that purpose; or
(b) the court may impose sentence for the offence for which the offender has been convicted.

(6) R.S., 1985, c. C-46, s. 753;

1997, c. 17, s. 4;

2008, c. 6, s. 42.

Application for remand for assessment — later conviction

753.01 (1) If an offender who is found to be a dangerous offender is later convicted of a serious personal injury offence or an offence under subsection 753.3(1), on application by the prosecutor, the court shall, by order in writing, before sentence is imposed, remand the offender, for a period not exceeding 60 days, to the custody of a person designated by the court who can perform an assessment or have an assessment performed by experts for use as evidence in an application under subsection (4).

Report

(2) The person to whom the offender is remanded shall file a report of the assessment with the court not later than 30 days after the end of the assessment period and make copies of it available to the prosecutor and counsel for the offender.

Extension of time

(3) On application by the prosecutor, the court may extend the period within which the report must be filed by a maximum of 30 days if the court is satisfied that there are reasonable grounds to do so.

Application for new sentence or order

(4) After the report is filed, the prosecutor may apply for a sentence of detention in a penitentiary for an indeterminate period, or for an order that the offender be subject to a new period of long-term supervision in addition to any other sentence that may be imposed for the offence.

Sentence of indeterminate detention

(5) If the application is for a sentence of detention in a penitentiary for an indeterminate period, the court shall impose that sentence unless it is satisfied by the evidence adduced during the hearing of

the application that there is a reasonable expectation that a sentence for the offence for which the offender has been convicted — with or without a new period of long-term supervision — will adequately protect the public against the commission by the offender of murder or a serious personal injury offence.

New long-term supervision

(6) If the application is for a new period of long-term supervision, the court shall order that the offender be subject to a new period of long-term supervision in addition to a sentence for the offence for which they have been convicted unless it is satisfied by the evidence adduced during the hearing of the application that there is a reasonable expectation that the sentence alone will adequately protect the public against the commission by the offender of murder or a serious personal injury offence.

2008, c. 6, s. 43.

Victim evidence

753.02 Any evidence given during the hearing of an application made under subsection 753(1) by a victim of an offence for which the offender was convicted is deemed also to have been given during any hearing held with respect to the offender under paragraph 753(5)(a) or subsection 753.01(5) or (6).

2008, c. 6, s. 43.

Application for finding that an offender is a long-term offender

753.1 (1) The court may, on application made under this Part following the filing of an assessment report under subsection 752.1(2), find an offender to be a long-term offender if it is satisfied that
(a) it would be appropriate to impose a sentence of imprisonment of two years or more for the offence for which the offender has been convicted;
(b) there is a substantial risk that the offender will reoffend; and
(c) there is a reasonable possibility of eventual control of the risk in the community.

Substantial risk

(2) The court shall be satisfied that there is a substantial risk that the offender will reoffend if
(a) the offender has been convicted of an offence under section 151 (sexual interference), 152 (invitation to sexual touching) or 153 (sexual exploitation), subsection 163.1(2) (making child pornography), 163.1(3) (distribution, etc., of child pornography), 163.1(4) (possession of child pornography) or 163.1(4.1) (accessing child pornography), section 170 (parent or guardian procuring sexual activity), 171 (householder permitting sexual activity), 171.1 (making sexually explicit material available to child), 172.1 (luring a child) or 172.2 (agreement or arrangement — sexual offence against child), subsection 173(2) (exposure) or section 271 (sexual assault), 272 (sexual assault with a weapon) 273 (aggravated sexual assault) or 279.011 (trafficking — person under 18 years) or subsection 279.02(2) (material benefit — trafficking of person under 18 years), 279.03(2) (withholding or destroying documents — trafficking of person under 18 years), 286.1(2) (obtaining sexual services for consideration from person under 18 years), 286.2(2) (material benefit from sexual services provided by person under 18 years) or 286.3(2) (procuring — person under 18 years), or has engaged in serious conduct of a sexual nature in the commission of another offence of which the offender has been convicted; and
(b) the offender
(i) has shown a pattern of repetitive behaviour, of which the offence for which he or she has been convicted forms a part, that shows a likelihood of the offender's causing death or injury to other persons or inflicting severe psychological damage on other persons, or
(ii) by conduct in any sexual matter including that involved in the commission of the offence for which the offender has been convicted, has shown a likelihood of causing injury, pain or other evil to other persons in the future through similar offences.

Sentence for long-term offender

(3) If the court finds an offender to be a long-term offender, it shall
(a) impose a sentence for the offence for which the offender has been convicted, which must be a minimum punishment of imprisonment for a term of two years; and

(b) order that the offender be subject to long-term supervision for a period that does not exceed 10 years.

Exception — if application made after sentencing

(3.1) The court may not impose a sentence under paragraph (3)(a) and the sentence that was imposed for the offence for which the offender was convicted stands despite the offender's being found to be a long-term offender, if the application was one that

(a) was made after the offender begins to serve the sentence in a case to which paragraphs 753(2)(a) and (b) apply; and

(b) was treated as an application under this section further to the court deciding to do so under paragraph 753(5)(a).

(4) and (5) If offender not found to be long-term offender

(6) If the court does not find an offender to be a long-term offender, the court shall impose sentence for the offence for which the offender has been convicted.

1997, c. 17, s. 4;
2002, c. 13, s. 76;
2008, c. 6, s. 44;
2012, c. 1, s. 36;
2014, c. 25, s. 30.

Long-term supervision

753.2 (1) Subject to subsection (2), an offender who is subject to long-term supervision shall be supervised in the community in accordance with the

Corrections and Conditional Release Act

(a) the sentence for the offence for which the offender has been convicted; and

(b) all other sentences for offences for which the offender is convicted and for which sentence of a term of imprisonment is imposed on the offender, either before or after the conviction for the offence referred to in paragraph (a).

Sentence served concurrently with supervision

(2) A sentence imposed on an offender referred to in subsection (1), other than a sentence that requires imprisonment, is to be served concurrently with the long-term supervision.

Application for reduction in period of long-term supervision

(3) An offender who is required to be supervised, a member of the Parole Board of Canada or, on approval of that Board, the offender's parole supervisor, as defined in subsection 99(1) of the Corrections and Conditional Release Act

Notice to Attorney General

(4) The applicant must give notice of an application under subsection (3) to the Attorney General at the time the application is made.

1997, c. 17, s. 4;
2008, c. 6, s. 45;
2012, c. 1, ss. 147, 160.

Breach of long-term supervision

753.3 (1) An offender who, without reasonable excuse, fails or refuses to comply with long-term supervision is guilty of an indictable offence and liable to imprisonment for a term not exceeding 10 years.

Where accused may be tried and punished

(2) An accused who is charged with an offence under subsection (1) may be tried and punished by any court having jurisdiction to try that offence in the place where the offence is alleged to have been committed or in the place where the accused is found, is arrested or is in custody, but if the place where the accused is found, is arrested or is in custody is outside the province in which the offence is alleged to have been committed, no proceedings in respect of that offence shall be instituted in that place without the consent of the Attorney General of that province.

1997, c. 17, s. 4;
2008, c. 6, s. 46.

New offence
753.4 (1) If an offender who is subject to long-term supervision commits one or more offences under this or any other Act and a court imposes a sentence of imprisonment for the offence or offences, the long-term supervision is interrupted until the offender has finished serving all the sentences, unless the court orders its termination.
Reduction in term of long-term supervision
(2) A court that imposes a sentence of imprisonment under subsection (1) may order a reduction in the length of the period of the offender's long-term supervision.
1997, c. 17, s. 4;
2008, c. 6, s. 47.
Hearing of application
754 (1) With the exception of an application for remand for assessment, the court may not hear an application made under this Part unless
(a) the Attorney General of the province in which the offender was tried has, either before or after the making of the application, consented to the application;
(b) at least seven days notice has been given to the offender by the prosecutor, following the making of the application, outlining the basis on which it is intended to found the application; and
(c) a copy of the notice has been filed with the clerk of the court or the provincial court judge, as the case may be.
By court alone
(2) An application under this Part shall be heard and determined by the court without a jury.
When proof unnecessary
(3) For the purposes of an application under this Part, where an offender admits any allegations contained in the notice referred to in paragraph (1)(b), no proof of those allegations is required.
Proof of consent
(4) The production of a document purporting to contain any nomination or consent that may be made or given by the Attorney General under this Part and purporting to be signed by the Attorney General is, in the absence of any evidence to the contrary, proof of that nomination or consent without proof of the signature or the official character of the person appearing to have signed the document.
R.S., 1985, c. C-46, s. 754;
R.S., 1985, c. 27 (1st Supp.), s. 203;
2008, c. 6, s. 48.
Exception to long-term supervision — life sentence
755 (1) The court shall not order that an offender be subject to long-term supervision if they have been sentenced to life imprisonment.
Maximum length of long-term supervision
(2) The periods of long-term supervision to which an offender is subject at any particular time must not total more than 10 years.
R.S., 1985, c. C-46, s. 755;
1997, c. 17, s. 5;
2008, c. 6, s. 49.
756 Evidence of character
757 Without prejudice to the right of the offender to tender evidence as to their character and repute, if the court thinks fit, evidence of character and repute may be admitted
(a) on the question of whether the offender is or is not a dangerous offender or a long-term offender; and
(b) in connection with a sentence to be imposed or an order to be made under this Part.
R.S., 1985, c. C-46, s. 757;
1997, c. 17, s. 5;
2008, c. 6, s. 50.
Presence of accused at hearing of application
758 (1) The offender shall be present at the hearing of the application under this Part and if at the

time the application is to be heard

(a) he is confined in a prison, the court may order, in writing, the person having the custody of the accused to bring him before the court; or

(b) he is not confined in a prison, the court shall issue a summons or a warrant to compel the accused to attend before the court and the provisions of Part XVI relating to summons and warrant are applicable with such modifications as the circumstances require.

Exception

(2) Notwithstanding subsection (1), the court may

(a) cause the offender to be removed and to be kept out of court, where he misconducts himself by interrupting the proceedings so that to continue the proceedings in his presence would not be feasible; or

(b) permit the offender to be out of court during the whole or any part of the hearing on such conditions as the court considers proper.

R.S., c. C-34, s. 693;
1976-77, c. 53, s. 14.

Appeal — offender

759 (1) An offender who is found to be a dangerous offender or a long-term offender may appeal to the court of appeal from a decision made under this Part on any ground of law or fact or mixed law and fact.

(1.1) Appeal — Attorney General

(2) The Attorney General may appeal to the court of appeal from a decision made under this Part on any ground of law.

Disposition of appeal

(3) The court of appeal may

(a) allow the appeal and

(i) find that an offender is or is not a dangerous offender or a long-term offender or impose a sentence that may be imposed or an order that may be made by the trial court under this Part, or

(ii) order a new hearing, with any directions that the court considers appropriate; or

(b) dismiss the appeal.

(3.1) and (3.2) Effect of decision

(4) A decision of the court of appeal has the same force and effect as if it were a decision of the trial court.

(4.1) to (5) Commencement of sentence

(6) Notwithstanding subsection 719(1), a sentence imposed on an offender by the court of appeal pursuant to this section shall be deemed to have commenced when the offender was sentenced by the court by which he was convicted.

Part XXI applies re appeals

(7) The provisions of Part XXI with respect to procedure on appeals apply, with such modifications as the circumstances require, to appeals under this section.

R.S., 1985, c. C-46, s. 759;
1995, c. 22, s. 10;
1997, c. 17, s. 6;
2008, c. 6, s. 51.

Disclosure to Correctional Service of Canada

760 Where a court finds an offender to be a dangerous offender or a long-term offender, the court shall order that a copy of all reports and testimony given by psychiatrists, psychologists, criminologists and other experts and any observations of the court with respect to the reasons for the finding, together with a transcript of the trial of the offender, be forwarded to the Correctional Service of Canada for information.

R.S., 1985, c. C-46, s. 760;
1997, c. 17, s. 7.

Review for parole

761 (1) Subject to subsection (2), where a person is in custody under a sentence of detention in a penitentiary for an indeterminate period, the Parole Board of Canada shall, as soon as possible after the expiration of seven years from the day on which that person was taken into custody and not later than every two years after the previous review, review the condition, history and circumstances of that person for the purpose of determining whether he or she should be granted parole under Part II of the
Corrections and Conditional Release Act
Idem
(2) Where a person is in custody under a sentence of detention in a penitentiary for an indeterminate period that was imposed before October 15, 1977, the Parole Board of Canada shall, at least once in every year, review the condition, history and circumstances of that person for the purpose of determining whether he should be granted parole under Part II of the
Corrections and Conditional Release Act
R.S., 1985, c. C-46, s. 761;
1992, c. 20, s. 215;
1997, c. 17, s. 8;
2012, c. 1, s. 160.

PART XXV

PART XXV
Effect and Enforcement of Recognizances

Applications for forfeiture of recognizances
762 (1) Applications for the forfeiture of recognizances shall be made to the courts, designated in column II of the schedule, of the respective provinces designated in column I of the schedule.
Definitions
(2) In this Part,
clerk of the court
schedule
R.S., c. C-34, s. 696.
Recognizance binding
763 Where a person is bound by recognizance to appear before a court, justice or provincial court judge for any purpose and the session or sittings of that court or the proceedings are adjourned or an order is made changing the place of trial, that person and his sureties continue to be bound by the recognizance in like manner as if it had been entered into with relation to the resumed proceedings or the trial at the time and place at which the proceedings are ordered to be resumed or the trial is ordered to be held.
R.S., 1985, c. C-46, s. 763;
R.S., 1985, c. 27 (1st Supp.), s. 203.
Responsibility of sureties
764 (1) Where an accused is bound by recognizance to appear for trial, his arraignment or conviction does not discharge the recognizance, but it continues to bind him and his sureties, if any, for his appearance until he is discharged or sentenced, as the case may be.
Committal or new sureties
(2) Notwithstanding subsection (1), the court, justice or provincial court judge may commit an accused to prison or may require him to furnish new or additional sureties for his appearance until he is discharged or sentenced, as the case may be.
Effect of committal
(3) The sureties of an accused who is bound by recognizance to appear for trial are discharged if he is committed to prison pursuant to subsection (2).
Endorsement on recognizance

(4) The provisions of section 763 and subsections (1) to (3) of this section shall be endorsed on any recognizance entered into pursuant to this Act.

R.S., 1985, c. C-46, s. 764;
R.S., 1985, c. 27 (1st Supp.), s. 203.

Effect of subsequent arrest

765 Where an accused is bound by recognizance to appear for trial, his arrest on another charge does not vacate the recognizance, but it continues to bind him and his sureties, if any, for his appearance until he is discharged or sentenced, as the case may be, in respect of the offence to which the recognizance relates.

R.S., c. C-34, s. 699.

Render of accused by sureties

766 (1) A surety for a person who is bound by recognizance to appear may, by an application in writing to a court, justice or provincial court judge, apply to be relieved of his obligation under the recognizance, and the court, justice or provincial court judge shall thereupon issue an order in writing for committal of that person to the prison nearest to the place where he was, under the recognizance, bound to appear.

Arrest

(2) An order under subsection (1) shall be given to the surety and on receipt thereof he or any peace officer may arrest the person named in the order and deliver that person with the order to the keeper of the prison named therein, and the keeper shall receive and imprison that person until he is discharged according to law.

Certificate and entry of render

(3) Where a court, justice or provincial court judge issues an order under subsection (1) and receives from the sheriff a certificate that the person named in the order has been committed to prison pursuant to subsection (2), the court, justice or provincial court judge shall order an entry of the committal to be endorsed on the recognizance.

Discharge of sureties

(4) An endorsement under subsection (3) vacates the recognizance and discharges the sureties.

R.S., 1985, c. C-46, s. 766;
R.S., 1985, c. 27 (1st Supp.), s. 203.

Render of accused in court by sureties

767 A surety for a person who is bound by recognizance to appear may bring that person into the court at which he is required to appear at any time during the sittings thereof and before his trial and the surety may discharge his obligation under the recognizance by giving that person into the custody of the court, and the court shall thereupon commit that person to prison until he is discharged according to law.

R.S., c. C-34, s. 701.

Substitution of surety

767.1 (1) Notwithstanding subsection 766(1) and section 767, where a surety for a person who is bound by a recognizance has rendered the person into the custody of a court pursuant to section 767 or applies to be relieved of his obligation under the recognizance pursuant to subsection 766(1), the court, justice or provincial court judge, as the case may be, may, instead of committing or issuing an order for the committal of the person to prison, substitute any other suitable person for the surety under the recognizance.

Signing of recognizance by new sureties

(2) Where a person substituted for a surety under a recognizance pursuant to subsection (1) signs the recognizance, the original surety is discharged, but the recognizance and the order for judicial interim release pursuant to which the recognizance was entered into are not otherwise affected.

R.S., 1985, c. 27 (1st Supp.), s. 167.

Rights of surety preserved

768 Nothing in this Part limits or restricts any right that a surety has of taking and giving into custody any person for whom, under a recognizance, he is a surety.

R.S., c. C-34, s. 702.
Application of judicial interim release provisions
769 Where a surety for a person has rendered him into custody and that person has been committed to prison, the provisions of Parts XVI, XXI and XXVII relating to judicial interim release apply, with such modifications as the circumstances require, in respect of him and he shall forthwith be taken before a justice or judge as an accused charged with an offence or as an appellant, as the case may be, for the purposes of those provisions.
R.S., c. C-34, s. 703;
R.S., c. 2(2nd Supp.), s. 14.
Default to be endorsed
770 (1) Where, in proceedings to which this Act applies, a person who is bound by recognizance does not comply with a condition of the recognizance, a court, justice or provincial court judge having knowledge of the facts shall endorse or cause to be endorsed on the recognizance a certificate in Form 33 setting out
(a) the nature of the default;
(b) the reason for the default, if it is known;
(c) whether the ends of justice have been defeated or delayed by reason of the default; and
(d) the names and addresses of the principal and sureties.
Transmission to clerk of court
(2) A recognizance that has been endorsed pursuant to subsection (1) shall be sent to the clerk of the court and shall be kept by him with the records of the court.
Certificate is evidence
(3) A certificate that has been endorsed on a recognizance pursuant to subsection (1) is evidence of the default to which it relates.
Transmission of deposit
(4) Where, in proceedings to which this section applies, the principal or surety has deposited money as security for the performance of a condition of a recognizance, that money shall be sent to the clerk of the court with the defaulted recognizance, to be dealt with in accordance with this Part.
R.S., 1985, c. C-46, s. 770;
R.S., 1985, c. 27 (1st Supp.), s. 203;
1997, c. 18, s. 108.
Proceedings in case of default
771 (1) Where a recognizance has been endorsed with a certificate pursuant to section 770 and has been received by the clerk of the court pursuant to that section,
(a) a judge of the court shall, on the request of the clerk of the court or the Attorney General or counsel acting on his behalf, fix a time and place for the hearing of an application for the forfeiture of the recognizance; and
(b) the clerk of the court shall, not less than ten days before the time fixed under paragraph (a) for the hearing, send by registered mail, or have served in the manner directed by the court or prescribed by the rules of court, to each principal and surety named in the recognizance, directed to the principal or surety at the address set out in the certificate, a notice requiring the person to appear at the time and place fixed by the judge to show cause why the recognizance should not be forfeited.
Order of judge
(2) Where subsection (1) has been complied with, the judge may, after giving the parties an opportunity to be heard, in his discretion grant or refuse the application and make any order with respect to the forfeiture of the recognizance that he considers proper.
Judgment debtors of the Crown
(3) Where, pursuant to subsection (2), a judge orders forfeiture of a recognizance, the principal and his sureties become judgment debtors of the Crown, each in the amount that the judge orders him to pay.
Order may be filed
(3.1) An order made under subsection (2) may be filed with the clerk of the superior court and if an

order is filed, the clerk shall issue a writ of
Transfer of deposit
(4) Where a deposit has been made by a person against whom an order for forfeiture of a recognizance has been made, no writ of
R.S., 1985, c. C-46, s. 771;
R.S., 1985, c. 27 (1st Supp.), s. 168;
1994, c. 44, s. 78;
1999, c. 5, s. 43.
Levy under writ
772 (1) Where a writ of
Costs
(2) Where this section applies, the Crown is entitled to the costs of execution and of proceedings incidental thereto that are fixed, in the Province of Quebec, by any tariff applicable in the Superior Court in civil proceedings, and in any other province, by any tariff applicable in the superior court of the province in civil proceedings, as the judge may direct.
R.S., c. C-34, s. 706.
Committal when writ not satisfied
773 (1) Where a writ of
Notice
(2) Seven clear days notice of the time and place fixed for the hearing pursuant to subsection (1) shall be given to the sureties.
Hearing
(3) The judge shall, at the hearing held pursuant to subsection (1), inquire into the circumstances of the case and may in his discretion
(a) order the discharge of the amount for which the surety is liable; or
(b) make any order with respect to the surety and to his imprisonment that he considers proper in the circumstances and issue a warrant of committal in Form 27.
Warrant to committal
(4) A warrant of committal issued pursuant to this section authorizes the sheriff to take into custody the person in respect of whom the warrant was issued and to confine him in a prison in the territorial division in which the writ was issued or in the prison nearest to the court, until satisfaction is made or until the period of imprisonment fixed by the judge has expired.
Definition of
Attorney General
(5) In this section and in section 771,
Attorney General
R.S., 1985, c. C-46, s. 773;
1995, c. 22, s. 10.

PART XXVI

PART XXVI
Extraordinary Remedies

Application of Part
774 This Part applies to proceedings in criminal matters by way of
R.S., 1985, c. C-46, s. 774;
R.S., 1985, c. 27 (1st Supp.), s. 169.
Appearance in person —
774.1 Despite any other provision of this Act, the person who is the subject of a writ of
2002, c. 13, s. 77.
Detention on inquiry to determine legality of imprisonment

775 Where proceedings to which this Part applies have been instituted before a judge or court having jurisdiction, by or in respect of a person who is in custody by reason that he is charged with or has been convicted of an offence, to have the legality of his imprisonment determined, the judge or court may, without determining the question, make an order for the further detention of that person and direct the judge, justice or provincial court judge under whose warrant he is in custody, or any other judge, justice or provincial court judge, to take any proceedings, hear such evidence or do any other thing that, in the opinion of the judge or court, will best further the ends of justice.
R.S., 1985, c. C-46, s. 775;
R.S., 1985, c. 27 (1st Supp.), s. 203.

Where conviction or order not reviewable

776 No conviction or order shall be removed by
(a) where an appeal was taken, whether or not the appeal has been carried to a conclusion; or
(b) where the defendant appeared and pleaded and the merits were tried, and an appeal might have been taken, but the defendant did not appeal.
R.S., c. C-34, s. 710.

Conviction or order remediable, when

777 (1) No conviction, order or warrant for enforcing a conviction or order shall, on being removed by
(a) that an offence of the nature described in the conviction, order or warrant, as the case may be, was committed,
(b) that there was jurisdiction to make the conviction or order or issue the warrant, as the case may be, and
(c) that the punishment imposed, if any, was not in excess of the punishment that might lawfully have been imposed,
but the court or judge has the same powers to deal with the proceedings in the manner that the court or judge considers proper that are conferred on a court to which an appeal might have been taken.

Correcting punishment

(2) Where, in proceedings to which subsection (1) applies, the court or judge is satisfied that a person was properly convicted of an offence but the punishment that was imposed is greater than the punishment that might lawfully have been imposed, the court or judge
(a) shall correct the sentence,
(i) where the punishment is a fine, by imposing a fine that does not exceed the maximum fine that might lawfully have been imposed,
(ii) where the punishment is imprisonment, and the person has not served a term of imprisonment under the sentence that is equal to or greater than the term of imprisonment that might lawfully have been imposed, by imposing a term of imprisonment that does not exceed the maximum term of imprisonment that might lawfully have been imposed, or
(iii) where the punishment is a fine and imprisonment, by imposing a punishment in accordance with subparagraph (i) or (ii), as the case requires; or
(b) shall remit the matter to the convicting judge, justice or provincial court judge and direct him to impose a punishment that is not greater than the punishment that may be lawfully imposed.

Amendment

(3) Where an adjudication is varied pursuant to subsection (1) or (2), the conviction and warrant of committal, if any, shall be amended to conform to the adjudication as varied.

Sufficiency of statement

(4) Any statement that appears in a conviction and is sufficient for the purpose of the conviction is sufficient for the purposes of an information, summons, order or warrant in which it appears in the proceedings.
R.S., 1985, c. C-46, s. 777;
R.S., 1985, c. 27 (1st Supp.), s. 203.

Irregularities within section 777

778 Without restricting the generality of section 777, that section shall be deemed to apply where

(a) the statement of the adjudication or of any other matter or thing is in the past tense instead of in the present tense;
(b) the punishment imposed is less than the punishment that might by law have been imposed for the offence that appears by the evidence to have been committed; or
(c) there has been an omission to negative circumstances, the existence of which would make the act complained of lawful, whether those circumstances are stated by way of exception or otherwise in the provision under which the offence is charged or are stated in another provision.
R.S., c. C-34, s. 712.
General order for security by recognizance
779 (1) A court that has authority to quash a conviction, order or other proceeding on
Provisions of Part XXV
(2) The provisions of Part XXV relating to forfeiture of recognizances apply to a recognizance entered into under this section.
R.S., c. C-34, s. 713.
Effect of order dismissing application to quash
780 Where a motion to quash a conviction, order or other proceeding is refused, the order of the court refusing the application is sufficient authority for the clerk of the court forthwith to return the conviction, order or proceeding to the court from which or the person from whom it was removed, and for proceedings to be taken with respect thereto for the enforcement thereof.
R.S., c. C-34, s. 714.
Want of proof of order in council
781 (1) No order, conviction or other proceeding shall be quashed or set aside, and no defendant shall be discharged, by reason only that evidence has not been given
(a) of a proclamation or order of the Governor in Council or the lieutenant governor in council;
(b) of rules, regulations or by-laws made by the Governor in Council under an Act of Parliament or by the lieutenant governor in council under an Act of the legislature of the province; or
(c) of the publication of a proclamation, order, rule, regulation or by-law in the
Canada Gazette
Judicial notice
(2) Proclamations, orders, rules, regulations and by-laws mentioned in subsection (1) and the publication thereof shall be judicially noticed.
R.S., c. C-34, s. 715.
Defect in form
782 No warrant of committal shall, on
(a) it is alleged in the warrant that the defendant was convicted; and
(b) there is a valid conviction to sustain the warrant.
R.S., c. C-34, s. 716.
No action against official when conviction, etc., quashed
783 Where an application is made to quash a conviction, order or other proceeding made or held by a provincial court judge acting under Part XIX or a justice on the ground that he exceeded his jurisdiction, the court to which or the judge to whom the application is made may, in quashing the conviction, order or other proceeding, order that no civil proceedings shall be taken against the justice or provincial court judge or against any officer who acted under the conviction, order or other proceeding or under any warrant issued to enforce it.
R.S., 1985, c. C-46, s. 783;
R.S., 1985, c. 27 (1st Supp.), s. 203.
Appeal in
784 (1) An appeal lies to the court of appeal from a decision granting or refusing the relief sought in proceedings by way of
Application of Part XXI
(2) Except as provided in this section, Part XXI applies, with such modifications as the circumstances require, to appeals under this section.

Refusal of application, and appeal
(3) Where an application for a writ of
Where writ granted
(4) Where a writ of
Appeal from judgment on return of writ
(5) Where a judgment is issued on the return of a writ of
Hearing of appeal
(6) An appeal in
R.S., 1985, c. C-46, s. 784;
1997, c. 18, s. 109.

PART XXVII

PART XXVII
Summary Convictions

Interpretation

Definitions
785 In this Part,
clerk of the appeal court
informant
information
(a) a count in an information, and
(b) a complaint in respect of which a justice is authorized by an Act of Parliament or an enactment made thereunder to make an order;
order
proceedings
(a) proceedings in respect of offences that are declared by an Act of Parliament or an enactment made thereunder to be punishable on summary conviction, and
(b) proceedings where a justice is authorized by an Act of Parliament or an enactment made thereunder to make an order;
prosecutor
sentence
(a) a declaration made under subsection 199(3),
(b) an order made under subsection 109(1) or 110(1), section 259 or 261, subsection 730(1) or 737(3) or section 738, 739, 742.1 or 742.3,
(c) a disposition made under section 731 or 732 or subsection 732.2(3) or (5), 742.4(3) or 742.6(9), and
(d) an order made under subsection 16(1) of the
Controlled Drugs and Substances Act
summary conviction court
(a) is given jurisdiction over the proceedings by the enactment under which the proceedings are taken,
(b) is a justice or provincial court judge, where the enactment under which the proceedings are taken does not expressly give jurisdiction to any person or class of persons, or
(c) is a provincial court judge, where the enactment under which the proceedings are taken gives jurisdiction in respect thereof to two or more justices;
trial
R.S., 1985, c. C-46, s. 785;
R.S., 1985, c. 27 (1st Supp.), ss. 170, 203;
1992, c. 1, s. 58;

1995, c. 22, s. 7, c. 39, s. 156;
1996, c. 19, s. 76;
1999, c. 25, s. 23(Preamble);
2002, c. 13, s. 78;
2006, c. 14, s. 7;
2013, c. 11, s. 4.

Application of Part

786 (1) Except where otherwise provided by law, this Part applies to proceedings as defined in this Part.

Limitation

(2) No proceedings shall be instituted more than six months after the time when the subject-matter of the proceedings arose, unless the prosecutor and the defendant so agree.
R.S., 1985, c. C-46, s. 786;
1997, c. 18, s. 110.

Punishment

General penalty

787 (1) Unless otherwise provided by law, everyone who is convicted of an offence punishable on summary conviction is liable to a fine of not more than five thousand dollars or to a term of imprisonment not exceeding six months or to both.

Imprisonment in default where not otherwise specified

(2) Where the imposition of a fine or the making of an order for the payment of money is authorized by law, but the law does not provide that imprisonment may be imposed in default of payment of the fine or compliance with the order, the court may order that in default of payment of the fine or compliance with the order, as the case may be, the defendant shall be imprisoned for a term not exceeding six months.
(3) to (11) R.S., 1985, c. C-46, s. 787;
R.S., 1985, c. 27 (1st Supp.), s. 171;
2008, c. 18, s. 44.

Information

Commencement of proceedings

788 (1) Proceedings under this Part shall be commenced by laying an information in Form 2.

One justice may act before the trial

(2) Notwithstanding any other law that requires an information to be laid before or to be tried by two or more justices, one justice may
(a) receive the information;
(b) issue a summons or warrant with respect to the information; and
(c) do all other things preliminary to the trial.
R.S., c. C-34, s. 723.

Formalities of information

789 (1) In proceedings to which this Part applies, an information
(a) shall be in writing and under oath; and
(b) may charge more than one offence or relate to more than one matter of complaint, but where more than one offence is charged or the information relates to more than one matter of complaint, each offence or matter of complaint, as the case may be, shall be set out in a separate count.

No reference to previous convictions

(2) No information in respect of an offence for which, by reason of previous convictions, a greater punishment may be imposed shall contain any reference to previous convictions.
R.S., c. C-34, s. 724.

Any justice may act before and after trial
790 (1) Nothing in this Act or any other law shall be deemed to require a justice before whom proceedings are commenced or who issues process before or after the trial to be the justice or one of the justices before whom the trial is held.
Two or more justices
(2) Where two or more justices have jurisdiction with respect to proceedings, they shall be present and act together at the trial, but one justice may thereafter do anything that is required or is authorized to be done in connection with the proceedings.
(3) and (4) R.S., 1985, c. C-46, s. 790;
R.S., 1985, c. 27 (1st Supp.), s. 172.
791 792

Defects and Objections

793 No need to negative exception, etc.
794 (1) No exception, exemption, proviso, excuse or qualification prescribed by law is required to be set out or negatived, as the case may be, in an information.
Burden of proving exception, etc.
(2) The burden of proving that an exception, exemption, proviso, excuse or qualification prescribed by law operates in favour of the defendant is on the defendant, and the prosecutor is not required, except by way of rebuttal, to prove that the exception, exemption, proviso, excuse or qualification does not operate in favour of the defendant, whether or not it is set out in the information.
R.S., c. C-34, s. 730.

Application

Application of Parts XVI, XVIII, XVIII.1, XX and XX.1
795 The provisions of Parts XVI and XVIII with respect to compelling the appearance of an accused before a justice, and the provisions of Parts XVIII.1, XX and XX.1, in so far as they are not inconsistent with this Part, apply, with any necessary modifications, to proceedings under this Part.
R.S., 1985, c. C-46, s. 795;
R.S., 1985, c. 27 (1st Supp.), s. 176;
1991, c. 43, s. 7;
2011, c. 16, s. 16.
796 and 797

Trial

Jurisdiction
798 Every summary conviction court has jurisdiction to try, determine and adjudge proceedings to which this Part applies in the territorial division over which the person who constitutes that court has jurisdiction.
R.S., c. C-34, s. 733.
Non-appearance of prosecutor
799 Where, in proceedings to which this Part applies, the defendant appears for the trial and the prosecutor, having had due notice, does not appear, the summary conviction court may dismiss the information or may adjourn the trial to some other time on such terms as it considers proper.
R.S., c. C-34, s. 734.
When both parties appear
800 (1) Where the prosecutor and defendant appear for the trial, the summary conviction court shall proceed to hold the trial.
Counsel or agent
(2) A defendant may appear personally or by counsel or agent, but the summary conviction court may require the defendant to appear personally and may, if it thinks fit, issue a warrant in Form 7 for

the arrest of the defendant and adjourn the trial to await his appearance pursuant thereto.
Video links
(2.1) Where the court so orders and the defendant agrees, the defendant who is confined in prison may appear by closed-circuit television or any other means that allow the court and the defendant to engage in simultaneous visual and oral communication, if the defendant is given the opportunity to communicate privately with counsel, in a case in which the defendant is represented by counsel.
Appearance by organization
(3) Where the defendant is an organization, it shall appear by counsel or agent and, if it does not appear, the summary conviction court may, on proof of service of the summons, proceed
R.S., 1985, c. C-46, s. 800;
1997, c. 18, s. 111;
2003, c. 21, s. 21.
Arraignment
801 (1) Where the defendant appears for the trial, the substance of the information laid against him shall be stated to him, and he shall be asked,
(a) whether he pleads guilty or not guilty to the information, where the proceedings are in respect of an offence that is punishable on summary conviction; or
(b) whether he has cause to show why an order should not be made against him, in proceedings where a justice is authorized by law to make an order.
Finding of guilt, conviction or order if charge admitted
(2) Where the defendant pleads guilty or does not show sufficient cause why an order should not be made against him, as the case may be, the summary conviction court shall convict the defendant, discharge the defendant under section 730 or make an order against the defendant accordingly.
Procedure if charge not admitted
(3) Where the defendant pleads not guilty or states that he has cause to show why an order should not be made against him, as the case may be, the summary conviction court shall proceed with the trial, and shall take the evidence of witnesses for the prosecutor and the defendant in accordance with the provisions of Part XVIII relating to preliminary inquiries.
(4) and (5) R.S., 1985, c. C-46, s. 801;
R.S., 1985, c. 27 (1st Supp.), s. 177, c. 1 (4th Supp.), s. 18(F);
1995, c. 22, s. 10.
Right to make full answer and defence
802 (1) The prosecutor is entitled personally to conduct his case and the defendant is entitled to make his full answer and defence.
Examination of witnesses
(2) The prosecutor or defendant, as the case may be, may examine and cross-examine witnesses personally or by counsel or agent.
On oath
(3) Every witness at a trial in proceedings to which this Part applies shall be examined under oath.
R.S., c. C-34, s. 737.
Limitation on the use of agents
802.1 Despite subsections 800(2) and 802(2), a defendant may not appear or examine or cross-examine witnesses by agent if he or she is liable, on summary conviction, to imprisonment for a term of more than six months, unless the defendant is a corporation or the agent is authorized to do so under a program approved by the lieutenant governor in council of the province.
2002, c. 13, s. 79.
Adjournment
803 (1) The summary conviction court may, in its discretion, before or during the trial, adjourn the trial to a time and place to be appointed and stated in the presence of the parties or their counsel or agents.
Non-appearance of defendant
(2) If a defendant who is tried alone or together with others does not appear at the time and place

appointed for the trial after having been notified of that time and place, or does not appear for the resumption of a trial that has been adjourned in accordance with subsection (1), the summary conviction court
(a) may proceed
(b) may, if it thinks fit, issue a warrant in Form 7 for the arrest of that defendant and adjourn the trial to await their appearance under the warrant.
Consent of Attorney General required
(3) If the summary conviction court proceeds in the manner described in paragraph (2)(a), no proceedings under section 145 arising out of the defendant's failure to appear at the time and place appointed for the trial or for the resumption of the trial shall, without the consent of the Attorney General, be instituted or be proceeded with.
Non-appearance of prosecutor
(4) Where the prosecutor does not appear at the time and place appointed for the resumption of an adjourned trial, the summary conviction court may dismiss the information with or without costs.
(5) to (8) R.S., 1985, c. C-46, s. 803;
1991, c. 43, s. 9;
1994, c. 44, s. 79;
1997, c. 18, s. 112;
2008, c. 18, s. 45.

Adjudication

Finding of guilt, conviction, order or dismissal
804 When the summary conviction court has heard the prosecutor, defendant and witnesses, it shall, after considering the matter, convict the defendant, discharge the defendant under section 730, make an order against the defendant or dismiss the information, as the case may be.
R.S., 1985, c. C-46, s. 804;
R.S., 1985, c. 27 (1st Supp.), s. 178, c. 1 (4th Supp.), s. 18(F);
1995, c. 22, s. 10.
805 Memo of conviction or order
806 (1) Where a defendant is convicted or an order is made in relation to the defendant, a minute or memorandum of the conviction or order shall be made by the summary conviction court indicating that the matter was dealt with under this Part and, on request by the defendant, the prosecutor or any other person, the court shall cause a conviction or order in Form 35 or 36, as the case may be, and a certified copy of the conviction or order to be drawn up and shall deliver the certified copy to the person making the request.
Warrant of committal
(2) Where a defendant is convicted or an order is made against him, the summary conviction court shall issue a warrant of committal in Form 21 or 22, and section 528 applies in respect of a warrant of committal issued under this subsection.
Admissibility of certified copy
(3) Where a warrant of committal in Form 21 is issued by a clerk of a court, a copy of the warrant of committal, certified by the clerk, is admissible in evidence in any proceeding.
R.S., 1985, c. C-46, s. 806;
R.S., 1985, c. 27 (1st Supp.), s. 185(F);
1994, c. 44, s. 80.
Disposal of penalties when joint offenders
807 Where several persons join in committing the same offence and on conviction each is adjudged to pay an amount to a person aggrieved, no more shall be paid to that person than an amount equal to the value of the property destroyed or injured or the amount of the injury done, together with costs, if any, and the residue of the amount adjudged to be paid shall be applied in the manner in which other penalties imposed by law are directed to be applied.

R.S., c. C-34, s. 742.
Order of dismissal
808 (1) Where the summary conviction court dismisses an information, it may, if requested by the defendant, draw up an order of dismissal and shall give to the defendant a certified copy of the order of dismissal.
Effect of certificate
(2) A copy of an order of dismissal, certified in accordance with subsection (1) is, without further proof, a bar to any subsequent proceedings against the defendant in respect of the same cause.
R.S., c. C-34, s. 743.
Costs
809 (1) The summary conviction court may in its discretion award and order such costs as it considers reasonable and not inconsistent with such of the fees established by section 840 as may be taken or allowed in proceedings before that summary conviction court, to be paid
(a) to the informant by the defendant, where the summary conviction court convicts or makes an order against the defendant; or
(b) to the defendant by the informant, where the summary conviction court dismisses an information.
Order set out
(2) An order under subsection (1) shall be set out in the conviction, order or order of dismissal, as the case may be.
Costs are part of fine
(3) Where a fine or sum of money or both are adjudged to be paid by a defendant and a term of imprisonment in default of payment is imposed, the defendant is, in default of payment, liable to serve the term of imprisonment imposed, and for the purposes of this subsection, any costs that are awarded against the defendant shall be deemed to be part of the fine or sum of money adjudged to be paid.
Where no fine imposed
(4) Where no fine or sum of money is adjudged to be paid by a defendant, but costs are awarded against the defendant or informant, the person who is liable to pay them is, in default of payment, liable to imprisonment for one month.
Definition of
(5) In this section,
costs
R.S., c. C-34, s. 744.

Sureties to Keep the Peace

If injury or damage feared
810 (1) An information may be laid before a justice by or on behalf of any person who fears on reasonable grounds that another person
(a) will cause personal injury to him or her or to his or her spouse or common-law partner or child or will damage his or her property; or
(b) will commit an offence under section 162.1.
Duty of justice
(2) A justice who receives an information under subsection (1) shall cause the parties to appear before him or before a summary conviction court having jurisdiction in the same territorial division.
Adjudication
(3) If the justice or summary conviction court before which the parties appear is satisfied by the evidence adduced that the person on whose behalf the information was laid has reasonable grounds for the fear, the justice or court may order that the defendant enter into a recognizance, with or without sureties, to keep the peace and be of good behaviour for a period of not more than 12 months.
Refusal to enter into recognizance

(3.01) The justice or summary conviction court may commit the defendant to prison for a term of not more than 12 months if the defendant fails or refuses to enter into the recognizance.

Conditions in recognizance

(3.02) The justice or summary conviction court may add any reasonable conditions to the recognizance that the justice or court considers desirable to secure the good conduct of the defendant, including conditions that require the defendant

(a) to abstain from the consumption of drugs except in accordance with a medical prescription, of alcohol or of any other intoxicating substance;

(b) to provide, for the purpose of analysis, a sample of a bodily substance prescribed by regulation on the demand of a peace officer, a probation officer or someone designated under paragraph 810.3(2)(a) to make a demand, at the place and time and on the day specified by the person making the demand, if that person has reasonable grounds to believe that the defendant has breached a condition of the recognizance that requires them to abstain from the consumption of drugs, alcohol or any other intoxicating substance; or

(c) to provide, for the purpose of analysis, a sample of a bodily substance prescribed by regulation at regular intervals that are specified, in a notice in Form 51 served on the defendant, by a probation officer or a person designated under paragraph 810.3(2)(b) to specify them, if a condition of the recognizance requires the defendant to abstain from the consumption of drugs, alcohol or any other intoxicating substance.

Conditions

(3.1) Before making an order under subsection (3), the justice or the summary conviction court shall consider whether it is desirable, in the interests of the safety of the defendant or of any other person, to include as a condition of the recognizance that the defendant be prohibited from possessing any firearm, cross-bow, prohibited weapon, restricted weapon, prohibited device, ammunition, prohibited ammunition or explosive substance, or all such things, for any period specified in the recognizance and, where the justice or summary conviction court decides that it is so desirable, the justice or summary conviction court shall add such a condition to the recognizance.

Surrender, etc.

(3.11) Where the justice or summary conviction court adds a condition described in subsection (3.1) to a recognizance order, the justice or summary conviction court shall specify in the order the manner and method by which

(a) the things referred to in that subsection that are in the possession of the accused shall be surrendered, disposed of, detained, stored or dealt with; and

(b) the authorizations, licences and registration certificates held by the person shall be surrendered.

Reasons

(3.12) Where the justice or summary conviction court does not add a condition described in subsection (3.1) to a recognizance order, the justice or summary conviction court shall include in the record a statement of the reasons for not adding the condition.

Idem

(3.2) Before making an order under subsection (3), the justice or the summary conviction court shall consider whether it is desirable, in the interests of the safety of the informant, of the person on whose behalf the information was laid or of that person's spouse or common-law partner or child, as the case may be, to add either or both of the following conditions to the recognizance, namely, a condition

(a) prohibiting the defendant from being at, or within a distance specified in the recognizance from, a place specified in the recognizance where the person on whose behalf the information was laid or that person's spouse or common-law partner or child, as the case may be, is regularly found; and

(b) prohibiting the defendant from communicating, in whole or in part, directly or indirectly, with the person on whose behalf the information was laid or that person's spouse or common-law partner or child, as the case may be.

Forms

(4) A recognizance and a committal to prison in default of recognizance may be in Forms 32 and 23,

respectively.
Modification of recognizance
(4.1) The justice or the summary conviction court may, on application of the informant or the defendant, vary the conditions fixed in the recognizance.
Procedure
(5) The provisions of this Part apply, with such modifications as the circumstances require, to proceedings under this section.
R.S., 1985, c. C-46, s. 810;
1991, c. 40, s. 33;
1994, c. 44, s. 81;
1995, c. 22, s. 8, c. 39, s. 157;
2000, c. 12, s. 95;
2011, c. 7, s. 7;
2014, c. 31, s. 25.
Fear of certain offences
810.01 (1) A person who fears on reasonable grounds that another person will commit an offence under section 423.1 or a criminal organization offence may, with the Attorney General's consent, lay an information before a provincial court judge.
Appearances
(2) A provincial court judge who receives an information under subsection (1) may cause the parties to appear before a provincial court judge.
Adjudication
(3) If the provincial court judge before whom the parties appear is satisfied by the evidence adduced that the informant has reasonable grounds for the fear, the judge may order that the defendant enter into a recognizance to keep the peace and be of good behaviour for a period of not more than 12 months.
Duration extended
(3.1) However, if the provincial court judge is also satisfied that the defendant was convicted previously of an offence referred to in subsection (1), the judge may order that the defendant enter into the recognizance for a period of not more than two years.
Refusal to enter into recognizance
(4) The provincial court judge may commit the defendant to prison for a term not exceeding twelve months if the defendant fails or refuses to enter into the recognizance.
Conditions in recognizance
(4.1) The provincial court judge may add any reasonable conditions to the recognizance that the judge considers desirable for preventing the commission of an offence referred to in subsection (1), including conditions that require the defendant
(a) to participate in a treatment program;
(b) to wear an electronic monitoring device, if the Attorney General makes the request;
(c) to remain within a specified geographic area unless written permission to leave that area is obtained from the judge;
(d) to return to and remain at their place of residence at specified times;
(e) to abstain from the consumption of drugs, except in accordance with a medical prescription, of alcohol or of any other intoxicating substance;
(f) to provide, for the purpose of analysis, a sample of a bodily substance prescribed by regulation on the demand of a peace officer, a probation officer or someone designated under paragraph 810.3(2)
(a) to make a demand, at the place and time and on the day specified by the person making the demand, if that person has reasonable grounds to believe that the defendant has breached a condition of the recognizance that requires them to abstain from the consumption of drugs, alcohol or any other intoxicating substance; or
(g) to provide, for the purpose of analysis, a sample of a bodily substance prescribed by regulation at regular intervals that are specified, in a notice in Form 51 served on the defendant, by a probation

officer or a person designated under paragraph 810.3(2)(b) to specify them, if a condition of the recognizance requires the defendant to abstain from the consumption of drugs, alcohol or any other intoxicating substance.

Conditions — firearms

(5) The provincial court judge shall consider whether it is desirable, in the interests of the defendant's safety or that of any other person, to prohibit the defendant from possessing any firearm, cross-bow, prohibited weapon, restricted weapon, prohibited device, ammunition, prohibited ammunition or explosive substance, or all of those things. If the judge decides that it is desirable to do so, the judge shall add that condition to the recognizance and specify the period during which the condition applies.

Surrender, etc.

(5.1) If the provincial court judge adds a condition described in subsection (5) to a recognizance, the judge shall specify in the recognizance how the things referred to in that subsection that are in the defendant's possession shall be surrendered, disposed of, detained, stored or dealt with and how the authorizations, licences and registration certificates that are held by the defendant shall be surrendered.

Reasons

(5.2) If the provincial court judge does not add a condition described in subsection (5) to a recognizance, the judge shall include in the record a statement of the reasons for not adding the condition.

Variance of conditions

(6) A provincial court judge may, on application of the informant, the Attorney General or the defendant, vary the conditions fixed in the recognizance.

Other provisions to apply

(7) Subsections 810(4) and (5) apply, with any modifications that the circumstances require, to recognizances made under this section.

Definition of

Attorney General

(8) With respect to proceedings under this section,

Attorney General

1997, c. 23, ss. 19, 26;
2001, c. 32, s. 46, c. 41, ss. 22, 133;
2002, c. 13, s. 80;
2009, c. 22, s. 19;
2011, c. 7, s. 8;
2015, c. 20, s. 24.

Fear of terrorism offence

810.011 (1) A person who fears on reasonable grounds that another person may commit a terrorism offence may, with the Attorney General's consent, lay an information before a provincial court judge.

Appearances

(2) The provincial court judge who receives an information under subsection (1) may cause the parties to appear before a provincial court judge.

Adjudication

(3) If the provincial court judge before whom the parties appear is satisfied by the evidence adduced that the informant has reasonable grounds for the fear, the judge may order that the defendant enter into a recognizance, with or without sureties, to keep the peace and be of good behaviour for a period of not more than 12 months.

Duration extended

(4) However, if the provincial court judge is also satisfied that the defendant was convicted previously of a terrorism offence, the judge may order that the defendant enter into the recognizance for a period of not more than five years.

Refusal to enter into recognizance

(5) The provincial court judge may commit the defendant to prison for a term of not more than 12 months if the defendant fails or refuses to enter into the recognizance.
Conditions in recognizance
(6) The provincial court judge may add any reasonable conditions to the recognizance that the judge considers desirable to secure the good conduct of the defendant, including conditions that require the defendant
(a) to participate in a treatment program;
(b) to wear an electronic monitoring device, if the Attorney General makes that request;
(c) to return to and remain at their place of residence at specified times;
(d) to abstain from the consumption of drugs, except in accordance with a medical prescription, of alcohol or of any other intoxicating substance;
(e) to provide, for the purpose of analysis, a sample of a bodily substance prescribed by regulation on the demand of a peace officer, a probation officer or someone designated under paragraph 810.3(2)(a) to make a demand, at the place and time and on the day specified by the person making the demand, if that person has reasonable grounds to believe that the defendant has breached a condition of the recognizance that requires them to abstain from the consumption of drugs, alcohol or any other intoxicating substance; or
(f) to provide, for the purpose of analysis, a sample of a bodily substance prescribed by regulation at regular intervals that are specified, in a notice in Form 51 served on the defendant, by a probation officer or a person designated under paragraph 810.3(2)(b) to specify them, if a condition of the recognizance requires the defendant to abstain from the consumption of drugs, alcohol or any other intoxicating substance.
Conditions — firearms
(7) The provincial court judge shall consider whether it is desirable, in the interests of the defendant's safety or that of any other person, to prohibit the defendant from possessing any firearm, cross-bow, prohibited weapon, restricted weapon, prohibited device, ammunition, prohibited ammunition or explosive substance, or all of those things. If the judge decides that it is desirable to do so, the judge shall add that condition to the recognizance and specify the period during which it applies.
Surrender, etc.
(8) If the provincial court judge adds a condition described in subsection (7) to a recognizance, the judge shall specify in the recognizance how the things referred to in that subsection that are in the defendant's possession shall be surrendered, disposed of, detained, stored or dealt with and how the authorizations, licences and registration certificates that are held by the defendant shall be surrendered.
Condition — passport
(9) The provincial court judge shall consider whether it is desirable, to secure the good conduct of the defendant, to include in the recognizance a condition that the defendant deposit, in the specified manner, any passport or other travel document issued in their name that is in their possession or control. If the judge decides that it is desirable, the judge shall add the condition to the recognizance and specify the period during which it applies.
Condition — specified geographic area
(10) The provincial court judge shall consider whether it is desirable, to secure the good conduct of the defendant, to include in the recognizance a condition that the defendant remain within a specified geographic area unless written permission to leave that area is obtained from the judge or any individual designated by the judge. If the judge decides that it is desirable, the judge shall add the condition to the recognizance and specify the period during which it applies.
Reasons
(11) If the provincial court judge does not add a condition described in subsection (7), (9) or (10) to a recognizance, the judge shall include in the record a statement of the reasons for not adding it.
Variance of conditions
(12) A provincial court judge may, on application of the informant, the Attorney General or the defendant, vary the conditions fixed in the recognizance.

Other provisions to apply
(13) Subsections 810(4) and (5) apply, with any modifications that the circumstances require, to recognizances made under this section.
Definition of
Attorney General
(14) With respect to proceedings under this section,
Attorney General
2015, c. 20, s. 25.
Fear of forced marriage or marriage under age of 16 years
810.02 (1) A person who fears on reasonable grounds that another person will commit an offence under paragraph 273.3(1)(d) or section 293.1 or 293.2 may lay an information before a provincial court judge.
Appearances
(2) The judge who receives the information may cause the parties to appear before a provincial court judge.
Adjudication
(3) If the provincial court judge before whom the parties appear is satisfied by the evidence adduced that the informant has reasonable grounds for the fear, the judge may order that the defendant enter into a recognizance to keep the peace and be of good behaviour for a period of not more than 12 months.
Duration extended
(4) However, if the provincial court judge is also satisfied that the defendant was convicted previously of an offence referred to in subsection (1), the judge may order that the defendant enter into the recognizance for a period of not more than two years.
Refusal to enter into recognizance
(5) The provincial court judge may commit the defendant to prison for a term not exceeding 12 months if the defendant fails or refuses to enter into the recognizance.
Conditions in recognizance
(6) The provincial court judge may add any reasonable conditions to the recognizance that the judge considers desirable to secure the good conduct of the defendant, including conditions that
(a) prohibit the defendant from making agreements or arrangements for the marriage, whether in or outside Canada, of the person in respect of whom it is feared that the offence will be committed;
(b) prohibit the defendant from taking steps to cause the person in respect of whom it is feared that the offence will be committed to leave the jurisdiction of the court;
(c) require the defendant to deposit, in the specified manner, any passport or any other travel document that is in their possession or control, whether or not such passport or document is in their name or in the name of any other specified person;
(d) prohibit the defendant from communicating, directly or indirectly, with any specified person, or refrain from going to any specified place, except in accordance with any specified conditions that the judge considers necessary;
(e) require the defendant to participate in a treatment program, including a family violence counselling program;
(f) require the defendant to remain within a specified geographic area unless written permission to leave that area is obtained from the provincial court judge; and
(g) require the defendant to return to and remain at their place of residence at specified times.
Conditions — firearms
(7) The provincial court judge shall consider whether it is desirable, in the interests of the defendant's safety or that of any other person, to prohibit the defendant from possessing any firearm, cross-bow, prohibited weapon, restricted weapon, prohibited device, ammunition, prohibited ammunition or explosive substance, or all of those things. If the judge decides that it is desirable to do so, the judge shall add that condition to the recognizance and specify the period during which the condition applies.

Surrender, etc.
(8) If the provincial court judge adds a condition described in subsection (7) to a recognizance, the judge shall specify in the recognizance how the things referred to in that subsection that are in the defendant's possession are to be surrendered, disposed of, detained, stored or dealt with and how the authorizations, licences and registration certificates that are held by the defendant are to be surrendered.

Variance of conditions
(9) A provincial court judge may, on application of the informant or the defendant, vary the conditions fixed in the recognizance.
2015, c. 29, s. 11.

Where fear of sexual offence
810.1 (1) Any person who fears on reasonable grounds that another person will commit an offence under section 151 or 152, subsection 153(1), section 155 or 159, subsection 160(2) or (3), section 163.1, 170, 171, 171.1, 172.1 or 172.2, subsection 173(2), section 271, 272, 273 or 279.011, subsection 279.02(2) or 279.03(2), section 280 or 281 or subsection 286.1(2), 286.2(2) or 286.3(2), in respect of one or more persons who are under the age of 16 years, may lay an information before a provincial court judge, whether or not the person or persons in respect of whom it is feared that the offence will be committed are named.

Appearances
(2) A provincial court judge who receives an information under subsection (1) may cause the parties to appear before a provincial court judge.

Adjudication
(3) If the provincial court judge before whom the parties appear is satisfied by the evidence adduced that the informant has reasonable grounds for the fear, the judge may order that the defendant enter into a recognizance to keep the peace and be of good behaviour for a period that does not exceed 12 months.

Duration extended
(3.01) However, if the provincial court judge is also satisfied that the defendant was convicted previously of a sexual offence in respect of a person who is under the age of 16 years, the judge may order that the defendant enter into the recognizance for a period that does not exceed two years.

Conditions in recognizance
(3.02) The provincial court judge may add any reasonable conditions to the recognizance that the judge considers desirable to secure the good conduct of the defendant, including conditions that
(a) prohibit the defendant from having any contact — including communicating by any means — with a person under the age of 16 years, unless the defendant does so under the supervision of a person whom the judge considers appropriate;
(a.1) prohibit the defendant from using the Internet or other digital network, unless the defendant does so in accordance with conditions set by the judge;
(b) prohibit the defendant from attending a public park or public swimming area where persons under the age of 16 years are present or can reasonably be expected to be present, or a daycare centre, schoolground or playground;
(b.1) prohibit the defendant from communicating, directly or indirectly, with any person identified in the recognizance, or refrain from going to any place specified in the recognizance, except in accordance with the conditions specified in the recognizance that the judge considers necessary;
(c) require the defendant to participate in a treatment program;
(d) require the defendant to wear an electronic monitoring device, if the Attorney General makes the request;
(e) require the defendant to remain within a specified geographic area unless written permission to leave that area is obtained from the provincial court judge;
(f) require the defendant to return to and remain at his or her place of residence at specified times;
(g) require the defendant to abstain from the consumption of drugs except in accordance with a medical prescription, of alcohol or of any other intoxicating substance;

(h) require the defendant to provide, for the purpose of analysis, a sample of a bodily substance prescribed by regulation on the demand of a peace officer, a probation officer or someone designated under paragraph 810.3(2)(a) to make a demand, at the place and time and on the day specified by the person making the demand, if that person has reasonable grounds to believe that the defendant has breached a condition of the recognizance that requires them to abstain from the consumption of drugs, alcohol or any other intoxicating substance; or

(i) require the defendant to provide, for the purpose of analysis, a sample of a bodily substance prescribed by regulation at regular intervals that are specified, in a notice in Form 51 served on the defendant, by a probation officer or a person designated under paragraph 810.3(2)(b) to specify them, if a condition of the recognizance requires the defendant to abstain from the consumption of drugs, alcohol or any other intoxicating substance.

Conditions — firearms

(3.03) The provincial court judge shall consider whether it is desirable, in the interests of the defendant's safety or that of any other person, to prohibit the defendant from possessing any firearm, cross-bow, prohibited weapon, restricted weapon, prohibited device, ammunition, prohibited ammunition or explosive substance, or all of those things. If the judge decides that it is desirable to do so, the judge shall add that condition to the recognizance and specify the period during which the condition applies.

Surrender, etc.

(3.04) If the provincial court judge adds a condition described in subsection (3.03) to a recognizance, the judge shall specify in the recognizance how the things referred to in that subsection that are in the defendant's possession should be surrendered, disposed of, detained, stored or dealt with and how the authorizations, licences and registration certificates that are held by the defendant should be surrendered.

Condition — reporting

(3.05) The provincial court judge shall consider whether it is desirable to require the defendant to report to the correctional authority of a province or to an appropriate police authority. If the judge decides that it is desirable to do so, the judge shall add that condition to the recognizance.

Refusal to enter into recognizance

(3.1) The provincial court judge may commit the defendant to prison for a term not exceeding twelve months if the defendant fails or refuses to enter into the recognizance.

Judge may vary recognizance

(4) A provincial court judge may, on application of the informant or the defendant, vary the conditions fixed in the recognizance.

Other provisions to apply

(5) Subsections 810(4) and (5) apply, with such modifications as the circumstances require, to recognizances made under this section.

1993, c. 45, s. 11;
1997, c. 18, s. 113;
2002, c. 13, s. 81;
2008, c. 6, ss. 52, 54, 62;
2011, c. 7, s. 9;
2012, c. 1, s. 37;
2014, c. 21, s. 4, c. 25, s. 31.

Where fear of serious personal injury offence

810.2 (1) Any person who fears on reasonable grounds that another person will commit a serious personal injury offence, as that expression is defined in section 752, may, with the consent of the Attorney General, lay an information before a provincial court judge, whether or not the person or persons in respect of whom it is feared that the offence will be committed are named.

Appearances

(2) A provincial court judge who receives an information under subsection (1) may cause the parties to appear before a provincial court judge.

Adjudication

(3) If the provincial court judge before whom the parties appear is satisfied by the evidence adduced that the informant has reasonable grounds for the fear, the judge may order that the defendant enter into a recognizance to keep the peace and be of good behaviour for a period that does not exceed 12 months.

Duration extended

(3.1) However, if the provincial court judge is also satisfied that the defendant was convicted previously of an offence referred to in subsection (1), the judge may order that the defendant enter into the recognizance for a period that does not exceed two years.

Refusal to enter into recognizance

(4) The provincial court judge may commit the defendant to prison for a term not exceeding twelve months if the defendant fails or refuses to enter into the recognizance.

Conditions in recognizance

(4.1) The provincial court judge may add any reasonable conditions to the recognizance that the judge considers desirable to secure the good conduct of the defendant, including conditions that require the defendant

(a) to participate in a treatment program;

(b) to wear an electronic monitoring device, if the Attorney General makes the request;

(c) to remain within a specified geographic area unless written permission to leave that area is obtained from the provincial court judge;

(d) to return to and remain at his or her place of residence at specified times;

(e) to abstain from the consumption of drugs except in accordance with a medical prescription, of alcohol or of any other intoxicating substance;

(f) to provide, for the purpose of analysis, a sample of a bodily substance prescribed by regulation on the demand of a peace officer, a probation officer or someone designated under paragraph 810.3(2)

(a) to make a demand, at the place and time and on the day specified by the person making the demand, if that person has reasonable grounds to believe that the defendant has breached a condition of the recognizance that requires them to abstain from the consumption of drugs, alcohol or any other intoxicating substance; or

(g) to provide, for the purpose of analysis, a sample of a bodily substance prescribed by regulation at regular intervals that are specified, in a notice in Form 51 served on the defendant, by a probation officer or a person designated under paragraph 810.3(2)(b) to specify them, if a condition of the recognizance requires the defendant to abstain from the consumption of drugs, alcohol or any other intoxicating substance.

Conditions — firearms

(5) The provincial court judge shall consider whether it is desirable, in the interests of the defendant's safety or that of any other person, to prohibit the defendant from possessing any firearm, cross-bow, prohibited weapon, restricted weapon, prohibited device, ammunition, prohibited ammunition or explosive substance, or all of those things. If the judge decides that it is desirable to do so, the judge shall add that condition to the recognizance and specify the period during which the condition applies.

Surrender, etc.

(5.1) If the provincial court judge adds a condition described in subsection (5) to a recognizance, the judge shall specify in the recognizance how the things referred to in that subsection that are in the defendant's possession should be surrendered, disposed of, detained, stored or dealt with and how the authorizations, licences and registration certificates that are held by the defendant should be surrendered.

Reasons

(5.2) If the provincial court judge does not add a condition described in subsection (5) to a recognizance, the judge shall include in the record a statement of the reasons for not adding the condition.

Condition — reporting

(6) The provincial court judge shall consider whether it is desirable to require the defendant to report to the correctional authority of a province or to an appropriate police authority. If the judge decides that it is desirable to do so, the judge shall add that condition to the recognizance.

Variance of conditions

(7) A provincial court judge may, on application of the informant, of the Attorney General or of the defendant, vary the conditions fixed in the recognizance.

Other provisions to apply

(8) Subsections 810(4) and (5) apply, with such modifications as the circumstances require, to recognizances made under this section.

1997, c. 17, s. 9;
2002, c. 13, s. 82;
2008, c. 6, s. 53;
2011, c. 7, s. 10.

Video conference

810.21 If a defendant is required to appear under any of sections 83.3 and 810 to 810.2, a provincial court judge may, on application of the prosecutor, order that the defendant appear by video conference if the judge is satisfied that it would serve the proper administration of justice, including by ensuring a fair and efficient hearing and enhancing access to justice.

2015, c. 20, s. 26.

Transfer of order

810.22 (1) If a person who is bound by an order under any of sections 83.3 and 810 to 810.2 becomes a resident of — or is charged with, convicted of or discharged under section 730 of an offence, including an offence under section 811, in — a territorial division other than the territorial division in which the order was made, on application of a peace officer or the Attorney General, a provincial court judge may, subject to subsection (2), transfer the order to a provincial court judge in that other territorial division and the order may then be dealt with and enforced by the provincial court judge to whom it is transferred in all respects as if that provincial court judge had made the order.

Attorney General's consent

(2) The transfer may be granted only with

(a) the consent of the Attorney General of the province in which the order was made, if the two territorial divisions are not in the same province; or

(b) the consent of the Attorney General of Canada, if the information that led to the issuance of the order was laid with the consent of the Attorney General of Canada.

If judge unable to act

(3) If the judge who made the order or a judge to whom an order has been transferred is for any reason unable to act, the powers of that judge in relation to the order may be exercised by any other judge of the same court.

2015, c. 20, s. 26.

Samples — designations and specifications

810.3 (1) For the purposes of sections 810, 810.01, 810.011, 810.1 and 810.2 and subject to the regulations, the Attorney General of a province or the minister of justice of a territory shall, with respect to the province or territory,

(a) designate the persons or classes of persons that may take samples of bodily substances;

(b) designate the places or classes of places at which the samples are to be taken;

(c) specify the manner in which the samples are to be taken;

(d) specify the manner in which the samples are to be analyzed;

(e) specify the manner in which the samples are to be stored, handled and destroyed;

(f) specify the manner in which the records of the results of the analysis of the samples are to be protected and destroyed;

(g) designate the persons or classes of persons that may destroy the samples; and

(h) designate the persons or classes of persons that may destroy the records of the results of the analysis of the samples.

Further designations

(2) Subject to the regulations, the Attorney General of a province or the minister of justice of a territory may, with respect to the province or territory, designate the persons or classes of persons

(a) to make a demand for a sample of a bodily substance for the purposes of paragraphs 810(3.02)(b), 810.01(4.1)(f), 810.011(6)(e), 810.1(3.02)(h) and 810.2(4.1)(f); and

(b) to specify the regular intervals at which a defendant must provide a sample of a bodily substance for the purposes of paragraphs 810(3.02)(c), 810.01(4.1)(g), 810.011(6)(f), 810.1(3.02)(i) and 810.2(4.1)(g).

Restriction

(3) Samples of bodily substances referred to in sections 810, 810.01, 810.011, 810.1 and 810.2 may not be taken, analyzed, stored, handled or destroyed, and the records of the results of the analysis of the samples may not be protected or destroyed, except in accordance with the designations and specifications made under subsection (1).

Destruction of samples

(4) The Attorney General of a province or the minister of justice of a territory, or a person authorized by the Attorney General or minister, shall cause all samples of bodily substances provided under a recognizance under section 810, 810.01, 810.011, 810.1 or 810.2 to be destroyed within the period prescribed by regulation unless the samples are reasonably expected to be used as evidence in a proceeding for an offence under section 811.

Regulations

(5) The Governor in Council may make regulations

(a) prescribing bodily substances for the purposes of sections 810, 810.01, 810.011, 810.1 and 810.2;

(b) respecting the designations and specifications referred to in subsections (1) and (2);

(c) prescribing the periods within which samples of bodily substances are to be destroyed under subsection (4); and

(d) respecting any other matters relating to the samples of bodily substances.

Notice — samples at regular intervals

(6) The notice referred to in paragraph 810(3.02)(c), 810.01(4.1)(g), 810.011(6)(f), 810.1(3.02)(i) or 810.2(4.1)(g) must specify the places and times at which and the days on which the defendant must provide samples of a bodily substance under a condition described in that paragraph. The first sample may not be taken earlier than 24 hours after the defendant is served with the notice, and subsequent samples must be taken at regular intervals of at least seven days.

2011, c. 7, s. 11;

2015, c. 20, s. 34.

Prohibition on use of bodily substance

810.4 (1) No person shall use a bodily substance provided under a recognizance under section 810, 810.01, 810.011, 810.1 or 810.2 except for the purpose of determining whether a defendant is complying with a condition in the recognizance that they abstain from the consumption of drugs, alcohol or any other intoxicating substance.

Prohibition on use or disclosure of result

(2) Subject to subsection (3), no person shall use, disclose or allow the disclosure of the results of the analysis of a bodily substance provided under a recognizance under section 810, 810.01, 810.011, 810.1 or 810.2.

Exception

(3) The results of the analysis of a bodily substance provided under a recognizance under section 810, 810.01, 810.011, 810.1 or 810.2 may be disclosed to the defendant to whom they relate, and may also be used or disclosed in the course of an investigation of, or in a proceeding for, an offence under section 811 or, if the results are made anonymous, for statistical or other research purposes.

Offence

(4) Every person who contravenes subsection (1) or (2) is guilty of an offence punishable on summary conviction.

2011, c. 7, s. 11;
2015, c. 20, s. 34.

Breach of recognizance

811 A person bound by a recognizance under any of sections 83.3 and 810 to 810.2 who commits a breach of the recognizance is guilty of

(a) an indictable offence and is liable to imprisonment for a term of not more than four years; or

(b) an offence punishable on summary conviction and is liable to imprisonment for a term of not more than 18 months.

R.S., 1985, c. C-46, s. 811;
1993, c. 45, s. 11;
1994, c. 44, s. 82;
1997, c. 17, s. 10, c. 23, ss. 20, 27;
2001, c. 41, s. 23;
2015, c. 20, s. 27, c. 23, s. 19, c. 29, s. 12.

Proof of certificate of analyst — bodily substance

811.1 (1) In a prosecution for breach of a condition in a recognizance under section 810, 810.01, 810.011, 810.1 or 810.2 that a defend- ant not consume drugs, alcohol or any other intoxicating substance, a certificate purporting to be signed by an analyst that states that the analyst has analyzed a sample of a bodily substance and that states the result of the analysis is admissible in evidence and, in the absence of evidence to the contrary, is proof of the statements contained in the certificate without proof of the signature or official character of the person who appears to have signed the certificate.

Definition of

analyst

(2) In this section,

analyst

Notice of intention to produce certificate

(3) No certificate shall be admitted in evidence unless the party intending to produce it has, before the trial, given reasonable notice and a copy of the certificate to the party against whom it is to be produced.

Requiring attendance of analyst

(4) The party against whom a certificate of an analyst is produced may, with leave of the court, require the attendance of the analyst for cross-examination.

2011, c. 7, s. 12;
2015, c. 20, s. 34.

Appeal

Definition of

appeal court

812 (1) For the purposes of sections 813 to 828,

appeal court

(a) in the Province of Ontario, the Superior Court of Justice sitting in the region, district or county or group of counties where the adjudication was made;

(b) in the Province of Quebec, the Superior Court;

(c) in the Provinces of Nova Scotia, British Columbia and Prince Edward Island, the Supreme Court;

(d) in the Provinces of New Brunswick, Manitoba, Saskatchewan and Alberta, the Court of Queen's Bench;

(e) (f) (g) in the Province of Newfoundland and Labrador, the Trial Division of the Supreme Court;

(h) in Yukon and the Northwest Territories, a judge of the Supreme Court; and

(i) in Nunavut, a judge of the Nunavut Court of Justice.

When appeal court is Court of Appeal of Nunavut

(2) A judge of the Court of Appeal of Nunavut is the appeal court for the purposes of sections 813 to 828 if the appeal is from a conviction, order, sentence or verdict of a summary conviction court consisting of a judge of the Nunavut Court of Justice.
R.S., 1985, c. C-46, s. 812;
R.S., 1985, c. 11 (1st Supp.), s. 2, c. 27 (2nd Supp.), s. 10;
1990, c. 16, s. 7, c. 17, s. 15;
1992, c. 51, s. 43;
1998, c. 30, s. 14;
1999, c. 3, s. 55;
2002, c. 7, s. 149;
2015, c. 3, s. 56.

Appeal by defendant, informant or Attorney General

813 Except where otherwise provided by law,
(a) the defendant in proceedings under this Part may appeal to the appeal court
(i) from a conviction or order made against him,
(ii) against a sentence passed on him, or
(iii) against a verdict of unfit to stand trial or not criminally responsible on account of mental disorder; and
(b) the informant, the Attorney General or his agent in proceedings under this Part may appeal to the appeal court
(i) from an order that stays proceedings on an information or dismisses an information,
(ii) against a sentence passed on a defendant, or
(iii) against a verdict of not criminally responsible on account of mental disorder or unfit to stand trial,
and the Attorney General of Canada or his agent has the same rights of appeal in proceedings instituted at the instance of the Government of Canada and conducted by or on behalf of that Government as the Attorney General of a province or his agent has under this paragraph.
R.S., 1985, c. C-46, s. 813;
R.S., 1985, c. 27 (1st Supp.), s. 180;
1991, c. 43, s. 9.

Manitoba and Alberta

814 (1) In the Provinces of Manitoba and Alberta, an appeal under section 813 shall be heard at the sittings of the appeal court that is held nearest to the place where the cause of the proceedings arose, but the judge of the appeal court may, on the application of one of the parties, appoint another place for the hearing of the appeal.

Saskatchewan

(2) In the Province of Saskatchewan, an appeal under section 813 shall be heard at the sittings of the appeal court at the judicial centre nearest to the place where the adjudication was made, but the judge of the appeal court may, on the application of one of the parties, appoint another place for the hearing of the appeal.

British Columbia

(3) In the Province of British Columbia, an appeal under section 813 shall be heard at the sittings of the appeal court that is held nearest to the place where the adjudication was made, but the judge of the appeal court may, on the application of one of the parties, appoint another place for the hearing of the appeal.

Territories

(4) In Yukon, the Northwest Territories and Nunavut, an appeal under section 813 shall be heard at the place where the cause of the proceedings arose or at the place nearest to it where a court is appointed to be held.
R.S., 1985, c. C-46, s. 814;
1993, c. 28, s. 78;
2002, c. 7, s. 150.

Notice of appeal

815 (1) An appellant who proposes to appeal to the appeal court shall give notice of appeal in such manner and within such period as may be directed by rules of court.

Extension of time

(2) The appeal court or a judge thereof may extend the time within which notice of appeal may be given.

R.S., c. C-34, s. 750;
1972, c. 13, s. 66;
1974-75-76, c. 93, s. 89.

Interim Release of Appellant

Undertaking or recognizance of appellant

816 (1) A person who was the defendant in proceedings before a summary conviction court and by whom an appeal is taken under section 813 shall, if he is in custody, remain in custody unless the appeal court at which the appeal is to be heard orders that the appellant be released

(a) on his giving an undertaking to the appeal court, without conditions or with such conditions as the appeal court directs, to surrender himself into custody in accordance with the order,

(b) on his entering into a recognizance without sureties in such amount, with such conditions, if any, as the appeal court directs, but without deposit of money or other valuable security, or

(c) on his entering into a recognizance with or without sureties in such amount, with such conditions, if any, as the appeal court directs, and on his depositing with that appeal court such sum of money or other valuable security as the appeal court directs,

and the person having the custody of the appellant shall, where the appellant complies with the order, forthwith release the appellant.

Application of certain provisions of section 525

(2) The provisions of subsections 525(5), (6) and (7) apply with such modifications as the circumstances require in respect of a person who has been released from custody under subsection (1).

R.S., 1985, c. C-46, s. 816;
R.S., 1985, c. 27 (1st Supp.), s. 181(E).

Undertaking or recognizance of prosecutor

817 (1) The prosecutor in proceedings before a summary conviction court by whom an appeal is taken under section 813 shall, forthwith after filing the notice of appeal and proof of service thereof in accordance with section 815, appear before a justice, and the justice shall, after giving the prosecutor and the respondent a reasonable opportunity to be heard, order that the prosecutor

(a) give an undertaking as prescribed in this section; or

(b) enter into a recognizance in such amount, with or without sureties and with or without deposit of money or other valuable security, as the justice directs.

Condition

(2) The condition of an undertaking or recognizance given or entered into under this section is that the prosecutor will appear personally or by counsel at the sittings of the appeal court at which the appeal is to be heard.

Appeals by Attorney General

(3) This section does not apply in respect of an appeal taken by the Attorney General or by counsel acting on behalf of the Attorney General.

Form of undertaking or recognizance

(4) An undertaking under this section may be in Form 14 and a recognizance under this section may be in Form 32.

R.S., c. 2(2nd Supp.), s. 16.

Application to appeal court for review

818 (1) Where a justice makes an order under section 817, either the appellant or the respondent may,

before or at any time during the hearing of the appeal, apply to the appeal court for a review of the order made by the justice.
Disposition of application by appeal court
(2) On the hearing of an application under this section, the appeal court, after giving the appellant and the respondent a reasonable opportunity to be heard, shall
(a) dismiss the application; or
(b) if the person applying for the review shows cause, allow the application, vacate the order made by the justice and make the order that in the opinion of the appeal court should have been made.
Effect of order
(3) An order made under this section shall have the same force and effect as if it had been made by the justice.
R.S., c. 2(2nd Supp.), s. 16;
1974-75-76, c. 93, s. 91.1.
Application to fix date for hearing of appeal
819 (1) Where, in the case of an appellant who has been convicted by a summary conviction court and who is in custody pending the hearing of his appeal, the hearing of his appeal has not commenced within thirty days from the day on which notice of his appeal was given in accordance with the rules referred to in section 815, the person having the custody of the appellant shall, forthwith on the expiration of those thirty days, apply to the appeal court to fix a date for the hearing of the appeal.
Order fixing date
(2) On receiving an application under subsection (1), the appeal court shall, after giving the prosecutor a reasonable opportunity to be heard, fix a date for the hearing of the appeal and give such directions as it thinks necessary for expediting the hearing of the appeal.
R.S., c. 2(2nd Supp.), s. 16;
1974-75-76, c. 93, s. 92.
Payment of fine not a waiver of appeal
820 (1) A person does not waive his right of appeal under section 813 by reason only that he pays the fine imposed on conviction, without in any way indicating an intention to appeal or reserving the right to appeal.
Presumption
(2) A conviction, order or sentence shall be deemed not to have been appealed against until the contrary is shown.
R.S., c. C-34, s. 753.

Procedure on Appeal

Notification and transmission of conviction, etc.
821 (1) Where a notice of appeal has been given in accordance with the rules referred to in section 815, the clerk of the appeal court shall notify the summary conviction court that made the conviction or order appealed from or imposed the sentence appealed against of the appeal and on receipt of the notification that summary conviction court shall transmit the conviction, order or order of dismissal and all other material in its possession in connection with the proceedings to the appeal court before the time when the appeal is to be heard, or within such further time as the appeal court may direct, and the material shall be kept by the clerk of the appeal court with the records of the appeal court.
Saving
(2) An appeal shall not be dismissed by the appeal court by reason only that a person other than the appellant failed to comply with the provisions of this Part relating to appeals.
Appellant to furnish transcript of evidence
(3) Where the evidence on a trial before a summary conviction court has been taken by a stenographer duly sworn or by a sound recording apparatus, the appellant shall, unless the appeal court otherwise orders or the rules referred to in section 815 otherwise provide, cause a transcript

thereof, certified by the stenographer or in accordance with subsection 540(6), as the case may be, to be furnished to the appeal court and the respondent for use on the appeal.
R.S., c. C-34, s. 754;
1972, c. 13, s. 67;
1974-75-76, c. 93, s. 93.

Certain sections applicable to appeals
822 (1) Where an appeal is taken under section 813 in respect of any conviction, acquittal, sentence, verdict or order, sections 683 to 689, with the exception of subsections 683(3) and 686(5), apply, with such modifications as the circumstances require.

New trial
(2) Where an appeal court orders a new trial, it shall be held before a summary conviction court other than the court that tried the defendant in the first instance, unless the appeal court directs that the new trial be held before the summary conviction court that tried the accused in the first instance.

Order of detention or release
(3) Where an appeal court orders a new trial, it may make such order for the release or detention of the appellant pending the trial as may be made by a justice pursuant to section 515 and the order may be enforced in the same manner as if it had been made by a justice under that section, and the provisions of Part XVI apply with such modifications as the circumstances require to the order.

Trial
(4) Despite subsections (1) to (3), if an appeal is taken under section 813 and because of the condition of the record of the trial in the summary conviction court or for any other reason, the appeal court, on application of the defendant, the informant, the Attorney General or the Attorney General's agent, is of the opinion that the interests of justice would be better served by hearing and determining the appeal by holding a trial

Former evidence
(5) The appeal court may, for the purpose of hearing and determining an appeal under subsection (4), permit the evidence of any witness taken before the summary conviction court to be read if that evidence has been authenticated in accordance with section 540 and if
(a) the appellant and respondent consent,
(b) the appeal court is satisfied that the attendance of the witness cannot reasonably be obtained, or
(c) by reason of the formal nature of the evidence or otherwise the court is satisfied that the opposite party will not be prejudiced,
and any evidence that is read under the authority of this subsection has the same force and effect as if the witness had given the evidence before the appeal court.

Appeal against sentence
(6) Where an appeal is taken under subsection (4) against sentence, the appeal court shall, unless the sentence is one fixed by law, consider the fitness of the sentence appealed against and may, on such evidence, if any, as it thinks fit to require or receive, by order,
(a) dismiss the appeal, or
(b) vary the sentence within the limits prescribed by law for the offence of which the defendant was convicted,
and in making any order under paragraph (b), the appeal court may take into account any time spent in custody by the defendant as a result of the offence.

General provisions re appeals
(7) The following provisions apply in respect of appeals under subsection (4):
(a) where an appeal is based on an objection to an information or any process, judgment shall not be given in favour of the appellant
(i) for any alleged defect therein in substance or in form, or
(ii) for any variance between the information or process and the evidence adduced at the trial, unless it is shown
(iii) that the objection was taken at the trial, and
(iv) that an adjournment of the trial was refused notwithstanding that the variance referred to in

subparagraph (ii) had deceived or misled the appellant; and

(b) where an appeal is based on a defect in a conviction or an order, judgment shall not be given in favour of the appellant, but the court shall make an order curing the defect.

R.S., 1985, c. C-46, s. 822;

1991, c. 43, s. 9;

2002, c. 13, s. 83.

823 Adjournment

824 The appeal court may adjourn the hearing of an appeal from time to time as may be necessary.

R.S., c. C-34, s. 756.

Dismissal for failure to appear or want of prosecution

825 The appeal court may, on proof that notice of an appeal has been given and that

(a) the appellant has failed to comply with any order made under section 816 or 817 or with the conditions of any undertaking or recognizance given or entered into as prescribed in either of those sections, or

(b) the appeal has not been proceeded with or has been abandoned,

order that the appeal be dismissed.

R.S., c. C-34, s. 757;

R.S., c. 2(2nd Supp.), s. 18.

Costs

826 Where an appeal is heard and determined or is abandoned or is dismissed for want of prosecution, the appeal court may make any order with respect to costs that it considers just and reasonable.

R.S., c. C-34, s. 758.

To whom costs payable, and when

827 (1) Where the appeal court orders the appellant or respondent to pay costs, the order shall direct that the costs be paid to the clerk of the court, to be paid by him to the person entitled to them, and shall fix the period within which the costs shall be paid.

Certificate of non-payment of costs

(2) Where costs are not paid in full within the period fixed for payment and the person who has been ordered to pay them has not been bound by a recognizance to pay them, the clerk of the court shall, on application by the person entitled to the costs, or by any person on his behalf, and on payment of any fee to which the clerk of the court is entitled, issue a certificate in Form 42 certifying that the costs or a part thereof, as the case may be, have not been paid.

Committal

(3) A justice having jurisdiction in the territorial division in which a certificate has been issued under subsection (2) may, on production of the certificate, by warrant in Form 26, commit the defaulter to imprisonment for a term not exceeding one month, unless the amount of the costs and, where the justice thinks fit so to order, the costs of the committal and of conveying the defaulter to prison are sooner paid.

R.S., c. C-34, s. 759.

Enforcement of conviction or order by court of appeal

828 (1) A conviction or order made by the appeal court may be enforced

(a) in the same manner as if it had been made by the summary conviction court; or

(b) by process of the appeal court.

Enforcement by justice

(2) Where an appeal taken against a conviction or order adjudging payment of a sum of money is dismissed, the summary conviction court that made the conviction or order or a justice for the same territorial division may issue a warrant of committal as if no appeal had been taken.

Duty of clerk of court

(3) Where a conviction or order that has been made by an appeal court is to be enforced by a justice, the clerk of the appeal court shall send to the justice the conviction or order and all writings relating thereto, except the notice of intention to appeal and any recognizance.

R.S., c. C-34, s. 760.

Summary Appeal on Transcript or Agreed Statement of Facts

Definition of
829 (1) Subject to subsection (2), for the purposes of sections 830 to 838,
appeal court
Nunavut
(2) If the appeal is from a conviction, judgment, verdict or other final order or determination of a summary conviction court consisting of a judge of the Nunavut Court of Justice,
appeal court
R.S., 1985, c. C-46, s. 829;
R.S., 1985, c. 27 (1st Supp.), s. 182;
1999, c. 3, s. 56.
Appeals
830 (1) A party to proceedings to which this Part applies or the Attorney General may appeal against a conviction, judgment, verdict of acquittal or verdict of not criminally responsible on account of mental disorder or of unfit to stand trial or other final order or determination of a summary conviction court on the ground that
(a) it is erroneous in point of law;
(b) it is in excess of jurisdiction; or
(c) it constitutes a refusal or failure to exercise jurisdiction.
Form of appeal
(2) An appeal under this section shall be based on a transcript of the proceedings appealed from unless the appellant files with the appeal court, within fifteen days of the filing of the notice of appeal, a statement of facts agreed to in writing by the respondent.
Rules for appeals
(3) An appeal under this section shall be made within the period and in the manner directed by any applicable rules of court and where there are no such rules otherwise providing, a notice of appeal in writing shall be served on the respondent and a copy thereof, together with proof of service, shall be filed with the appeal court within thirty days after the date of the conviction, judgment or verdict of acquittal or other final order or determination that is the subject of the appeal.
Rights of Attorney General of Canada
(4) The Attorney General of Canada has the same rights of appeal in proceedings instituted at the instance of the Government of Canada and conducted by or on behalf of that Government as the Attorney General of a province has under this section.
R.S., 1985, c. C-46, s. 830;
R.S., 1985, c. 27 (1st Supp.), s. 182;
1991, c. 43, s. 9.
Application
831 The provisions of sections 816, 817, 819 and 825 apply, with such modifications as the circumstances require, in respect of an appeal under section 830, except that on receiving an application by the person having the custody of an appellant described in section 819 to appoint a date for the hearing of the appeal, the appeal court shall, after giving the prosecutor a reasonable opportunity to be heard, give such directions as it thinks necessary for expediting the hearing of the appeal.
R.S., 1985, c. C-46, s. 831;
R.S., 1985, c. 27 (1st Supp.), s. 182.
Undertaking or recognizance
832 (1) When a notice of appeal is filed pursuant to section 830, the appeal court may order that the appellant appear before a justice and give an undertaking or enter into a recognizance as provided in section 816 where the defendant is the appellant, or as provided in section 817, in any other case.

Attorney General
(2) Subsection (1) does not apply where the appellant is the Attorney General or counsel acting on behalf of the Attorney General.
R.S., 1985, c. C-46, s. 832;
R.S., 1985, c. 27 (1st Supp.), s. 182.
No writ required
833 No writ of
R.S., 1985, c. C-46, s. 833;
R.S., 1985, c. 27 (1st Supp.), s. 182;
1991, c. 43, s. 9.
Powers of appeal court
834 (1) When a notice of appeal is filed pursuant to section 830, the appeal court shall hear and determine the grounds of appeal and may
(a) affirm, reverse or modify the conviction, judgment, verdict or other final order or determination, or
(b) remit the matter to the summary conviction court with the opinion of the appeal court,
and may make any other order in relation to the matter or with respect to costs that it considers proper.
Authority of judge
(2) Where the authority and jurisdiction of the appeal court may be exercised by a judge of that court, the authority and jurisdiction may, subject to any applicable rules of court, be exercised by a judge of the court sitting in chambers as well in vacation as in term time.
R.S., 1985, c. C-46, s. 834;
R.S., 1985, c. 27 (1st Supp.), s. 182;
1991, c. 43, s. 9.
Enforcement
835 (1) Where the appeal court renders its decision on an appeal, the summary conviction court from which the appeal was taken or a justice exercising the same jurisdiction has the same authority to enforce a conviction, order or determination that has been affirmed, modified or made by the appeal court as the summary conviction court would have had if no appeal had been taken.
Idem
(2) An order of the appeal court may be enforced by its own process.
R.S., 1985, c. C-46, s. 835;
R.S., 1985, c. 27 (1st Supp.), s. 182.
Appeal under section 830
836 Every person who appeals under section 830 from any conviction, judgment, verdict or other final order or determination in respect of which that person is entitled to an appeal under section 813 shall be taken to have abandoned all the person's rights of appeal under section 813.
R.S., 1985, c. C-46, s. 836;
R.S., 1985, c. 27 (1st Supp.), s. 182;
1991, c. 43, s. 9.
Appeal barred
837 Where it is provided by law that no appeal lies from a conviction or order, no appeal under section 830 lies from such a conviction or order.
R.S., 1985, c. C-46, s. 837;
R.S., 1985, c. 27 (1st Supp.), s. 182.
Extension of time
838 The appeal court or a judge thereof may at any time extend any time period referred to in section 830, 831 or 832.
R.S., 1985, c. C-46, s. 838;
R.S., 1985, c. 27 (1st Supp.), s. 182.

Appeals to Court of Appeal

Appeal on question of law
839 (1) Subject to subsection (1.1), an appeal to the court of appeal as defined in section 673 may, with leave of that court or a judge thereof, be taken on any ground that involves a question of law alone, against
(a) a decision of a court in respect of an appeal under section 822; or
(b) a decision of an appeal court under section 834, except where that court is the court of appeal.
Nunavut
(1.1) An appeal to the Court of Appeal of Nunavut may, with leave of that court or a judge of that court, be taken on any ground that involves a question of law alone, against a decision of a judge of the Court of Appeal of Nunavut acting as an appeal court under subsection 812(2) or 829(2).
Sections applicable
(2) Sections 673 to 689 apply with such modifications as the circumstances require to an appeal under this section.
Costs
(3) Notwithstanding subsection (2), the court of appeal may make any order with respect to costs that it considers proper in relation to an appeal under this section.
Enforcement of decision
(4) The decision of the court of appeal may be enforced in the same manner as if it had been made by the summary conviction court before which the proceedings were originally heard and determined.
Right of Attorney General of Canada to appeal
(5) The Attorney General of Canada has the same rights of appeal in proceedings instituted at the instance of the Government of Canada and conducted by or on behalf of that Government as the Attorney General of a province has under this Part.
R.S., 1985, c. C-46, s. 839;
R.S., 1985, c. 27 (1st Supp.), s. 183;
1999, c. 3, s. 57.

Fees and Allowances

Fees and allowances
840 (1) Subject to subsection (2), the fees and allowances mentioned in the schedule to this Part are the fees and allowances that may be taken or allowed in proceedings before summary conviction courts and justices under this Part.
Order of lieutenant governor in council
(2) The lieutenant governor in council of a province may order that all or any of the fees and allowances mentioned in the schedule to this Part shall not be taken or allowed in proceedings before summary conviction courts and justices under this Part in that province and, when the lieutenant governor in council so orders, he or she may fix any other fees and allowances for any items similar to those mentioned in the schedule, or any other items, to be taken or allowed instead.
R.S., 1985, c. C-46, s. 840;
1994, c. 44, s. 83;
1997, c. 18, s. 114.

PART XXVIII

PART XXVIII
Miscellaneous

Electronic Documents

Definitions
841 The definitions in this section apply in this section and in sections 842 to 847.
data
electronic document
R.S., 1985, c. C-46, s. 841;
R.S., 1985, c. 31 (4th Supp.), s. 97;
2002, c. 13, s. 84.

Dealing with data in court
842 Despite anything in this Act, a court may create, collect, receive, store, transfer, distribute, publish or otherwise deal with electronic documents if it does so in accordance with an Act or with the rules of court.
2002, c. 13, s. 84.

Transfer of data
843 (1) Despite anything in this Act, a court may accept the transfer of data by electronic means if the transfer is made in accordance with the laws of the place where the transfer originates or the laws of the place where the data is received.

Time of filing
(2) If a document is required to be filed in a court and the filing is done by transfer of data by electronic means, the filing is complete when the transfer is accepted by the court.
2002, c. 13, s. 84.

Documents in writing
844 A requirement under this Act that a document be made in writing is satisfied by the making of the document in electronic form in accordance with an Act or the rules of court.
2002, c. 13, s. 84.

Signatures
845 If this Act requires a document to be signed, the court may accept a signature in an electronic document if the signature is made in accordance with an Act or the rules of court.
2002, c. 13, s. 84.

Oaths
846 If under this Act an information, an affidavit or a solemn declaration or a statement under oath or solemn affirmation is to be made by a person, the court may accept it in the form of an electronic document if
(a) the person states in the electronic document that all matters contained in the information, affidavit, solemn declaration or statement are true to his or her knowledge and belief;
(b) the person before whom it is made or sworn is authorized to take or receive informations, affidavits, solemn declarations or statements and he or she states in the electronic document that the information, affidavit, solemn declaration or statement was made under oath, solemn declaration or solemn affirmation, as the case may be; and
(c) the electronic document was made in accordance with the laws of the place where it was made.
2002, c. 13, s. 84.

Copies
847 Any person who is entitled to obtain a copy of a document from a court is entitled, in the case of a document in electronic form, to obtain a printed copy of the electronic document from the court on payment of a reasonable fee determined in accordance with a tariff of fees fixed or approved by the Attorney General of the relevant province.
2002, c. 13, s. 84.

Remote Appearance by Incarcerated Accused

Condition for remote appearance

848 Despite anything in this Act, if an accused who is in prison does not have access to legal advice during the proceedings, the court shall, before permitting the accused to appear by a means of communication that allows the court and the accused to engage in simultaneous visual and oral communication, be satisfied that the accused will be able to understand the proceedings and that any decisions made by the accused during the proceedings will be voluntary.
2002, c. 13, s. 84.

Forms

Forms
849 (1) The forms set out in this Part, varied to suit the case, or forms to the like effect are deemed to be good, valid and sufficient in the circumstances for which they are provided.
Seal not required
(2) No justice is required to attach or affix a seal to any writing or process that he or she is authorized to issue and in respect of which a form is provided by this Part.
Official languages
(3) Any pre-printed portions of a form set out in this Part, varied to suit the case, or of a form to the like effect shall be printed in both official languages.
2002, c. 13, s. 84.

SCHEDULE TO PART XX.1

SCHEDULE TO PART XX.1
SCHEDULE [to Part XXV]

SCHEDULE [to Part XXV] A judge of the Court of Appeal in respect of a recognizance for the appearance of a person before the Court
The Registrar of the Court of Appeal
The Superior Court of Justice in respect of all other recognizances
A Registrar of the Superior Court of Justice
The Court of Quebec, Criminal and Penal Division
The Clerk of the Court
The Supreme Court
A Prothonotary of the Supreme Court
The Court of Queen's Bench
The Registrar of the Court of Queen's Bench
The Supreme Court in respect of a recognizance for the appearance of a person before that Court or the Court of Appeal
The District Registrar of the Supreme Court
A Provincial Court in respect of a recognizance for the appearance of a person before a judge of that Court or a justice
The Clerk of the Provincial Court
The Supreme Court
The Prothonotary
The Court of Queen's Bench
The registrar or a deputy registrar of the Court of Queen's Bench
The Court of Queen's Bench
The Local Registrar of the Court of Queen's Bench
The Court of Queen's Bench
The Clerk of the Court of Queen's Bench
The Trial Division of the Supreme Court
The Registrar of the Supreme Court

The Supreme Court
The Clerk of the Supreme Court
The Supreme Court
The Clerk of the Supreme Court
The Nunavut Court of Justice
The Clerk of the Nunavut Court of Justice
R.S., 1985, c. C-46, Sch. to Part XXV;
R.S., 1985, c. 11 (1st Supp.), s. 2, c. 27 (2nd Supp.), s. 10;
1992, c. 1, s. 58, c. 51, ss. 40 to 42;
1998, c. 30, s. 14;
1999, c. 3, s. 54, c. 5, s. 44;
2002, c. 7, s. 148;
2015, c. 3, ss. 57 to 59.

SCHEDULE [to Part XXVII]

SCHEDULE [to Part XXVII]

Fees and Allowances That May Be Charged by Summary Conviction Courts and Justices

1 Information
2 Summons or warrant
3 Warrant where summons issued in first instance
4 Warrant where summons issued in first instance
5 Each subpoena or warrant to or for witnesses
(A subpoena may contain any number of names. Only one subpoena may be issued on behalf of a party in any proceeding, unless the summary conviction court or the justice considers it necessary or desirable that more than one subpoena be issued.)
6 Information for warrant for witness and warrant for witness
7 Each necessary copy of subpoena to or warrant for witness
8 Each recognizance
9 Hearing and determining proceeding
10 Where hearing lasts more than two hours
11 Where two or more justices hear and determine a proceeding, each is entitled to the fee authorized by item 9.
12 Each warrant of committal
13 Making up record of conviction or order on request of a party to the proceedings
14 Copy of a writing other than a conviction or order, on request of a party to the proceedings; for each folio of one hundred words
15 Bill of costs, when made out in detail on request of a party to the proceedings
(Items 14 and 15 may be charged only where there has been an adjudication.)
16 Attending to remand prisoner
17 Attending to take recognizance of bail

Fees and Allowances That May Be Allowed to Peace Officers

18 Arresting a person on a warrant or without a warrant
19 Serving summons or subpoena
20 Mileage to serve summons or subpoena or to make an arrest, both ways, for each mile
(Where a public conveyance is not used, reasonable costs of transportation may be allowed.)
21 Mileage where service cannot be effected, on proof of a diligent attempt to effect service, each way, for each mile

22 Returning with prisoner after arrest to take him before a summary conviction court or justice at a place different from the place where the peace officer received the warrant to arrest, if the journey is of necessity over a route different from that taken by the peace officer to make the arrest, each way, for each mile

23 Taking a prisoner to prison on remand or committal, each way, for each mile
(Where a public conveyance is not used, reasonable costs of transportation may be allowed. No charge may be made under this item in respect of a service for which a charge is made under item 22.)

24 Attending summary conviction court or justice on summary conviction proceedings, for each day necessarily employed
(Not more than $2.00 may be charged under this item in respect of any day notwithstanding the number of proceedings that the peace officer attended on that day before that summary conviction court or justice.)

Fees and Allowances That May Be Allowed to Witnesses

25 Each day attending trial
26 Mileage travelled to attend trial, each way, for each mile

Fees and Allowances That May Be Allowed to Interpreters

27 Each half day attending trial
28 Actual living expenses when away from ordinary place of residence, not to exceed per day
29 Mileage travelled to attend trial, each way, for each mile
R.S., c. C-34, Sch. to Part XXIV.
FORM 1

Information To Obtain a Search Warrant

Canada,
Province of
(
This is the information of A.B., of
The informant says that (
Wherefore the informant prays that a search warrant may be granted to search the said (
Sworn before me this
FORM 2

Information

Canada,
Province of
(
This is the information of C.D., of
The informant says that (
Sworn before me this
R.S., 1985, c. C-46, Form 2;
R.S., 1985, c. 27 (1st Supp.), s. 184.
FORM 3 FORM 4

Heading of Indictment

Canada,
Province of

(
In the (
Her Majesty the Queen
against
(
1 That he (
2 That he (
Dated this
R.S., 1985, c. C-46, Form 4;
R.S., 1985, c. 27 (1st Supp.), s. 184;
1999, c. 3, s. 58.
FORM 5
Warrant To Search

Canada,
Province of
(
To the peace officers in the said (
Whereas it appears on the oath of A.B., of
This is, therefore, to authorize and require you between the hours of (
Dated this
R.S., 1985, c. C-46, Form 5;
1999, c. 5, s. 45.
FORM 5.001
Preservation Demand

Canada,
Province of
(
To (
Because I have reasonable grounds to suspect that the computer data specified below is in your possession or control and that that computer data
will assist in the investigation of an offence that has been or will be committed under (
Criminal Code
(or)
will assist in the investigation of an offence that has been committed under (
you are required to preserve (
This demand is subject to the following conditions:
If you contravene this demand without lawful excuse, you may be subject to a fine.
You are required to destroy the computer data that would not be retained in the ordinary course of business, and any document that is prepared for the purpose of preserving the computer data, in accordance with section
Criminal Code
2014, c. 31, s. 26.
FORM 5.002
Information To Obtain a Preservation Order

Canada,
Province of
(
This is the information of (
The informant says that they have reasonable grounds to suspect that an offence has been or will be

committed under (
Criminal Code
The informant also says that a peace officer or public officer intends to apply or has applied for a warrant or order in connection with the investigation to obtain a document that contains the computer data (
The reasonable grounds are: (
Criminal Code
The informant therefore requests that (
Sworn before me on (
2014, c. 31, s. 26.
FORM 5.003

Preservation Order

Canada,
Province of
(
To (
Whereas I am satisfied by information on oath of (
(a) that there are reasonable grounds to suspect that an offence has been or will be committed under (
Criminal Code
(b) that a peace officer or public officer intends to apply or has applied for a warrant or order to obtain a document that contains the computer data (
Therefore, you are required to preserve the specified computer data that is in your possession or control when you receive this order until (
This order is subject to the following conditions:
If you contravene this order without lawful excuse, you may be subject to a fine, to imprisonment or to both.
You are required to destroy the computer data that would not be retained in the ordinary course of business, and any document that is prepared for the purpose of preserving the computer data, in accordance with section
Criminal Code
Dated (
2014, c. 31, s. 26.
FORM 5.004

Information To Obtain a Production Order

Canada,
Province of
(
This is the information of (
The informant says that they have reasonable grounds to suspect (
Criminal Code
(a) that an offence has been or will be committed under (
Criminal Code
(b) (
Criminal Code
(or)
(b) (
Criminal Code
(or)
(b) (
Criminal Code

(or)
(b) (
Criminal Code
(or)
(b) (
Criminal Code
The reasonable grounds are:
The informant therefore requests
(
Criminal Code
(or)
(
Criminal Code
(or)
(
Criminal Code
(or)
(
Criminal Code
(or)
(
Criminal Code
Sworn before me on (
2014, c. 31, s. 26.
FORM 5.005

Production Order for Documents

Canada,
Province of
(
To (
Whereas I am satisfied by information on oath of (
Criminal Code
Therefore, you are ordered to
produce a document that is a copy of (
(
prepare and produce a document containing (
The document must be produced to (
This order is subject to the following conditions:
You have the right to apply to revoke or vary this order.
If you contravene this order without lawful excuse, you may be subject to a fine, to imprisonment or to both.
Dated (
2014, c. 31, s. 26.
FORM 5.006

Production Order To Trace a Communication

Canada,
Province of
(
Whereas I am satisfied by information on oath of (
Criminal Code

Therefore, on being served with this order in accordance with subsection
Criminal Code
The document must be produced to (
This order is subject to the following conditions:
You have the right to apply to revoke or vary this order.
If you contravene this order without lawful excuse, you may be subject to a fine, to imprisonment or to both.
Dated (
Served on (
2014, c. 31, s. 26.
FORM 5.007

Production Order for Transmission Data or Tracking Data

Canada,
Province of
(
To (
Whereas I am satisfied by information on oath of (
Criminal Code
Therefore, you are ordered to prepare and produce a document containing the data specified that is in your possession or control when you receive this order.
The document must be produced to (
This order is subject to the following conditions:
You have the right to apply to revoke or vary this order.
If you contravene this order without lawful excuse, you may be subject to a fine, to imprisonment or to both.
Dated (
2014, c. 31, s. 26.
FORM 5.008

Production Order for Financial Data

Canada,
Province of
(
To (
Whereas I am satisfied by information on oath of (
Criminal Code
Therefore, you are ordered to prepare and produce a document setting out (
The document must be produced to (
This order is subject to the following conditions:
You have the right to apply to revoke or vary this order.
If you contravene this order without lawful excuse, you may be subject to a fine, to imprisonment or to both.
Dated (
2014, c. 31, s. 26.
FORM 5.0081

Information To Revoke or Vary an Order Made Under Any of Sections 487.013 to 487.018 of the Criminal Code

Canada,
Province of
(

This is the information of (
The informant says that on or after (
Criminal Code
The informant therefore requests that the order be revoked (or be varied as follows:
Sworn before me on (
2014, c. 31, s. 26.
FORM 5.009

Information To Obtain a Non-Disclosure Order

Canada,
Province of
(
This is the information of (
The informant says that they have reasonable grounds to believe that the disclosure of the existence (or any of the contents or any of the following portion or portions) of (
Criminal Code
(
The reasonable grounds are:
The informant therefore requests an order prohibiting (
Sworn before me on (
2014, c. 31, s. 26.
FORM 5.0091

Non-Disclosure Order

Canada,
Province of
(
To (
Whereas I am satisfied by information on oath of (
Criminal Code
Therefore, you are prohibited from disclosing the existence (or any of the contents or any of the following portion or portions) of the demand (or the order) during a period of (
(
You have the right to apply to revoke or vary this order.
If you contravene this order without lawful excuse, you may be subject to a fine, to imprisonment or to both.
Dated (
2014, c. 31, s. 26.
FORM 5.01

Information To Obtain a Warrant To Take Bodily Substances for Forensic DNA Analysis

Canada,
Province of
(
This is the information of (
The informant says that he or she has reasonable grounds to believe
(a) that (
Criminal Code
(b) that a bodily substance has been found
(i) at the place where the offence was committed,
(ii) on or within the body of the victim of the offence,

(iii) on anything worn or carried by the victim at the time when the offence was committed, or
(iv) on or within the body of any person or thing or at any place associated with the commission of the offence;
(c) that (
(d) that forensic DNA analysis of a bodily substance from (
The reasonable grounds are:
The informant therefore requests that a warrant be issued authorizing the taking from (
Criminal Code
Sworn to before me this
1998, c. 37, s. 24.
FORM 5.02

Warrant Authorizing the Taking of Bodily Substances for Forensic DNA Analysis

Canada,
Province of
(
To the peace officers in (
Whereas it appears on the oath of (
(a) that (
Criminal Code
(b) that a bodily substance has been found
(i) at the place where the offence was committed,
(ii) on or within the body of the victim of the offence,
(iii) on anything worn or carried by the victim at the time when the offence was committed, or
(iv) on or within the body of any person or thing or at any place associated with the commission of the offence,
(c) that (
(d) that forensic DNA analysis of a bodily substance from (
And whereas I am satisfied that it is in the best interests of the administration of justice to issue this warrant;
This is therefore to authorize and require you to take from (
Criminal Code
Dated this
1998, c. 37, s. 24.
FORM 5.03

Order Authorizing the Taking of Bodily Substances for Forensic DNA Analysis

Canada
Province of
(
To the peace officers in (
Whereas (
Criminal Code
Young Offenders Act
Youth Criminal Justice Act
Criminal Code
Therefore, you are authorized to take or cause to be taken from (
Criminal Code
This order is subject to the following terms and conditions that I consider advisable to ensure that the taking of the samples is reasonable in the circumstances:
Dated this

1998, c. 37, s. 24;
2002, c. 1, s. 185;
2005, c. 25, s. 12;
2007, c. 22, s. 23.

FORM 5.04

Order Authorizing the Taking of Bodily Substances for Forensic DNA Analysis

Canada
Province of
(
To the peace officers in (
Whereas (
(a) has been found not criminally responsible on account of mental disorder for (
Criminal Code
(b) has been convicted under the
Criminal Code
Young Offenders Act
Youth Criminal Justice Act
Criminal Code
[ ] (i) an offence under the
Criminal Code
[ ] (ii) an offence under any of sections 5 to 7 of the
Controlled Drugs and Substances Act
[ ] (iii) an offence under any of sections 145 to 148, subsection 173(1), sections 252, 264, 264.1, 266 and 270, subsection 286.1(1), paragraph 348(1)(e) and sections 349 and 423 of the
Criminal Code
[ ] (iv) an offence under section 433 or 434 of the
Criminal Code
[ ] (v) an attempt or a conspiracy to commit an offence referred to in subparagraph (i) or (ii) that was prosecuted by indictment (
Whereas I have considered the offender's criminal record, the nature of the offence, the circumstances surrounding its commission, whether the offender was previously found not criminally responsible on account of mental disorder for a designated offence, and the impact that this order would have on the offender's privacy and security of the person;
And whereas I am satisfied that it is in the best interests of the administration of justice to make this order;
Therefore, you are authorized to take or cause to be taken from (
Criminal Code
This order is subject to the following terms and conditions that I consider advisable to ensure that the taking of the samples is reasonable in the circumstances:
Dated this
1998, c. 37, s. 24;
2002, c. 1, s. 186;
2005, c. 25, s. 12;
2007, c. 22, s. 23;
2012, c. 1, s. 38;
2014, c. 25, s. 32.

FORM 5.041

Order to a Person To Have Bodily Substances Taken for Forensic DNA Analysis

Canada

Province of
(
To A.B., of
Whereas an order has been made under section 487.051, or an authorization has been granted under section 487.055, of the
Criminal Code
This is therefore to command you, in Her Majesty's name, to appear on
Criminal Code
You are warned that failure to appear in accordance with this order may result in a warrant being issued for your arrest under subsection 487.0551(1) of the
Criminal Code
Subsection 487.0551(1) of the
Criminal Code
If a person fails to appear at the place, day and time set out in an order made under subsection 487.051(4) or 487.055(3.11) or in a summons referred to in subsection 487.055(4) or 487.091(3), a justice of the peace may issue a warrant for their arrest in Form 5.062 to allow samples of bodily substances to be taken.
Subsection 487.0552(1) of the
Criminal Code
Every person who, without reasonable excuse, fails to comply with an order made under subsection 487.051(4) or 487.055(3.11) of this Act or under subsection 196.14(4) or 196.24(4) of the
National Defence Act
(a) an indictable offence and liable to imprisonment for a term of not more than two years; or
(b) an offence punishable on summary conviction.
Dated this
2007, c. 22, s. 23.
FORM 5.05

Application for an Authorization To Take Bodily Substances for Forensic DNA Analysis

Canada
Province of
(
I (
Criminal Code
Whereas (
(a) had been declared a dangerous offender under Part XXIV of the
Criminal Code
(b) had been declared a dangerous offender or a dangerous sexual offender under Part XXI of the
Criminal Code
(c) had been convicted of murder,
(c.1) had been convicted of attempted murder or conspiracy to commit murder or to cause another person to be murdered and is currently serving a sentence of imprisonment for that offence,
(d) had been convicted of a sexual offence within the meaning of subsection 487.055(3) of the
Criminal Code
(e) had been convicted of manslaughter and is currently serving a sentence of imprisonment for that offence;
Therefore, I request that an authorization be granted under subsection 487.055(1) of the
Criminal Code
Dated this
1998, c. 37, s. 24;
2005, c. 25, s. 12;

2007, c. 22, s. 23.
FORM 5.06
Authorization To Take Bodily Substances for Forensic DNA Analysis

Canada
Province of
(
To the peace officers in (
Whereas (
Criminal Code
Whereas (
(a) had been declared a dangerous offender under Part XXIV of the
Criminal Code
(b) had been declared a dangerous offender or a dangerous sexual offender under Part XXI of the
Criminal Code
(c) had been convicted of murder,
(c.1) had been convicted of attempted murder or conspiracy to commit murder or to cause another person to be murdered and, on the date of the application, was serving a sentence of imprisonment for that offence,
(d) had been convicted of a sexual offence within the meaning of subsection 487.055(3) of the
Criminal Code
(e) had been convicted of manslaughter and, on the date of the application, was serving a sentence of imprisonment for that offence;
And whereas I have considered the offender's criminal record, the nature of the offence, the circumstances surrounding its commission and the impact that this authorization would have on the offender's privacy and security of the person;
Therefore, you are authorized to take those samples or cause them to be taken from (
Criminal Code
This authorization is subject to the following terms and conditions that I consider advisable to ensure that the taking of the samples is reasonable in the circumstances:
Dated this
1998, c. 37, s. 24;
2005, c. 25, s. 12;
2007, c. 22, s. 23.
FORM 5.061
Summons to a Person To Have Bodily Substances Taken for Forensic DNA Analysis

Canada
Province of
(
To A.B., of
Whereas an authorization has been granted under section 487.055 or 487.091 of the
Criminal Code
This is therefore to command you, in Her Majesty's name, to appear on
Criminal Code
You are warned that failure to appear in accordance with this summons may result in a warrant being issued for your arrest under subsection 487.0551(1) of the
Criminal Code
Subsection 487.0551(1) of the
Criminal Code
If a person fails to appear at the place, day and time set out in an order made under subsection

487.051(4) or 487.055(3.11) or in a summons referred to in subsection 487.055(4) or 487.091(3), a justice of the peace may issue a warrant for their arrest in Form 5.062 to allow samples of bodily substances to be taken.

Subsection 487.0552(1) of the
Criminal Code

Every person who, without reasonable excuse, fails to comply with an order made under subsection 487.051(4) or 487.055(3.11) of this Act or under subsection 196.14(4) or 196.24(4) of the National Defence Act

(a) an indictable offence and liable to imprisonment for a term of not more than two years; or
(b) an offence punishable on summary conviction.

Dated this
2007, c. 22, s. 23.
FORM 5.062

Warrant for Arrest

Canada
Province of
(
To the peace officers in (
This warrant is issued for the arrest of A.B., of
Whereas the offender failed to appear at the place, day and time set out in an order made under subsection 487.051(4) or 487.055(3.11), or in a summons referred to in subsection 487.055(4) or 487.091(3), of the
Criminal Code
This is, therefore, to command you, in Her Majesty's name, to arrest the offender without delay in order to allow the samples of bodily substances to be taken.
Dated this
2007, c. 22, s. 23.
FORM 5.07

Report to a Provincial Court Judge or the Court

Canada
Province of
(
[ ] To (
Criminal Code
[ ] To the court that made an order under section 487.051 of the
Criminal Code
I (
Criminal Code
I have (
The samples were taken on the
I (
Criminal Code
[ ] individual hairs, including the root sheath
[ ] epithelial cells taken by swabbing the lips, tongue or inside cheeks of the mouth
[ ] blood taken by pricking the skin surface with a sterile lancet
Any terms or conditions in the (
Dated this
1998, c. 37, s. 24;
2007, c. 22, s. 24.
FORM 5.08

Application for an Authorization To Take Additional Samples of Bodily Substances for Forensic DNA Analysis

Canada
Province of
(
I (
Whereas samples of bodily substances were taken from (
Criminal Code
And whereas on (
(a) a DNA profile could not be derived from the samples for the following reasons:
(b) the information or bodily substances required by regulations made under the
DNA Identification Act
Therefore, I request that an authorization be granted under subsection 487.091(1) of the
Criminal Code
Dated this
1998, c. 37, s. 24;
2005, c. 25, s. 13;
2007, c. 22, s. 25.
FORM 5.09

Authorization To Take Additional Samples of Bodily Substances for Forensic DNA Analysis

Canada
Province of
(
To the peace officers in (
Whereas samples of bodily substances were taken from (
Criminal Code
Whereas on (
(a) a DNA profile could not be derived from the samples for the following reasons:
(b) the information or bodily substances required by regulations made under the
DNA Identification Act
And whereas (
Criminal Code
Therefore, you are authorized to take those additional samples, or cause them to be taken, from (
Criminal Code
This authorization is subject to the following terms and conditions that I consider advisable to ensure that the taking of the samples is reasonable in the circumstances:
Dated this
1998, c. 37, s. 24;
2005, c. 25, s. 13;
2007, c. 22, s. 25.
FORM 5.1

Warrant To Search

Canada,
Province of [
To A.B. and other peace officers in the [
Whereas it appears on the oath of A.B., a peace officer in the [
[

relevant to the investigation of the following indictable offence
[
are to be found in the following place or premises
[
This is, therefore, to authorize you to enter the said place or premises between the hours of [
Issued at [
You may obtain from the clerk of the court a copy of the report filed by the peace officer who executed this warrant. That report will indicate the things, if any, that were seized and the location where they are being held.
R.S., 1985, c. 27 (1st Supp.), s. 184, c. 1 (4th Supp.), s. 17.
FORM 5.2

Report to a Justice

Canada,
Province of
(
To the justice who issued a warrant to the undersigned pursuant to section 256, 487 or 487.1 of the Criminal Code
I, (
Criminal Code
1 searched the premises situated at
2 seized the following things and dealt with them as follows:
Property Seized
(
Disposition
(
(a) (b) In the case of a warrant issued by telephone or other means of telecommunication, the statements referred to in subsection 487.1(9) of the
Criminal Code
Dated this
R.S., 1985, c. 27 (1st Supp.), s. 184.
FORM 5.3

Report to a Judge of Property Seized

Canada,
Province of
(
To a judge of the court from which the warrant was issued (
I, (
Criminal Code
1 searched the premises situated at
2 seized the following property:
Property Seized
(
Location
(
Dated this
R.S., 1985, c. 42 (4th Supp.), s. 6.
FORM 6

Summons to a Person Charged with an Offence

Canada,

Province of
(
To A.B., of
Whereas you have this day been charged before me that (
This is therefore to command you, in Her Majesty's name:
(a) to attend court on
(b) to appear on
Identification of Criminals Act
You are warned that failure without lawful excuse to attend court in accordance with this summons is an offence under subsection 145(4) of the
Criminal Code
Subsection 145(4) of the
Criminal Code
"(4) Every one who is served with a summons and who fails, without lawful excuse, the proof of which lies on him, to appear at a time and place stated therein, if any, for the purposes of the Identification of Criminals Act
(a) an indictable offence and is liable to imprisonment for a term not exceeding two years; or
(b) an offence punishable on summary conviction."
Section 510 of the
Criminal Code
"510 Where an accused who is required by a summons to appear at a time and place stated therein for the purposes of the
Identification of Criminals Act
Dated this
R.S., 1985, c. C-46, Form 6;
R.S., 1985, c. 27 (1st Supp.), s.184.
FORM 7

Warrant for Arrest

Canada,
Province of
(
To the peace officers in the said (
This warrant is issued for the arrest of A.B., of
Whereas the accused has been charged that (
And whereas:
(a) there are reasonable grounds to believe that it is necessary in the public interest to issue this warrant for the arrest of the accused [507(4), 512(1)];
(b) the accused failed to attend court in accordance with the summons served on him [512(2)];
(c) (an appearance notice or a promise to appear or a recognizance entered into before an officer in charge) was confirmed and the accused failed to attend court in accordance therewith [512(2)];
(d) it appears that a summons cannot be served because the accused is evading service [512(2)];
(e) the accused was ordered to be present at the hearing of an application for a review of an order made by a justice and did not attend the hearing [520(5), 521(5)];
(f) there are reasonable grounds to believe that the accused has contravened or is about to contravene the (promise to appear or undertaking or recognizance) on which he was released [524(1), 525(5), 679(6)];
(g) there are reasonable grounds to believe that the accused has since his release from custody on (a promise to appear or an undertaking or a recognizance) committed an indictable offence [524(1), 525(5), 679(6)];
(h) the accused was required by (an appearance notice or a promise to appear or a recognizance entered into before an officer in charge or a summons) to attend at a time and place stated therein for

the purposes of the
Identification of Criminals Act
(i) an indictment has been found against the accused and the accused has not appeared or remained in attendance before the court for his trial [597];
(j) This is, therefore, to command you, in Her Majesty's name, forthwith to arrest the said accused and to bring him before (
(
This warrant is also issued to authorize you to enter the dwelling-house for the purpose of arresting or apprehending the accused, subject to the condition that you may not enter the dwelling-house unless you have, immediately before entering the dwelling-house, reasonable grounds to believe that the person to be arrested or apprehended is present in the dwelling-house.
Dated this
* ** R.S., 1985, c. C-46, Form 7;
R.S., 1985, c. 27 (1st Supp.), s.203;
1997, c. 39, s. 3;
1999, c. 5, s. 46.
FORM 7.1

Warrant To Enter Dwelling-house

Canada,
Province of
(
To the peace officers in the said (
This warrant is issued in respect of the arrest of A.B., or a person with the following description (
Whereas there are reasonable grounds to believe:
(a) a warrant referred to in this or any other Act of Parliament to arrest or apprehend the person is in force anywhere in Canada;
(b) grounds exist to arrest the person without warrant under paragraph 495(1)(a) or (b) or section 672.91 of the
Criminal Code
(c) grounds exist to arrest or apprehend without warrant the person under an Act of Parliament, other than this Act;
And whereas there are reasonable grounds to believe that the person is or will be present in (
This warrant is issued to authorize you to enter the dwelling-house for the purpose of arresting or apprehending the person.
Dated this
* 1997, c. 39, s. 3;
2002, c. 13, s. 85.
FORM 8

Warrant for Committal

Canada,
Province of
(
To the peace officers in the said (
This warrant is issued for the committal of A.B., of
Whereas the accused has been charged that (
And whereas:
(a) the prosecutor has shown cause why the detention of the accused in custody is justified [515(5)];
(b) an order has been made that the accused be released on (giving an undertaking or entering into a recognizance) but the accused has not yet complied with the order [519(1), 520(9), 521(10), 524(12), 525(8)];

(c) the application by the prosecutor for a review of the order of a justice in respect of the interim release of the accused has been allowed and that order has been vacated, and the prosecutor has shown cause why the detention of the accused in custody is justified [521];

(d) the accused has contravened or was about to contravene his (promise to appear or undertaking or recognizance) and the same was cancelled, and the detention of the accused in custody is justified or seems proper in the circumstances [524(4), 524(8)];

(e) there are reasonable grounds to believe that the accused has after his release from custody on (a promise to appear or an undertaking or a recognizance) committed an indictable offence and the detention of the accused in custody is justified or seems proper in the circumstances [524(4), 524(8)];

(f) the accused has contravened or was about to contravene the (undertaking or recognizance) on which he was released and the detention of the accused in custody seems proper in the circumstances [525(7), 679(6)];

(g) there are reasonable grounds to believe that the accused has after his release from custody on (an undertaking or a recognizance) committed an indictable offence and the detention of the accused in custody seems proper in the circumstances [525(7), 679(6)];

(h) This is, therefore, to command you, in Her Majesty's name, to arrest, if necessary, and take the accused and convey him safely to the (

I do hereby command you the said keeper to receive the accused in your custody in the said prison and keep him safely there until he is delivered by due course of law.

Dated this

* ** *** R.S., 1985, c. C-46, Form 8;

R.S., 1985, c. 27 (1st Supp.), ss. 184, 203.

FORM 9

Appearance Notice Issued by a Peace Officer to a Person Not Yet Charged with an Offence

Canada, Province of

To A.B., of

You are alleged to have committed (

1 You are required to attend court on

2 You are also required to appear on

Identification of Criminals Act

You are warned that failure to attend court in accordance with this appearance notice is an offence under subsection 145(5) of the

Criminal Code

Subsections 145(5) and (6) of the

Criminal Code

"(5) Every person who is named in an appearance notice or promise to appear, or in a recognizance entered into before an officer in charge or another peace officer, that has been confirmed by a justice under section 508 and who fails, without lawful excuse, the proof of which lies on the person, to appear at the time and place stated therein, if any, for the purposes of the

Identification of Criminals Act

(a) an indictable offence and liable to imprisonment for a term not exceeding two years; or

(b) an offence punishable on summary conviction.

(6) For the purposes of subsection (5), it is not a lawful excuse that an appearance notice, promise to appear or recognizance states defectively the substance of the alleged offence."

Section 502 of the

Criminal Code

"502 Where an accused who is required by an appearance notice or promise to appear or by a recognizance entered into before an officer in charge or another peace officer to appear at a time and place stated therein for the purposes of the

Identification of Criminals Act

Issued at
R.S., 1985, c. C-46, Form 9;
R.S., 1985, c. 27 (1st Supp.), s. 184;
1994, c. 44, s. 84;
1997, c. 18, s. 115.
FORM 10
Promise To Appear

Canada, Province of
I, A.B., of
In order that I may be released from custody,
1 I promise to attend court on
2 I also promise to appear on
Identification of Criminals Act
I understand that failure without lawful excuse to attend court in accordance with this promise to appear is an offence under subsection 145(5) of the
Criminal Code
Subsections 145(5) and (6) of the
Criminal Code
"(5) Every person who is named in an appearance notice or promise to appear, or in a recognizance entered into before an officer in charge or another peace officer, that has been confirmed by a justice under section 508 and who fails, without lawful excuse, the proof of which lies on the person, to appear at the time and place stated therein, if any, for the purposes of the
Identification of Criminals Act
(a) an indictable offence and liable to imprisonment for a term not exceeding two years; or
(b) an offence punishable on summary conviction.
(6) For the purposes of subsection (5), it is not a lawful excuse that an appearance notice, promise to appear or recognizance states defectively the substance of the alleged offence."
Section 502 of the
Criminal Code
"502 Where an accused who is required by an appearance notice or promise to appear or by a recognizance entered into before an officer in charge or another peace officer to appear at a time and place stated therein for the purposes of the
Identification of Criminals Act
Dated this
R.S., 1985, c. C-46, Form 10;
1994, c. 44, s. 84;
1997, c. 18, s. 115.
FORM 11
Recognizance Entered into Before an Officer in Charge or Other Peace Officer

Canada, Province of
I, A.B., of
In order that I may be released from custody, I hereby acknowledge that I owe $ (
(
In order that I may be released from custody, I hereby acknowledge that I owe $ (
1 I acknowledge that I am required to attend court on
2 I acknowledge that I am also required to appear on
Identification of Criminals Act
I understand that failure without lawful excuse to attend court in accordance with this recognizance to appear is an offence under subsection 145(5) of the
Criminal Code

Subsections 145(5) and (6) of the
Criminal Code
"(5) Every person who is named in an appearance notice or promise to appear, or in a recognizance entered into before an officer in charge or another peace officer, that has been confirmed by a justice under section 508 and who fails, without lawful excuse, the proof of which lies on the person, to appear at the time and place stated therein, if any, for the purposes of the
Identification of Criminals Act
(a) an indictable offence and liable to imprisonment for a term not exceeding two years; or
(b) an offence punishable on summary conviction.
(6) For the purposes of subsection (5), it is not a lawful excuse that an appearance notice, promise to appear or recognizance states defectively the substance of the alleged offence."
Section 502 of the
Criminal Code
"502 Where an accused who is required by an appearance notice or promise to appear or by a recognizance entered into before an officer in charge or another peace officer to appear at a time and place stated therein for the purposes of the
Identification of Criminals Act
Dated this
R.S., 1985, c. C-46, Form 11;
1992, c. 1, s. 58;
1994, c. 44, s. 84;
1997, c. 18, s. 115.
FORM 11.1

Undertaking Given to a Peace Officer or an Officer in Charge

Canada, Province of
I, A.B., of
In order that I may be released from custody by way of (a promise to appear or a recognizance), I undertake to (
(a) remain within (
(b) notify (
(c) abstain from communicating, directly or indirectly, with (
(d) deposit my passport with (
(e) to abstain from possessing a firearm and to surrender to (
(f) report at (
(g) to abstain from
(i) the consumption of alcohol or other intoxicating substances, or
(ii) the consumption of drugs except in accordance with a medical prescription; and
(h) comply with any other conditions that the peace officer or officer in charge considers necessary to ensure the safety and security of any victim of or witness to the offence.
I understand that I am not required to give an undertaking to abide by the conditions specified above, but that if I do not, I may be kept in custody and brought before a justice so that the prosecutor may be given a reasonable opportunity to show cause why I should not be released on giving an undertaking without conditions.
I understand that if I give an undertaking to abide by the conditions specified above, then I may apply, at any time before I appear, or when I appear, before a justice pursuant to (a promise to appear or a recognizance entered into before an officer in charge or another peace officer), to have this undertaking vacated or varied and that my application will be considered as if I were before a justice pursuant to section 515 of the
Criminal Code
I also understand that this undertaking remains in effect until it is vacated or varied.
I also understand that failure without lawful excuse to abide by any of the conditions specified above

is an offence under subsection 145(5.1) of the
Criminal Code
Subsection 145(5.1) of the
Criminal Code
"(5.1) Every person who, without lawful excuse, the proof of which lies on the person, fails to comply with any condition of an undertaking entered into pursuant to subsection 499(2) or 503(2.1)
(a) is guilty of an indictable offence and is liable to imprisonment for a term not exceeding two years; or
(b) is guilty of an offence punishable on summary conviction."
Dated this
1994, c. 44, s. 84;
1997, c. 18, s. 115;
1999, c. 25, s. 24;
2002, c. 13, s. 86(F).
FORM 12

Undertaking Given to a Justice or a Judge

Canada,
Province of
(
I, A.B., of
In order that I may be released from custody, I undertake to attend court on
(
I also undertake to (
(a) report at (
(b) remain within (
(c) notify (
(d) abstain from communicating, directly or indirectly, with (
(e) deposit my passport (
(f) (
I understand that failure without lawful excuse to attend court in accordance with this undertaking is an offence under subsection 145(2) of the
Criminal Code
Subsections 145(2) and (3) of the
Criminal Code
"(2) Every one who,
(a) being at large on his undertaking or recognizance given to or entered into before a justice or judge, fails, without lawful excuse, the proof of which lies on him, to attend court in accordance with the undertaking or recognizance, or
(b) having appeared before a court, justice or judge, fails, without lawful excuse, the proof of which lies on him, to attend court as thereafter required by the court, justice or judge,
or to surrender himself in accordance with an order of the court, justice or judge, as the case may be, is guilty of an indictable offence and liable to imprisonment for a term not exceeding two years or is guilty of an offence punishable on summary conviction.
(3) Every person who is at large on an undertaking or recognizance given to or entered into before a justice or judge and is bound to comply with a condition of that undertaking or recognizance, and every person who is bound to comply with a direction under subsection 515(12) or 522(2.1) or an order under subsection 516(2), and who fails, without lawful excuse, the proof of which lies on them, to comply with the condition, direction or order is guilty of
(a) an indictable offence and liable to imprisonment for a term not exceeding two years; or
(b) an offence punishable on summary conviction."
Dated this

R.S., 1985, c. C-46, Form 12;
R.S., 1985, c. 27 (1st Supp.), s. 184;
1994, c. 44, s. 84;
1999, c. 25, s. 25;
2008, c. 18, s. 45.1.
FORM 13
Undertaking by Appellant (Defendant)

Canada,
Province of
(
I, A.B., of
(
I also undertake to (
(a) report at (
(b) remain within (
(c) notify (
(d) abstain from communicating, directly or indirectly, with (
(e) deposit my passport (
(f) (
Dated this
R.S., 1985, c. C-46, Form 13;
1999, c. 25, s. 26.
FORM 14
Undertaking by Appellant (Prosecutor)

Canada,
Province of
(
I, A.B., of
Dated this
FORM 15
Warrant To Convey Accused Before Justice of Another Territorial Division

Canada,
Province of
(
To the peace officers in the said (
Whereas A.B., of
And Whereas I have taken the deposition of X.Y. in respect of the said charge;
And Whereas the charge is for an offence committed in the (
This is to command you, in Her Majesty's name, to convey the said A.B., before a justice of the (
Dated this
FORM 16
Subpoena to a Witness

Canada,
Province of
(
To E.F., of
Whereas A.B. has been charged that (
This is therefore to command you to attend before (

* and to bring with you anything in your possession or under your control that relates to the said charge, and more particularly the following: (
Dated this
(
R.S., 1985, c. C-46, Form 16;
R.S., 1985, c. 27 (1st Supp.), s. 184;
1999, c. 5, s. 47.
FORM 16.1

Subpoena to a Witness in the Case of Proceedings in Respect of an Offence Referred to in Subsection 278.2(1) of the Criminal Code

Canada,
Province of
(
To E.F., of
Whereas A.B. has been charged that (
This is therefore to command you to attend before (
You are only required to bring the things specified above to the court on the date and at the time indicated, and you are not required to provide the things specified to any person or to discuss their contents with any person unless and until ordered by the court to do so.
If anything specified above is a
record
Criminal Code
If anything specified above is a
record
Criminal Code
If anything specified above is a
record
Criminal Code
As defined in section 278.1 of the
Criminal Code
record
Dated this
(
1997, c. 30, s. 3.
FORM 17

Warrant for Witness

Canada,
Province of
(
To the peace officers in the (
Whereas A.B. of
And Whereas it has been made to appear that E.F. of
* (a) the said E.F. will not attend unless compelled to do so;
(b) the said E.F. is evading service of a subpoena;
(c) the said E.F. was duly served with a subpoena and has neglected (to attend at the time and place appointed therein or to remain in attendance);
(d) the said E.F. was bound by a recognizance to attend and give evidence and has neglected (to attend or to remain in attendance).
This is therefore to command you, in Her Majesty's name, to arrest and bring the witness forthwith before (

Criminal Code
Dated this
(
R.S., 1985, c. C-46, Form 17;
R.S., 1985, c. 27 (1st Supp.), s. 184.
FORM 18
Warrant To Arrest an Absconding Witness

Canada,
Province of
(
To the peace officers in the (
Whereas A.B., of
And Whereas I am satisfied by information in writing and under oath that C.D., of
This is therefore to command you, in Her Majesty's name, to arrest the witness and bring him forthwith before (
Criminal Code
Dated this
R.S., 1985, c. C-46, Form 18;
R.S., 1985, c. 27 (1st Supp.), s. 203.
FORM 19
Warrant Remanding a Prisoner

Canada,
Province of
(
To the peace officers in the (
You are hereby commanded forthwith to arrest, if necessary, and convey to the (
Person charged
And I hereby command you, the keeper of the said prison, to receive each of the said persons into your custody in the prison and keep him safely until the day when his remand expires and then to have him before me or any other justice at
Dated this
R.S., 1985, c. C-46, Form 19;
R.S., 1985, c. 27 (1st Supp.), s. 184.
FORM 20
Warrant of Committal of Witness for Refusing To Be Sworn or To Give Evidence

Canada,
Province of
(
To the peace officers in the (
Whereas A.B. of
And Whereas E.F. of
This is therefore to command you, in Her Majesty's name, to arrest, if necessary, and take the witness and convey him safely to the prison at
I do hereby command you, the said keeper, to receive the said witness into your custody in the said prison and safely keep him there for the term of
Dated this
R.S., 1985, c. C-46, Form 20;
R.S., 1985, c. 27 (1st Supp.), s. 184.

FORM 21
Warrant of Committal on Conviction

Canada,
Province of
(
To the peace officers in (
Whereas (
Offence
(
Sentence
(
Remarks
(
You are hereby commanded, in Her Majesty's name, to arrest the offender if it is necessary to do so in order to take the offender into custody, and to take and convey him or her safely to (
Dated this
R.S., 1985, c. C-46, Form 21;
R.S., 1985, c. 27 (1st Supp.), s. 184;
1995, c. 22, s. 9;
2009, c. 29, s. 4.
FORM 22
Warrant of Committal on an Order for the Payment of Money

Canada,
Province of
(
To the peace officers in the (
Whereas A.B., hereinafter called the defendant, was tried on an information alleging that (
I hereby command you, in Her Majesty's name, to arrest, if necessary, and take the defendant and convey him safely to the (
I hereby command you, the keeper of the said prison, to receive the defendant into your custody in the said prison and imprison him there for the term of
Dated this
R.S., 1985, c. C-46, Form 22;
R.S., 1985, c. 27 (1st Supp.), s. 184.
FORM 23
Warrant of Committal for Failure To Furnish Recognizance To Keep the Peace

Canada,
Province of
(
To the peace officers in the (
Whereas A.B., hereinafter called the accused, has been ordered to enter into a recognizance to keep the peace and be of good behaviour, and has (refused or failed) to enter into a recognizance accordingly;
You are hereby commanded, in Her Majesty's name, to arrest, if necessary, and take the accused and convey him safely to the (
You, the said keeper, are hereby commanded to receive the accused into your custody in the said prison and imprison him there until he enters into a recognizance as aforesaid or until he is discharged in due course of law.
Dated this

(
R.S., 1985, c. C-46, Form 23;
R.S., 1985, c. 27 (1st Supp.), ss. 184, 203;
1993, c. 45, s. 12.
FORM 24
Warrant of Committal of Witness for Failure To Enter into Recognizance

Canada,
Province of
(
To the peace officers in the (
Whereas A.B., hereinafter called the accused, was committed for trial on a charge that (
And Whereas E.F., hereinafter called the witness, having appeared as a witness on the preliminary inquiry into the said charge, and being required to enter into a recognizance to appear as a witness on the trial of the accused on the said charge, has (failed or refused) to do so;
This is therefore to command you, in Her Majesty's name, to arrest, if necessary, and take and safely convey the said witness to the (
I do hereby command you, the said keeper, to receive the witness into your custody in the said prison and keep him there safely until the trial of the accused on the said charge, unless before that time the witness enters into the said recognizance.
Dated this
R.S., 1985, c. C-46, Form 24;
R.S., 1985, c. 27 (1st Supp.), s. 184.
FORM 25
Warrant of Committal for Contempt

Canada,
Province of
(
To the peace officers in the said (
Whereas E.F. of
And Whereas in and by the said conviction it was adjudged that the defaulter (
And Whereas the defaulter has not paid the amounts adjudged to be paid; (
This is therefore to command you, in Her Majesty's name, to arrest, if necessary, and take the defaulter and convey him safely to the prison at
I do hereby command you, the said keeper, to receive the defaulter into your custody in the said prison and imprison him there
* (a) for the term of
(b) for the term of
(c) for the term of
Dated this
(
R.S., 1985, c. C-46, Form 25;
R.S., 1985, c. 27 (1st Supp.), s. 184.
FORM 26
Warrant of Committal in Default of Payment of Costs of an Appeal

Canada,
Province of
(
To the peace officers of (
Whereas it appears that on the hearing of an appeal before the (

And Whereas the Clerk of the Court has certified that the defaulter has not paid the sum within the time limited therefor;

I do hereby command you, the said peace officers, in Her Majesty's name, to take the defaulter and safely convey him to the (

I do hereby command you, the said keeper, to receive the defaulter into your custody in the said prison and imprison him for the term of

Dated this

FORM 27

Warrant of Committal on Forfeiture of a Recognizance

Canada,
Province of
(
To the sheriff of (

You are hereby commanded to arrest, if necessary, and take (A.B. and C.D.

You, the said keeper, are hereby commanded to receive the defaulters into your custody in the said prison and imprison them for a period of

Dated this
(
R.S., 1985, c. C-46, Form 27;
R.S., 1985, c. 27 (1st Supp.), s. 184.
FORM 28

Endorsement of Warrant

Canada,
Province of
(
Pursuant to application this day made to me, I hereby authorize the arrest of the accused (or defendant) (or execution of this warrant

Dated this
R.S., 1985, c. C-46, Form 28;
R.S., 1985, c. 27 (1st Supp.), s. 184.
FORM 28.1 FORM 29

Endorsement of Warrant

Canada,
Province of
(
Whereas this warrant is issued under section 507, 508 or 512 of the
Criminal Code
Dated this
R.S., 1985, c. C-46, Form 29;
1994, c. 44, s. 84.
FORM 30

Order for Accused To Be Brought Before Justice Prior to Expiration of Period of Remand

Canada,
Province of
(
To the keeper of the (

Whereas by warrant dated the
Now, therefore, I order and direct you to have the accused before
Dated this
FORM 31
Deposition of a Witness

Canada,
Province of
(
These are the depositions of X.Y., of
X.Y., having been duly sworn, deposes as follows: (
M.N., having been duly sworn, deposes as follows:
I certify that the depositions of X.Y., and M.N., written on the several sheets of paper hereto annexed to which my signature is affixed, were taken in the presence and hearing of the accused (and signed by them respectively, in his presence
FORM 32
Recognizance

Canada,
Province of
(
Be it remembered that on this day the persons named in the following schedule personally came before me and severally acknowledged themselves to owe to Her Majesty the Queen the several amounts set opposite their respective names, namely,
to be made and levied of their several goods and chattels, lands and tenements, respectively, to the use of Her Majesty the Queen, if the said A.B. fails in any of the conditions hereunder written.
Taken and acknowledged before me on the
1 Whereas the said
Now, therefore, the condition of this recognizance is that if the accused attends court on
And further, if the accused (
the said recognizance is void, otherwise it stands in full force and effect.
2 Whereas the said
Now, therefore, the condition of this recognizance is that if the appellant attends as required by the court in order to be dealt with according to law;
And further, if the appellant (
the said recognizance is void, otherwise it stands in full force and effect.
3 Whereas the said
Now, therefore, the condition of this recognizance is that if the appellant appears personally at the sittings of the appeal court at which the appeal is to be heard;
And further, if the appellant (
the said recognizance is void, otherwise it stands in full force and effect.
4 Whereas the said
Now, therefore, the condition of this recognizance is that if the appellant appears personally or by counsel at the sittings of the appeal court at which the appeal is to be heard the said recognizance is void, otherwise it stands in full force and effect.
5 Whereas the said
And whereas A.B. appeared as a witness on the preliminary inquiry into the said charge [550, 706, 707];
Now, therefore, the condition of this recognizance is that if the said A.B. appears at the time and place fixed for the trial of the accused to give evidence on the indictment that is found against the accused, the said recognizance is void, otherwise it stands in full force and effect.
6 The condition of the above written recognizance is that if A.B. keeps the peace and is of good

behaviour for the term of

7 Whereas a warrant was issued under section 462.32 or a restraint order was made under subsection 462.33(3) of the
Criminal Code
Now, therefore, the condition of this recognizance is that A.B. shall not do or cause anything to be done that would result, directly or indirectly, in the disappearance, dissipation or reduction in value of the property or otherwise affect the property so that all or a part thereof could not be subject to an order of forfeiture under section 462.37 or 462.38 of the
Criminal Code
(a) reports at (
(b) remains within (
(c) notifies (
(d) abstains from communicating, directly or indirectly, with (
(e) deposits his passport (
(f) (
Criminal Code
"763 Where a person is bound by recognizance to appear before a court, justice or provincial court judge for any purpose and the session or sittings of that court or the proceedings are adjourned or an order is made changing the place of trial, that person and his sureties continue to be bound by the recognizance in like manner as if it had been entered into with relation to the resumed proceedings or the trial at the time and place at which the proceedings are ordered to be resumed or the trial is ordered to be held.
Where an accused is bound by recognizance to appear for trial, his arraignment or conviction does not discharge the recognizance, but it continues to bind him and his sureties, if any, for his appearance until he is discharged or sentenced, as the case may be.
(2) Notwithstanding subsection (1), the court, justice or provincial court judge may commit an accused to prison or may require him to furnish new or additional sureties for his appearance until he is discharged or sentenced, as the case may be.
(3) The sureties of an accused who is bound by recognizance to appear for trial are discharged if he is committed to prison pursuant to subsection (2)."
R.S., 1985, c. C-46, Form 32;
R.S., 1985, c. 27 (1st Supp.), ss. 101, 184, 203;
c. 42 (4th Supp.), s. 7;
1993, c. 45, ss. 13, 14;
1999, c. 25, s. 27.
FORM 33

Certificate of Default To Be Endorsed on Recognizance

I hereby certify that A.B. (has not appeared as required by this recognizance or has not complied with a condition of this recognizance) and that by reason thereof the ends of justice have been (defeated or delayed,
The nature of the default is
The names and addresses of the principal and sureties are as follows:
Dated this
(
R.S., 1985, c. C-46, Form 33;
R.S., 1985, c. 27 (1st Supp.), s. 203;
1994, c. 44, s. 84.
FORM 34

Writ of Fieri Facias

Elizabeth II by the Grace of God, etc.

To the sheriff of (
You are hereby commanded to levy of the goods and chattels, lands and tenements of each of the following persons the amount set opposite the name of each:
Name
And you are further commanded to make a return of what you have done in execution of this writ.
Dated this
(
FORM 34.1

Statement on Restitution

Canada,
Province of
(
To the court that is sentencing (
Criminal Code
I, (

[ ] (i) I am not seeking restitution for the losses and damages I suffered as the result of the commission of the offence.

[ ] (ii) I am seeking restitution in the amount of $

I declare that I have suffered the following losses and damages as the result of the commission of the offence:
(
Description
(
Amount of loss and damage
(
1.
2.
3.
4.
I understand that the amount of my losses and damages must be readily ascertainable by the court. For that purpose, I am responsible for providing the court with all necessary documents, including bills, receipts and estimates, in support of my claim for restitution.
Dated this
Signature of declarant
2011, c. 6, s. 5;
2015, c. 13, s. 35.
FORM 34.2

Victim Impact Statement

This form may be used to provide a description of the physical or emotional harm, property damage or economic loss suffered by you as the result of the commission of an offence, as well as a description of the impact of the offence on you. You may attach additional pages if you need more space.

Your statement must not include

• any statement about the offence or the offender that is not relevant to the harm or loss you suffered;
• any unproven allegations;
• any comments about any offence for which the offender was not convicted;
• any complaint about any individual, other than the offender, who was involved in the investigation or prosecution of the offence; or
• except with the court's approval, an opinion or recommendation about the sentence.

You may present a detailed account of the impact the offence has had on your life. The following sections are examples of information you may wish to include in your statement. You are not required to include all of this information.

Describe how the offence has affected you emotionally. For example, think of
• your lifestyle and activities;
• your relationships with others such as your spouse, family and friends;
• your ability to work, attend school or study; and
• your feelings, emotions and reactions as they relate to the offence.

Describe how the offence has affected you physically. For example, think of
• ongoing physical pain, discomfort, illness, scarring, disfigurement or physical limitation;
• hospitalization or surgery you have had because of the offence;
• treatment, physiotherapy or medication you have been prescribed;
• the need for any further treatment or the expectation that you will receive further treatment; and
• any permanent or long-term disability.

Describe how the offence has affected you financially. For example, think of
• the value of any property that was lost or damaged and the cost of repairs or replacement;
• any financial loss due to missed time from work;
• the cost of any medical expenses, therapy or counselling;
• any costs or losses that are not covered by insurance.

Please note that this is not an application for compensation or restitution.

Describe any fears you have for your security or that of your family and friends. For example, think of
• concerns with respect to contact with the offender; and
• concerns with respect to contact between the offender and members of your family or close friends.

You may use this space to draw a picture or write a poem or letter if it will help you express the impact that the offence has had on you.

[?] I would like to present my statement in court.

To the best of my knowledge, the information contained in this statement is true.
Dated this
Signature of declarant
If you completed this statement on behalf of the victim, please indicate the reasons why you did so and the nature of your relationship with the victim.

Dated this
Signature of declarant
2015, c. 13, s. 35.
FORM 34.3

Community Impact Statement

This form may be used to provide a description of the harm or loss suffered by a community as the result of the commission of an offence, as well as a description of the impact of the offence on the community. You may attach additional pages if you need more space.

Your statement must not include
• any statement about the offence or the offender that is not relevant to the harm or loss suffered by the community;
• any unproven allegations;
• any comments about any offence for which the offender was not convicted;
• any complaint about any individual, other than the offender, who was involved in the investigation

or prosecution of the offence; or
• except with the court's approval, an opinion or recommendation about the sentence.
Name of community on whose behalf the statement is made:
Explain how the statement reflects this community's views:

You may present a detailed account of the impact the offence has had on the community. The following sections are examples of information you may wish to include in your statement. You are not required to include all of this information.
Describe how the offence has affected community members emotionally. For example, think of
• community members' lifestyles and activities;
• community members' relationships with others in the community and outside it;
• community members' ability to work, attend school or study;
• community members' feelings, emotions and reactions as they relate to the offence; and
• the community's sense of belonging to the region.

Describe how the offence has affected community members physically. For example, think of
• the ability of community members to access services; and
• changes in transportation and routes taken to and from school, work, shopping, etc.

Describe how the offence has affected the community financially. For example, think of
• any reduction in the number of visitors or tourists to the region;
• the value of any property that was lost or damaged and the cost of repairs or replacement; and
• any costs or losses that are not covered by insurance.
Please note that this is not an application for compensation or restitution.

Describe any fears that community members have for their security or that of their family and friends. For example, think of concerns with respect to contact with the offender.

You may use this space to draw a picture or write a poem or letter if it will help you express the impact that the offence has had on the community.

[?] I would like to present this statement in court.
To the best of my knowledge, the information contained in this statement is true.
Dated this
Signature of declarant
2015, c. 13, s. 35.
FORM 35
Conviction

Canada,
Province of
(
Be it remembered that on the
Criminal Code
* (a) that the said accused be imprisoned in the (
(b) that the said accused forfeit and pay the sum of
(c) that the said accused be imprisoned in the (
Dated this
(
R.S., 1985, c. C-46, Form 35;
R.S., 1985, c. 27 (1st Supp.), ss. 184, 203.
FORM 36

Order Against an Offender

Canada,
Province of
(
Be it remembered that on the
Dated this
R.S., 1985, c. C-46, Form 36;
R.S., 1985, c. 27 (1st Supp.), s. 184.
FORM 37

Order Acquitting Accused

Canada,
Province of
(
Be it remembered that on the
Dated this
(
R.S., 1985, c. C-46, Form 37;
R.S., 1985, c. 27 (1st Supp.), ss. 184, 203.
FORM 38

Conviction for Contempt

Canada,
Province of
(
Be it remembered that on the
Wherefore I adjudge the defaulter for his said default, (
Criminal Code
Dated this
(
FORM 39

Order for Discharge of a Person in Custody

Canada,
Province of
(
To the keeper of the (
I hereby direct you to release E.F., detained by you under a (warrant of committal or order) dated the
(
FORM 40

Challenge To Array

Canada,
Province of
(
The Queen
v.
C.D.
The (prosecutor or accused) challenges the array of the panel on the ground that X.Y., (sheriff or deputy sheriff), who returned the panel, was guilty of (partiality or fraud or wilful misconduct) on

returning it.
Dated this
FORM 41
Challenge for Cause

Canada,
Province of
(
The Queen
v.
C.D.
The (prosecutor or accused) challenges G.H. on the ground that (
Criminal Code
FORM 42
Certificate of Non-payment of Costs of Appeal

In the Court of
(
I hereby certify that A.B. (the appellant or respondent,
Dated this
(
FORM 43
Jailer's Receipt to Peace Officer for Prisoner

I hereby certify that I have received from X.Y., a peace officer for (
* Dated this
R.S., 1985, c. C-46, Form 43;
1995, c. 22, s. 18.
FORM 44 I, (
Criminal Code
(
Dated this
R.S., 1985, c. C-46, Form 44;
R.S., 1985, c. 27 (1st Supp.), s. 184, c. 1 (4th Supp.), s. 18;
1995, c. 22, s. 18;
2005, c. 10, s. 34.
FORM 45 I, (
Criminal Code
Dated this
R.S., 1985, c. C-46, Form 45;
R.S., 1985, c. 27 (1st Supp.), s. 184;
2005, c. 10, s. 34.
FORM 46
Probation Order

Canada,
Province of
(
Whereas on the
Criminal Code
And whereas on the
* (a) that the offender be discharged on the following conditions:

(b) that the passing of sentence on the offender be suspended and that the said offender be released on the following conditions:
(c) that the offender forfeit and pay the sum of
(d) that the offender be imprisoned in the (
(e) that following the expiration of the offender's conditional sentence order related to this or another offence, that the said offender comply with the following conditions:
(f) that following the expiration of the offender's sentence of imprisonment related to another offence, that the said offender comply with the following conditions:
(g) when the offender is ordered to serve the sentence of imprisonment intermittently, that the said offender comply with the following conditions when not in confinement:
Now therefore the said offender shall, for the period of
(
Criminal Code
Dated this
R.S., 1985, c. C-46, Form 46;
R.S., 1985, c. 27 (1st Supp.), s. 203;
1995, c. 22, s. 10;
2004, c. 12, s. 17.
FORM 47

Order To Disclose Income Tax Information

Canada,
Province of
(
To A.B., of
Whereas, it appears on the oath of C.D., of
Whereas there are reasonable grounds for believing that it is in the public interest to allow access to the information or documents, having regard to the benefit likely to accrue to the investigation if the access is obtained;
This is, therefore, to authorize and require you between the hours of (
Dated this
R.S., 1985, c. 42 (4th Supp.), s. 8.
FORM 48

Assessment Order of the Court

Canada,
Province of
(
Whereas I have reasonable grounds to believe that evidence of the mental condition of (
[ ] whether the accused is unfit to stand trial
[ ] whether the accused suffered from a mental disorder so as to exempt the accused from criminal responsibility by virtue of subsection 16(1) of the
Criminal Code
[ ] whether the balance of the mind of the accused was disturbed at the time of commission of the alleged offence, if the accused is a female person charged with an offence arising out of the death of her newly-born child
[ ] if a verdict of unfit to stand trial or a verdict of not criminally responsible on account of mental disorder has been rendered in respect of the accused, the appropriate disposition to be made in respect of the accused under section 672.54, 672.58 or 672.64 of the
Criminal Code
[ ] if a verdict of unfit to stand trial has been rendered in respect of the accused, whether the court should order a stay of proceedings under section 672.851 of the

Criminal Code
I hereby order an assessment of the mental condition of (
This order is to be in force for a total of
[ ] in custody at (
[ ] out of custody, on the following conditions:
(
* Check applicable option.
Dated this
1991, c. 43, s. 8;
1995, c. 22, s. 10;
2005, c. 22, s. 40;
2014, c. 6, s. 19.
FORM 48.1

Assessment Order of the Review Board

Canada,
Province of
(
Whereas I have reasonable grounds to believe that evidence of the mental condition of (
[ ] if a verdict of unfit to stand trial or a verdict of not criminally responsible on account of mental disorder has been rendered in respect of the accused, make a disposition under section 672.54 of the Criminal Code
[ ] if a verdict of unfit to stand trial has been rendered in respect of the accused, determine whether the Review Board should make a recommendation to the court that has jurisdiction in respect of the offence charged against the accused to hold an inquiry to determine whether a stay of proceedings should be ordered in accordance with section 672.851 of the
Criminal Code
I hereby order an assessment of the mental condition of (
This order is to be in force for a total of
[ ] in custody at (
[ ] out of custody, on the following conditions:
(
* Check applicable option.
Dated this
2005, c. 22, s. 40;
2014, c. 6, s. 20.
FORM 48.2

Victim Impact Statement — Not Criminally Responsible

This form may be used to provide a description of the physical or emotional harm, property damage or economic loss suffered by you arising from the conduct for which the accused person was found not criminally responsible on account of mental disorder, as well as a description of the impact that the conduct has had on you. You may attach additional pages if you need more space.
Your statement must not include
• any statement about the conduct of the accused that is not relevant to the harm or loss suffered by you;
• any unproven allegations;
• any comments about any conduct for which the accused was not found not criminally responsible;
• any complaint about any individual, other than the accused, who was involved in the investigation or prosecution of the offence; or
• except with the court's or Review Board's approval, an opinion or recommendation about the disposition.

The following sections are examples of information you may wish to include in your statement. You are not required to include all of this information.
Describe how the accused's conduct has affected you emotionally. For example, think of
• your lifestyle and activities;
• your relationships with others such as your spouse, family and friends;
• your ability to work, attend school or study; and
• your feelings, emotions and reactions as these relate to the conduct.

Describe how the accused's conduct has affected you physically. For example, think of
• ongoing physical pain, discomfort, illness, scarring, disfigurement or physical limitation;
• hospitalization or surgery you have had because of the conduct of the accused;
• treatment, physiotherapy or medication you have been prescribed;
• the need for any further treatment or the expectation that you will receive further treatment; and
• any permanent or long-term disability.

Describe how the accused's conduct has affected you financially. For example, think of
• the value of any property that was lost or damaged and the cost of repairs or replacement;
• any financial loss due to missed time from work;
• the cost of any medical expenses, therapy or counselling; and
• any costs or losses that are not covered by insurance.
Please note that this is not an application for compensation or restitution.

Describe any fears you have for your security or that of your family and friends. For example, think of
• concerns with respect to contact with the accused; and
• concerns with respect to contact between the accused and members of your family or close friends.

You may use this space to draw a picture or write a poem or letter if it will help you express the impact that the accused's conduct has had on you.

[?] I would like to read or present my statement (in court or before the Review Board).
To the best of my knowledge, the information contained in this statement is true.
Dated this
Signature of declarant
2015, c. 13, s. 36.
FORM 49
Warrant of Committal

Disposition of Detention

Canada,
Province of
(
To the peace officers in the said (
This warrant is issued for the committal of A.B., of
Whereas the accused has been charged that (
And whereas the accused was found
☐ unfit to stand trial
☐ not criminally responsible on account of mental disorder
This is, therefore, to command you, in Her Majesty's name, to take the accused in custody and convey the accused safely to the (
I do therefore command you the said keeper (

The following are the conditions to which the accused shall be subject while in your (
The following are the powers regarding the restrictions (
* Check applicable option.
Dated this
1991, c. 43, s. 8.
FORM 50
Warrant of Committal

Placement Decision

Canada,
Province of
(
To the peace officers in the said (
This warrant is issued for the committal of A.B., of
Whereas the accused has been charged that (
And whereas the accused was found
☐ unfit to stand trial
☐ not criminally responsible on account of mental disorder
And whereas the Review Board has held a hearing and decided that the accused shall be detained in custody;
And whereas the accused is required to be detained in custody pursuant to a warrant of committal issued by (
This is, therefore, to command you, in Her Majesty's name, to
☐ execute the warrant of committal issued by the court, according to its terms
☐ execute the warrant of committal issued herewith by the Review Board
* Check applicable option.
Dated this
1991, c. 43, s. 8.
FORM 51
Notice of Obligation To Provide Samples of Bodily Substance

To A.B., of
Because, on (
Criminal Code
You are provided with this notice to inform you of your obligations with respect to providing samples.
1 On (
2 Every (
3 You have the right to apply to a court to terminate the obligation to provide samples, and the right to appeal any decision of that court.
4 If you are found to have not complied with your obligation to provide samples as set out in this notice, you may be subject to a fine or imprisonment, or to both (
Criminal Code
5 The results of the analysis of the bodily substances may be used or disclosed in accordance with the
Criminal Code
Served on (
1991, c. 43, s. 8;
1995, c. 22, s. 10 (Sch. I, item 37);
2005, c. 22, s. 41;
2011, c. 7, s. 13;

2015, c. 20, s. 34.
FORM 52
Order To Comply with Sex Offender Information Registration Act

Canada,
Province of
(
To A.B., of
You have been convicted of or found not criminally responsible on account of mental disorder for (
Criminal Code
1 You must report for the first time to the registration centre referred to in section 7.1 of the
Sex Offender Information Registration Act
2 You must subsequently report to the registration centre referred to in section 7.1 of the
Sex Offender Information Registration Act
Criminal Code
3 Information relating to you will be collected under sections 5 and 6 of the
Sex Offender Information Registration Act
4 Information relating to you will be registered in a database, and may be consulted, disclosed and used in the circumstances set out in the
Sex Offender Information Registration Act
5 If you believe that the information registered in the database contains an error or omission, you may ask a person who collects information at the registration centre referred to in section 7.1 of the
Sex Offender Information Registration Act
6 You have the right to apply to a court to terminate this order, and the right to appeal the decision of that court.
7 If you are found to have contravened this order, you may be subject to a fine or imprisonment, or to both.
8 If you are found to have provided false or misleading information, you may be subject to a fine or imprisonment, or to both.
Dated this
2004, c. 10, s. 21;
2007, c. 5, s. 30;
2010, c. 17, s. 26;
2013, c. 24, s. 117(F).
FORM 53
Notice of Obligation To Comply with Sex Offender Information Registration Act

Canada,
Province of
(
To A.B., of
Criminal Code
Because, on
designated offence
Criminal Code
designated offence
National Defence Act
Sex Offender Information Registration Act
1 You must report for the first time to the registration centre referred to in section 7.1 of the
Sex Offender Information Registration Act
2 You must subsequently report to the registration centre referred to in section 7.1 of the

Sex Offender Information Registration Act
Criminal Code
3 Information relating to you will be collected under sections 5 and 6 of the
Sex Offender Information Registration Act
4 Information relating to you will be registered in a database, and may be consulted, disclosed and used in the circumstances set out in the
Sex Offender Information Registration Act
5 If you believe that the information registered in the database contains an error or omission, you may ask a person who collects information at the registration centre referred to in section 7.1 of the
Sex Offender Information Registration Act
6 You have the right to apply to a court to exempt you from the obligation to comply with the
Sex Offender Information Registration Act
7 You have the right to apply to a court to terminate the obligation, and the right to appeal any decision of that court.
8 If you are found to have contravened the obligation, you may be subject to a fine or imprisonment, or to both.
9 If you are found to have provided false or misleading information, you may be subject to a fine or imprisonment, or to both.
Dated this
2004, c. 10, s. 21;
2007, c. 5, s. 31;
2013, c. 24, s. 117(F);
2014, c. 25, s. 33.
FORM 54

Obligation To Comply with Sex Offender Information Registration Act

To A.B., of
Because, on (
Criminal Code
You are provided with this to inform you that you are required to comply with the
Sex Offender Information Registration Act
1 You must report for the first time to the registration centre referred to in section 7.1 of the
Sex Offender Information Registration Act
2 You must subsequently report to the registration centre referred to in section 7.1 of the
Sex Offender Information Registration Act
Criminal Code
3 Information relating to you will be collected under sections 5 and 6 of the
Sex Offender Information Registration Act
4 Information relating to you will be registered in a database, and may be consulted, disclosed and used in the circumstances set out in the
Sex Offender Information Registration Act
5 If you believe that the information registered in the database contains an error or omission, you may ask a person who collects information at the registration centre referred to in section 7.1 of the
Sex Offender Information Registration Act
6 You have the right to apply to a court to exempt you from the obligation to comply with the
Sex Offender Information Registration Act
7 You have the right to apply to a court to terminate the obligation to comply with the
Sex Offender Information Registration Act
8 If you are found to have not complied with the
Sex Offender Information Registration Act
9 If you are found to have provided false or misleading information, you may be subject to a fine or imprisonment, or to both.

Served on (
Sentence imposed or verdict of not criminally responsible on account of mental disorder rendered on
(
2010, c. 17, s. 27.

RELATED PROVISIONS

— 1991, c. 43, ss. 10(1) to (7), as amended by 2005, c. 22, s. 43

Lieutenant Governor warrants or orders remain in force
10 (1) Any order for detention of an accused or accused person made under section 614, 615 or 617 of the
Criminal Code
National Defence Act
Criminal Code
Review of inmates held in custody on lieutenant governor warrants or orders
(2) The Review Board of a province shall, within twelve months after the coming into force of this section, review the case of every person detained in custody in the province by virtue of an order of detention referred to in subsection (1).
Application of sections 672.5 to 672.85 to reviews under subsection (2)
(3) Sections 672.5 to 672.85 of the Criminal Code apply, with such modifications as the circumstances require, to a review under subsection (2) as if
(a) the review were a review of a disposition conducted pursuant to section 672.81 of that Act; and
(b) the warrant issued by the lieutenant governor pursuant to which the person is being detained in custody were a disposition made under section 672.54 of that Act.
(c) and (d) (4) to (7)

— 2004, c. 12, s. 22

Interpretation of 2001, c. 32, ss. 82(1), (2) and (4)
22 For greater certainty, section 82 of
An Act to amend the Criminal Code (organized crime and law enforcement) and to make consequential amendments to other Acts
Criminal Law Amendment Act, 2001
(a) the reference in subsection 82(1) of the Act to "Bill C-15" refers, with respect to subsections 82(2) and (4) of the Act, to Bill C-15A, which resulted from the division of Bill C-15 and has the same title;
(b) the reference in subsection 82(2) of the Act to "section 25 of the other Act" refers to section 16 of Bill C-15A; and
(c) the reference in subsection 82(4) of the Act to "section 62 of the other Act" refers to section 52 of Bill C-15A.

— 2004, c. 12, s. 23

Interpretation of 2001, c. 32, ss. 82(1) and (3)
23 For greater certainty, section 82 of
An Act to amend the Criminal Code (organized crime and law enforcement) and to make consequential amendments to other Acts
Criminal Law Amendment Act, 2001
An Act to amend the Criminal Code (cruelty to animals and firearms) and the Firearms Act
(a) the reference in subsection 82(1) of the Act to "Bill C-15" refers, with respect to subsection 82(3) of the Act, to Bill C-10A, which resulted from the division of Bill C-10 and is entitled
An Act to amend the Criminal Code (firearms) and the Firearms Act

(b) the reference in subsection 82(3) of the Act to "section 32 of the other Act" refers to section 8 of Bill C-10A.

— 2005, c. 32, s. 27.1

Review
27.1 (1) Five years after this section comes into force, a committee of the Senate, of the House of Commons or of both Houses of Parliament that is designated or established for the purpose shall undertake a comprehensive review of this Act and its operation.
Report
(2) The committee shall submit a report on the review to Parliament, including a statement of any changes that it recommends, within six months after it undertakes the review or within any further time authorized by the Senate, the House of Commons or both Houses of Parliament, as the case may be.

— 2009, c. 28, s. 12

Review
12 Within five years after the day on which this Act receives royal assent, a comprehensive review of its provisions and operation shall be undertaken by the committee of the Senate, of the House of Commons or of both Houses of Parliament that is designated or established by the Senate or the House of Commons, or by both Houses of Parliament, as the case may be, for that purpose.

— 2009, c. 29, s. 5

Application — persons charged after coming into force
5 Subsections 719(3) to (3.4) of the Act, as enacted by section

— 2011, c. 2, s. 7

Existing applications
7 (1) Applications that were made under section 745.6 of the
Criminal Code
Further applications
(2) A person who has made an application referred to in subsection (1) and who is the subject of a determination made under subsection 745.61(4) of the
Criminal Code
Further applications
(3) A person who has made an application referred to in subsection (1) and in respect of whom a time is set under paragraph 745.61(3)(a) or 745.63(6)(a) of the
Criminal Code

— 2012, c. 1, par. 163(a)

Pending applications — references in other legislation
163 A reference to an application for a record suspension in the following provisions, as enacted by this Part, is deemed also to be a reference to an application for a pardon that is not finally disposed of on the day on which this section comes into force:
(a) paragraph 672.35(c) and subsection 750(4) of the
Criminal Code

— 2012, c. 1, par. 165(b)

Pardons in effect — references in other legislation
165 A reference to a record suspension in the following provisions, as enacted by this Part, is deemed also to be a reference to a pardon that is granted or issued under the
Criminal Records Act
(b) the definition
record suspension
Criminal Code

— 2014, c. 6, s. 20.1

Review
20.1 (1) Within five years after sections 2 to 20 come into force, a comprehensive review of the operation of sections 672.1 to 672.89 of the
Criminal Code
Report
(2) Within a year, or such further time as authorized by the Senate, the House of Commons or both Houses of Parliament, as the case may be, after the review is undertaken, the Committee referred to in subsection (1) must submit a report on that review to the Senate, the House of Commons or both Houses of Parliament, as the case may be, including a statement of any changes recommended by the Committee.

— 2014, c. 25, s. 45.1

Review
45.1 (1) Within five years after this section comes into force, a comprehensive review of the provisions and operation of this Act shall be undertaken by such committee of the House of Commons as may be designated or established by the House for that purpose.
Report
(2) The committee referred to in subsection (1) shall, within a year after a review is undertaken pursuant to that subsection or within such further time as the House may authorize, submit a report on the review to the Speaker of the House, including a statement of any changes the committee recommends.

— 2015, c. 13, s. 37

Hearing — subsection 278.3(5)
37 Subsection 278.3(5) of the Act, as that subsection read immediately before the day on which section

— 2015, c. 13, s. 38

Restitution requests — section 380.3
38 Section 380.3 of the Act, as that section read immediately before the day on which section

— 2015, c. 13, s. 39

Community impact statements — section 380.4
39 Section 380.4 of the Act, as that section read immediately before the day on which section

— 2015, c. 13, s. 40

Section 423.1
40 Section 423.1 of the Act, as amended by section

— 2015, c. 13, s. 41

Victim impact statements — section 672.5
41 Section 672.5 of the Act, as that section read immediately before the day on which section

— 2015, c. 13, s. 42

Section 718
42 The amendments to section 718 of the Act made by section

— 2015, c. 13, s. 42.1

Paragraph 718.2(e)
42.1 The amendment to paragraph 718.2(e) of the Act made by section 24 of this Act applies only in respect of sentences imposed in respect of conduct engaged in on or after the day on which that section 24 comes into force.

— 2015, c. 13, s. 43

Victim impact statements — section 722
43 Section 722 of the Act, as that section read immediately before the day on which section

— 2015, c. 13, s. 44

Sections 737.1 and 739.1 to 739.4
44 Section 737.1 of the Act, as enacted by section

— 2015, c. 20, s. 28

Information — terrorism offence
28 If an information has been laid under subsection 810.01(1) of the Criminal Code

— 2016, c. 3, s. 9.1

Mature minors, advance requests and mental illness
9.1 (1) The Minister of Justice and the Minister of Health must, no later than 180 days after the day on which this Act receives royal assent, initiate one or more independent reviews of issues relating to requests by mature minors for medical assistance in dying, to advance requests and to requests where mental illness is the sole underlying medical condition.
(2) The Minister of Justice and the Minister of Health must, no later than two years after the day on which a review is initiated, cause one or more reports on the review, including any findings or recommendations resulting from it, to be laid before each House of Parliament.

— 2016, c. 3, s. 10

Review by committee

10 (1) At the start of the fifth year after the day on which this Act receives royal assent, the provisions enacted by this Act are to be referred to the committee of the Senate, of the House of Commons or of both Houses of Parliament that may be designated or established for the purpose of reviewing the provisions.

Report

(2) The committee to which the provisions are referred is to review them and the state of palliative care in Canada and submit a report to the House or Houses of Parliament of which it is a committee, including a statement setting out any changes to the provisions that the committee recommends.

AMENDMENTS NOT IN FORCE

— 2001, c. 32, ss. 82(1), (3)

Bill C-15
82 (1) If Bill C-15 [C-10A]
Criminal Law Amendment Act, 2001
Criminal Code
(3) On the later of the coming into force of subsection 37(1) of this Act and section 32 [8]
Criminal Code
Condition additionnelle
(4.1) Lorsqu'il rend une ordonnance en vertu du paragraphe (2) dans le cas d'une infraction perpétrée avec usage, tentative ou menace de violence contre autrui, de l'infraction visée aux articles 264 (harcèlement criminel) ou 423.1 (intimidation d'une personne associée au système judiciaire), d'une infraction aux paragraphes 5(1) ou (2), 6(1) ou (2) ou 7(1) de la
Loi réglementant certaines drogues et autres substances
* [Note: See 2004, c. 12, s. 23.]

— 2014, c. 20, s. 366(1)

Replacement of "trade-mark" in other Acts
366 (1) Unless the context requires otherwise, "trade-mark", "trade-marks", "Trade-mark", "Trade-marks", "trade mark" and "trade marks" are replaced by "trademark", "trademarks", "Trademark" or "Trademarks", as the case may be, in the English version of any Act of Parliament, other than this Act and the
Trademarks Act

— 2015, c. 16, s. 1

1 Section 279.01 of the
Criminal Code
Presumption
(3) For the purposes of subsections (1) and 279.011(1), evidence that a person who is not exploited lives with or is habitually in the company of a person who is exploited is, in the absence of evidence to the contrary, proof that the person exercises control, direction or influence over the movements of that person for the purpose of exploiting them or facilitating their exploitation.

— 2015, c. 16, s. 2

2 Subsection 279.04(1) of the French version of the Act is replaced by the following:
Exploitation

279.04 (1) Pour l'application des articles 279.01 à 279.03, une personne en exploite une autre si elle l'amène à fournir — ou à offrir de fournir — son travail ou ses services, par des agissements dont il est raisonnable de s'attendre, compte tenu du contexte, à ce qu'ils lui fassent croire qu'un refus de sa part mettrait en danger sa sécurité ou celle d'une personne qu'elle connaît.

— 2015, c. 16, s. 3

3 The Act is amended by adding the following after section 279.04:
Sentences to be served consecutively
279.05 A sentence imposed on a person for an offence under sections 279.01 to 279.03 shall be served consecutively to any other punishment imposed on the person for an offence arising out of the same event or series of events and to any other sentence to which the person is subject at the time the sentence is imposed on the person for an offence under any of those sections.

— 2015, c. 16, s. 4

4 Subsection 462.37(2.02) of the Act is amended by striking out "and" at the end of paragraph (a), by adding "and" at the end of paragraph (b) and by adding the following after paragraph (b):
(c) an offence under any of sections 279.01 to 279.03.

— 2015, c. 23, s. 30

2010, c. 17, s. 21(2)
30 Subsection 490.031(3) of the
Criminal Code
Proof of certain facts by certificate
(3) In proceedings under subsection (1), a certificate of a person referred to in paragraph 16(2)(b) of the
Sex Offender Information Registration Act

— 2015, c. 23, s. 31

2007, c. 5, s. 29
31 The portion of section 490.0311 of the Act before paragraph (a) is replaced by the following:
Offence
490.0311 Every person who knowingly provides false or misleading information under subsection 5(1) or 6(1) or (1.01) of the
Sex Offender Information Registration Act

— 2017, c. 7, s. 54

54 (1) Paragraphs 83.13(4)(a) and (b) of the
Criminal Code
(a) the power to make an interlocutory sale of perishable or rapidly depreciating property;
(b) the power to destroy, in accordance with subsections (5) to (8), property that has little or no value; and
(c) the power to have property, other than real property or a conveyance, forfeited to Her Majesty in accordance with subsection (8.1).
(2) Subsection 83.13(5) of the Act is replaced by the following :
Application for destruction order
(5) Before a person who is appointed to manage property destroys property that has little or no value,

they shall apply to a judge of the Federal Court for a destruction order.

(3) Subsection 83.13(6) of the English version of the Act is replaced by the following :

Notice

(6) Before making a destruction order, a judge shall require notice in accordance with subsection (7) to be given to and may hear any person who, in the judge's opinion, appears to have a valid interest in the property.

(4) Subsections 83.13(7) to (9) of the Act are replaced by the following :

Manner of giving notice

(7) A notice shall

(a) be given in the manner that the judge directs or that may be specified in the rules of the Federal Court; and

(b) specify the effective period of the notice that the judge considers reasonable or that may be set out in the rules of the Federal Court.

Destruction order

(8) A judge shall order that the property be destroyed if they are satisfied that the property has little or no financial or other value.

Forfeiture order

(8.1) On application by a person who is appointed to manage the property, a judge of the Federal Court shall order that the property, other than real property or a conveyance, be forfeited to Her Majesty to be disposed of or otherwise dealt with in accordance with the law if

(a) a notice is given or published in the manner that the judge directs or that may be specified in the rules of the Federal Court;

(b) the notice specifies a period of 60 days during which a person may make an application to the judge asserting their interest in the property; and

(c) during that period, no one makes such an application.

When management order ceases to have effect

(9) A management order ceases to have effect when the property that is the subject of the management order is returned in accordance with the law, destroyed or forfeited to Her Majesty.

For greater certainty

(9.1) For greater certainty, if property that is the subject of a management order is sold, the management order applies to the net proceeds of the sale.

— 2017, c. 7, s. 58

58 (1) Paragraphs 462.331(3)(a) and (b) of the Act are replaced by the following :

(a) the power to make an interlocutory sale of perishable or rapidly depreciating property;

(b) the power to destroy, in accordance with subsections (4) to (7), property that has little or no value; and

(c) the power to have property, other than real property or a conveyance, forfeited to Her Majesty in accordance with subsection (7.1).

(2) Subsections 462.331(4) and (5) of the Act are replaced by the following :

Application for destruction order

(4) Before a person who is appointed to manage property destroys property that has little or no value, they shall apply to a court for a destruction order.

Notice

(5) Before making a destruction order, a court shall require notice in accordance with subsection (6) to be given to and may hear any person who, in the court's opinion, appears to have a valid interest in the property.

(3) Paragraphs 462.331(6)(a) and (b) of the Act are replaced by the following :

(a) be given in the manner that the court directs or that may be specified in the rules of the court; and

(b) specify the effective period of the notice that the court considers reasonable or that may be set out in the rules of the court.

(4) Subsections 462.331(7) and (8) of the Act are replaced by the following :
Destruction order
(7) A court shall order that the property be destroyed if it is satisfied that the property has little or no financial or other value.
Forfeiture order
(7.1) On application by a person who is appointed to manage the property, a court shall order that the property, other than real property or a conveyance, be forfeited to Her Majesty to be disposed of or otherwise dealt with in accordance with the law if
(a) a notice is given or published in the manner that the court directs or that may be specified in the rules of the court;
(b) the notice specifies a period of 60 days during which a person may make an application to the court asserting their interest in the property; and
(c) during that period, no one makes such an application.
When management order ceases to have effect
(8) A management order ceases to have effect when the property that is the subject of the management order is returned in accordance with the law, destroyed or forfeited to Her Majesty.
For greater certainty
(8.1) For greater certainty, if property that is the subject of a management order is sold, the management order applies to the net proceeds of the sale.

— 2017, c. 7, s. 59

59 (1) Subsections 462.37(1) and (2) of the Act are replaced by the following :
Order of forfeiture of property
462.37 (1) Subject to this section and sections 462.39 to 462.41, if an offender is convicted, or discharged under section 730, of a designated offence and the court imposing sentence on or discharging the offender, on application of the Attorney General, is satisfied, on a balance of probabilities, that any property is proceeds of crime obtained through the commission of the designated offence, the court shall order that the property be forfeited to Her Majesty to be disposed of as the Attorney General directs or otherwise dealt with in accordance with the law.
Proceeds of crime — other offences
(2) If the evidence does not establish to the satisfaction of the court that property in respect of which an order of forfeiture would otherwise be made under subsection (1) was obtained through the commission of the designated offence of which the offender is convicted or discharged, but the court is satisfied, beyond a reasonable doubt, that the property is proceeds of crime, the court may make an order of forfeiture under subsection (1) in relation to that property.
(2) Subsection 462.37(2.01) of the French version of the Act is replaced by the following :
Confiscation — circonstances particulières
(2.01) Dans le cas où le contrevenant est condamné pour une infraction mentionnée au paragraphe (2.02), le tribunal qui détermine la peine à infliger est tenu, sur demande du procureur général et sous réserve des autres dispositions du présent article et des articles 462.4 et 462.41, d'ordonner la confiscation au profit de Sa Majesté des biens du contrevenant précisés par le procureur général dans la demande et de prévoir dans l'ordonnance qu'il est disposé de ces biens selon les instructions du procureur général ou autrement en conformité avec le droit applicable, s'il est convaincu, selon la prépondérance des probabilités, de l'un ou l'autre des faits suivants :
a) le contrevenant s'est livré, dans les dix ans précédant l'inculpation relative à l'infraction en cause, à des activités criminelles répétées visant à lui procurer, directement ou indirectement, un avantage matériel, notamment pécuniaire;
b) le revenu du contrevenant de sources non liées à des infractions désignées ne peut justifier de façon raisonnable la valeur de son patrimoine.

— **2017, c. 7, s. 60(1)**

60 (1) Paragraph 462.38(2)(b) of the Act is replaced by the following :
(b) that property was obtained through the commission of a designated offence in respect of which proceedings were commenced, and

— **2017, c. 7, s. 61**

61 The portion of subsection 462.41(2) of the Act before paragraph (c) is replaced by the following :
Manner of giving notice
(2) A notice shall
(a) be given in the manner that the court directs or that may be specified in the rules of the court;
(b) specify the period that the court considers reasonable or that may be set out in the rules of the court during which a person may make an application to the court asserting their interest in the property; and

— **2017, c. 7, s. 64**

64 Subsections 490.1(1) and (2) of the Act are replaced by the following :
Order of forfeiture of property on conviction
490.1 (1) Subject to sections 490.3 to 490.41, if a person is convicted, or discharged under section 730, of an indictable offence under this Act or the
Corruption of Foreign Public Officials Act
(a) if the prosecution of the offence was commenced at the instance of the government of a province and conducted by or on behalf of that government, order that the property be forfeited to Her Majesty in right of that province to be disposed of or otherwise dealt with in accordance with the law by the Attorney General or Solicitor General of that province; and
(b) in any other case, order that the property be forfeited to Her Majesty in right of Canada to be disposed of or otherwise dealt with in accordance with the law by the member of the Queen's Privy Council for Canada that is designated by the Governor in Council for the purpose of this paragraph.
Property related to other offences
(2) Subject to sections 490.3 to 490.41, if the evidence does not establish to the satisfaction of the court that property in respect of which an order of forfeiture would otherwise be made under subsection (1) is related to the commission of the indictable offence under this Act or the Corruption of Foreign Public Officials Act

— **2017, c. 7, s. 65**

65 Paragraphs 490.2(4)(a) and (b) of the Act are replaced by the following :
(a) if the prosecution of the offence was commenced at the instance of the government of a province and conducted by or on behalf of that government, order that the property be forfeited to Her Majesty in right of that province to be disposed of or otherwise dealt with in accordance with the law by the Attorney General or Solicitor General of that province; and
(b) in any other case, order that the property be forfeited to Her Majesty in right of Canada to be disposed of or otherwise dealt with in accordance with the law by the member of the Queen's Privy Council for Canada that is designated by the Governor in Council for the purpose of this paragraph.

— **2017, c. 7, s. 66**

66 The portion of subsection 490.4(2) of the Act before paragraph (c) is replaced by the following :
Manner of giving notice

(2) A notice shall
(a) be given in the manner that the court directs or that may be specified in the rules of the court;
(b) specify the period that the court considers reasonable or that may be set out in the rules of the court during which a person may make an application to the court asserting their interest in the property; and

— 2017, c. 7, s. 67

67 Paragraphs 490.41(2)(a) and (b) of the Act are replaced by the following :
(a) be given in the manner that the court directs or that may be specified in the rules of the court;
(b) specify the period that the court considers reasonable or that may be set out in the rules of the court during which a member of the immediate family who resides in the dwelling-house may make themselves known to the court; and

— 2017, c. 7, s. 68

68 (1) Paragraphs 490.81(3)(a) and (b) of the Act are replaced by the following :
(a) the power to make an interlocutory sale of perishable or rapidly depreciating property;
(b) the power to destroy, in accordance with subsections (4) to (7), property that has little or no value; and
(c) the power to have property, other than real property or a conveyance, forfeited to Her Majesty in accordance with subsection (7.1).
(2) Subsections 490.81(4) and (5) of the Act are replaced by the following :
Application for destruction order
(4) Before a person who is appointed to manage property destroys property that has little or no value, they shall apply to a court for a destruction order.
Notice
(5) Before making a destruction order, a court shall require notice in accordance with subsection (6) to be given to and may hear any person who, in the court's opinion, appears to have a valid interest in the property.
(3) Paragraphs 490.81(6)(a) and (b) of the Act are replaced by the following :
(a) be given in the manner that the court directs or that may be specified in the rules of the court; and
(b) specify the effective period of the notice that the court considers reasonable or that may be set out in the rules of the court.
(4) Subsections 490.81(7) and (8) of the Act are replaced by the following :
Destruction order
(7) A court shall order that the property be destroyed if it is satisfied that the property has little or no financial or other value.
Forfeiture order
(7.1) On application by a person who is appointed to manage the property, a court shall order that the property, other than real property or a conveyance, be forfeited to Her Majesty to be disposed of or otherwise dealt with in accordance with the law if
(a) a notice is given or published in the manner that the court directs or that may be specified in the rules of the court;
(b) the notice specifies a period of 60 days during which a person may make an application to the court asserting their interest in the property; and
(c) during that period, no one makes such an application.
When management order ceases to have effect
(8) A management order ceases to have effect when the property that is the subject of the management order is returned in accordance with the law, destroyed or forfeited to Her Majesty.
For greater certainty
(8.1) For greater certainty, if property that is the subject of a management order is sold, the

management order applies to the net proceeds of the sale.

— 2017, c. 27, s. 61

61 The
Criminal Code
Preclearance officers
117.071 Despite any other provision of this Act, but subject to section 117.1, no
Preclearance Act, 2016
Firearms Act
(a) possesses a firearm, a prohibited weapon, a restricted weapon, a prohibited device or any prohibited ammunition in the course of or for the purpose of their duties or employment;
(b) transfers or offers to transfer a firearm, a prohibited weapon, a restricted weapon, a prohibited device, any ammunition or any prohibited ammunition in the course of their duties or employment;
(c) exports or imports a firearm, a prohibited weapon, a restricted weapon, a prohibited device or any prohibited ammunition in the course of their duties or employment; or
(d) fails to report the loss, theft or finding of any firearm, prohibited weapon, restricted weapon, prohibited device, ammunition, prohibited ammunition or explosive substance that occurs in the course of their duties or employment or the destruction of any such thing in the course of their duties or employment.

— 2017, c. 27, s. 62

62 The Act is amended by adding the following after section 579:
Instruction to stay
579.001 (1) The Attorney General or counsel instructed by him or her for that purpose shall, at any time after proceedings in relation to an act or omission of a
Preclearance Act, 2016
Stay
(2) The clerk or other officer of the court shall make the entry immediately after being so directed, and on the entry being made the proceedings are stayed and any recognizance relating to the proceedings is vacated.
Recommencement
(3) The proceedings may be recommenced without laying a new information or preferring a new indictment, if the Attorney General or counsel instructed by him or her gives notice to the clerk or other officer of the court that
(a) the Government of the United States has provided notice of waiver under paragraph 15 of Article X of the Agreement; or
(b) the Government of the United States has declined, or is unable, to prosecute the accused and the accused has returned to Canada.
Proceedings deemed never commenced
(4) However, if the Attorney General or counsel does not give notice under subsection (3) on or before the first anniversary of the day on which the stay of proceedings was entered, the proceedings are deemed never to have been commenced.
Definition of
(5) In this section,
Agreement

— 2017, c. 33, s. 255

255 (1) Paragraph 188(4)(c) of the
Criminal Code

(c) in the Provinces of Nova Scotia, British Columbia and Prince Edward Island, and in the Yukon and the Northwest Territories, the Chief Justice of the Supreme Court;

(2) Paragraph 188(4)(f) of the Act is replaced by the following:

(f) in Nunavut, the Chief Justice of the Nunavut Court of Justice.